Intelligent Computing on IoT 2.0, Big Data Analytics, and Block Chain Technology

The book is designed as a reference text and explores the concepts and techniques of IoT, artificial intelligence (AI), and blockchain. It also discusses the possibility of applying blockchain for providing security in various domains. The specific highlight of this book is focused on the application of integrated technologies in enhancing data models, better insights and discovery, intelligent predictions, smarter finance, smart retail, global verification, transparent governance, and innovative audit systems.

- The book discusses the potential of blockchain to significantly increase data while boosting accuracy and integrity in IoT-generated data and AI-processed information.
- It elucidates definitions, concepts, theories, and assumptions involved in smart contracts and distributed ledgers related to IoT systems and AI approaches.
- The book offers real-world uses of blockchain technologies in different IoT systems and further studies its influence in supply chains and logistics, the automotive industry, smart homes, the pharmaceutical industry, agriculture, and other areas.
- It also presents readers with ways of employing blockchain in IoT and AI, helping them to understand what they can and cannot do with blockchain.
- The book is aimed primarily at advanced undergraduates and graduates studying computer science, computer engineering, electrical engineering, information systems, computational sciences, artificial intelligence, and information technology. Researchers and professionals will also find this book very useful.

Intelligent Computing on IoT 2.0, Big Data Analytics, and Block Chain Technology

Edited by
Mohammad S. Obaidat
Padmalaya Nayak
Niranjan K. Ray

CRC Press
Taylor & Francis Group
Boca Raton London New York

CRC Press is an imprint of the
Taylor & Francis Group, an **Informa** business

A CHAPMAN & HALL BOOK

Designed cover image: ShutterStock Images

First edition published 2024
by CRC Press
2385 NW Executive Center Drive, Suite 320, Boca Raton FL 33431

and by CRC Press
4 Park Square, Milton Park, Abingdon, Oxon, OX14 4RN

CRC Press is an imprint of Taylor & Francis Group, LLC

© 2024 selection and editorial matter, Mohammad S. Obaidat, Padmalaya Nayak and Niranjan K. Ray; individual chapters, the contributors

ISBN: 978-1-032-35123-0 (hbk)
ISBN: 978-1-032-35295-4 (pbk)
ISBN: 978-1-003-32623-6 (ebk)

DOI: 10.1201/9781003326236

Typeset in Times New Roman
by SPi Technologies India Pvt Ltd (Straive)

Contents

Preface

As the editors of this book, we intend to help the readers to deeply understand the widespread IoT technology, big data analytics, and blockchain technology and how all these technologies can be integrated for societal benefit as these technologies are highly diverse, rapidly changing, and economically emergent in the global context. All the authors are involved in sharing their ideas about the enhanced versions of IoT, the integration of big data in IoT, the role of blockchain in securing IoT networks, and the overall applications of machine learning in IoT network systems.

Chapter 1 is an introductory chapter that discusses the challenges involved in IoT 2.0, the integration of IoT and big data, and the role of blockchain in IoT networks to ensure security.

In Chapter 2, the authors have provided a detailed review of blockchain technology and its impact on the IoT network. However, several challenges are discussed in this chapter that need to be addressed and overcome before exploiting the full potential of the blockchain in IoT applications. Chapter 3 presents an overview of cloud architecture, services, and applications of cloud technology. A real-time cloud-based weather forecasting system is presented.

Chapter 4 proposes a blockchain-based method to solve security and privacy issues. This chapter emphasizes blockchain technology as a possible solution to several IoT security and privacy issues.

An onion routing protocol is proposed in Chapter 5 along with blockchain technology to handle security and privacy in IoT networks. Blockchain technology verifies the authenticity of the IoT data at each stage of the OR network.

Chapter 6 presents the development of blockchain in the banking and financial industry while Chapter 7 presents a blockchain-based warranty system solution that can be enforced to stop return abuse.

In Chapter 8, a mathematical queuing model is proposed for blockchain applications while Chapter 9 discusses different types of components in IoT networks and the role of sensors in the IoT industry. This latter chapter also addresses the software and hardware issues in IoT networks and emerging trends in smart systems.

Blockchain development in various industries such as the financial industry, logistics industry, healthcare industry, and manufacturing industry is discussed in Chapter 10.

In Chapter 11, the authors have given exposure to smart agricultural systems using IoT 2.0.

A smart health monitoring and management system is discussed in Chapter 12 while Chapter 13 discusses the types of pollution in the city and how they affect the environment's natural cycles (bearing in mind that many of these pollutants also affect rural areas).

In addition, relevant environmental processes produced by the contamination of human beings and nature have been described.

In Chapter 14, sensor technology in IoT is explored in various domains. Furthermore, the challenges, innovations, and characteristics of the data generated by the sensors in each domain are discussed. Chapter 15 deals with the problem of scheduling in the Internet of Things requests for energy optimization. So, an objective function using delay and maximum response time is defined. Then, to solve this problem, an improved evolutionary algorithm using linear scaling is used.

In Chapter 16, the authors introduced AI-based off-loading schemes in a cloud environment, which can reduce time delay, energy consumption, and packet loss in IoT networks. In the event of emergencies, such as fires, chemical spills, and earthquakes, evacuating people out of a building promptly is critical to ensuring their safety.

Chapter 17 reviews the state-of-the-art approaches in emergency evacuation research and practice and discusses the application of the recent advances in IoT technologies to dynamically guide the evacuation process. Stochastic timed Petri nets (STPN) are used to model the evacuation process of teaching buildings.

Chapter 18 conveys information about the detailed networking technologies used in IoT.

In Chapter 19, the authors highlight the importance of properly evaluating the security level of Industrial Control Systems (ICS) focusing on the agricultural scenario and propose an software defined radio (SDR)-based framework to assess the cybersecurity of these systems.

Chapters 20 and 21 present an intensive study and analysis of machine learning and deep learning methods to track malicious behaviors, network intrusion, and malware detection in IoT applications.

The above chapters represent a good coverage of recent advances in intelligent computing on IoT 2.0, big data analytics, and blockchain technology that we believe will lead the readers to a great understanding of the state of the art of these fascinating technologies. We hope that this will represent a good resource for readers from academia, industry, and business in pursuing future research and developing new applications.

The book will be an ideal reference to practitioners and researchers in the areas of Intelligent Computing on IoT 2.0, Big Data, and Block Chain Technology as well as a good textbook for graduate and senior undergraduate courses in these domains.

We would like to thank the reviewers of the original book proposal for their constructive suggestions. Special thanks go to all authors of the chapters for their contributions and cooperation. Many thanks go to the editors and editorial assistants for their cooperation and fine work.

The Book Editors
Mohammad S. Obaidat, Life Fellow of IEEE, Fellow of AAIA,
Fellow of FTRA, and Fellow of SCS
Padmalaya Nayak,
Niranjan K. Ray,

About the Editors

Professor Mohammad S. Obaidat is an internationally known academic, researcher, scientist, and scholar. He received his Ph.D. degree in Computer Engineering with a minor in Computer Science from the Ohio State University, Columbus, USA. He has received extensive research funding and published to date (2023) over one thousand and three hundred (1,300) refereed technical articles – about half of them are journal articles, 110 books, and over 70 book chapters. He is Editor-in-Chief of three scholarly journals and an editor of many other international journals. He is the founding Editor-in-Chief of Wiley *Security and Privacy Journal*. Moreover, he is the founder or co-founder of five IEEE International Conferences. Among his previous positions are Advisor to the President of Philadelphia University for Research, Development and Information Technology, President and Chair of Board of Directors of the Society for Molding and Simulation International (SCS), Senior Vice President of SCS, SCS VP for Membership and SCS VP for Conferences, Dean of the College of Engineering at Prince Sultan University, Founding Dean of the College of Computing and Informatics at the University of Sharjah, Chair and tenured Professor at the Department of Computer and Information Science and Director of the MS Graduate Program in Data Analytics at Fordham university, Chair and tenured Professor of the Department of Computer Science and Director of the Graduate Program at Monmouth University, Chair and Professor of Computer Science Department at the University of Texas-Permian Basin, Distinguished Professor at IIT-Dhanbad, Distinguished Professor at SRM University, tenured Full Professor at King Abdullah II School of Information Technology (KASIT), University of Jordan, the PR of China Ministry of Education Distinguished Overseas Professor at the University of Science and Technology Beijing, China, and an Honorary Distinguished Professor at the Amity University – A Global University. He is now a Distinguished Professor at KASIT, University of Jordan.

He has chaired numerous (over 190) international conferences and has given numerous (over 190) keynote speeches worldwide. He has served as ABET/CSAB evaluator and on the IEEE CS Fellow Evaluation Committee. He has served as an IEEE CS Distinguished Speaker/Lecturer and an ACM Distinguished Lecturer. Since 2004 has been serving as an SCS Distinguished Lecturer. He received many best paper awards for his papers including ones from IEEE ICC, IEEE GLOBECOM, AICSA, CITS, SPECTS, DCNET, IEEE ICCCA, and international conferences. He also received Best Paper awards from *IEEE Systems Journal* in 2018 and in 2019 (2 Best Paper Awards). In 2020, he received four Best Paper awards from *IEEE Systems Journal* and also in 2021 received the Best Paper award from *IEEE Systems Journal*.

During his tenure as Founding Dean of the College of Computing and Informatics at the University of Sharjah, the Computer Sciences program has been ranked by *Times for Higher Education* (THE) as number one in UAE and for the first time in the history of the University. He also received many other worldwide awards for his technical contributions including the 2018 IEEE ComSoc-Technical Committee on Communications Software 2018 Technical Achievement Award for contribution to Cybersecurity, AI, Wireless Networks, Computer Networks and Modeling and Simulation, SCS prestigious McLeod Founder's Award, Presidential Service Award, SCS Hall of Fame – Lifetime Achievement Award for his technical contribution to modeling and computer simulation and for his outstanding visionary leadership and dedication to increasing the effectiveness and broadening the applications of modeling and simulation worldwide. He also received the SCS Outstanding Service Award. He was awarded the IEEE CITS Hall of Fame Distinguished and Eminent Award. He also received the Nokia Distinguished Fellowship Award and Fulbright

Distinguished Scholar Award, among others. He was ranked recently by research.com agency as the number one Computer Scientist and number one Scholar in Electronics and Electrical Engineering in Jordan.

Dr. Obaidat is a Life Fellow of IEEE, Fellow of AAIA, Fellow of FTRA, and SCS. In recognition of his significant scientific contribution, Springer published in 2022 a book honoring his contributions to computing, informatics, networking, and cybersecurity. It is entitled *Advances in Computing, Informatics, Networking and Cybersecurity – A Book Honoring Professor Mohammad S. Obaidat's Significant Scientific Contributions.*

Dr. Padmalaya Nayak is working as a Professor and Head of the Department of CSE/IT at Gokaraju Lailavathi Womens Engineering College, Hyderabad. Prior to that, she had been working as a Professor in the Department of Computer Science Engineering at Gokaraju Rangaraju Institute of Engineering and Technology, Hyderabad since 2009.

Dr. Padmalaya Nayak obtained her doctoral degree from the National Institute of Technology, Tiruchirappalli, India, in 2010. She has 20 years of teaching and research experience in the areas of Ad hoc and Sensor Networks, Network Security, etc. She has published more than 65 research papers in various International Journals and Conferences and also contributed six book chapters. She visited many countries to present her research paper at International Conferences. She received many National/International Level awards for her academic contributions to the education system and research. She worked on various funding projects sponsored by AICTE, UGC, and TEQIP Projects. She is a member of IEEE, IETE, CSI, and IEANG professional bodies. Prof. Nayak is the Editor of two books published by Taylor and Francis. She has one Indian Patent and one Australian Patent to her credit. She is also a member of the advisory committee and Technical Program Committee for several International Conferences and Professional bodies like IEEE, CSI, IETE, IAENG, etc. Prof. Nayak is the Convenor of an International Conference (ICWSNUCA), proceedings approved by Springer. Her Google Scholar h-index is 15 and her i-10 index is 21. She has 1,268 citations for her research credit.

Dr. Niranjan K. Ray received his PhD from National Institute of Technology, Rourkela, India. He is an Associate Professor of the School of Computer Engineering at the Kalinga Institute of Industrial Technology (KIIT-DU), India, where he teaches undergraduate and post-graduate courses. He has three books and over 80 published papers and four patents. He has received the IEEE Outstanding Service Award for 2022 from IEEE Computer Society, Bio-inspired Computing STC. He was the Associate Editor of IEEE Consumer Electronics Magazine and currently serves as Section Editor of SN Computer Science and serves as Guest Editor for several special issues of distinguished journals. At present, he is serving as Chair of the IEEE Kolkata Section-Consumer Technology Society Chapter, Bhubaneswar and executive council member of IEEE Bhubaneswar Subsection. He has worked as Program Chair/ Co-Chair and TPC member for several noted international conferences sponsored by IEEE. His main research interests are Internet of Things, Edge/Fog Computing, sensor and ad hoc networks. He is a senior member of IEEE and secretary of Odisha IT Society, India.

List of Contributors

Nosherwan Adilb
Riphah International University
Pakistan

Fatih Alagöz
Bogazici University
Istanbul, Turkiye

Ruhul Amin
National Institute of Technology
Jamshedpur, India

Iqra Aslam
Riphah International University
Pakistan

Vasileios Asteriou
Aristotle University of Thessaloniki
Greece

Fatemeh Bahrani-pour
Yazd University
Yazd, Iran

Konstantina Banti
University of Western Macedonia
Kozani, Greece

Peristera Baziana
University of Thessaly
Lamia, Greece

Georgia Beletsioti
Aristotle University of Thessaloniki
Greece

Roberto Caviglia
University of Genoa
Italy

Srinivas R. Chakravarthy
Kettering University
USA

Sanskar Chandra
International Institute of Information
    Technology Naya Raipur
Atal Nagar-Nava, Raipur, India

Yue Chen
University of Science and Technology Beijing
Beijing, China

Franco Davoli
University of Genoa
Italy

Mohammad Farshi
Yazd University
Yazd, Iran

Misbah Fatima
Riphah International University
Pakistan

Alessandro Fausto
University of Genoa
Italy

Giovanni Gaggero
University of Genoa
Italy

Laura García
Universitat Politècnica de València
Valencia, Spain

Aditya Goel
International Institute of Information
    Technology Naya Raipur
Atal Nagar-Nava, Raipur, India

Shruti Goel
Jaypee Institute of Information and Technology
India

Debasis Gountia
Odisha University of Technology and Research
    Bhubaneswar
India

Meghan Granit
Monmouth University
New Jersey, USA

M. Junaid Gul
Yeungnam University, Daegu
South Korea

Nivine Guler
University of Technology Bahrain

Yu Guo
University of Science and Technology Beijing
Beijing, China

Alberto Ivars-Palomares
Universitat Politècnica de València
Valencia, Spain

Nilesh Kumar Jadav
Nirma University
Ahmedabad, India

Vidyottama Jain
Central University of Rajasthan
India

Hasan Javed
Riphah International University
Pakistan

Jose Miguel Jiménez
Universitat Politècnica de València
Valencia, Spain

Konstantinos Kantelis
Aristotle University of Thessaloniki
Greece

Mucheol Kim
Chung-Ang University
South Korea

Jaime Lloret
Universitat Politècnica de València
Valencia, Spain

Malamati Louta
University of Western Macedonia
Kozani, Greece

Khalid Mahmood
National Yunlin University of Science
    and Technology
Taiwan

Mario Marchese
University of Genoa
Italy

Aya Moheddine
University of Genoa
Italy

Sepehr Ebrahimi Mood
Yazd University
Yazd, Iran

Vaidik Murarka
Shri Ramdeobaba College of Engineering
    and Management
Nagpur, India

Devishree Naidu
Shri Ramdeobaba College of Engineering
    and Management
Nagpur, India

Manjit Kumar Nayak
Odisha University of Technology and Research
Bhubaneswar, India

Padmalaya Nayak
Gokaraju Lailavathi Womens Engineering
    College
Hyderabad, India

Petros Nicopolitidis
Aristotle University of Thessaloniki
Greece

Mohammad S. Obaidat
University of Jordan
Amman, Jordan

Serife Ozkar
Balikesir University
Balikesir, Turkey

Pankaj Pal
Indian Institute of Technology (ISM)
Dhanbad, India

Georgios Papadimitriou
Aristotle University of Thessaloniki
Greece

Maitri Patel
Nirma University
Ahmedabad, India

Fabio Patrone
University of Genoa
Italy

Anand Paul
Kyungpook National University
Daegu, South Korea

Giancarlo Portomauro
University of Genoa
Italy

Raina Raj
Central University of Rajasthan
India

Niranjan K. Ray
KIIT University
Bhubaneswar, India

Seungmin Rho
Chung-Ang University
Seoul 06974, South Korea

Javier Rocher
Universitat Politècnica de València
Valencia, Spain

Christos Roumeliotis
University of Western Macedonia
Kozani, Greece

Sandesh Sachdev
Shri Ramdeobaba College of Engineering
    and Management
Nagpur, India

Ilgın Şafak
Fibabanka R&D Center
Turkey

Mohammed Salamah
Eastern Mediterranean University
Turkey

Sandra Sendra
Universitat Politècnica de València
Valencia, Spain

Iqra Shafique
Riphah International University
Pakistan

Salman Shamshad
The University of Lahore
Pakistan

Alireza Souri
Halic University
İstanbul, Turkey

Konstantina Spathi
Aristotle University of Thessaloniki
Greece

Jordan Strobing
Monmouth University
New Jersey, USA

Muhammad Zeeshan Tanveer
Riphah International University
Pakistan

Sudeep Tanwar
Nirma University
Ahmedabad, India

Shubhangi Tirpude
Shri Ramdeobaba College of Engineering
    and Management
Nagpur, India

Athanasios Tsakmakis
Aristotle University of Thessaloniki
Greece

Anastasios Valkanis
Aristotle University of Thessaloniki
Thessaloniki, Greece

Sandra Viciano-Tudela
Universitat Politècnica de València
Valencia, Spain

Jiacun Wang
Monmouth University
New Jersey, USA

Yuanyan Xie
University of Science and Technology Beijing
Beijing, China

Swarup Yeole
International Institute of Information
    Technology Naya Raipur
Atal Nagar-Nava Raipur, India

1

Introduction to Intelligent Computing on IoT 2.0, Big Data, and Block Chain Technology

Padmalaya Nayak
Gokaraju Lailavathi Womens Engineering College, Hyderabad, India

Niranjan K. Ray
KIIT University, Bhubaneswar, India

Mohammad S. Obaidat
University of Jordan, Amman, Jordan

1.1 Introduction

The definition of IoT proposed by Kevin Ashton has remained as it is since 1999. IoT is formally defined by the International Telecommunication Union (ITU) thus: "A global infrastructure for the information technology society by interconnecting things (physical as well as virtual) by allowing interoperable services, and communication technologies" [1]. This definition is believed to be the basic definition of IoT networks. In [2], it is predicted that there will be a huge increase in interconnected devices from 18 billion to 29 billion during the period 2017 to 2022 and that machine-to-machine (M2M) connectivity will reach 15 billion in 2022. Now, our eyewitness agrees with the increase in IoT devices. It is also expected that about 8 billion to 25 billion active smart gadgets will be interconnected by 2030 and controlled by a single huge information network [3]. As we are on the edge of the 5G era, IoT follows the natural course of improvement that leads to IoT 2.0; that is, high-speed and ultra-latency networks motivate further development of IoT technologies and applications [4]. In [5], several features like interoperability, connectivity, security, and automation are discussed as the major fields of IoT applications. All these features are required to be improved in the context of IoT 2.0. However, the recent development of other technologies and applications such as machine learning (ML), edge computing, fog computing, and Industry 4.0 demands updating and redefining the concept of IoT to IoT 2.0 [4, 6]. The articles published in the public domain focus on the users' point of view by improving the productivity and service quality of IoT applications [7–9]. In the view of AI-based service development, the quality of service can be enhanced through IoT [10]. IoT interoperability is a crucial issue that has to be enhanced in IoT 2.0 [11]. Apart from this, security and privacy factors are major concerns that have to be resolved in IoT echo systems [12]. In summary, current IoT technology comprises seven domains such as intelligence of machine learning, 5G communication, scalability, security, sustainability, interoperability, and user-friendly IoT [13]. Further, ML-based algorithms are applied in all layers of IoT applications. As per the Joint Research Centre (JRC) report of the European Commission [14], IoT 2.0 should make use of ML techniques to enhance the intelligence of the network and knowledge available to users. The motive of IoT 2.0 is that contents, code, and data delivery should be attained at a higher speed with intensely lower costs. The big picture of IoT 2.0 is the evolutionary progress from custom-built systems to tremendously

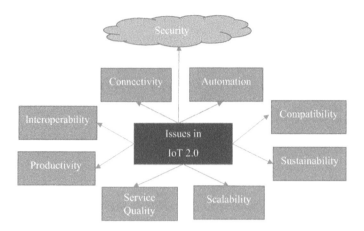

FIGURE 1.1   Domains in IoT 2.0.

scalable and broadly applicable product ecosystems. Blockchain could be the probable resolution to ensure IoT security and privacy. The various domains involved in IoT 2.0 are depicted in Figure 1.1.

The contributions of this chapter are summarized as follows:

1) Overview of IoT 2.0
2) Discussion on IoT big data
3) The role of blockchain in IoT
4) Discussion on open research issues

The rest of the chapter is structured as follows. Section 1.2 discusses the underlying principle of IoT 2.0 technology, Section 1.3 discusses the significance of big data in IoT 2.0 architecture, Section 1.4 discusses the role of blockchain in IoT, and Section 1.5 concludes the chapter.

1.2   Underlying Technologies in IoT 2.0

- Fifth-Generation Mobile Systems (5G)
  5G stands for fifth generation mobile network, followed by previous first generation (1G) (2G), third generation (3G), and fourth generation (4G) networks that empower a new kind of network to provide larger capacity with lower latency and higher speed than the 4G LTE network [15]. The 5G network aims to connect virtually everything including devices, machines, and objects. It is designed to have massive network capacity, more capable air interface, higher data rates in multi-Gbps, ultra-low latency, more availability, and more reliability, while also meeting customers' expectations without compromising quality. It is also designed to abide by new deployment models and deliver new services. Therefore, 5G could support next-generation IoT deployment models to provide better services by moving the data at a faster rate over more secure communication channels. The underlying technologies in IoT 2.0 is shown in Figure 1.2.
- Industry 4.0
  Industry 4.0 is the fourth industrial revolution that adds two more ingredients: digitation and automation of industry [16]. Many technological developments like robotics, 3-D printing, machine learning, big data analytics, and networking are transforming industrial processes and reducing human labor and judgment. The main goal of Industry 4.0 is to enhance the productivity of manufacturing companies by integrating all advanced technologies into a single platform. Cyber-Physical System (CPS) is the heart of Industry 4.0, which has huge potential to influence technology for industry automation [17]. The main challenge is that the

CPS workforce must have the expertise to handle heterogeneous data from multiple sources and other related technologies to sustain the growth of the industrial process. Hence, the application of ML and big data analytics is the most important task for the advancement of Industry 4.0. CPS generates a huge amount of data, which is certainly difficult for a centralized cloud architecture to process. Certainly, the role of edge computing is crucial as the devices involved in edge computing are placed closer to end users. Therefore, it distributes the load among the devices evenly by ensuring the lower latency of a service.

- **Tactile Internet**
  Mobile Internet has made it possible to connect people at any place at any time to exchange any form of information such as text, image, audio, and video. IoT connects every object, thing, and machine anywhere, anytime through the Internet. The next wave of the Internet is the Tactile Internet equipped with various features like ultra-low-latency, high-availability, human-to-human (H2H) and machine-to-machine (M2M), data-centric technologies, and security. In [17], the Tactile Internet is considered the integrated battlespace network of human-to-machine (H2M) communications through haptic devices using the same Internet technology. The Tactile Internet uses IP protocol with variable message formats (VMF) that are common across the Tactical Internet. Tactile Internet has various features like electronic messaging, directory, network management, and security. These facilities are vital for the *Tactical Internet* in support of warfighters. In modern battlespace, it is expected that the three primary army tactical communications systems such as EPLRS, SINCGARS, and MSE/TPN will move the ever-increasing amount of digital data associated with command-and-control applications. It is also interpreted that features of Tactile Internet are identical to IoT and 5G [18]. It can support the low-latency requirement of 5G caused by the wireless infrastructure of IoT. The challenges in Tactile Internet are listed as communication, AI, haptics, and computation. Further, there are many communication challenges like higher data rates, ultra-low latency, high consistency, and fewer outlays to support cloud/fog networks. These challenges are similar to 5G networks and can be handled in the 5G environment. Artificial intelligence and computation power is the key feature for preserving low-latency services. Artificial intelligence helps predict future activities in order to reduce latency. Similarly, faster computation also minimizes latency.

- **Machine Learning**
  Data processing in IoT networks is a challenging task due to the 6V features of these data (volume, velocity, variety, veracity, value, and variability) [19]. Similar to machine learning techniques, data analytic techniques can process complex data with 6V features [38]. Moreover, when ML techniques are applied to diverse IoT data for intelligent applications, they provide better and more efficient services that lead to data visualization. Overall, ML techniques are partitioned into three groups: supervised learning, unsupervised learning, and reinforcement learning [20]. As the name implies, supervised learning methods work based on supervision. The machine is trained based on the labeled dataset, and it produces the output as per the training model. The labeled dataset means the machine is trained with a given set of input data followed by output data, then the machine is asked to predict the output based on the test data. On the other hand, the machine is not trained for an expected outcome when an unsupervised learning model is trained. As the name signifies, an unsupervised learning model works without any supervision. The ML model works on unsorted datasets based on similarities, differences, and patterns, and finds hidden patterns. Reinforcement learning models work based on the feedback process, learn from their experience, and improve through trial and error.

- **Edge Computing**
  Edge computing is one of the core enablers in real-time applications that refers to a range of networks and devices near the users. Edge is about processing the data where it is being generated, and at greater speeds and volume, producing action-oriented results in real-time applications. The main components of edge computing are edge devices, network edge, and

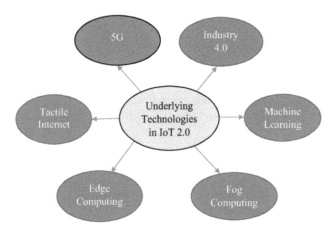

FIGURE 1.2 Underlying technologies in IoT 2.0.

on-premises infrastructure. Smart speakers, smartwatches, and smartphones are examples of edge devices. Similarly, sensors, robots, and vehicles are edge devices if they are connected to the cloud. Edge network does not require separate infrastructure. When a separate network is involved, this is just another location where connectivity occurs between the users and the cloud. Here, the 5G network comes into the picture. It integrates AI and edge computing to enhance IoT services, thus satisfying users' experience [21].

- **Fog Computing**
  Fog computing is a distributed computing architecture that computes the data, storage, and applications somewhere in between the data source and the cloud. In a fog network, the system works on control, configuration, and management over the Internet infrastructure, whereas gateways and switches attached to the network have primary control over the 4G LTE network. The fog computing framework is treated as a highly virtualized tiered computing architecture that provides services near the end users with the support of edge server nodes. Sometimes, edge computing and fog computing are used interchangeably as both types of computing use intelligence and processes near the data. The major difference between these architectures is the location where the computation and intelligence power are placed in the cloud computing framework. In both structures, data is sent by physical devices like sensors, gadgets, motors, relays, and pumps. All those devices perform physical activities such as sensing, electrical circuits, pumping water, and switching tasks around them.

1.3 Significance of Big Data in IoT 2.0

The Internet of Things has become a pinpointed technology at a global pace. For instance, a huge number of mixed devices such as sensors, automobiles, household electrical appliances, and different types of transducers are connected to the Internet and generate a huge volume of data known as IoT big data. As IoT applications generate a large amount of data, the current IoT data-processing techniques are becoming unproductive. So, at a global pace, managing such a large volume of data is a challenging task. So, there is a necessity to integrate big data technologies in the IoT domain to sustain the overall development of IoT. It is worth noting that the success of IoT applications depends on big data analytics. As IoT and big data are interdependent, big data analysts and data scientists have more opportunities to propose new techniques for the development and application of big data. On the other hand, the integration of big data analytics and IoT provides a platform for researchers to develop Industry 4.0. Any successful technology like IoT requires standardization that maintains interoperability, reliability, compatibility, and efficiency of the developments on a global scale. IoT data like environmental data, astronomical data, geographical data, and logistic data are

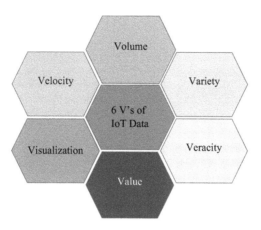

FIGURE 1.3 6Vs of IoT data.

stored and processed in the cloud. On the other side, data generated by economics, urban planning, and informatics requires intelligent analytic systems to analyze and predict the output; this is in order to resolve problems like air pollution, business decisions, and the selection of optimization techniques for a particular problem. As per the prediction by IDC, data volume will reach 175 ZB by 2025 [12] and the number of IoT devices will reach 20 billion by 2025 on a global scale [22]. Therefore, there is a growing demand for data scientists to analyze a huge volume of diversified data generated by widespread IoT devices. IoT big data have identical characteristics to standard big data which are discussed below [23]. The 6Vs of IoT data is shown in Figure 1.3.

- Volume: As the number of devices connected through the internet is increasing rapidly, the diverse volume of data is also increasing exponentially.
- Velocity: The data-generating devices do not generate the data at the same speed. Even many IoT devices generate data at high speed.
- Variety: As different varieties of IoT devices are used in IoT, the structure of the data is not similar for all the devices.
- Veracity: IoT data does not contain always structured data. It contains noise and error.
- Value: The value of IoT data is very important in optimized applications.
- Variability: The data gathering speed differs from one device to another. It is always associated with a particular incident. For instance, the data collection rate from GPS sensors used in vehicles differs from GPS sensors used in the body of birds. Further, the data format may differ from device to device.
- Visualization: It implies the interlink between different types of data.

Big data analytics has been a trending factor in the IoT domain. The learning experience from this massive amount of data through ML techniques is expected to bring substantial beginnings and transformative changes in various sectors. However, most conventional ML models are not certainly capable or scalable enough to deal with different types of data with different features like different speeds, vagueness, incompleteness, and low-value density. In response, ML techniques need to reinvent themselves for big data analysis. In addition to this, IoT data contains spatial and temporal information.

1.3.1 IoT Data Properties

The IoT data collected from various sensors or webs can be categorized based on their spatial, temporal, and sensing properties [13, 24]. The IoT data properties is shown in Figure 1.4.

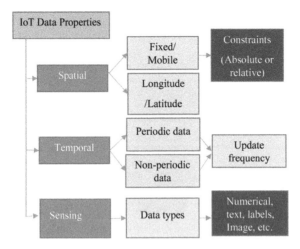

FIGURE 1.4 Properties of IoT data.

- Spatial Properties
  IoT devices are used to measure various parameters tagged in a particular application. These
  devices have to be verified first, whether they are static or mobile. For instance, sensors used
  in environmental sensing are static by nature; they carry fixed spatial information whereas
  moving vehicles are tagged with mobile spatial information. Next, we consider mobile devices
  and moving vehicles must be checked for constraints. Then, the shape of the IoT data comes
  into the picture. The spatial data consists of many points such as areas having rectangles
  and polygonal shapes, straight lines, multiple points, and areas that are not connected (based
  on longitude and latitude). For example, road networks and weather forecasting systems
  are represented by polygons and line strings. The spatial information in the data can be
  treated in the following ways: (a) two-dimensional or three-dimensional (b) relative or absolute
  positions. For instance, drones are equipped with 3-D absolute positions, and vehicles in
  factories are equipped with 2-D relative positions. Finally, spatial information needs to
  be checked for possible constraints. For instance, cars can travel only on roads. Likewise,
  constraints are frequently handled by pre-processing techniques to avoid erroneous analytics
  results.

- Temporal Properties
  IoT data contains both temporal information and spatial information. For instance, it can
  be updated in a periodic or non-periodic manner. When IoT data update is periodic, efficient
  methods must be defined to store these data and load-balancing must be done for the streaming
  process. Periodic data has the benefit of data partitioning as it does not contain temporal
  skew. Otherwise, in order to avoid the temporal skew, some techniques need to be applied for
  partitioning the periodic data. Next, the data should be updated frequently. When data are
  frequently updated in a periodic manner, data compaction can be achieved easily because the
  quality of data is likely to be similar. In the IoT data streaming process, high-frequency data
  collection is preferred in order to maintain low latency.

- Sensing Properties
  Mostly, IoT data is obtained from different types of sensors. These sensing values are of
  different types, such as numerical, text, labels, and images. Even if, for the same data, the names
  and units of the attributes are often different. Further, the quality of sense varies for each
  IoT device as IoT devices are deployed independently. Some sensors provide accurate results,
  whereas others do not. Sensed values often contain noise, errors, and invalid data. Systems,
  specifically, ML models should be efficient enough to handle these types of erroneous data
  and produce correct results.

1.4 Moving Ahead (Integrating Blockchain in IoT)

The main purpose of IoT is to connect people, products, and places at any time via the Internet in real time. Starting from tiny sensors, servers are capable of sensing and the sensed data is gathered for data analysis. The idea is to turn each object into smart object and the everyday environment into a smart environment so that they will be able to process and provide real-time information. However, with significant advancements in the IoT domain, the problem comes with data security. Not only the technologies are improving, but also hackers and cybercriminals are finding their own paths to crack private data and extract information. For instance, patient information is collected through IoT devices, which is sent back to doctors for analysis through the Internet. The collected data provides an opportunity for cybercriminals to create an entry point and gain access control to such private information. To provide data privacy and security, blockchain comes into the picture. Blockchain can keep track of data collected by sensors and thus prevent cybercriminals from doing malicious activities in order to sustain their business. IoT also has some features to exchange data through a specific blockchain, rather than exchanging the data through a third-party system. A third-party system always creates an open-door opportunity for hackers to manipulate/duplicate the data or information, which is almost eradicated with a blockchain. Since blockchains are stamped with a unique signature and cannot be manipulated, this makes it difficult for cybercriminals to access and gain control over the information. The information in a blockchain is also stored in a distributed manner, which really helps to keep private data from being leaked and hacked. As discussed earlier, the major problem with the current IoT ecosystem is a centralized client-server model without any standard security architecture, which makes the system vulnerable to a single point of failure. These problems can be addressed through blockchain technology by distributed decision-making capability to a consensus-based shared network of devices.

1.4.1 Major Challenges Adopting Blockchain in IoT

A few major challenges that need to be considered while designing IoT architecture in conjunction with a blockchain ledger are discussed below.

- **Scalability:** Scalability is one of the major challenges in IoT, that is, how to handle a large network of sensors that produce huge amounts of data, and how this data can be processed with lower latency. It is always necessary to define a clear data model before executing the model in real time so that productivity can be obtained easily. As the number of devices is growing day by day in an IoT network, the existing centralized model will turn into a bottleneck in authenticating, authorizing, and providing connectivity to different nodes. Data transactions in IoT networks are done across multiple devices. The owners and administrators are from different organizations, which makes it very hard to find out the source of any data leakages caused by any cybercriminals. In IoT, multiple stakeholders are involved, and the ownership of the data is not always known.

- **Security:** Security is a major concern in IoT networks as it involves the devices on a large scale. Many IoT devices carry default passwords during manufacturing, which makes the attackers an easy target for Distributed Denial of Service (DDoS) attacks. For instance, in a DDoS attack, a central server receives multiple requests at a time from different compromised systems which causes a denial of service for the authorized users of the targeted system. Weak password-protected IoT devices create an opportunity for cybercriminals to exploit the devices and perform DDoS attacks. In recent years, a number of DDoS attacks have taken place at the organization as well as individual levels.

- **Network privacy and transaction confidentiality:** The privacy of the transaction history of IoT networks cannot be easily granted on public blockchains. The reason is that one can interpret the identities of users or devices by analyzing the transaction patterns through the public keys. Organizations should recognize their privacy requirements to check whether private blockchains or hybrid blockchain could satisfy their requirement.

- **Sensors:** In general, sensors are used in almost all IoT devices. Maintaining the integrity of IoT devices is the major issue so that they cannot be altered by external influences. This can secure a safe environment for data recording and transactions.

1.4.2 Advantages of using Blockchain in IoT

Blockchain is an emerging technology that involves secure transactions and interactions. Blockchain and IoT-integrated solutions enable machine-to-machine transactions by keeping records of every transaction made across a network. These two technologies together offer many potential benefits and permit smart devices to operate autonomously without any assistance from any centralized control. They are not conflicting technologies, rather, they complement each other. IoT devices are empowered by blockchain to enhance transparency and security in IoT ecosystems. For example, smart contracts are automatically carried out when specific conditions are satisfied. Further, monitoring the environmental conditions or any smart applications that support specific IoT processes includes private data like user locations and business data. These processes when embedded with the IoT devices must be encrypted before being sent to the servers for data analysis, for instance, streaming Box-TZ provides security. Another concern is that even if data is secured during transmission, data is stored after the decryption process. The reason is that the system assumes that only authentic users can access the system and obtain IoT data. However, in the current scenario, many systems are hacked and their private info is leaked. In the current situation, it is better to (a) store encrypted data without decrypting it for security purposes and (b) put requests on encrypted data. The extended version of IoT still poses many issues regarding vulnerabilities and governance in various sectors related to policy, standards, quality of information, retention, privacy, and security. So, by integrating blockchain into IoT, many advantages can be obtained, which are discussed below.

- The distributed ledger in a blockchain system is **tamper-proof**; thus, it eliminates the necessity for a trust factor among the involved parties. The amount of data generated by IoT devices cannot be controlled by a single organization.
- **Blockchain-protected** IoT data embeds another layer of security into the IoT network. So, hackers need to cross one extra layer in order to get access to the network, and it is nearly impossible for the hackers to overwrite the existing data records due to robust encryption.
- **Transparency** is another feature of blockchain that allows anyone who is authorized to access the network to keep records of past transactions. This provides an authentic way to find out the data leakage source and take early corrective measures.
- It is possible to have **fast processing of transactions** and connectivity among a huge number of devices through blockchain. It is viewed that distributed ledger technology could provide a feasible solution to process a large number of transactions.
- IoT companies will benefit from blockchain applications by eliminating the overheads required for IoT gateway processing in terms of traditional protocol, hardware, communication costs, etc.
- Smart contract is an agreement between two parties, normally stored in the blockchain. It has an added feature of execution of contractual arrangements among stakeholders when a certain condition is satisfied. For example, smart contracts can authorize payments automatically without any human presence when certain conditions are reached to provide the service.

1.5   Use Cases of a Few Current Blockchain-IoT Groups

The integrated technology of smart chips and sensors is evolving rapidly, making the device portable and applicable for real-time communications. The growing number of IoT devices and connections susceptible to cybercrimes has provoked the development of blockchain technology. The combination of IoT and blockchain has a wide potential to ensure transparency and security, thus having a huge impact on business processes. The combined opinion of blockchain protocol developers and IoT device developers indicates that there is a good match for both technologies. Some current blockchain-IoT companies and their use cases are described below.

- **Chain of Things (CoT)** was designed by a group of scientists in connection with IoT hardware manufacturing and blockchain applications. Chain of Things is a research lab and venture studio that is dedicated to investigating the fundamental problems associated with IoT and blockchain companies through joint ventures, corporate partnerships, etc. for effective futuristic applications. CoT investigates the best possible use cases where blockchain technology can provide security for any type of IoT-related (environmental, industrial, and humanitarian) applications. As per our knowledge, an integrated blockchain and IoT hardware solution known as "Maru" is developed by CoT to address security, the identity of the device from birth, and interoperability issues.
- **IOTA** is a distributed ledger designed to record the transaction execution between machines and connected devices in IoT ecosystems. Tangle is a system of groups of nodes that confirms the transactions, M2M communication, and quantum-resistant data. Tangle is the key feature of IOTA that claims that the execution is faster than cryptocurrency and provides a promising infrastructure for IoT devices to process large amounts of data.
- **Riddle & Code** works on the blend between IoT devices and distributed ledger networks. It offers both patented hardware and software solutions with machines in the IoT domain by assigning a "trusted digital identity" to each machine or IoT device. It provides the highest security standards for blockchains in smart logistics and supply chain management.
- **Modum.io** integrates IoT sensors with blockchain technology to maintain data integrity for transactions involving physical products. Modum offers digital supply chain monitoring and analytics solutions that are easy to use and handle a wide range of applications.

1.5.1 Companies That Use Smart Packaging

Several companies use intelligent packing schemes in order to keep the product safe for a long period.

- **Amcor:** Amcor is a leading intelligent packaging company that aims to package anything from food, beverages, and household items to pharmaceuticals. Amcor is committed to protecting products, extending their shelf life, and reducing waste. They have Australia's first advanced recycling facilities.
- **Ball Corporation:** Ball Corporation serves metal packaging techs for foods, household items, beverages, and many more for both government and commercial clients. They focus on creating products that are environmentally friendly, and decomposable, and have added a few features to preserve food freshness.
- **Crown Holdings:** Crown Holdings is a leading food packaging company that is committed to enhancing the customer experience. They have developed loads of food and beverage packaging techniques to create a compelling brand, specifically, they use sustainable metal packaging to preserve perishable items in the safest possible way.

1.6 Conclusion and Open Research Issues

This chapter presents an open discussion on IoT 2.0, the correlation between IoT and big data, and the role of blockchain over IoT in maintaining security and privacy. In summary, IoT and blockchain are both emerging technologies with huge potential, but there are several technical issues and security concerns to adopt worldwide. Many issues are discussed in this chapter, and many still-hidden issues need to be extracted while implementing real-time systems. Several companies in the market already started working on integrating the two technologies, as together they offer a way to lessen the security and associated business risks. We discuss here a few open research issues that need to be addressed.

1. How to guarantee data privacy and security in IoT? Is the blockchain only a potential solution for IoT security?
2. How blockchain can be adopted with IoT on a global scale?
3. How can ML techniques be more intelligent to achieve context awareness and how to avoid overfitting during the process of training patterns?
4. Which big data analytics requires ML application?

REFERENCES

1. Y. Zhang, "Technology framework of the Internet of Things and its application," in Proc. Int. Conf. Electr. Control Eng., Sep. 2011, pp. 109–112.
2. V. Cisco, "*Cisco visual networking index: Forecast and trends, 2017–2022*," Cisco, San Jose, CA, USA, White Paper, 2018, Vol. 1.
3. Z. Zhou, S. Yu, W. Chen, and X. Chen, "CE-IoT: Cost-effective cloud-edge resource provisioning for heterogeneous IoT applications," *IEEE. Internet Things. J.*, 2020, https://doi.org/10.1109/jiot.2020.2994308
4. G. A. Akpakwu, B. J. Silva, G. P. Hancke, and A. M. Abu-Mahfouz, "A survey on 5G networks for the Internet of Things: Communication technologies and challenges," *IEEE Access*, vol. 6, pp. 3619–3647, 2018.
5. Samsung. (2019). IoT 2.0: The next phase of SmartThings engagement and growth. Youtube. Accessed: Sep. 16, 2020. [Online]. Available: https://www.youtube.com/watch?v=8hGkB6AQA38
6. G. Sun, V. Chang, S. Guan, M. Ramachandran, J. Li, and D. Liao, "Big data and Internet of Things_Fusion for different services and its impacts," *Future Gener. Comput. Syst.*, vol. 86, pp. 1368–1370, Sep. 2018.
7. Techiexpert. (2017). *What is coming in IoT 2.0?* Techiexpert. Accessed: Sep. 16, 2020. [Online]. Available: https://www.techiexpert.com/what-iscoming-in-iot-2-0/
8. J. Goldfein. (2019). *The Internet of Things 2.0_the technology revolution*. Mercury. Accessed: Sep. 16, 2020. [Online]. Available: https://mercury.one/online-business/internet-things-2-0-technologyrevo%lution/
9. D. Litwin. (2020). *Industrial IoT: How IoT has evolved and moved into the IoT 2.0 era*. MarketScale. Accessed: Sep. 16, 2020. [Online]. Available: https://marketscale.com/industries/industrial-iot/iot-2-0-era/
10. J. Gomez. (2020). *IoT 2.0: The Intelligence of Things*. Koombea. Accessed: Sep. 16, 2020. [Online]. Available: https://www.koombea.com/blog/iot-2-0-the-intelligence-of-things/
11. J. Carter. (2017). *A closer look at the Internet of Things 2.0 and Why it's Inevitable*. TechRadar. Accessed: Sep. 16, 2020. [Online]. Available: https://www.techradar.com/news/a-closer-look-at-the-internet-of-things-20-and-why-its-inevitable
12. Web Summit. (2018). IoT2.0. Youtube. Accessed: Sep. 16, 2020. [Online]. Available: https://www.youtube.com/watch?v=00K0AWbMe_U
13. Ian Zhou et al., "Internet of Things 2.0: Concepts, applications, and future directions," *IEEE Access*, 2021. doi:10.1109/ACCESS.2021.3078549
14. S. Nativi, A. Kotsev, P. Scudo, K. Pogorzelska, I. Vakalis, A. D. Benetta, and A. Perego, "IoT 2.0 and the Internet of transformation," publications of_ce Eur. Union, Luxembourg, Tech. Rep. JRC120372, 2020.
15. S. Li, L. Da Xu, and S. Zhao, "5G Internet of Things: A survey," *J. Ind. Inf. Integr.*, vol. 10, pp. 1–9, Jun. 2018.
16. D. Lukač, "The fourth ICT-based industrial revolution 'industry 4.0'— HMI and the case of CAE/CAD innovation with eplan p8," in Proc. 23rd Telecommun. Forum Telfor (TELFOR), Belgrade, Serbia, Nov. 2015, pp. 835–838.

17. M. Maier, M. Chowdhury, B. P. Rimal, and D. P. Van, "The tactile internet: Vision, recent progress, and open challenges," *IEEE Commun. Mag.*, vol. 54, no. 5, pp. 138–145, May 2016.
18. G. P. Fettweis, "5G and the future of IoT," in Proc. Conf. 42nd Eur. Solid State Circuits Conf. (ESSCIRC), Sep. 2016, pp. 21–24.
19. L. Farhan, S. T. Shukur, A. E. Alissa, M. Alrweg, U. Raza, and R. Kharel, "A survey on the challenges and opportunities of the Internet of Things (IoT)," in Proc. 11th Int. Conf. Sens. Technol. (ICST), Dec. 2017, pp. 1–5.
20. M. Z. Alom, T. M. Taha, C. Yakopcic, S. Westberg, P. Sidike, M. S. Nasrin, B. C. Van Esesn, A. A S. Awwal, and V. K. Asari, "The history began from AlexNet: A comprehensive survey on deep learning approaches," 2018, arXiv:1803.01164. [Online]. Available: http://arxiv.org/abs/1803.01164
21. S. Li, L. Da Xu, and S. Zhao, "5G Internet of Things: A survey," *J. Ind. Inf. Integr.*, vol. 10, pp. 1–9, Jun. 2018.
22. M. Abbas. (2018). IoT 2.0: Revolutionize the Internet of Things (IoT 2.0) using blockchain. IoTWorld. Accessed: Sep. 16, 2020. [Online]. Available: https://iotworld.co/2018/01/iot-2-0-revolutionize-internet-ofthings-us%ing-blockchain/
23. H. Ramazanali, A. Mesodiakaki, A. Vinel, and C. Verikoukis, "Survey of user association in 5G HetNets," in Proc. 8th IEEE Latin-Amer. Conf. Commun. (LATINCOM), Nov. 2016, pp. 1–6
24. A. Morgado, K. M. S. Huq, S. Mumtaz, and J. Rodriguez, "A survey of 5G technologies: Regulatory, standardization and industrial perspectives," *Digit. Commun. Netw.*, vol. 4, no. 2, pp. 87–97, Apr. 2018.

2

A Comprehensive Survey of Blockchain in IoT

Konstantina Banti and Christos Roumeliotis
University of Western Macedonia, Kozani, Greece

Peristera Baziana
University of Thessaly, Lamia, Greece

Malamati Louta
University of Western Macedonia, Kozani, Greece

2.1 Introduction

Recently, one of the most important technological advances of the 21st century has been the Internet of Things (IoT), which has received significant attention from society, industry, and academia. IoT is a term used to describe the network of devices equipped with sensors, software, and other technologies for data transmission over the Internet without the need for human interaction [1]. IoT offers sensing and computing capabilities to connect a wide range of things to the Internet, such as home appliances, cars, and lights. IoT devices can share all their data for the deployment of innovative services and applications that will improve people's lives. The number of devices connected to the Internet has significantly increased as a result of the IoT's rapid development. Some of the most prevalent IoT applications include smart homes, healthcare, smart cities, traffic monitoring, agriculture, smart grid, smart water, manufacturing, and transportation. These applications acquire data from heterogenous sources that produce huge amounts of heterogeneous data generated at high speed that should be analyzed, interpreted, utilized, and visualized in real time.

However, the complexity of IoT systems, the large volumes and heterogeneity of data, the massive number of devices, and the diversity of IoT devices and systems are increasing the challenges and limitations [2, 3] such as efficient data management and poor interoperability since it is difficult to exchange data among IoT systems due to their heterogeneous nature. Another challenge is that IoT devices are resource-constrained, with sensors or actuators having limited computing, communication, storage, and battery power resources. As a result of this challenge, IoT devices are vulnerable to malicious attacks [3]. It is extremely difficult to maintain data security because of the heterogeneity and complexity of IoT systems. Finally, scalability and reliability of IoT systems should be efficiently addressed.

To address the aforementioned IoT challenges, blockchain technology is thought to be a promising approach. Most IoT systems are built using centralized architectures, making them vulnerable to a variety of security and privacy issues. A decentralized, blockchain-based approach has the potential to address many of the issues associated with the centralized method. In cases where centralized architectures are used to manage sensitive data, privacy is especially at risk. Due to its inherent characteristics, blockchain technology is an ideal option for developing a secure and decentralized framework for IoT systems. Blockchain enhances IoT's interoperability, privacy, security, reliability, and scalability. This study focuses on how blockchain technology can be used to handle the key aspects and constraints of the IoT. Blockchain has a number of key characteristics including

DOI:10.1201/9781003326236-2

decentralization, immutability, and transparency without requiring a reliable third party. Blockchain is a distributed digital ledger that records and verifies transactions. Transactions are essentially immutable as they cannot be subsequently altered or removed. Also, blockchain is shared and synchronized across all involved nodes. A blockchain ensures data traceability by attaching a timestamp to every transaction. Blockchain offers a high level of encryption that can ensure data integrity and reliability.

Numerous research papers that have been published discussing the integration of blockchain and IoT. In the study by Dai et al. [3], the authors investigate blockchain and IoT integration, present blockchain-based IoT applications, and discuss the opportunities and open research directions of blockchain and IoT integration. In particular, Atlam et al. [4] outline blockchain and IoT integration, concentrating on the benefits and challenges arising from this integration. In the study by Alamri et al. [5], the authors outline several challenges and future directions of blockchain and IoT integration. In the study by Ferrag etal. [6], the authors present application domains, open research issues, and potential future research directions on blockchain and IoT integration regarding security and privacy preservation. Reyna et al. [7] present blockchain-based IoT applications and platforms and discusses IoT and blockchain integration, along with its advantages and disadvantages. Zafar et al. [8] analyzes the advantages and challenges of combining blockchain and IoT, as well as their solutions, and lists some of the most prominent blockchain-related IoT applications. In the study by Fernández-Caramés etal. [9], the current issues and potential improvements are described in detail as well as blockchain-based IoT applications are presented. In the study by Cui et al. [10], blockchain applications in IoT are presented, the utilization of blockchain for security is introduced, and the challenges and limitations associated with blockchain in the IoT are presented. Abdelmaboud et al. [11] present blockchain-based IoT applications and platforms. Also, it surveys recent literature and presents benefits, limitations, and future trends of the integration of blockchain with IoT. Finally, in [12], the authors discuss on objectives and challenges of blockchain and IoT integration and present recent blockchain-based IoT applications. Unlike the presented works, the focus of this study is the utilization of blockchain technology in the IoT to address data quality and reliability issues.

The key contributions of this chapter are as follows:

1. Review of blockchain technology and analysis of its unique concepts
2. Examine the challenges and benefits of blockchain and IoT integration
3. Analyze of current blockchain-based IoT platforms and applications
4. Survey of state-of-the-art works on blockchain and IoT integration.

The rest of the chapter is organized as follows. The blockchain technology is introduced in Section 2.2 and its key features are analyzed. In Section 2.3, the integration of IoT and blockchain is addressed and the benefits as well as the challenges of this integration are discussed. In Section 2.4, we present the blockchain-based IoT platforms, and in Section 2.5 the IoT-blockchain applications. Section 2.6 discusses how the blockchain can address issues related to data quality and reliability in IoT systems. Our conclusions and directions for the future are presented in Section 2.7.

2.2 Blockchain

Blockchain was originally designed to timestamp digital documents in a way that prevents tampering or backdating. However, blockchain started to gain importance in 2008 with the introduction of the Bitcoin cryptocurrency system [13], which allows online payments to be sent directly among parties without the involvement of a financial institution. Since then, blockchain technology has been one of the leading innovations in the financial industry and has revolutionized the way financial transactions operate. Blockchain is essentially a distributed ledger, a decentralized database, and there is no central authority in the network. Generally, it supports transactions among untrusted

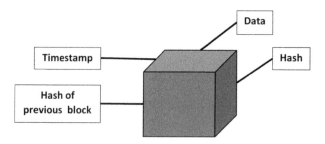

FIGURE 2.1   Block structure.

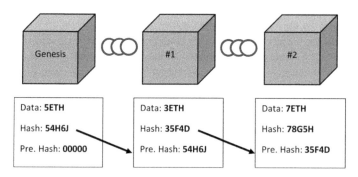

FIGURE 2.2   Blockchain structure.

entities and aims to provide security, transparency, traceability, and immutability to transactions as well as data integrity.

A blockchain transaction represents an action initiated by a participant and is the minimum fundamental data unit in the blockchain [10]. Blockchain is based on asymmetric cryptography. Thus, each entity has a private and a public key, which it uses to produce a digital signature. Each transaction is authorized by the sender's digital signature (private key) [14], which authenticates the transaction and makes it impossible for other users to change the data without a specific digital signature. The distributed ledger stores every transaction that requires confirmation by the majority of participants. As transactions are carried out, a blockchain expands continuously. Specifically, blockchain stores all the transaction information between two parties into a data structure called block. Once transaction data has been recorded in a block, it cannot be changed, manipulated, or forged. Each block contains the following elements [15], as shown in Figure 2.1:

1. Hash: A unique stamp or fingerprint used to identify each block and all of its contents.
2. Hash of previous block: Because each block (except the first block) carries the header of the previous block, the chain becomes very secure as it prevents any block from being altered or a block inserted between two existing blocks. As a result, if someone attempts to tamper with one block, this will require tampering with all the previous blocks.
3. Timestamp: Contains the block creation time to track the block's creation and update time.
4. Data: The transaction data. The data depends on the service and the application.

Blocks include certain numbers of transactions with cryptographic hashing and are linked together in chronological order, forming a chain. Blocks that are validated are automatically appended to the chain's end. One block is linked to another block with reference to its fragmentation. A blockchain is formed when each existing block has a valid reference to the block that preceded it. The initial block is called the genesis block, which lacks a parent block. Figure 2.2 shows how blocks are linked together in a blockchain.

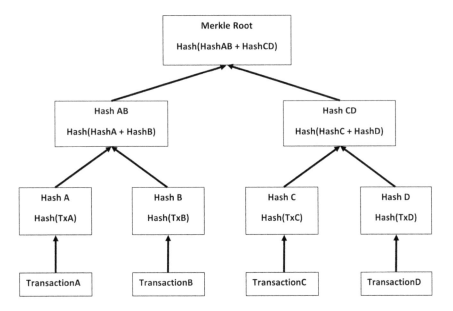

FIGURE 2.3 Merkle tree structure.

Blockchain transactions are organized and stored in blocks in a tree-like manner known as the Merkle tree, named after its creator, Ralph Merkle [16]. It is a binary tree structure formed by hash pointers. It allows all transactions to be hashed/linked and provides proof of membership in a time-effective way. A Merkle tree groups transactions into pairs. The hash is calculated for each pair and stored in its parent node. The parent nodes are paired, and their hashes are recorded one level up the tree as shown in Figure 2.3. Until the tree's root is reached, this process continues. To correctly build the Merkle tree, the number of leaf nodes must be even. The Merkle tree is very important to the blockchain because without it, the data would have to be transferred across the network to be verified. Merkle trees also allow transactions to be compared and verified with sustainable processing power and bandwidth [17, 18].

2.2.1 Consensus Algorithms

As aforementioned, each new block can only be added to the blockchain if the majority of the network's nodes agree to its inclusion, that is, if a consensus is reached among the users of the blockchain, as shown in Figure 2.4. Mining is the process of validating transactions by specialized nodes known as miners. Using their computing power, miners must solve difficult cryptographic mathematical equations. A consensus algorithm then determines the data to be added to a new block [9]. Consensus is an extremely important concept for the blockchain. It is essentially a mechanism for defining the conditions under which blocks are validated and included in a blockchain [19]. The most commonly used consensus algorithms include Proof of Work (PoW) and Proof of Stake (PoS) presented below.

Proof of Work: PoW is commonly used on blockchain networks like Bitcoin. Each block of transactions has a specific hash. To confirm the block, a miner must calculate a hash value lower than or equal to the block's value. As soon as a node reaches the desired value, it sends the block to the other nodes, who then confirm the accuracy of the hash. Once a block is authenticated, other nodes add it to their own blockchain. The first miner who adds a new block after it has been verified by 51% of the network is rewarded with cryptocurrency for his work. PoW consumes a significant amount of energy [20–22] as there is an excessive amount of computational overhead involved in mining blockchains, which prevents all nodes from participating.

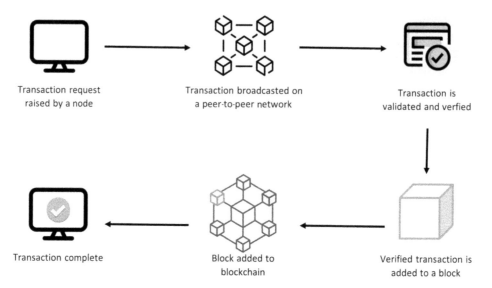

FIGURE 2.4   Transaction lifecycle on blockchain.

Proof of Stake: PoS is another type of consensus mechanism for achieving distributed consensus. The concept for this came from the need to handle the PoW issue of high-energy consumption and intensive computation. Peercoin was the first cryptocurrency to implement PoS, followed by Nextcoin, Crave, and Ethereum [23]. The algorithm's underlying concept is straightforward: instead of requiring miners to demonstrate how much work they have completed, miners must demonstrate how much stake they have in the system, and the block designer is chosen depending on the stakes that each miner owns. However, this selection process is unfair because the wealthiest miners can always take over the blockchain. Currently, many proof-based algorithms are reported in literature and articles to address consensus, speed, scalability, and cost problems [24].

2.2.2   Smart Contracts

Smart contracts are a combination of user interfaces and protocols that enable secure transactions on a blockchain over a network of computers. The object-oriented language "Solidity" that Gavin Wood proposed in 2014 is used to write smart contracts. [25]. A smart contract essentially works like a real legal contract in the sense that until a certain set of conditions issued by the creator of the smart contract are met, the outcome of a transaction by the parties involved will not begin or be completed. Only a transaction can initiate the execution of a smart contract. However, one contract can call for another, which can call for another, and so on. This is the so-called interaction between smart contracts in the blockchain where they can call other contract functions and are still able to create and develop other contracts (e.g., token issuance). Figure 2.5 shows the workflow of a smart contract.

To make it clearer, the example of an Ethereum-decentralized platform [26] will be explained since it is the first project that used smart contracts. The Ethereum blockchain acts as a transactional state machine. Smart contracts are the method by which developers interact with the Ethereum Virtual Machine (EVM). Ethereum uses the EVM runtime environment, which allows arbitrarily complex computations to be performed. Ethereum nodes validate blocks and run the EVM, that is, run code triggered by transactions. There are two distinct account types in Ethereum: Contract Accounts (CA), which contain EVM code and are controlled by the EVM code, and Externally Owned Accounts (EOA), which are managed by their Private Key but cannot contain EVM code [27]. Every system, in the context of security, must verify the sender's identity so that the transactions are valid between the sender and the recipient. A transaction is a specially formatted data structure signed by an EOA and transmitted to a node on the blockchain.

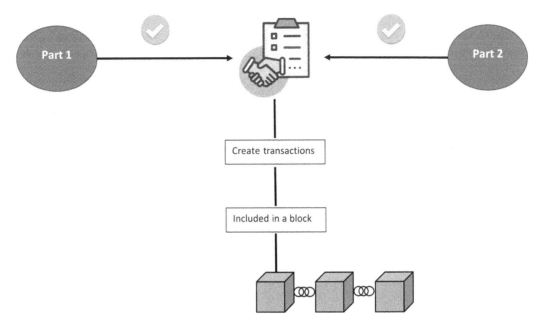

FIGURE 2.5 Smart contract workflow.

In particular, Ethereum supports smart contracts, which are programs that run as planned without the risk of downtime, fraud, or outside interference. Because all parts of the transaction are done on the blockchain and smart contracts are fully automated, no third party is required to maintain or guarantee its integrity. This is the trustless factor demonstrated in Ethereum's architecture but also in many other projects such as Solana [28] and Tezos [29]. Involved parties need not worry about the status of their funds, as all the factors of transactions or transfer of funds are agreed before the start of the transaction; therefore, only if all the parameters of the transaction are met it is completed. Otherwise, all the money will be returned to their respective parties [30].

The Ethereum blockchain uses the PoW algorithm. PoW enables the decentralized Ethereum network to reach an agreement on account balances, the sequence of transactions, etc. However, Bitcoin and Ethereum's PoW networks have slowed probabilistic time to finality and do not scale well. New solutions have already been implemented to reduce blockchain transaction time and cost. Ethereum has already executed the merge (Ethereum 2.0) in September 2022, according to the official website [26], which will be the most significant upgrade in the history of the Ethereum blockchain as PoW will be replaced by PoS.

A very important feature and prerequisite in blockchain is whether it can scale. The volume of transactions a blockchain can verify each second is a common metric for determining its scalability. For instance, a trading block on the Ethereum blockchain is intended every 12 to 14 seconds on average and can only hold a certain number of transactions [31]. This means that the frequency of transactions is bound by the time required to create the blocks. Each blockchain transaction consumes gas fees, and each block has a limit called the block gas limit. The smart contract developer should be aware that better contract development planning can lead to transactions that require less gas to execute, thus creating space for more transactions to be placed on a block, while at the same time it will be cheaper for the end user to execute a transaction.

To comprehend the blockchain's concept of gas better, we need to think about the scenario of a malicious user attempting to create network congestion. An attacker could maliciously flood the network with computer-intensive transactions and force the nodes to perform costly operations for extended periods. Thus, all the nodes in the blockchain process unnecessary transactions and contract executions. Ethereum uses gas to enter a cost to execute the calculations of the executed transactions something like the fees that the sender must pay to complete a transaction and record it in the blockchain. Each gas unit costs a certain amount of gas price which is determined by the person performing the transaction [32].

2.2.3 Blockchain Types

There are various blockchain types which can be classified as follows:

1. Public or permissionless: There is a low barrier to entry, and they have full transparency and immutability. This type of blockchain is frequently used for anonymous transactions. All network nodes should be able to access it and validate it. Every node on a public blockchain network has the ability to verify transactions and keep a local copy of the blockchain. However, the system has a slow speed for transaction validation because it needs to perform a certain amount of computation to guarantee the creation of an unbiased block. An example of a public blockchain is Ethereum.

2. Private or permissioned: Participation is limited based on the rules set by a group of operators. Usually, a single entity has control over a private blockchain, and authorized nodes are given access and transaction verification rights via a central controller. There are additional privacy features and immutability is not absolute. A permissioned network is created when only authorized nodes can access specific blockchain transactions or take part in the process of publishing new blocks. This greatly enhances transaction privacy, and decentralization is under the control of the organization. Examples of a private blockchain are Hyperledger Fabric and Ripple.

3. Consortium blockchain: A semi-decentralized type in which several organizations oversee a blockchain. Similar to a private blockchain, it is also maintained on a permissioned network. The main distinction is that a consortium blockchain involves numerous entities that verify transactions. The issue here is that there may not be complete trust between these organizations. However, they collaborate by adapting the consensus algorithm in accordance with their level of mutual trust. Examples of this type of blockchain are R3 and Energy Web Foundation (Energy Web Chain).

4. Hybrid blockchain: This is a blockchain that combines both private and public types. A hybrid blockchain is not open to everyone, but its members can decide who can participate in it or what transactions will be publicly disclosed, thus providing blockchain features such as integrity, transparency, and security. Due to the flexibility of this type of blockchain, users can quickly link a private blockchain to a number of public blockchains. An example of this type of blockchain is Dragonchain, and XinFin a hybrid blockchain developed based on Ethereum (public) and Quorum (private).

2.2.4 Blockchain x.0

The blockchain created by Nakamoto was a completely decentralized distributed ledger of Bitcoin (the first cryptocurrency in history) financial transactions. Further advancements have been made along the way to boost transaction speeds while preserving information integrity by developing rule sets unique to each application. The foundation of blockchain technology is Blockchain 1.0: it all started with Bitcoin. Blockchain 1.0 is used for financial transactions like currency exchange and transfer. Blockchain 2.0: smart contracts used for bonds and loans. Blockchain 3.0: decentralized enterprise-level applications. Blockchain 3.0, combined with the smart contracts of Blockchain 2.0, expands its reach beyond the financial system to include more industries and sectors. As a result, it addresses all facets of human social life, including IoT, energy, healthcare, social management, philanthropy, and public welfare. [33]. Also, there are reports of the advent of Blockchain 4.0, which will have some improvements to blockchain 3.0; however, some features of version 4.0 remain unclear [34, 35].

2.3   IoT and Blockchain Integration

Combining blockchain and IoT can greatly enhance the success of new business models and distributed applications. Many issues could be solved by a decentralized approach to the IoT. The costs associated with establishing and maintaining massive data centers as well as the distributed computing and storage requirements of the hundreds of millions of devices that make up IoT networks will be greatly reduced by using a peer-to-peer communication model for processing inter-device transactions. This will shield the network from the failure of a single node, thus preventing the network's collapse [36].

Blockchain technology is the missing key component in addressing privacy, scalability, reliability, and trust concerns related to the IoT. IoT solutions can utilize blockchain technology to enable reliable, secure messaging between connected devices on a network. Studies and experts have shown that blockchain can ensure system security and reliability in IoT. The vast majority of interactive devices used in today's IoT systems use centralized servers for data storage, authentication, and analysis [37]. Blockchain would offer a decentralized solution for the IoT.

In contrast to centralized architectures, which have made significant advancements to the growth of the IoT but do not provide transparency on where and how the information they collect will be used, blockchain can enhance the IoT by offering a trusted sharing service with trusted and traceable information [7]. The IoT optimizes manual processes, acquiring volumes of data that enable unprecedented knowledge, and facilitates the development of intelligent applications that improve life quality and management. By passing the data through the blockchain, an immutable record of interactions is recorded, making it possible to trace all selected interactions due to the fact that their details can be searched.

2.3.1   Benefits of IoT and Blockchain Integration

Blockchain and IoT integration has numerous advantages, as illustrated in Figure 2.6. These advantages can be summed up as follows:

- **Decentralization and scalability**: A decentralized blockchain network does not have a central authority. Thus, blockchain eliminates central servers and central points of failure but also

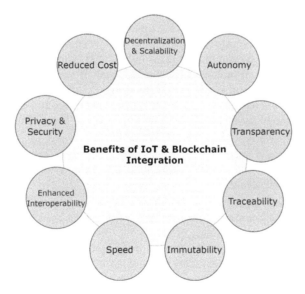

FIGURE 2.6   Benefits of IoT-blockchain integration.

improves fault tolerance and scalability. Through the use of all participating nodes' resources and the elimination of many-to-one networks, blockchain ensures scalability and robustness. Individual nodes are used by distributed ledgers to record, synchronize, as well as share transactions in every ledger (instead of keeping the data centrally). Additionally, blockchain is based on nodes, each of which keeps a local copy of the ledger and can independently verify transactions before they are included in a new block. A transaction can only be approved and entered into the blockchain if consensus is reached among the majority of nodes. This ensures that control and decision-making are distributed evenly across a network to eliminate the possibility of bias or misjudgment. Consequently, the blockchain will offer an IoT device platform that is secure.

- **Autonomy**: Smart contracts enable transactions to be completed automatically and without human intervention. IoT nodes will be able to execute smart contracts by simply sending transactions to their addresses. Each network node independently and automatically executes each smart contract. Smart contracts are integrated into the blockchain and are straightforward programs that execute when specific criteria are met. Smart contracts enable the automated execution of multi-step processes in the IoT, opening the door for new solutions based on automated transactions initiated by IoT devices. Based on the results of a smart contract's execution, each node that takes part in it updates its status. Smart contracts add value to automation and provide transaction security, thus strengthening the position of decentralized applications in the blockchain.

- **Transparency**: Blockchain makes data open – transparent. Every user has equal access to and interaction in a public blockchain like Bitcoin or Ethereum, and every node has access to the stored transactions and can confirm the committed transactions. Every transaction that has been verified and added to a blockchain block is accessible to all users. This does not imply that anyone can see the content of a transaction because the owner's private key protects it. The reliability, trustworthiness, and transparency of data on the blockchain are improved.

- **Traceability**: Every transaction on the blockchain is marked with a timestamp that reflects the moment the block was created. Blockchain stores all of the previous transactions, which are all traceable. Through the examination of timestamped blockchain data, nodes can quickly confirm and identify the source of historical blocks.

- **Immutability**: IoT data is more secure, thanks to blockchain technology because it can be distributed and kept immutable over time. Also, the blockchain can maintain an unchanged history of smart devices on IoT. Immutable means that the blockchain is a permanent and unchanging network. A blockchain is made up of sequentially linked blocks, where each link functions as the previous block's reverse hash point. Any changes made to the previous block render all newly created blocks invalid. This means that every user on the network cannot edit, change, or delete a transaction. Since the root hash of the Merkle tree contains the hash of every transaction, any modifications to transactions result in the creation of a new Merkle root. As a result, any misrepresentation can be quickly identified, and data leaks can be quickly identified and remedied by identifying the specific source. Thus, blockchains' immutability guarantees the reliability of IoT.

- **Speed**: Blockchain-based peer-to-peer systems allow messaging between devices and coordination among billions of connected devices but also make peer-to-peer messaging faster than the current IoT core structure.

- **Privacy and Security**: Blockchain can maintain a certain degree of privacy by anonymizing blockchain addresses. Systems that use advanced cryptography to hide transaction information from non-transacting parties already exist [38–40]. Bitcoin utilizes pseudonyms to hide the identity of an individual behind a random address; however, research has shown that this is not always a reliable privacy preservation measure [41, 42]. Blockchain is based on asymmetric cryptography and the fragmentation of any information and its recording in a block connected to the next and the previous. Any block of data cannot be changed or altered unless the fragmentation of that block and all preceding blocks has been recalculated, which is nearly impossible. Because the blockchain can store data on IoT devices, this cryptographic structure improves the security of IoT systems. Asymmetric encryption, which necessitates the use of a private and public key pair, ensures that data can only be accessed by the designated receiver that controls the private key. As a result, privacy is achieved only if the data are controlled by the entity that owns the private key. Blockchain would increase the privacy of personal information by using cryptographic algorithms. Additionally, blockchain enables decentralized, trusted IoT device authentication and authorization, and participants in large-scale IoT systems can uniquely identify each device. It is also possible to identify data provided by a device. Smart contracts can validate device message exchanges as blockchain transactions, securing communications between devices. Due to the network's decentralized structure, the system is also extremely resilient to failures and malicious attacks. Finally, consensus mechanisms are used to implement security procedures and confirm that the blockchain protocol works in its entirety. Consensus is an automated process to ensure that there is only a single valid copy of a record shared by all nodes. Nodes may not trust each other, but they can trust the algorithm running at the core of the network to make decisions. Consensus mechanisms are used to maintain data consistency.

- **Reduced Cost**: IoT systems demand high costs for infrastructure deployment and maintenance, and continuous network upgrades to support the connectivity of IoT devices. In contrast, blockchain, with its decentralized structure eliminates the need for such continuous upgrades and unnecessary costs.
- **Enhanced Interoperability**: The blockchain can also improve IoT interoperability by enabling communication between these devices and physical systems.

Thus, the blockchain and IoT integration is crucial as it adds value to the entire process of exchanging and storing information, since blockchain provides reliability, immutability, scalability, transparency, and security of transactions [36, 43].

2.3.2 Challenges in IoT and Blockchain Integration

Nevertheless, blockchain and IoT, like anything new, face various problems that in some cases their composition brings a headache to the creators of applications and services. However, blockchain and IoT can offer many benefits as long as the problem that most IoT devices lack cryptographic, computing, and storage capabilities for blockchain use is properly addressed [44].

The blockchain is built on the general principle that all transactions are verified and validated within the blocks, preventing errors because the blocks are connected. This mechanism requires transaction records to be maintained and stored by all entities that participate in a blockchain network. A new entity joining the blockchain network must download all previous blocks. However, this feature is becoming an obstacle to the growth of blockchain technology in IoT. The majority of devices have limited capacity for processing and storing blockchain transactions, and the connections between IoT nodes are constantly dynamic, making it nearly impossible to maintain or retrieve history blocks. In this section, we will briefly outline the challenges of integrating blockchain and IoT [7, 45].

A. Security

IoT faces serious security issues due to centralized infrastructure that prove to be fatal as it is resistant to attacks and internal leaks. As a decentralized technology, blockchain's main advantage is that it reduces the need for a third party to verify the validity of transactions. In the study by Li et al. [46], the authors suggest a secure scheme for storing and protecting IoT data based on blockchain. Through the use of numerous miners, the scheme eliminates the centralized server and ensures data security. However, this is also a matter of research as security is the most significant feature of any system [47]. Given that nodes are in charge of verifying transactions and generating blocks, a 51% attack on the blockchain network is possible if some attacker nodes cooperate. Additionally, even though blockchain can guarantee that data are immutable and can track their modifications, data that enters the blockchain already corrupted remains corrupted. Many different reasons, including the environment, users, vandalism, and device failure, can lead to corrupted IoT data. Sometimes the devices' sensors and actuators, as well as the devices themselves, either fail to function properly right away, or they function properly for a while before their behavior changes as a result of a short circuit, disconnection, etc. IoT devices should first go through a thorough testing process before being integrated with blockchain, placed in the proper location, and secured against malicious acts to prevent physical damage [48–50]. They should also have techniques to detect device failures.

B. Speed and Scalability

Network scalability and speed are two major obstacles for integrated IoT-blockchain solutions. Speed and scalability are both impacted by the size of the ledger and the rate at which transactions can be processed. A blockchain's ability to scale is often measured by the number of transactions it can verify each second. For instance, Bitcoin, which uses the consensus PoW protocol to support decentralized network governance, has a limited block size of 1 megabyte and can mine a block approximately every 10 minutes as a result, the yield of transactions is bound by the frequency of new blocks and the number of transactions in them. The network is limited to seven transactions per second (TPS), so it cannot handle high transaction frequencies, and as the use of blockchain has increased recently, the issue of scalability has increased, leading to research into solutions such as rollups and other concatenation algorithms. Scalability is key to managing the explosive growth of IoT applications, which means that applications must be able to support an increased number of connected devices. This problem implies the scalability of the blockchain. Blockchain is not designed to store large amounts of data, like IoT-generated data. As the number of nodes rises, the blockchain scales poorly. This problem is very serious because many nodes are anticipated in IoT networks. In [51], the authors propose a decentralized system based on blockchain that stores and distributes access control data for the many billions of restricted devices. With the exception of IoT devices and management nodes, all entities are integrated into the blockchain. Due to the fact that most IoT devices cannot directly support blockchain technology, they do not belong in the network. The solution shows that the situation escalates smoothly because many limited networks can be interconnected and there is flexibility due to the different node management nodes distributed in the blockchain.

C. Anonymity and Privacy

With regard to blockchain, anonymity refers to a party's ability to exchange data without disclosing their off-chain identities or other transactions. For transparent access control in the IoT, Ouaddah et al. [52] suggest a new blockchain-based privacy-preserving management system that gives users ownership and control over their data. Each device connected to the blockchain network would have its own asymmetric key pair. Each blockchain user could be recognized using their public key or hash. Each user is responsible for maintaining the privacy of his private key as an attacker can use it with the public key to pose as someone or steal something. A simple example would be Bitcoin, which is partially anonymous because each address looks random but knows all transactions to and from this address. Both the recent Manhattan bust and the Colonial Pipeline hack from the previous year show that it is possible to track Bitcoin transactions. In both cases, the authorities were able to recover some of the ransom money from the attackers [53].

Transactions are recorded permanently on the blockchain and cannot be changed, as was already mentioned. The security of a user's privacy may be jeopardized by permanently storing their transaction history across all of their devices on the blockchain. Even if the transaction's content is encrypted, the frequency at which a user saves transactions can be tracked, providing insight into how IoT devices interact with one another. As a result, users may decide to exercise their right not to store data from specific IoT devices on the blockchain due to privacy concerns. It also allows the user's identity to be anonymized if, for example, multiple transactions created by the user are linked, also known as linking attack [54, 55]. However, a design principle is proposed in [56] that enables IoT devices to directly communicate with smart contracts, allowing them to alter their security settings and change the entity they serve.

D. Capacity and Storage

IoT device proliferation will undoubtedly result in a sizable volume of transactions, which will significantly increase the memory requirements of the nodes that store the ledger. Blockchain reduces the requirement for a centralized server to keep track of transactions, but the ledger must be kept on the nodes. Distributed ledgers will expand in size as the number of network nodes rises. IoT devices can produce an enormous amount of data in real time, but they have very limited computational capabilities and storage capacity. Blockchain is not designed for large-scale data storage. However, numerous data compression, normalization, and filtration techniques have been suggested in the literature for IoT data.

E. Energy Efficiency

The majority of Internet of Things (IoT) devices are battery-powered, so energy efficiency is a crucial factor in the integration of IoT and blockchain. Blockchain architectures, however, are typically energy consuming. Blockchain energy consumption is primarily influenced by two factors: (a) mining, such as PoW, wastes a tremendous amount of energy and (b) edge devices must be powered on during peer-to-peer (P2P) communication, which also consumes a considerable amount of energy. In [57], the authors suggest a lightweight consensus algorithm. IoT devices with limited computational resources can benefit from the proposed algorithm since it reduces the time it takes to compute and permits higher transactions. They also provide a ledger distribution technique that reduces the amount of memory needed by IoT devices. Also, in [58], the authors suggest a resource-efficient, lightweight blockchain system ideal for industrial IoT (IIoT) environments with limited power without compromising traceability and non-repudiation. In particular, they present a lightweight data structure to streamline broadcast content and a green consensus mechanism to lower the consumption of computing power. Finally, in [46], authors suggest a blockchain system for large-scale IoT that uses edge computing to assist with data storage management and IoT devices to carry out computations.

F. Smart Contracts

Smart contracts can be used in IoT, but there are differences in how they are integrated into IoT applications. IoT can detect and actuate via the internet. A smart contract is technically a code that contains data and functions that are stored at a particular blockchain address. Applications can listen to events that are fired by functions so they can respond to the event in the proper way. For the IoT, smart contracts can offer a secure and reliable data processing system that records and manages all of its interactions. Upon being implemented on blockchain, smart contracts become immutable. Since devices are added and removed simultaneously during run-time, smart contracts must consider the dynamic nature of IoT applications. The erratic nature of IoT data, however, poses a risk to validating smart contracts. Additionally, these contracts might become overloaded if multiple data sources are accessed. It is important that legal advisors and developers establish procedures so that there are no gaps or errors between the two technologies [59, 60].

G. Legal Issues

The Data Protection Directive is one example of a piece of legislation that significantly affects the IoT sector. Many of these laws are out-of-date, making it challenging to integrate new technologies like blockchain into existing systems. It will be more challenging to address data privacy and information management laws given that blockchain is being used in conjunction with IoT. The absence of precise financial regulations and policies regarding digital currencies or cryptocurrencies is the main barrier. The IoT space has been clouded with legal uncertainties regarding data ownership, access, and privacy, despite some nations and regulatory regimes swaying in or out of the blockchain market. It is also challenging for mechanisms to recover or restore a private key or roll back transactions in the event of an error due to the absence of regulation.

2.4   Blockchain in IoT Applications

In many cases the blockchain resolves privacy or reliability flaws in the IoT, making it appropriate for use in various scenarios such as "Smart Home," "E-Health," "Smart Agriculture," "Smart Cities," and "Energy" [61]. Below, we illustrate some use-cases of blockchain concerning IoT.

2.4.1   Energy

There have been numerous studies on the application of blockchain smart contracts in the smart grid [59, 60]. An energy consumption transparency and provenance system based on smart contracts was introduced in the study by IOTA [62]. The use of blockchain to safely monitor and record energy consumption is suggested in [80, 86] in a similar manner. Additionally, the blockchain's cryptographic algorithms and consensus mechanism guarantee the immutability of any electricity transaction that is added to it. Due to this, consumers and power companies will benefit from greater pricing transparency regarding the production and consumption of electrical energy provided by blockchain-based trading infrastructure.

2.4.2   Healthcare

IoT devices may be able to deliver patient sensory data for processing and analysis in the healthcare sector. In [63], authors suggest using blockchain smart contracts to manage medical equipment and patient data. More specifically, a remote healthcare system is presented that uses sensors to track patients' health status and stores the records on the blockchain. This guarantees the security of the privacy of healthcare data, which is very critical. Mobile devices are used in hospitals to collect and transfer data, and IoT devices play a catalytic role in remote patient monitoring [64] as they provide important information such as a person's breathing patterns, blood glucose level, blood pressure, and even patient's emotions, as mentioned in [65]. In the study by Rahman et al. [66], a blockchain-based system to manage the health of dyslexic people was suggested. The dyslexic pattern can be stored and accessed using this system in the context of information sharing for dyslexic individuals and the people who care for them. Additionally, the management of the drug supply chain makes use of blockchain and IoT because human error or malicious behavior can often lead to mistakes that cause a lot of patients to suffer or even die from taking fake medications. To ensure transparency throughout, a blockchain architecture based on IoT is used. The records of a drug's supply chain can easily be entered into the blockchain without modification and are immutable and decentralized. In [67], the authors propose the use of IoT-embedded blockchain for counterfeit pharmaceuticals and innovative drug supply chain management to avoid counterfeit drugs that negatively affect the health of patients as well as the financial situation of real producers.

2.4.3   Agriculture

IoT has recently grown to be an essential part of the modern agricultural system. In [68], a blockchain-based smart agriculture IoT framework is proposed, where IoT sensors in greenhouses serve as a local private blockchain that is centralized owned-controlled. The framework's core is a blockchain-based platform that promotes actor trust. Additionally, real-time information about crops and livestock can be transmitted using blockchain. Lastly, crop and food supply chains can be transparent and traceable using blockchain-based IoT agriculture applications [69, 70].

2.4.4   Smart Cities

The idea of smart cities is based on the concept of IoT devices that can operate autonomously. Since IoT devices will be able to interact and coordinate more easily with one another and can reliably query trusted information with blockchain, it can increase the autonomy of devices. Blockchain technology has been introduced as an IoT component to address privacy and security concerns and is coming to provide solutions to issues related to smart cities. IoT security issues are dominated by blockchain technology, enabling services like accurate data collection and secure data distribution. In [71], the authors suggest a blockchain-based smart city system to efficiently and securely sense and control IoT data. Additionally, blockchain can be used in smart transport systems to address the issue of communication and collaboration among vehicles, roadside-connected devices, and smartphones (owned by pedestrians).

2.4.5 Smart Home

Another sector that has growing demand and applications is the smart home. The demand for enhancing information technology infrastructure to ensure data privacy, security, and transparency has increased with the rise of smart home applications. The smart home network consists of various interconnected IoT devices that communicate with one another through the local network at home and with remote servers through a gateway, jeopardizing the privacy of each device. Blockchain in IoT creates new possibilities to address serious problems of privacy, security, and data integrity in smart homes [72]. In [73] research on an IoT architecture in a smart home environment using blockchain and smart contracts is described. However, some of the challenges it faces are that home IoT devices lack powerful computing capabilities and plenty of storage space, so every home serves as a local blockchain, and every IoT device has a private distributed ledge. Applications that we can distinguish in the smart home are power control, object management, user preferences, etc.

2.5 Blockchain-Based Platforms for IoT

Many blockchain platforms are widely used in various fields with the most widespread being Ethereum. In this section, we will focus more on those platforms that enable, mostly, the development of IoT applications and services.

2.5.1 Bitcoin

The original cryptocurrency and blockchain platform was Bitcoin. It has been used and is used in many aspects of the electrical world and affects most of the cryptocurrency market. Bitcoin is involved in many IoT applications in the field of financial transactions. The problem here is that Bitcoin does not have smart contracts for secure management and recording of all interactions [14].

2.5.2 Ethereum

Ethereum, on the other hand, is the second-largest blockchain open-source framework and the first to use smart contracts to develop decentralized applications. It is a flexible and adaptable platform that supports the development of applications in several different languages, including Solidity, Python, Go, and C++, thus simplifying the development of applications. The platform uses consensus mechanisms to develop and customize IoT applications while reducing the latency of blockchain approaches [74].

2.5.3 Hyperledger Fabric

An open-source platform called Hyperledger Fabric is used to create modular blockchain applications and solutions. The platform can expand across multiple components, thanks to its modular design, which also makes it a good choice for supporting various other blockchain platforms and business solutions. The foundation of Hyperledger Fabric is permissions, which guarantee data confidentiality for encrypting transactions to prevent their modification by unauthorized parties. However, associating it with IoT has numerous drawbacks and restrictions. It has poor scaling of the consent algorithms necessary to establish a dependable multi-device network of an organization, is less or only partially decentralized and more trust-sensitive [75].

2.5.4 Multichain

Multichain is an enterprise open-source platform that helps organizations build and develop blockchain applications quickly and supports many languages including Java, C, C++, and Python. The platform offers command-line interfaces as well as application programming interfaces (API) to support Multichain configuration. Depending on business requirements, Multichain can be a private or public blockchain. In spite of the fact that Multichain is an authorized blockchain that offers an effective IoT approach for data collection in the event of data deletion concerns, but it does not provide protection against unauthorized data access. In addition, communicating smart devices with other resources between an authorized Multichain has poor performance and is expensive [76].

2.5.5 Quorum

Quorum is a platform for businesses and organizations and addresses specific challenges while enabling businesses to leverage Ethereum for their high-value blockchain applications within the financial industry and beyond. It is ideal for any application that needs to process private transactions quickly and efficiently among a fully controllable group of participants [77].

2.5.6 Lisk

Lisk is a blockchain application platform. Lisk can define sub-blockchains with decentralized blockchain applications and various cryptocurrency options (e.g. Bitcoin, Ethereum). Lisk products are developed completely in open-source and are especially easy to use for JavaScript developers. Through its support for the creation and development of decentralized applications that end users can use directly, Lisk enables the development of an ecosystem of interoperable blockchain services. The Lisk platform is considering whether it can be an efficient solution for IoT integration through its partnership with Chain of Things [78].

2.5.7 Litecoin

On the other hand, Litecoin functions exactly like Bitcoin but with quicker confirmation times for transactions and better storage performance. It is also based on the PoW algorithm, which has the highest security in transaction validity while Litecoin validation nodes require less computing power compared to Bitcoin, making it a better solution for blockchain and IoT applications [79].

2.5.8 IOTA

IOTA is an open-source, unlimited data and value transfer protocol that has redesigned blockchain technology to allow the secure exchange of both value and data at no charge. IOTA uses the MIOTA cryptocurrency to calculate transactions on its network. Tangle, a node system used to validate transactions that stands out as IOTA's most significant innovation, claims to be quicker and more effective than traditional blockchains. The Tangle is an attached data structure that is replicated at every node in an IOTA network. Tangle stores all data in objects known as transactions using a Directed Acyclic Graph (DAG) structure as opposed to blocks like Bitcoin and Ethereum. Parallel validation and acceptance of transactions ensure that they cannot be changed and remain unchanged. Billions of IoT devices are connected to IOTA. Devices can exchange data and payment information with a variety of other devices within this network during daily transactions. However, the IOTA platform lost some of its credibility when it was attacked by a phishing attack on its network. So, the team proceeded to integrate the SHA-256 hash method as well as Bitcoin [62].

2.5.9 Energy Web Chain

One of the most powerful presences in the field of energy and the devices that perform the work of smart cities owns the Energy Web Chain (EWC) of the Energy Web Foundation. With the

TABLE 2.1

Comparison of Blockchain Platforms

Platform	Type of Blockchain	Cryptocurrency	Smart Contracts	Block Time (sec)	Transaction per Second
Bitcoin	Public	Bitcoin (BTC)	No	600	3–7
Ethereum	Public and private	Ether (ETH)	Yes	12–14	30
Hyperledger Fabric	Private	None	Yes	0.5–3	3,000
Multichain	Private	Multi-currency	Yes	10–11	2,000
Quorum	Private	ETH	Yes	10	100+
Lisk	Public and private	LSK	Yes	10	5
Litecoin	Public	Litecoin (LTC)	No	150	56
IOTA	Public	MIOTA	Yes	No blocks	7
Energy Web Chain	Public and private	Energy Web Token (EWT)	Yes	5.3	76

EWC, network operators, customers, and physical assets will be connected digitally. EWC is a public open-source blockchain that uses the Proof-of-Authority hybrid algorithm derived from Ethereum blockchain technology [80].

Because there are so many blockchain platforms currently available, including Bitcoin, Ethereum, Hyperledger Fabric, and IOTA, a comparison of the platforms is provided in Table 2.1.

2.6 Data Quality and Reliability in IoT and Blockchain

Data quality and reliability are also important considerations when dealing with IoT data. Through the use of a sensing device, the IoT collects sensory data from the real world. In IoT systems, low quality may result due to data that originate from heterogeneous sources, and different sensors can provide data with different precision, ranges, units, specifications, etc., and with inherent uncertainties. Low-quality/inaccurate data may also be attributed to the potential faulty installation of sensors. One of the biggest worries is also how to prevent tampering, illegal access, and theft of IoT data coming from sensors. Some nodes may act selfishly and even maliciously, providing low-quality and even falsified data. Untrusted nodes can even modify information, so the provided information might not be reliable.

Based on the aforementioned, it is of utmost importance to confirm that the provided information has not been changed. The problem of data reliability might be resolved by blockchain technology. IoT data can be collected by blockchain and stored in a distributed manner to prevent data tampering. Because it is so complicated to change or falsify any transactions stored in blockchain, IoT data remains immutable, allowing users to confirm its authenticity and be sure that it hasn't been altered. Changes can be viewed and examined, as well as when and from whom they were made. Thus, malicious attempts to access data will be recorded and revealed, potentially resulting in a significant decrease in malicious attacks. Moreover, blockchain enables data traceability. This makes it possible to examine and confirm the data's originality and quality. Furthermore, trustworthiness and reputation mechanisms proposed in research literature could serve as a softer security mechanism to identify and mitigate nodes' malicious behavior [81]. IoT systems can integrate mechanisms to evaluate the trust and the behavior of the entities [82, 83]. Trust ensures that an IoT entity can act reliably and securely during collaborations by building trust relationships among nodes. If all participants have access to the same data and can confirm that it has not been altered, then the system will be trustworthy. Additionally, a smart contract on the blockchain controls each device's trust and reputation based on characteristics specified by the author [84]. There are reputation systems that compute a reputation value for each participant and store this value in a blockchain system to ensure credibility. In [84], authors propose a decentralized blockchain reputation model for IoT nodes. The findings demonstrate that using decentralized reputation management based on blockchain could be more efficient than currently used centralized trust models. In [85], authors present a blockchain review system for IoT, where users' reputations and reviews of their data are maintained in blockchain. The blockchain can be used by new system users to retrieve reviews and ratings of the data. In [86], authors suggest a cloud-fog-edge architecture to manage reputation values of IoT devices in order to guarantee the consistency and fault tolerance of the reputation management system. Thus, we believe that blockchain can ensure that IoT information is transparent and trustworthy. The blockchain ensures data storage and transmission, enhances the data quality, and prevents data tampering. Also, the blockchain system can improve authenticity and reliability of the information. Thus, the data recorded in the blockchain can be assured as reliable, eliminating potential errors in the sensor accuracy or detecting false data.

2.7   Conclusion

Among the most promising technologies are blockchain and the IoT. We believe blockchain will provide a solution to many issues faced by IoT technology. However, there are several problems to be explored and overcome before exploiting the full potential of the blockchain approach in IoT applications. In this chapter, we provided a thorough overview of blockchain technology. A detailed analysis of the advantages and challenges of blockchain and IoT integration followed. We also presented the potential of using blockchain in different IoT applications as well as the blockchain platforms that have been utilized for IoT applications. Finally, recognizing that data quality and reliability constitute key success factors for IoT; we discussed the potential solutions of blockchain-IoT integration to address these critical aspects. In the future, we intend to conduct a comprehensive investigation of the data quality challenge of NG-IoT systems, especially in IoT with human-centric sensing (HCS), in order to improve data quality and reliability by assessing the quality and trustworthiness of data collected by humans. We will propose the integration of blockchain into HCS-based NG-IoT systems due to its numerous advantages, since it will provide a secure platform for HCS systems, eliminate the weaknesses of a centralized platform, guarantee data integrity, and improve system reliability.

REFERENCES

1. Panda SS, et al. A blockchain based decentralized authentication framework for resource con-strained IOT devices. 2019 10th Int Conf Comput Commun Netw Technol ICCCNT 2019. 2019 Jul 1.
2. Zhang ZK, et al. IoT security: ongoing challenges and research opportunities. Proc - IEEE 7th Int Conf Serv Comput Appl SOCA 2014. 2014 Dec 5; 230–4.
3. Dai HN, et al. Blockchain for Internet of Things: a survey. *IEEE Internet Things J.* 2019 Oct 1;6(5):8076–94.
4. Atlam HF, et al. Blockchain with Internet of Things: benefits, challenges, and future directions. *Int J Intell Syst Appl.* 2018 Jun 1;10(6):40–8.
5. Alamri M, et al. Blockchain for Internet of Things (IoT) research issues challenges & future directions: a review. *IJCSNS Int J Comput Sci Netw Secur.* 2019;19(5):244.
6. Ferrag MA, et al. Blockchain technologies for the internet of things: research issues and challenges. *IEEE Internet Things J.* 2019;6(2):2188–204.
7. Reyna A, et al. On blockchain and its integration with IoT. Challenges and opportunities. *Futur Gener Comput Syst.* 2018;88(2018):173–90.
8. Zafar S, et al. Integration of blockchain and Internet of Things: challenges and solutions. *Ann des Telecommun Telecommun.* 2022;77(1–2):13–32.
9. Fernández-Caramés TM, et al. A review on the use of blockchain for the Internet of Things. *IEEE Access.* 2018 May 30;6:32979–3001.
10. Cui P, et al. Blockchain in IoT: current trends, challenges, and future roadmap. *J Hardw Syst Secur.* 2019;3(4):338–64.

11. Abdelmaboud A, et al. Blockchain for IoT applications: taxonomy, platforms, recent advances, challenges and future research directions. *Electron*. 2022;11(4):1–35.
12. Uddin MA, et al. A survey on the adoption of blockchain in IoT: challenges and solutions. *Blockchain Res Appl*. 2021;2(2):100006.
13. Adam IO, et al. Bridging the global digital divide through digital inclusion: the role of ICT access and ICT use. In: *Transforming Government: People, Process and Policy*, Anna Visvizi, editor. Leeds, England: Emerald Publishing Limited; 2020. pp. 580–96.
14. Bitcoin [Internet]. [accessed Jun 9 2022]. Available from: https://bitcoin.org/en/
15. Bosamia M, et al. Comparisons of blockchain based consensus algorithms for security aspects. *Int J Emerg Technol*. 2020 Jun 1;11:427–34.
16. Merkle RC. A digital signature based on a conventional encryption function. Vol. 293 LNCS, Lecture Notes in Computer Science (including subseries Lecture Notes in Artificial Intelligence and Lecture Notes in Bioinformatics). 1988. pp. 369–78.
17. Lee D, et al. Blockchain based privacy preserving multimedia intelligent video surveillance using secure Merkle tree. *Multimed Tools Appl*. 2021;80(26):34517–34.
18. Sáez De Ocáriz Borde H. An overview of trees in blockchain technology: Merkle trees and Merkle Patricia tries. 2022. Available from: https://www.researchgate.net/publication/358740207_An_Overview_of_Trees_in_Blockchain_Technology_Merkle_Trees_and_Merkle_Patricia_Tries
19. Zheng Z, et al. An overview of blockchain technology: architecture, consensus, and future trends. Proc - 2017 IEEE 6th Int Congr Big Data, BigData Congr 2017. 2017 Sep 7; 557–64.
20. Gemeliarana IGAK, et al. Evaluation of proof of work (POW) blockchains security network on selfish mining. 2018 Int Semin Res Inf Technol Intell Syst ISRITI 2018. 2018 Feb; 126–30.
21. Porat A, et al. Blockchain consensus: an analysis of proof-of-work and its applications. 2017; 1–6. Available from: http://www.scs.stanford.edu/17au-cs244b/labs/projects/porat_pratap_shah_adkar.pdf
22. Gervais A, et al. On the security and performance of proof of work blockchains. Proceedings of the 2016 ACM SIGSAC Conference on Computer and Communications Security. New York, NY, USA: Association for Computing Machinery; 2016. pp. 3–16. (CCS '16).
23. Kiayias A, et al. PPCoin: peer-to-peer crypto-currency with proof-of-stake. Proc 2016 ACM SIGSAC Conf Comput Commun Secur - CCS'16. 2017 Jan;1919. pp. 1–27.
24. Mingxiao D, et al. A review on consensus algorithm of blockchain. 2017 IEEE International Conference on Systems, Man, and Cybernetics (SMC). 2017. pp. 2567–72.
25. Bauer DP. Solidity. In: *Getting Started With Ethereum: A Step-by-Step Guide to Becoming a Blockchain Developer*, Bauer DP, editor. Berkeley, CA: Apress; 2022. pp. 13–6.
26. Ethereum blockchain [Internet]. [accessed Jun 9 2022]. Available from: https://ethereum.org/en/upgrades/merge/
27. Al-Emari S, et al. A labeled transactions-based dataset on the Ethereum network. International Conference on Advances in Cyber Security. Singapore: Springer; 2021. pp. 61–79.
28. Scalable blockchain infrastructure: billions of transactions & counting |Solana: build crypto apps that scale [Internet]. [accessed Aug 17 2022]. Available from: https://solana.com/
29. Tezos: A blockchain designed to evolve [Internet]. [accessed Aug 17 2022]. Available from: https://tezos.com/
30. Liang YC. Blockchain for dynamic spectrum management. In: *Dynamic Spectrum Management: From Cognitive Radio to Blockchain and Artificial Intelligence*, Liang YC, editor. Singapore: Springer Singapore; 2020. pp. 121–46.
31. Ethereum blocks [Internet]. [accessed Jun 12 2022]. Available from: https://ethereum.org/en/developers/docs/blocks/
32. Ethereum gas [Internet]. [accessed Jun 12 2022]. Available from: https://ethereum.org/en/developers/docs/gas/
33. Wu M, et al. A comprehensive survey of blockchain: from theory to IoT applications and beyond. *IEEE Internet Things J*. 2019;6(5):8114–54.
34. Purnama S, et al. Design of educational learning management cloud process with blockchain 4.0 based E-portfolio. *J Educ Technol*. 2021;5(4):628.
35. Mukherjee P, et al. Blockchain 1.0 to Blockchain 4.0—the evolutionary transformation of blockchain technology. In: *Blockchain Technology: Applications and Challenges*, Panda SK,

Jena AK, Swain SK, Satapathy SC, editors. Cham: Springer International Publishing; 2021. pp. 29–49.

36. Sadawi A Al, et al. A survey on the integration of blockchain with IoT to enhance performance and eliminate challenges. *IEEE Access*. 2021;9:54478–97.
37. Makridakis S, et al. Blockchain: current challenges and future prospects/applications. *Future Internet*. 2019;11:1–16.
38. Monero [Internet]. [accessed Jun 7 2022]. Available from: https://www.getmonero.org/
39. Zcash [Internet]. [accessed Jun 7 2022]. Available from: https://z.cash/
40. PivX [Internet]. [accessed Jun 14 2022]. Available from: https://pivx.org/
41. Reid F, et al. An analysis of anonymity in the Bitcoin system. In: *Security and Privacy in Social Networks*, Yaniv Altshuler, Yuval Elovici, Armin B. Cremers, Nadav Aharony, Alex Pentland, editors. New York: Springer; 2013. pp. 197–223.
42. Goodell G, et al. Can cryptocurrencies preserve privacy and comply with regulations? *Front blockchain*. 2019 (November 2018);2:1–14.
43. Islam MR, et al. A review on blockchain security issues and challenges. 2021 IEEE 12th Control and System Graduate Research Colloquium (ICSGRC). 2021. pp. 227–32.
44. EU blockchain works [Internet]. [accessed Jun 2 2022]. Available from: https://ses.jrc.ec.europa.eu/node/31978
45. Lin F, et al. Survey on blockchain for internet of things. *J Internet Serv Inf Secur*. 2019;9(2):1–30.
46. Li R, et al. Blockchain for large-scale internet of things data storage and protection. *IEEE Trans Serv Comput*. 2019;12(5):762–71.
47. Guo H, et al. A survey on blockchain technology and its security. *Blockchain Res Appl* [Internet]. 2022;3(2):100067. Available from: https://www.sciencedirect.com/science/article/pii/S2096720922000070
48. Roman R, et al. Mobile edge computing, Fog et al.: a survey and analysis of security threats and challenges. *Futur Gener Comput Syst* [Internet]. 2018;78:680–98.
49. Banerjee M, et al. A blockchain future for internet of things security: a position paper. *Digit Commun Netw*. 2018;4(3):149–60.
50. Roman R, et al. On the features and challenges of security and privacy in distributed internet of things. *Comput Netw*. 2013;57(10):2266–79.
51. Novo O. Blockchain meets IoT: an architecture for scalable access management in IoT. *IEEE Internet of Things J*. 2018 Mar 5;5:1184–95.
52. Ouaddah A, et al. FairAccess: a new blockchain-based access control framework for the Internet of Things. *Secur Commun Netw*. 2016;9(18):5943–64.
53. Colonial pipeline cryptocurrency [Internet]. [accessed Jun 5 2022]. Available from: https://www.thomsonreuters.com/en-us/posts/investigation-fraud-and-risk/colonial-pipeline-ransom-funds/
54. Feng Q, et al. A survey on privacy protection in blockchain system. *J Netw Comput Appl* [Internet]. 2019;126:45–58. Available from: https://www.sciencedirect.com/science/article/pii/S1084804518303485
55. Mohanta BK, et al. Blockchain technology: a survey on applications and security privacy Challenges. *Internet of Things* [Internet]. 2019;8:100107. Available from: https://www.sciencedirect.com/science/article/pii/S2542660518300702
56. Pouraghily AI et al. Poster abstract: privacy in blockchain-enabled IoT devices. 2018 IEEE/ACM Third International Conference on Internet-of-Things Design and Implementation (IoTDI). 2018. pp. 292–3.
57. Biswas S, et al. PoBT: a lightweight consensus algorithm for scalable IoT business blockchain. *IEEE Internet Things J*. 2020;7(3):2343–55.
58. Liu Y, et al. Lightchain: a lightweight blockchain system for industrial internet of things. *IEEE Trans Ind Informatics*. 2019;15(6):3571–81.
59. Rashid A, et al. Smart contracts integration between blockchain and internet of things: opportunities and challenges. 2019 2nd International Conference on Advancements in Computational Sciences (ICACS). 2019. pp. 1–9.
60. Tandon A. Challenges of integrating blockchain with internet of things. *Int J Innov Technol Explor Eng*. 2019;8(9 Special Issue 3):1476–89.

61. Panarello A, et al. Blockchain and IoT integration: a systematic survey. *Sensors (Switzerland)*. 2018;18:1–37.
62. IOTA [Internet]. [accessed Jun 3 2022]. Available from: https://www.iota.org/
63. Pham HL, et al. A secure remote healthcare system for hospital using blockchain smart contract. 2018 IEEE Globecom Work GC Wkshps 2018 - Proc. 2019.
64. Naresh VS, et al. Internet of things in healthcare: architecture, applications, challenges, and solutions. *Comput Syst Sci Eng*. 2020;35(6):411–21.
65. Chen T, et al. EEG emotion recognition model based on the LIBSVM classifier. *Meas J Int Meas Confed*. 2020;164:1–13.
66. Rahman MA, et al. Spatial blockchain-based secure mass screening framework for children with dyslexia. *IEEE Access*. 2018;6:61876–85.
67. Rayan R, et al. IoT-integrated blockchain in the drug supply chain. In: *Blockchain Applications in IoT Ecosystem*, Tanupriya Choudhury, Abhirup Khanna, Teoh Teik Toe, Madhu Khurana, Nguyen Gia Nhu, editors. Cham, Berlin, Germany: Springer2021. pp. 105–117.
68. Lin J, et al. Blockchain and IoT based food traceability for smart agriculture. Proceedings of the 3rd International Conference on Crowd Science and Engineering. New York, NY, USA: Association for Computing Machinery; 2018. (ICCSE'18).
69. Lin J, et al. Blockchain and IoT based food traceability for smart agriculture. *ACM Int Conf Proceeding Ser*. 2018. pp. 1–6.
70. Caro MP, et al. Blockchain-based traceability in agri-food supply chain management: a practical implementation. 2018 IoT Vert Top Summit Agric - Tuscany, IOT Tuscany 2018. 2018. p. 1–4.
71. Ibba S, et al. CitySense: blockchain-oriented smart cities. Proceedings of the XP2017 Scientific Workshops. 2017. pp. 1–5.
72. Moniruzzaman M, et al. Blockchain for smart homes: review of current trends and research challenges. *Comput Electr Eng*. 2020;83:1–16.
73. Zhou Y, et al. Improving IoT services in smart-home using blockchain smart contract. 2018 IEEE International Conference on Internet of Things (iThings) and IEEE Green Computing and Communications (GreenCom) and IEEE Cyber, Physical and Social Computing (CPSCom) and IEEE Smart Data (SmartData). 2018. pp. 81–7.
74. Ethereum [Internet]. [accessed Jun 3 2022]. Available from: https://ethereum.org/en/
75. Hyperledger fabric [Internet]. [accessed Jun 3 2022]. Available from: https://www.hyperledger.org/use/fabric
76. Multichain [Internet]. [accessed Jun 3 2022]. Available from: https://www.multichain.com/
77. Quorum [Internet]. [accessed Jun 3 2022]. Available from: https://consensys.net/quorum/
78. Lisk [Internet]. [accessed Jun 8 2022]. Available from: https://lisk.com/
79. Litecoin [Internet]. [accessed Jun 13 2022]. Available from: https://litecoin.org/
80. Energy Web [Internet]. [accessed Jun 8 2022]. Available from: https://www.energyweb.org/
81. Banti K, et al. Data quality in mobile crowd sensing systems: challenges and perspectives. 2018 9th Int Conf Information, Intell Syst Appl IISA 2018. 2019.
82. Asiri S, et al. An IoT trust and reputation model based on recommender systems. 2016 14th Annu Conf Privacy, Secur Trust PST 2016. 2016. pp. 561–8.
83. Arseni Ştefan C, et al. Resfit: A reputation and security monitoring platform for IoT applications. *Electron*. 2021;10(15):1–23.
84. Debe M, et al. IoT public fog nodes reputation system: a decentralized solution using Ethereum blockchain. *IEEE Access*. 2019;7:178082–93.
85. Abubaker Z, et al. Trustful data trading through monetizing IoT data using blockchain based review system. *Concurr Comput Pract Exp*. 2022;34(5):1–19.
86. Weerapanpisit P, et al. A decentralised location-based reputation management system in the IoT using blockchain. *IEEE Internet Things J*. 2022;9(16):15100–15.

3

Real-time Cloud Applications

Mohammed Salamah
Eastern Mediterranean University, Turkey

Nivine Guler
University of Technology Bahrain

3.1 Introduction

The revolution of Internet of Things (IoT) technologies, especially the advances in mobile communications brought by 5G and 6G standards, allows innovative application domains to enter the cloud world gradually such as real-time applications. Real-time applications that require data to be captured and processed under stringent time constraints are becoming more popular. With the use of the Internet to access these applications, cloud computing has become a main tool for the realization of utility model of computing. The main strengths of cloud computing include standardized platforms and management support services, massive scalability, global access, flexible infrastructure, incremental usage controls, and pricing. Cloud computing has become a viable technological means to provide a scalable, demand-driven, and ubiquitous computing infrastructure for many applications. It is the driving force for the major evolutionary technical developments in the information technology world and the IT marketplace. Along with ultra-reliable and low-latency communication infrastructures, computing and machine learning (ML) algorithms are the most important enablers of cloud various domains such as the navy, where efficient alarm systems for critical situations and remote monitoring should be supported in real time. Besides the navy domain, unmanned vehicle is another type of real-time application that runs on the cloud.

Along with cloud computing, artificial intelligence (AI) and ML are becoming very appealing and impactful in several applications such as the Internet of Things, Power Grid, Telecommunications, Healthcare, Business Analytics, and many more. However, critical issues that arise with ML algorithms include computational complexity, processing power required for running such algorithms, and huge storage requirements. These issues make it even more challenging to deploy ML algorithms for real-time applications. The key solution is to use cloud computing as a common strategy for deploying such applications in real-time systems. The aim of this chapter is to fundamentally demonstrate how ML algorithms and cloud computing, which are dominating the IT landscape, can be combined to provide powerful solutions for such applications. Chapter 3 is divided into four sections: Section 3.2 explains the fundamental concepts, paradigms, and architectures of cloud computing, and it describes the different types of cloud computing services and platforms. Section 3.3 gives deep explanations of the combined ML and cloud computing technologies in real-time applications. In addition, this section describes cloud resource management and scheduling. Section 3.4 presents a detailed explanation of developing a cloud computing application for a real-time weather forecasting system. Section 3.5 describes the main challenges faced by real-time cloud applications and the future of cloud computing.

DOI:10.1201/9781003326236-3

3.2 Cloud Computing: Terminologies, Infrastructure, Applications and Paradigms

In the previous decades, computing power was limited and considered an expensive means. Soon after cloud computing came into existence, this scarce resource become more available at an affordable price, and a noticeable shift toward an intense model evolution to adopt the cloud computing concept was seen. This innovation in computer technology accelerates the accessibility of business products, facilities, and models. Cloud computing deals are convenient to the customers or companies as the customers pay only for the utilized computing facilities, in other words, pay-as-you-go concept. In traditional computing, resources were over-provisioned to handle the possible business operation ultimate levels. With cloud computing, the required resources are available to the users, and these resources can be easily expanded or shrunk based on the company's demands. This section covers the cloud computing vision, key features, and the advances behind the existence of cloud computing.

3.2.1 An Overview of the Cloud

In 1960, John McCarthy, a computer scientist, defined the concept of computing in the cloud as follows:

> If computers of the kind I have advocated become the computers of the future, then computing may someday be organized as a public utility just as the telephone system is a public utility... The computer utility could become the basis of a new and important industry.

Leonard Kleinrock [1] said in 1969:

> as of now, computer networks are still in their infancy, but as they grow up and become sophisticated, we will probably see the spread of 'computer utilities' which, like present electric and telephone utilities, will service individual homes and offices across the country.

The idea behind making use of computing services enables the concept of cloud computing industry in this era. This concept is based on easily utilizing the computing services, perceived as a "cloud," and providing on-demand access to applications and services just like our daily commodities anywhere and anytime. So, the customers must pay the cloud service providers like Amazon, Microsoft, and Google to access their computing resources such as applications and storage, and at the same time, the cloud customers will not face any hassle with any infrastructure setup and maintenance. As a result, this is a big business that holds competence for cloud suppliers by offering the same services to a broad range of clients. Hence, cloud computing has become an innovative supplier model of computing services by utilizing the underlying network resources, and data centers can be done efficiently. In fact, cloud computing supports simultaneous virtualization and convergence by having several systems running on server platforms. As shown in Figure 3.1, historically, the emergence of cloud computing started when IBM developed the first virtual machine (VM) and the cloud symbol was used in 1972 and 1977, respectively. Then, after the Internet and the World Wide Web came into the picture, in 1992, online disk space, which is a place to keep the users' files, was provided by many telecommunication companies. The word cloud itself was coined by Ramesh Chellappa in 1997 in which the word "cloud" was used as an allegory for the Internet, whereas the symbol of the cloud was used to symbolize the network of computing equipment. In 1999, cloud companies started to exist such as Salesforce and VM Ware. In 2002, Amazon launched Amazon Web Services (AWS) and in 2006 Hadoop was released. In 2008, Google launched Google App Engine (GAE), and in 2010 Microsoft released Microsoft Azure. In 2016, IBM released the first quantum computing system (IBM Q System) for scientific and commercial purposes. Starting in 2017 and beyond, two significant events happened. The first is processing outside the cloud became possible, and the second is having heterogeneous cloud resources. Afterward, the "cloud in a box" concept was initiated. This concept simply allowed the possibility of computing on network devices,

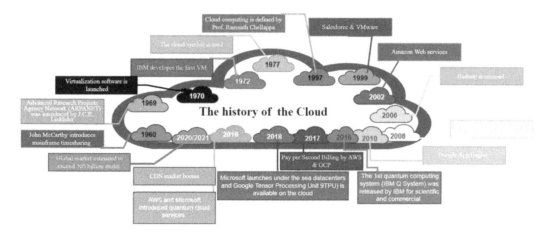

FIGURE 3.1   Cloud computing history.

such as routers and base stations, which was named "edge computing" at the beginning of 2010. Later, additional interest in edge computing technology evolved especially by Cisco, which released the concept of "fog computing," where computing is assisted along the entire cloud-edge continuum. Fog/edge computing is a good mechanism to alleviate challenges that are anticipated with the increase in network traffic and communication latency. Thus, to support this concept, the underlying hardware in data centers has to be heterogeneous. Since most applications on the cloud require execution speed that can't be met by traditional CPUs, accelerators such as graphics processing units (GPUs) are added to data centers. Also, Google has incorporated tensor processor units (TPUs) in the cloud to meet the workload need and even support complex probabilistic algorithms for predicting user preference such as ML algorithms. It seems that many companies have embraced the edge technology, even Microsoft has launched micro data centers undersea.

The advancement in several technologies such as hardware, Internet technologies, distributed computing, and autonomous computing forms the basis of the novelty of cloud computing. Figure 3.2 highlights the advances in different areas of technology that led to the advent of cloud computing. At an early stage of development, some of the mentioned technologies were considered as speculations. Later, they received considerable attention when standardization was needed, which led to more interest in cloud computing technology. By using the Internet to access applications, cloud computing has strengthened the understanding of the utility model of computing. Standardized platforms and management support services, massive scalability, global access, flexible infrastructure, incremental usage controls, and pricing are among the main strengths of cloud computing.

3.2.2 Basic Definitions and Terminologies

Cloud computing is considered a model that incorporates an advanced set of computational facilities mainly offered on an on-demand basis by common providers, such as Amazon, Google, and Microsoft. The "cloud" reflects a powerful and scalable computing system framework that provides applications and services worldwide in an on-demand manner to organizations and individual users [2]. Various definitions and characteristics have been stated by different researchers and professionals for cloud computing. For instance, the National Institute of Standards and Technology (NIST) [2] defined cloud computing as "a pay-per-use" model for accessing the shared network resources when needed such that provisioning and releasing such resources can be performed at minimal management work. McKinsey and Co. [3] claim that clouds are considered service providers for hardware utilities that include storage, power, and capacity, while customers are completely isolated from managing such hardware. To be precise, the consumers incur the infrastructure costs as

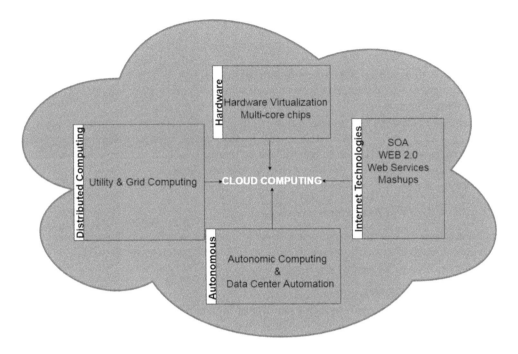

FIGURE 3.2 Cloud computing fundamentals.

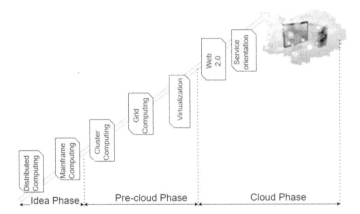

FIGURE 3.3 Evolution of the cloud computing.

a variable operational expenditure, with an elastic capacity. Also, Buyya et al. [4] have defined cloud computing as follows:

> Cloud is a parallel and distributed computing system consisting of a collection of inter-connected and virtualized computers that are dynamically provisioned and presented as one or more unified computing resources based on service-level agreements (SLA) established through negotiation between the service provider and consumers.

3.2.3 Cloud Computing Paradigm

The cloud computing paradigm emerged because of the maturity and convergence [1] of several of its supporting models and technologies that belong to one of the three phases illustrated in Figure 3.3.

3.2.3.1 Phase 1 – Idea Phase

It consists of the practical progress prior to the Internet epoch. This is described as follows:

- ***Distributed Computing*** refers to multi-independent entities connected such that essential characteristics of cloud computing such as network scalability and guaranteed connectivity are provided.
- ***Mainframe Computing*** is a supercomputer with good characteristics in terms of power and storage, which can be considered as several systems on the user side. Though it offers high processing and storage facilities, the problem of the geographical location couldn't be solved. This was the reason behind the existence of cluster computing.

3.2.3.2 Phase 2 – Pre-Cloud Phase

This phase refers to the Internet phase, where fewer numbers of systems located in different regions were connected; thus, this invention gave opportunities for new technologies to exist.

3.2.3.2.1 Cluster Computing

Here each computer is connected through a network of high bandwidth. Thus, by reducing the cost caused by mainframe, cluster computing is considered a great substitute. With the advent of the Internet, local networks around the globe could be interconnected and share resources under certain restrictions. This was termed Internet computing.

3.2.3.2.2 Grid Computing

It refers to a network of systems, located at different physical regions, connected via the Internet. These systems are controlled by specialized software such as middleware that allows resources to be accessed and used externally. Simply the grid service is the process of managing the access to the grid resources via the middleware. Several access controls and security services characterize the grid services, starting from the permissions to retrieve data from libraries and databases to the permissions to use wide storage facilities. The main problem of distance is solved; however, problems related to providing high bandwidth for far-away nodes became a limitation.

3.2.3.2.3 Virtualization

Virtualization separates software environments from physical infrastructures so that multiple operating systems and applications can run simultaneously on the same machine. Virtualization is a technique used by Amazon, Google, and many more cloud providers.

3.2.3.3 Phase 3 – Cloud Phase

Following the integration of grid computing with virtualization techniques, good hardware and Internet resources are needed. Consequently, the development of the cloud has just started.

3.2.3.3.1 Web 2.0 and Web 3.0

Web applications mostly benefit from the on-demand applications provided by cloud computing, in particular, Web 2.0 and Web 3.0, where improving creativity, sharing of information, and user collaboration are provided by such applications by leveraging the Internet as the main utility and the user platform. The uninterrupted connectivity of a user accessing services via the Internet with a broadband connection is enabled by Web 3.0 technology. Web 3.0 technology accredits the services in cloud computing.

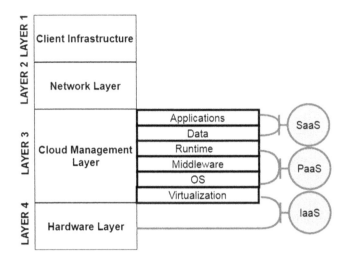

FIGURE 3.4 Cloud computing architecture.

3.2.3.3.2 Service Orientation

Service orientation combines cloud resources with various business services that include components designed to reduce dependency. Therefore, business processes need to adopt service orientation to utilize existing resources.

3.2.3.3.3 Cloud Computing

Many companies have started to provide cloud storage, infrastructure, and management services. Initially, it was termed utility computing. Today, cloud computing is brought into action. There are many types of cloud models and services, which are described in detail in the upcoming sections.

3.2.4 Cloud Computing Architecture and Services

The architecture of the cloud incorporates four main layers, as shown in Figure 3.4.

Layer 1 is referred to as the client infrastructure, which allows the interaction between the Graphical User Interface (GUI) with the cloud. In other words, it is considered the front end, which is, in most cases, a simple web browser. This layer represents devices with sufficient power referred to as users or clients, requesting cloud access.

Layer 2 is referred to as the network layer, which maintains the connection between the users and the cloud. This layer is considered the cloud backbone, where all the network services are delivered to the customers when connecting to the cloud; hence, all the cloud services are highly dependent on this layer. For instance, this layer is in fact the Internet in the public cloud that is normally located in a place that is unknown to the cloud users but is accessible worldwide through the Internet. Private clouds, on the other hand, can be connected to the cloud users through the Local Area Network (LAN).

Layer 3 is referred to as the cloud management layer, which is responsible for all the cloud entities. These include the users and access control, data, applications, and services. Precisely, this layer persuades the service-level agreements between the user and the cloud operator [5]. According to NIST, three basic service models are defined, namely, SaaS, PaaS, and IaaS, as shown in Table 3.1. The classification of the user service model is defined in Layer3 based on the agreement of sharing the cloud components with cloud users such as Software-as-a-Service (SaaS), Platform-as-a-Service (PaaS), and Infrastructure-as-a-Service (IaaS) [5]. This layer integrates software that is responsible for sharing the cloud resources and managing the cloud such as scheduling and provisioning,

TABLE 3.1

Cloud Service Models

Service Model	User Type	Resource Managed	Examples
Software-as-a-Service SaaS	Business users	Business applications, web services, multimedia	Google Apps, emails, billing and payroll, Facebook, YouTube
Platform-as-a-Service PaaS	Developers, network architects, deployers	Software framework (Java, .Net), storage, databases, OS, runtimes.	Microsoft Azure, Google App Engine
Industry-as-a-Service IaaS	System administrators	Virtual machines, CPU, memory, OS, load balancing, Internet, bandwidth provisioning	Amazon EC2, GoGrid, Flexiscale, data centers

optimization at the level of the server and workload, as well as cloud control within the organization. Figure 3.4 shows the six components of this layer:

(i) Applications: Various types of application software are provisioned.

(ii) Data: Two kinds of data exist, either structured or unstructured, depending on the client's requirements. It can be observed from Figure 3.4 that SaaS is associated with the applications and data components. Examples of applications that form part of SaaS include Gmail, Facebook, YouTube, and Dropbox.

(iii) Runtime: This component supplies the runtime and execution environments to the VMs.

(iv) Middleware: This component is a kind of software that provides the necessary services and features, such as verification, messages, and API supervision, to the applications.

(v) Operating System (OS): It is the core software that handles all the fundamental management jobs related to storage, execution, and peripheral devices. PaaS is associated with the runtime, middleware, and OS components. Software frameworks such as GAE and Microsoft Azure are part of this service.

(vi) Virtualization: It is defined as the creation of a virtual abstraction instead of the actual version of a hardware or software resource such as an OS, a server, a storage device, or a network. The IaaS forms part of the virtualization component and layer 4. Examples of services offered that fall under IaaS include VMs, Amazon Web Services, Go Greed, Rack Space, etc. It is a service level meant for administrators.

Layer 4 is referred to as the hardware layer, which consists of the actual hardware resources. For instance, a data center can be used at the back end for both public cloud and private cloud. A data center includes various network systems and infrastructures to be utilized by companies to deal with huge data volumes. Since organization data centers aim to keep resources protected, cloud providers and different organizations always work in harmony.

A closer view of each of the cloud service models is provided below:

(i) Software-as-a-Service (SaaS): The Cloud Service Provider (CSP) releases the applications running on the cloud to the Cloud Service Customer (CSC). The applications can be accessed through different types of client systems such as client email, a dedicated programming interface, or even an Integrated Development Environment (IDE). The CSC does not have the facility to manipulate or control the fundamental cloud setup structure represented by the network entities, power, storage, and systems and applications. Applications entailing a quick and on-time response cannot benefit from the SaaS. On the contrary, the most likely applicants for SaaS are, for example, those that are used by different competitors, such as email; on-demand applications that happen periodically in a peak form like billing and payroll; mobile sales management software; and short-term projects incorporating collaborative software.

(ii) Platform-as-a-Service (PaaS): In this service model, an instance of the platform owned by the CSP is leased to the CSCs to deploy their own programming applications onto the CSP's platform. Apart from the deployed applications and some restricted user-defined configurations and settings for the application, which can be set by the CSC, the core cloud infrastructure, which includes the network, servers, processors, and operating systems, is fully managed by the CSP [12]. The user can control cloud applications and, probably, those integrating management and configurations. Such facilities include Universal Description Discovery and Integration (UDDI), contents, session and knowledge management, device integration and testing, and sandboxes.

(iii) Infrastructure-as-a-Service (IaaS): In this service class, an instance of the infrastructure (typically virtualized processing, storage, and other resources) owned by the CSP is made available to the CSC. The CSC can deploy and execute different types of software such as operating systems and programming environments on that leased infrastructure. The core cloud infrastructure remains under full control of the CSP, but the CSC can control all the applications it has deployed on the CSP's infrastructure including some security and network settings that are specific to the host device. Dynamic distribution of scaled resources, convenient pricing facility, and shared hardware among several cloud users are the essential IaaS model characteristics. In cases where the demands are unstable, the company is growing quickly, or a new business requires only the computing resources, the IaaS model becomes useful. Cloud service models have also evolved, and other more specific service classes include Analytics as a Service (AaaS), Network-as-a-Service (NaaS), Mobile Backend-as-a-Service (MBaaS), Mobile Network-as-a-Service (MNaaS), and Communications as a Service (CaaS).

The existing services and enablers are the motives for the success of cloud computing technology or in other words correspond to the benefits of cloud computing. These enablers can be listed as:

(i) Virtualization – The main function of virtualization is to provide cloud service providers with flexibility by minimizing the amount of actual physical hardware and their required software resources. VM technologies, such as VMware and Xen, and Virtual Networks (VN), such as VPN, are the core tools of virtualization. Virtualization can take different forms as application virtualization, desktop virtualization, storage virtualization, server virtualization, and network virtualization.

(ii) Massive scalability – The massive scalability of cloud computing is characterized by multi-core processors in addition to VMs to provide the highest possible scalability to the customer as required. By doing so, customers do not need to have any additional hardware and do not even face any hassle accompanied by all the management issues. Instead, the cloud service providers provide fast provisioning of virtual servers, standardized hardware, and persistent cloud storage.

(iii) Universal access: This is a major feature of cloud computing where accessing the same cloud services provided by a cloud provider is done worldwide by many customers and from any place using the Internet. Although cloud resources are shared by different customers worldwide, their data and operations performed on the cloud are kept confidential and distinct from each other. This is a common feature in public computing providing IaaS, PaaS, and SaaS services.

(iv) Usage management and fees: The economic benefits are associated with the adoption of cloud computing. Hence, usage management and fees or charges are the main characteristics that provide cloud computing providers with this benefit. With cloud computing, users can, for instance, rent processing power and storage facilities based on their own requirements and on a *pay-as-you-go* basis. For example, at some specific period of time, if there is a need for a high processing power, the consumer will only pay for that high processing power for that specific period.

(iv) Standardized resources – Cloud computing provides standardized hardware, virtualization, and application platforms. However, the hardware and software facilities don't need to be homogeneous or standard. Instead, there is a lot of flexibility in terms of server configurations; programming languages like Java, Python, and C++; operating systems such as Linux or Windows; and application stacks such as LAMB or Microsoft.Net. Cloud computing providers intend to provide a wide variety of options to meet the customers' needs and at the same time to benefit from their services. Hence, their aim is to provide a balance between their customers' requirements and the available options of services.

(v) Management support services – Management support services of cloud computing are the core components for providing comprehensive services, where these services are proprietary and support both the operational and management features. Hence, cloud users get access to the facilities they need without any assistance from technical operators as the cloud operational support services will do the job. Web Services and Service Oriented Architecture (SOA) are the backbone services of cloud computing. Cloud services are typically designed as Web services that employ industry standards including Web Services Description Language (WSDL), Simple Object Access Protocol (SOAP), and UDDI. The SOA is responsible for organizing and managing Web services within the cloud. It also provides a series of cloud services that can be accessed from several distributed platforms. An important feature beneficial to cloud users is that the management support services provide the users with the necessary informative reports. For instance, the CPU utilization reports give the user a clear view of unnecessary deployment of additional servers for tasks that could have been performed with fewer servers. Similarly, the storage and bandwidth reports help cloud users to optimize the use of these resources.

(vi) Broadband Network: Since the network is the key element for connecting the clouds over the Internet, the cloud requirements ranging from high-speed networking and low-latency communication to Data Center Bridging (DCB) and Data Center Transmission Control (DCTC) should be supported by the network technologies. As these requirements are attained, the potential of the cloud networking system is enhanced. In addition to the mentioned requirements, maintaining load balancing is another important feature that aggregates the server bandwidth. Furthermore, providing backup operational modes for data transmission is another requirement that must be supported by the network. With the network technology advances especially those of 5G/6G, cloud computing services are benefiting from such enhancements as 5G/6G technology provides ultra-low latency and high reliability.

3.2.5 Cloud Computing Deployment Models

Cloud computing is extensive as it embraces infrastructures of various sizes with different management for different models, and it defines different attributes and cloud resources as shown in Figure 3.5.

Different cloud categories outlined by NIST are as follows:

- Private cloud. The cloud services function privately, located either onsite or offsite an organization as shown in Figures 3.6(a) and 3.6(b), respectively. The software executed on the cloud is confined to a specific domain.
- Community cloud. The infrastructure is not private to one organization as in private cloud. Instead, different organizations having common concerns such as mission and security requirements can benefit from the community cloud. Hence, cloud management is carried out by either the organization or a third party and by means of either on-premises or off-premises. Figure 3.7 illustrates the off-premises community model.
- Public cloud. The cloud offers its services to the public by which various customers such as academic institutions, government organizations, and business owners make use of cloud

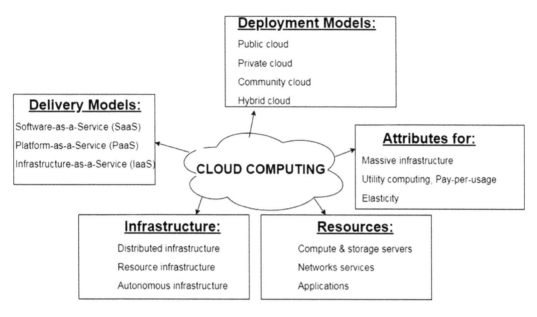

FIGURE 3.5 Fundamentals of the cloud computing.

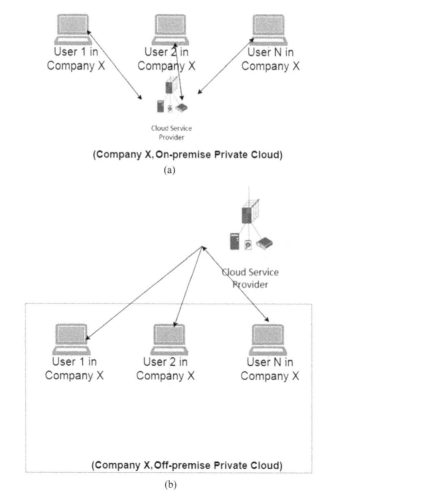

FIGURE 3.6 (a) Private cloud deployment on premise, (b) private cloud deployment off-premises.

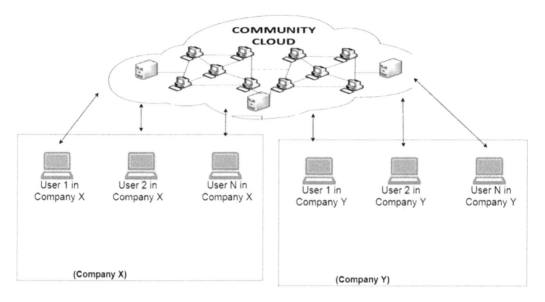

FIGURE 3.7   Community cloud deployment.

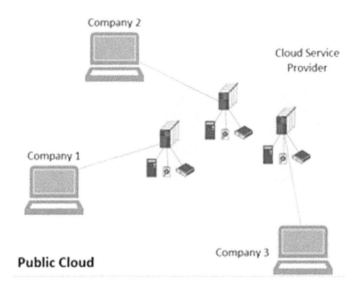

FIGURE 3.8   Public cloud deployment model.

services. The convenient purchase of cloud computing and storage services is done on a pay-as-you-go basis. Figure 3.8 illustrates a typical public cloud model whereby users from N different companies located worldwide could access the cloud.

- Hybrid cloud. A combination of different types of the cloud such as private, community, or public is referred to as hybrid cloud. This type of cloud enables data and application transferability, for instance, using cloud bursting to ensure load balancing between clouds.

Besides, there is an argument stating that the private cloud doesn't support utility computing since an organization has to invest in the infrastructure and the cloud consumer must spend money for utilized cloud resources. Figure 3.9 illustrates the hybrid cloud where Company X uses its own on-premises private cloud but uses public cloud for extra services.

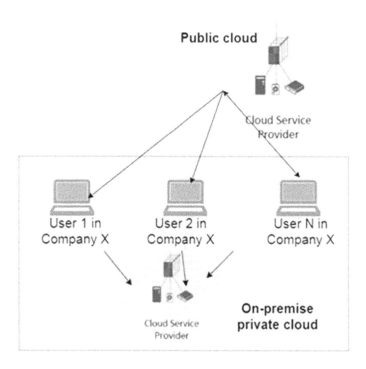

FIGURE 3.9 Hybrid cloud deployment model.

3.2.6 Google's Cloud Platform

Firebase is a mobile and web application development platform developed by Google. It was originally an independent company founded in 2011 by James Tamplin and Andrew Lee, named initially Envolve, which enabled developers to integrate online chat capability into their website via an API. In addition to chat messages, other forms of application data could be passed by Envolve. For example, application data such as a game state could be synced in real time between users by the developers of Envolve. Subsequently, the chat system was separated from the real-time architecture. Firebase developed from Envolve in April 2012 and was set up as a distinct company that offered Backend-as-a-Service (BaaS) with real-time capability. Firebase then quickly developed into a multifunctional mobile and web platform, following its acquisition by Google in 2014. It offers a wide spectrum of technologies and services for developers to assist them in the development of sophisticated apps, expand their customer pool, and become more profitable. Firebase is a comprehensive mobile/web development platform with the following benefits:

- Build better applications with Cloud Firestore, Machine Learning Kit, Cloud Functions, Authentication, Hosting, Cloud Storage, and Realtime Database.
- Improve application quality with Crashlytics, Performance Monitoring, and Test Lab.
- Grow your business with Google Analytics, Predictions, A/B Testing, Cloud Messaging, Remote Config, Dynamic Links, and App Indexing.

3.2.7 IBM's Cloud Platform

Two services are offered by the IBM Cloud platform: PaaS and IaaS. Virtualization of network and the required resources are enabled with the use of IaaS. However, the PaaS helps users to create and execute various applications, written in Python or PHP codes, for public use and in-house use.

3.2.8 Amazon's Cloud Platform

AWS owned by Amazon includes different services as IaaS, PaaS, and SaaS [4]. Tools to be used by the organization such as power, storage, and delivery services are granted by AWS [6]. AWS first launched the service of pay-on-demand where the user pays for the needed storage space and computation services. Amazon services are provided not only to users but also to software developers and companies worldwide.

3.2.9 Features of Google, IBM, and Amazon Cloud Platforms

Table 3.2 shows the different features of the three platforms: Firebase, IBM Cloud, and AWS.

TABLE 3.2

Main Features of Firebase, IBM Cloud, and AWS Platforms

	Name	Firebase	IBM Cloud	AWS
Platform Supported	SaaS	✓	✓	✓
	PaaS	✓	✗	✓
	IaaS	✗	✗	✓
Audience	Organizations looking for:	compute power, database storage, and content delivery	tools to build successful apps	cloud solution
Support	Online	✓	✓	✓
	Business hours	✗	✗	✓
	24/7 Live support	✗	✗	✓
Ratings	Overall	4.8/5	4.6/5	4.6/5
	Ease	4.7/5	4.9/5	4.6/5
	Features	5.0/5	4.6/5	4.3/5
	Design	4.5/5	4.8/5	4.5/5
	Support	4.9/5	4.7/5	4.6/5
Training	Documentations	✓	✓	✓
	Webinars	✗	✗	✓
	Live Online	✗	✗	✓
	In Person	✗	✗	✓
Company Information	Amazon	Founded: 1994 United States aws.amazon.com	✗	✗
	Google	✗	Founded: 1998 United States www.google.com	✗
	IBM	✗	✗	Founded: 1911 United States www.ibm.com/cloud

(Continued)

TABLE 3.2

(Continued)

	Name	Firebase	IBM Cloud	AWS
Alternatives	Hostinger		⊗	⊗
		⊗	Frontegg	⊗
		⊗	⊗	Maxihost Bare Metal
	Microsoft Azure		⊗	⊗
		⊗	Singular	⊗
		⊗	⊗	Storecove
	DigitalOcean		⊗	⊗
		⊗	FusionAuth	⊗
		⊗	⊗	ArchiverFS
	Oracle Cloud Infrastructure		⊗	⊗
		⊗	Twilio	⊗
		⊗	⊗	IBM Db2
	UpCloud		⊗	⊗
		⊗	Backendless	⊗
		⊗	⊗	Microsoft Access

TABLE 3.2

(Continued)

	Name	Firebase	IBM Cloud	AWS
Categories	Cloud Hosting	✓	✗	✓
	Cloud Management	✓	✗	✗
	Cloud Storage	✓	✗	✗
	DevOps	✓	✗	✓
	Hybrid Cloud	✓	✗	✓
	IT Management	✓	✗	✗
	Server Management	✓	✗	✗
	Web Hosting	✓	✗	✗
	Mobile App Development	✗	✓	✗
	Push Notifications	✗	✓	✗
	Relational Database	✗	✗	✓
Integrations	Mio	✓	✓	✓
	Pipedream	✓	✓	✓
	Affirmed Cloud Edge	✓	✗	✗
	AppBilling	✓	✗	✓
	Artifakt	✓	✗	✗
	Azure Pipelines	✓	✗	✗
	Canonical Juju	✗	✗	✓
	Cloudcraft	✓	✗	✗
	Coalfire	✗	✗	✓
	Coding Rooms	✓	✗	✗
	FNA	✓	✗	✗
	Grumatic	✓	✗	✗
	Jira Software	✗	✓	✗
	LendingWise	✓	✗	✗
	Onde	✗	✓	✗
	SOLIXCloud CDP	✓	✗	✓
	SaltStack	✓	✗	✗
	Trakzee	✓	✗	✗
	Virtana Platform	✓	✗	✗
	diDNA	✓	✗	✗

3.2.10 Related Cloud Computing Applications

Cloud computing has been integrated into various fields such as telecommunications, governments, enterprises, backups, big data analytics, education, and healthcare, which demand a lot of computing services. The following companies have proven the viability of cloud computing by simply taking advantage of the cloud services and expanding the company's business.

- *The New York Times* is based on the guaranteed services provided by cloud computing. By gathering old magazines dating back to the 18th century, the *New York Times* had to assemble these images in a portable document format, which was successfully processed using 100 EC2 instances within 24 hours at a low cost. In addition to the *New York Times*, the *Washington Post* also had the same experience by converting thousands of images into a database using a cloud server.

- **DISA:** The Defense Information Systems Agency (DISA) has mentioned the cost of using the Amazon EC2 to be 10 cents on an hourly basis.

- **SmugMug** is a type of web application for posting images that uses Amazon's S3 cloud storage service. With the use of cloud service, SmugMug saved thousands of dollars by reducing storage costs in half.

- **Eli Lily** is dedicated to research purposes and benefits from cloud computing services to provide promising performance for required processes, where execution time for a process is limited to a few seconds compared to the number of weeks when traditional methods were used.

- **TC3**, which stands for Total Claims Capture & Control and cares for health, also benefits from cloud computing service by maintaining service-level agreement (SLA).

- **Industry 4.0** is a digitalization process that has altered the natural basis of those organizations associated mainly with the manufacturing sector, by totally distorting the value and production chain. Industry 4.0 is a novel high-tech intelligent framework that is powered by the cloud and exhibits the characteristics of ubiquity and pervasiveness. The critical enabler of the Industrial Revolution 4.0 is cloud technology. Research commissioned by Oracle found that 60% of businesses see an integrated enterprise Cloud Platform as the route to unlocking the potential of disruptive technologies such as robotics or AI at the heart of Industry 4.0. This is due to the scale and the speed provided by the cloud that proves to be the connection backbone of Industry 4.0. Enterprises adopting Industry 4.0 are thus able to bring about the digital transformation process faster with the help of the cloud.

- **Cloud-Radio Access Networks (C-RAN):** C-RAN is a central cloud computing architectural framework in which these networks are based on emerging standards such as 5G/6G. C-RAN provides real-time virtualization functionalities, collaborative radio system support, and massive deployment. With the mobile network architecture advances, it becomes possible to manage complex features such as network resource slicing, statistical multiplexing, energy efficiency, and high capacity. The main state-of-the-art technologies that enable the realization of C-RAN are Software-Defined Networking (SDN) and Network Function Virtualization (NFV). By using the same infrastructure with different access technologies, operators can achieve more rapid deployment of mobile networks in C-RAN. To this end, the deployment cost is reduced, the network resources are effectively utilized, and the maintenance cost is minimized. The rationale of C-RAN is to split the functions of the base stations by separating the base station into a Base Band Unit (BBU) and a Remote Radio Head (RRH). After that, using cloud computing and virtualization techniques, the BBUs from several sites are centralized into a common geographical location such as a data center. BBUs are responsible for Baseband signal processing, and signal amplification and modulation are performed by RRHs. A front haul link connects the BBU pool to the RRHs that are deployed at the cell site using an antenna. In a virtualized BBU pool, baseband processing is centralized. Hence, adaptation to random traffic and effective utilization of the resources becomes possible.

The same BBU pool can be shared by several operators, by leasing it as a cloud service. Additionally, with a reduction in the handover delay, an improvement in network performance has been achieved.

- **Big data analytics:** Big data is related to gigantic volumes of data produced by operational systems such as Enterprise Resource Planning (ERP), Customer Relationship Management (CRM), Supply Chain Management (SCM) systems, as well as IoT sensors and mobile traffic. The tremendous combination of both structured and non-structured data is referred to as big data in contrast with the conventional data structures. The main characteristics of big data can be portrayed by volume, velocity, variety, and veracity. Plenty of advanced quantitative techniques such as AI, machine learning, deep learning, statistics, and numerical methods are used for data mining and pattern discovery in big data. Cloud computing provides flexible, efficient use of data, and enhanced communication; thus, it can significantly promote the capacity of scalable analytics solutions.

- **Cloud Private Branch Exchange (PBX):** A low-cost, scalable, secure, and reliable office phone system can be obtained via an Internet connection by using a cloud or virtual PBX. A PBX system is a private phone system deployed inside a company or organization. New business phone systems have shifted away from conventional phone systems, which are now being replaced by PBX systems that make use of an Internet connection. By connecting IP phones to a PBX server, major cost savings and enhanced phone features are obtained. In contrast, a cloud phone system is hosted on a cloud server although it operates in a similar fashion. Given the availability of efficient network connectivity in most organizations, the cloud PBX has become a viable option.

- **Processing Pipelines:** Processing pipelines represent huge segments of data applications running on the cloud at the present time. Such applications for data processing support:
  - Datasets recording created by browsers.
  - Relevant data prediction and analysis.
  - Image processing, for image conversion to support image enhancement and thumbnails, in addition to image compression and encryption.
  - Video transcoding, to support the conversion from one video format to another.
  - Document processing, to encrypt documents and convert one format to another. Data processing also supports optical character recognition (OCR) to allow editable PDF files.

- **Batch Processing:** Batch processing systems also cover a broad spectrum of data-intensive applications in enterprise computing. Such applications typically have deadlines, and the failure to meet these deadlines could have serious economic consequences. Security is also a critical aspect for many applications of batch processing. A non-exhaustive list of batch processing purposes involves:
  - Creating detailed reports for various economic, health, and other types of divisions based on a specific period.
  - Inventory management for large corporations.
  - Handling invoicing statements.
  - Updating software sources.
  - Authenticating software and hardware systems.

- **Web Access:** The access of websites is done on an episodic period or for an occasional event only; precisely, some websites occur during a conference, Christmas, or summer season. Other limited-time websites used for promotional activities, "sleep" during the night and auto-scale during the day, store their data close to the premise of the computational servers. Hence, the cost of the storage (per GB) is low with more efficient data processing.

- **E-Learning:** The days when the search for information required a library are gone. These days, digitally enabled classrooms are available to allow students to create and submit presentations online, attend classes remotely through web conferencing, and collaborate and participate in globally distributed projects. Examples of e-learning cloud systems are SlideRocket and Ratatype.

- **Healthcare:** Traditionally, searching for a patient's history among the bulk of hospital records is considered a big hassle to experience. On the contrary, with the presence of health management systems such as the healthcare cloud, all data is found on secure cloud solutions and can be retrieved with just a button. With the cloud service, all information on the cloud is shared and accessed among all relevant investors. In addition to information sharing, the cloud guarantees no delay, which is preferable and needed for resolving critical situations. Also, remote surgery can now be real with the integration of cloud services, by which a revolution in the healthcare sector will be a promising progress.

- **Anti-Virus Applications:** In the past, anti-virus software was installed in the company's system. With the presence of the cloud, the company doesn't need to install the anti-virus as the anti-virus is found in the cloud. Hence, the software monitors the company's system remotely, identifies the security risks, and fixes them.

- **E-commerce Application:** Cloud-based e-commerce permits a quick response to any emerging possibilities and challenges in the market in the least possible time. Users respond quickly to market opportunities and traditional e-commerce responds to the challenges quickly. Cloud-based e-commerce gives a new approach to doing business in the minimum time possible. Customer data, product data, and other operational systems are managed in cloud environments. For example, Hepsiburada, Gittigidiyor, and n11 are Turkish e-commerce platforms that use Google Cloud's Big Query platform to leverage data and insights and identify customers' needs more precisely. This improves the business' data-driven decision-making environment.

- **E-Governance Application:** Cloud computing offers its services to several activities carried out by the government. It helps the government to provide services professionally by expanding the availability of the environment, making the environment more scalable and customized. It helps the government to cut down on unnecessary costs related to managing, installing, and upgrading applications.

- **Personal Storage:** The cloud offers an unrestricted feature related to storing personal data on the cloud, and even sharing these files becomes possible through applications running on the cloud such as Dropbox.

- **Navigation:** Most modern vehicles, such as Tesla, come with navigation programs. Cloud computing has enabled these navigation programs to store large amounts of map data and regularly update it to assist the drivers. Whenever the driver uses these tools, he/she is indirectly utilizing the cloud to reach the destination. Also, these vehicle companies provide an option of synchronizing the owner's info and preferences on other vehicles if they own more than one vehicle.

3.3   Cloud-based Real-Time Weather Forecasting System

This section focuses on real-time weather forecasting systems using cloud computing in detail. Weather forecasting refers to the prediction of the state of the atmosphere at a future time and specific location. Physical models are mostly used to simulate and predict meteorological dynamics, known as Numerical Weather Prediction (NWP). In NWP, the atmosphere is modeled as a fluid with numerical solutions of atmospheric hydrothermodynamic equations to provide the future state of the atmosphere. The initial conditions directly affect the accuracy of the prediction where the instability of the differential equations under perturbations and uncertainties in the initial measurements can affect the reliability of the NWP [5]. Nowadays, with IoT evolution and techniques such as neural networks, Fuzzy logic, time series, and regression analysis, it becomes possible to predict the weather. Several forecasting systems that provide short-term forecasts for small regions mainly rely

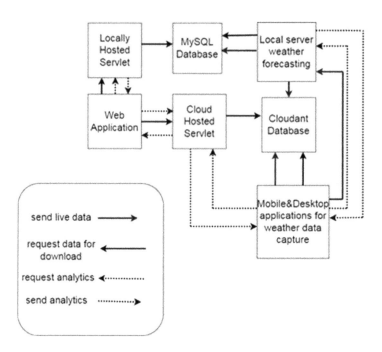

FIGURE 3.10 Weather-forecast system data flow.

on localized sensors connected to cloud services. The data flow of the real-time weather forecasting system is shown in Figure 3.10.

The description of each block of the data flow system is as follows:

1. Locally Hosted Servlet: The servlet is located on an Apache Tomcat server unlike the cloud-hosted servlet but with similar tasks. Connection to the servlet is done after verifying the server IP Address.

2. MySQL Database: This database locally stores data requested by different applications. Apart from the cloud-hosted servlet, it carries out prediction locally on the local server.
   • Local Server: The functionalities of the local server are as follows:
     • Displays a live graph that monitors the current weather conditions.
     • Collects various application's data locally or on the Cloudant platform.
     • Performs prediction locally and displays the result to the client.
     • Transfers the requested data either from its database or Cloudant platform.
     • Serves requests for data or analytics results from the mobile and desktop clients.

3. Cloudant Database: The **IBM** Cloud platform offers the Cloudant database as a service where the weather data is collected in the cloud and accessible worldwide.

4. Cloud Hosted Servlet: The requests issued by the clients visiting a webpage are served by the servlet. The servlet performs the following tasks:
   • Updates the real-time graph on the webpage accessed by the client.
   • Retrieves data from the Cloudant database upon client requests.
   • Carries out analytical reviews and sends them back to the client.

5. Web Application: Different real-time weather data is provided to the user with variations on a graph, enabling the user to access and save the data for a specific date or for several monitored data. More details on the above blocks can be obtained from Chapter 7 of [5].

6. Mobile and Desktop Applications for Weather Data Capture: This part explains an Android application development to capture weather data from an API that allows users to monitor

TABLE 3.3

Library Functionality for Desktop Applications

Library	Purpose	Repository	Jar Files
Cloudant Manager	Contains several classes to interact with the Cloudant database programmatically.	https://github.com/cloudant/java-cloudant	• cloudant-client-2.19.2.jar • cloudant-http-2.19.2.jar • commons-codec-1.6.jar • commons-io-2.4.jar • gson-2.8.6.jar
JSON	Used to parse JSON documents into Java objects and to generate new JSON documents from the Java classes.	https://github.com/stleary/JSON-java	json-20210307.jar
JSOUP	JSOUP is a Java library for working with real-world HTML. It provides a very convenient API for fetching URLs and extracting and manipulating data, using the best of HTML5 DOM methods and CSS selectors.	https://mvnrepository.com/artifact/org.jsoup/jsoup	jsoup-1.13.1.jar
JFreeChart	JFreeChart is a comprehensive free chart library for the Java platform that is used in the project to create a chart that is updated with new values.	https://github.com/jfree/jfreechart	• hamcrest-core-1.3.jar • jcommon-1.0.23.jar • jfreechart-1.0.19.jar • jfreechart-1.0.19-experimental.jar • jfreechart-1.0.19-swt.jar • jfreesvg-2.0.jar • junit-4.11.jar • orsoncharts-1.4-eval nofx.jar • orsonpdf-1.6-eval.jar • servlet.jar • swtgraphics2d.jar

the current weather conditions in real time. Also, by integrating traditional regression analysis and neural networks into the application, it is possible to predict the weather conditions for the next N minutes. First, the desktop application is created in NetBeans IDE using the steps described in Appendix 3A.

A detailed description of various library functionality for desktop applications can be found in Table 3.3.

7. Secondly, the steps for creating a new Cloudant database to store weather forecasting observations are given in Appendix 3B.

3.4 Challenges and Future of Real-Time Cloud Applications

This section highlights various challenges that might face real-time cloud applications and the future of cloud applications. In fact, any new technology starts simply as an idea and provides benefits at its time, but it faces various limitations and challenges. This is also true for cloud computing, where its main challenges can be listed as follows.

3.4.1 Main Challenges

The integration of real-time applications with the cloud is not as easy as it sounds; on the contrary, this entails prediction features of real-time virtualization. Hence, the adoption of real-time applications in the cloud faces essential challenges. The key barrier faced by predictability is directly related to the restricted access to hardware resources. These challenges are listed as follows:

- Cloud computing heavily depends on the underlying network infrastructure. Hence, the challenges that network elements face might be encountered on the cloud as well, such as server failures, denial of services and malware attacks, power-off instances, communication latencies, and security [7].
- Cloud providers should maintain a decent SOA to efficiently provide different services.
- Data storage that deals with bandwidth, capacity, and location should be carefully considered where the performance of applications is directly affected by data storage.
- Cloud computing with its services is not yet fully mature due to the presence of various vendors with their own terms and assistances.
- Cloud environments can impose portability/interoperability limitations. Sometimes, it becomes necessary to migrate from one cloud provider to another due to certain operations. Since services offered by each cloud provider are proprietary, the customer will face what is called vendor locked-in costs associated with such migration.
- Balancing workloads evenly among servers becomes difficult, where each physical server can host many virtual servers and sometimes receives workloads more than its neighboring physical servers.
- Sometimes cloud service becomes unavailable when:
  - Runtime usage demands exceed the cloud's processing capacity.
  - Maintenance update mandates a temporary outage.
  - Permanent migration to a new physical server host is required.
  - Meeting the deadline in real-time systems is classified as soft and hard real-time systems. Failure to meet the deadline in soft real-time systems is just annoying to the customer. However, this would result in catastrophic results in hard real-time systems.
- Some challenges must be considered when dealing with C-RAN. Since in the C-RAN, there is centralization of the BBUs at a single site (data center), this raises the awareness for preventing the single point of failure. In addition, data consistency must be maintained since BBU data are shared by many cloud providers. Also, channel connectivity must always be available between BBU and RRHs and must be resistant to any external factor.
- Scaling or elasticity of the cloud: The cloud's main service is to provide the applications with the necessary number of resources whereas in the public cloud, the users pay for such resources, and this provides the user guarantee for accessing such resources. In the case of excessive and unpredictable external load and server failures, resource reallocation that guarantees a smooth and continuous application runtime is a must. For instance, Amazon offers an adaptive load-balancing service to distribute the incoming load from different applications among its multiple instances.
- Load balancing: Most cloud applications use the horizontal scaling mode where the number of VMs is either increased or decreased based on the existing workload. Therefore, load balancing among the VMs should be efficiently maintained between the front-end servers and back-end servers.
  - Mapping a computation: An important aspect of the cloud is to successfully map an application to a suitable server to maintain a reduction in computing time and network traffic.
  - Virtualization: Virtualization is one of the key challenges faced by real-time applications where guaranteeing isolation among them is to be achieved. Hence, this means a smooth

translation of SLAs to resource assignment such as network bandwidth, latency, memory, and so on, should be carried out. However, guaranteeing the timing requirements in real-time applications is needed. Specifically, resource virtualization should be detached from the application execution and cloud resources. The demand for the existence of real-time virtual machines (RT-VMs) is remarkably increasing especially for distributed real-time virtualized environments, where the virtualized network performance becomes unpredictable.

- Resource sharing: Resources such as network, storage, power, and computing resources are usually shared among different VMs. Hence, running software in predictable means becomes a difficult task, especially in real-time cloud computing settings. Likewise, setting up new VMs or even migrating from one machine to another adds an enormous load that not only directly affects the performance but also induces interference among VMs even worse. Since the performance of a VM depends on its load and the load of VMs of other network members.

- Security and privacy: Usually data is internally located in data centers in different countries, where laws for data protection and data privacy differ from one country to another. This makes many CIOs not fully satisfied.

3.4.2 Future Directions

The most important target to be achieved in cloud computing is related to enhancing the network that embraces high bandwidth, high speed, and more reliable and secure networks – in addition to ensuring confidentiality in data centers with more effective data access algorithms. Achieving the target encourages many businesses in the market to join the cloud. Since everything will be executed on the cloud, guaranteeing good network performance is a requirement, especially in cases where scalability is needed. Ethernet can also make use of the cloud since its critical challenge, which is to prevent contention at the cost of decreasing the network throughput, can be resolved. Video streaming is one of the applications that can benefit from real-time cloud computing that can guarantee the required network resources. X-Gigabit solutions are becoming promising solutions not only for network throughput enhancement but also to easily adapt to the increase in VMs running on the cloud.

REFERENCES

1. [Online]. Available: https://networkinterview.com/evolution-of-cloud-computing/
2. [Online]. Available: https://mu.ac.in/wp-content/uploads/2021/01/Cloud-Computing.pdf
3. W. Forrest and C. Barthold, "Clearing the Air on Cloud Computing," 2009, M. &. Co.
4. R. Buyya, C. S. Yeo, S. Venugopal, J. Broberg and I. Brandic, "Cloud computing and emerging IT platforms: Vision, hype, and reality for delivering computing as the 5th utility," *Future Generation Computer Systems*, 25, 599–616, 2009.
5. T. P. Fowdur, L. Babooram, M. Indoonundon and M. Rosun, *Real-Time Cloud Computing and Machine Learning Applications*, New York: Nova Science Publisher, 2021.
6. "SourgeForge," *Slashdot Media*, 2022. [Online]. Available: https://sourceforge.net/software/compare/Amazon-Web-Services-AWS-vs-Firebase-vs-IBM-Cloud/
7. M. D. Dikaiakos, D. Katsaros, P. Mehra and G. Pallis, "Cloud computing: Distributed Internet computing for IT and scientific research," *IEEE Internet Computing*, 13(5), 10–13, 2009.

4

The Role of Blockchain in IoT

Khalid Mahmood
National Yunlin University of Science and Technology, Douliu, Yunlin, Taiwan

Hasan Javed, Nosherwan Adil, and Iqra Aslam
Riphah International University, Lahore, Pakistan

Salman Shamshad
The University of Lahore, Lahore, Pakistan

Mohammad S. Obaidat
King Abdullah II School of Information Technology University of Jordan, Amman, Jordan
University of Science and Technology Beijing, Beijing, China
SRM University, India
Amity University, Noida, India

4.1 Introduction

The Internet of Things (IoT) is a emerging, inventive, and revolutionary computing paradigm that connects any object with storage, computation, and communication capabilities to the Internet. Securing gadgets to the Internet leads to several applications, including smart homes, smart grids, smart cities, smart transportation, intelligent logistics, innovative healthcare, and smart industries. According to Global System for Mobile Communications Association (GSMA), IoT will bring about a trillion worldwide by 2025, giving vendors, companies, and manufacturers a vast investment opportunity [1].

The IoT has a wide range of applications. For example, IoT devices worn by patients can be directly linked to healthcare organizations through a network continuously transmitting information such as blood pressure and heart rate. This could allow for remote patient monitoring and faster healthcare responses. Additionally, in the transportation sector, IoT has expanded to the "Internet-of-Vehicles" (IoV), which can enhance transportation efficiency by promoting safer driving, optimizing fuel usage, providing entertainment to vehicle users, and improving travel times. By installing IoT sensors on logistics containers and connecting them via advanced network technologies such as LTE Advanced (LTE-A) or 5G, global logistics could be improved [2]. In summary, IoT is a new technology that offers benefits to numerous stakeholders and individuals. IoT is a new technology that benefits many stakeholders and people.

IoT applications carry crucial information; for example, IoV handles automobile safety notifications. E-health directly affects human lives, and logistics might include essential information regarding things' durability and delivery schedules. IoT networks need security and privacy [3].

Blockchain (BC) was initially advocated for cryptocurrencies and the financial sector may be used to secure IoT networks. The BC aims to establish a public "open ledger" where any participating node may receive needed information without a third party [4]. BC is an entirely decentralized method, which makes the network more secure and open because every node has the same correct, up-to-date information. Upon successfully completing a challenging consensus process, miners have

DOI:10.1201/9781003326236-4

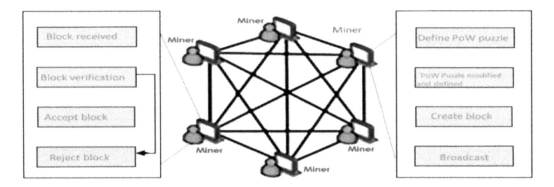

FIGURE 4.1 PoW technique in BC systems.

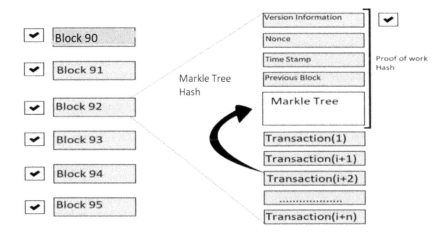

FIGURE 4.2 BC made using linked blocks.

the ability to modify and append data on the blockchain network. This process involves solving complex algorithms or puzzles. There are several existing consensus algorithms used in blockchain, such as Proof-of-Work (PoW), Proof-of-Stake (PoS), Delegated Proof-of-Stake (DPoS), Ripple, Tendermint, and others. The PoW algorithm is employed by Bitcoin and Ethereum, is illustrated in Figure 4.1, where each miner creates a puzzle as part of the blockchain system. Next, the node publishes a puzzle in BC, which is available to all nodes. Nodes that solve PoW may retain, access, and alter BC data [5].

Figure 4.2 shows a BC made using linked blocks. Each block consists of two sections: a PoW hash and transactions. The PoW hash includes various elements such as a nonce, timestamps, previous block, and Merkle trees, while the transactions contain user data that is stored on the blockchain. One of the advantages of using blockchain in IoT-based networks is that it provides inherent trust, facilitates distributed content sharing, ensures privacy-aware communication, is designed with security in mind, and offers high levels of resilience and dependability.

4.2 Overview of the IoT

Recently, academics and business experts have paid a lot of attention on the progress of Internet of Things (IoT). IoT is exciting because it may make new ways of doing things available to us. On a personal level, it presents a society of the future where everything is linked to the Internet and converses with one another to operate intelligently. The ultimate goal is to improve the environment around us by giving things the ability to instantaneously sense their surroundings, interact with one another without incurring substantial expenditures, and react to our wants and preferences without our guidance. The IoT has more commercial potential [6].

It involves the automatic discovery and fast analysis of hundreds of elements relating to services or commodities, as well as the automatic response to any problems before they have an influence on client experiences or the functionality of objects. In order to gain a competitive advantage through improved service delivery and optimized business processes, it is necessary to obtain and analyze large amounts of both structured and unstructured data from a variety of sources, including internal and external sources as well as social media [7]. Consider how the Internet has impacted people, businesses, science, governments, and even our capacity to control the environment before you dismiss this as a bold assertion. Many believe that the IoT will be the greatest technical challenge in history.

In 1999, Kevin Ashton created the term IoT. Linking the innovative idea of Radio Frequency Identification (RFID) in Procter & Gamble's supply chain to the Internet at the time was more than just a clever way to attract the ex-executives. IoT has the potential to bring about a transformation in the world comparable to the impact of the Internet. The MIT Auto-ID Center presented their vision for the IoT in 2001, while the Internet of Things was officially named and recognized by the International Telecommunication Union (ITU) Internet Report in 2005. IoT use is growing, particularly in wireless communications.

The increase of smart objects or things in our surroundings, such as smartphones, smart watches, advanced home automation systems, etc., that can interact with one another and work with other systems to complete certain tasks, serves as evidence of this [8]. IoT's biggest strength is without a doubt the significant improvements it has already made to businesses and people's daily lives. IoT is presently used by businesses to create new business models, improve operational processes, lower costs, and mitigate risks, among many other things. A few examples of how people's lives are improving include in the areas of learning, security, and health monitoring [9].

IoT is based on the idea that physical connections may be created through the Internet to monitor and manage processes involving people, animals, objects, and even trees. People may access "things" via connections and take control as required. They go beyond being just informative Internet connections [10]. As a result, connecting things together is not the major goal. Instead, information gleaned from related objects is used to improve products and services. Before offering a definition, it would be beneficial to first list the essential components that make up the IoT. Essentially, the IoT is a network of actual physical objects. Sensors are used to obtain data.

Identifiers: In order to study the data, identifiers are instruments for locating the source of the data (such as sensors or devices). All things considered, the IoT is a network of objects that are easily recognizable, equipped with software intelligence and sensors, and permanently connected to the Internet for communication and message delivery [11]. Things may interact with their maker, owner, or other connected devices using the IoT to share information. It makes it possible to remotely sense things (to offer exact information) and operate real-world objects online. This makes it possible for computer-based systems and the outside world to interact more closely, boosting productivity, accuracy, and financial advantages. Each one differs from the others and can work with the present Internet infrastructure thanks to its own computer system. Industry experts and businesses project that the IoT will facilitate the connection of numerous devices. According to Gartner's prediction [12], the number of devices in use will reach 20 billion by the year 2020. Cisco also forecasts that by that time, there will be 26.8 billion connected devices, including laptops, mobile phones, tablets, televisions, and machine-to-machine gadgets.

Others consider this prediction to be underwhelming since it makes the assumption that any gadget with a simple microcontroller, an easy on/off switch, or even a QR (Quick Response) code would someday be able to connect to the Internet [13]. The theory of Moore's Law [14], which states that the number of transistors in a densely packed integrated circuit doubles roughly every 18 months, supports this claim. The term IoT is also referred to as the "Internet of Everything" (IoE), which encompasses people, data, processes, and things. Therefore, the IoE is an extension of the IoT.

- People: Bringing people together may help individuals integrate more thoroughly.
- Data: Making decisions by using data to obtain understanding.
- Process: Transferring the proper info to the proper device or person at the proper moment.
- Things: Things are genuine objects and machinery that communicate using the Internet and other technology to reach intelligent conclusions.

IoT seeks to link "things" so that they can take appropriate action by deftly communicating with one another. The Internet of Things is then integrated with the Internet of People (IoP). However, this book and modern literature claim that "IoT" refers to everything (including people). Given this, the IoT may be described as follows: With the use of the IoT, or IoT, devices may identify themselves, have internal intelligence, and be able to sense and take action. It connects people and things over the Internet. We'll use the term "IoT" to refer to anything that is connected to the Internet, as we have in the past. This includes equipment, buildings, automobiles, people, pets, and other creatures, as well as trees and other plants. IoT is based on the idea that "things" may be seen and controlled from anywhere in the world.

4.3   Internet of Things(IoT)

4.3.1   Background

IoT was initially conceived approximately 20 years ago, although its technology had been under development for years. Let's trace the emergence of IoT and its supporting and linked technologies [15].

- 1969—The Internet, the primary technology behind IoT, emerged as the Advanced Research Project Agency Network (ARPANET), which was used by the academic and research fraternity to share research work, develop new interconnection techniques, and link computers to many general-purpose computer centers of the U.S. defense department, public, and private sector.
- 1973—RFID is another IoT necessity. RFID technology has existed since World War II, but in 1973, Mario W. Cardullo was awarded the first U.S. patent for a rewritable RFID tag. That same year, a California businessman named Charles Walton also obtained a patent for a passive transponder capable of opening distanced doors.
- Embedded computers were another IoT technology. These embedded systems use single-board processors and microcontrollers.
- 1984—IoT usage before it was named [16] A Coke machine linked to the Internet reported availability and temperature.
- 1990: The Internet spreads in commercial and consumer areas. Low network connectivity hindered its utilization.
- In 1991, Mark Weiser proposed ubiquitous computing. Advanced embedded computing allows ubiquitous computing to be everywhere but undetectable. It was replaced by pervasive computing.
- In the mid-1990s—sensor nodes were created to detect data from uniquely recognized embedded devices and easily share information.

- Bill Joy created a device-to-device communication in 1999, and Ashton came up with the phrase "Internet of Things." The Auto-ID Center at MIT created a low-cost chip that can store data and link devices to the Internet.
- In the year 2000, Internet connectivity had become commonplace for many purposes, and it was necessary for all companies and products to be online and to give information.

These Internet-connected gadgets still need human intervention and supervision through applications and interfaces. The IoT's ultimate promise will be fulfilled when technology works behind the scenes and responds in real time to our expectations or needs.

4.3.2 Applications of IoT

The IoT refers to things that can transport data across a network without human intervention. Gartner predicts that by 2020, 20.4 billion connected devices will be in use. The IoT industry is projected to see growth in its market value, reaching 1.7 trillion USD by 2020, compared to its value of 655.8 billion USD in 2014. IoT systems will generate this much income. An IoT platform collects data from any source item utilizing circuits and sensors, processes and transmits it across a network, and stores, visualizes and processes it using artificial intelligence. Recent advancements in sensors, efficient communication protocols, open-source server programs, state-of-the-art web development tools, and dashboards of IoT are being used to address numerous social concerns, as illustrated in Figure 4.3.

4.3.2.1 Military

The IoT has military uses. ZigBee and GSM networks were utilized to monitor and track armed personnel's health. These systems have downsides such as restricted bandwidth, high operating costs, and sophisticated infrastructure. Upgrade armed personnel's health monitoring and tracking systems to IoT architecture to solve these shortcomings. IoT may increase military situational

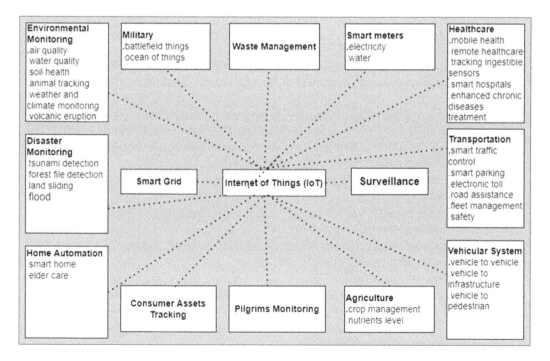

FIGURE 4.3 Applications of IoT.

awareness, risk assessment, and reaction time. IoT-based technologies may help the military detect adversaries, monitor soldiers' physical and mental health, and coordinate troops with defensive systems. Military outfits and helmets with built-in sensors can track soldiers' positions and vitals. The command center can rescue armed people in real time. Bright military clothes and helmets might have a temperature, pulse rate, acceleration, ECG, movement, and oxygen level sensors.

4.3.2.2 Healthcare

IoT applications for treating chronic illnesses, tracking ingestible sensors, mobile health, and smart hospitals are covered in this area.

4.3.2.2.1 Remote Health Monitoring

Patients may enjoy their usual lives while being continually monitored, thanks to remote health monitoring. With the help of the remote health monitoring system, falls in elderly, cardiac, neurological, and diabetic patients are detected. The patient's body is equipped with sensors to collect vital signs, accelerometers, sensors that measure respiration rates, a t-shirt with integrated sensors, a Kinect camera, wireless body sensors, Pulse Amped sensor, a defibrillator device, pulsometers, and pedometers, as well as a textile-based autonomous nervous system. These signals are then amplified, filtered, and packetized in accordance with the communication network. On a central server, the processed data is saved and examined. Physicians may keep track of patients' health using a graphical user interface.

4.3.2.2.2 Tracking Ingestion Sensors

Capsule endoscopy uses ingestible sensors to communicate pictures of the body's interior to hospital software. Ingestible capsules may also detect nutrient uptake and gas production during digestion.

4.3.2.2.3 Smart Hospitals

IoT makes hospitals more luminous. Smartphone-based appointment scheduling, mobile application-based inquiry, test result reporting, etc., are the initial steps toward an intelligent hospital. Medical devices intelligently transmit real-time sensed data (e.g., ECG, blood pressure, blood sugar, etc.) to a remote medical server. accessible to a medical physician. It's possible to monitor very expensive medical equipment using chips.

4.3.2.3 Home Automation

Control of home appliances has been redefined by the IoT. A network device, a microcontroller, and a relay switch may be used to connect any appliance to the Internet. Appliances may be controlled remotely, thanks to a graphical user interface. IoT-based home automation systems utilize a variety of sensors, including those for temperature measurement (such as DHT11/22, DS18B20, and LM35), light measurement (such as TSL2591 and BH1750), water level detection (such as HC-SR04 and LM1830), air quality measurement (such as MiCS-5525, MQ-8, and MQ135), and humidity measurement (such as HIH6100 and Dig RH). The focus is on utilizing IoT technology in home automation initiatives that deliver an AI-optimized lighting system. This system, based on the geolocation of home automation nodes, provides a cloud-based system for detecting intrusion that notifies the police. An email or SMS alert to the fire department may be sent by a gas or smoke detection system.

4.3.2.4 Solid Waste Management

Unfilled trash can waste time, fuel, and labor if solid waste is scheduled to be collected daily. Additionally, if trash bins are picked up weekly, spillage pollutes the environment. IoT garbage bin monitoring solutions tackle solid waste management challenges by utilizing sensor-based bin level monitoring systems. The end sensor node is made up of an ultrasonic sensor for tracking the amount of garbage that is still unfilled, a microcontroller for processing that data, a solar panel for charging the battery, and a radio for disseminating the unfilled data online. Bin levels are managed via central monitoring using an app.

4.3.2.5 Smart Metering

Every home needs water, gas, and electricity. End-of-month bills are usually sent. IoT-based smart metering allows service providers to monitor resource utilization from a central station and helps users track daily usage. A smart meter sends usage data to a central server through the Internet. Main monitoring stations, including electricity, gas, and water distribution centers, relay information to clients over the Internet. After receiving paperless bills, customers can view and pay them online.

4.3.2.6 Surveillance

Human behavior and activity monitoring are vital. Surveillance systems are essential for monitoring worker behaviors, workplace amenities, and security-sensitive areas. Surveillance lets the user monitor and lead individuals and gathers evidence during an inquiry, presenting an IoT-based surveillance system. This Internet-connected surveillance equipment collects data constantly. Audio or video data is acceptable. A cloud server shares collected information remotely. It is feasible to conduct continuous remote monitoring, offering real-time insights into the records of individuals entering and exiting a location. In the event of theft, security alerts will be instantly sent to a mobile device through motion detection, facial recognition, and identification of vehicle license plates, allowing for quick action to be taken. It controls and coordinates real-time workplace labor.

4.3.2.7 Consumer Asset Tracking

IoT identifies physical items uniquely. This feature uses IoT to monitor customer assets. Most mobile phones include Global Positioning System (GPS) tracking technology that helps find misplaced phones. IoT gives consumer items a unique identity and an online connection. E-commerce enterprises may track their in-transit merchandise to ensure delivery. Sensors include accelerometers, GPS, vibration sensors, and RFID. Nano network processors link to cloud services.

4.3.2.8 Smart Grid

Conventional power systems have low dependability, high outages, carbon emissions, safety issues, etc. The IoT can turn a traditional power infrastructure into an intelligent grid. A smart grid is an IoT system that detects multiple grid components and controls power supply based on demand. The smart grid enables accurate and rapid consumer interactions. Due to online monitoring, failure recovery is automated by gaining pre-control.

4.3.2.9 Vehicle Communication System (VCS)

Including sensor-to-vehicle, vehicle-to-vehicle, and vehicle-to-network communications, the IoT adds a new level to vehicular communications. There is additional communication between and inside vehicles. The temperature of the water in the cooling system, the pressure of the tyres, and other factors are all monitored via in-vehicle communication systems. A large number of sensors must be connected to the ECU, which makes use of CAN, FlexRay, Ethernet, etc. The design, deployment, and ECU communication may employ short-range protocols since the sensors are fixed and supplied by the vehicle's power source. The ability to communicate among vehicles enables them to avoid collisions, convey lane-changing instructions, etc. Using simple communication protocols and thoughtful architecture, the IoT may swiftly transform automobiles into intelligent cars.

4.3.2.10 Pilgrims Monitoring

A pilgrimage session draws more people. Many pilgrims go together. So, misplacing valuables or losing a group member is likely. If a pilgrim becomes separated from their group, it causes worry for their family and challenges crowd-control officials. An IoT-based pilgrim monitoring systems can identify missing, dead, and injured pilgrims, guide and connect them to their groups, and manage and regulate pilgrim crowds.

4.3.3 Architecture of IoT

Digital IoT A perfect IoT architecture that can incorporate all its attributes is unattainable due to the multi- and inter-disciplinary nature of the IoT. Several IoT architectures have been explored. Figure 4.4 shows our simplified four-layer design for capturing major IoT application features. Figure 4.4's architecture has four layers: device, edge, cloud, and cross. Describe each layer briefly. In this section, existing fog computing architecture, existing load balancing, and fault tolerance approaches have been described.

4.3.3.1 Layer-1—Device-Layer

This layer measures detects, and controls the environment. This layer comprises an (extensive) network of heterogeneous IoT end-devices such as sensors, actuators, transceivers, and processor units to accomplish application tasks. Various Original Equipment Manufacturers (OEMs) provide these gadgets with differing capacities. Because of varied application, hardware, and software requirements, selecting a device or hardware technology is not straightforward. This layer has several communication and networking protocols. No protocol can meet the needs of all IoT areas; hence there is a wide variety. Figure 4.4 shows examples of how a layer-1 IoT end-systems network may connect with the rest of the subsystem. This layer contains the most heterogeneous hardware, software, communication, and network protocols.

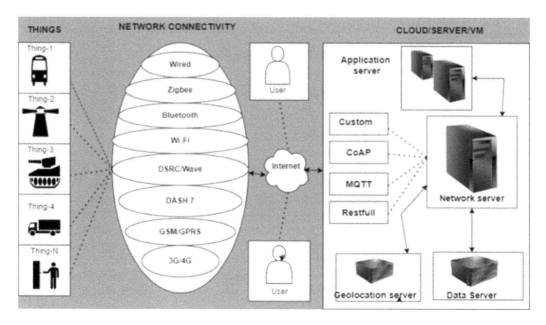

FIGURE 4.4 Architecture of IoT.

4.3.3.2 Layer-2 — Edge-Layer

Without any data processing, this layer serves as a bridge for data transfer between the device and cloud layers. Nevertheless, it may carry out challenging cloud tasks referred to as "edge computing" or "fog computing." Layer-1 porting of complex cloud services lowers bandwidth and latency for key applications. The hardware in this layer is capable of supporting current operating systems. For application developers, the operating system at this layer hides hardware heterogeneity. At the application layer, traditional Internet protocol suite protocols such as HTTP, MQTT, CoAP, etc., are employed for data exchange. This spans across both wired and wireless technologies, encompassing standards from 3GPP (3G, LTE, 5G, etc.), IEEE (802.11, 802.2), and others. The development of sophisticated operating systems (Linux, Windows, etc.) that enable the construction of hardware-independent, compute-intensive features or services is made possible by the use of resource-rich hardware devices at this layer.

4.3.3.3 Layer-3 — Cloud-Layer

The cloud stores large amounts of data from the layer and offers various tools for building cloud-based applications and services, including AI, big data, cognitive computing, machine learning techniques, analytics, and cross-domain data exchange. Since IoT application developers employ cloud services like SaaS, PaaS, and IaaS from Amazon, Google, Microsoft, etc., this layer hides less hardware variability. Applications may be moved more easily at this tier thanks to consistent APIs (like Mesos, Terraform, etc.) and safe access protocols (like MQTT, AMQP, HTTP, etc.).

4.3.3.4 IoT Cross-Layer Management

IoT system management is crucial to its sustainability and is the backbone of its design. System management plays a crucial role in installing and maintaining IoT end-systems, addressing a commercial need by providing a comprehensive examination of IoT administration. This includes aspects such as service orchestration, software maintenance, deployment troubleshooting, and configuration. The design covered in this part, in contrast to previous work, emphasizes common application domain features that are useful for comprehending and developing IoT functions. It also adds an essential cross-layer for system management to help deploy and maintain IoT systems.

4.4 Invariant Functionality (IF) and Programming Patterns (PP) for IoT Applications

This portion analyzes IoT apps' IF and PP in each architectural layer. IF/PP-1 Layer-1 is a network of IoT end-systems such as sensors, actuators, transceivers, HMIs, and processors. As stated below and summarized in Figure 4.4, IoT end-systems perform crucial high-level activities. These memory-encoded functions influence IoT end-device behavior. PU may configure IoT end-device types. Other sections perform end-device-specific tasks. An HMI's read function reads human input, not sensor data.

A write function controls actuators and displays data on OLED screens. Depending on the underlying communication technology and network protocol, a PU may transmit and receive data at layer-2, layer-3, or layer-1. PUs invoke the library or user-defined functions using an execute command (For instance, an algorithm that processes sensor data locally before transmission). Waiting delays, disrupts, and sleeps. Layer 2-IF/PP: At this layer, gateways transmit and receive.

The first set uses low-power wireless to exchange layer-1 data (LR WPAN or LPWAN). The second set is for Internet backhaul via 3GPP/4G, LTE, WLAN, etc. This layer may operate layer-1 cloud services, so a gateway might give a high-level execute command that a user can bind to one or more services. This layer, like layers 1 and 2, sends and receives data with layer-2 or the layer-1 bypassing gateway.

Cloud services and on-demand cloud instance configuration are vital. Figure 4.5 shows 3PP. IF/PP Cross-layer problems include regulating application logic deployment and behavior, preserving

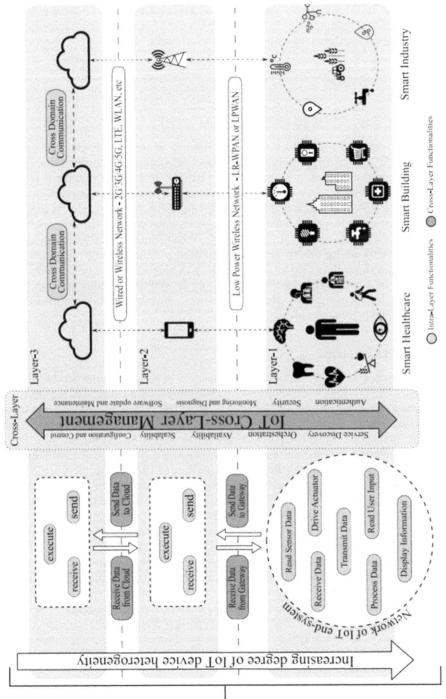

FIGURE 4.5

Invariant Functionality (IF) and Programming Pattern (PP).

firmware versions, and monitoring data sent during a network failure. These functionalities demand a continual network connection with send-and-receive instructions. System updates include setting devices with suitable firmware and monitoring the deployed software version. Devices should have a boot loader like Mender for OTA firmware updates. When building L3 cloud architectures (number of virtual machines, database type, machine learning algorithm, etc.) or setting up an Edge container or network access to pass data, the configuration logic has extra tiers.

4.5 Blockchain (BC)

4.5.1 Definition

"Blockchain is often connected with Bitcoin. It's a distributed, vetted, and maintained database of transactions by a global network of computers. Instead of a central authority like a bank, a vast community oversees the records, and no one can edit or delete transaction history. Unlike a centralized database, the blockchain's distributed structure and peer-verified assurances prevent information manipulation. A blockchain is distributed among software users, unlike a centralized database that resides on a single server. A blockchain enables everybody on the network to view everyone else's entries, making central control impossible. When someone executes a transaction, computer algorithms verify its legitimacy. Once a transaction is validated, it's connected to the preceding one, creating a chain It's called a blockchain [17]. A blockchain is a decentralized peer-to-peer network. Bitcoin, a blockchain-based digital ledger, is widespread. Bitcoin's complicated algorithm and decentralized network allow users to mine, store, and exchange bitcoins. Blockchains may be utilized as an asset register and inventory.

4.5.2 Blockchain—Background

"New Directions in Cryptography" explored distributed ledgers. Stuart Haber and Scott Stornetta's "Hot to Time-Stamp a Digital Document" proposed timestamping the data instead of the medium as cryptography advanced. "Electronic cash" or "digital currency," based on a model by David Chaum, also contributed to the creation of Blockchain, which was followed by protocols that enabled double spending detection. Adam Back created "hash cash" in 1997 to combat spam emails.

Wei Dai created "b-money" based on peer-to-peer networks. Satoshi Nakamoto invented blockchain technology when he released "Bitcoin: [18] A Peer-to-Peer Electronic Cash System" in 2008. The article's abstract was about direct Internet payments without a third party. The article described a cryptographic payment mechanism. Nakamoto proposed a digital currency that could not be duplicated or spent twice in his writing. According to the report, a public ledger should be used to track and verify the transaction history of an electronic coin, thereby preventing the occurrence of duplicate spending. Satoshi Nakamoto designed the first bitcoins in early 2009 and provided open-source software to implement the system a few months later. Bitcoins continued to be manufactured and marketed, and significant community-supported and addressed code flaws.

Bitcoins occupy the lion's market share, making them the most popular cryptocurrency [19]. It could keep users unified, but its openness made it famous. In 2013, investors began pouring money into Bitcoin start-ups. Bitcoins may be traded for cash or goods. Wallet software lets users transfer bitcoins through a PC, mobile, or web app. In 2015, Ethereum allowed Blockchain to function with loans and contacts. An intelligent contract algorithm ensures the two parties' actions. Its speed, safety, and efficiency made it famous [20].

4.5.3 Overview of Blockchain

The fundamentals of blockchain are covered in this section, including its concept, design elements, advantages, and kinds. The chapter introduced the concept of Blockchain Peer-to-Peer Electronic Cash, popularly known as Bitcoin, presenting two groundbreaking technologies by Nakamoto in

2008. The first blockchain is the first bitcoin, a decentralized digital currency. A blockchain is a network of cryptographically complex algorithms connecting individual blocks.

On a distributed database, this method stores digital assets in blocks connected by a hash, which is a type of digital fingerprint (Cirstea et al., 2018; Woodside et al., 2017). "A distributed ledger system that offers transparency and trust" is what blockchain is (Linn & Koo, n.d., p. 2). According to Koshechkin et al. [21], blockchain is a peer-to-peer network and open database without a centralized server. In essence, a blockchain is a secure ledger of previous transactions that has been reviewed and verified by blockchain parties. Business trust is built thanks to blockchain's accurate representation of reality at any given instant.

Similar to a state machine, a blockchain maintains a permanent record while storing and altering previous states. There is no going back in time (Adams et al., 2017). A strength of the blockchain is "hashing." Every new block that is added to the chain has a "hash" code that is determined by the block's creation date. A popular password security strategy is "hashing." The hash of each new block includes the hash of the preceding block. As a result, making phony blocks is difficult. Future block hashes are determined by previous block hashes, so altering a single block necessitates completely rewriting the blockchain. These barriers act as preventative valves against tampering (Hughes & Morrow, 2019; White, 2017).

The blockchain was created to trade and store bitcoin securely. This blockchain-based digital currency tool supports transactions, distribution, and issues. The ability to use Turing-complete programming languages has been added. Smart contracts can function on the blockchain thanks to Blockchain 2.0. The most popular smart contract blockchain platform is Ethereum (Li et al., 2017; Oh & Shong, 2017). Apart from financial and economic matters, Aras and Kulkarni (2017). According to Engelhardt (2017), the following businesses and organizations benefit the most from blockchain: There are many parties engaged. The parties also need to establish confidence. Eliminating a middleman could increase efficiency and confidence. Fourth, data upkeep and activity monitoring must be trustworthy.

4.5.4 Blockchain-Based Design Features

Blockchain's fundamental properties are what distinguish it. These design characteristics, according to Perkinson and Miller (2016), are crucial particularly when transaction verification, reconciling and settling, and addressing disputes require a lot of time and effort [22].

- Blockchain protocols need users to confirm transactions before publishing them, ensuring transaction legitimacy.
- Blockchain verifies pre-transaction asset ownership when counterparties come to an agreement on the transaction's specifics, simplifying asset transfer settlement as the transaction is finalized. After blocks are generated, uploaded to the chain, arranged in the correct sequence, and assigned a timestamp, a lasting documentation of their order and timing is established.
- Automation of smart contracts: Blockchain ledgers could make it possible for smart contracts to run automatically if certain conditions are met.

4.5.5 Characteristics of Blockchain Technology

The literature discusses blockchain's characteristics. Some blockchain qualities contribute to other particular features so that the list may be condensed.

4.5.5.1 Distributed

The distributed ledger's transactions may all be seen by users of the blockchain, who can also check the records of the parties in a transaction. No central authority or independent third-party checks or settles transactions (decentralization). On the data's integrity, all blockchain users concur (consensus-based data approval). There is no central node used by peers. The nodes of the network store and transmit data (peer-to-peer transmission).

4.5.5.2 Standardized Rules

Blockchain transactions must follow the same standards. It's hard to falsify or erase data on a blockchain (persistency) (immutability). This is due to the hashing algorithm and hash identifiers. Immutability doesn't imply blockchain data can't be changed. Modifiers may add new blocks to the chain to remove outdated data.

4.5.5.3 Privacy

The platform can't recognize users (nodes). Each party may utilize blockchain with a created address without revealing its identity. Users interact with blockchain addresses (anonymity). Due to intrinsic constraints, privacy on a blockchain cannot be appropriately kept.

4.5.5.4 Auditability

Transactions are confirmed and timestamped, making blockchain data transparent and traceable. Computational techniques assure the persistence and chronological order of ledger recordings for all network users (irreversibility of records).

4.5.5.5 Security

The sophisticated cryptography employed by Blockchain enables users to assert ownership of addresses and cryptographic assets through public and private keys. These addresses aren't linked to users' identities, preventing identity theft. Hashes relate to blocks; thus, tampering with one block affects others. Blockchain protects user data and transactions.

4.5.6 Benefits of Blockchain Technology

Even in its infancy, blockchain technology has altered many companies and been desirable to numerous sectors (Workie & Jain, 2017; Beck, 2018; Herlihy, 2019; Kumar, 2019).

- All network users have everlasting access to a blockchain's whole transaction history [23]. All users know any actions performed on data or transactions, encouraging transparency.
- Business continuity: All companies need service availability and continuity. Because blockchain technology doesn't have a single point of failure, and the system is never down, which keeps business going [24].
- Disintermediation: A decentralized blockchain infrastructure facilitates disintermediation. The technology could replace mediators, improving efficiency and cutting direct and indirect costs caused by friction between people and organizations.
- Trust: Blockchain creates a trustworthy record between untrustworthy parties. Good blockchain architecture ensures confidence and makes verification easier.
- Smart contracts: Most blockchain systems feature scripting languages so that ledgers may be enhanced. Bitcoin uses a stack-based vocabulary, whereas Ethereum uses JavaScript, a Turing-complete imperative language. Computer codes or software known as "smart contracts" are used to digitally facilitate, confirm, and enforce business logic negotiations and performances. When obligations are honored, smart contracts carry out reliable transactions and activities (Such as the transfer of goods, money, shares, or other valuable items, eliminating the necessity for an intermediary or a middleman. Traditional systems can employ smart contracts, but the blockchain is the greatest venue for them due to the high quality and accessibility of the data there.

4.5.7 Blockchain System Types

Nakamoto created the first blockchain-based system, Bitcoin, in 2008. It is a decentralized electronic cash system among peers and a decentralized public ledger. Different blockchain methods and options are presently available to both individuals and businesses. Blockchain data access (public and private blockchains) and access to blockchain systems (permissionless and permissioned blockchains) may be categorized (BitFury Group, 2015; Peter & Panayi, 2015).

- Unauthorized blockchains: Blockchains without permission enable transaction verification by all stakeholders. Blocks may be built by users without authority.
- Permissioned blockchain: Only pre-selected users can create and verify transaction blocks in permissioned blockchains.
- Public blockchain: Anyone can access data and contribute transactions on public blockchains.
- Private blockchain restricts data access, viewing, and reporting transactions to preset users inside an organization or specific organizations. The blockchain platform combines encryption, a consensus process, and a distributed ledger. This section discusses three blockchain technologies:
- To sign transactions, blockchain employs public-key cryptography. Users sign transactions using their private keys. Blockchain network recipients authenticate a transaction's signature using the sender's public key. Sources or end-devices sign transactions when created.
- Distributed Ledger: BC uses distributed storage to record transactions. All network systems store all trades or a subset of them. Before recording transactions into the ledger, all network nodes reach an agreement (using a consensus method). This makes the blockchain immutable.
- A centralized server does not verify blockchain transactions. Blockchain employs a peer-to-peer approach, and all network decisions are decided by consensus.

4.5.8 Applications of Blockchain

Blockchain's key characteristics are used beyond decentralized currency. It has the potential to revolutionize business transaction models and asset management protocols in various sectors such as e-voting, automobile rental, and movie viewing. Its applications span multiple fields such as FinTech, Healthcare, Governance, Supply Chain, Manufacturing, Insurance, Education, IoT, Big Data, and Machine Learning. In FinTech, for instance, blockchain could enable financial transactions and asset management based on distributed ledger technology. It eliminates trusted third parties and speeds up transactional services. In insurance, blockchain may help identify fraudulent claims and abandoned policies, creating a risk-free, transparent system.

Blockchain's encryption characteristics give insurers ownership of insured goods. IoT refers to any Internet-connected device. Blockchain's IoT use is enormous [25]. Smart Home apps, Cloud Integration, Smart Cities, etc. Healthcare generates a lot of data. Daily patient monitoring reports, clinical research management, insurance claims processing, and archiving of medical information.

Blockchain decentralizes recordkeeping for patients, doctors, and insurance companies in the healthcare sector. Blockchain in education is still in pilot and may be used for identity management, digital certificates, blockchain-enabled credentials, etc. It lets users share their academic accomplishments with those who wish to verify them. E-voting allows people to vote securely. Since blockchain data is tamperproof, it prevents faked voting.

The supply chain is another key industry where blockchain has tremendous potential. It can transmit products, track things, repay customers in case of defective delivery, and conduct quicker, cheaper transactions. Blockchain may improve supply chain efficiency. The applications as mentioned earlier are revolutionized by blockchain, but not only. Researchers are attempting to use blockchain in many more domains.

To describe its usage in aforesaid sectors in more detail.

4.5.8.1 *Economics*

- Processing payments quickly, securely, and affordably without intermediaries.
- Real-time transfer and settlement.

- Reduces worldwide payment friction.
- Lessens friction associated with international payments.
- Permits financial settlements without requiring a clearinghouse.
- Allows for trading digital stocks without the need for a broker.
- Enhanced trade finance through automation of procedures, payments, and settlements, and reduced fraud, quicker, cheaper shipment tracking, and faster document transmission).

4.5.8.2 Accounting

- Enables new ways to capture, process, validate, and store financial information.
- Allows real-time, verified, transparent accounting.
- Reduces costs, mistakes, and fraud; reduces reconciliations; [26] offers audit trail.

4.5.8.3 Insurance

- Prevents fraud and establishes a transparent marketplace for insurance.
- Claims automation.
- Improve sales, client onboarding, underwriting, claims processing, asset transfers, payments, and reinsurance.

4.5.8.4 Supply chain management

- Increases accountability, visibility, and transparency in the supply chain.
- Ensures supply chain compliance and fosters chain-wide trust.
- Verifies the validity and quality of the goods while monitoring their status.

4.5.8.5 Energy

- Promotes microgrid energy exchange.
- Facilitates microgrid transactions without a centralized authority.
- Improves smart grid energy trading security and privacy.
- Allows digital currency power transactions.

4.5.8.6 Advertising and Media

- Affordable Internet advertising.
- Connects digital advertising and media players directly, without middlemen.
- Reduces advertising and media fraud.
- Increases media transparency.
- Ensures content security and rights.
- Protects copyrights and media quality.

4.5.8.7 Legal

- Smart contracts help create and execute legal agreements, boosting confidence in online legal services.
- Boosts legal data integrity and openness.

4.5.8.8 Real estate

- No fees or commissions.
- Secured transactions.

- Reduces property fraud.
- Helps investors track real estate history when register and transfer data are recorded on the blockchain.

4.5.8.9 Healthcare

- Securely sharing medical information.
- It gives people access to their medical records.
- Enhances the interchange of health data.
- Ensures the integrity of the drug chain.
- Assists in building standard databases for health data and information.
- Facilitates clinical research and analysis via the exchange, monitoring, and maintenance of data.

4.5.8.10 Internet of Things(IoT)

- Smart contracts for IoT security.
- Increases device security and privacy.
- Creates a framework for managing IoT identification and access.

4.5.9 Architecture of Blockchain

A blockchain is a decentralized network supported by distributed consensus, computational hashing, and digital certificates. Figure 4.6 shows the six components of blockchain architecture.

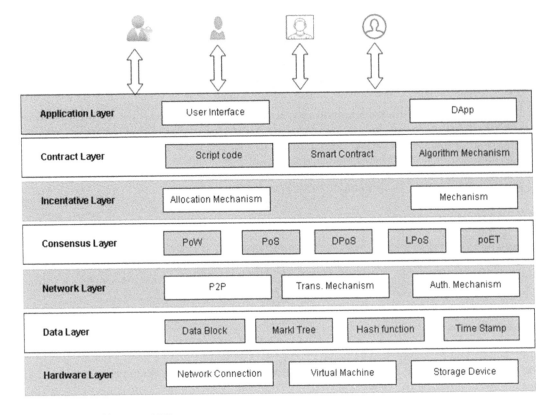

FIGURE 4.6 Architecture of BC.

4.5.9.1 This Data Layer Handles Hiverse Information

This module encapsulates time-scribbled data. The block body holds verified messages, while the genesis block contains the block's description, time, Nonce, Merkle root, and hash. The hash of the new block is connected to that of its parent block. Date-stamped blocks revealed when they were created. This layer's time stamp and Merkle tree are necessary for the blockchain. Time stamps place and track blockchain data. This might incorporate time-dimensioned blockchain data to facilitate data repetition. The Merkle tree will use a binary hash tree to check that these transactions are correct and exist.

4.5.9.2 A Layer of the Network

At the core of the architecture lies the network layer, also referred to as Point-to-Point (P2P). It regulates communication between nodes. It finds nodes, transactions, blocks that are always getting new information, and integrations to show how the blockchain system works.

4.5.9.3 The Consensus Layer

It's the blockchain's primary body. It discusses consensus mechanisms. A consensus method synchronizes communication entities and forces participants to establish a single contract, also known as a unanimous agreement, on cloud transaction data status. A standard wisdom method generates cryptographic keys for the most vital base station. Consensus mechanisms are safe and coherent, lively and affordable, and fault-sensitive.

4.5.9.4 Incentive Layer

The incentive module encourages modules to validate blockchain data security. A mining operation evaluates every other module in the public ledger using consensus calculations on the consensus layer. Even during authentication, a node uses CPU and energy. The blockchain incentivizes anticipated nodes to participate in the verification process with a cryptographic digital currency. The component's assembly and launch process includes two reward mechanisms.

4.5.9.5 Contract Layer

It monitors logic-based transaction Inquiries. It incurs contract aspects like scripting scripts, algorithms, logical contracts, etc. A consensus mechanism is a collection of company policies and processes in the form of technical programs that activate Ethereum blockchain devices when predetermined parameters are met. Smart contracts employ high-standard syntax like EVM, solidity, etc. The contract layer is well characterized. The contract layer may face threats to reentrancy, access control, structural rigidity increase, etc.

4.5.9.6 Application Layer

It gives customers functionality via an app. The software may be built in any computer language and on many platforms. Blockchain application safety is a challenge. Exchange server security holes, DDoS transfers, worker host protection, malicious code infections, attacks on weak passwords, selfish mining attacks, etc.

4.6 Blockchain in IoT: A Vital Transformation

The IoT sensors and edge devices are altering how businesses function. Enterprises must secure information at all levels of the IoT ecosystem. Data security has gotten more challenging as the number of connected devices grows. Blockchain helps with IoT security. Blockchain and IoT enable machine-to-machine transactions. It employs a collection of database-recorded, validated, and distributed ledger transactions. IoT and blockchain provide potential advantages and enable smart devices to work independently without a centralized authority.

It monitors device communication. The decentralized nature of blockchain might be a concern for IoT. IoT systems use a centralized client-server or hub-and-spoke architecture. Building a decentralized IoT platform makes sure that it can work with a blockchain network, but it might be hard to set up IoT sensors so that they can handle their own computing and data storage. Blockchain is used with IoT in banking, finance, automotive, and agriculture. Smart homes, supply chains, logistics, and smart contracts leverage IoT. Smart contracts use blockchain to execute contracts automatically in IoT environments. This permits smart devices to operate without a central authority.

This blockchain application helps organizations manage data on IoT edge devices, saving maintenance and transfer expenses. No centralized data repository and a cyberattack-resistant ledger lessen data management concerns. It gets rid of the IoT gateway or any other middleman for exchanging data, which cuts down on processing time.

Blockchain secures encrypted device data via decentralized, distributed ledgers. Distributed ledgers spread data processing and storage over millions of devices. In the conventional architecture, a device, server, or network failure might disrupt the whole IoT ecosystem. In many circumstances, a blockchain network is resilient enough to continue working even if nodes are down.

Many IoT ecosystems are easy to hijack due to inadequate access control and client/server designs. DDoS attacks interrupt regular traffic to connected devices by flooding the target or nearby infrastructure with Internet traffic. Mirai and Hajime IoT botnets revealed DDoS-vulnerable devices.

Blockchain's distributed security architecture protects the IoT against botnet-driven DDoS assaults. In this design, every network device uses a blockchain peer-to-peer network. IoT-blockchain technology is in its early phases, and several IT businesses are exploring it.

The IBM Blockchain Platform lets companies expand blockchain into cognitive IoT, which mixes IoT with cognitive computing. Technical issues and operational problems have slowed IoT-blockchain deployment. Scalability and storage are important challenges in blockchain systems with a big centralized ledger, and keeping the ledger on edge nodes is wasteful since smart devices at the edge can't handle enormous quantities of data or processing power.

The notion is still young, but it might have a big influence in the future. Standard security requirements will facilitate IoT-blockchain adoption. Blockchain may increase Internet security by enabling data openness and peer-to-peer connectivity.

Here are blockchain's components:

A full node is responsible for storing, validating, accepting, and rejecting all transactions. In contrast, a Partial or Lightweight Node does not store the entire blockchain ledger; instead, it retains only the transaction hash. This hash value serves as an entry point to access the complete transaction, making it suitable for environments with limited storage and CPU power.

A ledger refers to a digital database, particularly relevant in the context of cryptocurrency transactions between nodes. In this domain, three distinct ledgers coexist.

Ledger public Everyone has access. Anyone may read or write on the blockchain.

All nodes have a local copy of the database in a distributed ledger. Groups of nodes verify transactions and contribute blocks to the blockchain. No node or group of nodes controls this decentralized ledger. Each node executes the task.

Wallet: A digital wallet serves as a storage facility for bitcoins. Blockchain nodes all have wallets. Public and private key pairs protect a blockchain wallet's privacy. The money in a wallet is widely accepted, so no conversion is needed.

Hash Hashing reduces data size. It's used in cryptography. In blockchain networks, one transaction's hash value is another's input.

4.7 Difficulties in Implementing Blockchain Technology in IoT

Integrating IoT with blockchain gives tremendous possibilities and addresses numerous IoT difficulties. However, integration is challenged by freshly developed hurdles, which opens the way to modern research ideas. The literature focuses mostly on how blockchain might improve IoT design and application. IoT-Blockchain improves IoT security, traceability, transparency, efficiency, and trust. Before the integration's full potential can be exposed, researchers must address its flaws. Blockchain was originally built for powerful computers in an Internet paradigm, which is not the case for IoT. This section discusses many IoT-blockchain integration issues.

4.7.1 IoT Resource Constraints

Resource-constrained IoT devices include sensors, RFID tags, and smart meters. These gadgets have weak computational, network, storage, and battery power. Blockchains have unique needs. First, the consensus technique requires substantial computer resources, which is inefficient for low-power IoT devices. Second, blockchain data is large, so it's impractical to keep it in each IoT device, particularly because IoT creates vast amounts of data in real time.

Thirdly, blockchain assumes steady network connections, which may not be possible for IoT, which might have bad network connections or unstable networks owing to node failure (e.g., drained batteries) In most circumstances, the status of IoT devices cannot be discovered until they are tested. In other cases, the devices operate great for a while, but the situation changes due to disconnection, short circuits, or software obsolescence.

4.7.2 Security Susceptibility

Many industries use wireless networks because they are scalable and feasible. Wireless suffers from passive eavesdropping, jamming, denial of service, and more. Due to IoT devices' resource limits, it's hard to maintain public/private key encryption techniques in a dispersed setting. Many IoT systems involve devices with varying processing capabilities, so not all can run the encryption method at the same pace. Malicious nodes steal blockchain communications to postpone block broadcasting.

4.7.3 IoT Devices' Mobility and Naming

The blockchain network topology varies from the IoT in that nodes cannot discover one another. In the Bitcoin blockchain, senders' IP addresses are included in transactions and utilized to establish the network architecture. Many IoT devices are mobile, so this architecture is impractical.

4.7.4 Scalability of the Integrated System

Blockchain scalability is determined by the number of IoT nodes and concurrent workloads. Current blockchain scalability inhibits large-scale IoT applications. Terabytes of real-time data are generated by IoT devices, which blockchain cannot store. Bitcoin blockchains may not be scalable enough for IoT. Some blockchains perform a few transactions per second. This is an IoT bottleneck. Consortiums or private blockchains overcome this problem. Consortium blockchain systems include Hyperledger.

4.7.5 Network Privacy and Transaction Confidentiality

Public blockchains can't simply protect a network of IoT devices' transaction history. Because transaction pattern analysis may deduce user or device identities behind public keys. Organizations should choose hybrid or private blockchains based on their privacy needs.

4.8 Blockchain and IoT Use Cases

The portability and performance of smart chips and sensors are advancing, which allows for real-time interactions with blockchain technology. The integration of blockchain and IoT can enable a service marketplace between devices, allowing companies to derive value from the data collected.

The proliferation of blockchain protocols, alliances, and IoT device suppliers suggests the potential of blockchain in the IoT industry. The next section outlines some stakeholders and examples of use cases at the intersection of blockchain and IoT. It is important to note that the partnerships and firms mentioned in this section are not endorsed by Deloitte.

1. A group of blockchain experts known as "Chain of Things" (CoT) is working together to investigate the potential benefits of integrating blockchain and IoT in industrial, environmental, and humanitarian contexts. CoT has developed a hardware solution called Maru that leverages blockchain and IoT technology to enhance identification, security, and interoperability. CoT has also developed several use cases, including "Chain of Security," "Chain of Solar," and "Chain of Shipping."

2. The IOTA Tangle ledger reduces the need for costly mining, enabling quick transaction settlement and data integrity (validation of transactions). IOTA can handle massive volumes of microdata for IoT devices. The ledger provided by Tangle has features that allow for communication between machines, microtransactions without fees, and data that is resistant to quantum computing. IOTA has created a platform for buying and selling sensor data and is also growing its position in the market for insights obtained from data analysis.

3. Riddle & Code provides encrypted tagging to optimize logistics and supply chain management. By integrating IoT devices with distributed ledger networks, Riddle & Code enables secure and reliable interactions between machines in the IoT era. Their solution offers a "trusted digital identity" for physical objects and machines, thus bridging the gap between the physical and digital worlds and combining the benefits of blockchain with traditional paper documents.

4. The integration of blockchain and IoT sensors ensures the reliability of information in transactions involving physical goods. For instance, Modum sensors track environmental conditions, including temperature, during shipment. Upon the arrival of goods at their destination, sensor data is compared to a blockchain smart contract, which verifies that the delivery meets the requirements of the sender, client, or regulatory body. The smart contract triggers various actions, such as sending notifications to the sender and receiver, releasing the products, or initiating payment.

4.9 Blockchain's Role in IoT

The integration of blockchain and IoT technology creates new opportunities for reducing inefficiencies, enhancing security, and increasing transparency. These technologies make it feasible to monitor a physical asset throughout its lifecycle, from the mining of raw materials to the point of sale to the end-user, said Parekh. With these technologies, it is possible to track a physical asset from the time raw materials are mined to the time it is sold to the last customer.

1. **Safety:** Blockchain technology can authenticate and authorize transactions from a trustworthy source and encrypts data during transmission and storage. Blockchain technology gives openness regarding access, transactions, and interactions. Blockchain makes things safer by using encryption, not having a single point of failure, and being able to find a network's weak link right away.

2. **Cost-cutting by Automating:** The validation and processing of blockchain transactions, the ecosystem may be able to become more proactive for less money.

3. **Speed of Transaction:** This is particularly true with various suppliers, manufacturers, distributors, and customers. Through the blockchain, people who don't trust each other can share information right away. This cuts out time-consuming steps and speeds up transactions.

4. **Transparency:** The IoT can now analyze and process data in real-time, thanks to cloud computing. Cloud computing has helped the growth of IoT systems. Transparency in data is missing. Rarely are participants aware of the intended use of their data.

4.9.1 In Several Ways, Blockchain May Enhance IoT Security and Scalability

Blockchain's tamper-proof distributed ledger eliminates the need for trust. No one organization controls all IoT data. Using blockchain to store IoT data would offer another degree of network security. The blockchain's stronger encryption makes it almost impossible to erase data. Blockchain allows anybody with network access to trace prior transactions. This may help identify a data leak's source and take prompt action.

Blockchain allows quick transaction processing and device coordination. As the number of linked devices grows, distributed ledger technology can handle more transactions. Blockchain may help IoT enterprises decrease expenses by removing IoT gateway processing overheads (e.g., traditional protocol, hardware, or communication overhead costs). Smart contracts, a two-party agreement kept on the blockchain, may execute contractual agreements depending on specified parameters. Smart contracts may automatically allow payments when service requirements are met without human interaction.

4.10 Blockchain and IoT Integration

By transforming and streamlining manual operations in connection with IoT, the blockchain brings them into the digital age and collects vast amounts of data that enable previously unheard-of levels of knowledge. Undoubtedly, IoT and blockchain separately have a vital role in the advancement of the era. The combination of these both have an extreme role in the advancement of the digital world.

4.10.1 Possibilities for Combining Blockchain and IoT

The heterogeneity of IoT systems, poor interoperability, resource limitations on IoT devices, and security and privacy flaws are just a few of the issues IoT systems must deal with. IoT systems may benefit from blockchain technology's increased interoperability, greater privacy, and enhanced security. Furthermore, blockchain has the potential to improve the scalability and dependability of IoT systems. We refer to this kind of blockchain and IoT connection as BCoT in short. In contrast to existing IoT systems, BCoT provides the following potential advantages.

4.10.2 Improved IoT System Compatibility

IoT data may be transformed and stored on blockchains to fundamentally increase the interoperability of IoT devices. Diverse IoT data types are transformed, processed, retrieved, compressed, and then stored in blockchains throughout this process. Since blockchains are built on top of the P2P overlay network that gives everyone access to the Internet, interoperability is also shown by how easy it is to move between different kinds of fragmented networks.

4.10.3 Enhanced IoT System Security

IoT data may be safeguarded by blockchains, this involves storing the data as transactions that are secured with digital signatures and encryption using cryptographic keys like the elliptic curve digital signature algorithm. By utilizing blockchain technologies like smart contracts, IoT systems can also automatically update their firmware to fix security issues and improve overall security.

4.10.4 IoT Data Traceability and Reliability

Data on the blockchain may be located and validated at any time, anywhere. In the meantime, it is possible to track every past transaction that was kept on a blockchain. For instance, work has created a blockchain-based system for product traceability that offers suppliers and retailers traceable services. This makes it possible to examine and confirm the items' authenticity and quality. Since blockchain transactions can't be changed or faked, the immutability of blockchains ensures that IoT data is correct.

4.10.5 IoT Systems Have Interactions that Are Autonomous

IoT components or devices may be able to interact automatically through blockchain technology. For instance, the work suggests using Distributed Autonomous Corporations (DACs) to automate transactions when conventional roles like governments or businesses are not engaged with the payment. DACs may operate autonomously without human interaction thanks to smart contracts, which reduce costs.

4.11 Blockchain and IoT Opportunities

BC-IoT integration provides several advantages. It unlocks both doors. Here are some opportunities:

- Building trust between parties: BC-security IoT would establish confidence among linked devices. Only validated devices may interact on the network, and miners must verify each transaction block before entering the BC.
- Cost reduction is achieved by eliminating intermediaries, simplifying the process and removing any middlemen between the sender and the recipient, making it a straightforward transaction.
- Reduces time: Transactions take seconds instead of days.
- Provides security and privacy: It protects the security and privacy of devices and information.
- Social services: This method offers linked-devices for social and public functions. All linked gadgets are capable of communication and data exchange.
- Financial services: This method securely transfers money without involving a third party. It offers quick, secure, and confidential financial services. Transfer time and expense were decreased.
- Risk management: This strategy has been crucial in analyzing and lowering the danger of resources and transactions failing.

4.12 Conclusion

IoT has various benefits in transportation, healthcare, industry, logistics, grids, etc., since it links objects that can compute, communicate, and transfer critical information. IoT security is key. This chapter discussed how blockchain could safeguard IoT networks. We advocate for the symbiotic integration of Blockchain and IoT to enhance connectivity and security for IoT devices. We also discussed BC's IoT applications. We discussed obstacles and future research areas to enable BC to operate inside the IoT network. Putting BC into an IoT network is difficult and will need industry and research. This chapter offers a fresh perspective on BC and IoT. Opportunities and difficulties are mentioned. This page lists platforms. This technique may replace the present Internet system with one in which every smart device connects to other devices in real-time utilizing the peer-to-peer network. It saves time and money by transmitting real-time information to the proper device. It may be useful later. We'll create a blockchain-based IoT security solution in the future.

4.13 Future Work

The following points have been identified for consideration as part of our future work:

- In the future, we may see more integration between blockchain and AI/machine learning to create more intelligent and adaptive IoT systems. This could involve using blockchain to securely store and share data for AI training and inference, or using AI to improve the efficiency and scalability of blockchain networks.
- Edge computing is an emerging technology that involves processing data at the edge of the network, closer to where it is generated. In the future, we may see more integration between blockchain and edge computing, creating more efficient and scalable systems for IoT applications.
- As more and more data is generated by IoT devices, the need for privacy and security becomes increasingly important. In the future, we may see more advanced privacy-preserving techniques, such as zero-knowledge proofs and secure multi-party computation, to ensure the confidentiality of sensitive data.
- The energy consumption of blockchain networks is a major concern, especially as the number of devices connected to the IoT continues to grow. In the future, we may see more energy-efficient consensus mechanisms, such as proof-of-stake or proof-of-authority, to reduce the energy consumption of blockchain networks.
- Smart contracts are a key feature of blockchain technology, enabling the automation of complex processes. In the future, we may see more advanced smart contracts that can incorporate machine learning and other advanced technologies to create more intelligent and adaptive systems.

REFERENCES

1. A. Rayes and S. Salam, *Internet of things from hype to reality: The road to digitization*, vol. 2, Springer Cham, 2017.
2. A. Pal, "Internet of things: Making the hype a reality," *IT Professional*, vol. 17, no. 3, pp. 2–4, 2015.
3. A. Rayes and S. Salam, "Internet of things (IoT) overview," in Ammar Rayes and Samer Salam, ed., *Internet of Things from hype to reality*. Springer, 2019, pp. 1–35.
4. N. Kshetri, "Can blockchain strengthen the internet of things?," *IT Professional*, vol. 19, no. 4, pp. 68–72, 2017.
5. T. Alam, "Blockchain and its role in the internet of things (IoT)," *arXiv preprint arXiv:1902.09779*, 2019.
6. O. Alfandi, S. Khanji, L. Ahmad, and A. Khattak, "A survey on boosting iot security and privacy through blockchain," *Cluster Computing*, vol. 24, no. 1, pp. 37–55, 2021.
7. G. F. Hurlburt, J. Voas, and K. W. Miller, "The internet of things: A reality check," *IT Professional*, vol. 14, no. 3, pp. 56–59, 2012.
8. M. Dabbagh and A. Rayes, "Internet of things security and privacy," in A. Rayes and S. Salam, ed. *Internet of Things from hype to reality*. Springer, 2019, pp. 211–238.
9. B. P. Rao, P. Saluia, N. Sharma, A. Mittal, and S. V. Sharma, "Cloud computing for internet of things & sensing based applications," in *2012 Sixth International Conference on Sensing Technology (ICST)*. IEEE, 2012, pp. 374–380.
10. D. Singh, G. Tripathi, and A. J. Jara, "A survey of internet-of-things: Future vision, architecture, challenges and services," in *2014 IEEE World Forum on Internet of Things (WF-IoT)*. IEEE, 2014, pp. 287–292.

11. A. Saint, "Where next for the internet of internet of things?" *Engineering & Technology*, vol. 10, no. 1, pp. 72–75, 2015.

12. A. Gupta, T. Tsai, D. Rueb, M. Yamaji, and P. Middleton, "Forecast: Internet of things—Endpoints and associated services, worldwide, 2017," *Technical report*, 2017.

13. N. Sharma, M. Shamkuwar, and I. Singh, "The history, present and future with iot," in V. E. Balas, V. K. Solanki, R. Kumar and M. Khari, ed. *Internet of Things and Big Data Analytics for Smart Generation*. Springer, 2019, pp. 27–51.

14. G. E. Moore *et al.*, "Progress in digital integrated electronics," in *Electron devices meeting*, vol. 21. 1975, pp. 11–13.

15. S. Madakam, V. Lake, V. Lake, V. Lake *et al.*, "Internet of things (IoT): A literature review," *Journal of Computer and Communications*, vol. 3, no. 05, p. 164, 2015.

16. A. Gyrard, G. Atemezing, C. Bonnet, K. Boudaoud, and M. Serrano, "Reusing and unifying background knowledge for internet of things with lov4iot," in *2016 IEEE 4th International Conference on Future Internet of Things and Cloud (FiCloud)*. IEEE, 2016, pp. 262–269.

17. S. S. Sarmah, "Understanding blockchain technology," *Computer Science and Engineering*, vol. 8, no. 2, pp. 23–29, 2018.

18. M. Crosby, P. Pattanayak, S. Verma, V. Kalyanaraman *et al.*, "Blockchain technology: Beyond bitcoin," *Applied Innovation*, vol. 2, no. 6–10, p. 71, 2016.

19. S. Underwood, "Blockchain beyond bitcoin," *Communications of the ACM*, vol. 59, no. 11, pp. 15–17, 2016.

20. K. Omote, M. Yano *et al.*, "Bitcoin and blockchain technology," in Makoto Yano, Chris Dai, Kenichi Masuda and Yoshio Kishimoto, ed. *Blockchain and crypt currency*. Springer, 2020, p. 129.

21. K. Koshechkin, G. Lebedev, G. Radzievsky, R. Seepold, and N. M. Martinez, "Blockchain technology projects to provide telemedical services: Systematic review," *Journal of Medical Internet Research*, vol. 23, no. 8, p. e17475, 2021.

22. S. Ølnes and A. Jansen, "Blockchain technology as s support infrastructure in e-government," in *International conference on electronic government*. Springer, 2017, pp. 215–227.

23. D. Yaga, P. Mell, N. Roby, and K. Scarfone, "Blockchain technology overview," *arXiv preprint arXiv:1906.11078*, 2019.

24. P. Treleaven, R. G. Brown, and D. Yang, "Blockchain technology in finance," *Computer*, vol. 50, no. 9, pp. 14–17, 2017.

25. J. Wu and N. K. Tran, "Application of blockchain technology in sustainable energy systems: An overview," *Sustainability*, vol. 10, no. 9, p. 3067, 2018.

26. Y. Guo and C. Liang, "Blockchain application and outlook in the banking industry," *Financial Innovation*, vol. 2, no. 1, pp. 1–12, 2016.

5

AI and Blockchain-Enabled Onion Routing Protocol to Secure IoT Communication

Maitri Patel, Nilesh Kumar Jadav, and Sudeep Tanwar
Institute of Technology, Nirma University, Ahmedabad, India

Mohammad S. Obaidat
University of Jordan, Amman, Jordan
University of Science and Technology Beijing, Beijing, China
SRM University, India

5.1 Introduction

Modernization with groundbreaking technologies, such as the Internet of Things (IoT), artificial intelligence (AI), and blockchain, has uplifted the Internet. IoT technology has attracted many real-time applications, such as smart healthcare systems, smart cities, Industry 5.0, and many more, to strengthen the nation's economy and people's quality of life. Numerous IoT devices are interconnected with physical machines to offer diverse use cases at hyper-scale. Figure 5.1 shows the forecasting data, i.e., the number of IoT devices connected globally from 2019 to 2035 [1]. It consists of different small-scale physical devices that can sense their surrounding environment and collect and transmit the data to other physical devices to accomplish a shared task. For instance, temperature sensors are essential indicators for equipment checks in the smart industry. Any unexpected fluctuations or instabilities in the temperature reading indicate that the equipment is not working correctly. Such changes need to be sent to other temperature sensors and alert the administrator for predictive maintenance. Moreover, these sensors use IoT communication protocols, such as message queuing telemetry transport (MQTT), constrained application protocol (CoAP), data distribution service (DDS), and hypertext transfer protocol (HTTP), to communicate with each other. This enables different sensors to relay critical data via these communication protocols to offer proactive services.

5.1.1 IoT Promotes Smarter Computing

As IoT development progresses, knowledge systems and networks employed for autonomous communication also increase. We will then be surrounded, supported, and sustained by an increasing number of smarter systems in our classrooms, homes, businesses, food kiosks, and other vital locations. They will easily communicate, cooperate, corroborate, and correlate to comprehend our psychological, social, and physical requirements and meet them discreetly, securely, and unhurriedly. In other words, the appropriate information and services will be created, provided, and delivered to the right person at the proper time and location. The main drivers of this tectonic modernization and migration are primarily physical artifacts and assets. The world of conscious, linked, and cognitive computing will incorporate everything that is common, casual, and economical to benefit the users.

DOI:10.1201/9781003326236-5

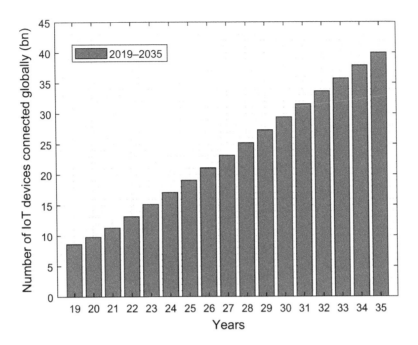

FIGURE 5.1   Number of IoT devices connected globally (2019–2035) [1].

5.1.2   IoT Paves the Way for Smarter Environments

A wide range of electronics with high-definition Internet protocol (IP) televisions is expected to be incorporated into our living, relaxing, and working spaces. Aside from these, all actual and concrete goods, articles, furniture, and packages have specially manufactured electronics that enable computation and communication. People-centric, smarter settings are what the IoT technologies and cloud infrastructure structures are supposed to produce [2].

5.1.3   IoT Stipulates Personal Convenience

IT specialists predict that commonplace technologies seamlessly and impulsively combine to form a technology cluster that instantly and intuitively satisfies our personal and professional needs. That is, there is a chance that our thoughts transparently integrate with robots. Because we will have constant access to the world's information resources and knowledge base through any of our auxiliary electronic gadgets, learning will become a 24 × 7 endeavor. On the flip side, we will have an unfailing backup of our brains on enormous digital storage systems. These seemingly mystical and cutting-edge technology themes allow us to connect our nervous systems to computers in a positive way. The transformation of all material and valuable things into intelligent and sentient digital artifacts strengthens the economic backbone of the nations.

5.2   Applications of IoT

5.2.1   Smart City

As the title implies, smart cities are intelligently controlled by using various technological systems, sensors, cutting-edge communication techniques, etc. The smart city is consistently regarded as one of the most prominent, promising, and inspiring applications of IoT. It is used to establish a substantial link between the sensors, physical equipment, and networks utilised in setting up

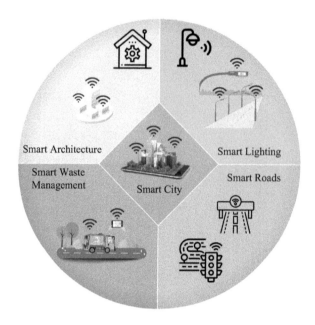

FIGURE 5.2 Applications of smart city.

and creating a smart city. The integration of IoT in smart cities significantly reduces the human efforts required for system control and monitoring [3]. Smart Cities are being considered as a new strategy for reducing the shortcomings caused by urban population expansion and fast urbanization. Different facets of individuals' lives can be made easier with the creation of smart transportation, smart homes, smart healthcare, and other infrastructure.

People can find the most efficient answers to their difficulties with the aid of smart cities. This system makes extensive use of wireless communication channels, such as Low Power Wide Area Networks (LPWANs), Radio Frequency Identification (RFID), Wireless Sensor Networks (WSNs), and Light Fidelity (Li-Fi) to seamlessly transmit the smart city-based IoT data to different applications of a smart city [4]. There are numerous smart city applications currently used and numerous potential avenues for further research in this field, as shown in Figure 5.2. Applications for smart cities are essentially constructed around four distinct building blocks, i.e., data collection, transmission or reception of data, data retention, and data analysis [5]. Data collection is application-dependent and has been a major driver for sensor development across various domains. Data transmission from the data gathering devices to the cloud for archival and analysis is the second step of the process. Next, the data must be arranged and organized using various storage techniques (e.g., cloud storage) to assist in the data analysis phase. Data analysis is the process of drawing conclusions and patterns from obtained data to be utilized in decision-making. In other circumstances, straightforward analysis, such as simple decision-making and aggregation, would also be effective. The availability of the cloud enables the collection, processing, and real-time analysis of heterogeneous data using statistical techniques, such as machine learning and deep learning algorithms, for more complex decision-making [6]. A few smart city applications are discussed as follows.

- Smart Architecture—Smart cities establish a long-term and adequate infrastructure for the nation's development. Designs and constructions were made more systematic, structured, and conservative by creating smart infrastructure. IoT applications are incorporated into smart infrastructure to make systems smart in various economic spheres like business, industry, environment, etc. For example, motion detectors are employed in smart architecture (e.g., elevators) to detect the presence of any person; if the person is in the elevator, then only the elevator operates; otherwise not; improve the system's energy efficiency [4].

- Smart Lighting—In setting up a smart lighting system, photodiodes, proximity sensors, and ambient lighting sensors are routinely used. The sensors built into the light nodes give instructions (commands) to the lights by detecting the light intensity, measured by light and motion sensors. The areas covering these smart lighting systems are divided based on the potential population or activity. The systems accurately determine illuminance levels after selecting the required level of light. So, it is simple to calculate and cut the power used to improve the system's efficiency.

- Smart Roads—Vehicles can be monitored, and traffic lights can be adjusted following vehicle traffic flow by employing smart road technology. The construction of smart roads utilising IoT and sensor technologies makes driving secure and comfortable. It provides vehicle drivers with up-to-date information on traffic, parking, road conditions, weather, the shortest route to their destination, and obstructions on the road. Smart roads can save lives when traveling through risky topographies and uneven terrains with the help of different sensors. It increases pedestrian security and reduces the likelihood of accidents, thereby improving public safety [7].

5.2.2 Smart Homes

Smart homes are an essential segment of smart cities since they serve as the focal point of city residents' lives. Since people spend most of their time at home, automating household tasks is very important. A wide range of peripheral and digital technologies are being modified so that they may be used to create and maintain smarter homes fast and easily. In order to sufficiently improve the quality of life, futuristic home environments make extensive and prominent use of technologies, such as wireless broadband communication, ambient, agile, and adaptive sensors integrated with other sophisticated systems [8]. It is a modern application of pervasive computing that incorporates intelligence into households' management and maintenance for convenience, well-being, security, and energy efficiency. By judiciously melding specific use cases, numerous compound applications for smart houses can be recognized. A few smart home applications are summarized as follows.

- Home security - While at home or the workplace, security, and surveillance components, such as security sensors embedded within different home components, like doors and windows, can protect against criminal activity. IP-enabled security and surveillance cameras provide rigid, indestructible, and impermeable security. Systems for detecting and preventing intrusions are other significant security components. Home security is also improved by using the building or home sensors that can immediately alert the owner, particular neighbors, or the police and fire departments. These facilities can also enable family members to check on the welfare of the elderly and children from a distance.

- Home networking - All inert and passive objects are becoming digitalized and being wirelessly and shrewdly networked with all different types of home electronics. This is done to connect, interact (peer-to-peer or via a middleware) and create suitable people-centric, interconnected, and embedded e-services. The ubiquitous Internet also allows a home network to interact with the outer world. This makes it possible to manage remotely, monitor, and maintain home appliances. Home systems are also connected to car electronics, navigation and multimedia systems, parking management systems, and other devices for real-time communication and engagement.

- Energy conservation - Future electrical grid demands will encourage minute-by-minute regulation of residential appliances to prioritize energy services while providing owners with automatic savings. Energy consumption is minimized by depending on the changing environmental conditions and consumption practices in the home by synchronizing lights, household appliances, and climatic and temperature sensors. Building automation systems (BAS) is crucial in simplifying occupant needs. The importance of BAS in preserving limited electrical energy increases considerably with the incorporation of smart grids.

- Health and wellness - Healthcare providers can keep a constant check on their clients' health and well-being by using biosensors or other medical equipment that can be implanted in the clients or used in their homes, without the need for hospitalization. Smart home sensors could consistently monitor advanced metrics, including fitness and well-being. These electronic health gadgets can gather evaluative data regarding current health conditions to maintain overall well-being and prevent diseases.

5.2.3 Smart Healthcare Systems

The healthcare industry is in the midst of technological advances that address many problems they are currently facing due to numerous factors, such as aging infrastructure and a lack of adequate technology adoption at the proper times in the past. The enormous quantities of large datasets produced by the healthcare industry are another major issue. These colossal volumes of data require storage infrastructure systems and technologies. The alteration in patients' attitudes and mindsets has added to this slew of issues. Regarding the quality of their interactions with their healthcare service providers, patients nowadays are not ready to make any compromises. Patients no longer tolerate long wait times caused by the absence of specific infrastructure components. By ensuring that patients receive the appropriate care at the proper moment, IoT holds a lot of promise for the healthcare sector.

5.2.3.1 *Clinical Monitoring and Remote Consultation*

Patients with particular chronic illnesses must constantly monitor their essential physiological indicators. These patients are typically housed in hospitals' intensive care units (ICU). IoT-driven noninvasive monitoring technology makes this type of monitoring possible, which uses sensors to gather detailed physiological data on patients' many essential bodily metrics (as shown in Figure 5.3). The information gathered by these sensors is transmitted to immediate family members and caregivers via wireless networks and gateways so they can handle the patient in the best way possible. The conventional constant in-person monitoring by medical staff and doctors at hospitals

FIGURE 5.3 Services offered by smart healthcare systems.

is replaced by IoT technology. It offers chronically ill patients better-automated home healthcare at a reasonable price. Furthermore, individuals who reside in distant locations usually lack access to ongoing health monitoring. For such patients, health monitoring is made possible through wireless technologies and sensors that are connected via the IoT. These wireless systems use sensors to gather data about the body, evaluate it using sophisticated algorithms, and share the results with medical specialists to provide patients with pertinent health advice. Depending on the patient and whether they require specialised care for elderly patients or particular care for patients with chronic conditions, the parameters, facilities, and procedures used may change. The following are the smart healthcare applications.

- Mobile health care—Mobile health care (mHealth) is the use of portable electronic devices for communication and health-related purposes. Around the world, there is a surge of interest in this topic. The main drivers driving the use of mobile devices in the healthcare industry are the proliferation of mobile devices, the accessibility of high-speed wireless networks, and their impact on the daily lives of vast populations. In addition to these factors, the government has been concerned about the severe lack of healthcare professionals that persists in many parts of the world. Surveys in the healthcare industry have also shown that mobile health services are more accessible and effective, especially in rural and resource-limited settings. eHealth, or the use of information and communication technology for services connected to healthcare, has given rise to mHealth.

- Remote Monitoring—The concept is to provide virtual medical treatment and consultation, medication delivery, and therapeutic procedures assuming that the patient has access to remote connectivity, teleconferencing, and other interactive technologies. Patients are now routinely screened remotely in many different nations throughout the world. The major goal is to offer people access to high-quality healthcare who would not otherwise have it owing to a variety of factors, such as living in rural areas or not having the time to physically visit doctors due to their busy work schedules. The development of telesurgery, which uses robots and nurse aides to do treatments, is another intriguing innovation.

- Convenience for aged people—This application's primary goal is to provide ongoing bodily parameter monitoring for an aging population. The wearable, which tracks patient, bodily parameters without requiring manual intervention, is one of the key devices utilized for this. The body measurements taken from the elderly are relayed to a typical mobile device, which serves as a node for the network to relay the data to a doctor in real time. If an abnormality is discovered, this knowledge may be used to give patients the proper medical care at the appropriate time. To assure engagement and the proper form of treatment at the right moment, this program also includes options for alert messages to be sent to local hospitals and patient families.

5.2.4 Smart Agriculture

One of the most crucial elements of the 2030 Sustainable Development Goals of the United Nations is food; security. The expanding global population and deteriorating climate change are causing unforeseeable weather patterns in different areas of the world that produce food, countries all over the world are racing to corroborate that food production is made sustainable and that dwindling natural resources like water are utilised optimally. Digitalisation helps with agriculture's need for sustainability. Smart agriculture utilizes sensors in farms and crops to measure various metrics to help with decision-making to prevent diseases, pests, and other problems [9]. The smart agriculture framework includes precision agriculture, which requires embedding sensors in crops to provide focused measurements and afterwards enable the deployment of customized care mechanisms. Precision agriculture is essential to the fight for sustainable agricultural production since it will be necessary for future food security. The IoT is revolutionizing the agriculture sector by supplying farmers with a variety of tools to address the various issues they face in the field. While sensors and actuators are used to regulate farming operations, WSNs are used to monitor the farm. With the help of IoT, farmers may use a mobile phone from any location to check on the condition of their farmland. IoT-enabled technologies can increase land productivity and decrease the cost of growing crops. Some of the key benefits of IoT-based smart agriculture are summarized below:

- Mobility—The enhanced adaptability of processes is one advantage of implementing IoT in agriculture. Farmers can respond promptly to any substantial shift in the weather or condition of the soil or crops because of real-time monitoring and forecasting tools. Attributable to emerging IoT technologies, agricultural workers can save crops in the face of catastrophic weather variations.
- Sustainable process—In addition to saving water and energy and making farming more environmentally friendly, precision farming also significantly lowers the use of pesticides and fertilizers. The end outcome is better and more organic with smart agriculture as opposed to conventional farming methods.
- Operations like planting, irrigation, and harvesting are automated to conserve resources, reduce human error, and cut expenses overall.
- The agriculture sector faces the issue of ensuring appropriate productivity while also providing a nutritious and balanced food supply. There have been several allegations of food theft, including forgeries, adulteration, and artificial manipulation [10]. One's health and financial security may be negatively impacted by such fraud [11]. Adoption of IoT technology can acknowledge different food theft issues discussed in Manning [12], including product authenticity, procedural integrity, individual integrity, and data integrity.
- Remote control of equipment is one of the purported advantages of IoT [13]. When compared to staff members manually surveying large fields by vehicle or foot, the penetration of IoT in agriculture would aid in saving substantial effort and expense. Cost and waste could be reduced by using IoT to decide when and how to apply pesticides or fertilizers.
- IoT enables real-time monitoring of farm assets and machinery to detect fraud, accelerate element substitution and assure timely maintenance.

5.2.5 Smart Supply Chain Management

By meticulously regulating the flow of suppliers, the idea of a smart supply chain operates the entire logistical chain from customer to client, regardless of where they are located. This control addresses both the requirement for quality and reduced costs. The IoT and blockchain are two developing technologies used to accomplish this performance. The first technology seeks to connect all the gadgets in a networked system. In contrast, the second technique seeks IoT operations that have already been completed and guarantees them by offering safe and dependable data communication. Coordination of multiple events, cycles, and resources is essential for supply chain management (SCM). As a result, blockchain permits security, authenticity, and ownership while saving time [14]. The supply chain has prompted solutions like tracking goods and communicating inventory data for many years. Devices and sensors embedded in the firm could transmit and receive data depending on a variety of characteristics like pressure, temperature, and machine usage while processing workflow data, equipment change settings, and optimal performance with the aid of IoT-enabled systems. In order for an industry to be responsive and flexible, the supply chain must be intelligent. IoT can help with retail operations and SCM by embedding RFID chips inside the products and utilizing smart ledges to monitor the availability of commodities in real time; the merchant can optimize various applications. When a consumer visits a store and cannot find the desired item on the shelves, it has been discovered that a sales loss has also occurred. With the aid of IoT, this retail store loss can be minimized. Moreover, by making data from the retail shop available, the logistics of the entire SCM can be optimized. The manufacturers will also be able to create and ship the right amount of merchandise with store sales data and stock availability. As a result, overproduction or underproduction can be avoided.

5.3 Security and Privacy Issues in IoT Communication

Cloud, big data, and mobile technologies are all amalgamated in the IoT infrastructure. Every one of those technological elements is vulnerable to numerous security flaws and attacks, which could make them inconsistent in operating. Corroborating that the IoT infrastructure elements are sufficiently protected from potential security threats is crucial. Integrity, privacy, and availability are among the most important security considerations for the security of information technology components that apply to an IoT architecture [15]. Following are the security parameters that need to be assessed while performing a security check on the IoT applications.

- Integrity—It guarantees that authorized users can only change the underlying data. It acknowledges that unauthorized users won't be able to reorient the data in any way. Write, remove, and update procedures are all part of data reorientation.
- Privacy—It guarantees that the underlying data will only be accessible to authorized users. In other words, it protects that privacy by limiting access to the data transferred and stored through IoT infrastructure.
- Availability—It assures that the underlying data is accessible to authorized users as and when needed. This involves ensuring that the fault tolerance capabilities are included in the IoT infrastructure. Fault tolerance is implemented into the IoT infrastructure by assuring that the backup components are provided in each of the IoT infrastructure's components, notably servers, storage, and networks. Clustering the servers to create a high-availability environment helps ensure server backup. Additionally, it is critical to confirm that the backup server is a replica of the primary server and can step in as the primary server if the primary server fails. Employing the highly scalable Redundant Array of Independent Disks (RAID) architecture for hard disks helps assure storage backup because the same data is striped and mirrored across numerous disks, meaning that even if one disk fails, data won't be lost because it will be kept in the other disks of the array. To guarantee that the failure of any network component won't impede the passage of data over the network, several switches, multiple ports, and numerous cables should be placed between the two connecting endpoints.

Moreover, IoT communication uses traditional routing algorithms and protocols, which attackers can easily target due to its trivial operating nature. For instance, the attacker knows that IoT communication uses the public Internet, which formally runs on the traditional routing algorithm that can be exploited by manipulating their routing tables [16]. An attacker can perform data link layer attacks, such as address resolution protocol (ARP), to manipulate the routing tables. Such an attack can jeopardize the performance of IoT communication. The following are the security and privacy challenges of IoT communication:

- Privacy concerns—In the IoT, devices are utilised in various spheres of life; for instance, smartwatches have the ability to gather, store, and analyze personal data. The majority of devices in IoT infrastructure allow for the collection of device credentials information. The logical inference made here is that devices transmit information over many networks without an encryption function which presents more privacy issues. When IoT objects acquire information but are not secure, privacy risks primarily escalate. Various user activities are being tracked anonymously in an effort to perform analytics to gather insights. If this data is shared with an unreliable third party, it might be tremendously dangerous for the users. Strict adherence to policies and procedures is required to ensure that only authorized users and apps have access to data.
- Lack of encryption—Devices habitually employ lightweight encryption techniques. Due to the implementation of a mild encryption approach, the majority of devices are unable to encrypt data. Therefore, a substantial and secure encryption method must be employed to create a secure architecture.

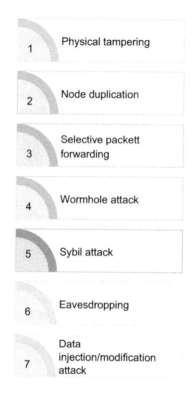

FIGURE 5.4   Security issues in WSN-based IoT systems.

- Default credentials—In most devices and sensors, default credentials (username or password) are generally utilized; however, this is inappropriate since, once a hacker obtains the details through any means, the network is in real jeopardy of being exploited. Default passwords are typically straightforward and easy so that users will find them easy to remember, but failing to update the credentials for an extended period of time poses a hazard to the network.

Due to the aforesaid security and privacy challenges, IoT applications are lured by attackers, wherein they target critical applications, such as healthcare, banking, nuclear power plants, water treatment plants, and critical infrastructure. Due to the large-scale development of IoT-based applications, it is integrated with an IP network where it is exposed to various cyberattacks (as illustrated in Figure 5.4). These networks are accessible via remote connections, and there is a wide possibility that an attacker can access one of the communication links to access private and sensitive data. It has been observed that most attacks in IoT systems are intrusion attacks, leading to other possible attacks, such as data injection, session hijacking, and malware that disrupt other services, such as servers and access control systems. Moreover, IoT uses weak protocols and does not support robust cryptography as it is computationally expensive. Devices in the IoT infrastructure are essentially embedded with WSNs [17]. Due to the broadcasting transmission medium being adopted, WSNs are particularly vulnerable to IoT security breaches. Some of the crucial WSN threats include:

- Physical Tampering—Recently, all physical devices have been equipped with sensing capabilities to function appropriately for societal benefits. However, it is challenging to physically safeguard the devices and prevent unnecessary physical accessibility. An attacker can indulge in altering the node's or sensor's information, putting the overall performance of the sensor network at risk.

- Node Duplication—In this attack, an existing sensor's node identification is duplicated in the same network. This replicated new sensor results in packet misrouting, exhibiting erroneous sensor values, or even a network crash [18].
- Selective Packet Forwarding—It is expected in WSN that all nodes deliver messages to the target. In selective forwarding, a malicious node randomly forward packets, i.e., floods the network. Some messages may be simply dropped without being forwarded. Since the attacker often modifies packets from a small number of distinct nodes and subsequently forward the message to other nodes, there is no reason to suspect that the malicious node modified the packets. The modified packets disrupt the regular day-to-day activities of IoT applications.
- Wormhole Attack—It is a malignant attack where the attacker tunnels the packets to a new destination after recording them at one point in the network. It is also possible to implement this process selectively. Additionally, regular business operation is disturbed when routing-based messages are tunneled [19].
- Sybil Attack—This attack is established where it concerns peer-to-peer topologies, wherein an attacker has multiple identities and is found at numerous places at once. This can be achieved if, prior to the attack, the system is taken over by the attacker. In such a network, a single node displays numerous identities, significantly reducing the effectiveness of fault tolerances like disparity, dispersed storage, and multipath [20].
- Eavesdropping—The invader perceives the information while it is being transferred between the two nodes via a public network interface. Information is unchanged, but here privacy is compromised. The intrusive party may use this knowledge against the user [18].

5.4 Theoretical Background

This section presents key enabler technologies that can reduce the effect of security threats in IoT applications.

5.4.1 Onion Routing

In order to maintain privacy in an IoT infrastructure, one must conceal the recipients of communications and their content, i.e., traffic analysis. A single-layer encryption strategy is used for most IoT connections, making it relatively simple for an adversary with powerful computing resources to break the cipher and reveal the message. As a result, stronger multi-layer encryption that guarantees anonymity becomes necessary. A general-purpose architecture called Onion Routing (OR) allows private communication over a public network [21]. It offers anonymous connections that are highly resistant to traffic analysis, data injection, and eavesdropping. Both connection-oriented and connectionless traffic can be employed on bidirectional, nearly real-time connections. Through specialized proxies, OR communicates with commercially available application software and systems, making it simple to implement into existing systems by using a pool of anonymous onion nodes, and encrypting data at several levels [22]. A few nodes (onion routers) from this pool are randomly selected depending on the communication from source to destination. Using its shared key (generated by Rivest–Shamir–Adleman (RSA) algorithm), each onion node removes one layer of encryption, much like an onion, and then transfers the remaining layers to the next onion node. Repetition of the entire procedure until the removal of all encryption levels is necessary to assure security in an IoT scenario.

5.4.2 Artificial Intelligence

A capable machine, under supervision or otherwise, of performing tasks of any human cognitive level can be said to possess intelligence. AI is a broad domain covering search algorithms to complex processes such as machine learning and deep learning. People initially had a skeptical response to AI in the early 1990s as the complex calculational processes could not be easily evaluated. However, with the advent of technology, AI has become an integrated part of everyday life. The fourth industrial revolution, often known as Industry 4.0, is a collection of IoT and AI technologies. The IoT paradigm comprises a wide range of sensors, actuators, data storage, and data processing capabilities. As a result, IoT-enabled devices to sense their surroundings, transmit data, store it, and analyze it. AI models learn from learning patterns (from the IoT data) provided by these devices [23]. These models employ algorithms that classify malicious and non-malicious sensor data or predict the chances of zero-day attacks so that the architecture retains only non-malicious data for analysis. AI systems collect massive amounts of data, and learning algorithms are employed to find patterns in the data that enable the provision of predictive services in the IoT paradigm [24]. It is a promising technology for efficiently organizing and processing massive amounts of data to assist decision-making processes [25]. It has attracted tremendous prominence with the growth of IoT devices. As a consequence of this expansion, IoT cybersecurity applications have started leveraging AI technologies like decision trees, linear regression, machine learning, deep learning, support vector machines, and neural networks to identify threats and prospective assaults.

5.4.3 Blockchain Technology

Blockchain is a tamper-proof ledger-based technology that is integrated with many IoT-based use-case scenarios, such as smart healthcare, smart banking, and smart industry. Considering developing factors and gathered data sample sets, the blockchain generally represents a consistently managed and regulated database. The participant-created transactions and the recorder blocks of these transactions are the foundational components of a blockchain. Here, the recorder block determines whether or not transaction details were preserved in the right sequence. This prevents any modifications to the available data. The preserved transaction is then shared with the blockchain participants. Here, each transaction is cryptographically secured, i.e., the transactions are encrypted using robust encryption methods, such as RSA, advanced encryption standards (AES), and hashing algorithms. Moreover, a smart contract is integrated into the blockchain network, which consists of various user-defined functions according to the application [26]. These functions offer permission and access control to the users; additionally, they validate the IoT application's data before storing it in the blockchain immutable ledger. Smart contracts eliminate the need for third-party intermediaries; instead, all third-party services are replaced with user-defined functions, thus strengthening trust in the blockchain network. The chronological sequence of time-stamped data is established by algorithms that are cryptographically connected to individual transaction sets, i.e., blocks, to one another. By using a hash reference to connect each block to the one before it, the chain of blocks is given both order and integrity. Participants must agree on the state of the chain through a decentralized majority voting procedure to maintain the blockchain's consistency. Blockchains can be distinguished as public and private, wherein public blockchain allows anyone to play a part in the blockchain network. On the contrary, the private blockchain is a permissioned blockchain, where each participant has read and write access control [27]. IoT enables Internet-connected devices to transmit data to private blockchain networks in order to construct tamper-proof records of shared transactions. This enhances our IoT data's security, adaptability, and sense of trust.

5.5 Proposed Architecture

Based on the above discussion on IoT security and privacy issues, we proposed a secure and intelligent framework by integrating AI models and blockchain-based OR to overcome various security vulnerabilities of IoT applications. We considered a smart home system as our IoT application, so in this section, we present a secure and end-to-end communication pipeline through which the smart home data can be securely routed from one sensor to another. The proposed architecture comprises of different layers, such as the sensing, intelligence, and data security layers (as shown in Figure 5.5). A summarized description of each layer is as follows:

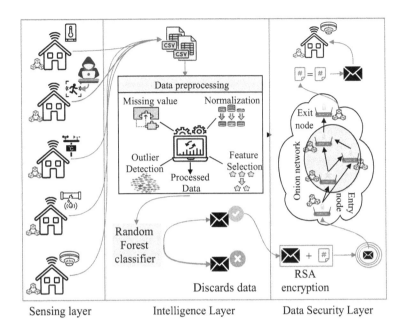

FIGURE 5.5 The proposed architecture.

5.5.1   Sensing Layer

This layer consists of different sensors, such as temperature, thermostat, weather, motion, and smoke, deployed in smart home systems. A sensor relays its data readings or instructions to another sensor to complete a shared task. For instance, in case of fire, turn on the smoke sensors in all the rooms of the smart home systems. Here, the sensors use traditional routing algorithms and communication protocols to transmit the sensor's reading; hence, the attackers can leverage this opportunity to increase their attack surface for their lucrative businesses. For example, the attacker can change the sensor reading, i.e., turn on smoke sensors to turn off smoke sensors by performing data injection attacks on the ongoing communication channel. Therefore, there is a stringent requirement for an intelligent, proactive mechanism to detect malicious behavior in IoT communication and discard such data readings from the smart home communication pipeline.

5.5.2   Intelligence Layer

This layer comprises of AI models which are incorporated in the proposed framework for classification purposes, i.e., classify malicious and non-malicious data readings from smart home systems. We used AI models, such as random forest (RF), naive Bayes (NB), bilayered neural network (BNN), support vector machine (SVM), and logistic regression (LR); they are chosen for their indispensable characteristics, such as faster training time, feasible with non-linear data, classify with fewer data preprocessing steps, and many more. First, a standard dataset of the smart home system is downloaded from the authentic website [28]. The dataset consists of different sensor readings for the thermostat, temperature, weather, and motion, wherein each row specifies the reading for a particular timestamp. The class label consists of categorical data, i.e., attack and non-attack data; this also implies that it is a binary classification problem. Then the dataset is preprocessed with different preprocessing steps, such as normalization with min-max scalar to resolve range problems, missing and not a number (NaN) values are replaced with central tendency, i.e., mean value, and type cast the data types (e.g., object to int data type). After that, the dataset is split into two, i.e., training and testing datasets. The training dataset is forwarded to the AI models to complete the training; once the training is completed, the testing dataset is applied to the trained models to validate the results of the training dataset. Finally, the AI models are assessed with different assessment parameters, such as accuracy, precision, recall, and F1 score, wherein the RF model outperforms others in terms of accuracy, i.e., 93.78%.

5.5.3   Data Security Layer

This section presents the integration of a triple-layered OR network in our proposed framework. As discussed in the previous sections, security threats deteriorate the regular operations of the smart home system. The attackers can intercept the sensor's communication to silently sniff the entire transmission or exploit it by using attacks, such as executing malware payload (e.g., trojans), performing injection attacks, and scanning the sensor communication to find the device vulnerabilities. Furthermore, if they find any loopholes in the smart home-based sensor communication, they can proliferate their attack by targeting that specific vulnerability. For example, if they found a severe vulnerability in the temperature sensors manufactured by a particular company, the attacker tried to attack all the temperature sensors made by that company, resulting in a devastating situation across the globe. Therefore, there must be an encrypted tunnel via all the sensors transmitting their data to tackle the aforementioned security and privacy concerns. The proposed framework uses an OR network, which uses RSA-enabled cryptography to secure the data readings from the attackers. It selects three onion routers, i.e., entry, middle, and exit nodes, from the pool of routers to form an onion circuit through which the data is securely relayed to its intended destination.

However, it is observed from the literature that the Internet service provider blocks the OR network for building transparency in communication. Moreover, the entry and exit nodes are publicly listed in the master node list, i.e., any person can view the meta information of that onion router and analyze the network traffic, resulting in an anonymity break for the IoT application. Therefore, in this section, we employ bridges and pluggable transport that are the secret onion routers, which are not publicly listed on the master node list of the OR network. We used *obfs4bridge*() to overcome the above-mentioned problem of anonymity break. First, the data is hashed using a message digest algorithm to perform an integrity check on the received data, i.e., whether the data has been tampered with in the OR network or not. Meanwhile, the RSA algorithm has generated public and private key pairs, by which the data will be encrypted and decrypted at subsequent stages of the OR network. Then, the data is triple-encapsulated, where each encapsulated layer is encrypted using the RSA-based public key algorithm. In addition, each encapsulated layer has a unique identifier (ID) generated by a pseudorandom number generator. Implying that each incoming sensor data has three unique IDs that are appended with the encapsulated layer.

We also want to mention that each onion router is associated with blockchain technology to strengthen the security of the OR network. This is because an attacker might manipulate the onion routers to exploit the entire OR network; therefore, each router is integrated with blockchain to confront the above-mentioned security concern. This is achieved by storing all the IDs inside the blockchain's immutable ledger, so if the attackers exploit any onion router, the particular IDs will also be exploited. Thus, when the incoming sensor data with its associated ID reaches the onion router, it first matches the ID with the blockchain-stored ID; if both IDs match, the onion router can decrypt the encrypted layer and forward it to the next onion router. So, encrypted data is forwarded to the OR network. It is first received by the entry router, which has the private key to decrypt the first layer of the encryption. Before that, the IDs are matched; on a successful match, the entry node can use its private key to decrypt the first layer of the encryption. Then it is forwarded to the middle node, where IDs are first matched; then, on a successful match, it decrypts the second layer encryption using its private key. Similarly, the third router decrypts the final encrypted layer using its private key. After that, the hashed is computed on the receiver side; if both, the sender and receiver hash match, the receiver sensor confirms the data integrity and accepts the data readings from the source sensor. This way, the smart home system data is securely transmitted from the source sensor to the destination sensor.

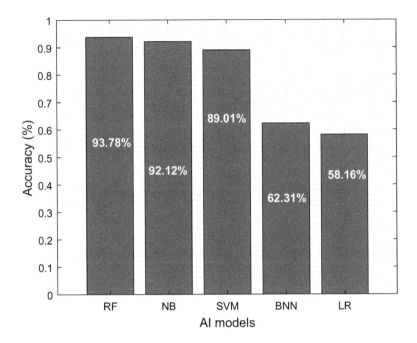

FIGURE 5.6 AI models accuracy comparison.

TABLE 5.1

Performance Evaluation of Intelligence Layer

AI Models	Accuracy (%)	Precision (%)	Recall (%)	F1 Score (%)
RF	93.78	93.12	91.11	94.27
NB	92.12	91.71	83.67	91.23
SVM	89.01	87.12	86.13	89.81
BNN	62.31	62.69	61.13	64.38
LR	58.16	56.86	56.34	56.1

5.5.4 Performance Evaluation of Proposed Framework

This section describes the performance analysis of the proposed framework by utilizing various performance metrics, such as accuracy, precision, recall, F1 score, preserving anonymity, and blockchain response time. Figure 5.6 displays the comparison of accuracy with different AI models (discussed in section 5). From the graph, one can observe that the RF achieves an accuracy of 93.78% compared to other AI models. This is because RF has an advantage over other AI models; for instance, it operates using an ensemble technique where it first splits the entire dataset into small subsets, and then each subset (acts as a decision tree) is individually trained with the RF algorithm iteratively. Finally, a performance score is computed based on the voting; the highest voting subset is selected as the best tree for that particular iteration. Moreover, unlike other AI models, the RF algorithm does not need preprocessed data, resulting in faster training time than others. Table 5.1 shows the comparison of precision, recall, and F1 scores of the adopted AI models.

From the security perspective, privacy is as important as security in the smart home system; for example, if the attacker discovers that a particular smart home user uses virtual assistant technology to operate his home. It can use privilege escalation attacks to find users' private information (most of the data is stored in the virtual assistant), such as contact information, friends, current location, etc. Therefore, preserving anonymity is an essential parameter to evaluate. Here, existing work, such as works in [30] and [29] use an OR network to securely disseminate IoT data to the intended destination. However, they have used onion routers whose identity is publicly available; hence, anonymity is not preserved in their work. In the proposed framework, we consider this intuitive observation and calculate the number of times the routers are exposed to the public Internet; this is achieved by utilizing the deep packet inspection (DPI) tool. Figure 5.7 shows the comparison

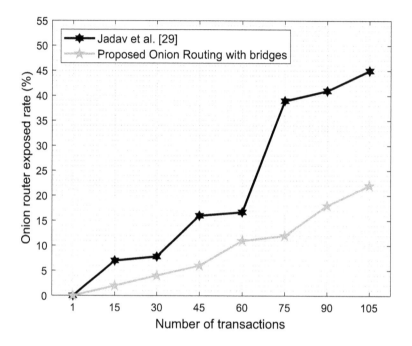

FIGURE 5.7 Anonymity check by analyzing onion router exposed rate.

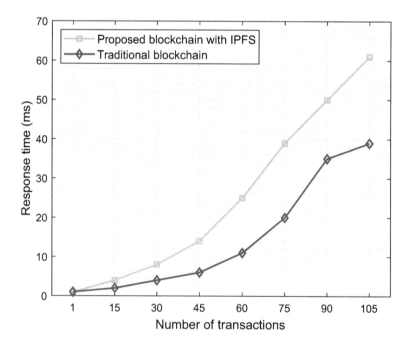

FIGURE 5.8 Blockchain response time comparison.

of the onion router exposed rate with the existing baseline works. As the proposed framework uses pluggable transport (obfs4 bridge), the onion routers are not exposed to the public Internet, resulting in higher anonymity than other existing works.

Figure 5.8 displays the performance of blockchain response time. We utilize the essential characteristics of an interplanetary file system (IPFS) in the blockchain to speed up the processing time. Here, it stores and fetches the data from multiple blockchain nodes at once; this reduces bandwidth wastage and improves the response time of the blockchain network. The graph shows the comparison between IPFS-based blockchain and traditional blockchain. It is evident from Figure 5.8 that the blockchain response is significantly improved due to the incorporation of the IPFS in the proposed framework.

5.6 Conclusion

IoT is an eminent technology that has seen unprecedented growth to become one of the most empowering technologies with the potential to transfigure the world forever. The IoT infrastructure is a conglomeration of technologies like cloud computing, big data, AI, and mobile devices to offer automated, intelligent, and predictive services. However, IoT-based communication links and their protocols are vulnerable to diverse security attacks and threats, such as DoS, data injection, interception, and man-in-the-middle attacks. Motivated by the aforementioned security challenges in the IoT environment, we reviewed different IoT applications and their services in this chapter. Then, we studied various security and privacy issues of IoT communication in real-world applications. After that, we highlighted a few groundbreaking technologies that can tackle IoT communication security issues. We also proposed a secure framework for the IoT environment, i.e., AI and blockchain-based OR protocol. The proposed framework is assessed using performance metrics, such as accuracy, precision, recall, onion router exposed rate, and blockchain response time.

In the future, we will enhance the performance of the proposed architecture by designing a hybrid routing network that involves the potential of both an onion and garlic routing network. This will not only ensures robust security but will also strengthen end-to-end anonymity in the smart home environment.

REFERENCES

1. Number of Internet of Things (IoT) Connected Devices Worldwide from 2019 to 2021, With Forecasts from 2022 to 2030. https://www.statista.com/statistics/1183457/iot-connected-devices-worldwide/, accessed: 2021-11-30.
2. Prasad, V.K., Bhavsar, M.D., Tanwar, S.: Influence of Montoring: Fog and Edge Computing. *Scalable Computing: Practice and Experience* **20**, 365–376 (2019).
3. Du, J.: Application Analysis of IoT Technology in Smart Cities. In: The proceedings of 2nd International Conference on E-Commerce and Internet Technology (ECIT), pp. 264–269 (2021). https://doi.org/10.1109/ECIT52743.2021.00064
4. Janani, R.P., Renuka, K., Aruna, A., Lakshmi Narayanan, K.: IoT in smart cities: A contemporary survey. *Global Transitions Proceedings* **2**(2), 187–193 (2021). https://doi.org/10.1016/j.gltp.2021.08.069
5. Syed, A.S., Sierra-Sosa, D., Kumar, A., Elmaghraby, A.: IoT in smart cities: A survey of technologies, practices and challenges. *Smart Cities* **4**(2), 429–475 (2021). https://doi.org/10.3390/smartcities4020024
6. Khan, Z., Anjum, A., Soomro, K., Tahir, M.A.: Towards Cloud Based Big Data Analytics for Smart Future Cities. *Journal of Cloud Computing* **4** (2015). https://doi.org/10.1186/s13677-015-0026-8
7. Bhogaraju, S.D., Korupalli, V.R.K.: Design of Smart Roads - A Vision on Indian Smart Infrastructure Development. In: 2020 International Conference on COMmunication Systems & NETworkS (COMSNETS). pp. 773–778 (2020). https://doi.org/10.1109/COMSNETS48256.2020.9027404
8. Obaidat, M.S., Nicopolitidis, P.: *Smart Cities and Homes Key Enabling Technologies*. Elsevier (2016). https://doi.org/10.1016/C2014-0-04875-7

9. Patil, K.A., Kale, N.R.: A Model for Smart Agriculture using IoT. pp. 543–545 (2016). https://doi.org/10.1109/ICGTSPICC.2016.7955360

10. Marvin, H.J., Bouzembrak, Y., Janssen, E.M., van der Fels- Klerx, H., van Asselt, E.D., Kleter, G.A.: A Holistic Approach to Food Safety Risks: Food Fraud as an Example. *Food Research International* **89**, 463–470 (2016). https://doi.org/10.1016/j.foodres.2016.08.028

11. Tahkapaa, S., Maijala, R., Korkeala, H., Nevas, M.: Patterns of food frauds and adulterations reported in the EU rapid alert system for food and feed and in Finland. *Food Control* **47**, 175–184 (2015).

12. Manning, L.: Food Fraud: Policy and Food Chain. *Current Opinion in Food Science* **10**, 16–21 (2016).

13. Kodali, R.K., Soratkal, S., Boppana, L.: IOT Based Control of Appliances. In: 2016 International Conference on Computing, Communication and Automation (ICCCA). pp. 1293–1297 (2016). https://doi.org/10.1109/CCAA.2016.7813918

14. Chbaik, N., Khiat, A., Bahnasse, A., Ouajji, H.: The Application of Smart Supply Chain Technologies in The Moroccan Logistics. *Procedia Computer Science* **198**, 578–583 (2022).

15. Obaidat, M., Boudriga, N.: *Security of e-Systems and Computer Networks.* Cambridge University Press (2007). https://doi.org/10.1017/CBO9780511536700

16. Obaidat, Mohammad, T.I., Woungang, I.: *Biometric-Based Physical and Cybersecurity Systems.* Springer International Publishing (2019). https://doi.org/10.1007/978-3-319-98734-7

17. Obaidat, M.S., Misra, S.: *Principles of Wireless Sensor Networks.* Cambridge University Press (2014). https://doi.org/10.1017/CBO9781139030960

18. Balte, A., Kashid, A., Patil, B.: Security Issues in Internet of Things (IoT): A Survey (2015).

19. Tatar, E.E., Dener, M.: Wormhole attacks in IoT based networks. In: 2021 6th International Conference on Computer Science and Engineering (UBMK), pp. 478–482 (2021). https://doi.org/10.1109/UBMK52708.2021.9558996

20. Rajan, A., Jithish, J., Sankaran, S.: Sybil Attack in IOT: Modelling and Defenses. In: 2017 International Conference on Advances in Computing, Communications and Informatics (ICACCI), pp. 2323–2327 (2017). https://doi.org/10.1109/ICACCI.2017.8126193

21. Reed, M., Syverson, P., Goldschlag, D.: Anonymous Connections and Onion Routing. *IEEE Journal on Selected Areas in Communications* **16**(4), 482–494 (1998). https://doi.org/10.1109/49.668972

22. Dutta, N., Jadav, N., Tanwar, S., Sarma, H.K.D., Pricop, E.: TOR–The Onion Router. *Cyber Security: Issues and Current Trends.* Springer, Singapore, pp. 37–55 (2022).

23. Patel, K., Mehta, D., Mistry, C., Gupta, R., Tanwar, S., Kumar, N., Alazab, M.: Facial Sentiment Analysis Using AI Techniques: State-of-the-art, Taxonomies, and Challenges. *IEEE Access* **8**, 90495–90519 (2020). https://doi.org/10.1109/ACCESS.2020.2993803

24. Gupta, R., Kumari, A., Tanwar, S.: Fusion of Blockchain and Artificial Intelligence for Secure Drone Networking Underlying 5g Communications. *Transactions on Emerging Telecommunications Technologies* **32**(1), e4176 (2021). https://doi.org/10.1002/ett.4176, https://onlinelibrary.wiley.com/doi/abs/10.1002/ett.4176

25. Duan, Y., Edwards, J.S., Dwivedi, Y.K.: Artificial Intelligence for Decision Making in the Era of Big Data – Evolution, Challenges and Research Agenda. *International Journal of Information Management* **48**, 63–71 (2019). https://doi.org/10.1016/j.ijinfomgt.2019.01.021

26. Singh, R., Tanwar, S., Sharma, T.P.: Utilization of blockchain for mitigating the distributed denial of service attacks. *Security and Privacy* **3**(3), e96 (2020). https://doi.org/10.1002/spy2.96, https://onlinelibrary.wiley.com/doi/abs/10.1002/spy2.96

27. Alkurdi, F., Elgendi, I., Munasinghe, K.S., Sharma, D., Jamalipour, A.: Blockchain in IoT Security: A Survey. In: 2018 28th International Telecommunication Networks and Applications Conference (ITNAC). pp. 1–4 (2018). https://doi.org/10.1109/ATNAC.2018.8615409

28. Moustafa, N.: ToN_IoT Datasets (2019). https://doi.org/10.21227/fesz-dm97

29. Jadav, N.K., Gupta, R., Alshehri, M.D., Mankodiya, H., Tanwar, S., Kumar, N.: Deep Learning and Onion Routing-Based Collaborative Intelligence Framework for Smart Homes Underlying 6G Networks. *IEEE Transactions on Network and Service Management* **19**(3), 3401–3412 (2022). https://doi.org/10.1109/TNSM.2022.3164715

30. Gupta, R., Jadav, N.K., Mankodiya, H., Alshehri, M.D., Tanwar, S., Sharma, R.: Blockchain and Onion Routing-based Secure Message Exchange System for Edge-enabled IIoT. *IEEE Transactions on Industrial Informatics*, 1–12 (2022). https://doi.org/10.1109/TII.2022.3191444

6

Blockchain Development in the Banking and Financial Industry

Ilgın Şafak
Fibabanka R&D Center, Istanbul, Turkiye

Fatih Alagöz
Bogazici University, Istanbul, Turkiye

6.1 Introduction

Although originally developed for financial services, blockchain technology has many other useful applications, including information management. It is currently generating excitement in various fields, such as banking, healthcare, the Internet of Things (IoT), and international trade, among others. A key characteristic of blockchain technology is that it facilitates trust between and among unknown parties, allowing them to transact business and share information without the involvement of an intermediary while ensuring data integrity and a full audit trail. Blockchain technology records, verifies, and settles transactions by recording details such as price, asset, and ownership within seconds across all nodes. Any verified change recorded in one ledger is simultaneously recorded in all other copies. Blockchain transactions are stored in blocks, which are groups of records. Transaction records are stored in a block of information. Blocks are linked to each other once they are complete, forming a chain. This makes it particularly suitable for tracking the movement of financial transactions and goods internationally. It can help provide accurate and quick information not only regarding where the financial transaction or goods originate but also tracing each step in the process. International buyers, sellers, and carriers could benefit from availability, accuracy, and precision, but also government customs agencies, who often face the same issues of origin and provenance of shipments, as well as how to handle the numerous transactions occurring simultaneously at ports of entry that are often widely dispersed.

In addition, blockchain systems automatically perform many of the functions currently performed by multiple middlemen, such as monitoring movements, payments, and other information. Consequently, international trade costs may be significantly reduced, both for traders and government agencies. Blockchain-based platforms have been developed to improve the existing systems, including the logistics chain. One such example is Tradelens, a joint initiative between MAERSK and IBM that allows all parties involved in an international shipment to exchange information in real time about events and transport documents [1, 2].

The banking and financial industry is often viewed as a conservative, well-regulated industry that slowly changes. However, banks are currently undergoing tremendous and fast changes concerning technology and regulations, and these changes are expected to continue in the future. By 2025, 90% of European Payments Council members expect blockchain technology to fundamentally transform the banking industry. As a result of blockchain technology, the financial sector is set to undergo a transformation. While some jobs, such as those of brokers, will be eliminated, new ones will also

DOI:10.1201/9781003326236-6

be created. In the extreme case, blockchain technology is predicted to eliminate banks. However, financial institutions are more likely to benefit from blockchain technology rather than disappear [3].

However, there are also barriers to blockchain's adoption in banking and finance. In comparison to a centralized solution, replicating data across multiple nodes will likely increase the cost of maintaining this data. Additionally, another factor to consider for blockchain costs is that one entity typically owns one node as opposed to a centralized database. As a result of replicating data across many nodes, scalability challenges arise since transactions must be broadcast and recorded on every node [4]. Banking and insurance are traditional industries due to their significant fiduciary responsibilities [5]. Therefore, these institutions may be hesitant to adopt blockchain due to the difficulty of explaining to regulators how data is shared among blockchain participants.

Many blockchain applications rely on mutual standards and cooperation among the financial sector's actors. An international collaboration between the financial technology start-up R3 [6] and a group of approximately 50 financial institutions aims to accelerate the adoption of blockchain technology in the financial sector. As the world of finance is highly competitive, it may be difficult to establish standards for its use [7].

6.2   Blockchain in the Banking and Financial Industry: An Overview

In this section, an overview of blockchain's application in banking and finance is provided, including existing blockchain applications, their benefits, and challenges. Additionally, a state-of-the-art (SoTA) analysis is provided of the blockchain platforms deployed within the industry.

6.2.1   Blockchain Applications in Banking and Finance Industry

*   *Payments, Clearing, and Settlement*
    Blockchain technology can be implemented by banks and financial institutions to automate payments nationally and internationally, as well as for trading of securities, non-fungible tokens (NFTs), etc. In today's banking systems, international payments are expensive and can take several days to be received. These types of payments can be transferred in near real time using blockchain technology, resulting in lower transaction costs. R3 and Ripple, among others, are collaborating with traditional banks to accelerate the settlement of payments between conventional and crypto assets within enterprise blockchains [8].
*   *Blockchain for Public, Interoperable, and Tamperproof Contracts, Records, and Models*
    Public and tamperproof contracts, records, and models, including land registry databases, ownership records of artworks, and luxury items, can be implemented with the aid of blockchain technology. This is particularly useful in countries with unreliable records. Using blockchain technology, traditional securities, such as stocks, bonds, and alternative valuable assets, can be tokenized and placed on public blockchain networks. Capital markets will be more efficient and interoperable as a result [9].

    The blockchain can be used for storing information, preventing theft, establishing property rights, or verifying ownership of the following [10]:
    i.   Cryptocurrencies (bitcoin)
    ii. Non-fungible tokens
    iii. Financial instruments (bills, bonds, equities)
    iv. Derivative instruments (future contracts, options, swaps, forwards)
    v.   Financial instruments voting rights
    vi. Commodities
    vii. Expenditure and trade records
    viii. Pledge-mortgage/credit records
    ix. Service records

  x. Land or property

  xi. Artwork and luxury goods

  xii. Crowdfunding

  xiii. Micro finance and Micro assistance

- Trading, Auditing and Certification
  Smart contracts can be used for any type of contract, including securities trading, audits, and certifications, as well as customs and trade processes. Smart contracts are programs that automatically verify and approve valid transactions that meet a prescribed protocol on the blockchain. A Bitcoin transaction may be executed under certain conditions, and companies can create contracts that provide dividends to their stakeholders upon achieving certain profit levels. Similarly, annual Payments Card Industry (PCI) Data Security Standard (DSS) [11] compliance testing of a crypto wallet server can be performed automatically. Unlike traditional contracts, smart contracts are cheaper, more reliable, and eliminate the need for an intermediary to verify the terms. Being tamper-proof is one of the key characteristics of the blockchain and contributes to its reliability. Investors can embed information and trading rules into their blockchain securities using smart contracts. Trades can be executed automatically if certain conditions are met, such as price demands. The ownership of the security remains unchanged if the terms do not materialize [12].

- *Peer-to-Peer (P2P) Lending and Crowdfunding*
  Initial Coin Offerings (ICOs) offer new methods of financing that disentangle traditional capital-raising services and firms from access to capital [13].

- *Consortium Banking*
  Consortium banks bring together several banks to finance large-scale projects that cannot be handled by an individual bank alone and to leverage their individual assets. A consortium bank is owned equally by all its members, and no bank has a controlling interest. Blockchain can be leveraged in the automatic forming of syndicates via smart contracts [14].

6.2.2 Blockchain Implementation in the Banking and Financial Industry

Despite numerous experiments and proofs of concept, the implementation of blockchain-based banking and financial solutions remains a challenge. The transition from individual to shared systems is associated with substantial capital costs. Due to the need for data sharing, banks must also adapt to a significant change in culture. In an industry accustomed to the precedence of confidentiality, this is a novel concept that raises issues of accountability: If Bank A completes the Know Your Customer (KYC) process and publishes the data on a blockchain, is Bank B responsible for errors or fraud on its own account? Moreover, will Bank A be sufficiently motivated to share its data, since sharing its data will hinder its ability to provide its customers with personalized services?

 In addition, several practical challenges exist. For example, for KYC and fraud detection purposes, as part of the setup process, the customer must consent to uploading their digital fingerprints and performing additional authentication steps. In addition to updating their authentication systems at the point of sale, merchants will have to modify their online checkout process. For benefits to be realized at scale, banks must establish large networks, which involve standardizing data and collaborating. Furthermore, it is unclear whether any bank would be willing to take the lead in developing a utility that does not provide any competitive advantages, which is also known as the coopetition paradox [15–17].

 Table 6.1 shows the most widespread blockchain platforms currently used by banks, including IBM Blockchain, R3, Komgo, and Hong Kong Monetary Authority (HKMA). IBM Blockchain Platform is IBM's commercial implementation of Hyperledger Fabric, which provides full support with service level agreements (SLAs). A comprehensive set of productivity tools is included for the development, administration, and operation of blockchain applications. Its flexible blockchain framework enables innovators to transform global businesses.

TABLE 6.1

Blockchain Platforms Used by Banks

Feature	IBM Blockchain	R3 Corda	Komgo	eTradeConnect
Blockchain type	Permissioned blockchain using Hyperledger Fabric framework	Permissioned blockchain based on Corda framework	Permissioned blockchain based on Ethereum framework	Permissioned blockchain
Data privacy and automated compliance	Yes, built-in support for GDPR compliance	Yes, privacy via Conclave integration; ISO 20022 and International Swaps and Derivatives Association (ISDA) Common Domain Model (CDM) compliant	Yes	Yes
Tracking and management of bank guarantees and letters of credit	Yes	?	Yes	?
International trade finance and trade support	Yes, via we.trade	Yes	Yes	Yes
KYC, Fraud Detection, and AML support	Yes	Yes	Yes	Yes
Exchange and settlement of tokenized financial assets	Yes, including government bonds	Yes	Yes	Yes

The R3 Group is a leading provider of enterprise technology and services that enable secure exchange of value in regulated industries, where trust is a critical component. Powered by R3, Corda is the largest private, permissioned distributed ledger platform in the world that also provides smart workflow and tokenization services. Hundreds of regulated financial institutions, including central banks, commercial banks, fintechs, financial market infrastructure providers, as well as exchanges, rely on R3's leading distributed digital platform, connected networks, and industry expertise to digitally transform their operations. Komgo is a blockchain-based open platform that optimizes financing processes and accelerates industry operations by digitizing transactions and supplying trusted documents to reduce fraud in commodity trade finance. HKMA supported the development of eTradeConnect, which is a distributed ledger technology (DLT)-based platform that enables the sharing of information between customers and their trading partners in an effective and efficient manner. By digitizing trade documents, automating trade finance processes, and utilizing blockchain technology, eTradeConnect allows trade participants to realize increased efficiency, build trust among themselves, reduce risks, and facilitate the procurement of financing in order to facilitate trade.

The SoTA on blockchain implementations for banking can be categorized as shown in Figure 6.1.

Relative advantages and disadvantages of some of the major SoTA blockchain-based banking systems are summarized below:

Ref. [15] proposes a KYC verification cost- and time-saving solution for customers based on blockchain technology. It presents a blockchain-based KYC architecture that offers a major improvement over conventional methods and enables secure sharing of verification results with customers. The feasibility and effectiveness of this strategy are evaluated with proof-of-concept (PoC) work based on the Ethereum platform and using an Android application. Compliance with regulations or certification testing is not studied.

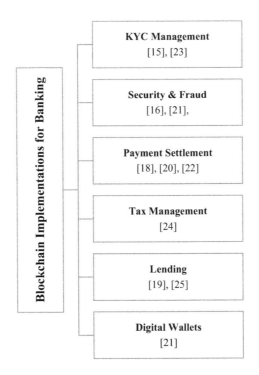

FIGURE 6.1 Categorizations of SoTA related to blockchain implementations for banking.

Ref. [18] discusses the use of a tokenless blockchain system to protect bank transaction information, such as transfer amounts, card numbers, and participant names. Additionally, it analyzes distributed database security mechanisms, offers recommendations about how blockchain technology can be used to maintain the uniqueness of information in distributed databases without using tokens or mining, and suggests integrating blockchain technology into modern banking systems. It introduces a centralized system in that only the bank can issue tokens. The end user or third party cannot issue their own tokens. The proposed algorithm is not validated through experimental work. Compliance with regulations or certification testing is not studied.

In ref. [19], the author examines and proposes a solution to address the challenges faced by traditional credit banks, as well as evaluating the feasibility of adopting blockchain technology in this context. Credit chains were developed using an experimental blockchain, where transaction speed, scalability, and credibility were improved through the use of domain indexing, dual-chain concurrency, and parallel Byzantine protocol. The proposed credit chain is applied to the credit bank architecture in order to provide an effective solution for the construction of credit banks. Compliance with regulations or certification testing is not studied.

Ref. [20] proposes a decentralized money lending system based on Ethereum blockchain platform for decentralized banking. The system provides a variety of services, including money deposit, money transfer, and loan checking. The proposed system's performance is evaluated with experimental work. Compliance with regulations or certification testing is not studied.

A peer-to-peer blockchain network based on swarms has been proposed by ref. [21] as a means of connecting e-wallets from different banks and other institutions. This network allows transfer of cash between bank accounts and e-wallets and minimizes the load on the core banking systems. Compliance with regulations or certification testing is not studied.

In ref. [22], a private blockchain platform using Practical Byzantine Fault Tolerance (PBFT) consensus and smart contracts is proposed for interbank transactions in order to provide banks with increased security and transparency without relying on a trusted third party. It also provides the software architecture, eliminates intermediary transaction costs, and enables banks to monitor and identify all banking activities. Compliance with regulations or certification testing is not studied.

In ref. [23], a framework based on Hyperledger Indy is proposed for the identification of fraudulent bank service calls and the prevention of possible losses in personal accounts. This framework provides architecture and sequence diagrams for improving KYC processes and enhancing third-party agency trust in handling financial services delegated by banks. The proposed algorithm is not validated through experimental work. Compliance with regulations or certification testing is not studied.

Ref. [24] presents a blockchain architecture that allows a tax bureau to build an interactive bank tax system and commercial banks to have access to businesses' tax information in an efficient and secure manner. System development and experiments are performed to demonstrate its effectiveness. Compliance with regulations or certification testing is not studied.

Ref. [25] proposes a distributed banking scheme based on blockchain for the distribution of financial transactions. The performance and effectiveness of the proposed architecture are evaluated using a prototype based on smart contracts. The prototype's performance is compared with Ethereum. Compliance with regulations or certification testing is not studied.

6.2.3   Benefits of Blockchain for Banking and Financial Industry

The benefits of the blockchain may be summarized as follows [26].

- *Cost Savings & Speed by Elimination of Intermediaries*
  Cryptographic proof is used instead of trust in blockchain technology, which enables two parties to transact directly without the involvement of third parties. This increases efficiency by reducing transaction fees and operational costs. Blockchain-based payment systems allow for near-real-time settlement of transactions, removing friction and reducing risk.

  By removing unnecessary intermediaries from the securities market, blockchain-based securities can be more efficient. As a result, less capital is at risk in transactions. The trade-and-settlement procedure is quite outdated and is a complicated process, where the ownership of the securities changes faster than the ownership of the money. Security ownership can change instantly in blockchains, which simplifies the trade-and-settlement process. Trade and settlement using blockchain technology increases trading efficiency and reduces costs.

- *Elimination of Single Point of Failures (SPOFs) via Decentralization*
  In technology, a single point of failure means that when a component in a system fails, it affects the entire system. Peer-to-peer (P2P) architecture of blockchain may help solve the problems caused by single points of failure and bottlenecks. The blockchain provides a high degree of availability due to its distributed nature, and its adoption can overcome SPOFs.

- *Transparency, Trust, and Anonymity*
  Transactions in the peer-to-peer network are recorded publicly. The blockchain does not store the identities of parties or transaction data but only records the existence of transactions, which ensures anonymity. Blockchain can also improve trade finance security and trust by replacing cumbersome, paper-free bill-of-lading processes. It provides visibility into the asset status in order to track merchandise, automates the completion of contract obligations through smart contracts, and ensures that networks are highly available and resilient in the event of a failure.

- *Auditability and Certification via Immutability*
  In the blockchain, each transaction has a permanent and verifiable record. By providing a single source of truth, the blockchain's consensus mechanism facilitates the issuance of financial assets (trade receivables and other payment obligations). As a result, it eliminates the issues of double spending and fraud, and hence the need for continuous reconciliation between trading and financing parties involved in the transfer of digital assets. Smart contracts can be used for auditing and certification purposes as well as to accomplish predefined business tasks and complete legally enforceable transactions without the involvement of an intermediary.

- *Know Your Customer (KYC), Fraud Prevention and Anti-Money Laundering (AML)*
  Blockchain technology permits easy and safe sharing of customer information between financial institutions by storing it in decentralized blocks. Blockchain technology allows users

to use a digital fingerprint that acts as a unique identifier similar to a physical fingerprint. Any bank in the network may reference it through a distributed ledger. Owners of digital fingerprints may use them to apply for new accounts and establish their identity universally. Blockchain technology eliminates the need for overlapping KYC and AML compliance checks since banks can share authentication information. As a result, banks are relieved of the burden of gathering information and are able to disseminate updated data immediately.

- *Collaboration and Joint Governance*
  Companies, countries, or regions may be subject to different regulations. Additionally, they may have different compliance, testing, user experience, and security requirements, regardless of the regulations. Therefore, it may be necessary to develop a blockchain-based software system that supports cross-collaboration. Through smart contracts that execute transactions automatically, blockchain mitigates the problem of cooperation failure at its source, human opportunism, and also reduces the probability of opportunistic behavior by requiring actors to adhere to the terms of the agreement.

6.2.4 Challenges in Blockchain Adoption in the Banking and Finance Industry

Potential technical and legislative challenges facing blockchain in its adoption by the banking and financial industries are listed below [27]:

- *Scalability and Transaction Authorization and Settlement Speed*
  Visa processes approximately 1700 transactions per second, whereas Bitcoin processes approximately seven transactions per second. Thus, there is a clear performance difference between Visa and blockchain-based technologies. The unresolved issue of scalability on the architectural level creates challenges with regard to blockchain adoption and its practical applications.

- *Merchant Adoption*
  For mass adoption, we must educate not only the public about the value of their data and about financial empowerment but also merchants and vendors about the advantages of accepting cryptocurrencies. Retail industry challenges include lengthy settlement processes and high processing fees for merchants. Funds take up to three to five days to settle for debit cards and within 60 days for credit cards. Accepting crypto payments can help reduce transaction costs and speed up the settlement process. In contrast to credit card payments, which require merchants to pay a 3% fee on each transaction, crypto payments do not incur any fees. The customer may pay a small fee to cover the "gas" needed for the transaction to be validated by the network nodes, but the merchant keeps all profits from the sale. The integration of merchant systems with the blockchain, however, may present a challenge for some merchants. Currently, chargebacks are another major issue facing the retail sector. Refunds can still be issued by merchants; however, chargebacks are not possible since cryptocurrency payments are final.

  Another barrier to merchant adoption is regulation. It is not sufficient for a merchant to embrace a blockchain strategy unless the country's regulator approves it. As a result, many merchants are reluctant to accept cryptocurrency payments in their online stores.

- *Energy Waste*
  Creating new blocks or verifying a transaction requires enormous amounts of electricity and mining equipment. Despite very intensive efforts to resolve this issue, energy is wasted. Energy consumption increases with the use of blockchain-based programs. Using efficient technology, miners could consume two terawatt-hours of electricity each year, which is equivalent to the electricity consumption of 150,000 people in California. It is therefore necessary to develop more environmentally friendly mining processes and to find secondary uses for waste energy. However, virtual mining can reduce the need for equipment by replacing the manual process of solving mathematical puzzles with software. Consequently, stakeholders concerned about the integrity of the system will be involved in the mining process.

- *Testing*
  Since blockchains are immutable, it is important to make sure that every aspect of the system functions correctly. In this regard, testing is crucial; however, the complex nature of blockchain systems makes testing a challenging process.
- *Security*
  The following measures must be taken so as to make sure of the safety of the blockchain.
  - Ledger-level security: It is recommended that only participants who have undergone the necessary scrutiny are permitted to participate in the blockchain. Members will typically be legal institutions with real-world legal credentials and are unlikely to disengage (unlike hostile users who are likely to withdraw from an event).
  - Network-level security: In addition to blockchain software, blockchain systems may include conventional "shadow" databases, messaging, and other services. Communication between components of various nodes should be secure from a networking standpoint. An organization's network must be resistant to a variety of external and internal threats.
  - Transaction-level security: In order to maintain accurate and immutable records, banks rely on transaction accuracy. Transaction details must be encrypted using Public Key Infrastructure (PKI) as a safeguard against unauthorized disclosure.
  - Contract security: Smart contract agreements can be pre-programmed with the capability of self-executing and self-enforcing. A program creator may introduce a flaw that exposes assets controlled by the smart contract to vulnerability, either intentionally or unintentionally. Therefore, there is a need to ensure smart contract security.
- *Selfish Mining*
  Blockchain technology can be misused, for example, with a 51% attack, or a majority attack, where over 50% of the blockchain's hashing power is controlled by a group of miners or an entity. This makes it impossible to verify transactions. This results in the chain being tainted with false information. However, this is unlikely, given the network size. Another way the system might be misled is by adding unreliable blocks to the blockchain and fooling the system into believing it is reliable.
- *Regulations*
  Strict regulatory requirements in banking and uncertainties around blockchain regulations have created a high barrier to entry. Various countries have banned the usage of cryptocurrencies altogether, including Algeria, Bangladesh, China, Egypt, Iraq, Morocco, Oman, Qatar, and Tunisia. Another 42 nations, including Algeria, Bahrain, Bangladesh, Bolivia, and Turkey, have prohibited cryptocurrency exchanges or banned digital currencies by restricting banks' ability to deal with cryptocurrencies.

  Data privacy in particular has attracted growing global attention as a policy and regulatory concern. The General Data Protection Regulation (GDPR) [28] establishes a high, harmonized standard for personal data protection in the European Union (EU) and the European Economic Area (EEA). Personal data is defined broadly in the GDPR to include information that would allow for the individual to be identified or identifiable. Aside from protecting EU citizens in the EU when providing them goods or services and when monitoring their online behavior, the GDPR also protects EU citizens in other countries.

  Several compliance requirements may pose the following challenges for blockchain users:
  - Ensuring legality of personal data processing, for example, by obtaining consent from individuals or through fulfillment of a contract.
  - Informing and fulfilling the rights of individuals, including access, rectification, and portability of their personal data; the right to object to processing, including automated decision-making; and the right to be forgotten.
  - Upholding risk-based data security.

On the other hand, the United States has not yet established a comprehensive federal framework for data protection, relying instead on sector-specific laws and regulations, such as the Gramm-Leach-Bliley Act (GLBA) for financial institutions and the California Consumer Privacy Act of 2018 (CCPA) (Pritesh Shah and Daniel Forester). Akin to GDPR, the CCPA also provides consumer protections and compliance obligations that may be challenging for blockchain technology users, including:

- Informing and protecting consumers' rights, including notice, access, and disclosure, including information on third-party disclosures and sales; allowing them to opt out of the sale of their personal information without discrimination or opt in for minors; and giving them the right to be forgotten.
- Maintaining risk-based data security standards and exercising a CCPA-granted right of action for data breaches that result from a failure by an organization to maintain adequate data security standards.

- *Taxation*
  Tax treatment of digital assets and cryptocurrencies does not follow a generalized one-size-fits-all approach. Each investment strategy will have certain peculiarities and characteristics that make it distinct from those involving traditional assets. Therefore, each digital asset needs to be understood and scrutinized not only in relation to its characteristics as a digital asset but also with respect to the protocols, terms, and conditions governing these transactions on the blockchain [29, 30].

- *Integration and Standardization*
  Occasionally, blockchain applications require significant changes to existing systems or their replacement. Additionally, due to the heterogeneous and low-complexity nature of IoT devices, there is a need for standardization of IoT communications and security protocols for blockchain-IoT integration [31].

- *Traceability*
  Due to the need for traceability in the banking and financial industry, payments cannot be anonymous like Bitcoin transactions (Jutila, 2017). This emphasizes the necessity of developing privacy-preserving cryptocurrencies that include regulatory functions in order to support both privacy protection and transparency for financial regulation regarding money flows, user addresses, and amounts involved in transactions [32]. A closer approach to decentralization will also require the system to be resilient to malicious auditors [33].

6.3 Blockchain Implementation Recommendations for Banks

Based on the challenges outlined in the previous section, Table 6.2 summarizes existing banking system components that are impacted, as well as new components that will be required in a blockchain-based banking system to mitigate those challenges. New system components are indicated with an asterisk (*).

TABLE 6.2

Recommended Mitigation Methods of Blockchain Challenges for Its Adoption

Challenge	Recommended Mitigation Technique	Relevant System Component
Scalability and Speed	• Provide cloud-based SaaS/PaaS/IaaS and out-of-the-box solutions for on-premise blockchain applications for easier deployment • Usage of lightweight consensus algorithms or methods, e.g., Proof of Authority (PoA) or lightning networks • Provide customer support for blockchain application deployment • Performance and load testing	• Blockchain application server* • Blockchain module* • Smart contract module* • Integration/communications • Testing module

(Continued)

TABLE 6.2

(Continued)

Challenge	Recommended Mitigation Technique	Relevant System Component
Merchant Adoption	• Provide standardized Application Programming Interfaces (APIs) that are easy to integrate with merchant systems • Create standardized rules for chargebacks/refunds for blockchain transactions • Provide customer and/or community support about blockchain integration, including training on regulatory and security compliance	• Merchant module* • Rules Engine • Tax module* • Integration/communications • Customer relationship management module • Smart contract module*
Selfish Mining	• Ensure decentralization is fully implemented, especially in private blockchains • Trust scoring of participating nodes • Blacklisting of untrustworthy nodes	• Data analytics module • Reporting module • Security module
Energy Waste	• Usage of lightweight consensus algorithms that do not require intensive computation as Proof of Work (PoW) • Usage of data analytics to check energy usage and computational load	• Blockchain module* • Data analytics module
Testing	• Perform end-to-end testing of blockchain system • Provide customer and/or community support for blockchain testing • Usage of blockchain for collaborative testing, compliance, and certification	• Testing module • Data analytics module • Smart contract module* • Compliance module* • All banking modules to be tested
Security	• Data and security design of end-to-end blockchain system, including API, bank systems, IoT devices integrations • Usage of lightweight and standardized security protocols and consensus mechanisms, including for bank systems and IoT device integration • Deployment of role-based and usage of risk-based, PKI, and strong authentication mechanisms, such as Fast ID Online (FIDO) [34] for ensuring ledger-level access only to authorized parties • Deployment of anomaly detection methods for ensuring internal and external network security • Usage of PKI-based encryption/decryption techniques to securely store and access data on ledger and other systems • Automated end-to-end testing to ensure blockchain and contract security • Anomaly detection, fraud detection, and AML	• Security module • User management module • Device management module* • Portfolio management module • Transaction management module • Data analytics module • Reporting module • Rules engine • Testing module • Smart contracts module* • Integration/communications • Databases • All existing banking components parts of the security design
Traceability	• Linking blockchain addresses with a reference identifier (ID), such as a customer ID, bank account number, digital wallet ID, phone number, or national ID off-chain on a bank/wallet server for audit purposes • Trust scoring of auditors using data analytics	• Portfolio management module • Transaction management module • Logging, tracing, and monitoring module • Data analytics module • Reporting module • Databases

(Continued)

TABLE 6.2

(Continued)

Challenge	Recommended Mitigation Technique	Relevant System Component
Taxation	• Development of a tax treatment for digital assets and cryptocurrencies, including in international trade and customs environments • Reporting of taxable assets and transactions • Standardized APIs for easy integration of the tax system with the blockchain	• Tax module* • Transaction management module • Portfolio management module • Rules engine • Reporting module • Smart contracts module* • Online banking • Mobile banking • Integration/communications
Integration and Standardization	• Standardized blockchain APIs for integration with bank systems • Standardized IoT communications and security protocols for IoT-blockchain integration • Standardized integration with governmental and other external systems	• Integration/communications • Device Management module* • All banking components that require integration
Regulations	• Development of a standardized cross-border/universal regulatory framework • Development of a blockchain-based distributed testing tool for automatic compliance testing	• Compliance module* • Rules engine • Smart contracts module* • Reporting module • Testing module • Databases • All existing banking components that process personal data

6.4 Blockchain-Based Banking System Architecture

The recommended blockchain-based banking system architecture is presented in Figure 6.2. The system comprises IoT devices, user interfaces (UIs), bank systems, merchant and Point-of-Sale (POS) systems, and governmental and other external systems that all connect to a blockchain application server. The blockchain server is part of the blockchain network and stores and accesses data via databases. A description of the blockchain-based banking system components is provided below.

- **IoT Device:** Any connected device accessing the blockchain-based banking system, including customer and employee devices such as a laptop, smartphone, smartwatch, and tablet.
- **User Interface (UI):** The interface between a user and a connected device used in accessing bank services, including touch screens, keyboards, mobile banking applications, or websites. UIs should be updated to support blockchain-based transactions, such as making a crypto payment in store or applying for a crypto-backed loan.
- **Bank systems:** Includes all software and hardware components used by a bank for its operation. Hardware components include servers, databases, Hardware Security Modules (HSMs), ATMs, etc. Banking system software is used to manage, monitor, and record banks and other financial institutions transactions. Sales of core banking products, customer engagement, and portfolio management functionalities are managed using the software. Additionally, back-office functions such as accounting, auditing, credit approvals, financial background checks, and system integrations are also supported.

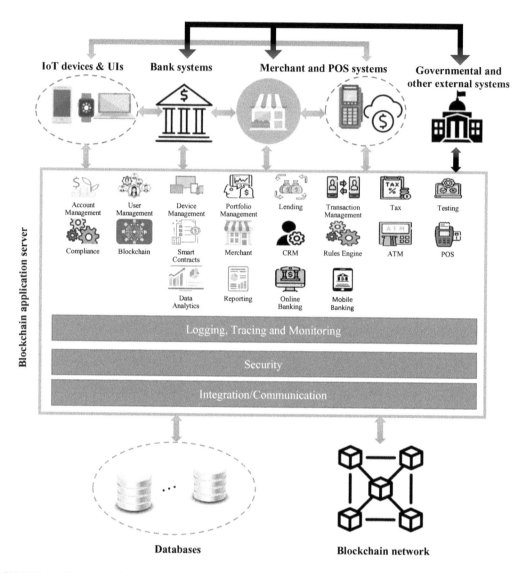

FIGURE 6.2 System architecture of recommended blockchain system.

- **Automated Teller Machine (ATM):** Allows bank or financial institution customers to perform financial transactions, such as withdrawing cash, making deposits, transferring funds, and checking their balance or accounts, at any time without having to interact directly with bank staff. Banks' existing ATM software could be updated to support crypto transactions. Crypto ATM machines are similar to traditional ATM machines; in order to exchange fiat currency into cryptocurrencies such as Bitcoin or Ether, consumers pay a fee. They can serve as a convenient way for people to invest in cryptocurrencies.

- **Point of Sale (POS):** Refers to a merchant device or software where a customer makes a payment for goods or services, as well as a place where sales tax may become due. POS transactions may take place offline or online, and receipts may be printed or generated electronically. Existing POS software must be updated to support crypto transactions. It is possible to integrate POS systems with blockchain-based banking systems using the Merchant module's support integrations, such as APIs for merchants.

- **Governmental systems:** The governmental systems that audit and ensure the compliance of the blockchain-based system, including customs.
- **External systems:** All other external systems that connect with the blockchain-based banking system, for example, payment gateways, payment networks, and private auditors.

The blockchain server and its components are described below.

- **Blockchain application server:** Application servers are software that interconnect operating systems (OS) with external resources, including databases, internet services and host communications, and user applications. Applications servers facilitate access to and performance of business applications by providing a host or container for the user's business logic. There are numerous and competing traffic conditions that must be handled by application servers, including the variable nature of client requests, hardware and software failures, distributed nature of large-scale applications, and heterogeneity of data and processing resources required to meet business needs. The blockchain application server differs from standard, centralized application servers in that blockchain-related activities are performed by a decentralized blockchain network. Data is stored on the blockchain, and smart contracts drive the logic of the blockchain-related activities.
- **Account management module:** Manages bank customers' debit, credit, savings accounts, including blockchain payment accounts. This module works together with the transaction management, blockchain, and smart contracts modules.
- **Blockchain module:** Performs blockchain-related activities and acts as an interface between the blockchain network and the blockchain application server.
- **Compliance module:** Performs legal, security, and contractual software compliance-related activities, including gathering, storing, and looking up requirements; updating the Rules Engine according to requirements; scheduling compliance tests with the Testing Module; providing recommendations for addressing non-compliance using the Data Analytics module; providing audit/compliance testing results using the Reporting Module; creating or revising smart contracts with the smart contracts module.
- **Customer relationship management (CRM) module:** Enables businesses to engage meaningfully with their customers, thereby improving profitability and reducing costs. Banks would need to update their existing CRMs in order to support blockchain-based banking services as follows:

    Every customer is provided with a unique ID by the bank for a unified and accurate view of customers' personal information, past transactions, account balances, etc. In order to eliminate inaccurate, obsolete, and duplicate data records, blockchain public addresses could be linked to customers' unique IDs, for example, for cryptocurrency transactions. This would help banks gain greater insights into their customers and engage them more effectively. Furthermore, blockchain technology could enable consumers to have a single, decentralized wallet that is compatible with all brands. As a result, they would be freed from the rules and limitations of individual brands, and point redemption would be simplified. As a result, consumers will have greater control over their shopping experience, and banks will be able to offer their customers better and personalized deals and enhance their user experience.
- **Data analytics module:** Analyzes large datasets mathematically for the purpose of making predictions, performing statistical analyses, or performing qualitative analyses. Using machine learning (ML) or artificial intelligence (AI) algorithms, this module performs all data analytics activities in the bank related to banking, security, and fraud, including credit scoring, trust scoring, risk-based authentication, and anomaly detection.
- **Device Management module:** Manages (performs device discovery, whitelisting, blacklisting, stores and updates device information, etc.) all devices connected to the blockchain-based banking system.

- **Integration/communications:** Manages all internal and external communications in the system, and performs necessary transformations required for correct data processing, for example, via an API gateway.
- **Lending module:** Performs all loan operations in the bank. A loan is an agreement where a lender, that is, the bank, gives money to a customer in return for a guarantee or trust that the customer will repay the borrowed money with some additional benefits, such as an interest rate. A bank's existing lending module could be revised to support crypto lending. Similar to a securities-based loan, a cryptocurrency-backed loan utilizes digital currency as collateral. This type of loan can be obtained through a cryptocurrency exchange or a crypto lending service provided by a bank's online or mobile banking system. Crypto lending differs from conventional lending in that the customer retains ownership of the crypto asset used as collateral but is excluded from certain rights, including the ability to trade it or use it for transactions. Additionally, if the value of the digital assets drops significantly, the customer may owe back significantly more than what was borrowed in the event of default.
- **Logging, tracing, and monitoring module:** Tracing and logging are powerful cross-cutting tools that can be used to monitor systems in real-time and investigate issues based on previous events. Logging facilitates the tracking of errors and data associated with them in a centralized manner. Tracing offers a more comprehensive overview of how an application is performing than logging, which is an event-triggered log. The purpose of tracing is to follow a program's flow and data progression. Monitoring involves instrumenting a program and collecting, aggregating, and analyzing metrics to determine how the program behaves. In order to ensure scalability and speed requirements of the blockchain-based system are met, relevant performance metrics must be included in the logging, tracing, and monitoring module.
- **Merchant module:** Merchant-related tasks are performed, and customer service is provided to merchants regarding online payments, billing, and POS integrations in accepting crypto payments in store, for example, via API integrations, plugins, payment buttons, and libraries. This module works together with the tax module for taxation of crypto sales.
- **Merchant systems:** Used in providing merchant services for accepting and processing payments, or merchant processing. Merchant systems are usually integrated with banks for reconciliation, and POS terminals for accepting online and in-store payments. Merchant systems may be integrated with the blockchain-based banking application server using the integration supported by the Merchant module.
- **Mobile banking:** Offered by a bank or financial institution for customers to carry out financial operations remotely via a mobile device, such as a smartphone or tablet. Unlike online banking, it uses a mobile application offered by the bank or financial institution. Mobile banking applications would need to be revised to support blockchain-based banking services, for example, for making crypto payments in store, P2P or cross-border payments, managing crypto assets, applying for a crypto-backed loan, for auto-insurance via smart contracts, and blockchain-based KYC.
- **Online banking:** Offers customers the ability to carry out a variety of financial transactions via the institution's website. Online banking applications would need to be updated to support blockchain-based banking services, for example, for making online crypto payments, online P2P or cross-border payments, managing crypto assets, applying for a crypto-backed loan, or applying for auto insurance.
- **Portfolio Management module:** Manages a group of investments, including crypto assets, to achieve a given set of financial objectives and risk tolerance. The investments can be selected and managed automatically based on the customer's risk profile using AI/ML methods or could be selected manually by the customer and/or investment advisor. This module works together with the blockchain and smart contracts modules for management of crypto assets and NFTs.
- **Reporting module:** Delivers a variety of operational reports to enterprises. Reports may include sales, production, ad hoc, or custom reports that allow the user to gain insight into a specific

problem by customizing the queries. The blockchain-based banking system would need to be able to report blockchain transactions, such as those related to interest rate fluctuations. As a data source for reports, smart contracts could be used to track fluctuations in interest rates, as well as the settlement and recording of transactions that resulted from these fluctuations. Additionally, it can also be used to report the exchange of assets such as titles and deeds, ownership of digital assets, such as music, or the collection of royalties.

- **Rules engine:** Executes business rules in a production environment as they occur. These rules may be derived from legal regulations, company policies, or any other source. Existing rules engines of banks should be updated to include (on-chain and off-chain) blockchain-related rules such as compliance, security, smart contracts, and merchant and taxation rules.

- **Security module:** In the banking and financial sector, security is of utmost importance. Security software is used by banks to secure and protect their systems end-to-end, including their application servers, their network, and any devices connected to them. It provides access control and data protection, protects the system from viruses and network-related intrusions, and evades other system-level security risks. The extent to which funds deposited by customers in their bank accounts and their personal information remain secure depends on how the solutions are implemented. Since the financial sector is particularly vulnerable to cybercrime, the security aspects are not governed by banks themselves but rather by state regulatory agencies. In order to support blockchain-based banking services, existing security software of banks must be modified to comply with regulations, such as personal data protection regulations. In addition, the security design of new software components such as smart contracts, device management, tax and compliance modules, and blockchain integrations must also be carefully considered.

- **Smart contracts module:** Smart contracts are programs or protocols designed to execute, control, or document legal events and actions based on the terms of a contract automatically. A smart contracts module could be developed in order to support blockchain-based banking services such as crypto asset trading, crypto-backed loans, or a digital insurance application (auto, health, home, life, etc.). This module would perform all activities related to smart contracts, including communicating with the blockchain network.

- **Tax module:** In order to support blockchain-based banking services, a new software component, namely tax module, will be needed for managing digital assets taxation and accounting in a compliant manner. It is necessary to incorporate taxation policies into the tax module, compliance module, merchant module, online/mobile banking, transaction management module, portfolio management module, rules engine, and all relevant integrations.

- **Testing module:** Software testing consists of validating and verifying the artifacts and behavior of the software under test. In addition to providing an objective, independent view of the software, software testing can enable the business to appreciate and understand the risks associated with the implementation of the software. Banks' existing testing software would need to be modified to include blockchain testing. The concept of blockchain testing is the systematic evaluation of components of the blockchain, such as blockchain APIs, smart contracts, and nodes. A key difference between blockchain testing and traditional software testing is that blockchain testing involves a variety of components – including blocks, mining, transactions, and wallets – that require a dedicated focus and specialized tools for testing.

- **Transaction management module:** Performs transaction processing of a bank's financial transactions, including bank cash management, credit/debit/prepaid card transaction processing, money order management, national and international transactions, check management, as well as preparing files for end-of-day processes, and reporting. This software should be modified to support crypto transactions.

- **User management module:** Software that is used in onboarding and managing bank customers. A bank's administrators and customers can access banking services through this module. This module would need to be modified to support blockchain transactions, for example, by linking a customer ID with its blockchain address (public key).

The databases and blockchain network are described below.

- **Databases:** A collection of structured information that is typically stored in an electronic format and controlled by a database management system (DBMS). Databases in the blockchain-based banking system would also need to store the following information:
  - Compliance rules and requirements
  - Blockchain testing requirements
  - Taxation rules
  - Merchant rules
  - Security rules and requirements of, for example, risk-based authentication of IoT devices
  - Blockchain integration rules and requirements of ATMs, POS terminals, merchants, governmental systems, IoT devices, etc.
  - Trust scoring models of auditors
- **Blockchain network:** Blockchain networks provide an infrastructure through which applications can access ledgers and smart contracts. Smart contracts are used to originate transactions, which are sent to peer nodes that then permanently record them on their copies of the ledger. The blockchain application server accesses the blockchain network using the blockchain module.

6.5   Conclusion and Future Work

In this chapter, we discussed blockchain's impact on the banking and financial industry, the state-of-the-art for blockchain-based banking applications, and architectural considerations for developing blockchain-based banking and financial applications.

Blockchain has the potential to revolutionize industries such as international trade and the world of banking. As crypto assets' market capitalization grows and institutional support for blockchains increases, banks that develop the infrastructure for blockchain-based banking services will gain a competitive advantage. In order to reap the benefits of next-generation technology, financial services companies will need to collaborate with regulators and develop standardized solutions. Standardizing industry solutions using public and private blockchains can improve transaction speed, reduce back-office costs, and decrease labor hours. Thus, the banking and financial sectors will be able to expand their product offerings, develop new profit centers, and enhance customer service for existing and previously unreachable customers.

A number of trends are expected to emerge in the banking industry as it continues to adopt blockchain technology. One of the new trends includes blockchain-based cross-border payments, which are already being tested by banks in order to increase their speed, security, and cost-effectiveness. As a result, international payments will be handled more efficiently and at lower cost. Blockchain is also becoming increasingly popular for verifying identities since it can be used by banks to store and verify customer identities and ensure compliance with anti-money laundering regulations. Blockchain technology can also be used by banks to verify third-party vendors, customers, and employees. Other future trends in blockchain use in the banking and financial industry include blockchain testing, blockchain integration with big data analytics platforms, compliance and certification using smart contracts, standardization of blockchain and IoT integrations, establishment of decentralization, collaboration on taxation and regulations for blockchain adoption, specifically for international trade and customs. Furthermore, we can expect to see more banks utilizing blockchain technology to manage assets in the future. In addition to improving security and transparency in asset management and reducing fraud by enhancing know-your-customer and anti-money laundering processes, blockchain technology can also assist banks in reducing costs and improving service quality by replacing the existing cross-border payments, lending, and trade finance infrastructure. It is anticipated that existing issues of blockchain scalability and feasibility will be resolved through the implementation of more energy-efficient consensus protocols.

Overall, blockchain technology is expected to have a profound impact on the banking industry. It provides a secure and cost-effective method for processing payments, verifying identity, managing assets, and more. In the near future, the banking industry is likely to continue exploring ways to use blockchain technology in order to achieve its goals.

REFERENCES

1. N. J. Birch, "Blockchains and Customs: Prospects and Possibilities," Primerus, [Online]. Available: https://www.primerus.com/business-law-articles/blockchains-and-customs-prospects-and-possibilities.htm
2. Y. Okazaki, "Unveiling the Potential of Blockchain for Customs," World Customs Organization (WCO), 2018.
3. E. Davradakis and R. Santos, "Blockchain, FinTechs and Their Relevance for International Financial Institutions," European Investment Bank (EIB), 2019.
4. F. Rega, N. Riccardi, J. Li and F. Di Carlo, "Blockchain in the Banking Industry: An Overview," *Research Gate,* 2018.
5. A. Khatri and A. Kaushik, "Systematic Literature Review on Blockchain Adoption in Banking," *Journal of Economics, Finance and Accounting (JEFA),* vol. 8, no. 3, pp. 126–145, 2021.
6. R3, [Online]. Available: https://www.r3.com/
7. D. L. Portilla, M. V. N. David J. Kappos, S. Rosenthal-Larrea, J. D. Buretta and C. K. Fargo, "Blockchain in the Banking Sector: A Review of the Landscape and Opportunities," 28 January 2022. [Online]. Available: https://corpgov.law.harvard.edu/2022/01/28/blockchain-in-the-banking-sector-a-review-of-the-landscape-and-opportunities/#respond
8. Y. Guo and C. Liang, "Blockchain application and outlook in the banking industry," *Financial Innovation,* vol. 2, no. 24, 2016. Available: https://jfin-swufe.springeropen.com/articles/10.1186/s40854-016-0034-9#citeas
9. L. Jutila, *The blockchain technology and its applications in the financial sector*, Aalto University School of Business, Department of Economics, 2017.
10. S. Albeshr, H. Nobanee and H. Nobanee, "Blockchain Applications in Banking Industry: A Mini-Review," *SSRN,* 2020.
11. PCI Security Standards Council, "PCI Security Standards," [Online]. Available: https://www.pcisecuritystandards.org/
12. S. Wang, L. Ouyang, Y. Yuan, X. Ni, X. Han and F. -Y. Wang, "Blockchain-Enabled Smart Contracts: Architecture, Applications, and Future Trends," *IEEE Transactions on Systems, Man, and Cybernetics: Systems,* vol. 49, no. 11, pp. 2266–2277, 2019.
13. D. K. C. Lee and L. Low, *Inclusive Fintech: Blockchain, Cryptocurrency and ICO*, World Scientific, 2018.
14. J. Zhang, R. Tan, C. Su and W. Si, "Design and application of a personal credit information sharing platform based on consortium blockchain," *Journal of Information Security and Applications,* vol. 55, p. 102659, 2020.
15. P. Yadav and R. Chandak, "Transforming the Know Your Customer (KYC) Process using Blockchain," in *2019 International Conference on Advances in Computing, Communication and Control (ICAC3),* 2019.
16. S. Islam, M. Obaidat, V. Rajeev and R. Amin, "Design of a Certificateless Designated Server Based Searchable Public Key Encryption Scheme," In: Giri, D., Mohapatra, R., Begehr, H., Obaidat, M. (eds), in *Mathematics and Computing. ICMC 2017. Communications in Computer and Information Science*, vol. 655, Singapore, Springer, 2017.
17. G. Salwan, P. Kaushal, S. Gupta and P. Nayak, "A Robust Cyber Security: Challenges and Opportunities," in *Artificial Intelligence, Machine Learning, and Data Science Technologies: Future Impact and Well-Being for Society 5.0*, Boca Raton, CRC, 2021, p. 310.
18. N. A. Popova and N. G. Butakova, "Research of a Possibility of Using Blockchain Technology without Tokens to Protect Banking Transactions," in *2019 IIEEE Conference of Russian Young Researchers in Electrical and Electronic Engineering (EIConRus),* 2019.
19. Y. Wang and C. Lin, "Research on the Application of Blockchain in Credit Bank," in *2020 International Conference on Information Science and Education (ICISE-IE),* 2020.

20. S. Joseph and S. Karunan, "A Blockchain Based Decentralized Transaction Settlement System in Banking Sector," in *Fourth International Conference on Microelectronics, Signals & Systems (ICMSS)*, 2021.

21. K. Singh, N. Singh and D. S. Kushwaha, "An Interoperable and Secure E-Wallet Architecture based on Digital Ledger Technology using Blockchain," in *2018 International Conference on Computing, Power and Communication Technologies (GUCON)*, 2018.

22. S. Sakho, Z. Jianbiao, F. Essaf and K. Badiss, "Improving Banking Transactions Using Blockchain Technology," in *IEEE 5th International Conference on Computer and Communications (ICCC)*, 2019.

23. K. A. M. Ahmed, S. F. Saraya, J. F. Wanis and A. M. T. Ali-Eldin, "A Self-Sovereign Identity Architecture Based on Blockchain and the Utilization of Customer's Banking Cards: The Case of Bank Scam Calls Prevention," in *2020 15th International Conference on Computer Engineering and Systems (ICCES)*, 2020.

24. Z. Lu, X. Wan, J. Yang, J. Wu, C. Zhang, P. C. K. Hung and S.-C. Huang, "Bis: A Novel Blockchain Based Bank-Tax Interaction System in Smart City," in *2019 IEEE Intl Conf on Dependable, Autonomic and Secure Computing, Intl Conf on Pervasive Intelligence and Computing, Intl Conf on Cloud and Big Data Computing, Intl Conf on Cyber Science and Technology Congress (DASC/PiCom/CBDCom/CyberSciTech)*, 2019.

25. W. Fan, S. -Y. Chang, S. Emery and X. Zhou, "Blockchain-based Distributed Banking for Permissioned and Accountable Financial Transaction Processing," in *2020 29th International Conference on Computer Communications and Networks (ICCCN)*, 2020.

26. L. Cocco, A. Pinna and M. Marchesi, "Banking on Blockchain: Costs Savings Thanks to the Blockchain Technology," *Future Internet,* vol. 9, no. 25, 2017. Available: https://www.mdpi.com/1999-5903/9/3/25

27. Z. Kawasmi, E. A. Gyasi and D. Dadd, "Blockchain Adoption Model for the Global Banking Industry," *Journal of Internastional Technology and Information Management,* vol. 28, no. 4, pp. 112–154, 2020.

28. European Parliament and the Council of the European Union, "Regulation (EU) 2016/679 of the European Parliament and of the Council," 2016. [Online]. Available: https://eur-lex.europa.eu/eli/reg/2016/679/oj

29. Board of Governors of the Federal Reserve System Federal Deposit Insurance Corporation Office of the Comptroller of the Currency, "Joint Statement on Crypto-Asset Policy Sprint Initiative and Next Steps," 2021. [Online]. Available: https://www.federalreserve.gov/newsevents/pressreleases/files/bcreg20211123a1.pdf.

30. Deloitte, "Crypto Asset Management: Managing the Tax Expectations Gap," 2022.

31. P. Nayak, N. Ray and P. Ravichandran, *IoT Applications, Security Threats, and Countermeasures*, Boca Raton, CRC Press, 2021.

32. P. Shah, D. Forester, D. Polk, W. LLP, M. Berberich, C. Raspe and H. Mueller, "Blockchain Technology: Data Privacy Issues and Potential Mitigation Strategies," *Practical Law,* 2019.

33. W. Li, Y. Wang, L. Chen, X. Lai, X. Zhang and J. Xin, "Fully Auditable Privacy-preserving Cryptocurrency Against Malicious Auditors," *Cryptology ePrint Archive,* 2019.

34. FIDO Alliance, [Online]. Available: https://fidoalliance.org/

7

Blockchain-Based eCommerce Warranty System using NFTs

Swarup Yeole
International Institute of Information Technology Naya Raipur, Naya Raipur, India

Mohammad S. Obaidat
University of Jordan, Amman, Jordan
SRM University, India
University of Science and Technology Beijing, China

Aditya Goel and Sanskar Chandra
International Institute of Information Technology Naya Raipur, Naya Raipur, India

Ruhul Amin
National Institute of Technology, Jamshedpur, India

7.1   Introduction

The Non-Fungible Tokens (NFT) market has expanded dramatically. The solution is a blockchain-based digital warranty system using NFTs that automates the warranty tracking and claim process and reduces the time consumed in processing the claims. The method is an automated process consisting of multiple ends. It can be used on multiple devices ranging from smartphones to personal laptops and desktops, thus making it easy to use for customers and vendors. The modular blockchain network creates a two-peer network for the warranty management system. One network is for the vendor, and the other is for the customer. The vendor will post his product and give details of the warranty claims. When a customer buys that product, its warranty claim (for example, it has a warranty for a year) will get triggered in the chain code. When the warranty date passes, the system automatically marks the warranty as *expired*, and the customer can no longer avail of the benefits of the listed product's warranty period. We aim to make the warranty system more robust and reliable.

Our architecture offers a guarantee in the form of a digital token upon product purchase, which serves as evidence of the purchase of the goods and the warranty that goes along with it.

7.2   Literature Review

7.2.1   Non-Fungible Token (NFT): Overview, Opportunities, Evaluation, and Challenges

This chapter introduces the Non-Fungible Token (NFT) concept and how the market has grown. It is stated that the concept of NFT originated from an Ethereum token standard, which means that each token must be distinguished by visible signs. As recognizable one-of-a-kind pieces of proof, this type of token can be bound with virtual/computerized properties. With NFTs, all noticeable properties can be freely exchanged for altered significances based on their ages, extraordinariness, liquidity, etc. The chapter emphasizes how NFTs have significantly boosted the success of the decentralized application (dApp) market.

DOI:10.1201/9781003326236-7

It examines NFT biological systems from various angles, starting with a summary of the best-in-class NFT solutions before offering information on their technological components, procedures, benchmarks, and desirable qualities. The security development that follows discusses the views, possibilities, and difficulties of such design paradigms.

According to a report, an NFT is a breakthrough in the blockchain sector. In this report, they investigate the best-in-class NFT arrangements that may reshape the market for computerized/virtual resources. It first analyzes the specialized parts and provides the plan models and properties. Then, it evaluates the security of current NFT frameworks and discusses the open doors and potential applications that embrace the NFT concept. The paper also discusses existing exploration challenges that are expected to be addressed before mass-market entry. The report conveys an appropriate examination and aggregate of current proposed arrangements and activities, making it more straightforward for newcomers to keep up with the ongoing advancement.

7.2.2   Non-Fungible Tokens: The Future of Digital Collectibles

This chapter investigates the concept of NFT concerning cryptocurrency and copyright, as well as its operation and various components. Its goal is to analyze the legal risks that affect its operations and the opportunities and challenges that the Indian legal framework faces in terms of cryptographic assets.

Like other virtual cryptocurrencies and assets, NFTs are digital certificates of authenticity based on blockchain technology. In recent years, interest in blockchain technology and cryptocurrency trading has increased. As has been evident lately, the NFT market is also growing. The Ethereum token standard, from which the idea of NFT is derived, seeks to separate and recognize each token by its distinctive signature, which is connected to digital characteristics.

India has seen a boom in interest in this digital industry because of the remarkable return on its quickly growing worldwide market, notably from up-and-coming new-age investors and innovators. There is, however, no regulatory legal structure in place to control such emerging digital crypto assets in India because the NFT ecosystem is still in its infancy. Their legal status and sanctity are unclear because of the various legal difficulties surrounding them. New artists can become lost in this chaotic growth without systematic descriptions.

7.3   Preliminaries

7.3.1   Blockchain

Blockchain is one of the advancing technologies, popularized by Satoshi Nakamoto in 2008 by publishing the paper "Bitcoin: A Peer-to-Peer Electronic Cash System". Due to its decentralized nature, a blockchain is a type of Distributed Ledger Technology (DLT) that renders digital transactions and records transparent and unchangeable. A block is a set of valid transactions. A valid transaction is one that has been approved by the consensus methods used in the validation process. Miners are the nodes in the blockchain network that operate these algorithms. A block is made up of the time-stamped, authenticated transactions that occur during a certain period of time. The current block is chained to the immediately preceding block through hashes, unique strings of letters, and numbers like fingerprints. The preceding block's hash is kept in each block for reference. Different messages produce different hashes by running algorithms like SHA256. A small change in the transaction will change the output hash and break the chain. Therefore, once a transaction is included in the block, it cannot be altered, making the blockchain immutable.

Records on the blockchain are chronologically organized, irreversible, and easily accessible to all nodes. Due to its advantages of cost savings, speed, transparency, privacy, visibility, less exposure, less fraud, less tampering, productivity, efficiency, quality, and outcomes, blockchain technology is quickly becoming popular in a variety of industries, including the financial sector, insurance, trade finance, digital identity, charity, and supply chain.

To date, there are four blockchain networks:

1) **Public blockchain**

   A public blockchain does not have entry requirements. Anyone with a Web connection may use it to transmit transactions and become a validator (i.e., partake in executing an agreement protocol). Such organizations often employ some Proof of Stake or Evidence of Work calculation and provide financial incentives to those who secure them. The Bitcoin and Ethereum blockchain are the two largest and best-known public blockchains.

2) **Private blockchain**

   Permitted blockchains are private blockchains. One cannot support it until the chairman of the organization gives their approval. Access is restricted to members and validators. Open blockchains and other shared, decentralized data set applications that are not accessible to designated process groups are sometimes distinguished by the term "Conveyed Record (DLT)."

3) **Hybrid blockchain**

   A hybrid blockchain combines decentralized and unified characteristics. Depending on how much centralization and how much decentralization are used, the chain's precise activities can change.

4) **Sidechain**

   A sidechain is an assignment for the blockchain record lined up with an essential blockchain. Records from the essential blockchain (where said sections regularly address computerized resources) can be connected to and from the sidechain; this permits the sidechain to, in any case, independently of the essential blockchain (e.g., by utilizing a substitute method for record-keeping, and substitute agreement calculation)

   Blockchain technology has uses in multiple fields some of which are as follows:

   a. **Financial services**

      According to a September 2016 **IBM** study, this is happening faster than anticipated. Many organizations divide their earnings between assisting businesses in creating private blockchains and processing transmitted data for use in banking. Banks are interested in this idea because it expedites administrative settlement procedures. Additionally, as the blockchain business has developed to an early level, institutional knowledge has risen that it is often the framework of an entirely new financial industry, with all its consequences.

      The blockchain has also made it feasible to contribute via initial coin offerings (ICOs), and security tokens (STOs), a separate class of digital assets sometimes referred to as improved security contributions (DSOs). Traditional resources like corporate shares and more irrational ones like licensed innovations, real estate, handiwork, or specific items are tokenized using STO/DSOs. STO/DSOs can be managed on managed stock exchanges in an open or covert manner. A large number of groups are involved in this field and support secure tokenization, public STOs, and private STOs.

   b. **Games**

      Blockchain innovation, like digital currencies and NFTs, has been utilized in computer games for adaptation. Some live-administration games let players purchase and trade in-game items with other players using in-game money, such as character skins or other in-game items. A few games likewise consider exchanging virtual things utilizing genuine cash, yet this might be unlawful in certain nations where computer games are viewed as likened to betting and have prompted dark market issues, for example, skin betting. Subsequently, distributors typically have avoided permitting players to procure certifiable assets from games. Blockchain games commonly permit players to exchange these in-game things for digital currency, which may then be converted into real money.

   c. **Supply chain**

      Shipping industry: Occupant delivering organizations and new businesses have started to use blockchain innovation to work with the rise of a blockchain-based stage environment that would make esteem across the worldwide transportation supply chains.

Mining for valuable goods: Blockchain technology has been used to track the sources of precious stones and additional items. The Money Road Diary reported in 2016 that IBM's blockchain-based technology was working with the blockchain innovation organization Everledger to track the source of diamonds to ensure that they were mined ethically. The Precious Stone Swapping Organization, direct to consumer (DTC), began working on developing a precious stone exchanging retail network item named Tracr in 2019.

Food supply: Starting in 2018, Walmart and IBM ran a test project to use a blockchain-based architecture for inventory network checking for spinach and lettuce. All blockchain hubs were under the control of Walmart and were hosted on IBM's cloud.

Design industry: In the fashion industry, there is a murky relationship between companies, distributors, and customers that will thwart its steady and consistent growth. Blockchain corrects this flaw and simplifies data, resolving the issue of controllable industry progress.

d. **Cryptocurrencies**

Cryptocurrencies are forms of digital money that may be exchanged on a computer network without the need for a centralized management or oversight body, like a government or bank.

Individual currency ownership records are stored in an advanced record, a computerized data set of strength regions, which may be used to get trade records, manage the production of more coins, and monitor the transfer of coin ownership. Despite their name, digital currencies are not thought of as traditional monetary standards. Digital currencies are widely viewed as a unique resource class in practice, despite the fact that they have been given several designations, including grouping as objects, safeguards, and monetary rules. Validators are used by certain crypto schemes to keep up with digital money. In a proof-of-stake paradigm, owners build security using their tokens. As a result, they have control over the token with regard to the bet they make. For the most part, these symbolic stakes get extra possession in the token over the long haul through network charges, shiny new tokens, or other such award mechanisms.

There is no such thing as digital currency in actual structure (like paper cash), and it is commonly not given by a focal power. Cryptographic forms of money normally utilize decentralized control rather than national bank computerized cash central bank digital currency (CBDC). When a digital currency is printed or made preceding issuance or given by a solitary guarantor, it is by and large thought to be concentrated. When executed with decentralized control, every cryptographic money manages disseminated record innovation, ordinarily, a blockchain that fills in as a public monetary exchange database. Conventional resource classes like monetary forms, items, and stocks, as well as macroeconomic elements, have unassuming openings to digital currency returns.

Most digital currencies use blockchain technology to track trades. Blockchain, for instance, is made available to the Ethereum and Bitcoin networks. David Marcus, who most recently handled Courier, will lead a new blockchain team that Facebook announced on May 8, 2018. The official introduction of Facebook's anticipated cryptographic currency platform, Libra (now known as Diem), was made on June 18, 2019.

Legislatures have blended approaches to the lawfulness of their residents or banks claiming digital forms of money. China executes blockchain innovation in a few enterprises, including computerized public money sent in 2020. To reinforce their particular monetary forms, Western legislatures, including the European Association and the United States, have started comparable undertakings.

e. **Domain names**

Several attempts exist to offer domain name administrations over the blockchain. These domain names can be controlled by using a secret key. Therefore, uncensorable websites must be taken into mind. Additionally, this would circumvent a recorder's capability to restrict websites that include extortion, abuse, or unlawful information.

Namecoin is a form of virtual currency that supports the high-level "piece" space (TLD). In 2011, Namecoin split off from Bitcoin. ICANN does not support the .piece TLD; it requires an alternative DNS root. Out of 120,000 registered names, 28 sites started using it around 2015. 2019 saw OpenNIC discontinue support for Namecoin owing to malware and potential legal problems.

Three explicit TLDs that are linked to the Ethereum blockchain via the Ethereum Name Administration are ".eth," ".luxury," and ".kred" (ENS). In addition to being more convenient than using regular digital currency wallet addresses, the .kred TLD is also useful for transferring money.

f. **Other Uses**

With blockchain technology, a dependable, transparent, and straightforward record-keeping system may be developed for gathering information on transactions, tracking computer use, and paying content providers like musicians or remote users. In the Gartner 2019 CIO Review, respondents in higher education made up 2% of the sample, while another 18% planned academic initiatives for the following 24 months. To implement blockchain technology for music distribution, IBM partnered with ASCAP and PRS for Music in 2017. Another blockchain-based option is Imogen Pile's Mycelia administration. This "gives artists greater control over how their music and related information circulate through listeners and other artists," according to the statement.

Following blockchain, new dispersion tactics are now available for the insurance industry, including distributed, parametric, and microinsurance. IoT and the sharing economy also benefit from blockchains since they encourage peer collaboration. A grant from the U.S. Foundation of Gallery and Library Services is being explored to use blockchain in libraries.

Hyperledger, a cooperative effort by the Linux Foundation to enable blockchain-based distributed records, is one of the other blockchain efforts. This initiative's projects include Hyperledger Texture and Hyperledger Tunnel (both by Monax) (led by IBM). Another is Majority, a private blockchain powered by JPMorgan Pursue with a private capacity for contract applications. This is shown in Figure 7.1.

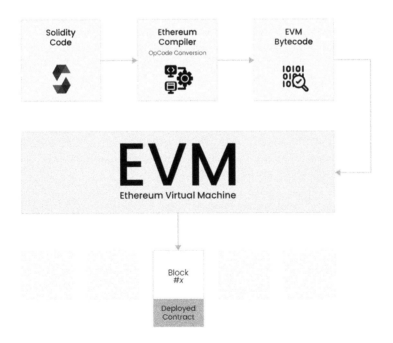

FIGURE 7.1   EVM.

7.3.2   Ethereum Virtual Machine (EVM)

Ether is the coin employed by the Ethereum blockchain. Ether represents any exchange of funds between accounts as a distributed currency. The currency used by Ethereum is called ether. This gives an extensive range of applications, from cryptocurrency exchange to financial software to the storage and management of digital assets and tokens, to traditional systems, voting software, and identity management, up to those that need traceable assets and resources. The runtime environment for smart contracts on Ethereum is called Ethereum Virtual Machine (EVM). The code running within EVM is wholly isolated and not simply sandboxed, so neither other processes nor the network can access it. Even alternate smart contracts can only be accessed under certain conditions.

By avoiding denial-of-service attacks, which are partially related to growing issues within the cryptocurrency industry, EVM ensures security. Second, EVM provides that communication may occur without interruption by interpreting and running the Ethereum programming language.

7.3.3   Smart Contracts

Blockchain-based smart contracts are computer programs that run when specific criteria are satisfied. They are used to automate the implementation of agreements so that everyone involved may be confident of the result without the need for a mediator or wasting any time. They can also automate the workflow so that when the conditions are met, the next step is initiated.

Smart contracts allow developers to build various decentralized apps and tokens. They are used in everything from financial tools to logistics and game experiences.

Smart contracts are "if/when...then" statements written in code and published on a blockchain. A network of computers will execute the activities if certain conditions have been confirmed to have been met. These include making the appropriate financial payments, registering a vehicle, distributing notices, or issuing a ticket. The blockchain is then updated when the transaction is complete. As a result, the transaction cannot be changed, and only those who have been given permission may see the results.

A smart contract can contain as many criteria as are necessary to provide assurance to the parties that the action will be completed successfully. In order to determine the conditions, participants must agree on the "if/when...then" rules that govern those transactions, take into account any potential exceptions, and provide a framework for resolving disputes. Also up for discussion among participants is how transactions and related data are stored on the blockchain.

A developer can then build the smart contract. Still, an increasing number of companies adopting blockchain for business are employing templates, web interfaces, and other online tools to make smart contract creation simpler.

Benefits of Smart Contract

- **Rapidity, effectiveness, and precision**
  If a requirement is met, the contract is swiftly carried out. As digital and automated contracts, smart contracts eliminate the need for paper documentation and the time-consuming errors that usually arise when forms are filled out manually.

- **Integrity and trust**
  There is no need to wonder whether information has been changed for one participant's gain because no third party is engaged, and participants exchange encrypted records of transactions.

- **Security**
  The encrypted blockchain transaction records make them extremely difficult to hack. On a distributed ledger, each record is connected to the entries that came before and after it. Thus, hackers would also need to change the entire chain to change a single record.

- **Savings**
  Smart contracts do away with the need for middlemen to manage transactions, along with the costs and time delays that go along with them.

- **Backup**
  The shared ledger is maintained by each node on the blockchain, making this service the best possible.

7.3.4 InterPlanetary File System

Blockchain is a safe way to store data. Still, it is not the best solution for handling vast amounts of data due to computational and network constraints. An alternative file system called InterPlanetary File System (IPFS) can be utilized for the cost-effective storage of massive amounts of data and content. The interplanetary file method, or IPFS, is a distributed, decentralized system and platform for securely storing data and files. It combines successful ideas from earlier peer-to-peer networks, including BitTorrent, DHT, SFS, and GIT. IPFS contributes by combining proven methods into a single, important system rather than just its parts. IPFS provides a completely new framework for creating and deploying large-scale applications.

The interplanetary file system, or IPFS, is a network and protocol created to create a distributed network with peer-to-peer hypermedia storing and sharing that is content-addressable because IPFS is peer-to-peer, and nodes have special privileges.

IPFS nodes use native storage to keep IPFS objects. These objects, which stand in for files and data structures, are connected and transferred by nodes. IPFS uses the content's hash to identify and distribute it among the nodes. It incorporates alternative technologies like Merkle DAG data structures for storing data and GIT for version control.

A peer-to-peer network disseminates the content, and IPFS aims to connect every computing device directly. Even the web itself can develop with IPFS. IPFS offers a content-addressed block storage format with high throughput and content-addressed hyperlinks. A self-certifying namespace, an incentive block exchange, and a distributed hash table are all combined in IPFS. Data transit on IPFS cannot be tampered with since there is no single point of failure. Hypertext Transfer Protocol (HTTP), which struggles with DDoS attacks, is protected by distributed content delivery and conserves bandwidth. There are numerous ways to access the filesystem, including FUSE or "File system in Userspace" over HTTP. The IPFS file system will incorporate a local file, making it accessible to everyone worldwide. Since hashes are used to identify files, it is cache friendly. Any user downloading the file makes the data available to other network users.

7.3.5 NFT

Non-fungible tokens are digital currency tokens that duplicate tangible properties of tangible things like uniqueness, shortage, and confirmation of possession. Simultaneously, they address novel, immaterial, and indispensable computerized stuff in light of the blockchain. NFTs are being applied to physical and virtual resources to adapt their worth.

NFTs are not tradable. They are distinguished from each other by metadata and unique identifiers like a scanner tag that permits them to connect themselves with specific on-chain addresses. Metadata makes them an optimal instrument for affirming responsibility. Since every token is exceptionally recognizable, NFTs contrast with blockchain cryptographic forms of money, like Bitcoin or Ethereum. For instance, one Bitcoin (BTC) is dependably equivalent in worth to another. Similar to this, one Ether (ETH) unit equals one more. Cryptographic money is rational as a secure medium of exchange in the digital economy because of its fungibility characteristic. By ensuring that each token is unique, NFTs change the crypto paradigm.

The ERC-721 standard gave rise to NFTs. ERC-721 specifies the minimal interface—ownership information, security, and metadata—needed to exchange and distribute gaming tokens. It was created by some of the same individuals that made the ERC-20 smart contract. By lowering the transaction and storage costs necessary for NFTs and batching many non-fungible token types into a single contract, the ERC-1155 standard expands on the idea.

To be clear, neither the concept of using unique identification nor the idea of digital representations of tangible goods is new. However, these ideas become a powerful force for change when combined with the advantages of a tamper-proof blockchain of smart contracts.

Market efficiency is arguably the most evident advantage of NFTs. A physical asset being transformed into a digital one simplifies procedures and eliminates middlemen. NFTs that represent actual or digital artwork on a blockchain do away with the necessity for agents, allowing artists to interact with their audiences directly. Additionally, they can enhance corporate procedures. For instance, an NFT for a wine bottle will make it simpler for various supply chain participants to communicate with it and assist in tracking its creation, provenance, and sale throughout the process. One of its clients, consulting company Ernst & Young, has already created such a solution.

Types of NFTs

1. **Art**
   The most common subset of NFTs is art. These are primarily digital works of art protected by a public certificate of ownership and authenticity issued by the digital ledger where they are kept. The most expensive NFT ever sold was a digital piece called "The First 5000 Days" by artist Beeple, which went for a staggering $69.3 million in a March 2021 Christie's auction.

2. **Music**
   One of the most recent developments in NFT madness is music. Before releasing their albums on typical streaming platforms, artists pre-release them on NFT markets. Customers can purchase a portion of the record, such as a share, and when it is published through conventional channels, they are entitled to a part of the album's revenues. Although this trading strategy for musical NFTs is still relatively new, many transactions follow this pattern. For instance, in March 2021, Kings of Leon's album "When You See Yourself" was offered for sale as several NFTs.

3. **Video game items**
   The world of video games is a Beyer NFT frontier. There aren't any full games being sold as NFTs by companies. Instead, they provide stuff like skins, characters, and other in-game content for sale. Players today purchase downloadable content (DLC) in millions of copies, while NFT assets are exclusive to one customer and are one-of-a-kind. The limited edition DLC can be sold on the NFT market after the standard DLC is sold by the developers.

4. **Trading cards/collectible items**
   The first NFT ever launched was a collectible. These digital collectibles are identical to tangible artifacts in physical forms, such as Pokemon cards or old, mint-condition toys. The first big NFT collectibles ever released were Curio Cards, and since then, various collectibles have

```
FUNCTIONS

balanceOf(owner)

ownerOf(tokenId)

safeTransferFrom(from, to, tokenId, data)

safeTransferFrom(from, to, tokenId)

transferFrom(from, to, tokenId)

approve(to, tokenId)

setApprovalForAll(operator, approved)

getApproved(tokenId)

isApprovedForAll(owner, operator)
```

FIGURE 7.2 ERC 721 function.

gained popularity, like Bored Ape Yacht Club, CryptoPunks, Cat Colony, and Meebits. Bored Ape Yacht Club has emerged as the market leader in digital treasures, and they are a treat for collectors.

5. **Big sports moments**
One of the most popular NFT categories is sports memorabilia, and the NBA Top Shot is the most well-known NFT in this niche. This kind of NFT contains a video clip of priceless athletic events. The LeBron James Dunk, Throwdowns (Series), which features footage of Lakers star LeBron James dunking the ball, is one of the most well-known NFTS in this category. One of the most expensive Sports Memorabilia NFTs, it sold for more than $380,000.

7.3.6 ERC 721

On the Ethereum blockchain, creating non-fungible or unique tokens is outlined in the free, open standard known as ERC-721. Most tokens are fungible, meaning that each token is identical to every other. However, ERC-721 tokens are all distinct. Despite the narrow emphasis of this study on video games, ERC-721 has uses in various fields, including documentation and art. To manage, own, and trade unique tokens, a smart contract must implement the minimal interface specified by ERC-721. It does not impose a standard for token information or place limitations on adding other features. ERC 721 is shown in Figure 7.2.

It offers features including the ability to move tokens between accounts, determine an account's current token balance, identify the owner of a particular token, and determine the total number of tokens that are currently in circulation on the network. In addition, it also offers certain additional features, such as the ability to authorize the transfer of a certain quantity of tokens from one account to another. An ERC-721 Non-Fungible Token Contract implements the methods and events listed below. Once it has been deployed, the contract is in charge of managing the tokens that have been produced on Ethereum.

7.3.7 ERC 1155

Another form of the token standard on the Ethereum blockchain is ERC-1155. Given that it follows the principles of ERC-20 (Fungible) and ERC-721, it is a widely accepted norm (Non-Fungible). Due to its ability to support several tokens in a single agreement, it enables goods to have genuine value. Exchanges and token production are now more acceptable because of the ERC-1155 specification. ERC 1155 also supports repurposing current tokens and creating new tokens from them; it has uses in several fields, such as documentation and fine art.

7.3.8 MetaMask

With MetaMask, users may send and receive Ethereum-based coins and tokens, broadcast transactions, save and manage account keys, and securely connect to decentralized applications using a suitable web browser or the built-in browser of the mobile app.

A user's MetaMask wallet (and any similar blockchain wallet browser extensions) can be connected to, authenticated, and/or integrated with other smart contract functionality by websites or decentralized applications using JavaScript code. This enables the website to utilize MetaMask as a middleman to deliver user action prompts, signature requests, or transaction requests.

Features

- **Ease of Use**
  MetaMask is quick, simple, and anonymous to use. It does not even require an email address. All you need to do is create a password and remember (and save) the secret recovery phrase.
- **Token Swaps**
  Peer-to-peer (P2P) token swaps may be carried out using the trade feature of MetaMask right from your wallet.

- **Security**

  Nobody can access your information since it is encrypted in your browser. You have the 12-word secret recovery phase (also known as a seed phrase) for recovery in the case of a forgotten password. Notably, even MetaMask has no knowledge of the seed phrase, making it imperative to keep it secure. It cannot be found after it is gone.

- **Built-In Crypto Store**

  Only Ethereum and tokens associated with Ethereum, including the well-known ERC-20 tokens, are supported with MetaMask. On Ethereum, all cryptocurrencies (apart from Ether) are created as ERC-20 tokens.

- **Backup and restore**

  The data you provide to MetaMask is locally stored. So, if you change browsers or computers, you may use your private recovery phrase to restore your MetaMask wallet.

- **Community support**

  There were 10 million monthly active users using MetaMask as of August 2021. These numbers continue to rise because of its clear and easy-to-use user interface, which has seen an 1800% growth since July 2020.

The MetaMask wallet is excellent for individuals familiar with cryptocurrencies, but it isn't the ideal choice for those just getting started. Due to the wallet's vulnerability to malware and social engineering assaults, users unaware of the warning signs run the danger of losing their money. Users risk losing access to their crypto assets permanently since there is no way to change a password without the 12-word secret seed phrase. Before using MetaMask or any other tool, new users must learn how to utilize Bitcoin wallets.

TechStack Used

1. MetaMask: It is a wallet-and-browser extension that installs similarly to other browser add-ons. After being installed, it gives users the ability to hold Ethereum and other ERC-20 tokens, enabling them to carry out transactions using any Ethereum address. By connecting MetaMask to Ethereum-based dApps, users may spend their money on games, stake tokens in gambling apps, and sell them on decentralized exchanges.

2. IPFS: For storing and accessing files, webpages, apps, and data, it is a distributed system. A more robust web is made possible by Infura's IPFS API and dedicated gateway, which link apps of all sizes to distributed safe storage quickly and easily.

3. React.js: Facebook created the front-end JavaScript framework known as React.js. We utilize React to declaratively construct composable user interfaces in a predictable and effective manner. The framework, which is open-source and component-based, is in charge of developing the application's display layer.

4. Hardhat: Hardhat is a development environment for Ethereum software. It is made up of many parts that may be used to edit, compile, debug, and deploy your dApps and smart contracts, together forming a whole development environment.

5. Ether.js: The ethers.js library for connecting with the Ethereum blockchain and its biological system. It was initially intended for use with ethers.io and has since ventured into a more universally useful library.

7.4   Implementation

The proposed architecture facilitates a decentralized marketplace and token infrastructure to list the product. The architecture also provides a warranty in the form of a digital token on product purchase, which acts as proof of product purchase and its associated warranty. It integrates IPFS to store the listed product metadata in decentralized storage cost-efficiently. The architecture uses

FUNCTIONS

```
constructor(uri_)

supportsInterface(interfaceId)

uri()

balanceOf(account, id)

balanceOfBatch(accounts, ids)

setApprovalForAll(operator, approved)

isApprovedForAll(account, operator)

safeTransferFrom(from, to, id, amount, data)

safeBatchTransferFrom(from, to, ids, amounts, data)

_safeTransferFrom(from, to, id, amount, data)

_safeBatchTransferFrom(from, to, ids, amounts, data)

_setURI(newuri)

_mint(to, id, amount, data)

_mintBatch(to, ids, amounts, data)

_burn(from, id, amount)

_burnBatch(from, ids, amounts)

_setApprovalForAll(owner, operator, approved)

_beforeTokenTransfer(operator, from, to, ids, amounts, data)

_afterTokenTransfer(operator, from, to, ids, amounts, data)
```

FIGURE 7.3 Functions for NFT smart contract.

Ethereum blockchain to deploy smart contracts. The decentralized token infrastructure uses the ERC 721 protocol to create unique token objects, including the product picture, product model number, and warranty duration. Once the product is purchased from the marketplace, these digital tokens are transferred to the buyer's account as a digital warranty. The implementation of the architecture involves the following steps:

1) **Customer and Seller Registration**
   MetaMask is a browser plugin that acts as an Ethereum wallet and can be installed in the same way that any other browser plugin would. It lets users store Ether and other ERC-20 tokens and transact with any Ethereum address once loaded. To begin, download and install the official MetaMask browser extension (also known as a plugin or add-on). The majority of individuals use the Google Chrome extension or the Firefox plugin. The seller or buyer would then need to connect their MetaMask wallet to dApp. After the connection has been established, the sellers will be able to list their products and the customers can buy the listed product.

2) **Smart Contract**
   The system employs two smart contracts to implement the architecture: This is shown in Figure 7.3.

7.4.1 NFT Smart Contract

The contract abides by the ERC 721 standard. The smart contract includes functions that involve minting of NFT. The smart contract has the following functions:

i. mint: This function helps in minting the NFT. It internally maintains the token count for the NFT being listed to uniquely identify each listed token. The function uses the *safeMint( )* function of the ERC721 standard to mint the NFT. It also internally uses another ERC721 function *SetTokenURI( )* to set the NFT MetaData for the particular NFT. The function returns the unique token ID of the NFT in the return statement.

7.4.2 MarketPlace and Warranty Contract

This smart contract allows sellers to list product information in the form of NFT on the marketplace for the items to be sold and then transfers the ownership of the NFT as warranty to the buyers on the product purchase. This smart contract also abides by the ERC721 token standard It also uses the reentrancy guard contract internally to protect the marketplace from reentrancy attacks. The smart contract sets the *feeAccount* to the deployer of the smart contract. The functions involved in the smart contract are:

a) MakeItem: The *makeItem( )* function takes input of the following variables:
    i.   *_nft*: Takes input of the NFT contract of the NFT to be listed.
    ii. *_tokenId*: Inputs the unique tokenId of the NFT being listed.
    iii. *_price*: Inputs the product price
    iv. *_warranty:* Inputs the product warranty period.
    v.   *_modelNum:* Inputs the product model number.
    The functions check if the necessary conditions like the *_ price, modelNum, _warranty* have valid inputs. The smart contract internally executes the *transferFrom( )* function transferring

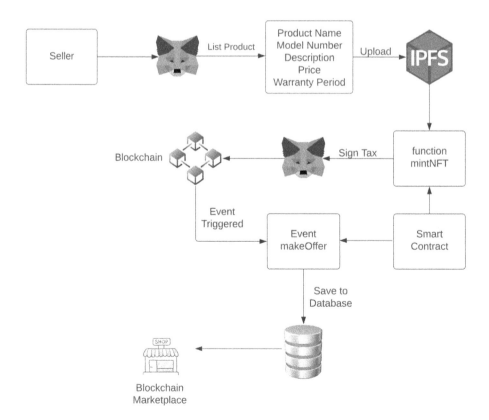

FIGURE 7.4 Product purchase flow chart.

the ownership of the listed product NFT from the seller to the smart contract. The listed product data is stored in map data structure *items*, which uniquely links each *ItemId* with its data. It emits the event *Offered* every time the function is executed.

b) PurchaseItem: This function takes the input of the unique *_itemId* of the token. It applies the *nonRentrant* modifier to prevent a reentrancy attack on the function. The function checks the conditions whether the *_ItemId* entered is in a valid format. It also checks the status of the item. If the item is unsold, then the transaction is allowed to move forward or else the transaction fails. It internally calls the *getTotalPrice* function to get the total price of the product and then calls the *transferFrom( )* function to transfer the ownership of NFT from the marketplace to the buyer as a form of warranty simultaneously it also updates the seller to deliver the requested product. The function finally transfers the money to the account of the marketplace and the seller.

c) getTotalPrice: The function returns the total price of the product, which is calculated by the formula: totalPrice $= (100 *$ feePercent)/100.

d) claimWarranty: This function updates the *_WarrantyClaimed* field to true once the buyer claims the warranty.

3) **Product Listing**

Product listing involves the following steps:

  I. The seller navigates to the list product section of the software.

  II. The seller uploads the below-mentioned details of the product:

    A. *Image:* Image of the product to be sold is provided.

    B. *Name:* Name of the product to be sold is added.

    C. *Model Number:* The product model number is listed.

    D. *Description:* In this field, the seller can add the product description.

    E. *Price:* In this field, the seller lists the product price in ETH.

    F. *Warranty:* In this field, the seller lists the warranty period of the product in years.

  III. The seller clicks on the list product and all the metadata is stored in a decentralized storage system known as IPFS. The *makeItem( )* function of the marketplace smart contract gets triggered. The MetaMask asks for the confirmation to list the product. After providing confirmation the transaction is signed and the data on the blockchain gets updated. The make Item function internally calls the *mintNFT* function to list the product NFT on the marketplace. The generated NFT ownerships get transferred to the marketplace.

4) **Product Purchase**

Product purchase involves the following steps:

  i. The customer navigates to the blockchain marketplace section of the software.

  ii. Customers can choose the product to buy out of the available products listed on the marketplace.

  iii. Once the customer buys the product the *PurchaseItem( )* function gets triggered. The MetaMask asks for a transaction confirmation after the confirmation of the transaction. The notification is sent to the seller for product delivery, and the product gets removed from the marketplace, the state of the blockchain is updated and the item is marked as sold. This is shown in Figure 7.4.

5) **Warranty Generation and Claim**

The *PurchaseItem( )* function internally calls the *_transferFrom( )* function, which passes the listed product NFT from the marketplace to the account of the buyer. The event *bought* is emitted once the ownership gets transferred. Now this NFT acts as a digital warranty and proof of product purchase. The NFT is displayed in the *myProductWarranties* section of the buyer with the following fields:

  i. Product Image

  ii. Product Name

iii.   Warranty Period

iv.   Warranty Claimed

If the customer claims the warranty, the *warranty Claimed* field gets updated to true, which shows that the warranty has been claimed for the product.

7.5   Deployment

Smart contracts have been deployed using hardhat. HardHat is an environment to test, compile, deploy, and debug dApps based on the Ethereum blockchain. When deployed, the Hardhat generates a local blockchain network with 20 accounts to simulate the Ethereum blockchain environment. Some of the accounts used in smart contract testing are given in Table 7.1.

Deploying smart contracts costs gas fees. Gas fees are payments to complete a transaction on a blockchain. These fees are used to compensate blockchain miners for the computing power they have to use to verify blockchain transactions. To analyze the gas fee the smart contracts were deployed on the remix IDE and the results are shown in Table 7.2.

7.5.1   Security Analysis

The smart contracts are immutable, that is, once deployed the code cannot be changed. Hence, smart contracts are highly susceptible to reentrancy attacks. A reentrancy assault takes place between two smart contracts, in which the attacking smart contract takes advantage of a weak contract's coding to steal its cash. The assault smart contract repeatedly calls the withdraw function before the weak smart contract has a chance to update the balance. This is how the exploit operates. This is shown in Figure 7.5.

Lendf.me is a decentralized finance protocol created to allow lending operations on the Ethereum platform. On April 18, 2020, a hacker used a reentrancy attack to steal $25 million from the protocol. The Lendf.me issue that allowed ERC777 tokens, an Ethereum token standard that permits more sophisticated interactions when trading tokens, to be utilized as collateral was abused by the hackers. The callback function that alerts users when money has been transmitted or received is included in ERC777 tokens, but the developers failed to take advantage of it. Hackers were able to take

TABLE 7.1

Contracts Accounts Used

Account Address	Private Keys
0xf39Fd6e51aad88F6F4ce6aB8827279cffFb92266	0x59c6995e998f97a5a0044966f0945389dc9e86dae88c7a8412f4603b6b78690d
0x70997970C51812dc3A010C7d01b50e0d17dc79C8	0x5de4111afa1a4b94908f83103eb1f1706367c2e68ca870fc3fb9a804cdab365a
0x90F79bf6EB2c4f870365E785982E1f101E93b906	0x7c852118294e51e653712a81e05800f419141751be58f605c371e15141b007a6
0x15d34AAf54267DB7D7c367839AAf71A00a2C6A65	0x47e179ec197488593b187f80a00eb0da91f1b9d0b13f8733639f19c30a34926a
0x9965507D1a55bcC2695C58ba16FB37d819B0A4dc	0x8b3a350cf5c34c9194ca85829a2df0ec3153be0318b5e2d3348e872092edffba

TABLE 7.2

Gas Fee Analysis of Smart Contracts

Smart Contracts	Transaction Cost (Gas)	Execution Cost (Gas)	Gas Fees (Gas)
NFT	1,020,805	1,020,805	2,208,524
MarketPlace	1,920,455	1,920,455	1,173,926

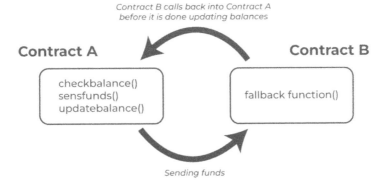

FIGURE 7.5 Security analysis.

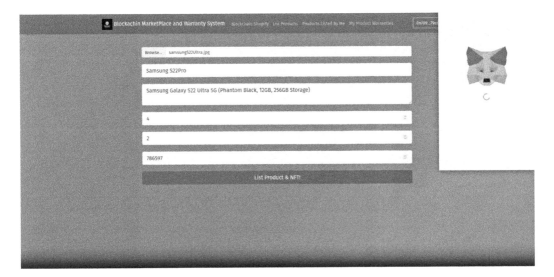

FIGURE 7.6 MetaMask credentials input.

advantage of this otherwise safe token standard by using a sophisticated reentrancy attack, emptying the Lendf.me platform of 99.5% of its cash, because the recipient was a smart contract.

Mutex (mutually exclusive flag) was built as a function modification for ReentrancyGuard to stop this attack. The function call is protected by a Boolean lock used by the modifier, which is susceptible to reentrancy. The value of "locked" is initially false (unlocked), but before the vulnerable function execution starts, it is set to true (locked), and it is then reset to false (unlocked) when it is finished.

7.6 Results

Before the initialization of the transaction, we have to connect our MetaMask wallet to the website.

It requires the login details of the associated MetaMask account.

To use a MetaMask account, we need to download the MetaMask extension and add the extension to our browser. When the extension is installed, we need to click on the icon in the upper right corner to open MetaMask and create a new account on it.

After opening the website, a popup shows up at the top right corner of the screen, which prompts us to connect our MetaMask account.

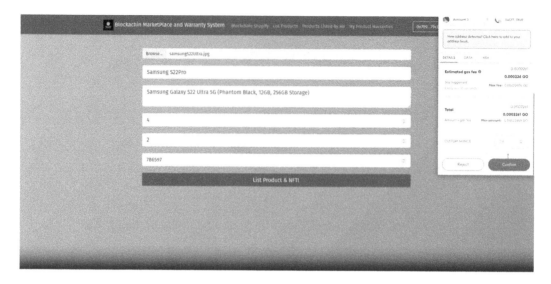

FIGURE 7.7　MetaMask transaction.

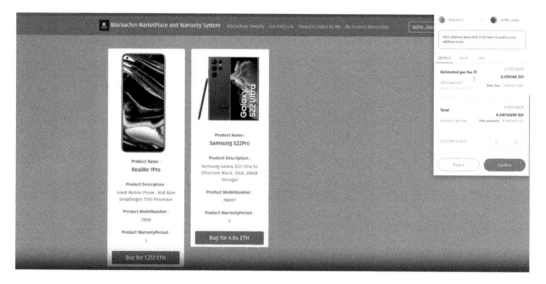

FIGURE 7.8　Listed product.

After connection establishment, we fill in all the product details, that is, name, model number, description, price, warranty, and image.

Then we click on the list product and NFT button, and the MetaMask wallet prompts us to confirm the transaction. It also states all the fees related to the transaction.

The product is sold and the NFT warranty is transferred to the account linked at the start of the transaction.

We can see all the listed products along with their prices that are available for sale under the blockchain Shopify section.

After buying a product, we can go to *my product warranty* section and see all the product's details, including the model number, the warranty period, and the warranty status, that is, if the warranty has been claimed or not.

If the user wants to claim a warranty, he can access it using the claim warranty button. The product's details will be visible on the user's *My Product Warranty* page. All these is illustrated in Figures 7.6, 7.7, 7.8 and 7.9.

FIGURE 7.9 My product warranties section.

7.7 Future Works

Our proposed solution aims to solve the current warranty system in the sales industry by introducing a blockchain-based warranty system using NFTs that automates the warranty tracking and claim process and reduces the time consumed in processing the claims. When the warranty date passes, the system automatically marks the warranty as *expired*. We have developed a marketplace system using various functions like *mintNFT, PurchaseItem*, and many other functions that facilitate retailers or merchants to sell their products and customers to purchase them. Customers can claim a warranty for their product using the system by providing the necessary details regarding the product.

This system thus enables customers to claim warranties easily and keep track of them. All the products purchased by the customer would be visible in his profile section. This chapter highlights the benefits of using a blockchain-based warranty system over the traditional one. This work can be further expanded in the following ways in future:

1. Providing Warranty on Customer Smartphone

   We can send a warranty card to the customer's smartphone via a text message or email upon purchase. This would make things easier for the customer as they can see all the product details at any point in time, and it can also act as a virtual receipt for future reference. With the increasing use of smartphones and digital devices, customers can easily access the warranty card at any time, eliminating the need to carry a physical warranty card or receipt. Additionally, by providing a virtual warranty card, you can ensure that the customer always has access to the most up-to-date information about their product. This is particularly important if there are any updates or changes to the warranty terms or product details, as the customer will receive notifications of any changes in real time.

   One popular type of blockchain-based game is a "play-to-earn" game, where users can earn tokens or other rewards for playing the game. These tokens can then be used to purchase products on your platform or traded on cryptocurrency exchanges. This can be a great way to create a secondary market for your platform's currency and increase its overall value.

2. Usage of Soulbound NFTs

   NFTs are non-transferable. It is not strange that some people find the use of a non-transferable token confusing. Especially given that NFTs have varied purposes because a significant part of them is due to their transportable nature.

Soulbound tokens, according to co-founder of Ethereum Vitalik Buterin, are non-transferable NFTs that may be used to reflect a person's identity and accomplishments on Web3. New non-transferable, publicly validated digital tokens called Soulbound NFTs can be used in Web 3.0 to represent social standing. This functions as a person's digital resume. SBTs would include all information on a person's memberships, affiliations, and credentials.

These SBTs were inspired by the popular video game World of Warcraft, where "Soulbound" goods are those that are "Soulbound" to the game's characters. Such items cannot be bought, sold, or traded by players with other players or characters. In a similar vein, SBTs guarantee that users cannot exchange their social position for the chance to advance.

The constant and permanent attachment to a wallet is what makes SBTs unique. Users who have a blockchain account store their personal data as well as records pertaining to their past, present, and future. This is like a CV in the real world. SBTs are a crucial instrument for creating a user's reputation on the Ethereum blockchain in the future.

SBTs have several applications that can be enumerated. We might start with something fundamental and straightforward, like a college degree. An SBT, as opposed to a certificate, might be given to university graduates.

The possibility of trading or selling such NFTs exists, despite the claim that NFTs are sufficient for the process. However, if the university provides a soul NFT, the students would not be able to transfer or sell it.

3. Expanding the Scope by Adding Blockchain-Based Games

We can add blockchain-based games to our platform through which users can earn points. These can be later redeemed by users while purchasing other products. One popular type of blockchain-based game is a "play-to-earn" game, where users can earn tokens or other rewards for playing the game. These tokens can then be used to purchase products on your platform or traded on cryptocurrency exchanges. This can be a great way to create a secondary market for the platform's currency and increase its overall value. We can also give loyalty points to customers who frequently purchase products from our website. These points can then be redeemed for discounts, free products, or other rewards. This can be a great way to incentivize repeat business and encourage customers to make larger purchases.

REFERENCES

1. A. Park, J. Kietzmann, L. Pitt and A. Dabirian, "The Evolution of Nonfungible Tokens: Complexity and Novelty of NFT Use-Cases," *IT Professional*. 2022;24(1): pp. 9–14, doi: 10.1109/MITP.2021.3136055
2. Shih D-H, Huang F-C, Chieh C-Y, Shih M-H and Wu T-W. Preventing Return Fraud in Reverse Logistics—A Case Study of ESPRES Solution by Ethereum. *Journal of Theoretical and Applied Electronic Commerce Research*. 2021;16(6):2170–2191. https://doi.org/10.3390/jtaer16060121
3. H. R. Andrian, N. B. Kurniawan and Suhardi, "Blockchain Technology and Implementation : A Systematic Literature Review," 2018 International Conference on Information Technology Systems and Innovation (ICITSI), 2018, pp. 370–374, doi: 10.1109/ICITSI.2018.8695939
4. F. Khan, R. Kothari, M. Patel and N. Banoth, "Enhancing Non-Fungible Tokens for the Evolution of Blockchain Technology," 2022 International Conference on Sustainable Computing and Data Communication Systems (ICSCDS), 2022, pp. 1148–1153, doi: 10.1109/ICSCDS53736.2022.9760849
5. Z. Zheng, S. Xie, H. Dai, X. Chen and H. Wang, "An Overview of Blockchain Technology: Architecture, Consensus, and Future Trends," 2017 IEEE International Congress on Big Data (BigData Congress), 2017, pp. 557–564, doi: 10.1109/BigDataCongress.2017.85
6. W. Li, M. He and S. Haiquan, "An Overview of Blockchain Technology: Applications, Challenges and Future Trends," 2021 IEEE 11th International Conference on Electronics Information and Emergency Communication (ICEIEC)2021 IEEE 11th International Conference on Electronics Information and Emergency Communication (ICEIEC), 2021, pp. 31–39, doi: 10.1109/ICEIEC51955.2021.9463842

7. H. R. Andrian, N. B. Kurniawan and Suhardi, "Blockchain Technology and Implementation : A Systematic Literature Review," 2018 International Conference on Information Technology Systems and Innovation (ICITSI), Bandung, Indonesia, 2018, pp. 370–374, doi: 10.1109/ICITSI.2018.8695939

8. Q. E. Abbas and J. Sung-Bong, "A Survey of Blockchain and Its Applications," 2019 International Conference on Artificial Intelligence in Information and Communication (ICAIIC), Okinawa, Japan, 2019, pp. 001–003, doi: 10.1109/ICAIIC.2019.8669067

8

Analysis of a Queueing System with Batch Poisson Arrivals and Batch Services in Blockchain Applications

Srinivas R. Chakravarthy
Kettering University, Flint, MI, USA

Shruti Goel
Jaypee Institute of Information and Technology, Noida, India

Vidyottama Jain
Central University of Rajasthan, India

Serife Ozkar
Balikesir University, Balikesir, Turkey

Raina Raj
Central University of Rajasthan, India

8.1 Introduction

The blockchain has evolved into one of the most fiercely contested topics in the past few years with the advent of cryptocurrencies. The blockchain technology has made a significant progress in both theoretical framework and real-life applications since the launch of Bitcoin by Satoshi Nakamoto [1]. It appeals to a variety of businesses and industrial sectors such as transportation, healthcare, banking, and financial services because it not only allows for distributed and decentralized transactions but also provides trust and transparency in the information shared. For a comprehensive survey on blockchain technology, the readers may refer to the excellent books [2–4] and the survey articles [5–7]. Several real-world applications of blockchains have emerged, including blockchain banking [8, 9], blockchain business [10, 11], blockchain supply chain management [12–14], blockchain Internet of Things [15–17], blockchain sharing economy [18, 19], and blockchain healthcare [20]. Despite extensive real-world applications of blockchain technology, there have only been a few published mathematical studies on blockchain systems in the literature. These mathematical investigations generate stochastic models, offer performance analysis and optimization, and establish beneficial correlations between important factors or fundamental parameters.

Thus, the main contributions of this paper to study a two-stage queueing model with batch arrivals and batch services where the batch size is assumed to be generally distributed has been employed in blockchain application. Further, a qualitative study of this proposed model based on simplified state space description has been performed in steady-state. Using the Neuts' matrix-analytic method, the system's stationary distribution, stability condition, and formulas of key performance metrics have been derived. Some illustrative examples are discussed.

DOI:10.1201/9781003326236-8

The rest of the chapter has the following structure. Section 8.2 represents related works to the proposed queueing model. In Section 8.3, the two-stage blockchain queueing model is thoroughly described. Section 8.4 demonstrates the construction of an infinitesimal generator matrix for the underlying process and provides the steady-state analysis of the system. Expressions for a few essential performance measures to assess the system's efficiency are formulated in Section 8.5. Section 8.6 presents numerical analysis to highlight the qualitative behavior of the proposed queueing model. Finally, a few concluding remarks and insights for further research are presented in Section 8.7.

8.2 Related Works

In this work, a two-stage blockchain queueing model comprising the block-generation (BG) and blockchain-building (BB) processes is studied. A blockchain is kept up-to-date by the mining procedures, where multiple nodes, referred to as miners, compete with one another to solve a problem (or puzzle) that needs producing a hash with a constraint, and these miners will produce a new block. While the transactions are compiled into a block, the key nonce (no sense (nonsense) string also referred to as once only (random) number—64-bit hex number) is provided, and thereafter the block is pegged to the blockchain [6, 7].

An early research work on blockchain queue was reported by Li et al. [21]. They [21] studied a $M/M^{[b]}/1$ queueing model applicable to a blockchain application. In that model, they considered the transactions to occur according to a Poisson process with rate λ. These transactions entered into an infinite buffer, are to be processed so as to become a part of a block. It is assumed that no block could accommodate more than b transactions. Once a block is formed with at least one but not exceeding b transactions, a mining process starts. During this mining period, the authors assumed that the transactions, if any, waiting in the queue would not be processed until the block was pegged into a blockchain. The processing (or pegging) times of a block are assumed to be exponentially distributed with parameter μ_1.

It is important to bring up that the authors [21] assumed that while processing the transactions (to form a new block), new transactions are allowed to enter into the processing (subject to the number currently under service is below b). Thus, no block exceeded b transactions. The processing times are exponentially distributed with rate μ_2 irrespective of the number of transactions. While the assumption of allowing new transactions to enter into a processing block is justifiable in the case of exponential processing times of a block, it may be a difficult one to justify when dealing with non-exponential processing times. This was one of the motivating factors for us to assume that the block has to be of size b to begin processing of that block. Once a block is formed the processing (or mining) of a block begins. During this time no transactions will be processed until the mining is done. This assumption makes the number of blocks in the system to be at most one and the number of transactions waiting in the queue to be zero or any positive integer. The server will be available to process the next block of transactions if the pegging of a block into a blockchain is finished and the queue is positive; otherwise it will remain idle for a new transaction to arrive.

In Ref. [22], the authors extended their study [21] by considering that the transactions occurred in accordance with a Markovian arrival process (MAP) and the processing times of the transactions and the mining times of the blocks to be of (possibly different) phase-type (PH) distribution. One issue with this model is to let new transactions enter into service while the processing of the transactions is going on. This is due to the fact that the processing times no longer possess the memoryless property and hence the processing of newly "added" transactions in real-life applications will not get full processing. It is important to point out that in both papers [21, 22], the authors could have simplified the state space description (with some minor modifications in the boundary states) by using the convolution of the processing times of the transactions and the mining. This is due to the fact that the server after processing the transactions remains idle until the pegging of a block is done.

One can think of this "idle" time waiting for the pegging to be the continuation of the processing time no matter where and how the blocks are processed. As far as the latency and other measures are concerned this approach will not make any difference. However, for modeling purposes this approach reduces the book-keeping process. This approach is considered in this work.

Kawase and Kasahara [23] presented a rigorous analysis on a blockchain queue with general service times. They also presented numerical illustrations for the performance evaluation of the system. Memon et al. [24] analyzed a blockchain queue system through simulation. Further, a probabilistic model of the Bitcoin blockchain using a transaction & block graph was proposed by Jourdan et al. [25]. They developed certain conditional dependencies caused by the Bitcoin protocol at the block level. To study the Raft consensus algorithm's performance measures for a private blockchain, a Markov process with an absorbing state was set up by Huang et al. [26]. Then, Srivastava [27] presented a Markov model with a consensus mechanism for a faster inclusion and transaction. Fralix [28] analyzed the time-dependent behavior of the queueing systems with an infinite server in Bitcoin. Fan et al. [29] established an $M/(M_1, M_2)/1$ queueing model with vacation and optional services in blockchain systems. They used the matrix-geometric method to obtain the system's stationary distribution, and they provided formulations for the average transaction-confirmation time as well as other performance indices. Chen et al. [30] intended to understand the latency of the private Internet of Things (IoT) network using the proof of work (PoW) and proof of authority (PoA) consensus algorithms in blockchain queue.

In this model, we study batch arrivals in blockchain queueing system, which is often encountered in practice. Therefore, a $M^{[X]}/M^{[b]}/1$ queueing model has been proposed and tackled by using the matrix-analytic method [31]. The batch service (of fixed size b) of the two-stage processes, i.e., BG and BB, follow exponential distributions with rates μ_1 and μ_2, respectively. The server will wait until the number of transactions reaches b or greater, if it is less than b after the service is completed. The model is studied as an $M/G/1$ type that is exhaustively studied by Neuts and his colleagues. Authors suggest to read Neuts [31] and the latest 2-volume book by Chakravarthy [32, 33] for details on the general approach to $M/G/1$ paradigm. Further, a rigorous performance analysis has been presented through obtaining the formulas of key performance measures and illustrating their behavior with respect to the various system parameters.

In the sequel, the following standard notations are adopted:

- Bold-faced letters—Either row or column vectors as per the context.
- $'$—Transpose.
- $\otimes$—Kronecker product [34, 35].
- $\oplus$—Kronecker sum [34, 35].
- e'—$(1, 1, \cdots, 1)$, its dimension will be as per the context.
- $e(m)$—A column vector of 1's of dimension m.
- e_i'—$(0, 0, \cdots, 1, 0, \cdots, 0)$, where 1 is at the ith position.
- I—An identity matrix, its dimension will be as per the context.

8.3 Model Description

This section describes a practical blockchain queueing system. A detailed description is as follows.

- **Arrival Process:** The transactions' arrival occur according to a batch Poisson process with a batch arrival rate λ_g. Assume that the batch size follows a general probability mass function (PMF), $\{p_k\}$, and the mean batch size is denoted as μ_{BS}. The arrival rate λ is then given by $\lambda = \lambda_g \mu_{BS}$.

- **Service Process:** In the blockchain system, service times in two stages of batch services (BG and BB) are also simply assumed to be i.i.d. and exponentially distributed with rates μ_1 and μ_2, respectively. The first stage services (as well as for the second) are in groups of fixed size b; that is, a block consists of exactly b transactions. If there are less than b transactions at the time a service is completed, the server will wait for the number to reach b or more.

The transaction-confirmation (service) time of a block (BG + BB) can be modeled as a phase type (generalized Erlang) distribution with representation (β, S) of order 2 with

$$\beta = (1,0), \quad S = \begin{pmatrix} -\mu_1 & \mu_1 \\ 0 & -\mu_2 \end{pmatrix}.$$

For later use, we define $\mu = \dfrac{\mu_1 \mu_2}{\mu_1 + \mu_2}$ as the service rate, $\dfrac{1}{\mu} = \beta(-S)^{-1}e$ as mean and S^0 as the column vector satisfying $Se + S^0 = 0$.

8.4 The Steady-State Analysis

8.4.1 Generator Matrix

Let $N(t)$ and $J(t)$ denote the number of transactions and the phase of the service, if the server is busy, at time t, respectively. It can be simply verified that the process $\{(N(t), J(t)) : t \geq 0\}$ is a continuous-time Markov chain on the state space $\Omega = \{i : 0 \leq i \leq b-1\} \bigcup \{(i,j) : i \geq b, j = 1,2\}$. Note that, the states $0, 1, \cdots, b-1$ correspond to the server being idle with up to $b-1$ waiting in the queue; the state (i,j), for $i \geq b, j = 1, 2$, corresponds to the case when there are i transactions in the system and the server is busy with b transactions in jth service mode.

The generator matrix Q governing the system under study is of the form:

$$Q = \begin{pmatrix} C_0 & C_1 & C_2 & C_3 & C_4 & C_5 & \cdots \\ F & H_1 & H_2 & H_3 & H_4 & H_5 & \cdots \\ & H_0 & H_1 & H_2 & H_3 & H_4 & \cdots \\ & & H_0 & H_1 & H_2 & H_3 & \cdots \\ & & & \ddots & \ddots & \ddots & \ddots \end{pmatrix}. \tag{8.1}$$

The matrices F, C_0 and C_k, $k \geq 1$, have dimensions $(2b \times b)$, $(b \times b)$ and $(b \times 2b)$, respectively. The other matrices H_k, $k \geq 0$, are square matrices of order $2b$.

$$C_0 = \begin{pmatrix} -\lambda_g & \lambda_g p_1 & \lambda_g p_2 & \lambda_g p_3 & \cdots & \lambda_g p_{b-2} & \lambda_g p_{b-1} \\ & -\lambda_g & \lambda_g p_1 & \lambda_g p_2 & \cdots & \lambda_g p_{b-3} & \lambda_g p_{b-2} \\ & & -\lambda_g & \lambda_g p_1 & \cdots & \lambda_g p_{b-4} & \lambda_g p_{b-3} \\ & & & \ddots & \cdots & \vdots & \vdots \\ & & & & -\lambda_g & \lambda_g p_1 & \lambda_g p_2 \\ & & & & & -\lambda_g & \lambda_g p_1 \\ & & & & & & -\lambda_g \end{pmatrix},$$

$$C_k = \lambda_g \begin{pmatrix} p_{(k-1)b+b} & p_{(k-1)b+b+1} & \cdots & p_{kb+b-1} \\ p_{(k-1)b+b-1} & p_{(k-1)b+b} & \cdots & p_{kb+b-2} \\ \vdots & \vdots & \cdots & \vdots \\ p_{(k-1)b+1} & p_{(k-1)b+2} & \cdots & p_{kb} \end{pmatrix} \otimes \beta, \quad k \geq 1,$$

$$F = I \otimes S^0, \quad H_0 = I \otimes S^0 \beta,$$

$$H_1 = \begin{pmatrix} S - \lambda_g I & \lambda_g p_1 I & \lambda_g p_2 I & \lambda_g p_3 I & \cdots & \lambda_g p_{b-2} I & \lambda_g p_{b-1} I \\ & S - \lambda_g I & \lambda_g p_1 I & \lambda_g p_2 I & \cdots & \lambda_g p_{b-3} I & \lambda_g p_{b-2} I \\ & & S - \lambda_g I & \lambda_g p_1 I & \cdots & \lambda_g p_{b-4} I & \lambda_g p_{b-3} I \\ & & & \ddots & \cdots & \vdots & \vdots \\ & & & & & S - \lambda_g I & \lambda_g p_1 I \\ & & & & & & S - \lambda_g I \end{pmatrix},$$

$$H_{k+1} = \lambda_g \begin{pmatrix} p_{(k-1)b+b} & p_{(k-1)b+b+1} & \cdots & p_{kb+b-1} \\ p_{(k-1)b+b-1} & p_{(k-1)b+b} & \cdots & p_{kb+b-2} \\ \vdots & \vdots & \cdots & \vdots \\ p_{(k-1)b+1} & p_{(k-1)b+2} & \cdots & p_{kb} \end{pmatrix} \otimes I, \quad k \geq 1.$$

The continuous-time Markov process is clearly of $M/G/1-$ type. Therefore, results from Refs. [31–33] can be employed in this work.

8.4.2   The Stability Condition

In this section, using the matrix-analytic method, the system stability conditions are deduced and the stationary probability vector is represented in order to study the proposed blockchain queueing system.

Let

$$\hat{p}_r = \sum_{k=1}^{\infty} p_{(k-1)b+r}, \quad 1 \leq r \leq b.$$

The generator matrix $H = \sum_{k=0}^{\infty} H_k$ can easily be obtained as (note: $\tilde{S} = S + S^0 \beta$)

$$H = \begin{pmatrix} \tilde{S} - \lambda_g(1 - \hat{p}_b) I & \lambda_g \hat{p}_1 I & \lambda_g \hat{p}_2 I & \cdots & \lambda_g \hat{p}_{b-1} I \\ \lambda_g \hat{p}_{b-1} I & \tilde{S} - \lambda_g(1 - \hat{p}_b) I & \lambda_g \hat{p}_1 I & \cdots & \lambda_g \hat{p}_{b-2} I \\ \vdots & \vdots & \vdots & \ddots & \vdots \\ \lambda_g \hat{p}_2 I & \lambda_g \hat{p}_3 I & \lambda_g \hat{p}_4 I & \cdots & \lambda_g \hat{p}_1 I \\ \lambda_g \hat{p}_1 I & \lambda_g \hat{p}_2 I & \lambda_g \hat{p}_3 I & \cdots & \tilde{S} - \lambda_g(1 - \hat{p}_b) I \end{pmatrix}.$$

Note that, H is cyclic and hence, if π is the stationary probability vector of H satisfying

$$\pi H = \mathbf{0}, \pi e = 1,$$

then using the uniqueness of the invariant vector $\mu \beta(-S)^{-1}$ of the generator $\tilde{S}$, it can be easily verified that $\pi = \dfrac{\mu}{b}(e' \otimes \beta(-S)^{-1})$.

The stability condition of the blockchain queueing model under study is provided in Theorem 8.1 as follows.

Theorem 8.1: *The queueing model $M^{[X]}/M^{[b]}/1$ under study with the generator given in (8.1) is stable if and only if*

$$\lambda < b\mu. \tag{8.2}$$

Proof: Following the results from the $M/G/1-$type queues (see, Refs. [31–33]), the stability condition is given by $\pi \sum_{k=1}^{\infty} k H_{k+1} e < \pi H_0 e$. This implies, (see the generator matrix in (8.1))

$$\sum_{k=1}^{\infty} k H_{k+1} = \lambda_g \begin{pmatrix} \sum_{k=1}^{\infty} k p_{kb} & \sum_{k=1}^{\infty} k p_{kb+1} & \sum_{k=1}^{\infty} k p_{kb+2} & \cdots & \sum_{k=1}^{\infty} k p_{kb+b-1} \\ \sum_{k=1}^{\infty} k p_{kb-1} & \sum_{k=1}^{\infty} k p_{kb} & \sum_{k=1}^{\infty} k p_{kb+1} & \cdots & \sum_{k=1}^{\infty} k p_{kb+b-2} \\ \sum_{k=1}^{\infty} k p_{kb-2} & \sum_{k=1}^{\infty} k p_{kb-1} & \sum_{k=1}^{\infty} k p_{kb} & \cdots & \sum_{k=1}^{\infty} k p_{kb+b-3} \\ \vdots & \vdots & \vdots & \ddots & \vdots \\ \sum_{k=1}^{\infty} k p_{(k-1)b+1} & \sum_{k=1}^{\infty} k p_{(k-1)b+2} & \sum_{k=1}^{\infty} k p_{kb+3} & \cdots & \sum_{k=1}^{\infty} k p_{kb} \end{pmatrix} \otimes I,$$

from which, we see that $\pi \sum_{k=1}^{\infty} k H_{k+1} e = \dfrac{\mu}{b}\left(\dfrac{\mu_1 + \mu_2}{\mu_1 \mu_2}\right)\lambda_g \mu_{\mathrm{BS}} = \dfrac{\lambda}{b}$. Since $\pi H_0 e = \mu$, we get the stated result on the stability condition. $\square$

8.4.3   The Steady-State Probability Vector

Let y be the steady-state probability vector for the generator matrix Q. It is well-known that (see, Refs. [31–33]) the computation of the vector y requires the knowledge of key matrix, say, G. This matrix is obtained as follows. Note that Q is positive recurrent and irreducible. The stochastic matrix G is determined as the minimal non-negative solution to

$$\sum_{r=0}^{\infty} H_r G^r = 0. \tag{8.3}$$

Note that the (j, k)th entry of G provides the conditional probability that the system under study will eventually visit the state (i, k) for the first time starting in state $(i + 1, j)$, for $i \geq 1$ (away from the boundary). The vector g is the invariant vector of G, i.e., g satisfies

$$g G = g, \quad g e = 1. \tag{8.4}$$

The matrix G and the vector g play a crucial role in the computation of the vector y. The full details including the algorithmic procedures for all these quantities are spelled out in Refs. [32, 33] and are omitted here. It is worth pointing out that one of the structural properties (see, Ref. [33]) of G indicates that G has all even numbered columns to be zero due to H_0 possessing this property. The following result, which is intuitively clear, can be utilized as an internal accuracy check in numerical computation.

Lemma 8.1: *We have*

$$\frac{1}{\rho} \sum_{j=1}^{\infty} y_j (e \otimes I) = \frac{1}{\mu_1 + \mu_2}(\mu_2, \mu_1). \tag{8.5}$$

Proof: The steady-state equation for the vector y partitioned as $y = (y_0, y_1, y_2, \cdots)$ is obtained by solving

$$y_0 C_0 + y_1 F = \mathbf{0},$$

$$y_0 C_k + \sum_{j=1}^{k+1} y_j H_{k-j+1} = \mathbf{0}, \quad k \geq 1, \tag{8.6}$$

subject to the normalizing condition

$$y_0 e + \sum_{j=1}^{\infty} y_j e = 1. \tag{8.7}$$

Post-multiplying the first equation in (8.6) by $(I \otimes \beta)$ and adding to this the second equation over k from 1 to ∞, and after interchanging the summations, we get (note that $H_0 = F(I \otimes \beta)$),

$$y_0 C_0 (I \otimes \beta) + y_0 \sum_{j=1}^{\infty} C_j + \sum_{j=1}^{\infty} y_j H = \mathbf{0}. \tag{8.8}$$

Post-multiplying Equation (8.8) by $(e \otimes I)$ and noting that $\left[C_0(I \otimes \beta) + \sum_{j=1}^{\infty} C_j \right](e \otimes I) = \mathbf{0}$, we see

$$\sum_{j=1}^{\infty} y_j H(e \otimes I) = \sum_{j=1}^{\infty} y_j (e \otimes \tilde{S}) = \mathbf{0}, \tag{8.9}$$

which implies, due to the uniqueness of the invariant vector of $\tilde{S}$, that

$$\sum_{j=1}^{\infty} y_j (e \otimes I) = d(\mu_2, \mu_1), \tag{8.10}$$

where d is a constant obtained by using the normalizing condition given in (8.7) along with the fact that $y_0 e = 1 - \rho$. It is simple to assert that $d = \dfrac{\rho}{\mu_1 + \mu_2}$ and this produces the desired result right away. $\qquad\square$

8.4.4 Quasi-Birth Death Approach

Assume that the maximum batch size is fixed at K. If $b \geq K$, then we can use quasi-birth death (QBD) approach, which will simplify a number of computational aspects. In this case, we write down the generator as

$$Q^{(1)} = \begin{bmatrix} B_1 & B_0 & & & \\ E & A_1 & A_0 & & \\ & A_2 & A_1 & A_0 & \\ & & A_2 & A_1 & A_0 \\ & & & \ddots & \ddots & \ddots \end{bmatrix}. \tag{8.11}$$

The matrices E, B_0 and B_1 have dimensions $(2b \times b)$, $(b \times 2b)$ and $(b \times b)$, respectively. The matrices A_0, A_1 and A_2 are square matrices of order $2b$.

$$
B_1 = \begin{pmatrix}
-\lambda_g & \lambda_g p_1 & \lambda_g p_2 & \cdots & \lambda_g p_K & & & & \\
 & -\lambda_g & \lambda_g p_1 & \cdots & \lambda_g p_{K-1} & \lambda_g p_K & & & \\
 & & \ddots & \cdots & \vdots & & \vdots & & \\
 & & & & -\lambda_g & \lambda_g p_1 & \lambda_g p_2 & \cdots & \lambda_g p_K \\
 & & & & & -\lambda_g & \lambda_g p_1 & \cdots & \lambda_g p_{K-1} \\
 & & & & & & \ddots & \cdots & \vdots \\
 & & & & & & & & -\lambda_g
\end{pmatrix},
$$

$$
B_0 = \begin{pmatrix}
\lambda_g p_K \beta & & & \\
\lambda_g p_{K-1} \beta & \lambda_g p_K \beta & & \\
\vdots & \vdots & & \\
\lambda_g p_1 \beta & \lambda_g p_2 \beta & \cdots & \lambda_g p_K \beta
\end{pmatrix},
$$

$$
E = I \otimes S^0, \quad A_2 = I \otimes S^0 \beta,
$$

$$
A_1 = \begin{pmatrix}
S - \lambda_g I & \lambda_g p_1 I & \lambda_g p_2 I & \cdots & \lambda_g p_K I & & & \\
 & S - \lambda_g I & \lambda_g p_1 I & \cdots & \lambda_g p_{K-1} I & \lambda_g p_K I & & \\
 & & \ddots & \cdots & \vdots & & \vdots & \\
 & & & S - \lambda_g I & \lambda_g p_1 I & \lambda_g p_2 I & \cdots & \lambda_g p_K I \\
 & & & & S - \lambda_g I & \lambda_g p_1 I & \cdots & \lambda_g p_{K-1} I \\
 & & & & & \ddots & \cdots & \vdots \\
 & & & & & & & S - \lambda_g I
\end{pmatrix},
$$

$$
A_0 = \begin{pmatrix}
\lambda_g p_K & & & \\
\lambda_g p_{K-1} & \lambda_g p_K & & \\
\vdots & \vdots & & \\
\lambda_g p_1 & \lambda_g p_2 & \cdots & \lambda_g p_K
\end{pmatrix} \otimes I.
$$

Under the stability condition $\lambda < b\mu$ (This can be proven similar to the previous case), the steady-state probability vector of $Q^{(1)}$ exists. Let $y^{(1)} = (y_0^{(1)}, y_1^{(1)}, y_2^{(1)}, \cdots)$, with the vector $y_0^{(1)}$ of dimension K and each of the vectors $y_i^{(1)}$, $i \geq 1$, of dimension $2K$, be the steady-state probability vector such that

$$
y^{(1)} Q^{(1)} = \mathbf{0}, \quad y^{(1)} e = 1. \tag{8.12}
$$

The following theorem results directly from Neuts' conclusion regarding QBD process (see, Ref. [36]) and we register it here for the sake of completeness (see also Refs. [32, 33] for details on expressing $y_i^{(1)}$, in terms of $y_0^{(1)}$ and R).

Theorem 8.2: *When the stability condition $\lambda < b\,\mu$ is satisfied, the steady-state probability vector, $y^{(1)}$, of $Q^{(1)}$ is of the matrix-geometric type:*

$$y_i^{(1)} = y_0^{(1)} (I \otimes \beta)\, R^i, \quad i \geq 1, \tag{8.13}$$

where the rate matrix R is the minimal non-negative solution to

$$R^2 A_2 + R A_1 + A_0 = \boldsymbol{0}, \tag{8.14}$$

and the vector $y_0^{(1)}$ is obtained by solving:

$$y_0^{(1)}[B_1 + (I \otimes \beta)\, R(I \otimes S^0)] = 0, \quad y_0^{(1)}(I \otimes \beta)\,(I - R)^{-1} e = 1.$$

Lemma 8.2: *We have*

$$\frac{1}{\rho} \sum_{i=1}^{\infty} y_i^{(1)} (e \otimes I) = \frac{1}{\mu_1 + \mu_2}(\mu_2, \mu_1). \tag{8.15}$$

Proof: The equations in (8.12) can be rewritten as follows.

$$y_0^{(1)} B_1 + y_1^{(1)} E = \boldsymbol{0}$$

$$y_0^{(1)} B_0 + y_1^{(1)} A_1 + y_2^{(1)} A_2 = \boldsymbol{0} \tag{8.16}$$

$$y_{i-0}^{(1)} A_0 + y_i^{(1)} A_1 + y_{i+0}^{(1)} A_2 = \boldsymbol{0}, \quad i \geq 2,$$

and the normalizing condition with the help of Theorem 8.2 is given by,

$$y_0^{(1)} e + \sum_{i=1}^{\infty} y_i^{(1)} e = y_0^{(1)} e + y_0^{(1)}(I \otimes \beta) R(I - R)^{-1} e = 1. \tag{8.17}$$

Post-multiplying the first equation in (8.16) by $(I \otimes \beta)$ and adding to this the other two equations with one of them over i from 2 to ∞, we get (note that $A_2 = E(I \otimes \beta)$ and $A = A_0 + A_1 + A_2$),

$$y_0^{(1)} B_1 (I \otimes \beta) + y_0^{(1)} B_0 + \sum_{i=1}^{\infty} y_i^{(1)} A = \boldsymbol{0}. \tag{8.18}$$

Post-multiplying Equation (8.18) by $(e \otimes I)$ and noting that $\left[B_1(I \otimes \beta) + B_0\right](e \otimes I) = \boldsymbol{0}$, we see

$$\sum_{i=1}^{\infty} y_i^{(1)} A(e \otimes I) = \sum_{i=1}^{\infty} y_i^{(1)}(e \otimes \tilde{S}) = \boldsymbol{0}, \tag{8.19}$$

which implies, due to the uniqueness of the invariant vector of $\tilde{S}$, that

$$\sum_{i=1}^{\infty} y_i^{(1)}(e \otimes I) = d^{(1)}(\mu_2, \mu_1), \tag{8.20}$$

where $d^{(1)}$ is a constant obtained by using the normalizing condition given in (8.17) along with the fact that $y_0^{(1)}e = 1 - \rho$. Note that $d^{(1)} = \dfrac{\rho}{\mu_1 + \mu_2}$ and this immediately yields the stated result. □

8.5 Performance Metrics

In this section, various important system performance measures along with their expressions for the proposed $M^{[X]}/M^{[b]}/1$ model are listed as follows.

1. $P(\text{server being idle}) = y_0 e$.
2. $P(\text{server is idle with no transactions waiting}) = y_0 e_1$.
3. $P(\text{server is busy processing transactions}) = \sum_{i=1}^{\infty} y_i(e \otimes e_1) = \dfrac{\lambda}{b \mu_1}$.
4. $P(\text{system is busy pegging a block}) = \sum_{i=1}^{\infty} y_i(e \otimes e_2) = \dfrac{\lambda}{b \mu_2}$.
5. The mean, the variance, the median, and the mode of the number in the system for the QBD–approach study can be computed. While the mean and the variance can be computed using the following expressions, the other measures need to be obtained numerically from the steady-state vectors.

$$E(N) = \sum_{n=1}^{\infty} n\, y_n^{(1)} = y_0^{(1)}(I \otimes \beta)R(I - R)^{-2}e,$$

$$V(N) = E(N^2) - [E(N)]^2 = y_0^{(1)}(I \otimes \beta)R\Big((I + R)(I - R)^{-1} - (I - R)^{-2}(I \otimes \beta)\Big)(I - R)^{-2}e.$$

6. Since the model is work-conserving, the latency (or the mean waiting time in the system, $E(W)$) can be derived using Little's result, $E(N) = \lambda E(W)$.
7. The mean recurrence time (time between successive visits to **0**): $\mu'_{RT} = \dfrac{1}{y_1 Fe}$.
8. The mean idle time: $\mu'_I = \dfrac{1 - \rho}{y_1 Fe}$.
9. The mean busy period: $\mu'_{BP} = \dfrac{\rho}{y_1 Fe}$.
10. The mean number (of groups of size b) served $= \mu_{NS} = \mu\, \mu'_{BP}$.

8.6 Numerical Analysis

In this section, we will discuss about a few numerical illustrations that highlight the qualitative features of the model under consideration. In Example 8.1, we consider Poisson distribution for batch sizes in the arrival process.

8.6.1 Poisson Batch Size

We assume that the arriving batch is of size k and the probability is given by $e^{-\theta}\left(\dfrac{\theta^{k-1}}{(k-1)!}\right)$, $k \geq 1$. Note that $\theta + 1$ provides the mean batch size.

We show that when (how) batch size distribution has effect on performance measures by considering different distribution types such as uniform, Poisson, geometric, and discrete phase-type (DPH) distribution in Examples 8.2 and 8.3.

Example 8.1:

In this example, we fix $\theta = 1$, $\mu_2 = 1$ and look at the effect of the traffic intensity (ρ), the block sizes (b) and the transaction processing rate (μ_1) on some selected performance

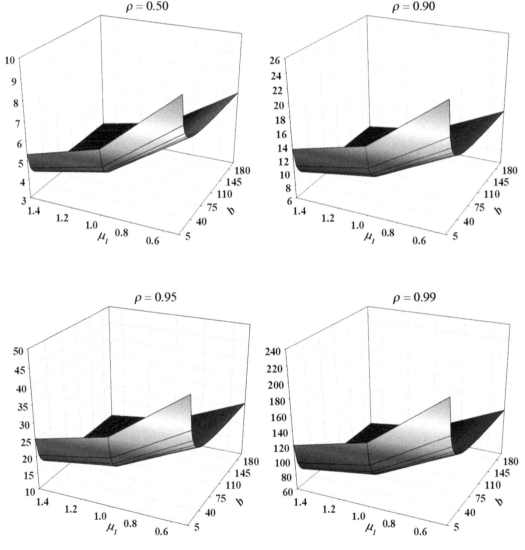

FIGURE 8.1   Mean recurrence time for *PbS* under different scenarios.

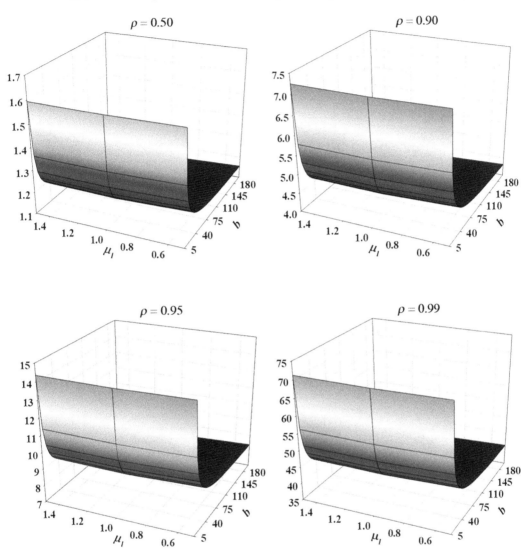

FIGURE 8.2 Mean number of blocks processed by the server during a busy period under different scenarios.

measures. Some key observations based on Figures 8.1–8.5, which contain the plots of these measures, are given below.

- An increase in μ_1 leads to a decrease in the mean recurrence time, for any fixed b. This holds for all values of *rho*, however for large values of *rho*, the decrease rate is significant. Besides, although this metric gradually decreases as batch size increases, the rate of decrease seems insignificant for high values of b.
- The mean number (of groups of size b) served, μ_{NS} appears to decrease with increasing values of b. It should be noted that μ_{NS} decreases as μ_1 is increased (for fixed b) for all four values of ρ considered; however the role gets reversed when μ_1 takes a large value.

Mean Idle Time (Poisson batches)

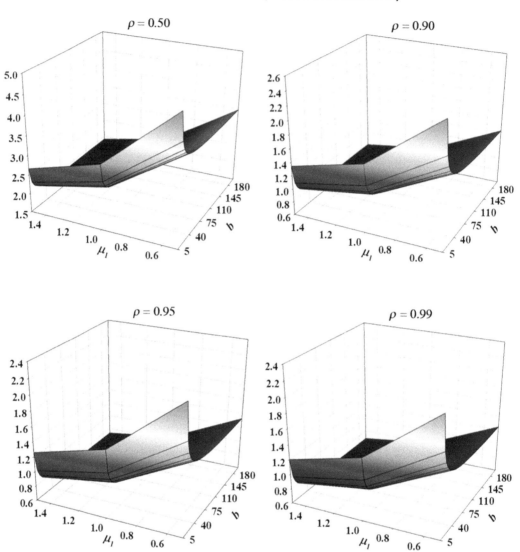

FIGURE 8.3   Mean idle time of the sever under different scenarios.

- Regarding the mean idle time of the server, we see that an increase in the block processing rate or in the batch size results in a decrease in this metric. This is obvious however, the degree of sensitivity to the value of μ_1 as well as b is high for large ρ.
- As the batch size increases, the mean number in system appears to increase monotonically (for any fixed μ_1) for all four values of ρ considered. It is noticed that this metric decreases with an increase in μ_1, however the role gets reversed for reasonably large values of μ_1. Moreover, this rate of change is significant for large ρ values.
- We also observe that the mean busy period of the server is a decreasing function of both b (for fixed μ_1) and μ_1 (for fixed b). This is the case for all values of ρ considered, however the rate of change is much significant for large values of ρ.

Mean Number in System (Poisson batches)

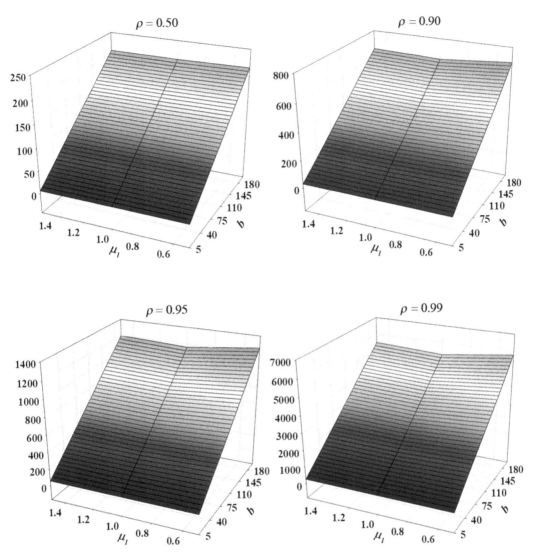

FIGURE 8.4 Mean number of blocks in the system under different scenarios.

Example 8.2:

The effect of batch size distributions, i.e., Poisson batch (PB), Geometric batch (GB), Uniform batch (UB), and Discrete Phase batch (DPB), on selected performance measures is investigated for $\rho = 0.5, 0.99$ by displaying the plots in Figures 8.6–8.13. For this purpose, we fix the block pegging rate $\mu_2 = 1$ and vary the transaction processing rate $\mu_1 = 0.2, 0.4, 0.6$ and the block size $b = 2, 3, \ldots, 100$.

- From Figure 8.6, it can be observed that the mean recurrence time decreases with respect to μ_1 for a particular value of b for $\rho = 0.50$. This behavior can be observed for all four types of batch size distributions. However, it can also be observed that the value of the

Mean Busy Period (Poisson batches)

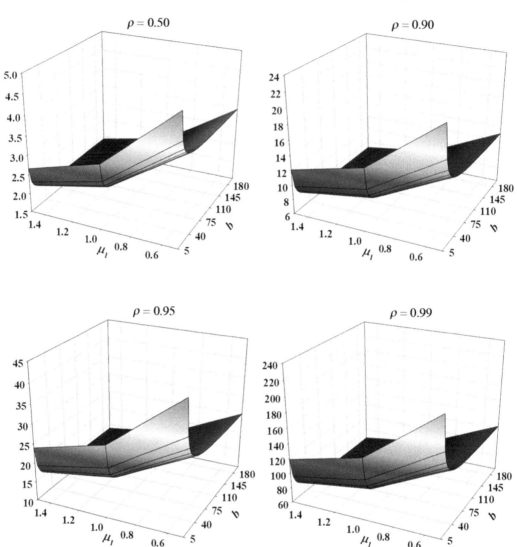

FIGURE 8.5 Mean busy period of the server under different scenarios.

mean recurrence time is the lowest for the UB and the highest for DPB for fixed values of b and μ_1. Similarly, the rate of decrease is high for DPB as compared to the other distributions. Also, an increment in the value of b shows a decrement in the value of the mean recurrence time for fixed values of μ_1.

- Figure 8.7 demonstrates a similar pattern of the mean recurrence time with respect to b and μ_1 or $\rho = 0.99$ for all four batch size distributions considered. The displayed graphs show that the value of the mean recurrence time is high for high value of ρ for some specific values of b and μ_1. This appears to be the case for all four batch size distributions considered here. As the traffic intensity increases, the mean recurrence time also increases and it starts decreasing once the service rate increases.

Mean Recurrence Time ($\rho = 0.50$)

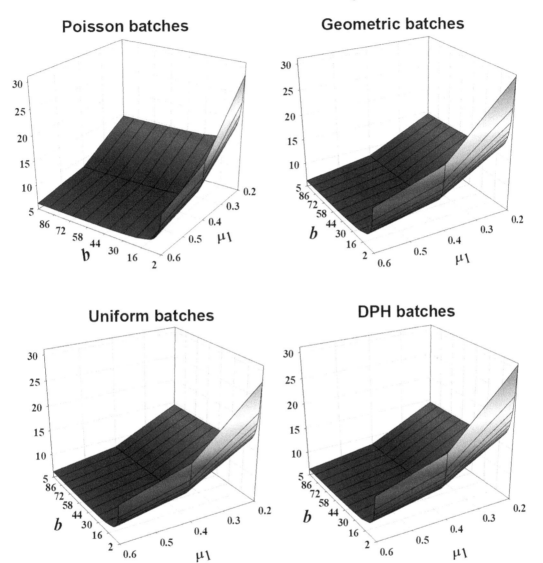

FIGURE 8.6 Mean recurrence time ($\rho = 0.50$) for different batch size distributions.

- From Figure 8.8, we once again notice a similar pattern of the mean busy period which is a decreasing function of both b and μ_1 for $\rho = 0.50$ for all four batch size distributions. If the service rate is increased, the mean busy time spent in the system decreases. This is the case for all four batch size distributions. The value of mean busy period is the lowest for UB and the highest for DPB.

- Figure 8.9, which displays the plots for the mean busy period for the case when $\rho = 0.99$. However, the value of the mean busy period is high for $\rho = 0.99$ as compared to $\rho = 0.50$.

Mean Recurrence Time ($\rho = 0.99$)

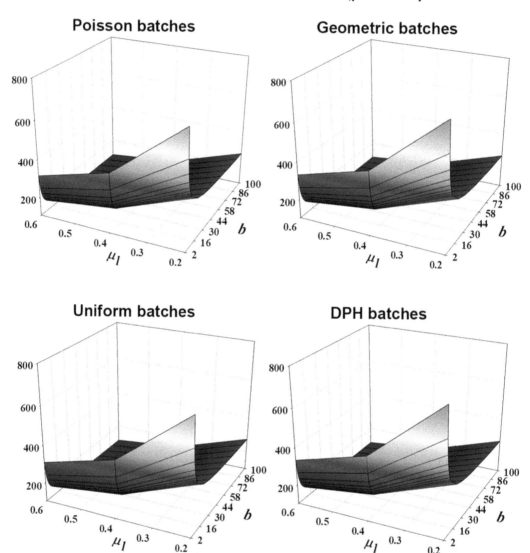

FIGURE 8.7 Mean recurrence time ($\rho = 0.99$) for different batch size distributions.

- The behavior of the mean number in the system can be seen in Figure 8.10 with respect to b and μ_1 for $\rho = 0.50$. With the increasing batch size, the performance measure seems to increase monotonically for a fixed value of μ_1, whereas it decreases with respect to μ_1 (for fixed b). The same pattern of behavior can be noticed for all four batch size distributions. Here, for DPB, the expected number in the system is large as compared to the other batch size distributions. If the service rate increases, the transactions in the system will be served at a fast rate, and consequently, the mean number in system will decrease.

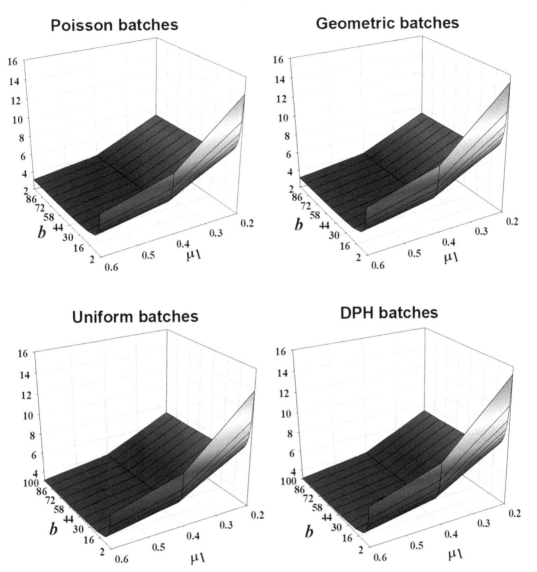

FIGURE 8.8 Mean busy period ($\rho = 0.50$) for different batch size distributions.

- In Figure 8.11 which contains the plots of the mean number in the system are displayed when $\rho = 0.99$, we see the insensitivity to the type of the batch size distributions with regard to the pattern. However, the value of the mean number in system is significantly large for $\rho = 0.99$ in comparison to $\rho = 0.50$.

- Figure 8.12 exhibits the behavior of the mean number served during a busy period μ_{NS} with respect to b and μ_1 for $\rho = 0.50$. The performance measure, μ_{NS}, appears to decrease with increase in b (for fixed μ_1) and it decreases as μ_1 is increased (for fixed b) for all four batch size distributions. The DPB has the highest value for μ_{NS} for fixed b and μ_1 but

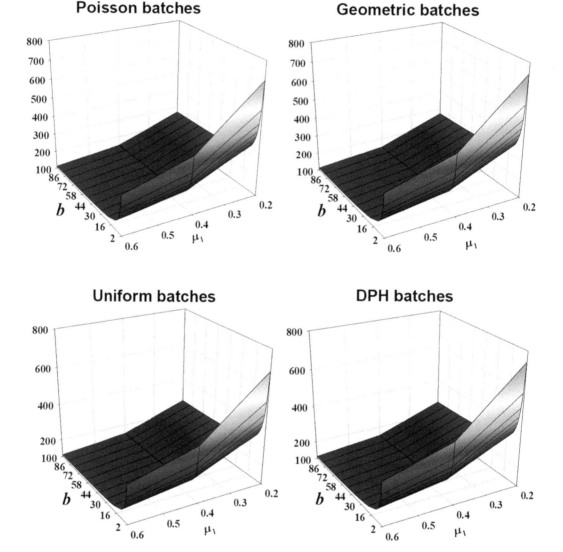

FIGURE 8.9   Mean busy period ($\rho = 0.99$) for different batch size distributions.

the difference between the values of μ_{NS} for DPB and GB is insignificant to make them look almost identical. Thus, it appears the behavior of this measure for DPH and GB are identical to each other.

- Figure 8.13 demonstrates a behavior of μ_{NS} with respect to the b and μ_1 for $\rho = 0.99$ that shows some level of insensitivity to the type of batch size distributions used. Here, the value of μ_{NS} is increased as the value of ρ is increased. Also, among all the four batch size distributions, DPB has the highest value of μ_{NS} and UB has the lowest value of μ_{NS}.

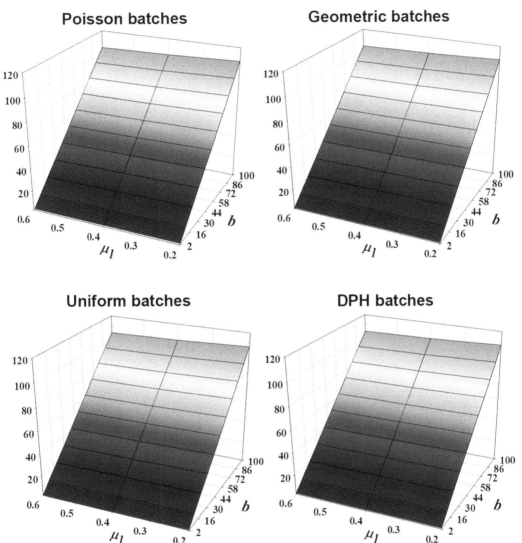

FIGURE 8.10 Mean number in system ($\rho = 0.50$) for different batch size distributions.

Example 8.3:

The effect of the batch size distribution on some performance measures under various scenarios is investigated by displaying the values in Tables 8.1–8.4. For this purpose, we fix the block pegging rate $\mu_2 = 1$ and vary the transaction processing rate $\mu_1 = 0.5, 1.5$; block size $b = 5, 50, 150, 200$ and the traffic intensity $\rho = 0.5, 0.90, 0.95, 0.99$.

We consider the parameter values of the uniform, Poisson, and geometric distribution are 3, 1 and 0.5, respectively. For a given tolerance level of 10^{-13}, the cut-off values of the batch sizes are 3, 13, and 34 for the uniform, Poisson, and geometric distribution, respectively.

Mean Number in System ($\rho = 0.99$)

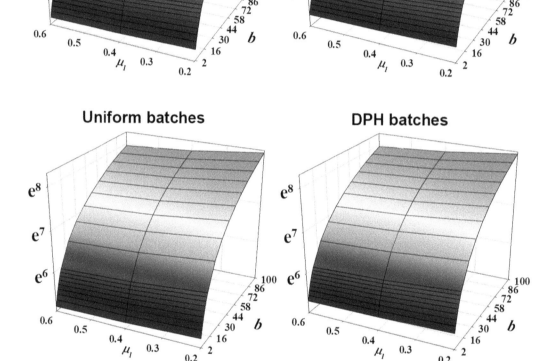
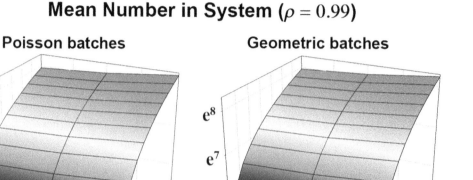

FIGURE 8.11   Mean number in system ($\rho = 0.99$) for different batch size distributions.

On the other hand, for the DPH distribution (see below for the representation of this DPH) has the maximum batch size is 50 for the same tolerance level.

$$\alpha = (0.4, 0.3, 0.3), \quad T = \begin{pmatrix} 0.3 & 0.11 & 0.01627 \\ 0.1 & 0.2 & 0.25 \\ 0.12 & 0.3 & 0.12 \end{pmatrix}.$$

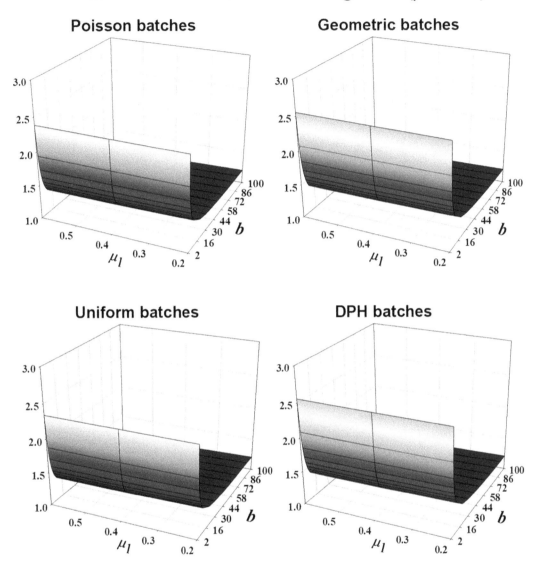

FIGURE 8.12 Mean number served during a BP ($\rho = 0.50$) for different batch size distributions.

For $\mu_1 = 0.5$ and Mean-RT, the effect of the batch size distribution is quite high for low b values ($b = 5$ and 50) as ρ increases (high ρ values). When the b values are large (150 and 200), the effect of the distribution is less in Table 8.1. When we look at $\mu_1 = 1.5$, the behavior just mentioned applies here as well. However, the differences between the four batch size distributions are somewhat less here. We can make similar comments for the other performance measures in Tables 8.2–8.4. In summary, we can say that smaller the b values and μ_1 values are, the larger the ρ values and hence greater the impact of the batch size distribution on the measures.

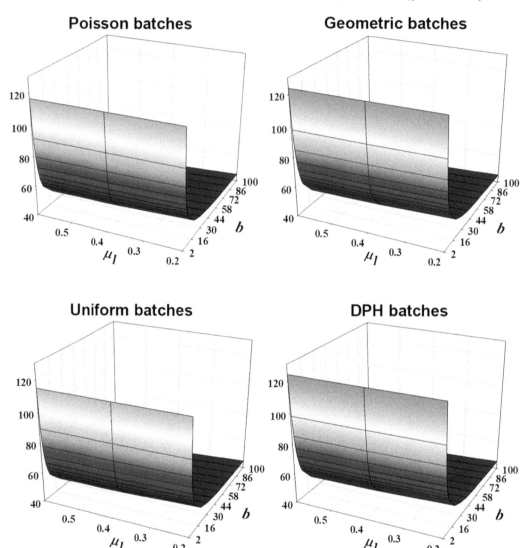

FIGURE 8.13 Mean number served during a BP ($\rho = 0.99$) for different batch size distributions.

TABLE 8.1

The Effect of Distribution Type on Mean-RT

μ_1	b	$\rho = 0.5$				$\rho = 0.90$			
		Uniform	Poisson	Geometric	DPH	Uniform	Poisson	Geometric	DPH
0.5	5	9.387	9.587	10.154	10.168	23.681	24.235	25.763	25.799
	50	7.100	7.117	7.167	7.169	15.101	15.169	15.373	15.379
	150	6.953	6.958	6.974	6.974	14.453	14.476	14.545	14.547
	200	6.935	6.939	6.951	6.951	14.372	14.389	14.441	14.442
1.5	5	5.203	5.315	5.631	5.638	13.110	13.418	14.267	14.287
	50	3.915	3.924	3.953	3.954	8.286	8.325	8.440	8.443
	150	3.831	3.834	3.843	3.844	7.920	7.933	7.972	7.973
	200	3.821	3.823	3.830	3.830	7.874	7.884	7.913	7.914
μ_1	b	$\rho = 0.95$				$\rho = 0.99$			
		Uniform	Poisson	Geometric	DPH	Uniform	Poisson	Geometric	DPH
0.5	5	44.448	45.493	48.371	48.438	211.724	216.716	230.452	230.774
	50	27.886	28.018	28.411	28.421	131.191	131.832	133.744	133.793
	150	26.629	26.674	26.808	26.811	125.062	125.279	125.933	125.950
	200	26.471	26.505	26.606	26.608	124.293	124.456	124.948	124.961
1.5	5	24.604	25.185	26.783	26.820	117.189	119.963	127.590	127.768
	50	15.297	15.372	15.593	15.599	71.951	72.312	73.388	73.416
	150	14.588	14.613	14.689	14.691	68.493	68.615	68.984	68.994
	200	14.499	14.518	14.574	14.576	68.059	68.151	68.428	68.436

TABLE 8.2

The Effect of Distribution Type on Mean-BP

μ_1	b	$\rho = 0.5$				$\rho = 0.90$			
		Uniform	Poisson	Geometric	DPH	Uniform	Poisson	Geometric	DPH
0.5	5	4.694	4.794	5.077	5.084	21.313	21.812	23.187	23.219
	50	3.550	3.558	3.584	3.584	13.591	13.652	13.836	13.841
	150	3.476	3.479	3.487	3.487	13.008	13.028	13.091	13.092
	200	3.468	3.469	3.475	3.475	12.934	12.950	12.997	12.998
1.5	5	2.602	2.657	2.815	2.819	11.799	12.076	12.840	12.858
	50	1.958	1.962	1.977	1.977	7.458	7.493	7.596	7.599
	150	1.916	1.917	1.922	1.922	7.128	7.140	7.175	7.176
	200	1.911	1.912	1.915	1.915	7.087	7.096	7.122	7.123
μ_1	b	$\rho = 0.95$				$\rho = 0.99$			
		Uniform	Poisson	Geometric	DPH	Uniform	Poisson	Geometric	DPH
0.5	5	42.226	43.218	45.952	46.016	209.607	214.549	228.148	228.466
	50	26.491	26.617	26.991	27.000	129.879	130.514	132.406	132.455
	150	25.298	25.340	25.467	25.471	123.811	124.026	124.673	124.690
	200	25.148	25.180	25.276	25.278	123.050	123.212	123.698	123.711
1.5	5	23.374	23.926	25.444	25.479	116.017	118.763	126.314	126.491
	50	14.532	14.603	14.814	14.819	71.231	71.589	72.654	72.681
	150	13.858	13.882	13.954	13.956	67.808	67.929	68.294	68.304
	200	13.774	13.792	13.846	13.847	67.378	67.469	67.744	67.751

TABLE 8.3

The Effect of Distribution Type on Mean

μ_1	b	$\rho = 0.5$				$\rho = 0.90$			
		Uniform	Poisson	Geometric	DPH	Uniform	Poisson	Geometric	DPH
0.5	5	5.528	5.603	5.839	5.845	26.600	27.343	29.577	29.635
	50	52.611	52.660	52.811	52.815	179.965	180.677	182.817	182.873
	150	157.545	157.590	157.728	157.732	521.088	521.795	523.919	523.975
	200	210.017	210.063	210.199	210.202	691.654	692.360	694.484	694.540
1.5	5	5.487	5.563	5.798	5.804	25.887	26.630	28.864	28.922
	50	52.270	52.318	52.467	52.471	172.891	173.602	175.742	175.797
	150	156.546	156.590	156.726	156.729	499.881	500.588	502.711	502.766
	200	208.690	208.734	208.868	208.871	663.383	664.089	666.210	666.265

μ_1	b	$\rho = 0.95$				$\rho = 0.99$			
		Uniform	Poisson	Geometric	DPH	Uniform	Poisson	Geometric	DPH
0.5	5	52.230	53.805	58.540	58.662	256.730	264.972	289.706	290.347
	50	331.299	332.845	337.485	337.606	1536.342	1544.544	1569.189	1569.832
	150	951.763	953.303	957.928	958.049	4380.231	4388.408	4413.047	4413.700
	200	1262.000	1263.541	1268.163	1268.283	5802.181	5810.350	5834.988	5835.646
1.5	5	50.633	52.208	56.942	57.065	248.026	256.268	281.002	281.642
	50	315.382	316.927	321.566	321.687	1449.351	1457.553	1482.197	1482.840
	150	904.027	905.565	910.190	910.310	4119.272	4127.452	4152.086	4152.738
	200	1198.356	1199.894	1204.514	1204.634	5454.237	5462.408	5487.046	5487.702

TABLE 8.4

The Effect of Distribution Type on MNS-BP

μ_1	b	$\rho = 0.5$				$\rho = 0.90$			
		Uniform	Poisson	Geometric	DPH	Uniform	Poisson	Geometric	DPH
0.5	5	1.565	1.598	1.692	1.695	7.104	7.271	7.729	7.740
	50	1.183	1.186	1.195	1.195	4.530	4.551	4.612	4.614
	150	1.159	1.160	1.162	1.162	4.336	4.343	4.364	4.364
	200	1.156	1.157	1.158	1.159	4.312	4.317	4.332	4.333
1.5	5	1.561	1.594	1.689	1.692	7.079	7.246	7.704	7.715
	50	1.175	1.177	1.186	1.186	4.475	4.496	4.558	4.559
	150	1.149	1.150	1.153	1.153	4.277	4.284	4.305	4.306
	200	1.146	1.147	1.149	1.149	4.252	4.257	4.273	4.274

μ_1	b	$\rho = 0.95$				$\rho = 0.99$			
		Uniform	Poisson	Geometric	DPH	Uniform	Poisson	Geometric	DPH
0.5	5	14.075	14.406	15.317	15.339	69.869	71.516	76.049	76.155
	50	8.831	8.872	8.997	9.000	43.293	43.505	44.135	44.152
	150	8.433	8.447	8.489	8.490	41.270	41.342	41.558	41.563
	200	8.383	8.393	8.425	8.426	41.017	41.071	41.233	41.237
1.5	5	14.024	14.355	15.266	15.288	69.610	71.258	75.788	75.894
	50	8.719	8.762	8.888	8.891	42.739	42.953	43.592	43.609
	150	8.315	8.329	8.372	8.374	40.685	40.758	40.976	40.982
	200	8.264	8.275	8.307	8.308	40.427	40.482	40.646	40.651

8.7 Conclusions and Future Directions

We analyzed a queueing model of the type $M^{[X]}/M^{[b]}/1$ useful in blockchain modeling. The modeling process captured the two different service stages that are inherent in the mining process of the miners pool and the building of a new blockchain. The proposed model utilizes the convolution of the processing times of the transaction and the mining, thus simplifying the analysis. By using the matrix-analytic method, a qualitative analysis of the model in steady-state through various performance metrics is presented. Illustrative and interesting numerical examples are given. The model under consideration here can be generalized to include BMAP transaction arrivals and phase type services in both stages. This extension is currently being studied, and the findings will be reported elsewhere.

REFERENCES

1. Nakamoto S. Bitcoin: A peer-to-peer electronic cash system; 2008. [Online]. Available: https://bitcoin.org/bitcoin.pdf
2. Kube N. *Daniel Drescher. Blockchain basics: A non-technical introduction in 25 steps.* Berkely: Apress; 2017.
3. Parker JF. *Blockchain technology simplified: The complete guide to blockchain management, mining, trading and investing cryptocurrency.* California: CreateSpace Independent Publishing Platform; 2018.
4. Wattenhofer R. *The science of the blockchain.* California: CreateSpace Independent Publishing Platform; 2016.
5. Lin IC, Liao TC. A survey of blockchain security issues and challenges. *Int J Netw Secur.* 2017;19(5):653–659.
6. Wang W, Hoang DT, Hu P, Xiong Z, Niyato D, Wang P, Wen Y, Kim DI. A survey on consensus mechanisms and mining strategy management in blockchain networks. *IEEE Access.* 2019;7:22328–22370.
7. Zheng Z, Xie S, Dai HN, Chen X, Wang H. Blockchain challenges and opportunities: A survey. *Int J Web Grid Serv.* 2018;14(4):352–375.
8. Nguyen QK. Blockchain-a financial technology for future sustainable development. In 2016 3rd International conference on green technology and sustainable development (GTSD); 2016. pp. 51–54.
9. Tsai WT, Blower R, Zhu Y, Yu L. A system view of financial blockchains. In 2016 IEEE Symposium on Service-Oriented System Engineering (SOSE). 2016; pp. 450–457.
10. Morabito V. *Business innovation through blockchain.* Cham: Springer International Publishing; 2017.
11. Mougayar W. *The business blockchain: Promise, practice, and application of the next internet technology.* Hoboken, NJ: John Wiley & Sons; 2016.
12. Hofmann E, Strewe UM, Bosia N. *Supply chain finance and blockchain technology: The case of reverse securitisation.* Heidelberg: Springer; 2017.
13. Korpela K, Hallikas J, Dahlberg T. Digital supply chain transformation toward blockchain integration. In proceedings of the 50th Hawaii International Conference on System Sciences. 2017.
14. Saberi S, Kouhizadeh M, Sarkis J, Shen L. Blockchain technology and its relationships to sustainable supply chain management. *Int J Prod Res.* 2019;57(7):2117–2135.
15. Bahga A, Madisetti VK. Blockchain platform for industrial internet of things. *J Soft Eng App.* 2016;9(10):533–546.
16. Conoscenti M, Vetro A, De Martin JC. Blockchain for the Internet of Things: A systematic literature review. In 2016 IEEE/ACS 13th International Conference of Computer Systems and Applications (AICCSA). 2016; pp. 1–6.
17. Dorri A, Kanhere SS, Jurdak R. Blockchain for IoT security and privacy: The case study of a smart home. In 2017 IEEE International Conference on Pervasive Computing and Communications Workshops, PerCom Workshops. 2017; pp. 618–623.
18. De Filippi P. What blockchain means for the sharing economy. *Harv Bus Rev.* 2017;15:1–5.
19. Pazaitis A, De Filippi P, Kostakis V. Blockchain and value systems in the sharing economy: The illustrative case of Backfeed. *Technol Forecast Soc Change.* 2017;125:105–115.

20. Rabah K. Challenges & opportunities for blockchain powered healthcare systems: A review. *Mara Res J Med Health Sci.* 2017;1(1):45–52.
21. Li QL, Ma JY, Chang YX. Blockchain queue theory. In International Conference on Computational Social Networks. Springer, New York; 2018. pp. 25–40.
22. Li QL, Ma JY, Chang YX, Ma FQ, Yu HB. Markov processes in blockchain systems. *Comput Soc Netw.* 2019;6(1):1–28.
23. Kawase Y, Kasahara S. Transaction-confirmation time for bitcoin: A queueing analytical approach to blockchain mechanism. In International Conference on Queueing Theory and Network Applications. Springer, Cham; 2017. pp. 75–88.
24. Memon RA, Li JP, Ahmed J. Simulation model for blockchain systems using queuing theory. *Electronics.* 2019;8(2):234–253.
25. Jourdan M, Blandin S, Wynter L, Deshpande P. A probabilistic model of the bitcoin blockchain. In Proceedings of the IEEE/CVF Conference on Computer Vision and Pattern Recognition Workshops; 2019.
26. Huang D, Ma X, Zhang S. Performance analysis of the raft consensus algorithm for private blockchains. *IEEE Trans Syst Man Cyber: Syst.* 2019;50(1):172–181.
27. Srivastava R. Mathematical assessment of blocks acceptance in blockchain using Markov model. *Int J Blockchains Crypto.* 2019;1(1):42–53.
28. Fralix B. On classes of bitcoin-inspired infinite-server queueing systems. *Queueing Systems.* 2020;95(1):29–52.
29. Fan J, Ma Z, Zhang Y, Zhang C. Analysis of blockchain system based on $M/(M_1, M_2)/1$ vacation queueing model. *J Supercomput.* 2021;77(4):3673–3694.
30. Chen X, Nguyen K, Sekiya H. On the latency performance in private blockchain networks. *IEEE Internet Things J.* 2022;9(19):19246–19259.
31. Neuts MF. *Structured stochastic matrices of $M/G/1$ type and their applications.* New York: Marcel Dekker, Inc.; 1989.
32. Chakravarthy SR. Introduction to matrix-analytic methods in queues 1: Analytical and simulation approach – basics. London; New York: ISTE Ltd; John Wiley and Sons; 2022.
33. Chakravarthy SR. Introduction to matrix-analytic methods in queues 2: Analytical and simulation approach – basics. London; New York: ISTE Ltd; John Wiley and Sons; 2022.
34. Marcus M, Minc H. A survey of matrix theory and matrix inequalities. Boston, MA: Allyn and Bacon; 1964.
35. Steeb WH, Hardy Y. *Matrix calculus and Kronecker product: A practical approach to linear and multilinear algebra* Second Edition. Singapore: World Scientific Publishing Company; 2011.
36. Neuts MF. *Matrix-geometric solutions in stochastic models: An algorithmic approach.* Baltimore, MD: The Johns Hopkins University Press; 1981.

9

Emerging Trends in Sensors, IoT, and Smart Systems

Mohammad S. Obaidat
King Abdullah II School of Information Technology University of Jordan, Amman, Jordan
University of Science and Technology Beijing, Beijing, China
SRM University, India
Amity University, Noida, India

Muhammad Zeeshan Tanveer, Misbah Fatima, and Iqra Shafique
Riphah International University, Lahore, Pakistan

Salman Shamshad
The University of Lahore, Lahore, Pakistan

Khalid Mahmood
National Yunlin University of Science and Technology, Douliu, Yunlin, Taiwan

9.1   Introduction

The Internet of Things (IoT), is a system of interconnected computers, mechanical and electrical devices, and both animate and inanimate objects that are able to exchange information (Figure 9.1). Examples of the IoT include individuals with heart monitors implanted, livestock fitted with biochip transponders, vehicles equipped with sensors that alert the driver to low tire pressure, and similar human-made or natural objects that can be assigned an Internet Protocol (IP) address and transmit data through a network.

Organizations in various industries are leveraging the IoT to improve efficiency, gain insights into consumer behavior, enhance customer experience, make informed decisions, and drive value for their businesses.

9.2   Internet of Things (IoT)

In this section, we will be more focused on the fundamentals of IoT and will look into in-depth details of IoT and its working to get a better idea about IoT itself.

9.2.1   Importance of IoT

People may live, work, and manage every aspect of their life with the IoT. IoT is essential for business and offers advanced home automation equipment. Businesses may monitor their systems and data in real time, including information on machine performance and logistical and supply chain activities. Thanks to IoT, businesses can automate operations and save labor costs. It also improves service quality and reduces waste. The IoT is one of the most significant technological developments of our time. It will only gather pace as more businesses realize how linked gadgets might help them stay competitive.

DOI:10.1201/9781003326236-9

FIGURE 9.1 An illustration of generic IoT environment.

The IoT is making it possible for individuals to live more efficiently, work more effectively, and have greater control over their daily lives. It is a valuable tool for businesses as well, offering the ability to monitor systems in real-time and gather data on various aspects such as machine performance and supply chain activities. By utilizing the IoT, businesses can automate processes and reduce labor costs, as well as implement strategies for reducing waste and improving service delivery, all while lowering manufacturing and delivery costs and increasing transparency in customer transactions.

The IoT has become a pivotal technology in today's world and its significance is only expected to grow as more companies recognize its importance in staying competitive.

9.2.2 Benefits of IoT to Organizations

The IoT offers several opportunities for businesses to gain significant advantages. While specific benefits are open to a range of businesses, others are industry-specific. Several of the most well-known IoT benefits allow businesses to:

- Monitoring internal and external business processes
- Save time
- Save money
- Enhance productivity of employees and organization
- Help in making better business decision
- Less expenditure and more revenue

The IoT is pushing companies to rethink their operations and giving them the tools they require to enhance their approach. IoT devices, such as sensors, are predominantly utilized in industries like transportation, utility, and industrial sectors. However, their use has also expanded to include agriculture, infrastructure, and home automation, leading to the widespread digital transformation of businesses. For farmers, the IoT has the potential to simplify their work through the use of sensors that collect data on factors such as temperature, humidity, soil composition, and rainfall, allowing for the automation of various tasks.

The IoT also offers the advantage of monitoring infrastructure operations. Sensors can be employed to keep track of buildings, bridges, and other structures for any changes or events. This leads to a paperless environment, improved work processes, and cost and time savings. A home automation company might utilize the IoT to oversee and regulate a building's electrical and mechanical systems. Residents of smart cities could also benefit from increased waste reduction and energy conservation.

9.2.3 IoT Background

The origins of IoT can be traced back to Norman Joseph Woodland and his creation of the bar code in the late 1940s. This marked the beginning of the IoT and was born from Woodland's drawings in the sand at Miami Beach. He was granted a patent for the linear bar code in 1952 [1]. In the 1950s, Morton Heilig introduced "Sensorama," the world's first head-mounted display that gave users an experience of taking a motorcycle ride through Brooklyn [2]. In 1955, Edward O. Thorp created the first wearable computer, which was housed inside a shoe. This device was designed to predict the outcome of roulette wheels [3]. The idea of interconnected devices had its roots in 1832 with the creation of the first telegraph using electromagnetic signals for communication between two machines. Nevertheless, the true origin of IoT can be traced back to the late 1960s with the invention of the Internet [4].

In 1967, ten years after the invention of the telegraph, Hubert Upton created a wearable computer that included an eyeglass display to assist with lip reading. The device was a type of analog computer [5]. In 1967, the US Department of Defense introduced the first message to be sent through ARPANET, the predecessor of the Internet [6]. Mario Cardullo was credited with obtaining the first patent for a passive, read-write RFID (Radio Frequency Identification) tag in early 1973, transforming the retail sector [7]. In 1974, the Universal Product Code (UPC) label was put into use for the first time to manage purchases at a supermarket, specifically for Wrigley's Chewing Gum, just a year after the invention of RFID technology [8].

9.2.3.1 The World's First IoT Device

The creation of the world's first IoT device happened at Carnegie Mellon University in the early 1980s. The team of students developed a system that enabled them to monitor the status of a Coca-Cola vending machine on their campus network, eliminating the need for manual checking. The vending machine was equipped with micro switches to report the availability of Coke cans and their temperature [9].

In 1990, John Romkey connected a toaster to the Internet for the first time [10]. A year after the Coca-Cola vending machine, a group of students from the University of Cambridge used a web camera to monitor the coffee in their computer lab. They devised a plan to use the first web camera prototype to keep track of the coffee pot's status. The camera was set to take three photos of the coffee pot every minute, which were then transmitted to local computers so that everyone could see if coffee was available in the 1990s [11].

LG introduced the world's first smart refrigerator in 2000 [12], the first iPhone was released in 2007 [13], and by 2008, the number of connected gadgets had increased dramatically. In 2009, Google began testing self-driving cars [14], and the Nest smart thermostat, which allowed remote control of central heating, was released in 2011. There are three types of connected devices:

- Consumer IoT, such as wearables
- Enterprise IoT, which includes intelligent factories and precision agriculture
- Public spaces IoT, waste management, for example, is an example of IoT in general settings

Businesses leverage IoT to enhance supply chains, streamline inventory management, and improve customer experience. At the same time, the availability of low-cost and low-power sensors has led to the widespread use of intelligent consumer devices, such as the Amazon Echo speaker, in homes. In the medical field, the IoT can support real-time remote patient monitoring, assist with robotic surgeries, and facilitate the use of intelligent inhaler devices. In 2015, faculty members from the Interaction Design Institute IVREA (IDII) in Italy designed the "Arduino," a user-friendly and reasonably priced microcontroller, to facilitate interaction between two objects [15]. Three years later, the Cisco Internet Business Solutions Group claimed that "The Internet of Things" was officially born, as there were more Internet-connected devices than people [16].

McKinsey reported that the use of IoT technologies among businesses increased from 13% in 2014 to nearly 25% in 2019 [17]. The "State of the Connected World" report states that according to a study by the World Economic Forum, by 2025, 41.6 billion devices will collect data on our daily activities, work, and urban travel, as well as manage and maintain the equipment we depend on [18]. The Fourth Industrial Revolution refers to the ongoing digital transformation brought about by the growth of innovative technologies such as robotics, the IoT, and artificial intelligence. The COVID-19 pandemic has hastened the implementation of these cutting-edge technologies.

According to the "State of the Connected World" study published by the World Economic Forum, the COVID-19 pandemic has seen a significant boost from the use of IoT technology in the past year. IoT devices such as connected thermal cameras, contact tracing equipment, and health monitoring wearables have provided essential data to aid in the fight against the disease. The study also states that temperature sensors and parcel tracking will help ensure the safe distribution of COVID-19 vaccines. Additionally, IoT and automation in industries beyond healthcare have made the fragmented COVID supply chains more reliable. In manufacturing and warehouse settings, the technology enables activities that keep people separated while providing secure remote access to the industries.

9.2.4   Architecture and Work in IoT

In this section, we will examine the architecture of IoT more thoroughly.

9.2.4.1   Architecture of IoT

The IoT has numerous applications and its utilization is growing rapidly. The architecture of the IoT is determined by the functioning and purpose in various domains where it is being used. However, there is a need for a universal standard to outline the workings of the IoT. The 4 Stage IoT Architecture, the primary and overarching IoT architecture, is founded on a fundamental process flow. This architecture consists of four levels that can be further categorized into the application layer, data processing layer, network layer, and sensing layer. This is further illustrated in Figure 9.2.

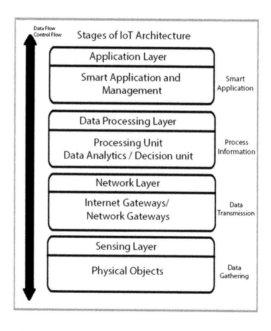

FIGURE 9.2   Stage of IoT architecture.

I. **Sensing Layer**

There are sensors, actuators, and gadgets in this sensory layer. Before delivering the information through a network, these sensors and actuators analyze the data (physical and environmental attributes) that they have just received.

II. **Network Layer**

The second tier in IoT infrastructure includes Internet or Network gateways and Data Acquisition Systems (DAS). The role of DAS is to gather and convert data, collecting information from various sources and converting analog sensor data into a digital format. These advanced gateways not only connect sensor networks to the Internet but also perform important functions such as virus protection, data filtering, and decision-making based on incoming data, as well as providing data management services.

III. **Data Processing Layer**

This is a component in the IoT infrastructure that handles data processing. The data collected from the IoT devices undergoes initial processing, such as examination and pre-processing, in this unit before being forwarded to a data center. Business applications can access the data after it has been prepped and made ready for action. Edge IT or edge analytics is also involved in this stage.

IV. **Application Layer**

The fourth tier of the IoT architecture involves data management, which takes place in either data centers or the cloud. This layer is where the collected data is utilized by various end-user applications across various industries such as agriculture, healthcare, aerospace, farming, and defense.

9.2.4.2 Working of IoT

The IoT consists of an extensive network of interconnected objects that generate and transfer vast amounts of information about their functioning and stored data. This information is gathered by these devices and sent to large cloud servers located globally, which then use the received data to issue appropriate commands. A demonstration of this is shown in Figure 9.3. The IoT is comprised of a vast network of interconnected objects that have sensors built into them. These sensors have

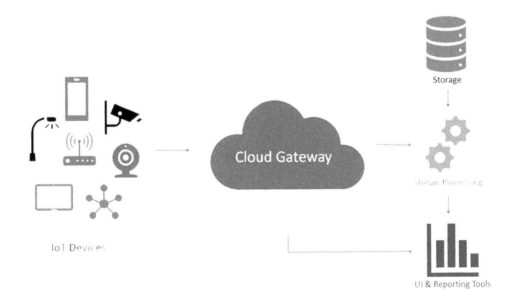

FIGURE 9.3 Illustration of IoT Architecture.

the capability to collect and sense information about the environment, with devices ranging from mobile phones, coffee makers, microwaves, water heaters, fire alarms, air conditioners, vehicles, and more storing this data in their storage. The data gathered by these devices is then transmitted to the IoT platform where it is processed and analyzed to extract valuable insights. Cloud servers and large databases are part of the IoT platform which then acts on the data by delivering appropriate commands. The platform uses the information to integrate, process, and analyze it to generate crucial details and then sends back instructions based on the provided data.

Data aggregation is then disseminated to other devices in order to improve performance and enhance the user experience in the future. The IoT has a promising future ahead. According to Business Insider, by 2020, there will be 24 billion IoT devices installed. ITC predicts that IoT sales will surpass 300 billion dollars in the coming years, providing numerous job opportunities in the technology industry as well as several other sectors [19].

9.2.4.3 Components of IoT

The main components based on which the IoT works are follow as in Figure 9.4.

I. **Devices and sensors**
   The connectivity layer of the IoT is comprised of a wide array of devices and sensors that continuously collect data from their environment. Some examples of these connected devices include phones, which have a range of sensors including GPS, cameras, motion sensors, and more. Advances in semiconductor fabrication technology have made it possible to create highly intelligent micro-sensors for a variety of applications.
   Some common sensors include the following:
   • Humidity/Moisture level
   • Pressure sensors
   • Temperature and thermostat sensors
   • Light intensity detectors
   • Proximity detection
   • Moisture sensors
   • RFID tags

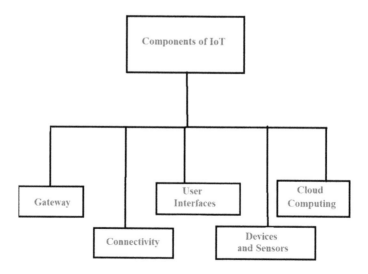

FIGURE 9.4 Components of IoT.

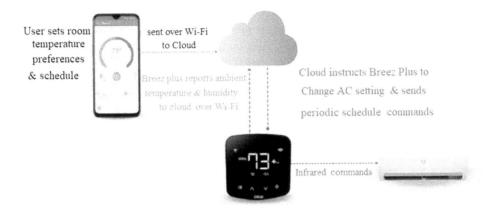

FIGURE 9.5 Example of air conditioner through sensor.

An example of an intelligent air conditioner (Figure 9.5) allows users to select their preferred room temperature between 73 and 77°F. The gadget instructs the air conditioner to switch on at a specific temperature when the room temperature rises above 77°. As soon as a room's temperature falls below 73°, a signal to turn off the AC will be issued. A conventional air conditioner is made intelligent by an IoT-enabled smart AC controller. It comprises a transmitter for signal transmission and a sensor for keeping track of environmental temperature changes. The direction of automated processes affects the entire IOT ecosystem.

II. **Cloud Computing**

The connectivity layer in the IoT architecture is comprised of devices and sensors that gather information about their environment and transmit it to the next layer. For example, a smartphone has many sensors, such as a GPS, camera, and motion sensor. Advanced semiconductor technology has allowed for the creation of compact and intelligent micro-sensors. Data collected from these devices is often stored in the cloud, which is a network of connected servers that operate 24/7. To effectively manage the large amounts of data generated by IoT systems, cloud storage is utilized. This also provides a platform for analysis.

The IoT cloud, made up of powerful computers, can quickly process huge volumes of data. The cloud plays a crucial role in managing and handling data, including data collection, processing, management, archiving, and remote access. IoT devices, including sensors, routers, gateways, user applications, and media, are connected through various connectivity paths, such as Wi-Fi, Bluetooth, Zigbee, and cellular networks like LTE or 5G. While the cloud is a popular option for the IoT, local processing with Edge or Fog computing is also possible. However, the cloud is often preferred due to its high performance, scalability, and low cost. Edge computing, on the other hand, is ideal for applications that require intensive local data processing and archiving.

III. **Connectivity**

Communication in IoT requires an Internet connection and the assignment of an IP address to each device connected to the Internet. However, the limited number of IP addresses has led researchers to explore a new IP address scheme that can accurately identify each physical device. Regardless of the medium used for transport, the collected data is transmitted to a cloud infrastructure. The sensors can connect to the cloud using various communication systems, such as wide-area networks, low-power wide-area networks, Bluetooth, Wi-Fi, and others, each of which has its own advantages and limitations in terms of power consumption, range, and bandwidth. The selection of the most appropriate connectivity solution is crucial for the proper functioning of the IoT system. Once the data is transmitted to the platform, it is processed to generate the necessary outputs and send them back to the devices. This step is critical for the success of IoT technology, as the processing must be efficient for optimal results. IoT refers to a network of interconnected objects, sensors, actuators, and clouds that must work together to process and act on data. Connectivity is an essential component of the complex IoT ecosystem.

IV.   **User Interface**

User interfaces (UIs) provide users with access to the visible and controllable components of the IoT system. The design of consumer interfaces is crucial as it often helps users choose a particular technology or device in today's competitive market. Devices with a simple and compatible design, aligned with current wireless standards, are more likely to attract users. With the advancements in technology, various interactive designs are available to make complex tasks easier on touchscreens. Physical buttons on equipment have been replaced by color touch displays and this trend is spreading to most smart home devices. For example, a user can change the temperature of their refrigerator remotely using their phone if they notice any changes.

In certain situations, certain processes can occur automatically. The IoT system can change its settings without human intervention by creating and implementing a few defined rules. The UI is the most accessible and controllable part of the IoT system, allowing users to modify and operate it. The more user-friendly this part of the IoT ecosystem is, the more convenient it becomes for users to interact with. Users can interact with the system both locally and remotely using laptops, tablets, and smartphones. They can even use smart home systems like Google Home or Amazon Alexa to communicate with their "things."

V.   **Gateway**

The IoT Gateway manages the two-way exchange of data between various networks and protocols, making sure the connected devices and sensors are compatible. With the use of advanced encryption methods, it provides a level of security for the network and data transmission. The gateway acts as a barrier between the devices and the cloud to prevent unauthorized access and malicious intrusion. In certain cases, it can also locally process the data from thousands of sensors before forwarding it, thereby reducing the amount of data being transmitted. The gateway serves as an extra layer of security for the data in transit with the latest encryption techniques. However, not all IoT gateways are capable of analyzing, aggregating, and only sending the relevant data to the cloud.

9.2.5   Resource of IoT

The IoT connects physical objects in the world to the global Internet. At the core of IoT is a diverse array of smart devices with sensors, actuators, and the ability to process and communicate information. These devices collect data about their surroundings through various types of sensors that measure things like pressure, temperature, and humidity. This information is then either directly uploaded to a server or transmitted through a gateway. Based on server feedback, IoT devices may also send commands to actuators. Applications of IoT in the real world include smart cities, intelligent transportation systems, smart homes, retail operations, health monitoring, and environmental and energy management. Due to the numerous benefits of IoT technology, industries, research and development facilities, and governments are investing large sums of money into IoT, resulting in intense competition and market fragmentation, hindered by compatibility issues with standards.

9.2.5.1   *Resources in IoT Ecosystems*

Resources of many kinds used in IoT contexts are displayed in Figure 9.6. The tools used for resource management can be applied to various tasks for the benefit of the system, network, or applications utilized by end users. There are two main types of resources: those focused on apps and those focused on infrastructure. Infrastructure-based resource management encompasses computing, networking, storage, and other resources. Resource management for energy is also important and includes

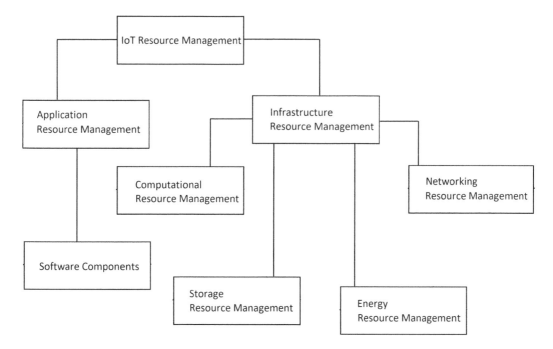

FIGURE 9.6 IoT resource modeling.

hardware such as sensors, CPUs, and memory, as well as firmware and software. From the system's perspective, hardware and software resources are differentiated, while from the network's perspective, resources could include radio antennas, channels, bandwidth, routing paths, or nodes. Storage resource management encompasses various components, such as memory and the file system. Energy resource management deals with energy sources and batteries. Resource management can impact any software components from an application or user perspective, including application management modules, resource databases, customer databases, resource identification, and resource modeling.

9.2.6 IoT Objects

This section will look into the devices and physical components we use to make an IoT ecosystem work. We will also profoundly analyze the type of these components.

9.2.6.1 *Introduction of IoT Devices*

The number of IoT devices has surpassed the global population. Currently, the world has a population of approximately 7.62 billion people, but by 2022, it is estimated that the number of IoT devices in operation will rise to 20 billion. This increase in IoT devices is driving the demand for 5G networks [17]. It is estimated that, in a few years, the average person in America will own more than ten IoT devices. The growth of IoT is increasing rapidly, with a multitude of devices available, including computers, smartphones, smart gadgets, smartwatches, and smart vehicles (Figure 9.7). These findings are further discussed in this section.

9.2.6.2 *Working of IoT Devices*

The functioning of various IoT devices may differ in purpose, but they share a similar operation mechanism. IoT devices are physical objects that detect events happening in the real world and are

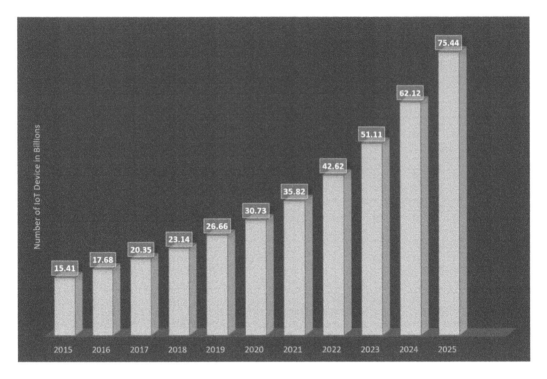

FIGURE 9.7   Number of IoT devices.

equipped with a Central Processing Unit (CPU), network adapter, firmware, and an IP address. To access the network, they connect to a Dynamic Host Configuration Protocol (DHCP) server.

Most IoT devices are operated and monitored through a software application, such as a smartphone app. For instance, using a smartphone app, one can control the lighting in their home. However, some devices come with an in-built web server and do not require an external program, like a light turning on when someone enters a room. Some examples of IoT Devices:

I.   **Home Security**
     IoT is a critical component in ensuring the safety and security of homes. A variety of sensors, alarms, and cameras can be connected through IoT and managed from a mobile device, providing constant protection.

II. **Activity Trackers**
     Health monitoring is made possible with the use of sensor-based activity trackers. These gadgets can continually keep track of vital health markers such as blood pressure, physical activity, appetite, and oxygen levels and provide updates.

III. **Industrial Security and Safety**
     The IoT is playing a significant role in maintaining the security of restricted areas by incorporating sensors and cameras in the form of detection systems. These devices can detect intruders as well as potential leaks and pressure buildups, allowing for timely rectification of these issues. In Augmented Reality (AR), wearable glasses equipped with computers allow users to enhance their real-world experiences by adding virtual information, such as animations in 3D and movies, to the scenes they see. The glasses provide access to Internet applications by incorporating the relevant information within their lenses.

IV. **Motion Detection**
     Motion sensors have the capability to detect movements or vibrations in large structures such as buildings, bridges, dams, and others. By doing so, they can identify any structural

anomalies or disruptions that could lead to a potential catastrophe. These sensors can also be deployed in areas prone to natural disasters such as earthquakes, landslides, and floods to provide early warning and preventative measures.

Let's have a look at some of the most popular IoT Devices:

I. **Google Home Voice Controller**
The Google Home voice controller is a popular IoT device that provides voice-activated control over various functions, including lighting, temperature control, and audio volume.

II. **Amazon Echo Plus Voice Controller**
The Amazon Echo Plus is a widely recognized and dependable IoT gadget that offers users numerous voice-activated functionalities such as answering calls, creating reminders and alarms, acquiring weather updates, and more.

III. **August Doorbell Cam**
The August Doorbell Cam is a smart device that provides remote monitoring and interaction with your front door. With its ability to continuously record activity, it helps you stay aware of any suspicious behavior that may occur at your doorstep.

IV. **August Smart Lock**
The August Smart Lock is a well-known and trustworthy IoT device that allows individuals to manage their door locks from anywhere.

V. **Foobot**
Foobot is an IoT device that accurately tracks indoor air pollution, helping to improve the air quality in homes, offices, coffee shops, and other indoor public spaces.

9.2.7 IoT Data

The term IoT encompasses physical objects that are equipped with sensors, computing power, software, and other technologies that allow them to communicate with each other through the Internet or other networks. Despite criticism that the name implies a connection to the entire Internet, it only refers to individual devices that can be accessed and connected to a network.

IoT refers to a network of interconnected objects, including computers, digital and mechanical equipment, living beings, or anything that can be assigned an IP address and exchange data over a network. Examples include people with implanted heart monitors, farm animals with biochip transponders, automobiles with built-in tire pressure sensors, and more.

9.3 Sensor

The IoT system is built on sensors, which act as the system's senses and gather useful information. These sensors can be seen as similar to human senses like eyes, ears, mouths, and noses, but they have the ability to collect much more data. The "brain" of the IoT system can move and change due to the information gathered by these sensors.

9.3.1 Introduction

The foundation of any IoT deployment is the use of sensors, which are the sources of data collection. These sensors provide the sensory information necessary for the software to function optimally. The group of intelligent devices that make up this system is known as a Wireless Sensor Network (WSN) or Micro-Electro-Mechanical Systems (MEMS). The nodes in this network have the capability to perform specific tasks due to the miniaturization of processing and sensing technologies, making it possible to create low-power and cost-effective equipment. The sensors are placed in the surrounding area to monitor or track objects of interest. They are in a dormant state but can create their own network topology, self-configure, and communicate with nearby nodes over short distances. The collection of detected nodes enables remote communication through multi-jump architecture, with exceptional nodes called cluster leaders combining the findings before forwarding them to the next hop. This helps prevent infrastructure failures, conserve resources, increase productivity, enhance security, and pave the way for new applications to emerge. The number of sinks and nodes in a network can vary, but they collect, organize, and distribute the necessary readings, monitoring physical factors such as temperature, humidity, sound, intensity, and vibration in real time. The ability of these devices to provide real-time environmental measurements also allows for global operation, though there are some limitations that need improvement, such as energy consumption, power requirements, security concerns, and storage space.

9.3.1.1 Role of Sensors in the IoT Industry

The IoT is a comprehensive network that brings together different information-gathering devices and the Internet. The Internet's advancement is the foundation for the information age, and the development of the IoT requires technical capabilities such as intelligent perception, identification, and communication. Sensors and related technologies play a crucial role in providing perception, and the expansion of the IoT would not be possible without their advancements. The use of sensors is essential to collect data and make a substantial contribution to the IoT's success. In the realm of sensors, there is expected to be tremendous growth.

9.3.2 Background

The WSN can facilitate short-range communication between devices within its network by constructing ad-hoc remote systems. However, connecting them to the Internet or other mobile communication systems is challenging as communication protocols are yet to be standardized. The limitations of WSN transmission protocols make it difficult to transmit data and detect technological advancements across long distances. This issue is addressed by the IoT, which provides a solution through the development of IoT Gateways. These gateways aim to reduce the heterogeneity between sensor and mobile communication systems, improve the management of WSNs with terminal devices, and support established communication systems with sensor systems. This makes managing the equipment of sensor systems much easier.

The IoT is a sophisticated and smart worldwide network infrastructure that consists of self-configuring nodes. With the help of various intelligent sensors, this network can perceive and modify the current reality, converting the collected data into a digital stream for transmission to a gateway. The IoT has gained popularity due to its versatility and the valuable information that microchip units can provide. It also helps conserve resources and alerts users when parameters fall outside acceptable limits. Although these devices have limited storage and processing power, they still provide an impressive representation of the real world while facing challenges in terms of privacy, performance, scalability, and reliability.

Another issue faced by sensors is the limited memory capacity. The cloud infrastructure offers a solution to this problem with sensor technology. Cloud computing is a vast and expanding arena, offering unlimited storage and powerful computation capabilities. It allows organizations to access a range of configurable computing resources on demand from any location. This includes storing data, providing services, managing servers, and developing programs that offer efficient administration. With its focus on enhancing Internet delivery, cloud computing has proven to be a highly innovative field. Mobile cloud computing takes the concept of distributed computing to the next level by making it accessible on the go.

The management of various services for clients using mobile devices is facilitated by the growth of mobile applications and cloud computing. Mobile applications provide users with a wealth of information about different services. These systems operate on both mobile devices and remote servers through isolated systems. There has been a proliferation of various application types centered on mobile devices, such as entertainment, games, business, casual chat, travel, and news. Fog computing expands the use of cloud technologies, enhancing edge computation and enabling new tasks and services to be performed. Devices in fog processing, like buildings or offices, serve as resources for local authorities near the network's edge and switches can function as modern servers.

9.3.3 Working of Sensors in Different Applications

Sensors play a crucial role in the operation of many contemporary businesses. Predictive maintenance is made possible through their use, allowing companies to minimize costly downtime by detecting potential problems before they escalate. By analyzing the trends in the sensor data, business owners can gain valuable insights and make informed decisions based on solid evidence. These sensors are designed to respond to specific physical conditions and generate signals that indicate the severity of the situation, such as temperature, sound, distance, pressure, or even the presence or absence of a gas or liquid. The typical IoT sensors used in this application include:

I. Intrusion Detection
II. Temperature Monitoring
III. Optical Sensor
IV. Humidity Sensor
V. Water Quality Monitoring
VI. Chemical Sensor
VII. Gyroscope Sensors
VIII. Gas Sensor

9.3.3.1 Intrusion Detection

An intrusion detection system detects and alerts of any potential intrusion within its monitoring area. It is commonly integrated with other physical security systems and utilizes IT systems with Internet access. The system consists of three crucial components: the sensor, control unit, and annunciator. The sensor employs various techniques to detect an intrusion and sends a warning signal to the control unit. The control unit, upon receiving the warning, triggers a discreet alarm or the annunciator issues a warning, such as a light or siren.

Different authors suggest various methods for detecting intrusions to protect the system. The technique of attack resistance is described as a non-zero-sum game between an attacker and a sensor. The game theory framework provides Nash equilibrium for the two players, the attacker and the IDS. The second method is the IDS, which requires Markov's decision-making. The IDS observes the behavior of the adversary while monitoring the system, trying to determine which hub requires protection. If the IDS confirms that the attacker is attempting to attack, it renders the attack unsuccessful, but if the attacker attacks an unexpected hub, the IDS considers it a successful attack. In the third approach, the IDS measures the amount of traffic and determines to secure the hub with the highest measured traffic load. In the simulation, 20–200 cluster heads are present in the required environment, and the simulation was run on a Pentium III running at 1133 MHz [20].

9.3.3.2 Temperature Monitoring

A temperature sensor is a device used to measure the temperature of a moving component in machinery. The thermocouple is one commonly used type of temperature sensor and is made up of two different conductors that come into contact at one or more points. When the temperature of one of these points differs from the reference temperature at other points in the circuit, the thermocouple measures this temperature variation.

Temperature Sensors are divided into the following subcategories:

I. **Thermocouples:**
   The voltage monitors detect changes in voltage levels. As the temperature increases, the output voltage of the thermocouple also rises.

II. **Resistor Temperature Detectors (RTD):**
   The resistance of the gadget increases in proportion to the rise in temperature, resulting in a positive correlation between the two. The resistor's resistance is altered due to changes in temperature, as it is designed to be temperature-sensitive.

III. **Semiconductor:**
   Linear devices utilize the changing resistance properties of semiconductors and exhibit linear increases in conductivity. Specifically, they have the ability to give a precise digital representation of temperature readings at low temperatures.

IV. **Infrared Sensors:**
   This method of temperature measurement is based on the transparency of gases. However, it only captures a portion of the temperature of solids and liquids. It is not effective in determining the infrared energy emitted by an object or substance, or in evaluating its strength.

9.3.3.3 *Optical Sensor*

An optical sensor converts the number of light rays into an electrical signal that can be easily interpreted by humans or electronic devices. Their ability to measure multiple factors simultaneously makes them popular among IoT experts. With the ability to monitor electromagnetic energy, such as electricity and light, these sensors have found applications in various industries including healthcare, environmental monitoring, energy, and aerospace. They greatly facilitate monitoring of ecological changes for mining, pharmaceutical, and oil corporations, while also ensuring the safety of their workers.

The following are examples of crucial optical sensor types:

I. **Photodetector:**
   This device operates as a photodetector by utilizing light-sensitive semiconductor components such as photocells, photodiodes, or phototransistors.

II. **Fiber Optics:**
   Fiber optics do not conduct electricity, making them immune to electrical and electromagnetic interference. They pose no risk of sparking or shock, even when damaged.

III. **Pyrometer:**
   The temperature of an object can be determined by analyzing the color of light it emits, as objects with the same temperature will produce the same color of light.

IV. **Proximity and Infrared:**
   Proximity sensors that use visible light can have limitations in detecting objects close by. To overcome this, sensors that work based on optical technology convert light waves into electrical signals. Such sensors play a crucial role in the field of autonomous vehicles as they are used to detect road signs, obstacles, and other objects that a driver would typically be able to see while driving or parking. They also have applications in extending battery life through ambient light sensing and in the biomedical industry, where they are used in devices such as heart-rate monitors and breath analyzers.

9.3.3.4 *Humidity Sensor*

The humidity in an environment composed of air or other gases is measured as the amount of water vapor present. The most widely used term is Relative Humidity (RH). As many industrial processes require controlled conditions, these sensors are often used in conjunction with temperature sensors to ensure everything is functioning as planned. A sudden change in humidity can be quickly detected by the sensors, allowing prompt action to be taken. They are used for controlling Heating, Ventilation, and Air Conditioning (HVAC) systems in both industrial and residential settings, as well as for protecting medications in a variety of settings such as automobiles, museums, greenhouses, industrial facilities, meteorological stations, paint and coating companies, hospitals, and the pharmaceutical industry.

9.3.3.5 Water Quality Sensor

The Wasp mote is a key characteristic among the top dozen water quality parameters measured by water quality sensors. Bright Water is the first platform for water quality monitoring that incorporates autonomous nodes capable of connecting to the cloud for real-time water monitoring, and it is primarily used to evaluate the quality of water sources such as rivers and the ocean.

I. **Chlorine Residual Sensor:**
   The residual chlorine levels in water, including free chlorine, mono chlorine, and total chlorine, are most often measured using this method, which is commonly used as a disinfectant.

II. **Total Organic Carbon (TOC) Sensor:**
   The presence of organic elements in water can be measured using a TOC sensor.

III. **Turbidity Sensor:**
   Turbidity sensors are commonly used for monitoring suspended particles in water, measuring river and stream levels, and assessing the quality of wastewater and effluent.

IV. **Conductivity Sensor:**
   In industrial processes, conductivity measurements are often used to determine the total concentration of ionic substances dissolved in water solutions.

V. **The pH Sensor:**
   The pH level of dissolved water, which indicates the degree of acidity or basicity, can be measured with this method.

VI. **Oxygen-Reduction Potential (ORP) Sensor:**
   The ORP measurement provides information about the oxidation and reduction reactions taking place in a solution.

9.3.3.6 Chemical Sensor

Chemical sensors play a vital role in numerous industries, with the goal of detecting any chemical changes in either gases or liquids. They are particularly important in urban areas where monitoring shifts and ensuring public safety are top priorities. These sensors are mainly utilized in industrial settings for process control and monitoring, detection of explosive and radioactive substances, and for operations in pharmaceutical industries, space stations, laboratories, and recycling facilities, among other uses.

The most popular types of chemical sensors are as follows:

- Glass pH electrode
- Electronic gas sensor
- Chemistry-based field-effect transistor
- Sulfur dioxide sensor
- Phosphorous chloride sensor
- Potentiometric detector
- Unbiased infrared sensor

- Nanorod zinc oxide sensor
- Chemiresistor

9.3.3.7   Gyroscope Sensor

Gyroscopic sensors are used to determine the speed of rotation around an axis. They are essential for measuring 3-axis rotational and angular velocity, which provides insights into an object's orientation. These sensors are used across various industries for a wide range of applications, including controlling vehicles, gaming devices, cameras, drones, helicopters, and unmanned aerial vehicles. The type of gyro sensor chosen depends on various factors, such as the environment, range of detection, output type, power requirements, and the underlying mechanism of operation.

- Optical gyroscopes
- Rotary (classical) gyroscopes
- MEMS
- Vibrating structure gyroscopes

Combining accelerometers with gyroscopic sensors enhances the system's performance. This combination provides ample feedback to the system. Devices equipped with gyroscopic sensors can help athletes improve their movements as they have access to information on the athlete's movements during sports activities.

9.3.3.8   Gas Sensor

Gas sensors, like chemical sensors, are designed specifically to detect and monitor changes in the presence of various gases. They have a wide range of applications in industries such as manufacturing, agriculture, and health. These sensors are used to monitor air quality, detect toxic or combustible gases, monitor hazardous gases in coal mines, the oil and gas industry, conduct research in chemical laboratories, and in the manufacturing of products such as paints, plastics, rubber, pharmaceuticals, and petrochemicals. The following examples of typical gas sensors are provided:

- Carbon dioxide sensor
- Carbon monoxide detector
- Oxygen sensor
- Hydrogen sensor
- Catalytic bead sensor
- Hygrometer
- Electrochemical gas sensor
- Nitrogen oxide sensor
- Breathalyzer
- Ozone monitor
- Gas detector
- Air pollution sensor

9.3.4   Issues And Challenges

Sensor has different types of Issues and challenges, some are discussed below:

  I.   Energy Consumption
 II.   Security Challenges
III.   Hardware-Related Issues

9.3.4.1 Energy Consumption

The primary objective of IoT in energy systems is to promote energy efficiency. IoT devices communicate data and connect to the system to make this possible. However, maintaining the IoT system and transmitting the vast amount of data produced by these devices consumes a significant amount of energy. To tackle this issue, reducing the energy consumption of IoT systems is crucial, and various methods have been developed to achieve this. For example, utilizing the sleep mode of the sensors and activating them only when required. Research has also led to the development of energy-efficient communication protocols and techniques like cooperative communication, modulation optimization, and adopting multi-path routing and cluster structures for energy-efficient routing.

9.3.4.2 Security Challenges

The integration of communication technologies in energy systems and the widespread use of IoT devices increases the risk of cyberattacks on user information and energy systems, from production to consumption. This creates a significant challenge for security in the energy industry. Energy sector companies often rely on IoT-based systems to provide services across large distances, making these systems more vulnerable to hacking attempts. To address this issue, researchers have proposed using encryption techniques to protect energy information from cyberattacks.

9.3.4.3 Hardware-related Issues

When designing hardware for IoT devices, it is crucial to consider the necessary features and specifications to meet the requirements of the device. IoT hardware design must take into account the specific needs of the device to ensure it is functional and efficient. IoT manufacturers must carefully consider these factors when creating the hardware for embedded devices.

I. **High Power Dissipation:**
   In order to design a successful embedded hardware system for IoT devices, it is important to balance the increasing number of transistors with manageable power consumption levels. The power usage per transistor increases as the density of gates increases, leading to an overall increase in the system's power consumption. If connected to an IoT gateway, an IoT device can exchange data remotely by having the gateway collect and transmit the data to the cloud while in operation.

II. **Security Concern:**
    Ensuring the security of IoT devices is of utmost importance, as it affects not only those who deal with the software aspect but also the hardware aspect, which must function securely in real-time embedded environments. The hardware design must meet the specifications and requirements of IoT devices, with manufacturers being mindful of these considerations. In order to execute various control operations securely and eliminate potential dangers, security must be integrated into the system architecture, including the use of cryptography. Protecting embedded systems requires the implementation of various strategies throughout the development process, from prototype to final deployment.

III. **Cost Considerations:**
     When developing embedded systems for the IoT, cost, flexibility, and security are major considerations. It's important to take a budget-conscious approach when selecting components for IoT devices, while still maintaining high levels of security. The design process must also be efficient and timely in order to bring embedded products to market quickly. This requires a comprehensive approach that includes system modeling and design, rapid prototyping, analytical verification, embedded system deployment, and consideration of cost limitations. The goal is to provide customers with a seamless experience from silicon design to embedded systems prototyping and from product development to deployment and maintenance.

IV. **Size Constraints:**

The design of IoT-embedded devices presents a challenge due to their compact size and low power requirements. Engineers must find a solution to these restrictions while ensuring the stability of the design. Another challenge arises when these devices are required to be installed in remote areas with limited access.

V. **Testing:**

The hardware design process of IoT products should include a mandatory testing phase. After the product has been developed, it is essential to evaluate its performance, accuracy, and conformity through hardware-based testing tools. This step is critical in determining if the functional verification has been effectively carried out and if the final product meets the specifications and quality standards.

9.3.4.4 *Localization*

The IoT is a technology that allows interconnected devices to communicate with one another, exchange information about our needs and habits, and even take on many of the tasks we currently perform manually. Examples are simple to come up with weather-tracking lawn-maintenance systems, food-recommendation refrigerators, emergency room-connected activity trackers, and intelligent car dashboards. Within the next five years, almost six trillion dollars in infrastructure investment will make IoT devices ubiquitous on every relevant site.

I. **IoT Industries:**

The Industrial IoT, which uses sensors to automatically track, optimize, and automate the operation of connected devices, is an example of IoT that currently exists to some extent in the manufacturing setting. Another sector that anticipates using innovative technology is the utility sector. Electrical grids, for instance, may be configured to precisely match power output to brief needs. Several businesses are already utilizing that technology with intelligent power metering.

II. **Localizing UIs:**

IoT devices will communicate with one another mainly through computer code, but many will still need UIs, or screens, for users to engage. When a particular market sells an IoT gadget, the following crucial aspects still need to be translated and localized:

- Icon labels
- Packaging directions
- Product information
- On-device help systems

III. **Software Development and Release in the IoT are Constant:**

IoT device software is likely to be updated often, unlike desktop PC software; it only needs localization for each release and may be shared for a long product refresh cycle. Manufacturers work in an "agile" atmosphere, constantly making incremental product enhancements. There is no need for user involvement or even awareness. When a bug is detected, the manufacturer can release a patch immediately and distribute it to networked devices. Of course, any time an update modifies the text that a user sees on a device, the updated text needs to be localized for every business client.

IV. **Connecting the IoT:**

By 2020, there will likely be 50 billion active linked IoT devices [21]. With interfaces that can communicate hundreds of languages, they will be everywhere. These pervasive devices constantly change remotely, which presents a massive issue for their providers. There has never been an enormous need for excellent localization services.

V. **Stay up-to-date:**

A new difficulty is keeping a product's UI up-to-date throughout all of one's markets with an ongoing release schedule. You can use the following two options:

- Think smaller, continual localization projects: For language service providers, adjusting to agile product development necessitates an unusually close working relationship with the vendor. To guarantee that localization keeps up with software development, the two must meet frequently and regularly to communicate. Even while the number of languages it demands is enhanced, the amount of text that needs to be unique at any given time is probably not very large. Turnaround times can be pretty short without sacrificing quality for a Language Server Protocol (LSP) like Morning side with a large pool of local language specialists.
- Machine Translation (MT) is another option for expediting IoT text updates when costs are a concern and standards permit.

VI. **Volume of Data:**

A vital component of the IoT is data collection. However, if the data cannot be transformed into a format that can be used, it is effectively useless. For instance, a sensor that detects snowy road conditions beneath your car's tyres is only helpful if it can adequately convey that information. Additionally, the amount of data that might be gathered could quickly become overwhelming. A sensor would produce 1440 data samples per day if it recorded data once every minute [22]. What happens if there are ten sensors, each of which records data once every second? The challenge of translating this volume of data for your international clientele.

Solution

Automated translation, often known as MT, enables higher cost reductions while increasing efficiency. Different from human translation has, which hitherto been financially unavailable, mass data may be handled instantly. The Common Sense Advisory asserts that the steadily increasing usage rates of MT are fundamentally altering the face of the language sector. Is it possible to manually post-edit the MT output for IoT volumes of this size? Unlikely. To increase productivity significantly without lowering quality, a combination of meticulous engine evaluation and adaptation and integrated terminology management will be helpful.

Best is a Two-Pronged Strategy:

i. Strive to produce more MT-friendly controlled source information by emphasizing accurate spelling, punctuation, and transparent structures.

ii. Adjustments and modify your MT engine to ensure high-level coding for rule-based systems or training with clear, high-quality, domain- or client-specific information (such as corpora) for data-driven or hybrid systems.

VII. **The Need for Speed:**

IoT will fundamentally alter how goods are created and distributed across all industries. Software developers will need to adapt to the lengthy release cycles that they have been used to and start responding to updates daily or even hourly. Localization will need to be agile. The IoT maelstrom is set to make things much faster for Language Service Providers (LSPs), who are already accustomed to agile approaches within mobile, cloud computing, and significant data paradigms. Time-sensitive content will be distributed regularly and quickly across various channels and devices. Utilizing automated technology and continuous translation workflows makes sense since your language strategy must be proactive.

Solution

Enable advanced scheduling of translators, reviewers, and engineers by integrating localization into development cycles. A modern, simplified, agile alternative to the more conventional waterfall localization process is provided by the newest Translation Management Systems (TMS), like Smartling.

An additional advantage is an in-context translation. The translation interface in the TMS displays the source text. By eliminating the guessing, translators may make edits in real time. Sizing concerns can be avoided because translators can see the available space; this is crucial for app and smartphone translation. Fewer QA cycles arise from eliminating time-consuming and expensive back-and-forth, or none at all if IoT time restrictions prevent it.

TMS and a qualified LSP will be worthwhile investments for businesses looking to change how their content is produced and consumed globally in an increasingly fast-paced, linked world of intelligent IoT devices.

VIII. **User Experience:**

It is one thing to have excellent tools, platforms, and integration. However, the user, who is the most crucial individual, is frequently overlooked. Success or failure with IoT technology may depend on how the user interacts with it. Users who speak a variety of languages must be able to use linked devices if they are to be widely embraced. IoT device manufacturers must transmit expertly localized content that considers regional idioms, current slang, and social and linguistic trends. Globality will be necessary.

XI. **What Role Does Localization Play?**

Users will demand IoT gadgets and applications that are culturally and linguistically appropriate for them. The user's target market must be reflected in the date, time, temperature scales, measuring systems, currency, and iconography. More audio, video, and animated material will undoubtedly be created to improve the user experience due to changes in digital marketing and consumer purchasing trends. On-screen text will need to be translated, subtitles inserted, and voice-over scripts will need to be transcribed, recorded, and possibly lip-synced. To fulfill IoT user expectations, your LSP will require the newest multimedia localization technologies, access to an immense pool of studios, sound engineers, and voice actors, and a well-planned procedure.

The IoT can enhance the quality of life, boost productivity, encourage safety, and more. The localization industry must prepare and advance in technology and automation to make rapid, efficient, and accurate IoT data translation a reality for all users worldwide. With increased IoT enablement comes accountability.

9.4 Smart System

Businesses that use automated processes, big data analytics, and the IoT are opening up new prospects for IoT. Integrated devices and networked applications are changing industries, as the fourth industrial revolution has shown in the manufacturing industry. By fusing physical and software components through computer-based algorithms, Industry 4.0 re-imagines factories as intelligent or conscious and enables decentralized decision-making and computer-controlled behavior. Utilizing Big Data analytics, recognition, discovery, and opportunity are made possible by incorporating IoT data from sensors, devices, media, apps, and the open web into context-aware systems known as Smart Systems. Predictive models can be built using statistical methods like data mining and algorithmic techniques like machine learning to forecast future events and identify non-events. Such analysis enables Smart Systems to command their surroundings or use actuators to perform physical actions. These technologies can be used to provide entirely specialized solutions for specific industrial sectors.

9.4.1 Emerging Trend of Smart System

A "smart city" is a location where residents use Information and Communication Technology (ICT) to enhance operational efficiency, share knowledge with the public, raise the bar for public services, and promote the welfare of their fellow citizens. A smart city uses data analytics and intelligent technology to optimize city services, promote economic growth, and improve the quality of life for its citizens; however, the precise definition varies. How a city uses technology, not how much of it has, determines how valuable a city it is. ICT is employed in smart cities to improve operational efficiency, share information with the public, and improve the standard of public services and the quality of life for its citizens. Several crucial characteristics define the intelligence of a person. They include the following characteristics:

- A technological base; environmental initiatives
- Solid system of public transportation
- The ability to plan cities
- City dwellers who work in the city

9.4.2 Success of Smart City

A fundamental element of a smart city's success is its capacity to forge strong bonds between the public and private sectors, including bureaucracy and regulations. It takes much work outside of government to create and maintain a digital, data-driven environment, which is why this relationship is required. The tools used to monitor congested roadways may include sensors, cameras, and various manufacturers' servers. The city administration may also pay outside consultants to review the data and produce a report. The challenges raised by big data may then be addressed by an application development team established using this data. This company might join the system if the solution requires frequent updating and maintenance. Therefore, the success of a smart city depends more on developing solid relationships than on completing a single project. The city administration may also pay independent contractors to analyze the data and produce a report. Correcting the difficulties revealed by the data analysis may then be assigned to an application development team created utilizing this data. If the system requires continuous updates and maintenance, this company might sign up for it. Because of this, the success of a smart city depends more on developing solid relationships than on completing a single project.

9.4.2.1 Benefits for Citizens

The advantages are available to residents of smart cities.

- Intelligent living environment
- Unreliable connectivity
- Services that are easy to access
- improved resource management
- intelligent government and making good decisions

9.4.2.2 Smart Grid and Energy Management

An electricity network that supports two-way communication is known as a smart grid. Electricity and data use digital communication technology to monitor, respond to, and take action on changes in usage and other issues. Electricity customers can take an active role in self-healing smart grids. The global "go green" movement and the energy crisis have encouraged the grid integration of renewable energy sources, plug-in electric automobiles, and energy storage technologies. Multiple energy sources are used in the grid; hence a robust energy management system is required to regulate the energy flow. Additional challenges for power engineers in achieving a demand-supply balance for a stable power system include the instability and volatility of renewable energy sources, the unknowns surrounding plug-in electric vehicles, the price of electricity, and time-varying load. The energy management system must properly coordinate energy trading across all available energy sources and provide loads affordably under all circumstances for the power to be dependable, secure, and efficient.

9.5   Conclusion and Future Work

The IoT improves people's lives by fusing the Internet with tangible objects. The IoT will improve human comfort while making things more innovative and effective. The versatility of IoT will soon surpass that of all other emerging technologies. This chapter discusses several IoT applications and their impacts on society. This study will also help academics and industry professionals understand potential IoT research problems that might result in future research trends.

IoT and its new tendencies were then covered. The world is becoming a "Smart Global Village" thanks to the rapid growth of smart systems. A few popular smart systems are also addressed. In conclusion, it can be said that the combination of 'sensors' and 'IoT' makes any system a 'smart system.'

There are still many future challenges that need some attention. Such as meeting the Universal Standards, in order to connect with such a diverse array of devices, universal standards are required. Despite the Internet Engineering Task Force (IETF) and European Telecommunications Standards Institute (ETSI) organizations creating standards for the IoT, finding a single, global communication standard remains a challenging research problem. Furthermore, Given the trillions of linked devices that exist globally, we want an identity management solution that offers effective global IoT device addressing. Moreover, the IoT can send sensitive financial data, such as PINs, for accounts and private information. Encryption is therefore required for secure communication. To avoid these eventualities, IoT security technology is essential. The writers concentrate on security-related problems.

Since data can be transported from one location to another, IOT will positively impact the automation business. Additionally, data analysis will enable us to predict them by comparing them to previous and present ones. IoT and cloud computing will work together in cities to analyze and make smart judgments to reduce car traffic and identify traffic. The IOT sector will offer an opportunity for entrepreneurs looking to start technological businesses and will surely help many individuals find work. There will be a high demand for IOT in the near future.

IoT can be used in any environment or sector. Anything we use daily can be made more intelligent, like a device connected to the grid or the Internet. It enhances the grid as a whole as well as that device's effectiveness, efficiency, and precision. IoT has many possible applications. The only sector that has advanced is home and industrial automation. Research and development are ongoing in several sectors, including biomedicine, security, smart cities, and others.

In the distant future, any device might be online, no matter how little. Digital security would become the newest in-demand skill because every tiny detail would be logged on enormous servers. Other predictions suggest that an increase in smart technology use might improve public infrastructure, encourage comparable investments in wireless power networks, and speed the development of transportation options like e-bikes and scooters, electric cars, and even driverless cars.

Lastly, IoT devices have far lesser processing and energy capacity than everyday Internet-connected devices; we must create encryption techniques suitable for IoT in the future. The IoT links different gadgets together so they may talk and exchange data. The energy requirements of devices would rise due to processing this massive data. The linked IoT devices will be affected. We need to use specialized energy-saving methods to improve IoT devices' energy efficiency. If IoT applications are to live up to their potential in the real world, these scientific issues need to be answered as quickly as is practical.

REFERENCES

1. A. Dugdale, "The inventor of the barcode, norman joseph woodland, dies at 92," Mar 2014.
2. Immerse, "A brief history of VR (and how it's set to change language education forever)," Jul 2022.
3. E. Thorp and E. Associates, "The invention of the first wearable computer," Jun 1999.
4. J. Scammells, "History of the Internet of Things (IoT): It blog," Dec 2020.
5. K. A. Popat and P. Sharma, "Wearable computer applications a future perspective," *International Journal of Engineering and Innovative Technology*, vol. 3, no. 1, pp. 213–217, 2013.

6. R. Rosenzweig, "Wizards, bureaucrats, warriors, and hackers: Writing the history of the internet," *The American Historical Review*, vol. 103, no. 5, pp. 1530–1552, 1998.

7. Y. Cheung, K. Choy, C. Lau and Y. Leung, "The impact of RFID technology on the formulation of logistics strategy," pp. 1673–1680, Aug 2008.

8. "A brief history of the barcode," Jul 2020.

9. M. Satyanarayanan, "The emergence of edge computing," *Computer*, vol. 50, no. 1, pp. 30–39, 2017.

10. J. Romkey, "Toast of the IoT: The 1990 interop internet toaster," *IEEE Consumer Electronics Magazine*, vol. 6, no. 1, pp. 116–119, 2016.

11. R. Kesby, "How the world's first webcam made a coffee pot famous," Nov 2012.

12. F. Bonaglia, A. Goldstein and J. A. Mathews, "Accelerated internationalization by emerging markets' multinationals: The case of the white goods sector," *Journal of World Business*, vol. 42, no. 4, pp. 369–383, 2007.

13. J. D. Akkara, A. Kuriakose, *et al.*, "Innovative smartphone apps for ophthalmologists," *Kerala Journal of Ophthalmology*, vol. 30, no. 2, p. 138, 2018.

14. E. R. Teoh and D. G. Kidd, "Rage against the machine? Google's self-driving cars versus human drivers," *Journal of Safety Research*, vol. 63, pp. 57–60, 2017.

15. D. Kushner, "The making of arduino," *IEEE Spectrum*, vol. 26, pp. 1–7, 2011.

16. R. Kester, "Demystifying the internet of things: Industry impact, standardization problems, and legal considerations," *Elon Law Review*, vol. 8, p. 205, 2016.

17. F. Dahlqvist, M. Patel, A. Rajko and J. Shulman, "Growing opportunities in the internet of things," *McKinsey & Company*, pp. 1–6, 2019.

18. M. A. Jan, J. Cai, X.-C. Gao, F. Khan, S. Mastorakis, M. Usman, M. Alazab and P. Watters, "Security and blockchain convergence with internet of multimedia things: Current trends, research challenges and future directions," *Journal of Network and Computer Applications*, vol. 175, p. 102918, 2021.

19. H. Espinoza, G. Kling, F. McGroarty, M. O'Mahony and X. Ziouvelou, "Estimating the impact of the internet of things on productivity in Europe," *Heliyon*, vol. 6, no. 5, p. e03935, 2020.

20. H. Yasuura, C.-M. Kyung, Y. Liu and Y.-L. Lin, *Smart sensors at the IoT frontier*. Springer, 2017.

21. J. Asharf, N. Moustafa, H. Khurshid, E. Debie, W. Haider and A. Wahab, "A review of intrusion detection systems using machine and deep learning in internet of things: Challenges, solutions and future directions," *Electronics*, vol. 9, no. 7, p. 1177, 2020.

22. J. Wimmer, M. Towsey, P. Roe and I. Williamson, "Sampling environmental acoustic recordings to determine bird species richness," *Ecological Applications*, vol. 23, no. 6, pp. 1419–1428, 2013.

10

Blockchain Development in Industries: A Systematic Review

Mohammad S. Obaidat
University of Jordan, Amman, Jordan
University of Science and Technology Beijing, Beijing, China
SRM University, India
Amity University, Noida, India

Pankaj Pal
Indian Institute of Technology(ISM), Dhanbad, India

10.1   Introduction

In recent times, blockchain technologies have become increasingly popular in both scientific and industrial domains because of their potential benefits across various sectors. This is because they can be applied practically to solve several issues that are currently hindering progress in many industrial fields [1]. These challenges include the secured gathering and exchange of large datasets, the establishment of intelligent and automated supply chain operations, and the improvement of transparency throughout the entire supply chain. Using decentralized, shared, permission-based, and secure transaction ledgers, blockchain efficiently addresses these concerns. Utilizing blockchain technology and the capacity to use it in a variety of contexts offers several commercial applications with a better level of security, improved accountability and transparency, and decreased costs. This chapter reviews the many commercial application fields where blockchain technology has been presented.

Numerous sectors and scholars have been drawn to blockchain technology due to its great potential. There are already over 3000 blockchain-based cryptocurrencies on the marketplace, and this figure continues to increase [2]. In addition to digital cryptocurrencies, blockchain technology has also been applied to the Internet of Things (IoT), medicine, finance, software, and academia, among others [3]. The rapid spread of the COVID-19 pandemic has brought to light the limitations of the technology that was previously in use. This has encouraged the implementation of blockchain technology in a variety of contexts, including the tracking of contacts, the sharing of medical information, the management of supply chains, and various immigration procedures. Deployments of blockchain-based platforms are now utilized by nearly every sector due to their capacity to offer time-stamped and irreversible transactional history [4]. Given that there is no centralized regulating authority over the blockchain, all the parties involved within the ecosystem are responsible for its maintenance. General agreement procedures are used to analyze and modify the information stored on the blockchain.

By leveraging a decentralized system of nodes, the blockchain significantly lowers the likelihood of a single point of failure as well as network intrusions. By time stamping entries, the usage of the decentralized network helps to decrease instances of fraud. Additionally, information about users is maintained in a public blockchain throughout the network via smart contacts. Blockchain

DOI:10.1201/9781003326236-10

removes manual operations such as reconciliation across several separate ledgers and administrative procedures, hence reducing the system's complexity. The transaction speed and degree of security are both significantly improved as a direct result of using a variety of cryptographic linked chains. As part of their investigation into how blockchain technology may facilitate Industry 4.0, the researchers have performed a number of surveys, the results of which are presented here.

Blockchain technology has changed healthcare, but there are still many unanswered questions and problems to be solved, as discussed in Refs. [3, 5, 6]. The present context of blockchain technology, as well as the open issues and challenges associated with it, was examined in Refs. [7, 8]. They have also examined the blockchain's usefulness for numerous intelligent applications. Authors in Ref. [9] examined the many elements of blockchains, including distributed procedures and the data integrity of the ledger, which makes the network hard to manipulate. Authors in Ref. [10] examined blockchain potential in public healthcare. Furthermore, they have explored the ways in which blockchain eliminates centralized control in the verification process, its use of digital certificates to ensure secure data storage, its structure, and the challenges that come with it. Authors in Ref. [11] studied the parameters of decentralized applications using blockchain technology. Authors in Ref. [12] investigated a sophisticated blockchain infrastructure for electronic healthcare systems. They centered their attention on the regulatory compliance of blockchain regarding data privacy, as well as its design, constraints, and advantages. Authors in Ref. [13] investigated the use of blockchain technology in educational settings.

The goal of this chapter is to examine the present studies in the field of blockchain based on several classifications and to highlight the opportunities where future blockchain development must be directed in order to keep up with the advancement of technology. Particularly, this chapter examines scholarly articles discussing blockchain published between 2016 and 2021 according to the SCI/SSCI database.

10.2 Blockchain Application in Industries

In this section, we have presented a brief survey on the use of blockchain technology in different industrial applications.

The IoT is a model establishes the groundwork for a future where numerous devices we engage with regularly will be connected to each other and their environment. This will enable them to gather data and simplify various tasks [14]. This goal necessitates, among many other factors, seamless certification, data protection, security, attack resilience, simple implementation, and self-maintenance [3]. At present, most IoT solutions rely on a centralized server-client architecture, where they communicate with cloud servers over the Internet. While this approach may work well currently, future growth suggests the need for alternative frameworks. In the past, decentralized designs, such as Peer-to-Peer (P2P) Wireless Sensor Networks (WSNs), have been suggested for creating large networks [15, 16]; however, there were gaps in terms of privacy and security. As a result, in recent years, pre IoT closed and centralized mainframe frameworks have transitioned toward IoT open-access cloud-centered alternatives [17]. This marks the next phase in the dispersal of cloud capabilities across multiple peers, and blockchain technology can aid in this regard.

In addition to cryptocurrencies and smart contracts, blockchain technologies have the potential to be implemented in a variety of other domains that involve the IoT. These encompass a range of applications such as sensing, storage of data, management of identity, provision of timestamp services, applications for smart living, systems for intelligent transportation, wearables, management of the supply chain, mobile crowd sensing, cybersecurity law, and security in critical scenarios.

Blockchain technology also has potential uses in IoF farming systems [1, 18–26]. For instance, a traceability system for tracing the suppliers of agricultural and food products in China is outlined in Ref. [27]. The system uses Radio Frequency Identification (RFID) tags and a blockchain to improve food quality and security while cutting down on logistical waste.

There has been some investigation into the potential use of blockchain technology in the administration of devices that are linked to the IoT [3]. This field of study provides a method that makes it possible to remotely operate and configure devices that are connected to the IoT. For instance, under the Ethereum architecture, public keys are stored by the system itself on Ethereum, whereas private keys are stored locally on each IoT device. According to literature, authors argue that blockchain adoption is critical because it enables them to develop their own programs that can operate on top of the network. Additionally, modifying the code on the blockchain alters the actions of IoT devices, simplifying the process of managing and resolving any problems that might occur.

As with other businesses, combining blockchain technology with the IoT will benefit the energy industry [28]. In the scientific literature, a number of academics have suggested a blockchain-based technology that would allow IoF devices to pay each other automatically for services rendered. In Ref. [29], the potential of this system is highlighted by showcasing an IoT framework that demonstrates how a smart cable connected to a smart socket can be utilized to pay for the electricity consumed. The researchers also present a micro-payment protocol that combines multiple small payments into one larger transaction, effectively lowering the transaction fees of cryptocurrencies [30].

Numerous blockchain-based IoF healthcare applications are discussed in published research. In Ref. [31], for instance, the authors describe a traceability application that uses IoT sensors and blockchain technology to verify the data's integrity and enable public access to temperature records in the pharmaceutical supply chain. This verification is crucial for the transportation of medical supplies, ensuring both their quality and the conditions in which they are kept. Therefore, each and every package that is sent out has a sensor that sends the data that it has gathered to the blockchain, where an intelligent contract checks to ensure that the measurements that have been received are still within the accepted level. In Ref. [32], another example of the use of BIoT technology in the healthcare sector is elaborated, wherein the authors outline the framework of a blockchain-based platform for clinical trials and precision medicine. Additionally, Ref. [33] explores the potential of IoT devices, the cloud, and fog computing in a comprehensive study that proposes an intelligent healthcare system.

10.2.1   Financial Industry

By adopting blockchain systems, banks and other financial institutions may avoid dealing with a number of persistent problems. A lack of credit score information is a major issue in the banking sector, making it hard for individuals and small and medium-sized enterprises (SMEs) to get loans [34]. Financial institutions also have trouble doing accurate customer profiling because they don't have enough accurate information. This makes it hard for them to differentiate their products and make them more personal. In a similar fashion, financial institutions' insurance products include a convoluted insurance claims procedure that calls for the participation of many parties prior to the claim's finalization and payment. Finally, the bulk of financial companies' transactions are facilitated by existing vital infrastructures, which are the main targets of cyberattacks.

When onboarding a client, all financial institutions begin Know Your Customer (KYC) and Know Your Business (KYB) procedures [35]. As a part of this activity, the client will be recognized and validated in accordance with the relevant laws and norms that have been established by authorities at both the national and international levels. Due to the fact that both client information and applicable laws are subject to change over time, the KYC/KYB procedure is a dynamic operation. As a result, the task of updating records and related documents may be fairly difficult. One solution is for a governing body to centrally store and update paperwork pertaining to individual customers. However, this is a solution that may easily be breached by attackers. By decentralizing and protecting the KYC operation, blockchain technology may help address the aforementioned problems. In particular, by storing customer information in a distributed ledger, blockchain participants will have a single, shared source of truth for all client data and may update it as required for a more complete view of each customer's profile.

These days, most banks see small and medium-sized businesses as high-risk clients. This is true not just for the smallest of businesses but also for those that are somewhat larger and more prosperous. It is mostly the result of more substantial restrictions that have been adopted as a response to the financial crisis that occurred in 2008. However, it is also a question of declining returns on equity, which has made it even more difficult for small and medium-sized businesses to get financing. In this setting, banks need creative methods for rating the creditworthiness of SMEs that don't rely only on traditional financial and accounting information. Methods like this may benefit not only from the possibilities of data sharing between financial institutions but also from the availability of large quantities of alternative data, like data from social media, news, and other Internet sources [36]. Technologies based on blockchain make it possible for numerous parties to share securely information on their credit scores. Each of the collaborating organizations provides data that may be used to evaluate the dependability of SMEs in order to ease the decision-making process about loans. The technique is distributed, which lowers the likelihood of information on credit risk scores being stolen or otherwise tampered with. In addition, the grading of credit risk is carried out without the disclosure of confidential information. It is essential to remember that the value of a blockchain of this kind improves not only with the number of people who contribute to it but also with the amount and quality of the information they supply. The accuracy of the credit risk assessments is directly correlated to the number of banks that participate in the blockchain project and work together [37].

10.2.2 Healthcare Industry

Healthcare is often cited as an area where blockchain might have a significant impact [3, 5, 6]. A number of experts have recently brought attention to the possibility of using blockchain technology to solve issues that already exist in healthcare applications.

In order to revolutionize healthcare, the primary emphasis must be placed on the processing of information, which stands to gain from the possibility of integrating previously separate units and boosting the precision of Electronic Health Records (EHR). Access control, data sharing, and keeping an audit trail of clinical practices are just some ways that blockchain technology may be used to assist prescriptions and supply chain management, pregnancy and any risk data management, and other areas of healthcare. Other sectors of healthcare that potentially benefit using blockchain technology include physician credentials, medical billing, contracts, patient records sharing, clinical trials, and anti-counterfeit medications. The evolution of healthcare services is facilitating a patient-centered strategy. Since individuals would be in charge of their own medical records, blockchain-based healthcare solutions might increase the security and dependability of patient information [10]. These technologies might also facilitate the consolidation of patient information, hence facilitating the transmission of medical information among various healthcare organizations. The storage of medical information about patients is crucial in healthcare. In addition to being vulnerable, this information is also a great target for cyberattacks. It is vital to safeguard all sensitive information. Another component is the optimum management of health information by the patient. Therefore, exchanging and obtaining control of patients' health records is another use instance that may profit from sophisticated current technology. The distributed ledger system is resistant to assaults and failures and includes several access control techniques. Consequently, blockchain offers a solid foundation for healthcare data. For private medical information, a private blockchain could be the best type of blockchain. According to the decision model developed by Würst and Gervais, a blockchain may be used in a circumstance in which several parties that do not trust each other are required to communicate and share common data but would prefer not to include a trusted third party in the process [38, 39]. The healthcare profession handles many sensitive information and records governed by strict regulations. These kinds of documents are often kept in a centralized database, which may give rise to a variety of problems, including those relating to security and interoperability. In Ref. [40], the authors offered a possible solution to this issue that utilizes Ethereum Blockchain Tools to develop a shared network architecture. The Network eliminates the restrictions of centralized archiving by giving all healthcare practitioners access to the identical healthcare data. This may aid in reducing the danger of medical negligence resulting from out-of-date information and in preventing any health problems that may develop as a result of this misinformation. It has been stated that Estonia has worked along with Guardtime, which is a service for healthcare that employs blockchain technology [41]. By using this technology, Estonian individuals, Estonian healthcare professionals, and Estonian health insurance companies are able to recover any medical procedures that have been carried out inside Estonia.

10.2.3   Logistics Industry

The use of blockchain technology by the freight logistics sector is currently in its inception. There has been a lot of research into the use of blockchains in other contexts, such as supply chain management, healthcare record keeping, and transparent government elections, but how freight logistics managers would utilize blockchains is less apparent [37]. Freight logistics may have a significant demand for digital advancements since its activities are often dispersed across regions and organizations, and information management flows are crucial for operational effectiveness. Recently, as a result of the proliferation of digital technology, the logistical freight industry's operating environment has been undergoing significant changes.

Many logistics experts believe that blockchains provide immense opportunities to revolutionize supply chains, and their adoption is anticipated to have far-reaching ramifications for the logistics industry. Although it is reasonable to anticipate that blockchains will bring about significant benefits that could provide a push in the adoption of technology, it is typical for freight logistics companies to make use of technologies that are straightforward and well-established rather than advanced technologies. The limited existing literature on the integration of blockchains into the freight logistics sector implies that adoption may prove challenging, with distinct contextual prospects that remain to be fully understood. According to Ref. [42], blockchains have the potential to assist shipping and logistics companies in real-time monitoring of material movements, improving transport handling, and enabling precise risk control. The combination of IoTs and blockchains has great potential for freight logistics and may be one of its most promising applications. With IoT sensors gathering real-world data, the regular tracking of shipment locations becomes more convenient. The utilization of IoT, AI, and smart contracts in logistics has produced a significant revolution, particularly in the transport of sensitive pharmaceuticals. A Swiss business created air freight carriers for chilled biopharmaceuticals using SkyCell sensors that track temperature, humidity, and location, therefore lowering temperature variation to less than 0.1% [43]. In the domain of freight logistics, the use of smart contracts enabled by blockchain technology has the potential to bring about significant cost reductions and improvements in operational efficiency. Using Ethereum-based smart contracts, for instance, a proof of delivery model for physical assets in the logistics industry has been developed to enable the tracking of items along with the incentive and payment process for clients and carriers. However, the majority of logistics experts must comprehend the idea of blockchain and learn how to use the technology to the advantage of their organizations. It is of the utmost importance to give concrete insights and a comprehensive knowledge of the key parameters that might support the effective implementation of blockchains by the freight logistics business.

10.2.4   Manufacturing Industry

In the Industry 4.0 blueprint, the need for intelligent, personalized, and sustainable goods resulted in the rise of new creative manufacturing paradigms [44]. The Industrial Internet will enable machines with a certain level of interaction capabilities to collaborate with one another under the Industry 4.0 concept. Data pertaining to production on a massive scale will be shared constantly. It will be possible for machines to make autonomous judgments at the local level, which will undoubtedly have an impact on the production process as a whole. However, further resources are required to address security concerns in these developing Industry 4.0 production models [45]. Existing industrial automation systems often include security flaws that make production data vulnerable to attack or tampering. Erroneous and manipulated data will result in inaccurate controls or decisions, posing a severe hazard to interconnected, and sophisticated production systems. Existing production management often depends on a centralized platform that lacks proper information traceability and is susceptible to system breakdowns.

Utilizing blockchain is one option for addressing this security problem; blockchain's features provide prospective advances for industrial systems, particularly to ensure cybersecurity. Blockchain might eliminate involvement from third parties that may not contribute direct value via intelligent contracts with inherent and strong cybersecurity measures, allowing for cheaper transaction costs. Practitioners must be well aware of the benefits of blockchain in disrupting the control and administration of industrial processes.

In terms of manufacturing systems, blockchain could serve as an enabler for existing factory information systems such as enterprise resource planning (ERP) and manufacturing execution system (MES), according to Ref. [46]. At the workshop level, the blockchain functions as an indexing server to monitor component production and facilitate factory automation. The utilization of blockchain in business facilitates the creation of a trustworthy environment for distributed manufacturers to organize their interconnectivity and service interactions through a transparent credit mechanism and decentralization. Nodes from various manufacturers can easily exchange data with each other, with all relevant information about orders, transactions, and product tracking being securely recorded on an unalterable distributed ledger. Smart contracts can also be utilized to automate scheduling and planning processes, increasing overall efficiency.

As more socialized capabilities, stakeholders, and technological expertise are included in the product lifecycle, the product management viewpoint on lifecycle activities is getting more complicated [44]. The necessity for the protection of intellectual property, security concerns, and difficulties of trust make the transmission and administration of product-related information difficult. Blockchain may offer the product lifecycle management community a mechanism to construct a centralized database for sharing product information and concluding transactions, allowing untrusted manufacturers to freely trade their capabilities and needs. This measure enables manufacturers to establish improved connections with each other and with end customers. At this level of blockchain integration, decisions are not made by the board of directors but rather by a set of consensus algorithms and smart contracts. The deal-making process of product lifecycle management, including preliminary bidding, the billing system, utilization monitoring, and resource management, can be automated using smart contracts and cryptocurrencies [44].

10.2.5 Energy Industry

As a result of the energy revolution, the use of renewable energy is fast expanding. The architecture of energy distribution networks is getting more decentralized [28]. Prosumers/consumers, who create and use their own power, might become new participants in the electricity market [47]. However, owing to their limited capacity, prosumers cannot engage economically in power trading at this time. The digitization of the energy revolution is particularly necessary due to the rising complexity of control, the burden on network infrastructure, the strict requirements for data security, and the links between the trade of power and the related electricity bills.

The energy sector will likely see a big influence from blockchain in the mid and long-term. The potential economic worth of blockchain technology is based on the qualities of the technology itself, which include decentralization, security, transparency, and automation. But in addition to technical difficulties like the impending rollout of smart meters, the necessity of a smart meter gateway for information exchange, and the interoperability of smart metering systems with the blockchain, there are also regulatory and legal barriers that make the use of the blockchain challenging in the short term. The peer-to-peer trade of decentralized power from renewable sources is probably the most frequently debated use of blockchain in the energy industry.

10.2.6 Agriculture and Food Industry

There has been a massive rise in the flow of goods and data across international borders as a result of the globalization of Food Supply Chains (FSC) and marketplaces [22, 48, 49]. Strong vertical integration and cooperation among supply chain stakeholders define traditional FSC, which benefits the community by reducing transaction, operational, and marketing expenses and satisfying customer expectations for food quality and safety. Consequently, FSC exchange partners are under growing demand to increase the openness of global supply chains, boost the sharing of trustworthy information, and enhance the monitoring and tracing capabilities of agricultural goods from farmers to shops [50].

The necessity for adequate traceability has increased as standards mandate that the origin of each component in a food product can be traceable. Many agricultural goods are now available year-round in response to consumer demand, which has increased the need for firms to provide information about the product quality, authenticity, traceability, origin, and supply circumstances. New technologies are being introduced as a result of the increased need for information. RFID technology is one tool used in FSCs to improve transparency and traceability, cut down on food waste, enable forward monitoring, streamline operations, collect data automatically, avoid mistakes when fulfilling orders, and keep supply chain circumstances and methods under intelligent control. Cloud computing systems are used to store information about food goods, and this information is made available to merchants and customers through websites or mobile barcode scans. The authors of Ref. [51] stated that cloud computing provides brief messaging services in agricultural supply chains, which include information on weather conditions, the correct application of pesticides, disease outbreak notifications, and government incentives. Despite the fact that these technologies are driving FSC toward a technological and data-driven food economy, some basic issues remain unsolved. For instance, the FSC is not continuously monitored, and the remaining shelf life of fresh goods cannot be predicted. Similarly, the traditional food monitoring system is hampered by data fragmentation, a lack of transparency due to data discrepancies and inconsistencies, inadequate interoperability, and a lack of information traceability. FSC experts and practitioners envisage using blockchain technology in the food business to transform how FSC are conceived, created, structured, and maintained to solve these issues. According to the authors of [50], blockchain technology has the capacity to influence future supply chain rules and practices by enhancing visibility and traceability. Similarly, it may enhance conventional supply chain processes defined by a dominant player operating as a central third-party provider imposing their own rules, governance framework, and centralized structures.

10.3   Conclusion

In this chapter, the use of blockchain technology in various industries was introduced. The review of several case studies revealed that blockchain has received considerable investments. However, despite its benefits, scalability concerns remain an issue. The industry has been relying on the traditional centralized approach for data sharing, which is considered to be safer compared to the decentralized approach that blockchain offers. The centralized approach has been in practice for a long time now. The current scenario is set to transform with the advent of blockchain that offers potential solutions for security and integrity concerns. The suitability of blockchain in several sectors such as healthcare, manufacturing, logistics, and agriculture has been examined, along with its applicability in IoT-related industries. Furthermore, challenges faced by these industries while implementing blockchain were also discussed. To ensure blockchain is fully usable and customizable, there needs to be industry-oriented research to overcome these challenges such as ensuring personal data protection and the scalability of block data.

REFERENCES

1. M. N. M. Bhutta, A. A. Khwaja, A. Nadeem, H. F. Ahmad, M. K. Khan, M. A. Hanif, H. Song, M. Alshamari, and Y. Cao, "A survey on blockchain technology: Evolution, architecture and security," *IEEE Access*, vol. 9, pp. 61 048–61 073, 2021.
2. J. Wu, J. Liu, Y. Zhao, and Z. Zheng, "Analysis of cryptocurrency transactions from a network perspective: An overview," *Journal of Network and Computer Applications*, vol. 190, p. 103139, 2021.
3. P. Ratta, A. Kaur, S. Sharma, M. Shabaz, and G. Dhiman, "Application of blockchain and internet of things in healthcare and medical sector: Applications, challenges, and future perspectives," *Journal*

of Food Quality, vol. 2021, pp. 1–20, 2021.

4. E. Karafiloski, and A. Mishev, "Blockchain solutions for big data challenges: A literature review," in *IEEE EUROCON 2017-17th International Conference on Smart Technologies*. IEEE, 2017, pp. 763–768.

5. I. Yaqoob, K. Salah, R. Jayaraman, and Y. Al-Hammadi, "Blockchain for healthcare data management: Opportunities, challenges, and future recommendations," *Neural Computing and Applications*, vol. 34, no. 14, pp. 11 475–11 490, 2022.

6. H. Fatoum, S. Hanna, J. D. Halamka, D. C. Sicker, P. Spangenberg, S. K. Hashmi *et al.*, "Blockchain integration with digital technology and the future of health care ecosystems: Systematic review," *Journal of Medical Internet Research*, vol. 23, no. 11, p. e19846, 2021.

7. E. Kapassa, M. Themistocleous, K. Christodoulou, and E. Iosif, "Blockchain application in internet of vehicles: Challenges, contributions and current limitations," *Future Internet*, vol. 13, no. 12, p. 313, 2021.

8. S. Alam, M. Shuaib, W. Z. Khan, S. Garg, G. Kaddoum, M. S. Hossain, and Y. B. Zikria, "Blockchain-based initiatives: Current state and challenges," *Computer Networks*, vol. 198, p. 108395, 2021.

9. A. T. Sherman, F. Javani, H. Zhang, and E. Golaszewski, "On the origins and variations of blockchain technologies," *IEEE Security & Privacy*, vol. 17, no. 1, pp. 72–77, 2019.

10. M. Weiss, A. Botha, M. Herselman, and G. Loots, "Blockchain as an enabler for public mhealth solutions in south africa," in *2017 IST-Africa Week Conference (IST-Africa)*. IEEE, 2017, pp. 1–8.

11. R. Zhang, R. Xue, and L. Liu, "Security and privacy on blockchain," *ACM Computing Surveys (CSUR)*, vol. 52, no. 3, pp. 1–34, 2019.

12. T. McGhin, K.-K. R. Choo, C. Z. Liu, and D. He, "Blockchain in healthcare applications: Research challenges and opportunities," *Journal of Network and Computer Applications*, vol. 135, pp. 62–75, 2019.

13. R. Raimundo, and A. Rosário, "Blockchain system in the higher education," *European Journal of Investigation in Health, Psychology and Education*, vol. 11, no. 1, pp. 276–293, 2021.

14. R. P. Sharma, D. Ramesh, P. Pal, S. Tripathi, and C. Kumar, "IoT-enabled IEEE 802.15.4 WSN monitoring infrastructure-driven fuzzy-logic-based crop pest prediction," *IEEE Internet of Things Journal*, vol. 9, no. 4, pp. 3037–3045, 2022.

15. S. Pandey, P. Pal, and A. Mukherjee, "IRF-NMB: intelligent route formation technique in Ad Hoc network using node mobility behaviour," *National Academy Science Letters*, vol. 38, no. 3, pp. 213–219, 2015.

16. S. Pandey, and P. Pal, "SPIN-MI: Energy saving routing algorithm based on spin protocol in WSN," *National Academy Science Letters*, vol. 37, no. 4, pp. 335–339, 2014.

17. M. A. Aleisa, A. Abuhussein, F. S. Alsubaei, and F. T. Sheldon, "Examining the performance of fog-aided, cloud-centered iot in a real-world environment," *Sensors*, vol. 21, no. 21, p. 6950, 2021.

18. P. Pal, R. P. Sharma, S. Tripathi, C. Kumar, and D. Ramesh, "NSGA-III based heterogeneous transmission range selection for node deployment in IEEE 802.15.4 infrastructure for sugarcane and rice crop monitoring in a humid sub-tropical region," *IEEE Transactions on Wireless Communications*, vol. 22, p. 1, 2022.

19. P. Pal, S. Tripathi, and C. Kumar, "Single probe imitation of multi-depth capacitive soil moisture sensor using bidirectional recurrent neural network," *IEEE Transactions on Instrumentation and Measurement*, vol. 71, pp. 1–11, 2022.

20. P. Pal, R. P. Sharma, S. Tripathi, C. Kumar, and D. Ramesh, "Machine learning regression for RF path loss estimation over grass vegetation in IOWSN monitoring infrastructure," *IEEE Transactions on Industrial Informatics*, vol. 18, no. 10, pp. 6981–6990, 2022.

21. R. Priya, D. Ramesh, and V. Udutalapally, "NSGA-2 optimized fuzzy inference system for crop plantation correctness index identification," *IEEE Transactions on Sustainable Computing*, vol. 7, no. 1, pp. 172–188, 2022.

22. R. Priya, and D. Ramesh, "Ml based sustainable precision agriculture: A future generation perspective," *Sustainable Computing: Informatics and Systems*, vol. 28, p. 100439, 2020 [Online]. Available: https://www.sciencedirect.com/science/article/pii/S2210537920301669

23. E. Khosla, R. Dharavath, and R. Priya, "Crop yield prediction using aggregated rainfall-based modular artificial neural networks and support vector regression," *Environment, Development and*

Sustainability, vol. 22, no. 6, pp. 5687–5708, 2020.

24. R. Priya, D. Ramesh, and E. Khosla, "Biodegradation of pesticides using density-based clustering on cotton crop affected by xanthomonas malvacearum," *Environment, Development and Sustainability*, vol. 22, no. 2, pp. 1353–1369, 2020.

25. R. Priya and D. Ramesh, "Adaboost. RT based soil NPK prediction model for soil and crop specific data: A predictive modelling approach," in *International Conference on Big Data Analytics*. Springer, 2018, pp. 322–331.

26. R. Priya, D. Ramesh, and E. Khosla, "Crop prediction on the region belts of india: A naïve bayes mapreduce precision agricultural model," in *2018 International Conference on Advances in Computing, Communications and Informatics (ICACCI)*, 2018, pp. 99–104.

27. B. Yan, P. Shi, and G. Huang, "Development of traceability system of aquatic foods supply chain based on RFID and EPC internet of things," *Transactions of the Chinese Society of Agricultural Engineering*, vol. 29, no. 15, pp. 172–183, 2013.

28. M. Andoni, V. Robu, D. Flynn, S. Abram, D. Geach, D. Jenkins, P. McCallum, and A. Peacock, "Blockchain technology in the energy sector: A systematic review of challenges and opportunities," *Renewable and Sustainable Energy Reviews*, vol. 100, pp. 143–174, 2019.

29. P. K. Sharma, N. Kumar, and J. H. Park, "Blockchain technology toward green IoT: Opportunities and challenges," *IEEE Network*, vol. 34, no. 4, pp. 263–269, 2020.

30. T. Lundqvist, A. De Blanche, and H. R. H. Andersson, "Thing-to-thing electricity micro payments using blockchain technology," in *2017 Global Internet of Things Summit (GIoTS)*. IEEE, 2017, pp. 1–6.

31. W. Y. Ng, T.-E. Tan, P. V. Movva, A. H. S. Fang, K.-K. Yeo, D. Ho, F. S. San Foo, Z. Xiao, K. Sun, T. Y. Wong *et al.*, "Blockchain applications in health care for covid-19 and beyond: A systematic review," *The Lancet Digital Health*, vol. 3, no. 12, pp. e819–e829, 2021.

32. I. A. Omar, R. Jayaraman, K. Salah, I. Yaqoob, and S. Ellahham, "Applications of blockchain technology in clinical trials: Review and open challenges," *Arabian Journal for Science and Engineering*, vol. 46, no. 4, pp. 3001–3015, 2021.

33. S. Shukla, S. Thakur, S. Hussain, J. G. Breslin, and S. M. Jameel, "Identification and authentication in healthcare internet-of-things using integrated fog computing based blockchain model," *Internet of Things*, vol. 15, p. 100422, 2021.

34. V. Hassija, G. Bansal, V. Chamola, N. Kumar, and M. Guizani, "Secure lending: Blockchain and prospect theory-based decentralized credit scoring model," *IEEE Transactions on Network Science and Engineering*, vol. 7, no. 4, pp. 2566–2575, 2020.

35. N. Kapsoulis, A. Psychas, G. Palaiokrassas, A. Marinakis, A. Litke, and T. Varvarigou, "Know your customer (KYC) implementation with smart contracts on a privacy-oriented decentralized architecture," *Future Internet*, vol. 12, no. 2, p. 41, 2020.

36. R. Wang, Z. Lin, and H. Luo, "Blockchain, bank credit and SME financing," *Quality & Quantity*, vol. 53, no. 3, pp. 1127–1140, 2019.

37. A. R. Harish, X. Liu, R. Y. Zhong, and G. Q. Huang, "Log-flock: A blockchain-enabled platform for digital asset valuation and risk assessment in e-commerce logistics financing," *Computers & Industrial Engineering*, vol. 151, p. 107001, 2021.

38. K. Wüst and A. Gervais, "Do you need a blockchain?" in *2018 Crypto Valley Conference on Blockchain Technology (CVCBT)*. IEEE, 2018, pp. 45–54.

39. D. Ramesh, R. P. Sharma, and D. R. Edla, "HHDSSC: Harnessing healthcare data security in cloud using ciphertext policy attribute-based encryption," *International Journal of Information and Computer Security*, vol. 13, nos. 3-4, pp. 322–336, 2020.

40. P. Zhang, J. White, D. C. Schmidt, and G. Lenz, "Applying software patterns to address interoperability in blockchain-based healthcare apps," *arXiv preprint arXiv:1706.03700*, 2017.

41. A. Farouk, A. Alahmadi, S. Ghose, and A. Mashatan, "Blockchain platform for industrial healthcare: Vision and future opportunities," *Computer Communications*, vol. 154, pp. 223–235, 2020.

42. A. Sturmanis, J. Hudenko, and M. Juruss, "The challenges of introducing the blockchain technology in logistic chains," in *Proceedings of the 22nd World Multi-Conference on Systemics, Cybernetics and Informatics (WMSCI 2018)*, vol. 2, 2018, pp. 37–42.

43. M. Dobrovnik, D. M. Herold, E. Fürst, and S. Kummer, "Blockchain for and in logistics: What to adopt and where to start," *Logistics*, vol. 2, no. 3, p. 18, 2018.

44. J. Leng, G. Ruan, P. Jiang, K. Xu, Q. Liu, X. Zhou, and C. Liu, "Blockchain-empowered sustainable manufacturing and product lifecycle management in industry 4.0: A survey," *Renewable and sustainable energy reviews*, vol. 132, p. 110112, 2020.

45. Z. Shahbazi and Y.-C. Byun, "Integration of blockchain, IoT and machine learning for multistage quality control and enhancing security in smart manufacturing," *Sensors*, vol. 21, no. 4, p. 1467, 2021.

46. L. Sislian and A. Jaegler, "Linkage of blockchain to enterprise resource planning systems for improving sustainable performance," *Business Strategy and the Environment*, vol. 31, no. 3, pp. 737–750, 2022.

47. Y. Jiang, K. Zhou, X. Lu, and S. Yang, "Electricity trading pricing among prosumers with game theory-based model in energy blockchain environment," *Applied Energy*, vol. 271, p. 115239, 2020.

48. P. Pal, R. P. Sharma, S. Tripathi, C. Kumar, and D. Ramesh, "2.4 GHz RF received signal strength based node separation in WSN monitoring infrastructure for millet and rice vegetation," *IEEE Sensors Journal*, vol. 21, no. 16, pp. 18 298–18 306, 2021.

49. P. Pal, R. Sharma, S. Tripathi, C. Kumar, and D. Ramesh, "Genetic algorithm optimized node deployment in IEEE 802.15.4 potato and wheat crop monitoring infrastructure," *Scientific Reports*, vol. 11, no. 1, pp. 1–12, 2021.

50. A. Kamilaris, A. Fonts, and F. X. Prenafeta-Boldú, "The rise of blockchain technology in agriculture and food supply chains," *Trends in Food Science & Technology*, vol. 91, pp. 640–652, 2019.

51. S. Dey, S. Saha, A. K. Singh, and K. McDonald-Maier, "FoodsQRBlock: Digitizing food production and the supply chain with blockchain and QR code in the cloud," *Sustainability*, vol. 13, no. 6, p. 3486, 2021.

11

Smart Agricultural System Using IoT 2.0

Pankaj Pal
Department of Computer Science and Engineering, Indian Institute of Technology(ISM), Dhanbad, India

Mohammad S. Obaidat
King Abdullah II School of Information Technology, University of Jordan, Amman, Jordan
University of Science and Technology Beijing, Beijing, China
SRM University, India
Amity University, Noida, India

11.1   Introduction

Contemporary agriculture faces numerous difficulties, such as the growing demand for food caused by the world's surging population, climate fluctuations, depletion of natural resources, changes in eating habits, and concerns regarding health and safety. Weather plays a crucial role in agriculture and has significant consequences in terms of variances in nutrient dynamics due to crop growth, development, and yield, the occurrence of pests and diseases, water scarcity, and the timely application of water and fertilizer, as well as the efficiency of preventative and cultural measures applied to crops [1]. Climate change can cause physical damage to crops and can also degrade soil quality. The quality of crop production depends on the planting season and is different depending on the region. During inclement weather, poor storage and transportation can affect the viability of seed and planting material, hence resulting in a reduction in crop yield. To tackle the challenges faced by the agricultural sector and the increasing demands placed upon it, there is a pressing need to enhance the efficiency of agricultural practices while simultaneously minimizing their environmental impact. This has led to the development of precision agriculture, which aims to optimize farming methods by focusing on these two crucial factors. There are various reasons for applying precision agriculture to agri-business and farming at the local scale. In this current reality where the Internet of Things (IoT) is accelerating the reception of information and robotization, basic occupations and social opportunities, like agriculture, can certainly witness progress. The advancement of farming techniques has significant potential to promote sustainability, maximize productivity, and ensure a safe environment. Smart farming, which aims to address growing demands, is generally founded on four main pillars: (a) efficient management of natural resources, (b) preservation of ecosystems, (c) appropriate service development, and (d) utilization of modern technologies.

The incorporation of Information and Communication Technology (ICT) is an essential need for contemporary agriculture, and global policymakers are promoting its adoption. ICT tools can involve various devices like farm management information systems, sensors for soil and moisture, accelerometers, wireless sensor networks, cameras, drones, low-cost satellites, online services, and automated guided vehicles. The digital transformation of agriculture generates a vast volume of data, and as intelligent machines and sensors become more prevalent on farms, agricultural processes are becoming more data-oriented.

DOI:10.1201/9781003326236-11

Precision agriculture relies on the use of multiple information technologies. One of the more popular techniques is remote sensing, which is highly efficient at detecting variations in crop growth within and between fields. Ground-based sensors with real-time monitoring capabilities are currently emphasized in the literature on precision agriculture. Wireless sensor networks (WSNs) of various types are used to monitor agricultural environments and crop growth status. While satellites, drones (UASs), and sensors provide crucial data, it's the automated actions of actuators and intelligent machinery that truly drive precision agriculture. The emergence of the IoT has brought about significant changes in various sectors worldwide. Precision agriculture is one area where the application of IoT 2.0 techniques has the potential to increase yields, improve quality, and promote sustainability. The use of IoT-assisted Wireless Sensor Networks (IoWSN) for monitoring agricultural data is a cost-effective and dependable approach that enables scalable data collection and remote access. The IoT, which combines several techniques mentioned above, is a recent and popular research focus in the field of precision agriculture [2–11].

We conducted a literature review of the last decade on the topic of IoT and IoT 2.0 in agriculture to assist in its implementation. By using visualization analysis, we were able to identify research fronts and intellectual bases, which revealed new developments in applied IoT techniques and agricultural issues. We determined the leading countries, institutions, and authors through analyzing the quantity of contributions in cooperation networks. Moreover, we used citation networks to identify influential studies and scholars, thereby highlighting the current research and trends in agriculture IoT literature from 2010 to 2022.

11.2   Importance of Precision Agriculture

To meet the food demands of a projected global population of nine billion by 2050, the Food and Agriculture Organization (FAO) of the United Nations has estimated that food production needs to increase by 60%. This necessitates enhancing crop productivity to address food scarcity and improve farm profitability. To accomplish this objective, a comprehensive understanding of crop performance and accurate forecasting under diverse environmental, soil, fertilization, and irrigation circumstances is crucial. Boosting farm productivity is an essential element of any strategy aimed at addressing these challenges. The farming practices in India are carried out manually and in a traditional manner, which does not match data acquisition standards and is not adequate to deal with the current scenarios of a climate shift. Currently, crop recommendations rely on data gathered through agricultural studies conducted in the field. However, the process of collecting this data is often difficult as these studies are conducted in remote and dispersed locations, and the data is usually collected manually. Moreover, this data collection process is not easily scalable since it is gathered only from a limited number of locations in farms, which is inadequate for creating a digital twin of the farm conditions. Additionally, there is a lack of accessible databases that record soil-related parameters such as soil temperature, soil moisture, and soil salinity. Additionally, using current solutions necessitates significant effort to combine and correlate data collected from various sensor nodes, such as combining data from a fertilizer sprayer on a tractor with data from soil moisture sensors.

Data-driven precision agriculture approaches are the modern world tool that is enhancing the productivity of crop yield and also addresses climate change and resource constraints issues (water, labor, and energy shortages). A taxonomy of Precision Agriculture is shown in Figure 11.1. Precision agriculture strives to enhance and refine agricultural processes to achieve maximum productivity. This involves fast, dependable, and distributed measurements to provide growers with a more comprehensive understanding of the current status of their cultivation area. Additionally, it enables the coordination of automated machinery to optimize energy consumption, water usage, and the application of chemicals for pest control and plant growth. Smart algorithms can also organize well-evaluated scientific knowledge to provide deeper insights into ongoing processes. Moreover, these algorithms can perform current situation reasoning and predict potential threats to crops, produce early warnings, and improve automated control signals based on plant responses.

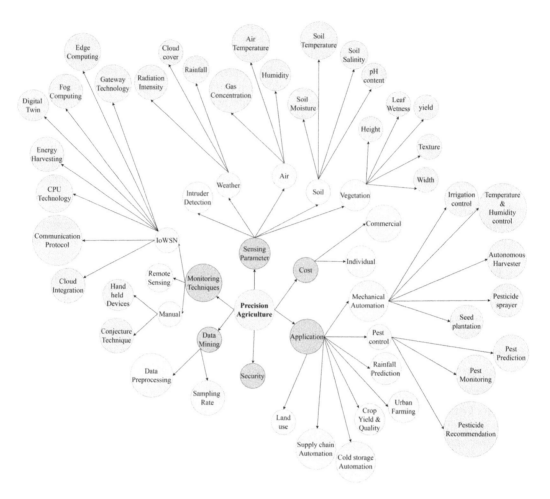

FIGURE 11.1 Taxonomy of precision agriculture.

Precision agriculture involves utilizing Information and Communication Technologies (ICT) and big data analytics to connect crop data with specific crop varieties' genetic and phenotypic characteristics. Figure 11.2 illustrates the flow of information in precision agriculture infrastructure. Wireless technologies have recently been introduced into agriculture, with high-value sectors such as greenhouse crops, horticulture, and vineyards taking priority. Wireless sensors are particularly useful in short-range indoor applications for greenhouses and small parcels of perennial crops with infrastructure for vineyards. Soil moisture measurement is mainly used to optimize crop irrigation, and wireless sensors are also commonly used as advanced weather stations to measure various parameters necessary for crop management. WSN are included in control loops and also used as actuators, such as in irrigation applications. The complexity of the algorithms needed to handle real-time distributed data is too great for low-power nodes in WSNs. However, with IoT, all objects are connected, making it easier to move computational overhead to the cloud or distribute it among interconnected devices.

11.2.1   Crop Management and Produce Quality

Crop growth and quality can be tracked using sensor data taken on the farm and processed in Python with OpenCV, Matplotlib, Scikit-image, and other image processing tools [12]. We can measure the crop attribute like the growing stage and quality and also predict the yield by extracting the unique

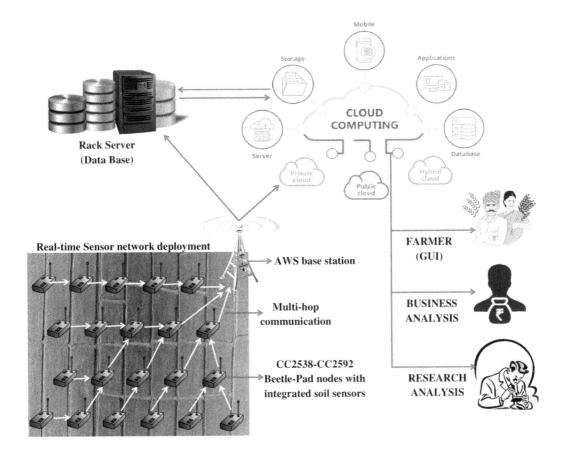

FIGURE 11.2   Flow of information in precision agriculture infrastructure.

properties like elevation, density, and leaf greenness index of vegetation from the captured data. The advancement in state-of-the-art IoT hardware technology made it possible to deploy economical monitoring infrastructures in large farms and collect and process big data on remote rack servers and cloud platforms [13]. As an illustration, IoT networks are set up in the food processing industries to gather information about each step of the food manufacturing process. This includes the quality of the raw materials used and the additives needed to produce the end product. The data collected can be saved in various file formats, like CSV, and stored on the cloud [14]. The objective of estimating crop yields is to analyze the various factors that influence and shape crop production. These factors comprise irrigation, topography, natural composition and physical characteristics of soil, weather and climatic conditions, crop diseases and pests, as well as crop stress [9]. Following an initial study and evaluation of the significance of the retrieved crop attribute, Machine learning and deep learning models can be trained with some of the abstracted data to estimate the yield of the crop. It facilitates effective resource management; fast and exact yield estimation can give a credible foundation for decision-makers to assess whether there will be a shortage or surplus and respond accordingly as per conditions [15].

11.2.2   Sustainable Use of Resources

There is a possibility for practical and scalable solutions for natural resource conservation and sustainable agriculture through the use of precision agriculture techniques [16–18]. Innovation in the agricultural sector is being driven by technologies like artificial intelligence (AI), drones, and the IoT, which leverage big data to enhance sustainability [19, 20]. As arable land is limited, groundwater levels are dropping, and soil quality is decreasing, these technologies could help optimize the utilization of land, water, and other resources to fulfill global demands while ensuring resources are preserved for future generations.

Agribusinesses can employ AI to manage weeds using state-of-the-art computer vision, machine learning, and robotics techniques [21, 22]. Based on data obtained from farms through IoT sensors, AI can help find weeds in fields through data abstraction and spray pesticides where weeds are located. As a result, the amount of pesticide used to spray the entire field can be reduced, and fewer chemicals are left on the agricultural product compared to the amount of chemicals sprayed regularly [23–25].

11.2.3 Plant Disease Detection

Plant illnesses pose a substantial risk to agricultural output and quality [26]. Recently, several neural network-based models have been developed to diagnose plant diseases [27–29]. Nonetheless, these models are limited in that they can only detect diseases after they have fully developed in the crop, and they do not have a significant impact on improving product quality. Identifying and monitoring plant diseases in the early stages in the field can be difficult, time-consuming, and costly. However, using deep learning algorithms for early disease detection and categorization is necessary to improve crop production and quality. To accomplish this, datasets on plant pathology diseases must be compiled throughout the vegetation's growth cycle.

11.2.4 Agriculture Management System

In recent years, farmers have exchanged data and collaborated more effectively, thanks to emerging information and communications technologies. Agriculture practitioner's connectivity enables the emergence of software-defined management systems [30]. New frameworks for rural administration are being developed to offer accounting services, link farmers with farm owners and managers, and enable agriculturalists to benchmark their performance by connecting them in a network [31]. The aim of the agriculture management system is to support farm managers and agribusinesses globally by collecting and analyzing a vast amount of data from real-time sources to aid them in making informed business decisions.

An agricultural Decision Support System (DSS) stores data collected at each agricultural manufacturing and distribution stage [32–35]. The data required for making informed decisions in agriculture comes from various sources, such as soil moisture, environmental conditions, crop yield, supply chain demand and supply data, food processing industry production data, and pesticides used by farmers [36–38]. This data is stored in both cloud-based and local databases and is used to understand critical factors like soil nutrient levels, seed characteristics, and their correlation with pathogens, pests, and toxic substances. Farmers and agricultural practitioners analyze biotic and abiotic data in conjunction with the probability of pest and pathogen development to make informed decisions. A DSS is employed to help practitioners choose crops based on market demand. The system tracks and maps crops with estimated demand, enabling farmers to avoid over-harvesting crops with low demand.

11.3 Role of Wireless Sensor Technologies and IoT in Agriculture

Recent advancements in wireless sensor technologies provide a plethora of research and development options. This is due to low cost and advancements in radio frequency technology of sensor nodes [39]. Wireless Regional Area Networks (Cognitive Radio/WRAN), Wireless Personal Area Networks (WPAN), Mesh, Point-to-Point (P2P), and Low-Power Wide-Area Networks (LPN/LPWAN) are the most widely used wireless technologies in the IoT arena [40–42]. GSM is segmented further into the GSM EDGE Radio Access Network (GERAN) and the UMTS Terrestrial Radio Access

Network (UMTS TRAIN) (UTRAN) [43, 44]. In recent academic literature, there has been a surprisingly significant number of references to embedded programmable devices [45–47]. Some equipment used in IoT research is custom-built, while others are commercially available systems that are pre-programmed or have closed-source monitoring capabilities. Researchers choose their equipment based on their specific research goals or focus areas. Commercial systems come with various functions that allow researchers to concentrate on other aspects of IoT deployment, such as intelligent algorithms, cloud compatibility, and metaprocessing. On the other hand, programmable and open solutions provide developers with complete control over node and network behavior, as well as the ability to program additional peripheral devices, such as new sensors or actuator modules, to make them compatible with the nodes. This information comes from various sources [48–53].

The WSN is one of the most important technologies of the twenty-first century [51]. Although RFID (Radio Frequency Identification) was originally designed to identify and track tags attached to objects, growing interest in a variety of other applications has resulted in the evolution of a new spectrum of RFID-based wireless sensor devices [54]. When comparing a WSN with an RFID system, the most significant distinction is that RFID devices do not provide cooperative communication. However, WSNs support a variety of network types and multi-hop communication [55]. The widespread use of standards such as Bluetooth and ZigBee for WSN and several ISO (International Organization for Standards) standards for RFID (ISO 15693, ISO/IEC 18000, ISO 11784, and others) has drawn significant attention to these technologies in recent years [56].

The IoT and WSN devices have a broad range of applications, including environmental monitoring, irrigation, livestock and greenhouse management, and cold chain. Agricultural infrastructure such as greenhouses are monitored and controlled using scalar sensor networks, while multimedia sensor networks are used to collect and process images remotely to detect insects and crop diseases. Product tracking and remote identification are accomplished using tag-based networks like RFID and NFC. Typically, the monitoring infrastructure consists of a small number of sinks and a large number of sensors. Wireless sensor nodes consist of three primary components: sensing, processing, and communication. These nodes communicate with a gateway unit, which can then communicate with other computers through LAN, WLAN, Internet, CAN, or WWAN using industry-standard protocols like GSM or GPRS. This information is based on various sources [56, 57].

In a variety of agricultural production systems, the WSN-based monitoring infrastructure allows for the collection of numerous crop-related parameters while minimizing damage to animals and the environment. Farmers may make crop-related choices based on real-time data obtained from the fields, which can boost crop output or assist them in water management. Precision farming involves identifying variations in crops and adjusting management techniques accordingly, rather than relying on an imaginary average state that may not reflect the reality of the situation. This idea is based on research cited in Ref. [58].

Sensor nodes mounted on off-road vehicles like tractors or combined harvesters enable data sharing with static infrastructure or other vehicles, resulting in the establishment of a mobile WSN [59, 60]. In Ref. [61], authors deployed a capacitance moisture sensor inside a forage harvester to monitor soil water content (SWC) during harvesting. Similarly, in Ref. [62], authors integrated Bluetooth-enabled sensor node in a fertilizer applicator that enabled on-site data acquisition. The data was used to calculate the right quantities and spread patterns for a fertilizer. In Ref. [63], a WSN is deployed to identify and control phytophthora in a potato farm. The phytophthora is caused by a fungal attack that depends on environmental factors. Humidity and temperature were measured using 868/916 MHz motes. The system aims to detect vegetation exposure to phytophthora and recommends treatment if necessary. Phytomonitoring, which is the process of keeping an eye on plants, is easier with WSN monitoring infrastructure. For example, with the assistance of WSN, a vineyard owner can manage vineyard operations more efficiently and automatically. For example, in Ref. [64], authors proposed a number of WSN configurations and implementations that can address various vineyard attributes. In Ref. [65], Zigbee motes were utilized by the authors to establish a WSN within a vineyard, and temperature data was gathered over a duration of one month. The aim was to examine two significant elements of winemaking, namely heat summation and potential frost damage, using the data collected. Similarly, the authors of Ref. [66] also demonstrated the effectiveness of using a remote sensing network based on Zigbee for precision viticulture. In their study, the network's nodes were powered by batteries that were recharged using solar cells.

In many crop systems, efficient irrigation management is a significant concern. WSN has the potential to accurately show how SWC changes in a field. The SWC data may be utilized to create a decision support system that assists farmers in increasing output while conserving water [67, 68]. Additionally, WSN eliminates the difficulties associated with wiring sensor nodes across the farm and lowers maintenance overhead. Because WSN is easier to set up than wired solutions, more sensors can be used to get more detailed information about what is going on in a specific area. Rather than irrigating a whole field, each region could be watered as needed and recognized based on the data obtained by the sensor that was strategically positioned on the field. A research study described in Ref. [69] involved the evaluation of two WSNs comprising infrared thermometers that were deployed on a center pivot irrigation system with six spans. They compared the performance of mesh and non-mesh WSN systems on a center pivot platform. Similarly, in [70], the authors developed an intelligent sensor array prototype for scheduling cotton irrigation. The system includes moisture sensors, thermocouples, and RFID tags. In Ref. [71], the authors deployed a WSN-based groundwater monitoring infrastructure. The monitoring data is processed by an embedded single-chip, and a GSM data module wirelessly transfers the data. The authors of Ref. [72] demonstrated the use of a WSN for site-specific irrigation control in a linear move irrigation system. Bluetooth radio connectivity enabled the sensors and irrigation controller to communicate with the base station. In Ref. [73], the author presented a study over an underground system that can monitor soil conditions like water and mineral content and give information about how to water and fertilize the soil in the right way. Additionally, the system may be used to monitor the presence and quantity of a wide variety of harmful compounds in soils near rivers and aquifers, where chemical runoff may affect drinking water sources.

It is vital for WSN in agriculture to consider the details of the circumstance and surroundings in which nodes will be deployed. The movement of crops and other objects in farmland can cause serious problems with connecting nodes in a network. These obstacles move unpredictably, which affects the quality of the link connection, causing it to fluctuate over time and space. This can affect various aspects of the network, including its deployment, routing, and failure diagnostics, among others, as noted in Ref. [74]. Various environmental factors, such as temperature, rainfall, humidity, solar radiation, shading from plant leaves, and noise from buildings like greenhouses, can also contribute to spatiotemporal climatic fluctuations, which further affect the links between nodes and the quality of communication, according to Ref. [74]. These issues are particularly relevant for automated agricultural installations, which rely on reliable connections between nodes. This characteristic outlines the requirements for advanced duty-cycle control, scheduling of data samples, data reconstruction, storage, and retrieval, as well as intelligent management, among other things. Therefore, selecting an appropriate IoT platform to plan the deployment may influence the project's overall achievement.

For farmers deploying a large network of soil moisture sensors across their fields, choosing the right wireless transceiver hinges on key parameters like number of nodes, communication range, and antenna mounting options. Multiple paths, shadowing, and attenuation all contribute to the complexity of real-world radio propagation [75]. We need WSNs to function flawlessly in diverse environments, from empty fields and vineyards to rolling hills and rugged mountains, all while braving diverse weather conditions. These factors, in turn, significantly impact radio performance. Radio propagation in farmlands is hindered by vegetation's differing height and density in a cropping cycle. The link power budget in these farm scenarios is determined by crop growth, geography, and more conventional considerations like node spacing and antenna height. Other agricultural applications, such as barns, greenhouses, or warehouses, include impediments like walls, windows, pallets, machinery, and so on, resulting in a significant loss of signal strength [76]. In these settings, a received signal intensity of 10–20 dB above the receiver's sensitivity limit is considered an acceptable link budget value [77].

Agricultural deployments commonly experience high temperatures and humidity. When the temperature rises from 25°C to 65°C, the received signal strength (RSS) can be significantly impacted. Additionally, humidity levels in agricultural settings can be very high, with wireless nodes exposed to rain or irrigation systems in open fields and humidity levels above 80% in greenhouses. This high humidity has been shown to have a notable effect on the propagation of radio waves [78]. Interference between devices operating in the same or neighboring bands is a potential problem in wireless communications. The IoT model offers a wide range of choices for bandwidth, communication distance, energy usage, and security protocols. Nevertheless, interoperability can be limited at the networking level due to varying technologies, standards, and unique demands of IoT projects [79].

Although there have been numerous investigations into the theoretical aspects of WSN in the literature, creating real-time IoT/WSN deployments in agricultural contexts remains challenging. Sensor modules must be highly accurate, have a suitable measurement range for the specific environment, and be protected against external factors that could result in incorrect readings or cause lasting damage to the sensor. Because of the dispersed nature of the WSN infrastructure, it may be difficult, if not impossible, to change the power source of battery-powered nodes that are located in open fields or other agricultural facilities. Therefore, when developing new sensor nodes, the selection of hardware is significantly influenced by strict power constraints, and the low-power attributes of peripheral devices are carefully considered. In addition, the software components that will be used to build the functionality of the end device must be thoroughly assessed. In order to avoid problems in the field, the final functional code must be developed with substantial embedded software engineering expertise and subjected to intensive testing [80]. Several factors determine the appropriateness of using a low-power embedded device, including its stability over extended periods, the number of digital and analog input/output channels available to support peripheral devices like sensors and actuators, its ability to sustain itself through power harvesting modules, and the level of programming complexity required.

11.4 Application of IoT 2.0

IoT 2.0 refers to a new era where devices and their data are utilized to generate actionable insights. It is driven by a massive network of interconnected devices, sensors, and actuators, making it more significant, resilient, and established than its predecessor, IoT. The next stage of IoT is often referred to as the "Internet of Transformation" or IoT 2.0. IoT 2.0 has the capability to extract valuable insights from device data and sharing, similar to how the Internet provided valuable information through document exchange. IoT 2.0 will include not only device technology and gateways but also the related IT technologies, processes, people, benefits, outcomes, and vast potential of the real world. Experts suggest that achieving this will require three essential attributes. To improve IoT, three factors need to be taken into account: (a) using standard protocols, (b) shifting from a centralized hub-and-spoke platform structure to a more decentralized peer-to-peer model, and (c) increasing device autonomy to boost cognitive, adaptive, and predictive capabilities both at the device and network levels. This is essential to manage the numerous diverse objects functioning on different platforms.

The term "IoT 2.0" encompasses various technological applications and transformative processes, making it the most significant technology driving digital transformation in society. In order to differentiate between different application contexts, challenges, and opportunities, more specific terms are often used. For instance, "Industrial IoT" (IIoT) or "Industrial Internet" refers to the use of IoT in industrial processes, while "Consumer IoT" (CIoT) refers to the billions of personal physical devices that utilize IoT technology. IoT 2.0 is sometimes referred to as the Internet of Everything (IoE) due to its extensive and multi-device nature. It encompasses technology, processes, people, benefits, results, and enormous potential for real-world applications, representing an Internet of Transformation. Regardless of the specific term used to describe it, IoT 2.0 is ultimately concerned with these aspects.

The fourth industrial revolution, known as Industry 4.0, brings together advanced technologies such as IoT, Big Data, robots, AI, and blockchain. These technologies have made industrial processes and supply chains more sophisticated and self-sufficient. By merging Industry 4.0 with agriculture, Agriculture 4.0 can be achieved, leading to sustainable and intelligent industrial agriculture.

In all aspects of the agricultural industry, from food production and processing to distribution and consumption, real-time data that is highly detailed and spatially and temporally variable can be collected, processed, and analyzed. Such an industrial agriculture ecosystem would involve a high level of digitization, real-time farm management, and data-driven autonomous decision-making processes, leading to increased productivity, efficiency in the agri-food supply chain, food safety, and conservation of natural resources. IoT's agricultural applications comprise precision agriculture, animal surveillance, artificial greenhouses, fisheries management, and weather monitoring. The authors of Ref. [81] described these implications on a broad scale, including the Space-Air-Ground-Undersurface Integrated Network for ubiquitous agricultural monitoring and networking.

The implementation of a remote sensing satellite constellation utilizing existing national and commercial space infrastructure could facilitate the extensive collection of agricultural data, resulting in significant benefits for tasks like crop production predictions, yield modeling, and pest identification. Additionally, advanced UASs equipped with hyperspectral sensors, multispectral cameras, and other specialized equipment may allow for swift emergency responses and improve observational accuracy through high-throughput 3D surveillance in various geographical locations. Ground and subsurface observation, which are responsible for several agricultural sensor nodes, autonomous farm tractors, and mobile crowdsensing, also play a vital role. Due to advancements in communication technologies, various wireless devices can now be selected to meet the diverse service requirements of agricultural applications, such as real-time remote hardware control and high-throughput plant phenotyping, for enhanced coverage, connection density, bandwidth, and end-to-end latency.

11.5   IoT 2.0 Challenges

Environmental sensing in agriculture can lead to several problems. Precision farming requires the deployment of multiple sensors on farmland, field crops, animals, and farming equipment. However, the lack of competent sensors poses a significant barrier to fine-grained agricultural monitoring, particularly in biosensing livestock and phenotyping plants. To address this issue, it is crucial to create and establish professional agricultural sensors with high standards, sensitivity, and dependability for assessing agricultural production settings and the physiological indicators of animals and plants. Another research direction could be the examination of sensorless agricultural sensing using radio waves.

In farming contexts, it is challenging to replace batteries of sensors installed underground, underwater, on trees, and animals, thus low-power sensing is critical. Wireless power transmission via electromagnetic waves has the potential to eliminate the need for battery replacement by recharging batteries. Long-distance wireless charging is required for most agricultural applications. Furthermore, research needs to be conducted to investigate wireless power transmission in severe conditions, such as underground and underwater. In the photovoltaic agricultural IoT [82], agriculture operations and power generation coexist on the same land. Scattered wireless chargers provide energy to sensing devices, but the adaptive task scheduling of energy transfer is challenging due to the variety of sensing devices utilized in agricultural applications. Another sustainable IoT alternative for agriculture is ambient energy harvesting. Pilot investigations have demonstrated that sensor nodes can collect energy from rivers, fluid flow, vehicle movement, and ground surface. However, power conversion efficiency must be increased to overcome the current restrictions on converted electrical energy.

Due to the diverse agricultural conditions, it is impossible to have a universal network solution that can cater to all applications. Agricultural sensing devices are located in various environments, such as indoor greenhouses, outdoor farmlands, subterranean spaces, and even marine areas. The heterogeneous nature of these environments necessitates the use of diverse wireless communication technologies based on radio frequency, sonar, vibration, and other signals for information sharing. Therefore, it is essential to evaluate the performance of different wireless communication techniques in each situation to select the most appropriate technology. In addition, for successful implementation of smart sensing in agricultural settings, cross-media communication between underground, underwater, and air is crucial. Furthermore, different agricultural applications have varying network sizes, node density, transmission distance, throughput, and latency requirements. Due to the variety of IoT applications in agrarian settings, cellular-based networks, 802.15.4 mesh networks, Bluetooth low energy networks, and LoRa networks would coexist in the same area. Hence, research into cross-technology communication across different physical layers is of utmost importance.

11.6   Conclusion

The current agricultural supply chain is partly automated and digitized, but lacks complete digital transformation and understanding, which limits its automation potential. Additionally, the current agri-food distribution system is not properly regulated. To address these issues, it is crucial to integrate new IoT 2.0 technology into agriculture. IoT 2.0 platforms utilize AI and machine learning to generate insights and provide actionable information to customers. The Internet is the driving force behind society and the economy, facilitating more efficient communication between the physical and digital worlds and creating digital representations of real objects and transactions to understand their behavior. As a result, this chapter presents an in-depth analysis of the most significant applications and research challenges associated with applying these technologies to agriculture.

REFERENCES

1. D. Ramesh, R. P. Sharma, and D. R. Edla, "HHDSSC: Harnessing healthcare data security in cloud using ciphertext policy attribute-based encryption," *International Journal of Information and Computer Security*, vol. 13, nos. 3–4, pp. 322–336, 2020.
2. P. Pal, R. P. Sharma, S. Tripathi, C. Kumar, and D. Ramesh, "NSGA-III based heterogeneous transmission range selection for node deployment in IEEE 802.15.4 infrastructure for sugarcane and rice crop monitoring in a humid sub-tropical region," *IEEE Transactions on Wireless Communications*, vol. 22, no. 6, pp. 1–1, 2022.
3. P. Pal, S. Tripathi, and C. Kumar, "Single probe imitation of multi-depth capacitive soil moisture sensor using bidirectional recurrent neural network," *IEEE Transactions on Instrumentation and Measurement*, vol. 71, pp. 1–11, 2022.
4. M. N. M. Bhutta, A. A. Khwaja, A. Nadeem, H. F. Ahmad, M. K. Khan, M. A. Hanif, H. Song, M. Alshamari, and Y. Cao, "A survey on blockchain technology: Evolution, architecture and security," *IEEE Access*, vol. 9, pp. 61 048–61 073, 2021.
5. P. Pal, R. P. Sharma, S. Tripathi, C. Kumar, and D. Ramesh, "Machine learning regression for rf path loss estimation over grass vegetation in iowsn monitoring infrastructure," *IEEE Transactions on Industrial Informatics*, vol. 18, no. 10, pp. 6981–6990, 2022.
6. R. Priya, D. Ramesh, and V. Udutalapally, "NSGA-2 optimized fuzzy inference system for crop plantation correctness index identification," *IEEE Transactions on Sustainable Computing*, vol. 7, no. 1, pp. 172–188, 2022.
7. R. Priya and D. Ramesh, "Ml based sustainable precision agriculture: A future generation perspective," *Sustainable Computing: Informatics and Systems*, vol. 28, p. 100439, 2020.
8. E. Khosla, R. Dharavath, and R. Priya, "Crop yield prediction using aggregated rainfall-based modular artificial neural networks and support vector regression," *Environment, Development and Sustainability*, vol. 22, no. 6, pp. 5687–5708, 2020.
9. R. Priya, D. Ramesh, and E. Khosla, "Biodegradation of pesticides using density-based clustering on cotton crop affected by xanthomonas malvacearum," *Environment, Development and Sustainability*, vol. 22, no. 2, pp. 1353–1369, 2020.
10. R. Priya and D. Ramesh, "Adaboost. RT based soil NPK prediction model for soil and crop specific data: A predictive modelling approach," in *International Conference on Big Data Analytics*. Springer, 2018, pp. 322–331.

11. R. Priya, D. Ramesh, and E. Khosla, "Crop prediction on the region belts of india: A naïve bayes mapreduce precision agricultural model," in *2018 International Conference on Advances in Computing, Communications and Informatics (ICACCI)*, 2018, pp. 99–104.

12. J. Doshi, T. Patel, and S. Kumar Bharti, "Smart farming using IoT, a solution for optimally monitoring farming conditions," *Procedia Computer Science*, vol. 160, pp. 746–751, 2019.

13. X. Shi, X. An, Q. Zhao, H. Liu, L. Xia, X. Sun, and Y. Guo, "State-of-the-art internet of things in protected agriculture," *Sensors*, vol. 19, no. 8, p. 1833, 2019.

14. N. Misra, Y. Dixit, A. Al-Mallahi, M. S. Bhullar, R. Upadhyay, and A. Martynenko, "IoT, big data and artificial intelligence in agriculture and food industry," *IEEE Internet of Things Journal*, vol. 9, no. 9, pp. 6305–6324, 2020.

15. T. N. Liliane and M. S. Charles, "Factors affecting yield of crops," *Agronomy-Climate Change & Food Security*. London, UK: IntechOpen, p. 9, 2020.

16. J. A. Delgado, N. M. Short Jr, D. P. Roberts, and B. Vandenberg, "Big data analysis for sustainable agriculture on a geospatial cloud framework," *Frontiers in Sustainable Food Systems*, vol. 3, p. 54, 2019.

17. J. N. Pretty, "Supportive policies and practice for scaling up sustainable agriculture," *Facilitating Sustainable Agriculture: Participatory Learning and Adaptive Management in Times of Environmental Uncertainty*. UK: Cambridge University Press, pp. 23–45, 1998.

18. A. Dobermann and R. Nelson, "Opportunities and solutions for sustainable food production," *Sustainable Development Solutions Network: Paris, France*, 2013.

19. S. A. Bhat and N.-F. Huang, "Big data and ai revolution in precision agriculture: Survey and challenges," *IEEE Access*, vol. 9, pp. 110 209–110 222, 2021.

20. K. Spanaki, E. Karafili, U. Sivarajah, S. Despoudi, and Z. Irani, "Artificial intelligence and food security: Swarm intelligence of agritech drones for smart agrifood operations," *Production Planning & Control*, vol. 33, pp. 1–19, 2021.

21. O. Bongomin, A. Yemane, B. Kembabazi, C. Malanda, M. Chikonkolo Mwape, N. Sheron Mpofu, and D. Tigalana, "Industry 4.0 disruption and its neologisms in major industrial sectors: A state of the art," *Journal of Engineering*, vol. 2020, 2020. https://www.hindawi.com/journals/je/2020/8090521/

22. T. Duckett, S. Pearson, S. Blackmore, B. Grieve, W.-H. Chen, G. Cielniak, J. Cleaversmith, J. Dai, S. Davis, C. Fox *et al.*, "Agricultural robotics: The future of robotic agriculture," *arXiv preprint arXiv:1806.06762*, 2018.

23. C. A. Damalas and S. D. Koutroubas, "Farmers' exposure to pesticides: Toxicity types and ways of prevention," *Toxics*, vol. 4, p. 1, 2016.

24. M. Kishi, N. Hirschhorn, M. Djajadisastra, L. N. Satterlee, S. Strowman, and R. Dilts, "Relationship of pesticide spraying to signs and symptoms in indonesian farmers," *Scandinavian Journal of Work, Environment & Health*, vol. 21, pp. 124–133, 1995.

25. J. Luck, S. Pitla, S. Shearer, T. Mueller, C. Dillon, J. Fulton, and S. Higgins, "Potential for pesticide and nutrient savings via map-based automatic boom section control of spray nozzles," *Computers and Electronics in Agriculture*, vol. 70, no. 1, pp. 19–26, 2010.

26. S. Chakraborty and A. C. Newton, "Climate change, plant diseases and food security: An overview," *Plant Pathology*, vol. 60, no. 1, pp. 2–14, 2011.

27. S. Mishra, R. Sachan, and D. Rajpal, "Deep convolutional neural network based detection system for real-time corn plant disease recognition," *Procedia Computer Science*, vol. 167, pp. 2003–2010, 2020.

28. A. F. Fuentes, S. Yoon, J. Lee, and D. S. Park, "High-performance deep neural network-based tomato plant diseases and pests diagnosis system with refinement filter bank," *Frontiers in Plant Science*, vol. 9, p. 1162, 2018.

29. B. Liu, Y. Zhang, D. He, and Y. Li, "Identification of apple leaf diseases based on deep convolutional neural networks," *Symmetry*, vol. 10, no. 1, p. 11, 2017.

30. H. El Bilali and M. S. Allahyari, "Transition towards sustainability in agriculture and food systems: Role of information and communication technologies," *Information Processing in Agriculture*, vol. 5, no. 4, pp. 456–464, 2018.

31. L. Jack, *Benchmarking in Food and Farming: Creating Sustainable Change*. Farnham, Surrey, UK: Gower Publishing, Ltd., 2009.

32. J. Jones, "Decision support systems for agricultural development," in *Systems Approaches for Agricultural Development*. Springer, 1993, pp. 459–471.

33. P. Kanatas, I. S. Travlos, I. Gazoulis, A. Tataridas, A. Tsekoura, and N. Antonopoulos, "Benefits and limitations of decision support systems (dss) with a special emphasis on weeds," *Agronomy*, vol. 10, no. 4, p. 548, 2020.

34. M. Kukar, P. Vračar, D. Košir, D. Pevec, Z. Bosnić *et al.*, "Agrodss: A decision support system for agriculture and farming," *Computers and Electronics in Agriculture*, vol. 161, pp. 260–271, 2019.

35. M. Bange, S. Deutscher, D. Larsen, D. Linsley, and S. Whiteside, "A handheld decision support system to facilitate improved insect pest management in australian cotton systems," *Computers and Electronics in Agriculture*, vol. 43, no. 2, pp. 131–147, 2004.

36. C. M. Herrera, "Defense of ripe fruit from pests: Its significance in relation to plant-disperser interactions," *The American Naturalist*, vol. 120, no. 2, pp. 218–241, 1982.

37. A. Alengebawy, S. T. Abdelkhalek, S. R. Qureshi, and M.-Q. Wang, "Heavy metals and pesticides toxicity in agricultural soil and plants: Ecological risks and human health implications," *Toxics*, vol. 9, no. 3, p. 42, 2021.

38. S. A. Younis, K.-H. Kim, S. M. Shaheen, V. Antoniadis, Y. F. Tsang, J. Rinklebe, A. Deep, and R. J. Brown, "Advancements of nanotechnologies in crop promotion and soil fertility: Benefits, life cycle assessment, and legislation policies," *Renewable and Sustainable Energy Reviews*, vol. 152, p. 111686, 2021.

39. M. Kocakulak and I. Butun, "An overview of wireless sensor networks towards internet of things," in *2017 IEEE 7th Annual Computing and Communication Workshop and Conference (CCWC)*. IEEE, 2017, pp. 1–6.

40. N. Tadayon and S. Aissa, "Modeling and analysis of cognitive radio based IEEE 802.22 wireless regional area networks," *IEEE Transactions on Wireless Communications*, vol. 12, no. 9, pp. 4363–4375, 2013.

41. Y. Türk and A. Akman, "A management model for low powered wireless personal area networks," in *2018 IEEE 19th International Symposium on "A World of Wireless, Mobile and Multimedia Networks"(WoWMoM)*. IEEE, 2018, pp. 14–16.

42. A. Ikpehai, B. Adebisi, K. M. Rabie, K. Anoh, R. E. Ande, M. Hammoudeh, H. Gacanin, and U. M. Mbanaso, "Low-power wide area network technologies for internet-of-things: A comparative review," *IEEE Internet of Things Journal*, vol. 6, no. 2, pp. 2225–2240, 2018.

43. E. Gritsai and I. Daudov, "Evolution and improvement trends of radio interfaces in geran/utran/e/utran networks," in *Journal of Physics: Conference Series*, vol. 2032, no. 1. IOP Publishing, 2021, p. 012009.

44. D. Kakadia, J. Yang, and A. Gilgur, "Evolved universal terrestrial radio access network (eutran)," in *Network Performance and Fault Analytics for LTE Wireless Service Providers*. Springer, 2017, pp. 61–81.

45. M. C. Martínez-Rodríguez, E. Camacho-Ruiz, P. Brox, and S. Sánchez-Solano, "A configurable RO-PUF for securing embedded systems implemented on programmable devices," *Electronics*, vol. 10, no. 16, p. 1957, 2021.

46. F. Renzini, M. Cuppini, C. Mucci, E. Franchi Scarselli, and R. Canegallo, "Quantitative analysis of multistage switching networks for embedded programmable devices," *Electronics*, vol. 8, no. 3, p. 272, 2019.

47. M. Martina, C. Condo, G. Masera, and M. Zamboni, "A joint source/channel approach to strengthen embedded programmable devices against flash memory errors," *IEEE Embedded Systems Letters*, vol. 6, no. 4, pp. 77–80, 2014.

48. F. J. Ferrández-Pastor, J. M. García-Chamizo, M. Nieto-Hidalgo, J. Mora-Pascual, and J. Mora-Martínez, "Developing ubiquitous sensor network platform using internet of things: Application in precision agriculture," *Sensors*, vol. 16, no. 7, p. 1141, 2016.

49. S. Didla, A. Ault, and S. Bagchi, "Optimizing aes for embedded devices and wireless sensor networks." in *TridentCom*. Citeseer, 2008, p. 4.

50. G. Strazdins, A. Elsts, and L. Selavo, "Mansos: Easy to use, portable and resource efficient operating system for networked embedded devices," in *Proceedings of the 8th ACM Conference on Embedded Networked Sensor Systems*, 2010, pp. 427–428.

51. K. M. Modieginyane, B. B. Letswamotse, R. Malekian, and A. M. Abu-Mahfouz, "Software defined wireless sensor networks application opportunities for efficient network management: A survey," *Computers & Electrical Engineering*, vol. 66, pp. 274–287, 2018.

52. L. Galluccio, S. Milardo, G. Morabito, and S. Palazzo, "SDN-wise: Design, prototyping and experimentation of a stateful sdn solution for wireless sensor networks," in *2015 IEEE Conference on Computer Communications (INFOCOM)*. IEEE, 2015, pp. 513–521.

53. P. M. Egidius, A. M. Abu-Mahfouz, and G. P. Hancke, "Programmable node in software-defined wireless sensor networks: A review," in *IECON 2018-44th Annual Conference of the IEEE Industrial Electronics Society*. IEEE, 2018, pp. 4672–4677.

54. X. Jia, Q. Feng, T. Fan, and Q. Lei, "RFID technology and its applications in internet of things (IoT)," in *2012 2nd International Conference on Consumer Electronics, Communications and Networks (CECNet)*. IEEE, 2012, pp. 1282–1285.

55. J. V. Sobral, J. J. Rodrigues, R. A. Rabelo, J. C. Lima Filho, N. Sousa, H. S. Araujo, and R. Holanda Filho, "A framework for enhancing the performance of internet of things applications based on RFID and WSNS," *Journal of Network and Computer Applications*, vol. 107, pp. 56–68, 2018.

56. L. Ruiz-Garcia, L. Lunadei, P. Barreiro, and I. Robla, "A review of wireless sensor technologies and applications in agriculture and food industry: State of the art and current trends," *Sensors*, vol. 9, no. 6, pp. 4728–4750, 2009.

57. D. Kandris, C. Nakas, D. Vomvas, and G. Koulouras, "Applications of wireless sensor networks: An up-to-date survey," *Applied System Innovation*, vol. 3, no. 1, p. 14, 2020.

58. D. Thakur, Y. Kumar, A. Kumar, and P. K. Singh, "Applicability of wireless sensor networks in precision agriculture: A review," *Wireless Personal Communications*, vol. 107, no. 1, pp. 471–512, 2019.

59. K. Sarvela *et al.*, "Development of a real-time measurement method for analyzing the influence of tire-soil contact on agricultural tractor mobility," The University of Helsinki, 2020, pp. 1–37.

60. I. I. Sunusi, J. Zhou, Z. Z. Wang, C. Sun, I. E. Ibrahim, S. Opiyo, S. A. Soomro, N. A. Sale, T. Olanrewaju *et al.*, "Intelligent tractors: Review of online traction control process," *Computers and Electronics in Agriculture*, vol. 170, p. 105176, 2020.

61. W. S. Lee, T. F. Burks, and J. K. Schueller, "Silage yield monitoring system," in *2002 ASAE Annual Meeting*. American Society of Agricultural and Biological Engineers, 2002, p. 1.

62. S. Cugati, W. Miller, and J. Schueller, "Automation concepts for the variable rate fertilizer applicator for tree farming," in *The proceedings of the 4th European Conference in Precision Agriculture*, 2003, pp. 14–19.

63. D. Goense and J. Thelen, "Wireless sensor networks for precise phytophthora decision support," in *2005 ASAE Annual Meeting*. American Society of Agricultural and Biological Engineers, 2005, p. 1.

64. J. Burrell, T. Brooke, and R. Beckwith, "Vineyard computing: Sensor networks in agricultural production," *IEEE Pervasive Computing*, vol. 3, no. 1, pp. 38–45, 2004.

65. J. D. F. Selvaraj, P. M. Paul, and I. D. J. Jingle, "Automatic wireless water management system (AWWMS) for smart vineyard irrigation using iot technology," *International Journal of Oceans and Oceanography*, vol. 13, no. 1, pp. 211–218, 2019.

66. R. Morais, M. A. Fernandes, S. G. Matos, C. Serôdio, P. Ferreira, and M. Reis, "A zigbee multi-powered wireless acquisition device for remote sensing applications in precision viticulture," *Computers and Electronics in Agriculture*, vol. 62, no. 2, pp. 94–106, 2008.

67. L. Hamami and B. Nassereddine, "Application of wireless sensor networks in the field of irrigation: A review," *Computers and Electronics in Agriculture*, vol. 179, p. 105782, 2020.

68. T. Savić and M. Radonjić, "WSN architecture for smart irrigation system," in *2018 23rd International Scientific-Professional Conference on Information Technology (IT)*. IEEE, 2018, pp. 1–4.

69. S. A. O'Shaughnessy and S. R. Evett, "Integration of wireless sensor networks into moving irrigation systems for automatic irrigation scheduling," in *2008 Providence, Rhode Island, June 29–July 2, 2008*. American Society of Agricultural and Biological Engineers, 2008, p. 1.

70. G. Vellidis, M. Tucker, C. Perry, C. Kvien, and C. Bednarz, "A real-time wireless smart sensor array for scheduling irrigation," *Computers and Electronics in Agriculture*, vol. 61, no. 1, pp. 44–50, 2008.

71. D. Qian, Y. Shi, and K. Zhang, "Study of wireless-sensor-based groundwater monitoring instrument," in *Watershed Management to Meet Water Quality Standards and TMDLS (Total Maximum*

Daily Load) Proceedings of the 10–14 March 2007, San Antonio, Texas. American Society of Agricultural and Biological Engineers, 2007, p. 129.

72. Y. Kim, R. G. Evans, and W. M. Iversen, "Remote sensing and control of an irrigation system using a distributed wireless sensor network," *IEEE Transactions on Instrumentation and Measurement*, vol. 57, no. 7, pp. 1379–1387, 2008.

73. I. F. Akyildiz and E. P. Stuntebeck, "Wireless underground sensor networks: Research challenges," *Ad Hoc Networks*, vol. 4, no. 6, pp. 669–686, 2006.

74. Y. Liu, X. Ma, L. Shu, G. P. Hancke, and A. M. Abu-Mahfouz, "From industry 4.0 to agriculture 4.0: Current status, enabling technologies, and research challenges," *IEEE Transactions on Industrial Informatics*, vol. 17, no. 6, pp. 4322–4334, 2020.

75. D. L. Ndzi, A. Harun, F. M. Ramli, M. L. Kamarudin, A. Zakaria, A. Y. M. Shakaff, M. N. Jaafar, S. Zhou, and R. S. Farook, "Wireless sensor network coverage measurement and planning in mixed crop farming," *Computers and Electronics in Agriculture*, vol. 105, pp. 83–94, 2014.

76. S. Kurt and B. Tavli, "Path-loss modeling for wireless sensor networks: A review of models and comparative evaluations." *IEEE Antennas and Propagation Magazine*, vol. 59, no. 1, pp. 18–37, 2017.

77. S. Singh and S. Kumar, "IEEE 802.15. 4 zigbee based wireless sensor technology in agriculture-a survey." *Journal: International Journal of Electrical and Electronics Engineers (IJEEE)*, vol. 8, no. 01, pp. 269–273, 2016.

78. R. Khan, I. Ali, M. Zakarya, M. Ahmad, M. Imran, and M. Shoaib, "Technology-assisted decision support system for efficient water utilization: A real-time testbed for irrigation using wireless sensor networks," *IEEE Access*, vol. 6, pp. 25 686–25 697, 2018.

79. Y. Chen, M. Li, P. Chen, and S. Xia, "Survey of cross-technology communication for IoT heterogeneous devices," *IET Communications*, vol. 13, no. 12, pp. 1709–1720, 2019.

80. I. Almomani and A. Alromi, "Integrating software engineering processes in the development of efficient intrusion detection systems in wireless sensor networks," *Sensors*, vol. 20, no. 5, p. 1375, 2020.

81. Y. Liu, X. Ma, L. Shu, G. P. Hancke, and A. M. Abu-Mahfouz, "From industry 4.0 to agriculture 4.0: Current status, enabling technologies, and research challenges," *IEEE Transactions on Industrial Informatics*, vol. 17, no. 6, pp. 4322–4334, 2021.

82. F. Yang, L. Shu, Y. Liu, K. Li, K. Huang, Y. Zhang, and Y. Sun, "Poster: Photovoltaic agricultural internet of things the next generation of smart farming." in *EWSN*, 2019, pp. 236–237.

12

Smart Health Monitoring and Management System

M. Junaid Gul
Yeungnam University, Daegu, South Korea

Anand Paul
Kyungpook National University, Daegu, South Korea

Mucheol Kim and Seungmin Rho
Chung-Ang University, Seoul, South Korea

12.1   Introduction

Innovative technologies now encircle humans, and ever-advancing technologies affect our daily lives. Smart healthcare is a term that has gained hype in recent years and is helping communities worldwide. Smart healthcare, or e-healthcare, is subdivided into SHMMS. The fundamental functionalities of smart healthcare are to collect and process healthcare data into knowledge, which helps to take proper actions [1–3].

The Internet of Things (IoT) opens new standards for technology and changes your lifestyle. IoT is everywhere from bus stops to our gadgets. Smart cities get the most benefits out of IoT technologies. IoT is keeping an eye on pollution, electricity generation, and consumption and making us more effective in the decision-making process. Under the hood, IoT is a fancy term for sensors that are connected via a network to communicate between servers and themselves. IoT technology is vulnerable to security and privacy threats. Cyber-attacks can result in the malfunctioning of IoT devices and compromise security and privacy [4]. Data integrity is also a key factor in the IoT ecosystem as data is required to be encrypted, but IoT technology lacks such functionality. Researchers are working on this issue but implementing security measures across the communication channel [5] is still an open challenge and thus requires more exploration. To overcome some of the IoT issues, blockchain technology can be explored as it inherits security and privacy properties.

Blockchain is also a promising technology, providing solutions for data security and privacy issues. International Business Machines (IBM) creates an opportunity for businesses and executives to understand the propositions of emerging blockchain technology to enable organizations like healthcare to adopt blockchain-based frameworks easily. Blockchain shows multispectral potential to create a substantial number of reliable and versatile networks, offering feasible solutions and frameworks to explore new ways to interact with data and consumers with a substantial level of security and privacy. Hospitals and medical care organizations anticipate a cure and diagnose a disease as accurately as possible, but organizations heavily rely on available data to reach any conclusion. Medical record management systems are readily available nowadays, and record data can be transferred to respective medical care centers. Still, current systems lack confidentiality of data and are prone to data manipulation attacks, which makes it harder for the involved organization to depend on the data, so doctors re-examine the patients. To avoid any implications, the hospital re-conducts the tests, which results in an increase in cost and is a waste of time. Time and cost are crucial factors for the healthcare industry, and blockchain can provide a solid foundation for

DOI:10.1201/9781003326236-12

reliable data availability by communicating data with confidentiality across organizations. Data or, in medical terminology, "medical data," transmission and storage are the key challenges as data can be hacked through eavesdropping [6], man-in-the-middle attacks, or any other attack that can result in data leakage. Medical data is supposed to be private and should be shared only with the consent of the patient and the involved organization or persons. Such disclosure of medical data voids confidentiality and even could be fatal for the patient in scenarios where data is manipulated. Due to high-risk factors, medical data is supposed to be transmitted after encryption. Encryption of medical data ensures reliability [7] to the extent that doctors can rely on it while diagnosing the patient. Although blockchain provides a higher level of security, it lacks certain capabilities – capability such as understanding the data to process and finding anomalies in sent and received data. Blockchain with machine learning concepts can address this issue.

Machine learning (ML) is a sub-branch of artificial intelligence. ML concepts and algorithm enable a system to understand the data and produce results without programming explicitly. Once an ML model is trained with available data, it can be used for classification, clustering, regression, and ensembling. In the field of IoT, ML can be used to reduce dimensions and make it more appropriate to store in blockchain. As the importance of ML is increasing every day, it can solve underlying issues for blockchain management systems. ML concepts can automate the blockchain management processes that are supposed to be hard, thus requiring extra cost and increasing the probability of errors.

This chapter introduces the IoT, Medical IoT, blockchain, and ML concepts in the introduction section. Sections 12.2 and 12.3 on Medical IoT provide in-depth insights into current and future trends of IoT and MIoT. Sections 12.4 and 12.5, which discuss blockchain use cases in healthcare and management not only emphasize MIoT with blockchain but also provide some use cases that can be developed to streamline the Medical or healthcare sector-related procedures. After this, authors discuss the concept of ML in the blockchain, especially reinforcement learning. To provide a robust example, the author proposes a framework as a use case scenario that provides a higher level of insight into building blockchain and ML-based healthcare monitoring and management systems. The authors supported the information shared in the chapter use case results support at the end. In the end, the author concludes the chapter with a summary.

12.2   Background

Healthcare monitoring and management systems are fine tailored for specific functionalities [8–13]. Monitoring body temperature is essential during fever. Body temperature can change before reaching the medical facility. Especially in the time of the COVID-19 pandemic, an effective body temperature monitoring system requires real-time. A real-time body temperature monitoring system using heterogeneous MIoT devices along with cloud services has proven to be effective in sending data across respective hospitals [14–17]. Although cloud-based monitoring services are viable, processing load can be shifted nearer to the user with fog and edge computing, which results in faster communication with healthcare organization and frameworks introduced where the fog and edge computing seems reasonable choices [18–24]. Medical IoT also provides a healthcare system for monitoring blood pressure. Blood pressure (BP) monitoring requires another person and going to the hospital can result in invalid BP readings. MIoT monitors BP by reading patient pulses [25–29], and real-time BP data can be sent to the medical center to generate alerts to save lives.

12.3   The Emergence of Medical IoT

Kevin Ashton coined the term Internet of Things (IoT) while working for Procter & Gamble [30–32]. The idea proposed was to embed radio frequency identification (RFID) chips in the products to track them. The advantages of tracking products through the supply chain are realized by the world. Thus, the term "IoT" gets attention. IoT devices can be anything with sensors and should be able to transmit data across the internet. Such conglomeration makes IoT more feasible where heterogeneous devices can communicate with each other to acquire viable results. Smart home appliances like air conditioning units (AC) can be an example of such a scenario where a user can send a command to turn on the AC and sensors can turn it off automatically when the room reaches the desired temperature. This can save monthly electricity costs for consumers and help the power grid to reduce costs and time of electricity generation. This example elaborates on the effectiveness of IoT devices in the modern era where IoT devices can work in a loop to provide better services and help to keep the environment as much green as possible. Figure 12.1 shows the ecosystem of IoT devices. Such growth indicates the importance of IoT in the future. The IoT market is expected to reach 1.40 trillion dollars [33] by 2026. IoT enables the world to get more connected as machines are getting smaller and industries are focusing on devices to perform specific or limited tasks rather than doing all the work in a single unit. Creating a network of devices takes the load off and builds a collaborative environment where each device can perform its specified calculations. Devices that perform a single task are more desirable as they are easier to maintain and manufacture. The software development process is much more focused as devices perform a limited number of calculations.

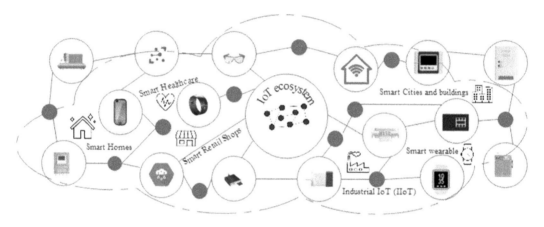

FIGURE 12.1   IoT ecosystem.

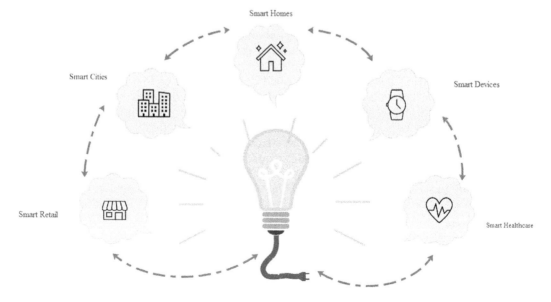

FIGURE 12.2   Key trends in IoT.

The boom of IoT can be felt across a broad spectrum of domains like smart cities, smart grids, IoT for healthcare, and many more. Some of the key emerging trends in IoT are shown in Figure 12.2. To emphasize the importance of IoT, we conducted an experiment with Google Trends to find when the term "IoT" gained more popularity.

Figure 12.3 shows the search trend of the term IoT in the Google search engine from January 2004 to February 2022. We can observe that for approximately ten years there has been no big leap. There is however an upward trend from 2015. Likewise, we also experimented with the term "Medical IoT" to analyze the recent developments in MIoT through Google search trends.

Figure 12.4 shows the search trends of the term "MIoT." As spikes are uncertain at the start, we are unable to conclude or provide any solid reasoning from 2004 to 2009. Since 2010, data lines have been stable, and a low upward trend can be observed. We can anticipate that the importance of MIoT is getting recognized but at a slow pace. Thus, more research and exploration are required in the field of MIoT. MIoT gathers medical data and in healthcare, the importance of timely and accurate data can make a difference between life and death. MIoT devices for heart patients can save them from impending heart attacks. Devices can sense the heart rate and other involved variables to alert the patient while sending an alert to the hospital to act before any serious heart damage. The elderly falling is also a prominent issue that has gained researchers' interest in recent years. Researchers have turned toward MIoT devices as they can sense that a patient might fall after detecting the blood sugar or oxygen level and send a pre-emptive alert so that the patient can sit or lie down before time. A few of the requirements for MIoT devices are latency, adequate bandwidth for required scenarios, security, and privacy.

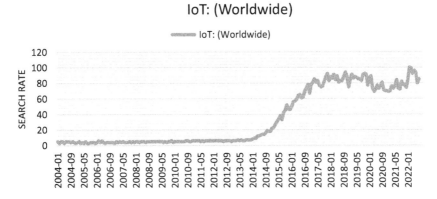

FIGURE 12.3 Search trend of the term IoT.

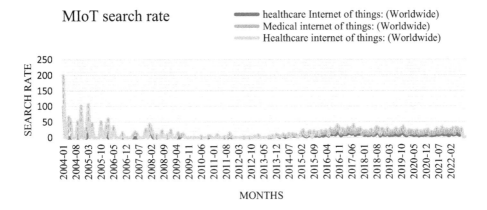

FIGURE 12.4 Search trends of the term MIoT.

TABLE 12.1

MIoT Data Rate, Range, and Frequency [34]

Technologies	Data Rate	Range	Frequency (Band)
RFID	106–424 Kbps	20 m	13.56 MHz
Bluetooth	1,2,3 Mbps	80–115 m	2.4 GHz
LoRa WAN	300 Bps–37.5 kbps	3–4 km	169–915 MHz
NFC	106–424 Kbps	20 cm	13.56 MHz
ZigBee	250 kbps	10–100 m	2.4 GHz
UWB	53–480 Mbps	10 m	3.1–10.6 GHz
WSN	80–250 kb/s	20–100 m	2.45 GHz
50 Network	5–10 Gibs	1,000 feet	28 GHz 39 GHz

TABLE 12.2

Limitation of MIoT Communication Technologies [34]

Technologies	Security	Drawbacks
RFID	Encryption (AES, DES)	No authorization
Bluetooth	Secure pairing 128-AES encryption	Blue jacking
LoRa WAN	Authentication, Encryption	Low bandwidth
Wi-Fi	Authentication, Authorization	Eavesdropping
NFC	Authentication	Hacking
ZigBee	encryption Integrity	Fixed key
UWB	Passive keyless entry	Need large frequency range
IrDA (Infrared)	Line of sight and exceptionally low bit error rate	Data transfer is very less
WSN	Encryption Authentication	DOS attack
50 Network	Authentication, Authorization	Distributed DoS. Intercell Interference

Table 12.1 shows some of the MIoT communication technologies with respect to their data rate, range, and operating frequencies. Such communication technologies can be used according to the patient's health and scenario. MIoT also includes wearable devices to monitor heart rate with Wi-Fi, Bluetooth, or both communication technologies to send and receive data. Such technologies play a vital role in creating a monitoring environment for the patient as the Bluetooth range is less, but Wi-Fi can send signal over a long range, compared to Bluetooth. If range and fast transmission are crucial factors, then a mesh network environment can be created where the patient can conduct their daily routines while the monitoring system can gather medical data.

Use cases for MIoT devices in the healthcare sector are but not limited to the automation of the medical sector through robotics, drug storage, anti-kidnapping monitoring systems for disabled persons, real-time monitoring through wearable devices, alert and alarm systems for sick persons, smart hospital, and healthcare centers.

While MIoT devices are helping people, they have their limitations – in terms of security and implementation drawbacks, as shown in Table 12.2.

Drawbacks pointed out in Table 12.2 are the topics of the research, and studies are conducted to address the overlaying security issue in MIoT. Other challenges faced by MIoT are security, data integrity and completeness, infrastructure development cost, lack of standards, and connectivity issues.

12.4   Role of Blockchain in Healthcare

Blockchain can play a vital role in transforming healthcare organizations. The health sector is facing challenges like secure data sharing across involved healthcare centers, integrity, availability, and reliability of data [35–38]. Blockchain technology enhances security, integrity, encrypted data sharing, and approximately real-time data accessibility. In conjunction with MIoT, data is generated from the MIoT devices. A new block is created to hold the received medical data. After making the desired size of a block, data is broadcast to the nodes. Nodes are miners who manage the calculation of the hash according to the business rules of a blockchain company. The size of the block can vary as different blockchain service providers enforce their own business rules. The difficulty level to calculate the hash also depends on the blockchain service providers. After the above-mentioned steps, nodes call for consensus. In simple words, consensus is the process to check whether all involved nodes reach the same hash. If all nodes are agreed for the hash, then the block is validated and sent to the blockchain. Blockchain is often a broader term but, in various books and papers, the author refers to the blockchain as a storage medium according to their context. The database used to save the validated block is also referred to as a ledger. A blockchain ledger or database holds the encrypted data and links it with the previous block to sustain continuity. The continuity of the blockchain creates a blockchain as all the blocks are chained together with the prior block's hash. If the hash of one block is changed then all blocks after it will be faulty. This phenomenon makes it easy to identify and locate where data is illegally changed, and proper countermeasures can be taken.

Figure 12.5 shows a search of the term "blockchain" on the Google search engine. Although we can observe from the line that the trend is somewhat constant, we cannot infer that there is a major decrease in the popularity of the blockchain. Researchers are exploring the paradigms where blockchain can provide solutions to enhance security and privacy.

The blockchain ecosystem is itself a complex architecture. Certain networking equipment is required to create a blockchain infrastructure. The cost of building blockchain infrastructure is very high, and businesses are still unsure about the feasibility of blockchain. Figure 12.6 shows the complexity of the blockchain infrastructure. The blockchain ecosystem and infrastructure can vary from business to business and security requirements. The basic blockchain of blockchain infrastructure can be divided into four sections. The user domain section in which where clients are connected to blockchain services. The client section is the blockchain services consumer section, and the mining domain consists of nodes to carry out hashing process and blockchain validation and storage section, where all consensus algorithms can reside.

Before we can proceed further, we must consider some key questions as mentioned in Table 12.3. These questions help identify the requirements, thus making the process of building blockchain much easier. In MIoT, we are going to track and record patient data. The value to capture is information and knowledge about the current condition of the patient, while blockchain is favorably built for healthcare organizations and medical centers. Figure 12.7 illustrates the basic building block of the blockchain.

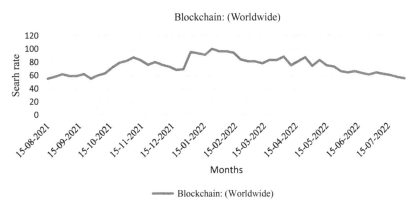

FIGURE 12.5 Blockchain search rate.

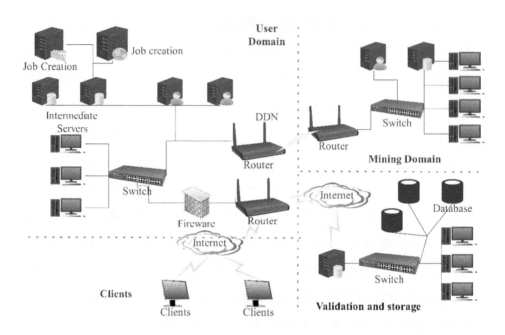

FIGURE 12.6 Workflow of blockchain.

TABLE 12.3

Key, Feasibility Questionnaire for Blockchain

Objective	What Value Do You Want to Capture?	For Whom?
• Record	• Information and knowledge	• Customers
• Track	• Attribution and responsibility	• Employees
• Verify	• Access or permission	• Suppliers
• Aggregate	• Decision rights or votes	• Producers or makers
	• Ownership or incentives	• Creditors or investors
	• Reputation and trust	• Governments
	• Contracts	• Citizens
	• Transactions	

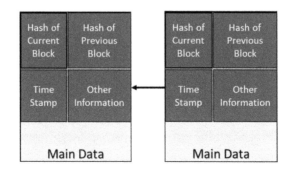

FIGURE 12.7 The basic structure of the block.

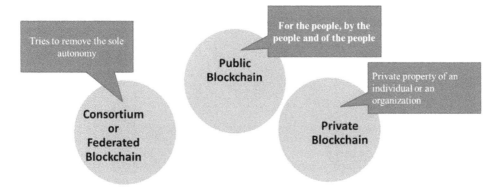

FIGURE 12.8 Types of blockchain.

TABLE 12.4

Functional Properties of the Blockchain

Public Blockchain	Private Blockchain	Consortium or Federated Blockchain
Anyone can run BTC/LTC full node	Anyone can't run a full node	Selected members of the consortium can run a full node
Anyone can make transactions	Anyone can't make transactions	Selected members of the consortium can make transactions
Anyone can review/audit the blockchain	Anyone can't review/audit the blockchain	Selected members of the consortium can review/audit the blockchain

There are three major types of blockchain, as shown in Figure 12.8. Any one or combination of these three types can be used to build a blockchain service for the healthcare sector. All three blockchains inhibit their specific properties, such as level of data exposure, consensus mechanism, and storage medium.

Healthcare organizations or patients might want to share their blockchain medical data across the country so doctors can easily access the medical history of the patient and prescribe accurate medicine. It is possible to create a trustworthy platform with blockchain in which medical data can be stored and shared with a higher level of security. As data in the blockchain is difficult to manipulate, doctors and medical centers rely on the information gathered from such a blockchain system. Blockchain healthcare management systems can provide features like healthcare data protection, tracking disease and source of origin, and interoperable medical records while making data and every step transparent. Before building the blockchain, we must identify the desired functionality, which is shown in Table 12.4.

12.5 Blockchain Healthcare Use Cases

One of the key features of blockchain in MIoT is that patients uphold the ownership of data. Medical data is documented along with a timestamp and other details to ensure transparency. As blockchain is already making its base in the financial domain, the patient can pay via a blockchain wallet. Blockchain-based healthcare system provides near real-time data about the patient so the doctor can prescribe medicine accordingly [39]. It is not that only healthcare organizations derive benefits from blockchain systems. The patient can sell or voluntarily provide data for research purposes and can take an active part in experiments and analysis. Furthermore, blockchain can record pharmaceutical records of the patients that can help healthcare researchers choose and track clinical trials for a new

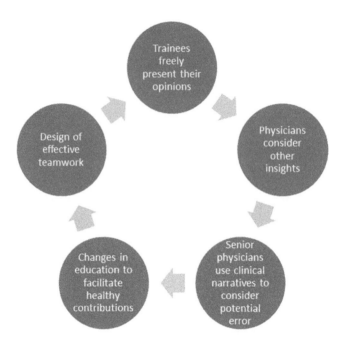

FIGURE 12.9   A potential model to improve patient care and facilitate.

medicine or vaccine by relying on blockchain data. If some patients get a chemical reaction due to some medicine, the doctor can easily prescribe alternative medicines.

12.5.1   Patient Centric MIoT data

Storing and maintaining patient history is a challenging task even for developed countries where infrastructure is well developed. Governments, local authorities, and healthcare medical centers are facing the challenge of incomplete data that is unreliable and unable to provide any insights into previous patient health. Due to this, many medical errors occur. Medical error happens when doctors make a mistake by relying on historical data that is either manipulated or poorly recorded. Due to such errors, numerous deaths occur every year in the United States. Figure 12.9 shows an abstract model to avoid such medical errors [40].

12.5.2   Cost Reduction

The introduction of blockchain in the healthcare ecosystem can reduce operational costs by streamlining underlying procedures. The study [41] shows that the healthcare sector can cut its operation costs by up to a hundred billion dollars in a few years. Such a reduction is possible as blockchain can reduce the cost of data security [42] as blockchain is not easy to hack, management and administration costs, insurance frauds, and other related operating costs. Figure 12.10 shows the annual expenditures of the United States, and we can observe that the graph exhibits a constant upward trend.

12.5.3   Identity and Credential Verification

Blockchain can help the healthcare system store and track medical staff data [43]. Thus, certain credentials of the medical staff can be verified on the go. In a use case where the doctor went to another medical institution, the institution can verify the doctor's credentials. This identity and credential can help healthcare organizations induct doctors easily. Likewise, if due to the unavailability of a specialized doctor, a hospital asks for help, blockchain can also verify the doctor's

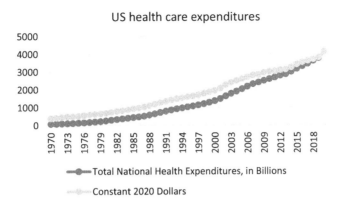

US health care expenditures

FIGURE 12.10 US per year healthcare expenditures.

credentials as it is very important in such a scenario. All the prescription and diagnosis records will be maintained on the blockchain for future reference.

12.5.4 Smart Contract-Based Insurance for Fraud Detection

Insurance fraud is common worldwide, and nations still facing to reduce such challenges [44]. Disputes over insurance contracts can be reduced by making a smart contract and connecting it with blockchain. Traditionally, a contract is made separately between customer and hospital and customer and insurance company, which results in many disputes like lack of coverage for certain diseases. Maintaining a single smart contract will be available to all parties and can be checked if required. Patients and hospitals can see a single version of the contract, which will result in less insurance fraud.

12.5.5 IoT-Based Secure Remote Monitoring

Remote monitoring is widely adopted and used and enables the healthcare sector to take initiative-taking measures. Blockchain can be deployed in this use case as it can ensure that only legitimate or authorized users can retrieve data from remote sensing devices [45].

12.6 Blockchain with Machine Learning

ML is a subcategory of artificial intelligence, as shown in Figure 12.11. ML is a process that teaches a computer (algorithm) to analyze and learn certain features from the provided data and make an algorithm decision-making process up to the level where no further human interaction is required.

Mostly, ML is used to solve regression and classification problems. ML is divided into four types:

- Supervised learning
- Unsupervised learning
- Semi-supervised learning
- Reinforcement learning

12.6.1 Supervised Learning

Supervised learning-based models try to build a relationship between predicted output and original output using a parametric hyper-tuning process. To train the supervised learning-based model, labeled data is required. Labeled data ensure that model extracts accurate features.

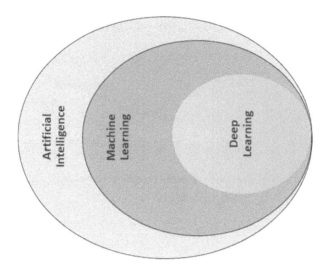

FIGURE 12.11   Artificial Intelligence in a glance.

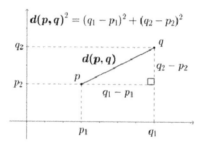

FIGURE 12.12   Two-dimensional Euclidean distance.

If after the first epoch, the error is high, the algorithm tunes its weights and tries to match the predicted output with provided labeled output. Some of the common error functions for regression problems are mean squared error and mean absolute error. Mathematical representations for both errors are represented in Eq. 12.1 and 12.2.

$$\text{Mean Squared Error} = \frac{\sum_{i=1}^{n}(y_i - \hat{y})^2}{n} \tag{12.1}$$

$$\text{Mean Absolute Error} = \frac{\sum_{i=1}^{n}|y_i - \hat{y}_i|}{n} \tag{12.2}$$

12.6.2   Unsupervised Learning

Unsupervised learning mostly deals with unlabeled clustering problems. Unlike supervised learning, where labeled data is required to train the model, here model try to understand the hidden pattern in the unlabeled data to assign or predict accurate cluster for data points. To create a robust model, usually, we try to reduce the Euclidean distance of the cluster center point. Figure 12.12 shows the formula to calculate Euclidean distance in two dimensions.

12.6.3   Semi-Supervised Learning

Semi-supervised learning benefits from both supervised and unsupervised ML techniques. Semi-supervised learning solves the issue of the unavailability of the labeled data and model error convergence due to no labeled data while training the model. Semi-supervised learning uses both labeled and unlabeled data to train the model, which saves the time and cost required to label a large dataset. Commonly a variant of the cross-entropy error function is used to evaluate the model as shown in mathematical in Eq. 12.3.

$$\text{loss} = \begin{cases} \text{crossentropy}(x_i, y_i) + \|f_\theta(x_i) - f_\theta(\text{augumented}(x_i)\|_2^2, x_i \in X_{\text{labelled}} \\ \|f_\theta(x_i) - f_\theta(\text{augumented}(x_i)\|_2^2, x_i \in X_{\text{unlabelled}} \end{cases} \tag{12.3}$$

12.6.4 Reinforcement Learning

Reinforcement learning (RL) is quite the same as the human learning process. Human learns from the feedback from their actions. Likewise, reinforcement learning relies on feedback from the environment to learn. Every action that humans take has consequences. Consequences or results can be good or bad. If the result of the action ends in good results, humans tend to follow that path; otherwise, they try to avoid bad actions in the future. Reinforcement learning does the same; for every good action or positive feedback a reward is given, and if an action results in bad or negative feedback, a penalty is given to ensure that after learning, the model will try to avoid action that results in negative feedback. Like supervised learning, reinforcement learning does not use labeled data, but it learns from feedback. Figure 12.13 illustrates the basic workflow of reinforcement learning. There are some specific terms related to reinforcement learning namely agent, environment, action, state, reward, policy, value, and Q-value.

Overall, an agent is programmed to act on the environment without knowing what the feedback will be. It is like the hit-and-trial method and only feedback provides insight if the action generates a positive reward, or the agent is going to face a penalty. Symbols used in RL are shown in Figure 12.14.

12.6.4.1 RL Agent

RL agent is described as an intelligent or smart piece of software or machine that can observe changes in the environment and act accordingly. Theoretically, an RL agent possesses a mental state that is belief or knowledge, which enables the RL agent to observe the change. There are several types of RL agents, for example, simple reflex, model-based reflex, goal-based, utility-based, and learning agents. At the abstract level, RL agents are divided into two categories, which are physical and virtual agents. Figure 12.15 shows the workflow and architecture of the simplex agent.

12.6.4.2 Bellman Equation

In 1953, Richard Ernest Bellman introduced an equation for the domain of dynamic programming to calculate certain values to decide at a specific point by incorporating previous states. Mathematically,

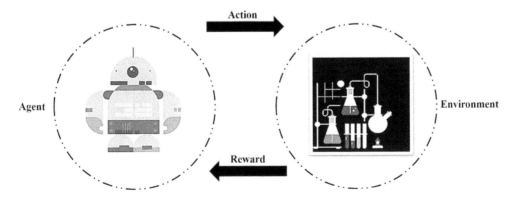

FIGURE 12.13 Reinforcement learning workflow.

Symbol	Meaning
$s \in S$	States.
$a \in A$	Actions.
$r \in R$	Rewards.
S_t, A_t, R_t	State, action, and reward at time step *t* of one trajectory. I may occasionally use s_t, a_t, r_t as well.
γ	Discount factor; penalty to uncertainty of future rewards; $0 < \gamma \leq 1$
G_t	Return; or discounted future reward; $G_t = \sum_{k=0}^{\infty} \gamma^k R_{t+k+1}$
$P(s', r \mid s, a)$	Transition probability of getting to the next state $s2$ from the current state s with action a and reward r.
$\pi(a \mid s)$	Stochastic policy (agent behavior strategy); $\pi_\theta(.)$ is a policy parameterized by θ.
$\mu(s)$	Deterministic policy; we can also label this as $\pi(s)$, but using a different letter gives better distinction so that we can easily tell when the policy is stochastic or deterministic without further explanation. Either π or μ is what a reinforcement learning algorithm aims to learn.
$V(s)$	State-value function measures the expected return of state s; $V_w(.)$ is a value function parameterized by w.
$V^\pi(s)$	The value of state s when we follow a policy π. $V^\pi(s) = \mathbb{E}_{a \sim \pi}[G_t \mid S_t = s]$
$Q(s, a)$	Action-value function is similar to $V(s)$, but it assesses the expected return of a pair of state and action (s, a); $Qw(.)$ is a action value function parameterized by w.
$Q^\pi(s, a)$	Similar to $V^\pi(.)$, the value of (state, action) pair when we follow a policy π; $Q^\pi(s, a) = \mathbb{E}_{a \sim \pi}[G_t \mid S_t = s, A_t = a]$.
$A(s, a)$	Advantage function, $A(s, a) = Q(s, a) \grave{} V(s)$; it can be considered as another version of Q-value with lower variance by taking the state-value off as the baseline.

FIGURE 12.14 Symbols in RL.

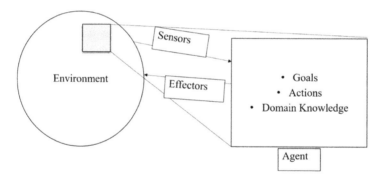

FIGURE 12.15 RL agent workflow and architecture.

the Bellman equation can be written as Eq. 12.4.

$$V(s) = \max \left[R(s, a) + \gamma V(s') \right] \tag{12.4}$$

where $V(s)$ is a value at a certain point, *a* is the action, *s* is the state that the agent reaches after taking the action, *R* is a reward after feedback, $V(s')$ value of the previous state and γ is the discount factor. The objective of the function is to maximize the reward by keeping track of rewards and previous states. Figure 12.16 shows some of the applications of reinforcement learning.

12.6.4.3 Markov Decision Process

Bellman equation builds the foundation for dynamic programming, and the Markov decision process (MDP) formalizes RL-related problems. Markov process can be used to model the dynamics if the environment is completely observable. This means the agent can observe all elements in the environment.

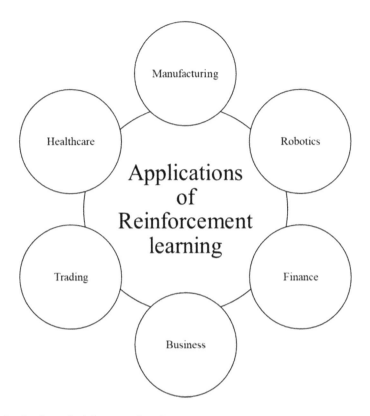

FIGURE 12.16   Applications of reinforcement learning.

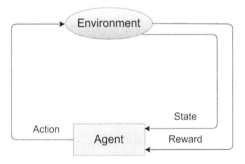

FIGURE 12.17   RL with Markov decision process workflow.

We can observe the difference between the simple workflow of the RL model in Figure 12.17, now with previous states are included. States keep tracking the position of the agent at a certain point. MDP requires four elements: a finite number of states, a finite number of actions, a reward or penalty while transitioning from one state to another, and the probability of the next state and action. The agent also learns from feedback which states are good and gives positive feedback and which are bad, and the agent starts learning to avoid it to maximize the reward. The optimization objective of the MDP is to choose the best policy to maximize the cumulative reward as mathematically shown in Eq. 12.5.

$$E\left[\sum_{t=0}^{\infty} \gamma^t R_{at}\left(s_t \rightarrow s_{t+1}\right)\right] \quad (12.5)$$

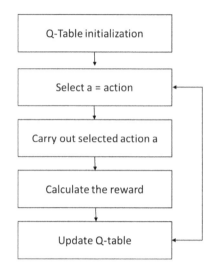

FIGURE 12.18   Workflow of the Q-learning algorithm.

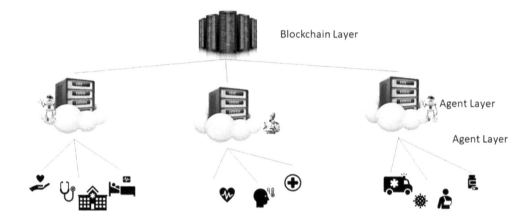

FIGURE 12.19   Abstract framework SHMMS.

12.6.4.4   *Reinforcement Learning Algorithms*

RL-based algorithms focus on teaching a computer to play intellectual games like chess, but other applications inspired by games like rover landing are available. Q-learning is the most famous and one of the first algorithms that took advantage of reinforcement learning. Q-learning is off-policy algorithm and can be used for temporal differencing where the algorithm can compare successive predictions. Figure 12.18 shows the workflow of the Q-learning algorithm.

12.6.4.5   *SHMMS*

In this section, we will evaluate smart health monitoring and management systems as a use-case scenario. Our SHMMS is generalized into three layers, as shown in Figure 12.19. Each layer possesses its functionalities. Agents are trained using a reinforcement learning algorithm as we discuss briefly in previous sections. To keep things simple for effective use case elaboration, we train our model with a neural network under the hood of reinforcement learning. An example of such neural net base reinforcement learning is Actor 2 critique (A2C). A2C is also now available in a more advanced version namely A3C. The job assigned to the neural network model is to identify any irregularities in wearable device data. Wearable device data is collected from secondary and primary sources to evaluate the effectiveness of the reinforcement learning model.

The blockchain layer consists of a database and miner node, which are responsible for calculating the cryptographic hash of the wearable device data. This layer is decentralized, but to communicate with the fourth layer, blockchain requires some central management system to enforce the smart contract along with the agent and MIoT layer.

Agent layers consist of multiagents that are trained via reinforcement learning to detect any anomaly in data. If an anomaly is detected agents stop the communication. It will prevent data from reaching miners where calculating cryptographic hash on wrong data can increase the cost. Already the cost of mining is not cheap and calculating wrong data is not desirable. In the second case where the agent detects an anomaly of medical emergency, the agent will inform the respective authority in advance. Finally, if there is no anomaly and the data is consistent then the agent will act according to the smart contract rule, which contains the severity or necessity of recording every observation in the blockchain. The medical situation can vary according to the conditions so smart contract and agent can prevent miner from working on unusable data, which also result in saving the storage capacity of the blockchain database.

The third and final layer is the MIoT layer. This layer is responsible for generating data. In our use case data is generated through a wearable device that is continuously monitoring the beat per minute.

To evaluate if your model is performing, as we anticipated, we devised an experiment. In the experiment, we fixed the number of episodes to 49 and ran the model seven times in seven sessions. The reward is the first variable to observe as it shows that the model is making good policies and decisions. If the model continuously accumulates rewards, then it will be reset after the termination point. It is a continuous scenario, which is why our termination points accumulate maximum reward at the end of the episode. Figure 12.20 provides insights into the model with respect to reward. In the figure, we can observe that rewards started from the lower end rise as the number of episodes increases. Such a slope in the figure shows that our model is accumulating the rewards and learning episode by episode until the termination point. One more fact is that the reward does not start from the same point for all sessions. In reinforcement, this is normal as at the beginning model or agent doesn't know anything and starts taking any random action. As the episode passes, the agent learns more and more until hyperparameters are tuned to the highest possible levels.

To confirm that our model is learning, we can also check the loss metric. Figure 12.21 provides information about the loss metric. Loss functions show a haphazard line across the graph. This can be due to random action at the start or any given time when an episode is terminated and started

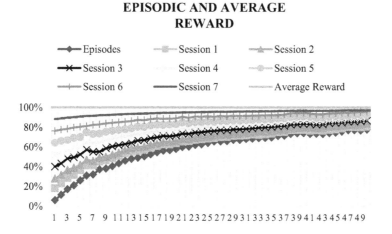

FIGURE 12.20 Episodic and average reward.

EPISODIC AND AVERAGE LOSS

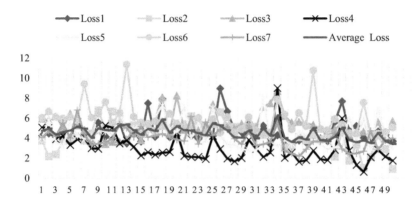

FIGURE 12.21   Episodic and average loss.

AVERAGE REWARD

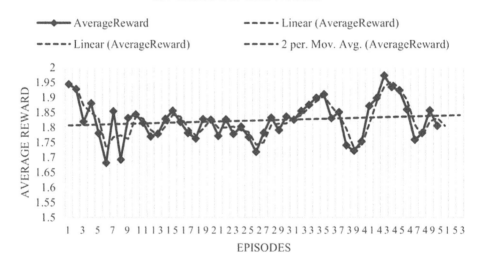

FIGURE 12.22   Trend line for the average reward with one and two step prediction.

again. From the above figures, it is noticeably clear that training is going well, and the model is learning. Reinforcement learning requires an extensive training process. Thus, 49 episodes might not provide in-depth information. To our hypothesis, we can perform one more experiment where we can check the reward first run in each session. This can tell us whether our model makes a mistake in the first step of every episode, or it implies the knowledge from the previous episode. To do this, we took an average of rewards at a certain point and tried to create a trend line. Figure 12.22 shows the trend line as well as the one-step and two-step prediction of the average reward. Slope is not that high but again it is due to the reason that reinforcement learning requires extensive training and obtaining this slope at 49 episodes is good.

Figure 12.23 provides information about the model loss. We can observe that loss is showing a downward trend. A slope of the trend line also seems to be quite good; thus, from these evaluations we can say that our model is learning and detecting anomalies in the data of wearable devices.

The overall framework is mostly dependent on the agent and blockchain security to provide a robust framework for the healthcare sector. ML concepts are viable for MIoT along with blockchain and can perform better once training is done. We can also see the shortcoming of the model – that the learning rate is slow and can be refined.

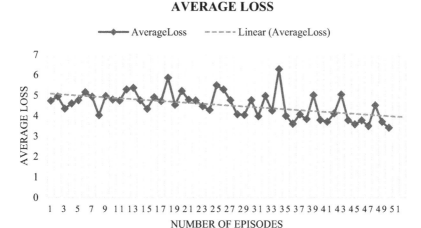

FIGURE 12.23 Trend line for average loss.

12.7 Chapter Summary

In this chapter, we discuss the challenges faced by the health sector and the importance of developing a framework where MIoT can work alongside blockchain and ML concepts. The chapter started with an example of an existing framework, but most of them are either using ML or blockchain. Moreover, we gather brief information about IoT, MIoT, blockchain, and ML concepts before going toward our use case. We discussed IoT, how IoT communicates in depth, and how more IoT-related domains are emerging. We covered the ML concept from starch and then studied reinforcement learning and its application. We also learned about blockchain and its properties and why it is more secure. The concept of mining is also presented in this chapter but up to a level so it remains more user readable as cryptography can lead to another mature domain to understand the functionality of the blockchain.

REFERENCES

1. M. M. Kamruzzaman, "Architecture of smart health care system using artificial intelligence", *2020 IEEE Int. Conf. Multimed. Expo Work. ICMEW 2020*. 2020, doi: 10.1109/ICMEW46912.2020.9106026
2. W. Li *et al.*, "A comprehensive survey on machine learning-based big data analytics for IoT-enabled smart healthcare system", *Mob. Networks Appl.* Volume 26(1), pp. 234–252, 2021, doi: 10.1007/S11036-020-01700-6/FIGURES/5
3. F. Ali *et al.*, "An intelligent healthcare monitoring framework using wearable sensors and social networking data", *Futur. Gener. Comput. Syst.* Volume 114, pp. 23–43, 2021, doi: 10.1016/J.FUTURE.2020.07.047
4. J. Li and Y. Hu, "Employing edge computing to enhance self-defense capabilities of IoT devices", *2022 IEEE World AI IoT Congr.* pp. 604–610, 2022, doi: 10.1109/AIIOT54504.2022.9817368
5. H. Moudoud, Z. Mlika, L. Khoukhi, and S. Cherkaoui, "Detection and prediction of FDI attacks in IoT systems via hidden Markov model", *IEEE Trans. Netw. Sci. Eng.* 2022, doi: 10.1109/TNSE.2022.3161479
6. M. H. Panahi Rizi and S. A. Hosseini Seno, "A systematic review of technologies and solutions to improve security and privacy protection of citizens in the smart city", *Internet of Things*. Volume 20 p. 100584, 2022, doi: 10.1016/J.IOT.2022.100584
7. C. H. Liu, T. L. Chen, C. Y. Chang, and Z. Y. Wu, "A reliable authentication scheme of personal health records in cloud computing", *Wirel. Netw.* pp. 1–11, 2021, doi: 10.1007/S11276-021-02743-7/TABLES/2

8. A. D. Jurik and A. C. Weaver, "Remote medical monitoring", *Computer (Long. Beach. Calif).* Volume 41(4), pp. 96–99, 2008, doi: 10.1109/MC.2008.133.

9. J. M. Ehrenfeld and M. A. Rehman, "Anesthesia information management systems: a review of functionality and installation considerations", *J. Clin. Monit. Comput.* Volume 25(1), pp. 71–79, 2010, doi: 10.1007/S10877-010-9256-Y.

10. A. Milenković, C. Otto, and E. Jovanov, "Wireless sensor networks for personal health monitoring: Issues and an implementation", *Comput. Commun.* Volume 29(13–14), pp. 2521–2533, 2006, doi: 10.1016/J.COMCOM.2006.02.011.

11. Y. Yang, H. Wang, R. Jiang, X. Guo, J. Cheng, and Y. Chen, "A review of IoT-enabled mobile healthcare: Technologies, challenges, and future trends", *IEEE Internet Things J.* Volume 9(12), pp. 9478–9502, 2022, doi: 10.1109/JIOT.2022.3144400.

12. A. Vaidyam, J. Halamka, and J. Torous, "Enabling research and clinical use of patient-generated health data (the mindLAMP platform): Digital phenotyping study", *JMIR Mhealth Uhealth.* Volume *10*(1), p. e30557, 2022, https//mhealth.jmir.org/2022/1/e30557; doi: 10.2196/30557.

13. K. B. Jyothilakshmi, V. Robins, and A. S. Mahesh, "A comparative analysis between hyperledger fabric and ethereum in medical sector: A systematic review", *Lect. Notes Data Eng. Commun. Technol.* Volume 93 pp. 67–86, 2022, doi: 10.1007/978-981-16-6605-6_5/COVER.

14. M. Sang *et al.*, "Ultrahigh sensitive Au-doped silicon nanomembrane based wearable sensor arrays for continuous skin temperature monitoring with high precision", *Adv. Mater.* Volume 34(4), p. 2105865, 2022, doi: 10.1002/ADMA.202105865.

15. V. Bhardwaj, Rajat Joshi, and A. M. Gaur, "IoT-based smart health monitoring system for COVID-19", *SN Comput. Sci.* Volume 3(2), pp. 1–11, 2022, doi: 10.1007/S42979-022-01015-1.

16. S. Ali and S. Parveen, "IoT-based smart healthcare monitoring system: A prototype approach", In Intelligent Communication Technologies and Virtual Mobile Networks: Proceedings of ICICV 2022. pp. 441–452, 2023, doi: 10.1007/978-981-19-1844-5_34.

17. R. M. Atta, "Cost-effective vital signs monitoring system for COVID-19 patients in smart hospital", *Health Technol. (Berl).* Volume 12(1), pp. 239–253, 2022, doi: 10.1007/S12553-021-00621-Y/FIGURES/9.

18. M. J. Gul, B. Subramanian, A. Paul, and J. Kim, "Blockchain for public health care in smart society", *Microprocess. Microsyst.* Volume 80 p. 103524, 2021, doi: 10.1016/J.MICPRO.2020.103524.

19. A. Singh and K. Chatterjee, "Securing smart healthcare system with edge computing", *Comput. Secur.* Volume 108 p. 102353, 2021, doi: 10.1016/J.COSE.2021.102353.

20. G. L. Santos *et al.*, "The internet of things for healthcare: Optimising e-health system availability in the fog and cloud", *Int. J. Comput. Sci. Eng.* Volume 21(4), pp. 615–628, 2020, doi: 10.1504/IJCSE.2020.106873.

21. R. Rajavel, S. K. Ravichandran, K. Harimoorthy, P. Nagappan, and K. R. Gobichettipalayam, "IoT-based smart healthcare video surveillance system using edge computing", *J. Ambient Intell. Humaniz. Comput.* Volume 13(6), pp. 3195–3207, 2022, doi: 10.1007/S12652-021-03157-1/TABLES/5.

22. I. S. B. M. Isa, T. E. H. El-Gorashi, M. O. I. Musa, and J. M. H. Elmirghani, "Energy efficient fog-based healthcare monitoring infrastructure", *IEEE Access.* Volume 8, pp. 197828–197852, 2020, doi: 10.1109/ACCESS.2020.3033555.

23. P. Verma, R. Tiwari, W. C. Hong, S. Upadhyay, and Y. H. Yeh, "FETCH: A deep learning-based fog computing and IoT integrated environment for healthcare monitoring and diagnosis", *IEEE Access.* Volume 10, pp. 12548–12563, 2022, doi: 10.1109/ACCESS.2022.3143793.

24. K. Lakshmanan and S. Arumugam, "An efficient data science technique for IoT assisted healthcare monitoring system using cloud computing", *Concurr. Comput. Pract. Exp.* Volume 34(11), p. e6857, 2022, doi: 10.1002/CPE.6857.

25. K. Sangeethalakshmi, U. Preethi, and S. Pavithra, "Patient health monitoring system using IoT", *Materials Today: Proceedings.* Volume 80, pp. 2228–2231, 2021, doi: 10.1016/J.MATPR.2021.06.188.

26. A. D. Acharya and S. N. Patil, "IoT based health care monitoring kit", *Proc. 4th Int. Conf. Comput. Methodol. Commun. ICCMC 2020.* pp. 363–368, 2020, doi: 10.1109/ICCMC48092.2020.ICCMC-00068.

27. M. A. Khan, M. T. Quasim, N. S. Alghamdi, and M. Y. Khan, "A secure framework for authentication and encryption using improved ECC for IoT-based medical sensor data", *IEEE Access.* Volume 8, pp. 52018–52027, 2020, doi: 10.1109/ACCESS.2020.2980739.

28. T. Mohanraj, B. Arunkumar, S. Shahulhammed, and R. Santhosh, "A review on Internet of Things (IoT) based pulse rate, blood pressure, body temperature monitoring system", *Proc. 4th Int. Conf. IoT Soc. Mobile, Anal. Cloud, ISMAC 2020.* pp. 78–79, 2020, doi: 10.1109/I-SMAC49090.2020.9243350.

29. N. Hashim, N. Norddin, F. Idris, S. Nur, I. M. Yusoff, and M. Zahari, "IoT blood pressure monitoring system", *Indones. J. Electr. Eng. Comput. Sci.* Volume 19(3), pp. 1384–1390, 2020, doi: 10.11591/ijeecs.v19.i3.pp1384-1390.

30. S. Albishi, B. Soh, A. Ullah, and F. Algarni, "Challenges and solutions for applications and technologies in the Internet of Things", *Procedia Comput. Sci.* Volume 124, pp. 608–614, 2017, doi: 10.1016/J.PROCS.2017.12.196.

31. K. Ashton, "Related content RFID-powered handhelds guide visitors at Shanghai expo despite sluggish growth, Taiwan's RFID industry remains committed mobile RTLS tracks health-care efficiency RFID journal live! 2010 Report, Part 2", *That "Internet Things" Thing-RFID J.* 2010, Accessed: Aug. 11, 2022. [Online]. Available: http://www.rfidjournal.com/article/print/4986

32. S. C. Mukhopadhyay and N. K. Suryadevara, "Internet of things: Challenges and opportunities", *Smart Sensors, Meas. Instrum.* Volume 9, pp. 1–17, 2014, doi: 10.1007/978-3-319-04223-7_1/COVER.

33. A. Rejeb, K. Rejeb, S. Simske, H. Treiblmaier, and S. Zailani, "The big picture on the internet of things and the smart city: A review of what we know and what we need to know", *Internet of Things.* Volume 19, p. 100565, 2022, doi: 10.1016/J.IOT.2022.100565.

34. T. Ramathulasi and M. Rajasekhara Babu, "Comprehensive survey of IoT communication technologies", *Adv. Intell. Syst. Comput.* Volume 1054, pp. 303–311, 2020, doi: 10.1007/978-981-15-0135-7_29/TABLES/2.

35. B. K. Sarkar, "Big data for secure healthcare system: A conceptual design", *Complex Intell. Syst.* Volume 3(2), pp. 133–151, 2017, doi: 10.1007/S40747-017-0040-1.

36. L. Zhang, J. Xu, P. Vijayakumar, P. K. Sharma, and U. Ghosh, "Homomorphic encryption-based privacy-preserving federated learning in IoT-enabled healthcare system", *IEEE Trans. Netw. Sci. Eng.* pp. 1–17, 2022, doi: 10.1109/TNSE.2022.3185327.

37. S. V. Akram, P. K. Malik, R. Singh, G. Anita, and S. Tanwar, "Adoption of blockchain technology in various realms: Opportunities and challenges", *Secur. Priv.* Volume 3(5), p. e109, 2020, doi: 10.1002/SPY2.109.

38. U. Satapathy, B. K. Mohanta, S. S. Panda, S. Sobhanayak, and D. Jena, "A secure framework for communication in Internet of Things application using hyperledger based blockchain", *2019 10th Int. Conf. Comput. Commun. Netw. Technol. ICCCNT 2019* 2019, doi: 10.1109/ICCCNT45670.2019.8944811.

39. T. Lavigne, B. Mbarek, and T. Pitner, "An intelligent blockchain application for emergency medical services", *Proc. 37th ACM/SIGAPP Symp. Appl. Comput.* 2022, doi: 10.1145/3477314.

40. J. Y. Park, Y. James, and H. Park, "The current state of medical error in South Korea", *Sch. J. Appl. Sci. Res.* Volume 1(4), 2018, Accessed: Aug. 11, 2022. [Online]. Available: www.innovationinfo.org

41. K. Kakhi, R. Alizadehsani, H. M. D. Kabir, A. Khosravi, S. Nahavandi, and U. R. Acharya, "The internet of medical things and artificial intelligence: Trends, challenges, and opportunities", *Biocybern. Biomed. Eng.* Volume 42(3), pp. 749–771, 2022, doi: 10.1016/J.BBE.2022.05.008.

42. J. Wang, J. Chen, Y. Ren, P. K. Sharma, O. Alfarraj, and A. Tolba, "Data security storage mechanism based on blockchain industrial Internet of Things", *Comput. Ind. Eng.* Volume 164, p. 107903, 2022, doi: 10.1016/J.CIE.2021.107903.

43. R. Cerchione, P. Centobelli, E. Riccio, S. Abbate, and E. Oropallo, "Blockchain's coming to hospital to digitalize healthcare services: Designing a distributed electronic health record ecosystem", *Technovation.* p. 102480, 2022, doi: 10.1016/J.TECHNOVATION.2022.102480.

44. G. Zhang, X. Zhang, M. Bilal, W. Dou, X. Xu, and J. J. P. C. Rodrigues, "Identifying fraud in medical insurance based on blockchain and deep learning", *Futur. Gener. Comput. Syst.* Volume 130, pp. 140–154, 2022, doi: 10.1016/J.FUTURE.2021.12.006.

45. G. Zhang and N. J. Navimipour, "A comprehensive and systematic review of the IoT-based medical management systems: Applications, techniques, trends and open issues", *Sustain. Cities Soc.* Volume 82, p. 103914, 2022, doi: 10.1016/J.SCS.2022.103914.

13

Pollution Monitoring and Governance in Smart City using IoT

Javier Rocher, Sandra Viciano-Tudela, Alberto Ivars-Palomares, and Jaime Lloret
Universitat Politècnica de València, Grao de Gandia, Spain

13.1 Introduction

Emigration from rural to urban areas (rural exodus) has increased considerably since the end of the twentieth century. However, this phenomenon started with the Industrial Revolution because new employment opportunities were generated in the cities. Today, 55% of people live in cities, and it is estimated that in 2050, 65% of people will live in cities [1]. This population increase in the cities has generated social conflict and environmental degradation. Different policies have been implemented to improve people's quality of life and reduce environmental damage. These policies and the introduction of new technology have given rise to what are known as smart cities. Parallel to smart cities, new forms of government related to governance have also been developed.

In this chapter, we analyse different pollutants that affect cities, how they are monitored from networks based on the Internet of Things (IoT), and the importance of governance.

13.1.1 Smart Cities

The smart city concept has developed in recent years. According to the European Commission, "[a] smart city is a place where traditional networks and services are made more efficient using digital solutions for the benefit of its inhabitants and business" [2]. Therefore, a smart city must have Information and Communication Technologies (ICT) solutions. The history of smart cities started in the late 1960s in Los Angeles, with the use of computational statistical analysis. With ICT improvement, more cities have developed plans to become smart cities in recent years. In this process, companies have an important role.

An example is Cisco Systems, which launched its Connected Urban Development programme in partnership with San Francisco, Amsterdam, and Seoul with $25 million from the Clinton Foundation in 2006. The main purpose of a smart city is to increase its sustainability through digitisation. It is important to highlight that sustainability is not only from an environmental point of view. It includes human and economic factors.

One of the pillars of smart cities is IoT, which has different definitions. However, most authors agree that IoT is based on smartphones, headphones, washing machines, lamps, wearable devices, etc. connected to the Internet and can receive and send information [3].

The IoT devices can monitor many parameters of cities, improving citizens' quality of life, and avoiding wastage of resource. Many resources were used to develop different technological systems that allow rapid and safe control of the other media that affect cities, such as water channels, lakes, water purification, discharge control, air pollution, light pollution, e-health, traffic, and others. The use of sensors and the communication and monitoring of these are essential to control

DOI:10.1201/9781003326236-13

these environments. IoT is used in smart cities to monitor the environment and improve decision performance. Examples are the use of noise sensors to establish noise maps [4], e-health devices to improve the health of people [5], control of the quality of drinking water [6], and control and prevention of forest fires [7].

The IoT devices used for monitoring have a microcontroller or microprocessor, which is in charge of obtaining the reading of the sensors and controlling their turn-on. Microprocessors have more RAM, flash memory, and computing power than microcontrollers. However, microcontrollers are cheaper than microprocessors [8]. The selection of one of them will depend on the calculation needs that we must have. IoT projects generally use microprocessors that send data to the Internet, where a device with more power computation proceeds to perform the analysis.

One problem with IoT devices is energy consumption. In some cases, these devices are powered by batteries. This implies that their energy consumption must be reduced to reduce energy costs. Different solutions have been proposed to reduce the energy use of these devices [9].

Smart cities are the future of urban development. However, important gaps need to be solved: (I) Smart city requires a considerable investment of capital. (II) There is an increase in dependence on technological services and new technologies. (III) Some groups are reluctant to use new technologies or feel uncomfortable. (IV) An increase in housing prices prevents the younger generation from accessing housing.

13.1.2 Pollution and Environmental Degradation

Pollution is the presence of substances, energy, or radiation harmful to life or infrastructure. People predominantly think that humans cause all pollution and environmental degradation. However, the pollution can have an anthropogenic or natural origin. Examples of natural pollution events are volcanic eruptions, which release huge amounts of sulphur oxides (SO_3) and carbon dioxide (CO_2) into the atmosphere and forest fires with natural origin (caused by electrical storms). However, natural environmental degradation is balanced with the environment, and different species have been adapted. An example is the Mediterranean forest, which has pyrophyte species. The environment can attenuate pollution with anthropogenic origin. However, in some cases, the environmental attenuation capacity must be improved to absorb human pollution.

Anthropogenic pollution is produced due to continuous pollution or as a result of an environmental catastrophe. There are many examples of environmental disasters: nuclear accidents, such as Fukushima (Japan) and Chornobyl (Ukrainian); oil spills, such as Prestige (Galician coast, Spain); Deepwater Horizon explosion (USA); Sanchi oil tanker collision (East China Sea); the spill of toxic sludge from mine such as Aznalcollar (Spain); Brumadinho dam disaster (Brazil); and Kingston Fossil Plant coal fly ash slurry spill (Tennessee, USA). In these accidents, large areas are immediately polluted, and its effects can last many years. The accumulation of pollutants over time can produce environmental disasters. Examples are excess fertilisers in soil that arrive in groundwater and cause nitrate pollution or groundwater, ozone layer holes produced by chlorofluorocarbon (CFC), and global warming. An example of the pollution of an area to the accumulation of pollutants is the eutrophication of water bodies such as the Mar Menor in Spain. Mar Menor has suffered various types of pollution over time. Due to urbanisation, sanitation networks became inadequate, and mining activities dumped waste in wetland areas. Agricultural and livestock activities increased with the arrival of the Tajo-Segura water transfer in 1979. The water masses of Mar Menor are deteriorating because of not complying with the regulations related to nitrates from agriculture and livestock and a lack of practical application of the legal system. Consequently, eutrophication of the waters of the Mar Menor was caused by discharges rich in nitrates, resulting in a lack of oxygen in the water and massive mortality of marine fauna [10].

In urban areas, pollution is a severe problem. According to the World Health Organization (WHO), nine out of ten people breathe polluted air, and seven million die each year [11]. Different studies have concluded that breathing polluted air has an effect equivalent to smoking tobacco. In urban areas, pollution is not only present in the air. Soil and water pollution affect human health. In the soil, the concentration of heavy metals, hydrocarbons, and other substances can come into contact with people by ingesting soil or inhaling vapours. In water, pollution reaches humans through the ingestion of water.

One pollution problem is that those who generate it may not feel its effects. Transboundary pollution is a critical problem, especially between countries in conflict [12]. An example of this is acid rain. It has devastating effects, including the disappearance of European forests, the eradication of life from lakes in Canada and the United States, and the harm it caused to humans and crops in China and India. Acid rain is caused by sulphur and nitrogen oxides that react in water and generate nitric acid, sulphurous acid, and sulphuric acid. These acids lower the pH of rainwater, which can cause acidification of water bodies affecting wildlife. In addition, acid rain risks human structures, artistic monuments, and respiratory problems [13].

Finally, pollution is not the only negative impact that an environment can have. The degradation of ecosystems can occur without the presence of pollutants in them. Habitat destruction, the reduction of water available, the compaction of soil, the extinction of wildlife, or the introduction of invasive species are examples of the degradation of natural environments.

13.1.3 Governance

Governance is about citizens participating in making decisions that can affect them. In traditional democracies, the people elect their representatives. These politicians make decisions without being obliged to consider people's opinions. Therefore, the political elites were at the top of the social pyramid. With the evolution of democracies, the concept of governance has been introduced. The governance tries to reduce the power pyramid between political elites and citizens. This implies that the new governments include citizen participation. The European Commission defined governance as the set of rules, procedures, and practices related to exercising powers in the European Union and bringing citizens closer to it. The principles are as follows: transparency of institutions, involving society in decision-making, implementing consistent policies, and administering a regulatory framework favouring employment [14]. For this reason, the public administration that applies governance has several complementary bodies that ensure the rights of citizens, such as accountability, public ethics guides, and public participation programmes.

The use of ICT has improved governance. Nowadays, it is a strange government that needs a webpage. On the webpage, the government can upload projects that affect different organisms, and interested people can consult more quickly than if these projects were only in paper format. Another improvement of ICT in governance is the possibility of organising electronic referendums. In these referendums, the citizens can vote between different projects allowing the government to choose those projects that citizens prefer.

Everything and the improvements that ICTs bring to governance can present problems that must be solved. (I) Some groups, such as the elderly, may not feel comfortable in a digital environment. That is why it is more likely that they will not participate in it. That is why their entry into or creation of physical spaces where they can interact and participate in the projects must be facilitated. (II) Security is an essential factor. Manipulation of public participation processes by third parties must be prevented. (III) Advertising campaigns should be carried out, so citizens know that public participation processes exist.

13.2 Pollution and Environment Degradation

In this part of the chapter, we will focus on exposing the different types of pollution in the city and the effects they produce.

13.2.1 Soil Pollution and Degradation

Soil pollution and degradation affect both agricultural and urban soils. One of the main problems is the soil compaction caused by civil engineering and agricultural machinery [15]. The soil compaction

FIGURE 13.1 Example of a desired path.

is the increase of its density caused by external stress, reducing, or eliminating the air pores. Soil compaction adversely affects soil's transpiration, reducing the oxygen available to animals, microorganisms, and plant roots found under the ground. Another effect is the reduction of rainwater infiltration and the soil's capacity to retain rainwater inside, increasing the flooding risk. Recovering compacted soil is difficult, so it is an intelligent use of civil engineering. Buildings and roads can cause soil compaction. Using agricultural machinery in the parks, the people transit, and rain on the bare ground produces compaction. An example of soil compaction is desire paths. Figure 13.1 shows an example of a desired path in a green area in Gandia (Spain) formed by the compaction and erosion of the soil by the people's transit. Another fact that causes environmental degradation is the elimination of flora in large cities. Some cities removed trees in the avenues and streets due to the cost of the maintenance of trees. This causes an increase in heat and a decrease in humidity. Trees have important advantages in cities because they absorb pollutants, reduce heat, and serve as a refuge for urban fauna.

Asphalting and buildings prevent the soil's natural renewal because the litter cannot be degraded. This fact causes an alteration in the cycle of soil decomposition and nutrient renewal. Figure 13.2 shows the soil decomposition cycle under normal conditions. Nitrogenous bacteria can fix atmospheric nitrogen in the roots or the soil and convert it to ammonium. Furthermore, animals feed on plants, and decomposers break down nitrogen. In turn, decomposer organisms also break down nitrogen from the plants themselves. Decomposers, through ammonification, convert it to ammonium. Due to the nitrifying bacteria, the ammonium is converted into nitrite and later into nitrate. Nitrate is incorporated into plants through the assimilation process. Alternatively, it can return to the atmosphere due to denitrification as denitrifying bacteria produce nitrogen. The soil degradation interference with the soil biota can affect food production for human consumption [16].

The pollution of urban areas causes the heat island effect [17]. This phenomenon consists of increased temperatures in the city's centre to the outside. This effect occurs, among other reasons, due to the construction of buildings, asphalt, pollutants, and the elimination of residual heat. The asphalt increases the heat in a city because sunlight heats the soil, releasing heat into the atmosphere through infrared radiation or reflected light. As the asphalt is black, the sunlight is absorbed, causing an accumulation of heat buildup that is released into the environment. The presence of buildings

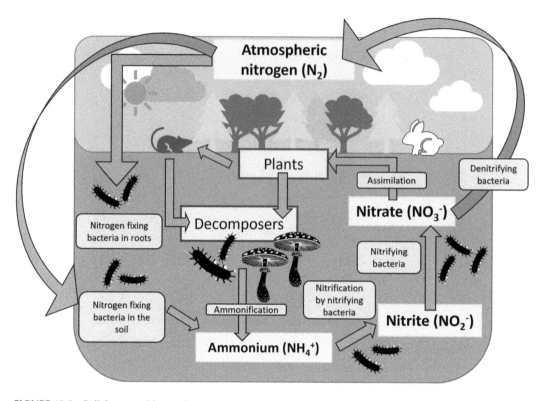

FIGURE 13.2 Soil decomposition cycle.

avoids the circulation of the wind, which causes heat to accumulate inside the city. Residual heat is produced in the towns and is released into the environment. Finally, pollutants have two effects: (I) Reactions between pollutants and the atmosphere generate heat. (II) Pollutants such as CO_2 absorb infrared radiation. This fact implies that the temperature increases between 1°C and 3°C.

Another problem in the soil is soil loss. Soil loss is due to the erosion and transport of soil by the wind and water. As we said previously, asphalt increases rainwater runoff, increasing soil loss. In addition, the reduction of vegetation increases due to the vegetation with its roots fixing the soil. The loss of soil reduces the fertility of soils. It is estimated that creating 1 cm of soil takes between 100 to 1,000 years.

So far, we have talked about land degradation. Now, we are analysing soil pollution. The soil pollutants can be found in three ways, depending on their concentration and physical characteristics. In low concentrations, the pollutants are adsorbed in the soil matrix. In addition, volatile pollutants such as hydrocarbons and mercury will be in equilibrium in the atmosphere of the soil. When the pollutant's concentration increases, the soil matrix will not be able to absorb them, and these go on to form a free sheet that descends through the ground until the water table. So if a pollutant is removed from the aquifer and the source of pollution is eliminated, the soil may be contaminated. Examples of soil pollutants are hydrocarbons, heavy metals, pesticides, fertiliser nitrates, and pathogenic microorganisms. Usually, heavy metals are found in industrial areas or deindustrialised areas. In the case of hydrocarbons, these can be found in the same areas as heavy metals, petrol stations, and near gas tanks. In industrial areas, the pollutants reach the soil due to discharges from companies or their dragging by water. Another source is the dragging of pollutants from the atmosphere by rainwater. In the case of hydrocarbons, these arrive in the soil due to the leaks of the combustible deposits. The other pollutants (nitrates, pesticides, and fertilisers) come from gardens, crops, or water transport. If the groundwater is polluted by these pollutants and is used for irrigation, these pollutants return to the soil.

Additionally, the greater use of plastics in all sectors has caused an increase in the accumulation of microplastics, which in most cases end up in the water or in the soil itself, increasing its contamination. Although microplastics are currently best known for their significant contamination of water, this excessive increase has caused them to infiltrate the soil considerably. These microplastics are ingested by small animals or deposited on plants, eventually becoming part of our food chain and ending inside our bodies [18]. We understand microplastics as any synthetic solid particle or polymeric matrix of regular or irregular shape with a size that ranges between 1 μm and 5 mm – of primary or secondary manufacturing origin – that are insoluble in water [19]. These microplastics are emerging and ubiquitous contaminants that have become an environmental challenge [20].

13.2.2   Water Pollution

This section will focus on water pollution. First, it is vital to know the water cycle. The water cycle has been known since ancient times. It is produced mainly by solar energy. The sun heats the water in the oceans, seas, and other water bodies, evaporating it. The water coalesces into heavier droplets through condensation and eventually falls back to the ground (rain). Rainwater will run through ravines and rivers until it returns to the sea. In this way, humans use this water for their industry, consumption, or irrigation. Currently, the annual global water requirement is around 6,000 to 7,000 km^3. However, there are about 7,000,000 km^3 of water reserves worldwide due to groundwater. This water accumulates annually, thanks to the rains and the percolation process. In recent years, this reserve has been affected by excessive extraction and low rainfall, causing a drop in the water table [21].

As mentioned above, the water cycle is vital on the planet for the life of organisms. An alteration in the water quality in this cycle can cause a significant system alteration. Urbanisation is one of the most characteristic examples that produce alterations in the quality of the water cycle (groundwater and surface water [22]). These mainly artificial alterations have given rise to various natural disasters. In the previous point, we discussed the effect of asphalt paving that causes alterations in the structure and quality of the soil.

Water has different pollutants, such as organic matter, solids, fertilisers, pesticides, nutrients, and endocrine disruptors. In organic matter, we can differentiate between Biochemical Oxygen Demand (BOD) and Chemical Oxygen Demand (COD). BOD is the organic matter that microorganisms can digest, and COD is the total organic matter [23]. The unit of these parameters is mg O_2/l because the amount of oxygen needed to degrade organic matter is measured. To measure the BOD, the sample must be placed in an airtight container with microorganisms for a while. Usually, in water analyses, the BOD_5 measure is performed. BOD_5 is the amount of oxygen consumed by microorganisms in five days. Another parameter is BOD_L. This is the amount of oxygen necessary to degrade all the biodegradable organic matter in the water. The use of BOD_5 is because five days is the average time that the water is in the rivers in the United Kingdom that were the first to implement these measures. To obtain the BOD_L, the sample is usually kept for 21 days. As the measurement of BOD is slow, COD is necessary many times. The COD is a measure that takes approximately two hours and can be related empirically to the values of BOD_L. In addition, the difference between COD and BOD gives us information about the contamination of organic matter that is not biodegradable in the water. Another parameter that can be introduced is total organic carbon (TOC), which measures the amount of CO_2 formed after the oxidation of organic matter in water. This parameter is related to the BOD and the COD. However, few studies still exist on its widespread use [24].

Solids are another pollutant present in water. The nature of solids can be very varied. Solids can be minerals, microorganisms, and soil. The solids can come from the presence of other contaminants or the drag produced by the water. Other water pollutants are nutrients, which are necessary for the growth of life. The presence of these in water can generate problems of eutrophication. The primary nutrients are nitrogen and phosphorus. These elements come from detergents, human and animal depositions, industry, etc. Finally, endocrine disruptors are one emerging pollutant. These are a group of pollutants detected nowadays with improved analytical techniques. There needs to be more information about these. The origin of these pollutants is due to the use of drugs and complex compounds. Endocrine disruptors generate hormonal changes in living beings, which cause changes in the sex of animals and can hinder reproduction.

Pollution of water bodies can occur by rainwater, which carries pollutants from the atmosphere or the soil surface, wastewater, illegal discharges produced by industry, or pollutant incidents. Wastewater is the result of the use of water by domestic, industrial, and public services, and due to its use, it ceases to be usable and therefore becomes waste. The sewerage infrastructure transports the wastewater from urban areas to a wastewater treatment plant (WWTP). Illegal discharges are when companies or individuals discharge wastewater without authorisation. These discharges cause significant pollution, increasing the poor quality of the water and becoming harmful to human health [18]. Pollution occurs when the sewerage does not work correctly and discharges its waters into the natural environment. Illegal discharges and pollution incidents affect flora and fauna. Wastewater must be treated before being released into the sea or rivers or reused. Hence, the WWTP eliminates pollution through physical–chemical processes. The purified wastewater (effluent from a WWTP) can be reused for other purposes or directly discharged into a water body. To dump the purified wastewater, WWTP must accomplish the legislation's values or discharge authorisation [25].

Moreover, the pollutants that affect the soil also affect the water. When these are introduced into the water cycle, they cause groundwater contamination. This contamination can be caused by sewage, which contains pathogenic microorganisms, such as bacteria, viruses, protozoa, and sometimes helminth eggs [26]. In addition to biological contaminants, chemical pollutants such as nitrates above 10 mg/L (10 ppm) produce essential diseases such as methemoglobinemia or blue baby syndrome. Currently, limits for nitrates in drinking water have been set at 50 mg/L by the European Community and the World Health Organization and at 10 mg/L (nitrate–nitrogen) by the US Environmental Protection Agency [27].

13.2.3   Air Pollution

With the increase in globalisation in recent years and the development of large cities, industrial areas, and transport systems, the production of gases harmful to the atmosphere has increased. An example is CO_2; although everyone knows that living beings expel this gas, using fossil fuels has caused this gas to reach the atmosphere and form part of the gases that produce the greenhouse effect [28]. In addition, there are other harmful gases, such as sulphur dioxide (SO_2) and nitrogen oxides. Sulphur dioxide is naturally emitted into the atmosphere by sulphur bacteria and volcanic eruptions. However, the increase in industry and power plants is the cause of the significant increase in the use of sulphur-rich fossil fuels. While volcanic eruptions also emit nitrogen oxides (NOx), the rise in motor vehicles causes a substantial increase in the atmosphere [29]. The emission of NOx is produced by the combustion of nitrogen components in the combustible and the dissociation of N_2 in the air used in the combustion. These gases are toxic and are precursors of acid rain.

SO_2 and NOx in contact with the atmosphere produced different acids (sulphuric, sulphurous, and nitric). These acids fall to the ground through water, fog, or snow. Acid rain is associated with a loss of biodiversity and decreased productivity in the environment [30]. In cities, it also affects heritage, with the corrosion of buildings, old streets, fountains, etc.

Another phenomenon due to air pollution is photochemical smog. Smog is associated with the presence of pollutants and light irradiation. It is represented by a lead-coloured or black cloud produced by gases originating in industrial areas that react upon exposure to sunlight [31]. Figure 13.3 shows the primary pollutant in the photochemical smog process. First, there are the primary pollutants that initiate the process. The emission of pollutants can come from natural or artificial sources. The primary pollutants are suspended particles, hydrocarbons (NOx), carbon monoxide (CO), and CO_2. These primary pollutants react, giving rise to secondary pollutants such as peroxyacetyl nitrates (PANs), ozone (O_3), H_2SO_4, and HNO_3. Figure 13.4 shows the reactions that occur in the photolytic process in smog. One of the reactions is ozone formation from NO_2, where the light falls on NO_2, giving rise to free radicals of NO and O. The oxygen atom unites with O_2, giving rise to O_3. Another reaction that occurs is the formation of free radicals from hydrocarbons.

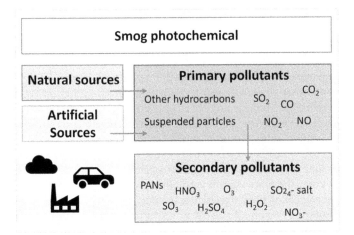

FIGURE 13.3 Smog photochemical.

PHOTOCHEMICAL SMOG REACTIONS	
Ozone formation from NO_2	**Formation of free radicals from hydrocarbons**
$NO_2 + Light \rightarrow NO + O$ $O + O_2 \rightarrow O_3$	$RH + O_2 \rightarrow RO^*$ (Free radical) $RO^* + O_2 \rightarrow RO^*_3$ $RO^*_3 + HC \rightarrow R^* CHO$ (Acetaldehyde)
Formation of PAN (Peroxyacetylene nitrate)	
$RO^*_3 + NO \rightarrow RO_2 + NO_2$ $RO^*_3 + O_2 \rightarrow RO_2 + O_3$ $RO^*_3 + NO_2 \rightarrow RCO_3NO_2$ (PAN)	

FIGURE 13.4 Photochemical smog reactions.

The hydrocarbon joins with the O_2, giving rise to a free radical. This merges with O_2 forming RO_3^*, which will join another hydrocarbon, giving rise to acetaldehyde. Finally, in photochemical smog, PAN is formed.

In this case, a molecule of RO_3^* joins with NO to give rise to RO_2 and NO_2. The RO_3^* molecule can bind with oxygen, leading to the formation of RO_2 and ozone. In addition to binding to NO and Ozone, this same molecule can bind to NO_2, giving rise to PAN. The reactions of smog are a cycle, where the final result is another NO_2. Therefore, once the chemical reactions are started, they will only stop once all the hydrocarbons are eliminated from the atmosphere. This, together with the generation of toxic compounds, makes this a hazardous event for human health. An example of its danger occurred in the Great Smog of London in 1952, where 4,000 people died and 100,000 suffered from respiratory problems.

Another pollutant is particles found in the air that are harmful to health. They can be classified into two types: primary and secondary. The primary particles are emitted directly from the exhaust pipes, dust, and sand particles. Secondary particles are formed in the atmosphere due to chemical reactions from gaseous materials called precursors. Particulate matter is a standard indicator of air pollution and affects more people than any other pollutant. Its main composition is nitrates, ammonia, sodium chloride, sulphates, mineral powders, water, and soot. The need to understand the danger of volatile particles has led scientists to characterise them according to size and origin. The dangerousness of the particles is affected by their size, causing different types of diseases. The particles more monitored in air stations are PM10 and PM2.5. The aerodynamic particle diameter size given its name is 10 micrometres and 2.5 micrometres, respectively [32]. We also find PM1 particles smaller than 1 micrometre. Bacteria, viruses, and ultrafine dust particles present this type of microparticle.

The WHO indicates that particles less than 2.5 micrometres cause the most severe diseases because it can reach the lungs, enter the bloodstream, and affect the heart [33]. Several studies focus on the importance and aggressiveness of PM2.5 particles. In addition to their danger due to their size, these particles contain pollutants. Their small size allows them to remain suspended in the air longer and be transported over long distances.

Although no threshold has been found in which particles do not affect health, WHO has established some values in which these particles must be found. The smallest particles (PM2.5) must be at 5 $\mu g/m^3$ annually and 15 $\mu g/m^3$ daily average. At the same time, coarse particles (PM10) should be found at 15 $\mu g/m^3$ as an annual average and 45 $\mu g/m^3$ 24 as a daily average.

13.2.4 Noise Pollution

Noise pollution is any type of vibration that implies an annoyance, risk, or damage to people; the development of their activities; or goods of any nature or causes damage to the environment without considering the acoustic emitter that originates them [34]. The WHO defines noise as more significant than 65 decibels (dB). If this noise exceeds 75 dB, it is considered harmful and painful from 120 dB.

The increase in the population, the decrease in the use of public transport and the increase in private vehicles, the construction of large buildings, and the increase in leisure areas have caused an increase in noise pollution in large cities. European Environment Agency (EEA) data shows that noise causes 72,000 hospitalisations and 16,600 premature deaths [35]. Some effects of noise in humans are decreased performance, aggressiveness, tiredness, stress, sleep disturbance, and stomach disorders. In animals, the cycles of sleep, mating, and social relationships between them can be affected due to noise – even leading to the extinction of some species.

13.2.5 Light Pollution

Light pollution is the emissions produced by artificial sources, which are not directed to the ground, and the reflection from the light on the ground towards the sky. Light pollution is caused by the excessive power of artificial lights and the poor design of streetlights or streetlamps [36]. The time these streetlights are connected should also be considered since a poor lighting control system can affect light pollution. In general, this type of pollution occurs in cities. Light pollution is energy wasted because the objective of light is not to light up the sky. Consequently, polluting residues are generated with this energy production.

The alteration in the luminosity indices causes an alteration in the biological cycles of living beings [37]. Plants and other animals see their circadian cycles affected. For example, birds deviate from their directions or their reproductive cycles. As for humans, artificial light causes sleep disturbances that can lead to the development of some diseases. As for the transport sector, glare can affect drivers' visibility and cause accidents. Furthermore, maritime and air traffic are affected by high light pollution.

Europe is one of the continents with the highest light pollution. This is partly due to its significant development compared to other continents. Spain is the third country with the most increased light pollution, followed by Greece and Malta. At a global level, it can be roughly observed that Europe is one of the continents with the highest rate of light pollution. On the opposite side, we find continents with less pollution, such as Africa, due to its low level of development.

13.3 Monitoring the Pollution

In this section, we analyse different methodologies and IoT technologies that can monitor the main pollutants in cities. We differentiate between the pollutants in soil, air, and water. In addition, we analyse the light and sound monitoring. These environments are related to them. For example, a pollutant can reach the soil by deposition from the air, and after this, it can be accumulated and carried by rainwater to another water body or infiltrated into groundwater.

13.3.1 Soil Monitoring

The monitoring of soil with IoT instrumentation is complex. The soil pollutants are hard to monitor because these are adsorbed in the soil matrix and are not evenly distributed in the soil. The application of analytic techniques in a laboratory or the use of analysers is necessary.

The techniques to monitor the hydrocarbons in the soil are based on the desorption of the hydrocarbons of the soil with a solvent and the analysis with gravimetry, chromatography, mass spectrometry, etc. These techniques require laboratory equipment and, in many cases, cannot be used in situ. To monitor the concentration of hydrocarbons in United States (US), the environmental protection agency (EPA) established the standard method (418.1 EPA). This traditional method is recommended to detect areas polluted and use more expensive methods to ensure the soil is clean [38]. One alternative is the detection of hydrocarbons in groundwater using materials that absorb the hydrocarbons and generate a change in one intrinsic property that can be measured. An example is presented by Yavari et al. [39]. They propose the use of optical fibre covered by a silicone rod. The silicone rod in contact with hydrocarbons absorbs them, generating a bending that affects the light's pass. However, this technique could be more precise; therefore, work must be done to prevent spills. Using a sensor to control the levels of oils in the deposits and correctly implementing the legislation are the best tools to control this parameter.

Like hydrocarbons, monitoring heavy metals in the soil is complex because the heavy metals are adsorbed to the ground. Different methodologies to monitor them have been proposed. One methodology is the use of spectrophotometry. Different studies have verified that artificially adding a number of heavy metals to the soil modifies its spectrum [40, 41]. This opens the possibility of using satellite imagery or drone flights to detect possible areas contaminated by heavy metals. However, spectrophotometry with the use of remote sensing presents essential gaps: (I) Remote sensing can detect the pollution of heavy metals on the surface. However, it is not adequate to detect pollution in the subsoil. (II) The presence of vegetation covers the soil, and measuring the reflectance of the soil is impossible. For these reasons, remote sensing can detect possible soil pollution but cannot be used to verify soil pollution. It is necessary to elaborate on in situ studies.

Technology is an essential instrument for reducing water use in green areas. Moisture sensors minimise the quantity of water used in irrigation. Because the moisture of the soil is maintained between field capacity (maximum amount of water that the soil can hold) and the permanent wilting point (minimum amount of water where the plant cannot obtain water from the soil). Recently, drones with Red, Green, Blue (RGB) and infrared cameras have been implemented to analyse plants' status and calculate the normalised difference vegetation index (NDVI).

13.3.2 Water Monitoring

Water is named a universal solvent because it dissolves most substances. Thus, many substances are detected in water. Water has been used to transport the pollutants of people from where they are generated. One problem with water is the presence of illicit discharges. The companies and people must only discharge the pollutant into the sewerage with a discharge permit. However, as we have previously discussed, illicit discharges are produced.

To detect the presence of illicit discharge in sewerage, it is essential to know the variation of pollutant concentration all day – the wastewater quality changes daily and yearly [42]. Sports events or holidays can affect the wastewater quality. In Figure 13.5, we represent the evolution of the

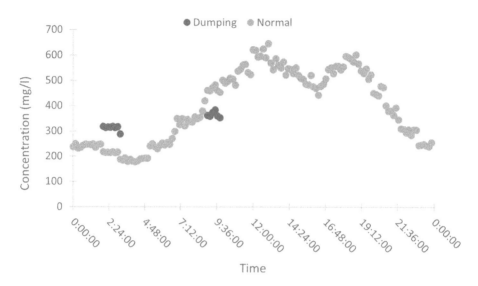

FIGURE 13.5 Evolution of solids throughout the day and the effect of two discharges.

concentration of a pollutant in wastewater (solids) and what happens in the case of two dumplings. The pollutant concentration at night is less than during the day. It is from 5:00 hours that it begins to see a rise in the concentration of pollutants until noon. At midday, there is a slight drop in the pollutant concentration until mid-afternoon. From this time, there is a constant drop until the next day. In the case of a discharge, this can be more, less, or the same concentration as the wastewater. With the monitoring of different parameters, the probability that the discharge concentration is the same as wastewater is reduced. The sensor will detect a change in wastewater concentrations in the other two cases. To discard the difference in the concentration due to daily fluctuations, the values must be sent to a central node where the values will be compared with the historical series and the values of other nearby sensors. With this information and the use of artificial intelligence, it is possible to detect the presence of a spill.

Integrating different sensors allows for the control of the physical water parameters [43, 44]. Turbidity is one of the parameters that can be used to detect the presence of illicit discharges [45]. Turbidity is defined as the transparency of water and depends on the solids and dissolved substances in water. Three methods to measure this parameter are Secchi disk, optical, and acoustic. Secchi disk is based on the introduction in the water of a disk and measuring the depth that disk is not visible. This method is complex of automatised. For this reason, it is not used for continuous monitoring. However, volunteers currently use it as a simple method to control water bodies [46]. The acoustic turbidity sensors are based on acoustic Doppler current profilers (ADCPs). These are based on emitting an acoustic pulse and measuring the acoustic backscatter. The optical turbidity sensors have a similar operation. This type of sensor emits light instead of an acoustic wave. A photoreceptor is located to capture the light (signal). The photoreceptor can be found at different angles concerning the light emitter. At a tip of 180°, it measures the absorbance of water (absorptiometer). If the angle differs from 180°, the photoreceptor measures the backscattering light (nephelometer). Usually, the photoreceptor of the nephelometer is at 90°. Figure 13.6 represents a turbidity sensor's function based on optical (a) and acoustic (b). The use of the two technologies is not impossible.

Conductivity can also be used to control the presence of illicit discharge. Water's conductivity is defined as water's ability to conduct electricity. Pure water is a poor conductor of electricity. However, the dissolved salts in water make water a good conductor of electricity. There are three methods to measure conductivity: (I) density methods, (II) conductivity cells, and (III) inductive sensors.

The density method is based on a tube's vibration containing the sample. The period of vibration is related to the density according to Equation 13.1. The instrument's calibration calculates the terms

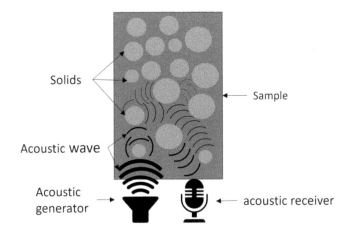

FIGURE 13.6 Operating an acoustic sensor.

A and *B* with samples of known density [47]. Nowadays, this method is not much used because cell methods are more reliable and easier to use.

$$\text{Density} = A + B \, \text{period}^2 \tag{13.1}$$

The conductivity cell method is based on two or more electrodes that measure the electrical current that the sample can carry. This method is the most used today due to its low cost and easier to use; however, it has disadvantages such as the hardiness of the elements. For this reason, there are studies on the use of inductive conductivity sensors. Inductivity sensors are based on generating an electromagnetic field that induces a coil. The induction will depend on the concentration of salt in the sample.

Other parameters such as pH, nitrates, ammonia, and organic matter indicate water pollution. To monitor the pH, the method used in IoT is the location of a specific membrane. The pH metre is similar to a conductivity cell but presents a membrane that does not allow the passage of substances other than protons. Similar methods are used for nitrates and ammonia. The use of membranes implies high maintenance cost, which makes use of these sensors on a large scale unfeasible. Regarding the organic matter, the most widely used method is ultraviolet spectrophotometry. In this case, it is difficult to generate ultraviolet light wavelengths for large-scale IoT-oriented equipment.

Other important groups of pollutants in water are biological pollutants. It is necessary to differentiate between biological pollution in drinking water and water bodies.

In drinking water, laboratory monitoring of biological pollutants of bacteria is produced with culture techniques. Different techniques are used, such as (I) multiple tube fermentation (MTF), (II) membrane filtration (MF), (III) DNA/RNA amplification, and (IV) fluorescence in situ hybridisation (FISH) [48]. The MTF is based on location in a glass tube of a culture medium and the sample we would analyse. Depending on the bacteria to be analysed, a specific culture medium will be placed at a specific temperature and time. Like MTF is the MF, in the MF technique, the samples are filtered, and the filter is located in a medium for the growth of the bacteria. These two techniques cannot be used to detect viruses because these cannot replicate without infecting a cell. The use of genetic techniques is used to detect viruses and bacteria. One technique is DNA and RNA amplification. This technique amplifies the DNA or RNA chain using reagents and thermocyclers. In the reagents, there is a fluorescent substance, that is the one that will mark the number of DNA or RNA chains generated. Finally, the FISH technique is based on fluorescent probes that hybridise into nucleic acid chains (the fluorescent probe is specific for a group of bacteria or viruses). When hybridisation occurs, the sample is fixed, and the excess probe is wiped off. The fluorescence of the sample is indicative of the number of bacteria or viruses present. Due to the precision demands necessary for these techniques and the fact that many are based on cultures, as far as we know, there are no sensors to monitor these parameters.

In water bodies, other microorganisms that can be developed are microalgae. This excessive growth can generate the eutrophication of water (bloom). It generally measures the concentration of chlorophyll A (green pigment) to detect eutrophication. Different studies have demonstrated that remote sensing can predict the values of these pigments in water. Because eutrophication causes a colour change in the water, the turbidity sensor is an option. Different wavelengths of light are used to differentiate between eutrophication turbidity and other turbidity sources. The different sources of turbidity presented different behaviours for each light wavelength. Therefore, it is possible to determine the source of turbidity [49].

13.3.3 Air Monitoring

Generally, the concentration of pollutants in the air is low, with orders of magnitude of $\mu g/m^3$ or mg/m^3. However, the amount of air consumed by a person is higher than in other routes of exposure.

In Europe, DIRECTIVE 2008/50/EC must create a network of station measures to control the air quality in the agglomerations and background pollution [50]. In other countries, there are similar laws. In US, the Clean Air Act ensures good air quality to protect public health and welfare and regulate emissions of air pollutants [51]. To ensure the correct air quality, the Environmental Protection Agency (EPA), with the federal government, performs and carries out air monitoring campaigns that include a series of fixed stations to monitor air quality (AirData Air Quality Monitors app). Other countries such as Australia [52], Singapore [53], and Japan [54] have similar networks. Usually, these networks provide information about air pollutant concentrations of O_3, NOx, CO_2, SO_2, NH_3, PM2.5, PM10, etc., and meteorological data such as rain, wind speed and direction, and sunlight.

These networks allow the control of pollution in cities. However, they cannot control the pollution inside buildings. Different sensors can be used to monitor indoor environments. Saini, Dutta, and Marques [55] analysed 40 papers about IoT in indoor environments and determined that 70% of the papers measured temperature and humidity, 65% measured CO_2, and 30% measured CO. PM10 and PM 2.5 are used in 27.5% of the papers, and, finally, 20% measured volatile organic compounds (VOCs). Most of the works use the MQ series sensors to monitor the gases. The DHT11 and DHT22 are the most common sensors to measure temperature and humidity.

DHT11 and DHT22 are two sensors to measure the relative humidity and temperature of the air. The temperature is measured with a thermistor, and humidity is measured with a capacitor sensor. The difference between these sensors is that DHT22 is more expensive than DHT11. However, the DHT22 is more precise. These sensors are used indoors to control the humidity and temperature. This helps to generate a more pleasant atmosphere and reduce the electrical consumption of appliances such as air conditioning. The control of these parameters is related to e-health.

The MQ sensors are a family of sensors that allow the monitoring of different gases. These sensors have a sensing element that reacts with the gas' changing properties. These sensors have a calefactor to heat the sensing element to react with the gas. In this sensor family, sensors that can contact explosive gases have a mesh covering the sensor to prevent explosions. Table 13.1 presents the different MQ sensors and the gases that can be monitored.

13.3.4 Sound Monitoring

Sound monitoring is essential to improve the health of citizens. Some cities have noise maps developed to know saturated areas and take measures. Sound maps are a tool that city governments use to reduce the sound level by applying specific regulations. However, more than the new regulation may be needed because it is difficult to enforce regulations. For this reason, the IoT is a good tool for reducing sound pollution [4].

The use of an IoT sound sensor detects places where excessive noise is produced. With this, the sensor can generate an alarm so that the police can stop the noise generation. This reduces noisy neighbours, spotting bar fights, and detecting illegal parties.

TABLE 13.1

Elements That Can Be Monitored with MQ Sensors

Sensor	Measure Element	Sensor	Measure Element	Sensor	Measure Element
MQ-2	Propane, butane, methane, hydrogen, alcohol	MQ-7	Carbon Monoxide	MQ-136	Hydrogen Sulfide
MQ-3	Alcohol	MQ-8	Hydrogen	MQ-137	NH3
MQ-4	Methane, natural gas	MQ-9	Carbon Monoxide	MQ-138	Benzene alcohol, NH3
MQ-5	LPG, LNG, natural gas, iso-butane, propane, town gas	MQ-131	Ozone	MQ-214	Methane, LPG, propane, butane
MQ-6	LPG, iso-butane, propane, LNG	MQ-135	Nh3, Benzene, alcohol	MQ-216	LPG, propane, butane, methane, alcohol

There are sound sensors such as LM386, KY-037, and DFR0034. These sensors have a microphone that detects the sound and transmits the information to a microcontroller.

13.3.5   Light Monitoring

There are few studies on monitoring light pollution with IoT. Usually, this type of pollution is detected with field studies. However, some authors introduce IoT sensors to monitor this pollution and take measures to reduce it. Pribadi et al. [56] used a sky quality metre model SQM-LU connected to a Raspberry Pi to control light pollution. The significant gap in the solution to continuous monitoring is that no solutions can be implemented to reduce light pollution quickly. The solutions to reducing it are based on improving the design of the lamps, reducing light intensity, eliminating the lights projected to the sky, etc. These solutions however need to be initiated by the administrations to come into effect.

13.4   Governance

As we said previously, governance is the interaction of all members of society in making decisions. In many cases, the laws require interaction with society for decision-making. In the European Union, Directive 2011/92/EU on assessing the effects of specific public and private projects on the environment in article 6 section 5 requires the submission to public participation of all projects that must undergo an environmental impact assessment [57]. In US, projects with environmental impacts are subjected to Environmental Impact Statement. The document includes the alternatives and the major impacts of the analysed project. The final and draft document is shared with the federal agency and the citizens [58].

Governance is a tool to include the different statements of the society and control the politician elites. Governance is a fundamental pillar of modern democracies. Citizens no longer only elect their rulers from time to time but also participate in decision-making. Proper governance can lead to conflicts. Aggravating these conflicts can lead to riots and even civil wars [59]. In addition, bad governance is related to corruption [60].

New technologies have improved governance with the introduction of e-governance. E-governance is the introduction of ICT in the different statements of the government to facilitate the exchange of information between the administration and citizens. The quality of e-government increases trust in government [61].

The data obtained from the different IoT systems present in a city help in decision-making. Hence, there are more and more cities that bet on smart cities. In addition, to help improve the city, financial expenses decrease with the reduction in the use of resources. In the following section, some of the smart cities are presented in which, thanks to good use of governance, the quality of the city and that of the citizens have been improved.

13.4.1 Projects in Cities Related to Governance

In this section, some examples of smart cities that are related to governance are cited. According to Telecommunication Standardization Sector of International Telecommunication Union (ITU-T) [62] "A Smart Sustainable City

> is an innovative city that takes advantage of Information and Communication Technologies (ICT) and other means to improve quality of life, competitiveness, operational efficiency, and urban services while ensuring that it responds to the needs of present and future generations in terms of economic, social, environmental and cultural aspects.

According to the IMD Smart City Index 2021 [63], Singapore is at the top of the list of the most intelligent cities. And within the top ten, we find Bilbao. According to this index, Madrid is in position 34, followed by Barcelona, and in position number 15, the city of Zaragoza appears on the list. Table 13.2 shows the top ten of the most innovative cities in the world in 2021, as well as the changes that have occurred in the positions of each city [64].

Next, we will comment on some of the smart cities in the Spanish state and examples of the projects they have associated with that allow them to develop smart cities.

First of all, we will talk about Valencia. In 2018, the intelligent city office was created in Valencia in the Local Government Board, where the necessary powers to carry out a smart city were established. For the development of this city, different projects have been carried out that have allowed the city of Valencia to develop as a smart city. Table 13.3 shows the classification followed by the projects depending on whether they affect services to citizens, the city, or municipal services [65].

TABLE 13.2

World Smart Cities Ranking in 2021

Position	1. Singapore	2. Zurich	3. Oslo	4. Taipei City	5. Lausanne
Rating	AAA	AA	AA	A	A
Structure	AAA	AAA	AAA	A	AAA
Technology	AAA	A	A	A	A
Position	6. Helsinki	7. Copenhagen	8. Geneva	9. Auckland	10. Bilbao
Rating	A	A	A	A	BBB
Structure	AA	AA	AA	A	A
Technology	A	A	A	A	BBB

TABLE 13.3

Projects Associated with the City of Valencia

Services to the citizenship	WiFi4EU, Web COVID 19 de información ciudadana, València al minut, AppValència, Geoportal, WiFiValencia, Open data, Connecta VLCi, Efficient management of places for reduced mobility-loading and unloading-taxi, and local civic network
City	VLCi Platform, ISO 37120 certification, development and evaluation of the implementation of Sustainable Development Goals, and smart tourism
Municipal services	Smart lighting, dashboards, urban waste and cleaning-sensorisation of vehicles, Russafa Market sensors pilot, noise management in Plaça del Tossal, effective social fund, smart management of municipal assets, EMT embedded environmental sensors, improvements in the GeoPortal – smart geoservices, AppValència – improvements and reuse, efficient urban noise management, solid waste management and cleaning, and smart clauses

TABLE 13.4

Some of the Projects Applied in Barcelona to Establish an Intelligent City

Some of the Projects Applied in Barcelona
The smart avenues
Bicing
The Barcelona City Council Tax System Renewal Plan
Connectivity in civic centres
Portal and urban information consultation services (PIU)
New SI management campaign for childhood aid
Deployment of citizen Wi-Fi in the bus fleet (Barcelona Wi-Fi services for citizens)
CityOS
Cloud4Cities (BCN Cloud)
Renovation of the Data Processing Centre of the City Council
PLEDGER
GrowSmarter
FLAME
Artificial Intelligence Threat Reporting and Incident Response System (IRIS)

On the other hand, in Spain, we find the city of Barcelona one of the most developed cities in terms of the use of technology to improve the quality of life of citizens in the town and in carrying out urban improvements. This presents different enhancements that make it on the list of the best smart cities. Table 13.4 shows how technology has been implemented in Barcelona and what changes the city is experiencing due to the implementation of different projects [66].

As mentioned above, Singapore is the best innovative country in the world. When Singapore decided to establish this country system, it was based on clearly defined pillars. These pillars guarantee a sustainable lifestyle, improve citizens' education, health, and mobility, reduce waiting times (end lines in public spaces), improve security, and strengthen public spaces.

Singapore presents what are called sustainable territories. These are territories in which many sensors are installed in different regions. These sensors allow data to be collected with exact information on how resources and services are used. In this way, it is possible to better distribute resources due to the identification of waste areas, reducing costs, and without forgetting to create awareness in the population [66].

On the other hand, it is worth highlighting the implementation of home telecare. They developed a programme called "Tele-Health." This system allows monitoring of the vital signs of older adults, people with reduced mobility, or chronic diseases. It allows for a follow-up of the patient's health to be able to adjust the medication administered and send an ambulance if necessary. This is because the medical centre receives the data. This programme has made it possible to decongest the country's emergency system [68].

In addition, Singapore works with the part of the city related to mobility, taking into account buses and establishing smart mobility. With the implementation of sensors and a georeferencing system, the public transport mobility network can indicate the number of passengers and the vehicle's location, among other parameters. This allows artificial intelligence to guarantee the optimal provision of services. At the same time, the data collected feeds the databases of the transit authorities, which complement the real-time management of mobility throughout the city with the traffic light network [69]. A modern security system has been implemented through surveillance cameras and sensors.

To keep all the active sensors in Singapore and to process the large amount of data received, extensive internet infrastructure is needed. Along with South Korea and Japan, Singapore offers one of the most significant low-cost connectivity capabilities, both for companies and users, with an average speed of 200 Mbps in homes [70].

13.5   Current Challenges and Future Trends

Nowadays, monitoring of the environment is a hot topic. Using low-cost sensors with open-source microcontrollers, such as Arduino and Raspberry, has increased the possibility of monitoring contaminants in the scientific community and by users.

In cities, the pollutant sources out of cities tend to be moved. An example is the electric car. Some European cities apply restrictions at the entrance of vehicles that run on fossil fuels. However, the batteries of these cars are charged in the electric network that in most countries continues to use fossil fuels for power generation. All in all, it is expected that green energy or cold fusion will displace fossil fuels and eliminate the emissions generated by energy production in the future.

As we said previously, developing countries have air quality networks to monitor the presence of pollutants in the air. Monitoring external air quality is essential to take measures of auto protection, such as using masks if the air contains too many particles, issuing health alerts, or implementing environmental policies. However, the internal atmosphere can present hazardous pollutant concentrations that are not monitored. In industrial environments, the monitoring of the internal atmosphere is produced as part of occupational risk prevention programmes. However, in homes monitoring the internal atmosphere presents deficiencies.

In the water, we can differentiate between monitoring drinking water and water bodies. In developed countries, the monitoring of drinking water is exhaustive, and the presence of chemical or biological is detected fast. However, in emerging countries, the pollution of drinking water is a challenge within Sustainable Development Goals. The use of sensors to monitor biological pollutants is a challenge. The current techniques are based on the cultivation of bacteria and DNA replication. These techniques need costly laboratory devices. However, it is expected that techniques will reduce their cost. This and improving developing countries' economic capacities can make the generalised application of these techniques possible.

The monitoring of soil pollution is difficult to improve. Being a heterogeneous environment where contaminants can be absorbed in different parts of the soil makes its monitoring complex. In the future, improvements in sensor monitoring techniques are expected. Using satellite images presents deficiencies in soil monitoring but helps monitor vegetation.

Finally, the different governments are dedicating efforts to governance. Nowadays, the use of ICT has allowed the government of cities or countries to be brought closer to the citizens, making them participate in decision-making. However, it is necessary to make more people aware of its usefulness to improve its implementation. Most older people do not use ICT, which means that their opinions may need to be considered in a city's governance processes.

13.6   Conclusion

The use of IoT in any field has increased considerably in recent years, mainly due to the amount of data provided by intelligent sensors. Hence, every day more cities apply the concept of governance, in which laws and decrees are established to reach the ideal well-being of the city and the citizens. This chapter has shown the types of pollution in the city and how they affect the environment's natural cycles (bearing in mind that many of these pollutants also affect rural areas). In addition, relevant environmental processes produced by the contamination of human beings and nature have been described. Examples of this are photochemical smog and acid rain. Finally, different ways of monitoring pollutants have been shown through low-cost systems through turbidity, conductivity, humidity, and temperature sensors. Examples of innovative city projects have been described under the governance references framework, such as Singapore, Barcelona, and Valencia. These guidelines can help implement governance in new cities.

REFERENCES

1. United Nations. 68% of the World Population is Projected to Live in Urban Areas by 2050, Says UN [Internet]. United Nations Department of Economic and Social Affairs 2018; Available from: https://www.un.org/development/desa/en/news/population/2018-revision-of-world-urbanization-prospects.html

2. European Commission. Smart cities [Internet]. European Commission 2019; Available from: https://ec.europa.eu/info/eu-regional-and-urban-development/topics/cities-and-urban-development/city-initiatives/smart-cities_en

3. Berte D-R. Defining the IoT. In: Proceedings of the International Conference on Business Excellence. Sciendo;2018. pp. 118–128.

4. Liu Y, Ma X, Shu L, Yang Q, Zhang Y, Huo Z, et al. Internet of Things for Noise Mapping in Smart Cities: State of the Art and Future Directions. *IEEE Network* 2020;34(4):112–8.

5. Rathee DS, Ahuja K, Hailu T. Role of Electronics Devices for E-Health in Smart Cities. In: Singh Rathee D, Ahuja K, Hailu T, editors. *Practice, Progress, and Proficiency in Sustainability*. Pennsylvania, USA. IGI global;2019. pp. 212–233.

6. Vijayakumar N, Ramya R. The real time monitoring of water quality in IoT environment. In: 2015 International Conference on Innovations in Information, Embedded and Communication Systems (ICIIECS). IEEE;2015.

7. Lloret J, Garcia M, Bri D, Sendra S. A Wireless Sensor Network Deployment for Rural and Forest Fire Detection and Verification. *Sensors* 2009;9(11):8722–8747.

8. Microsoft. Overview of Azure IoT Device Types [Internet]. *docs.microsoft.com* 2021 [cited 2022 Aug 13]; Available from: https://docs.microsoft.com/en-us/azure/iot-develop/concepts-iot-device-types

9. Mehmood A, Lv Z, Lloret J, Umar MM. ELDC: An Artificial Neural Network Based Energy-Efficient and Robust Routing Scheme for Pollution Monitoring in WSNs. *IEEE Transactions on Emerging Topics in Computing* 2020;8(1):106–114.

10. Velasco AM, Pérez-Ruzafa A, Martínez-Paz JM, Marcos C. Ecosystem Services and Main Environmental Risks in a Coastal Lagoon (Mar Menor, Murcia, SE Spain): The Public Perception. *Journal for Nature Conservation* 2018;43:180–189.

11. World Health Organization (WHO). 9 out of 10 People Worldwide Breathe Polluted Air, But More Countries Are Taking Action [Internet]. *WHO* 2018; Available from: https://www.who.int/news/item/02-05-2018-9-out-of-10-people-worldwide-breathe-polluted-air-but-more-countries-are-taking-action

12. Yim SHL, Gu Y, Shapiro MA, Stephens B. Air Quality and Acid Deposition Impacts of Local Emissions and Transboundary Air Pollution in Japan and South Korea. *Atmospheric Chemistry and Physics* 2019;19(20):13309–13323.

13. Grennfelt P, Engleryd A, Forsius M, Hov Ø, Rodhe H, Cowling E. Acid Rain and Air Pollution: 50 Years of Progress in Environmental Science and Policy. *Ambio* [Internet]. 2019, 49; Available from: https://link.springer.com/article/10.1007/s13280-019-01244-4

14. European Union. EUR-Lex - governance - EN - EUR-Lex [Internet]. *eur-lex.europa.eu*. 2018; Available from: https://eur-lex.europa.eu/EN/legal-content/glossary/eu-governance.html#

15. Batey T. Soil compaction and soil management – a review. *Soil Use and Management* 2009;25(4):335–345.

16. Bernhard A. The Nitrogen Cycle: Processes, Players, and Human Impact [Internet]. *Nature.com* 2010 [cited 2023 Feb 15]; Available from: https://www.nature.com/scitable/knowledge/library/the-nitrogen-cycle-processes-players-and-human-15644632/

17. Yang L, Qian F, Song D-X, Zheng K-J. Research on Urban Heat-Island Effect. *Procedia Engineering* [Internet]. 2016;169:11–18. Available from: https://www.sciencedirect.com/science/article/pii/S1877705816332039

18. Gall SC, Thompson RC. The Impact of Debris on Marine Life. *Marine Pollution Bulletin* 2015;92(1-2):170–179.

19. Frias JPGL, Nash R. Microplastics: Finding a Consensus on the Definition. *Marine Pollution Bulletin* 2019;138:145–147.

20. Afrin S, Uddin MdK, Rahman MdM. *Microplastics Contamination in the Soil from Urban Landfill Site*. Dhaka, Bangladesh. Heliyon 2020;6(11):e05572.

21. Dwivedi AK. Researches in Water Pollution: A Review. *Journal of Natural and Applied Sciences* 2017;4(1):118–142.
22. Hasan MdK, Shahriar A, Jim KU. Water Pollution in Bangladesh and Its Impact on Public Health. *Heliyon* [Internet]. 2019;5(8): e02145. Available from: https://www.heliyon.com/article/e02145/
23. Najafzadeh M, Ghaemi A, Emamgholizadeh S. Prediction of Water Quality Parameters Using Evolutionary Computing-Based Formulations. *International Journal of Environmental Science and Technology* 2018;16(10):6377–6396.
24. Lee J, Lee S, Yu S, Rhew D. Relationships between Water Quality Parameters in Rivers and Lakes: BOD5, COD, NBOPs, and TOC. *Environmental Monitoring and Assessment* 2016;188(4): 1–8.
25. Farid S, Baloch KM, Khan SAI. Water Pollution: Major Issue in Urban Areas. *International Journal of Water Resources and Environmental Engineering* [Internet]. 2012;4(3):55–65. Available from: https://academicjournals.org/journal/IJWREE/article-full-text-pdf/730CE7F2619
26. Official Journal of the European Communities. Council Directive 91/271/EEC of 21 May 1991 concerning urban wastewater treatment. 1991.
27. Chaudhry F, Malik M. Factors Affecting Water Pollution: A Review. *Journal of Ecosystem & Ecography* 2017;7(1): 225–231.
28. Ruiz-Beviá F, Fernández-Torres MJ. Effective Catalytic Removal of Nitrates from Drinking Water: An Unresolved Problem? *Journal of Cleaner Production* 2019;217:398–408.
29. Nicoletti G, Arcuri N, Nicoletti G, Bruno R. A Technical and Environmental Comparison Between Hydrogen and Some Fossil Fuels. *Energy Conversion and Management* [Internet] 2015;89:205–213. Available from: https://www.sciencedirect.com/science/article/pii/S0196890414008589
30. Lu Z, Streets DG, Zhang Q, Wang S, Carmichael GR, Cheng YF, et al. Sulfur Dioxide Emissions in China and sulfur Trends in East Asia since 2000. *Atmospheric Chemistry and Physics* 2010;10(13):6311–6331.
31. Grennfelt P, Engleryd A, Forsius M, Hov Ø, Rodhe H, Cowling E. Acid Rain and Air Pollution: 50 Years of Progress in Environmental Science and Policy. *Ambio* 2020;49(4):849–864. Available from: https://link.springer.com/article/10.1007/s13280-019-01244-4
32. Rani B, Singh U, Chuhan AK, Sharma D, Maheshwari R. Photochemical Smog Pollution and Its Mitigation Measures. *Journal of Advanced Scientific Research* 2011;2(4):28–33.
33. Barmpadimos I, Keller J, Oderbolz D, Hueglin C, Prévôt ASH. One Decade of Parallel Fine (PM2.5) and Coarse (PM10–PM2.5) Particulate Matter Measurements in Europe: Trends and Variability. *Atmospheric Chemistry and Physics* 2012;12(7):3189–3203.
34. World Health Organisation (WHO). WHO Global Air Quality Guidelines: Particulate Matter (PM2.5 and PM10), Ozone, Nitrogen Dioxide, Sulfur Dioxide and Carbon Monoxide [Internet]. www.who.int 2021 [cited 2022 Aug 8]; Available from: https://www.who.int/publications/i/item/9789240034228
35. Morillas JMB, Gozalo GR, González DM, Moraga PA, Vílchez-Gómez R. Noise Pollution and Urban Planning. *Current Pollution Reports* 2018;4(3):208–19.
36. European Environmental Agency. Noise [Internet]. *European Environment Agency* 2016 [cited 2022 Aug 8]; Available from: https://www.eea.europa.eu/themes/human/noise
37. Solano Lamphar HA, Kocifaj M. Light Pollution in Ultraviolet and Visible Spectrum: Effect on Different Visual Perceptions. *PLoS ONE* 2013;8(2):e56563
38. Mendoza J. Nighttime Light Hurts Mammalian Physiology: What Diurnal Rodent Models Are Telling Us. *Clocks & Sleep* 2021;3(2):236–250.
39. Schwartz G, Ben-Dor E, Eshel G. Quantitative Analysis of Total Petroleum Hydrocarbons in Soils: Comparison between Reflectance Spectroscopy and Solvent Extraction by 3 Certified Laboratories. *Applied and Environmental Soil Science* 2012;2012:1–11.
40. Yavari A, Georgakopoulos D, Stoddart PR, Shafiei M. Internet of Things-based Hydrocarbon Sensing for Real-time Environmental Monitoring. In: 2019 IEEE 5th World Forum on Internet of Things (WF-IoT). IEEE;2019.
41. Gholizadeh A, Borůvka L, Saberioon MM, Kozák J, Vašát R, Němeček K. Comparing Different Data Preprocessing Methods for Monitoring Soil Heavy Metals Based on Soil Spectral Features. *Soil and Water Research* 2015;10(4):218–227.

42. Liu K, Zhao D, Fang J, Zhang X, Zhang Q, Li X. Estimation of Heavy-Metal Contamination in Soil Using Remote Sensing Spectroscopy and a Statistical Approach. *Journal of the Indian Society of Remote Sensing* 2017;45(5):805–813.

43. Razif M, Yanuwiadi B, Rachmansyah A. Effects of Wastewater Quality and Quantity Fluctuations in Selecting the Wastewater Treatment Plant: A Case Study of 'Surabaya's Mall. *International Journal of ChemTech Research* 2015;8(2):534–540.

44. Parra L, Viciano-Tudela S, Carrasco D, Sendra S, Lloret J. Low-Cost Microcontroller-Based Multiparametric Probe for Coastal Area Monitoring. *Sensors* 2023;23(4):1871.

45. Rocher J, Parra M, Parra L, Sendra S, Lloret J, Mengual J. A Low-Cost Sensor for Detecting Illicit Discharge in Sewerage. *Journal of Sensors* 2021;2021:1–16.

46. Bigham Stephens DL, Carlson RE, Horsburgh CA, Hoyer MV, Bachmann RW, Canfield DE. Regional Distribution of Secchi Disk Transparency in Waters of the United States. *Lake and Reservoir Management* 2015;31(1):55–63.

47. Rice EW, Eaton AD, Baird R. 2520 C. Density method. In: American Public Health Association, American Water Works Association, Water Environment Federation, editors *Standard Methods for the Examination of Water and Wastewater*. Washington, DC: American Public Health Association, American Water Works Association, Water Environment Federation.

48. Zulkifli SN, Rahim HA, Lau W-J. Detection of Contaminants in Water Supply: A Review on State-of-the-Art Monitoring Technologies and Their Applications. *Sensors and Actuators B, Chemical* 2018;255:2657–2689.

49. Rocher J, Parra L, Jimenez JM, Lloret J, Basterrechea DA. Development of a Low-Cost Optical Sensor to Detect Eutrophication in Irrigation Reservoirs. *Sensors* 2021;21(22):7637.

50. European Council. Directive 2008/50/EC of the European Parliament and of the Council of 21 May 2008 on Ambient Air Quality and Cleaner Air for Europe [Internet]. 2008 [cited 2022 Aug 2]; Available from: https://eur-lex.europa.eu/legal-content/EN/TXT/PDF/?uri=CELEX:32008L0050&from=es

51. EEUU Congress EC. Clean Air Act. 2020.

52. Government of New South Wales. Monitoring Air Quality [Internet]. *NSW Environment, Energy and Science* 2022 [cited 2022 Aug 8]; Available from: https://www.environment.nsw.gov.au/topics/air/monitoring-air-quality

53. National Environmental Agency. How Does Singapore Monitor Its Ambient Air Quality? [Internet]. *va.ecitizen.gov.sg* 2022 [cited 2022 Aug 8]; Available from: https://va.ecitizen.gov.sg/CFP/CustomerPages/NEA_google/displayresult.aspx?MesId=1068830&Source=Google&url=va.ecitizen.gov.sg

54. Botta E, Yamasaki S. Policies, Regulatory Framework and Enforcement for Air Quality Management: The Case of Japan -Environment Working Paper N°156 [Internet]. OECD; 2020 [cited 2022 Aug 8]; Available from: https://www.oecd.org/officialdocuments/publicdisplaydocumentpdf/?cote=ENV/WKP(2020)3&docLanguage=En

55. Saini J, Dutta M, Marques G. Indoor Air Quality Monitoring Systems Based on Internet of Things: A Systematic Review. *International Journal of Environmental Research and Public Health* 2020;17(14):4942.

56. Pribadi P, Pramudya Y, Muchlas, Okimustava. The IoT implementation on the night sky brightness measurement in Banjar using the sky quality meter [Internet]. In: International Conference On Science And Applied Science (ICSAS) 2019. AIP Publishing; 2019 [cited 2022 Aug 9]; Available from: https://doi.org/10.1063/1.5141636

57. European parliament. Directive 2011/92/EU of the European Parliament and of the Council of 13 December 2011 on the assessment of the effects of certain public and private projects on the environment Text with EEA relevance [Internet]. 2011 [cited 2022 Jul 13]; Available from: https://eur-lex.europa.eu/legal-content/EN/TXT/?uri=celex%3A32011L0092

58. Code of Federal Regulations. Part 1502 - Environmental Impact Statement [Internet]. 2020 [cited 2022 Jul 14]; Available from: https://www.ecfr.gov/current/title-40/chapter-V/subchapter-A/part-1502

59. Walter BF. Why Bad Governance Leads to Repeat Civil War. *Journal of Conflict Resolution* 2014;59(7):1242–1272.

60. Jha S, Quising PF. Corruption in Asia and the Pacific: a manifestation of weak governance. In: Deolalikar AB, Jha S, Quising PF, editors. *Governance in Developing Asia*. Cheltenham: Edward Elgar Publishing Limited; 2015. pp. 101–136.
61. Myeong S, Kwon Y, Seo H. Sustainable E-Governance: The Relationship among Trust, Digital Divide, and E-Government. *Sustainability* 2014;6(9):6049–6069.
62. IT.U-T. An Overview of Smart Sustainable Cities and the Role of Information and Communication Technologies. In International Telecommunication Union (ITU-T) Focus Group on Smart Sustainable Cities (FGSSC) 2014. 3–3.
63. Smart Cities - Smart Cities World [Internet]. [cited 2022 Aug 10]; Available from: https://www.smartcitiesworld.net/smart-cities?topics=Singapore
64. Singapur vuelve a encabezar el Smart City Index de 2021, mientras que Bilbao escala al Top 10 - smartlighting (smart-lighting.es) [Internet]. [cited 2022 Aug 10]; Available from: https://smart-lighting.es/singapur-smart-city-index-2021-bilbao/
65. Oficina de Ciudad Inteligente - València Ciudad Inteligente (valencia.es) [Internet]. [cited 2022 Aug 10]; Available from: https://smartcity.valencia.es/oficina-ciudad-inteligente/
66. Nuevos proyectos para convertir Barcelona en una smart city — Nae [Internet]. [cited 2022 Aug 10]; Available from: https://nae.global/es/ultimos-proyectos-para-convertir-barcelona-en-una-smart-city/
67. Singapur, ¿la primera ciudad inteligente del mundo? | SG Buzz [Internet]. [cited 2022 Aug 10]; Available from: https://sg.com.mx/buzz/singapur-la-primera-ciudad-inteligente-del-mundo
68. gov.sg | Home (www.gov.sg) [Internet]. [cited 2022 Aug 10]; Available from: https://www.gov.sg/
69. Future mobility and transport | Growth sectors for collaboration |Enterprise Singapore (enterprisesg.gov.sg) [Internet]. [cited 2022 Aug 10]; Available from: https://www.enterprisesg.gov.sg/industries/hub/infrastructure-hub/build-on-singapores-infrastructure-ecosystem/growth-sectors/future-mobility-and-transport
70. Estos son los países que tienen mayor velocidad media de conexión a Internet (muycomputerpro.com) [Internet]. [cited 2022 Aug 10]; Available from: https://www.muycomputerpro.com/2020/06/10/paises-velocidad-media-conexion-internet

14

Sensor Technology in IoT

Laura García, Sandra Sendra, Jose Miguel Jiménez, and Jaime Lloret
Universitat Politècnica de València, Spain

14.1 Introduction

With the evolution of the technology of communications, interest in developing solutions to address the problems derived from deploying numerous people to perform monitoring and management activities increased. Wireless Sensor Networks (WSNs) allow the monitoring of vast areas conveniently from a personal computer. Later on, as communications continued to evolve, Internet of Things (IoT) solutions began to be implemented as convenient systems that helped people with their tasks, including interaction with the user. The first article on IoT was published in 2002 applying the concept to smart supermarkets [1]. From 2009 onward, IoT-related papers experienced rapid growth, and governments began to make plans and development directions to provide cities with smart capabilities. The big exponential growth began in 2015, and it is still growing.

The increase in interest and convenience of IoT has led to the application of IoT in a wide variety of domains. The domains of IoT comprise an extensive range of environments, functionalities, and applications. Industry, agriculture, homes, healthcare, cities, and seas are some of the environments where IoT has been deployed. The main functionality is obtaining information about the environment to obtain insights into its condition, perform predictions, or take actions to change the said environment or address detected problems through the use of actuators or notification alerts. This has led to countless efforts to create a classification to facilitate the comprehension of IoT and its concepts. Even though there is no consensus on the specific categories, most classifications include the same type of application [2–6].

For each application, the developer or researcher must consider the environmental physical parameters and their restrictions. Sensor devices for IoT should withstand high or low temperatures if deployed outdoors, deep pressures if deployed underwater, or be highly manipulated and tossed around if deployed on portable devices such as watches or toys. Furthermore, the main characteristic of IoT networks is that sensor nodes should be connected to a network to be able to share their data to process and/or store it on other external servers. Therefore, the best form of communication, wired or wireless, for the type of device and the environment it monitors needs to be determined when designing the device.

The requirements of the applications normally determine the type of wireless technology necessary to correctly develop the IoT solution. The list of current wireless technologies [7] for developing WSN and IoT solutions includes Bluetooth Low Energy (BLE), Zigbee, Z-Wave, 6LowPAN, Thread, WiFi, Sigfox, Neul, or LoRa/LoRaWAN, among others. Each of these technologies implies the consideration of a series of characteristics such as the use of a specific topology or effective data transfer rates, as well as maximum coverage, ranges that a single device can offer. Finally, and considering that we want to make effective use of the data collected, the type of application will mark the type of processing technique and storage of the information that we want to carry out.

DOI:10.1201/9781003326236-14

Therefore, depending on the needs of the application, an IoT solution can be sought with computing techniques such as edge computing, fog computing, or cloud computing [8].

This wide variety of IoT domains keeps increasing over time. Thus, sensor technologies must evolve to accommodate the requirements of these applications. Each of the domains may present specific needs such as the type of communication between sensing devices, the encapsulation (waterproof, impact-resistant), or power options (solar panels, direct connection to the grid, batteries), among other factors. Therefore, this chapter aims to address the differences between these domains and how they affect sensor technology, identify the main challenges for deploying sensor devices for each domain, determine the type of data generated by these sensors, and discuss the current innovations in sensor devices for IoT applications. It will provide the reader with an overview of the current state of sensor technologies for IoT as an introduction to this area of knowledge.

14.2   Definition of IoT

What time is it now? Did you pick up your phone to look at the hour? Did you look at your smartwatch? Perhaps the TV? I guess all those devices served the purpose but, what else do they do? Did they consider that movement as physical activity and add some burned calories to the app that you use for health management? Maybe the movement just made the screen light up. Or maybe there is more to it. There is no doubt technology is part of our lives. It is so intertwined with our everyday actions that we do not even think about it. But these devices have sensors that gather information and transmit it to provide us with all kinds of functionalities that we don't even think about. And as new advancements reach the market, new connections become part of the networks that comprise the Internet of Things (IoT).

The term "IoT" was coined in 1999 by a collaborator of the RFID (Radio Frequency Identification) development community [9]. The IoT is in essence a high number of objects interconnected through a private or public network. The word "object" is used in this definition to address devices of varied shapes, sizes, and types depending on their intended use. The aim of these devices is to collect and share information to monitor, manage, and control the environment where the device is located [9]. The devices interact and cooperate with each other to provide new services and applications to reach an established common goal. There is therefore something in common between a refrigerator, a doll, a food processor, your new car, or the medical equipment at the closest hospital. All of them may be IoT devices.

These devices that are located in our homes, that take us to places, that are used to heal us, and that we constantly carry with us – even our clothes, trees, animals, and the food on the shelves of our favorite supermarket – can also be part of an IoT network with the aid of wireless technologies such as WiFi, Bluetooth, or RFID. It is no wonder that some authors envision a world where all objects and people are equipped with some form of identifying device [10].

14.3   IoT Architecture

We now have some understanding of what IoT is. But how does it really work? How do these devices operate within the existing network? We will now look into a generic IoT architecture to assess the different elements that enable IoT.

Architecture is a scheme of the elements that constitute the system, their role within the system, and how they are related to each other. It is usually divided into layers that indicate the main purpose of the devices or software tools it contains. Figure 14.1 portrays this form of layered architecture. It is composed of four layers: the sensor layer, the communication layer, the service layer, and the application layer.

Sensor Layer: Sensors are the foundation of IoT. Without the devices that react to the environment and generate data, there would be nothing to communicate. Sensors are therefore devices that

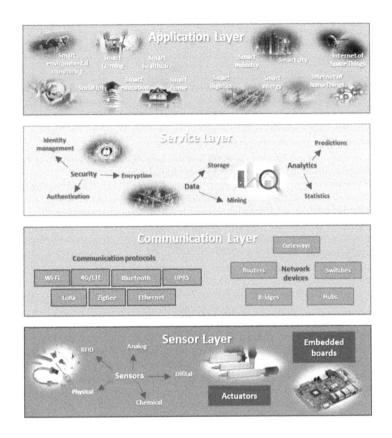

FIGURE 14.1 IoT generic architecture.

generate a response to the physical environment in which they are placed. The response is often a voltage that needs to be interpreted and converted into a value that can be understood by human users or the machines that are processing the data. However, the sensor itself is not able to store, display, or transmit the data. Other devices are necessary to perform all the functions to be considered an IoT device.

IoT devices are objects with computing capabilities not included in the standard devices for computation such as personal computers, tablets, or smartphones. This way, common objects can be equipped with connectivity to be part of a network and interact with other objects and the Internet. The sensors located within these devices that we use daily may not be easy to spot, but they are certainly there, reacting to the changes in their environment. PCs, tablets, and smartphones provide the necessary computing and communication capabilities to the sensors they integrate through different elements incorporated in the circuitry of the device. However, for developers, it is common practice to use embedded boards to provide these capabilities through the interconnection of the desired modules. Nevertheless, all of these devices share common elements (see Table 14.1), as displayed in Figure 14.2.

There are many embedded boards available in the market for different needs regarding processing capabilities, the number of I/O pins and their type (analog or digital), or the operating voltage (see Table 14.2). These aspects need to be considered when developing IoT devices to monitor different environments as we need to consider the characteristics of the employed sensors, the availability of a steady power supply or lack thereof, and even the weather conditions and the encapsulation that is required. IoT devices may get damaged by the environment and activities performed on them if they are not protected. Thus, it is necessary to cover the device and adapt the encapsulation to these specific conditions to enable proper operation. It should be weatherproof if it is located outdoors or endure high pressure if it is to be deployed deep underwater.

TABLE 14.1

Elements of an IoT Device

Element	Description
Processor	The processor is the part of the device that provides computing power. This computer power is used to run the program that dictates how the device should operate and process the information. If the IoT device needs to perform simple operations, the selection of an 8-bit processor may provide enough computing capabilities. However, 16-bit and 32-bit processors are available for higher processing requirements.
Memory	IoT devices are configured to perform a certain task through a software program. It may also be necessary to store the information gathered by the sensors until this information is transmitted. Therefore, memory is another important part of IoT devices with computing capabilities. The memory is part of the microcontroller. There are two types of memory for different types of information. The RAM (random access memory) stores short-term data that is lost when the device is not powered. The ROM (read-only memory) stores long-term data, such as the program, that can be accessed when necessary and is not lost when the device is restarted.
I/O pins	Sensors and other modules in the IoT device need to be connected to the processor to interact and perform their tasks. This connection is performed through the input and output pins. The pins read data or perform the actions established in the program of the device. The number of I/O pins and their specified use vary according to the type of board and should be consulted in the datasheet provided by the manufacturer.
Communication ports and antennas	IoT devices need a form of communication either to be configured or to exchange data with other devices. The communication ports enable wired communications with other devices. USB, UART, or the Ethernet port are examples of wired communication ports. Wireless communications are performed through antennas. The antennas may be as small as a printed circuit that is part of the embedded board, but oftentimes it is a bigger electronic device selected to meet the communication requirements in terms of coverage and transmission power that is connected to the embedded board.
Power supply	The power supply is necessary for the device to operate. Batteries, solar panels, or a connection to the power grid are some of the options for providing a steady power supply to the device. Typical voltages for powering small-sized devices comprised embedded boards are 5V and 3.3V. However, large-sized devices with higher processing and communication requirements may need more potent power supplies, including a connection to the power grid.
Circuitry	All the different elements of IoT devices are connected and integrated into a circuit with elements such as resistors, capacitors, diodes, or transistors, among others, to enable the correct operation of the device.

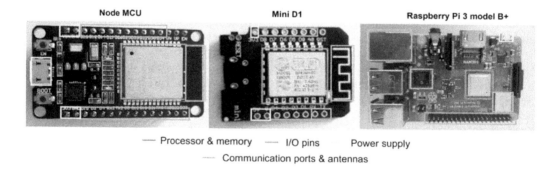

FIGURE 14.2 Parts of the embedded boards.

Depending on the purpose of the device, they may be consumer devices, such as smart watches, cars, home appliances, thermostats, lighting, and irrigation devices for gardens [11]; enterprise devices, such as security, lighting, locks, thermostats, cameras, TVs, monitors, and projectors; and industrial devices such as sensors and machinery.

TABLE 14.2

Commonly Embedded Boards and Their Characteristics

Controller	Analog Pins	Digital Pins	USB	Operating Voltage	Processor	FLASH	RAM	EEPROM	Frequency
Arduino Mega [12]	16	54	—	7–12 V	ATmega 2560	256 kB	8 kB	4 kB	16 MHz
Arduino UNO [13]	6	6+14	—	7–12 V	ATmega 328P	32 kB	2 kB	1 kB	16 MHz
WEMOS MINI D1 [14]	1	11	1	3.3 V	ESP8266	4 MB	—	—	80/160 MHz
Node MCU [15]	1	17	—	3.3 V	ESP8266	16 MB	32+80 kB	—	—
Raspberry Pi 2 Model B [16]		40	4	—	Broadcom BCM2837	900 MHz	—	1 GB	—
Raspberry Pi 3 Model B+ [17]		40	4	5 V	Broadcom BCM2837B0	1.4 GHz	—	1 GB	—

TABLE 14.3

Wired and Wireless Communication Protocols

Protocol	Distance	Data Rate/Bandwidth	Power Consumption
WiFi [18, 19]	70 m (indoor)/250 m (outdoor)	Up to 40 Mbps (802.11ah)	High
LoRa [19]	22 km	0.3 to 50 kbps	Low
RFID [20]	27 m (passive)/100 m(active)	Up to 640 kbps	Low
ZigBee [19]	75 m	Up to 250 kbps	Low
Bluetooth [19]	350 m	Up to 3 Mbps	Medium-Low
GPRS [21]	35 km	40 kbps	High
4G/LTE [19]	100 km	Upload 150 Mbps Download 50 Mbps	High
Ethernet [22]	Up to 100 m (without intermediate devices)	Up to 100 Gbps (Gigabit Ethernet)	Medium

Lastly, IoT devices may perform certain actions as a response to what has been sensed in the environment or the actions received from the user. A light might be turned on, the air conditioning may be turned off, a gate might be opened, or the plants may need some water. Actuators are devices that act according to the indications of the received signal. They have the opposite function from sensors, as sensors react to the environment whereas actuators modify the environment.

Communication Layer: Sensor devices cannot be considered IoT without the ability to communicate with other devices. They need to be part of a network. This network is comprised of different network devices such as gateways, routers, switches, hubs, or bridges that create the connections that enable communication. Communications can be wired or wireless, and depending on the communication protocol, the sensor device needs to include specific ports, antennas, or modules to communicate.

The available technologies are varied [9], thus using standards helps in the integration and interoperability of the devices. Table 14.3 presents the main characteristics of these technologies. The selection of the best technology varies according to the coverage, the amount of data that needs to be transmitted, or the power consumption requirements.

Service Layer: The service layer incorporates the varied functionalities provided by the network. Some of these functionalities are focused on data processing. This includes cloud services, local processing and analysis, and artificial intelligence (AI) techniques to perform predictions [9]. These techniques can, among other things, be employed to reduce the amount of information that needs to be forwarded and to obtain conclusions from the data to help users and systems make decisions or perform predictions. Other functionalities are focused on device management and security provision [11]. Devices may need to be registered and go through an activation process to establish the configuration, all of this after being authorized and authenticated. Furthermore, some applications may need special security, such as smart healthcare, due to the extremely private nature of the data. Other applications may need to manage high numbers of devices. Therefore, different applications may use different services, as it would be ineffective to apply all services to all applications. Smart farming would require less security than smart grids as farming data may not be as confidential. There are however some problems that need to be considered, such as interoperability, scalability, or availability. It is therefore important to use and develop standards that facilitate the implementation of IoT systems.

Application Layer: The last layer is the application layer. This layer includes the different functionalities of each smart environment to be monitored. Be it farming, environmental monitoring, healthcare, cities, space, nano things, logistics, education, energy, industry, or social IoT [9]. The interaction of the service and the user, or between people and devices can lead to people-to-people interactions, people-to-things interactions, and things-to-things interactions. Furthermore, access to the data by the user or things and the management of the smart applications can be performed from a remote location.

14.4   The Use of IoT Technology in Different Use Cases

In this section, the use cases for the different smart applications are presented. The concept for each smart application is described, and the architecture and sensor devices in each case are described.

14.4.1   IoT for Smart Environmental Monitoring

The increase in population has led to the detection of increased danger to the health of both people and ecological systems. A report of the Lancet Commission on pollution and health [23], where a two-year study was conducted, concludes that environmental pollution is currently the biggest culprit of disease and premature death in the world. The study states that, in countries with serious pollution problems, a quarter of the people who die do so from diseases directly related to pollution. They calculated that, in 2015, 9 million people died prematurely from diseases directly related to this serious problem. This reason is one of the main factors for the need to monitor the environment in cities, industrial areas, forests, rivers, lakes, seas, etc.

The combined action of sensors, IoT devices, and remote connectivity is used to monitor properly. In addition, we must be able to analyze, determine the accuracy, and present reports of the obtained data.

The use of sensor networks and IoT allows for protecting and cleaning our environment, thanks to the detection of harmful pollutants, harmful substances, chemical spills, etc. With the sensors that are integrated into weather stations, irrigation systems, ocean equipment, etc., we can easily and efficiently detect data such as temperature, humidity, water level, or physical properties, and facilitate monitoring air, soil, and water.

The data obtained from the sensors is transmitted through devices or nodes, which are connected to the cloud or external databases through different communication technologies. If data is processed using edge computing, critical information can be quickly classified and delivered. At other points, even from the very edge of the network, the information can be analyzed and evaluated. After that, the appropriate actions must be carried out in response to each of the anomalous situations.

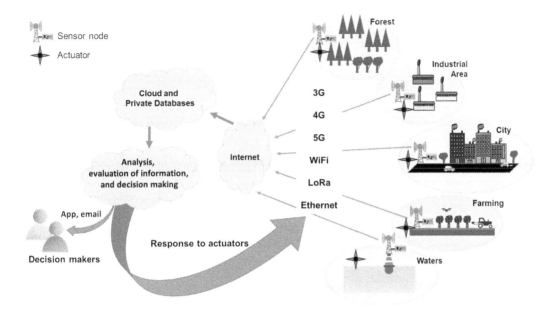

FIGURE 14.3 The network architecture of IoT for smart environmental monitoring.

The parameters that are most commonly monitored are the following:

- **Weather:** Temperature, humidity, rain, atmospheric pressure, the intensity of light, direction, and speed of the wind, solar radiation, UV radiation.
- **Air quality:** PM 2.5, PM 1, PM 10, CO_2, O_3, NO_2, SO_2.
- **Water pollution:** Turbidity, salinity, dissolved oxygen, temperature.
- **Forest fire detection:** smoke, flame, CO_2.

Figure 14.3 shows the network architecture of smart environmental monitoring. To carry out environmental monitoring, we must establish an architecture in which there will be:

- **Sensor network:** It continuously monitors the environment and generates data related to the observed variables.
- **Nodes:** The sensors will be connected to nodes that are capable of transmitting the data captured during monitoring.
- **Communications network:** Using different technologies, the data is sent from the nodes to the cloud or private databases to be processed.
- **Intelligent Systems:** They are responsible for processing the captured climate data to generate alerts and notifications in the event of dangerous situations.
- **Presentation of obtained information:** The results of the obtained information, once processed, must be sent to responsible actors or people so that they act appropriately.

There are public platforms that offer information with climatological data obtained in different locations, for example, Microsoft's Planetary Computer Data Catalog [24].

It is very interesting to use low-cost sensors that allow monitoring of the air and the exposure to pollution that people face [25] since they would allow its massive use. One of the biggest problems we have to face is the calibration of the sensors. They must be calibrated before their deployment. It would be advisable that, initially, its calibration is conducted in the laboratory following the manufacturer's instructions. Once the final implementation has been carried out, calibrations are performed again, since in this way the quality of the obtained data can be guaranteed. Access to environmental parameters using the web in remote areas would also be very interesting [26]. Citizens can access information on environmental parameters through the Internet, and in addition, alarms can be sent when the pollution parameters exceed the ranges considered appropriate. The control of marine pollution is of great interest as well. Using sensors and other technological means, it is possible to map and monitor aquatic environments, even seeing their distribution and evolution [27, 28].

14.4.2 Smart Farming: Smart Agriculture, Smart Breeding

According to the United Nations (UN) [29], the world population in 2050 will reach 9,700 million, given this forecast, the Food and Agriculture Organization of the United Nations (FAO) [30] indicates that world agricultural production should increase by 70% in 2050, compared to agricultural production in 2009.

Smart farming can be defined as the use of new technologies in agriculture to increase its yield efficiently, achieve better use of resources, and cause minimal environmental impact.

To achieve this objective, it is necessary to observe and analyze the conditions, to subsequently create an optimal plan of the actions to be taken. The available resources must be adjusted to the specific situations in each location. For all the reasons stated, it is necessary to use sensor technology to obtain the most precise information from the monitored data, which will be processed by intelligent systems to obtain optimal results.

The terms "smart farming" and "precision farming" are often used as similar terms, but they should be differentiated. Smart farming focuses on tillage agriculture, while precision farming takes more concepts into account, including smart electronics, to make the farmer's tasks more bearable and achieve additional cost savings.

The parameters that are usually monitored by different types of sensors are the following:

- Soil, plant, and water sensors: The parameters most controlled by these sensors are soil moisture, water level, pH (soil or water), water flow, soil temperature, water conductivity, leaf wetness, plant height, water temperature, and soil nutrients.
- Climate sensors: The parameters most controlled by these sensors are air temperature, air humidity, luminosity, rain, wind direction and velocity, ultraviolet radiation, CO_2, gas, atmospheric pressure, and smoke.

The use of actuators is also of vital importance. The data observed during monitoring is stored in the cloud or private databases and is processed by intelligent systems. With the produced response and based on pre-established reference values, appropriate decisions can be made in situations that may endanger crops. The actions can be carried out directly, acting automatically on the actuators, or the farmers themselves can make the decision they believe to be the best based on the received information.

In many situations, drones are being used [31] since they allow information to be collected through the sensors and cameras that are installed on a large surface. From the cameras, using infrared technology and multispectral images, information can be obtained on the state of the land, crops, water needs, etc. Furthermore, fumigation tasks can be carried out with the use of drones.

Another key point to monitor correctly is to use the appropriate communication technologies. The information must be sent from the field to the cloud or private databases, where it will be stored and can be accessed by farmers, even in real time. According to the Machina research report [32], the number of connected agricultural devices is expected to reach 225 million by 2024. The employed technologies are very numerous since multiple factors must be taken into consideration for their implementation. We can highlight the following factors, which will be of vital importance in the selection of the technology used for transmission: maximum data rate, maximum range, energy consumption, ease of installation, etc. Thus, we can find cellular technologies implemented

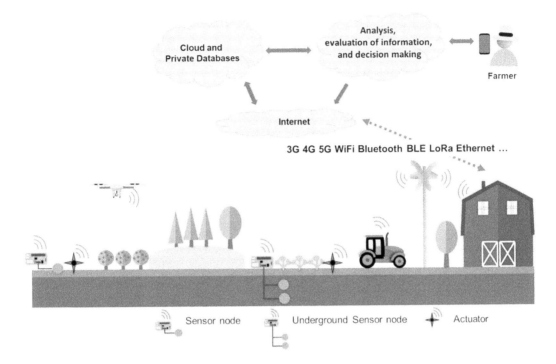

FIGURE 14.4 The network architecture of smart farming.

(3G, 4G, 5G), wireless (WiFi, Bluetooth BLE, RFDI, Zigbee, NB-IoT, IEEE 802.15.1) LPWAN (LTE-M, EC-GSM, Sigfox, LoRaWAN), and wired (Ethernet).

Due to climate change and its effects on precision farming, extremely efficient use of fresh water must be taken into account. In addition, water availability for food production and people, as well as to maintain ecosystems, must be ensured, as indicated by the authors [33]. A fundamental task when implementing soil moisture (or any other parameter) monitoring solutions in precision agriculture is the location of the nodes with their connected sensors since an observation will depend on its adequacy to the requirements. Authors such as [34] have submitted a proposal to fix this problem. The network architecture of smart farming is presented in Figure 14.4.

14.4.3 Smart Healthcare: eHealth, Smart Medical Management, Independent Living

In smart healthcare, the concept of IoT is applied to monitoring and managing people's health. The smart sensors deployed for these applications are often wearable devices (see Figure 14.5). Materials, people, and healthcare institutions are then connected to provide intelligent responses to medical needs [35]. It enables more interaction between the parties (hospitals, patients, doctors, and research facilities), helps allocate resources, improves medical research, prevents diseases, and facilitates making more informed decisions, diagnoses, and treatments. Smart healthcare functionalities can be classified into the categories of individual users, health institutions, and research institutions [35].

Traditional health management has been centered on the doctor–patient relationship and can be lacking in the management of chronic diseases. As a solution, IoT enables patient self-management. Patients can live in smart homes with sensor devices that help monitor possible health risks such as falls or air quality to improve quality of life and to provide assistance to elderly and disabled people. They can wear wearable devices, such as smartwatches, which contain advanced sensors that can monitor exercise, heart rate, or respiration patterns in real time without being uncomfortable to the patient. Hospitals can use RFID to identify and manage patients, personnel, and materials to improve performance; resource allocation; and reduce costs. Doctors can access information through

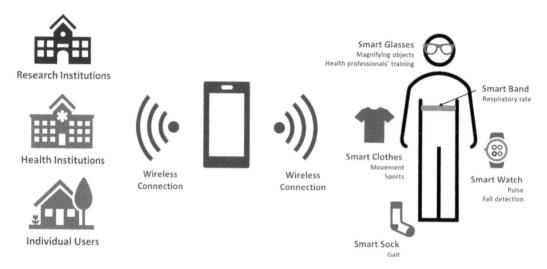

FIGURE 14.5 Network of smart wearable sensors for smart healthcare.

an integrated system or perform safer and more precise surgeries with the aid of medical robots. Lastly, research institutions can obtain more data and for longer periods to analyze and help in discovering new ways of helping patients.

Smart healthcare utilizes the common technologies for all IoT applications but may also include biotechnology with the incorporation of biosensors to smartphones and wearable devices [36].

Wearable sensors are usually external and wireless due to internal sensors being more uncomfortable and presenting more inconveniences if repair is needed. They measure physiological conditions such as vital signs like respiratory rate, temperature, pulse, blood pressure, and blood oxygen. Other special-purpose sensors of interest are fall detection, blood glucose, or joint angle sensors.

Accelerometers can be used for rehabilitation to detect movement in joints such as the knees or to determine the evolution of patients with Parkinson's disease. Pulse can be read from different parts of the body such as wrists, chest, fingertips, or earlobes. Many commercial devices monitor pulse, especially for sports. It can be measured using pressure, ultrasonic (RF), radio frequency, and photoplethysmographic (PPG) sensors. The latter utilizes an LED and a photodiode that observes the changes in light to determine the pulse. Respiratory rate can be monitored to detect apnea, airway obstructions, asthma, or hyperventilation, among other conditions. Thermistor-based nasal sensors are one form of monitoring respiratory rate and detecting the temperature of the air. Echocardiograms, microphones, optic fiber, pressure sensors, or stretch sensors can also be used to detect respiration. Body temperature is measured through thermistors. Blood pressure sensors can be utilized to manage patients with hypertension, but monitor regularly is difficult. It can be estimated to obtain the pulse transit time from pulse readings, though it is not as accurate as desired. Pulse oximetry sensors are used to monitor oxygen levels in the blood and are based on LED technology. Lastly, recent advances include smart pills that trigger a sensor when in contact with the gastric acid of the patient to generate a timestamp when the drug is consumed and contact lenses that monitor blood sugar from tear fluid and send information to an insulin pump [37]. Vision-based sensors could also be employed for smart healthcare solutions, but users may be reticent to install cameras at home.

On the other hand, AI is being applied to smart healthcare systems to analyze data for disease prevention, risk monitoring, precise diagnoses, and personalized treatment plans. It is based on analyzing the data gathered from all sensor devices and stored in a cloud system to determine the risk of suffering from a disease, evaluate the evolution of an illness, or make health and treatment suggestions. This helps in decision-making to improve the lifestyle of the patient and the behaviors that may increase the risk of disease or worsen the progression of current conditions. AI can also be used to implement virtual assistants that understand written or spoken language and respond accordingly, acting as the intermediary between patients, doctors, and institutions. It can be applied for mental health, to provide information, or for administrative tasks such as making appointments. Blockchain is implemented to provide security, privacy, transparency, immutability, fault tolerance, quality of service, and automation [38, 39]. Surgical robots such as the Da Vinci system help to improve results and recovery times. Furthermore, techniques such as mixed reality can be used to plan surgeries by modeling patients and their injuries.

There are however some challenges to the deployment of smart healthcare systems. There is no standard for smart healthcare, which leads to unclarity and lack of interoperability. Furthermore, legal regulations do not advance at the same speed as technology does, which can result in some problems that hinder the testing and deployment of these systems. A large quantity of data is generated from countless smart things, creating difficulty in managing and transmitting all the gathered information. Moreover, some users may have struggles when using technology, for example, elders and disabled people. Security of the data is also an important factor to consider. Lastly, some sensors may need to be recalibrated, and disconnections may happen due to coverage losses or being out of battery [36].

14.4.4 Smart Home: Smart Buildings, Smart Living

The fundamental objective of smart homes is the incorporation of sensors and actuators in homes and buildings to facilitate domestic life. A smart home can be created from the beginning during its construction stage, or the sensors, actuators, and necessary devices can be incorporated into older houses, which did not have them. A fundamental characteristic of smart homes is that residents can have local or remote access to the Internet to take control of information on the status of the home and act accordingly, based on their preferences and needs.

When automation is implemented in homes, higher levels of home control and security, higher levels of energy savings and efficiency, higher levels of comfort for its inhabitants, and even greater sustainability are achieved.

Currently, with the use of mobile devices, there are two options for controlling our home: Home Assistant or SmartThings. SmartThings [40] is a proprietary solution from Samsung. Through this solution, you can access an App to take control of Samsung and compatible devices. As a requirement for users of this option, they must be connected to the Samsung cloud service, which they will access through the Internet. If a user decides to use Home Assistant [41], they will be accessing open-source software automation. One of its main advantages is that we can control different devices and systems, which will work jointly and transparently from the user's point of view. This solution can be implemented using multiple systems, although among the best-known and most utilized are Google Home, Amazon Echo, and Alexa. From the point of view of its use, the Home Assistant option requires greater knowledge for its implementation.

To implement the Home Assistant or SmartThings solutions, it is necessary to use wireless or wired communication technologies to connect with the devices and controllers. The most used technologies are Ethernet, WiFi, Bluetooth low energy (BLE), Zigbee, etc.

If we have the necessary resources implemented in the smart home, from any place within the home with an Internet connection, we can take control of the heating, ventilation, and air conditioning (HVAC) systems, appliances, lighting, closed-circuit television (CCTV), etc. Among the most widely used sensors and actuators we can highlight:

- Intelligent opening and closing of doors and windows: We can open the access door to our home or garage from anywhere. It will also allow us to do it with the windows. This provides increased security and also facilitates access to other people at home.
- Smart lighting: The installation of these sensors and actuators allows us to remotely control household lights. Depending on the devices and controllers, we can even regulate the intensity of the light. Apart from significant energy savings, it can provide an additional security mode in homes.
- Smart energy consumption meters: These sensors and actuators allow for the control of energy consumption and can have a significant impact on cost reduction.

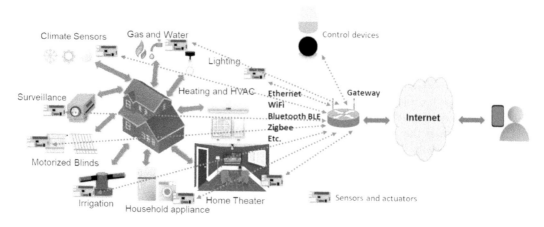

FIGURE 14.6   The network architecture of a smart home.

- Smart plugs: With their use, connected home appliances can be controlled. This will allow us to reduce consumption and avoid failures in case of electrical problems.
- Smoke and gas detection: The presence of smoke can be detected. It allows the prevention of fires by launching the appropriate alarms. In addition, this will prevent the great material losses that can occur in a fire. Also, gases harmful to health can be detected and the corresponding alarm activated.
- Smart HVAC systems: They will allow you to control the air conditioning of the home from anywhere. Its influence on reducing energy costs is unquestionable.
- Leak sensors: Sensors can be installed to report any loss that may occur in our piping system. They are usually used in kitchens and bathrooms, although detection can be extended to the entire home.
- Motion sensors: Their installation allows us to discover any anomalous movement that is taking place in our house. It is closely related to home security. Cameras and CCTV are often used to perform these functions.

An automation architecture should include at least:

- Sensors and actuators, which will be connected to all the devices and elements that you want to control.
- A network of smart sockets, which will have the function of energy management.
- A home communications network (wired or wireless).
- A central gateway, which will be in charge of the coordination and control of all the connected devices in the home.

Figure 14.6 shows the network architecture of the smart home.

14.4.5   Smart City: Traffic Management, Public Safety

Every day the population moving from living in rural environments to living in cities increases. According to the 2014 revision of the World Urbanization Prospects, of the Department of Economic and Social Affairs of the United Nations [42], it is expected that in 2050, 66% of the population will live in urban areas. To achieve adequate development, the premise of carrying out sustainable urbanization appears. Smart cities play a fundamental role in the future of cities.

A smart city uses digital solutions to achieve sustainability and efficiency in cities. Sensors and sensor networks are used in smart cities to monitor and improve their infrastructures, services, security, etc. Using sensor networks, cameras, wireless devices, and data centers, the data will be obtained, which helps transform traditional cities into smart cities.

The objective of a smart city, from an environmental point of view, is to become a sustainable city, and from the point of view of its inhabitants, it must be attractive due to the services they receive. To achieve the objectives, they must have:

- The necessary monitoring resources for decision-making.
- The appropriate communications technology.
- The ability to analyze the observed data to act, making the most appropriate decisions.
- Bet on future technologies, which will allow greater adaptation to improvement, based on our needs.

According to [43] the six key characteristics of a smart city are:

- **Smart Economy:** Economic growth will increase in smart cities by increasing their population. All this will influence the labor market, entrepreneurship, etc. There will be greater demand for products and services.
- **Smart People:** Entrepreneurship and entrepreneurship are encouraged in many smart cities. According to [44], the key to a city's success depends on the participation of people in exchanging knowledge.
- **Smart Governance:** Each smart city has a different way of organizing itself since each city has its objectives. Some of the most used forms of intelligent governance are transparency or participation in decision-making.
- **Smart Mobility:** Transport within the city is one of the key points in smart cities. Citizens need to have systems that allow them to move from one location to another as efficiently as possible.
- **Smart Environment:** This is another key point since the future of cities must reduce pollution, protect the environment, and manage waste more efficiently.
- **Smart Living:** Improving the quality of life of citizens will be essential. It will be achieved, among other things, by improving their health conditions, the quality of their homes, better educational and cultural facilities, etc.

Smart cities use a large number of sensors to obtain data. Some of the areas in which monitoring is necessary are the following:

- **Pollution management or air quality:** Using sensors strategically installed in cities, ambient air quality can be monitored to alert citizens of dangerous pollution levels, as well as influence and improve environmental awareness.
- **Structural health management:** Buildings are controlled to increase their safety and reduce maintenance costs. The structural deterioration of a building, which may be due to various causes such as the action of the environment and the degradation of construction materials, can be observed. Parameters such as temperature, humidity, stresses, accelerations, and material degradation are monitored.
- **Transportation and traffic management:** Using intelligent transport and traffic monitoring systems makes the transport network more efficient. Some of the advantages that it will bring us are the management and optimization of traffic, the improvement of road infrastructure, the increase in road safety, the reduction of environmental pollution, and the management of public transport. More efficient mobility of citizens will be generated, and commuting will become more agile, improving safety and reducing pollution levels.
- **Water management:** It is necessary to monitor the hydraulic infrastructure. Major cities waste a lot of water due to leaks in their pipes.

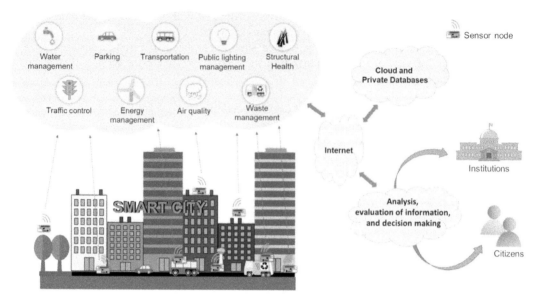

FIGURE 14.7 The network architecture of a smart city.

- **Energy management:** It is necessary to use sensors to perform intelligent control of the electrical network. When they detect any anomaly or failure, they alert the service company. You can proceed to quick repair or redirection of energy through another path. In addition, it provides information to companies and customers, so that they can improve the use and management of resources.

- **Public lighting management:** Using sensors that monitor the status of streetlights and public lighting, administrations can receive alerts at the moment a failure occurs. In this way, you can control the energy that is sometimes being wasted. For example, when the lights stay on during the day. Also, it will allow for the detection of thefts and manipulation of lighting.

- **Waste management:** By installing sensors in the garbage containers, it is possible to monitor and notify when they have been filled. In addition, citizens can have information on the level of filling of the ones closest to their location. Furthermore, it will allow the planning of collection routes, with consequent savings in the management of vehicles and landfills. Moreover, waste management can be controlled. They can even provide fire alerts by monitoring their temperature level.

Figure 14.7 shows the network architecture of the smart city.

14.4.6 Smart Logistics: Transport, Mobility, Smart Tourism, Product Lifetime Management, Smart Sea Transport, Smart Ports, Smart Ships

Logistics is defined as the set of resources and methods necessary to carry out the organization of a company, or a service, especially distribution. Over the years, the main objective has been maintained, however, the means and resources used to achieve this aim have been changing. Figure 14.8 shows the different generations that logistics have had [45].

Smart logistics is known as the application of the principles of cyber-physical systems for better control, self-organization, and optimization of this function in the supply chain. Logistics management is a developing innovative approach as a result of the constant changes that are taking place in the sector. Factors such as technological innovation, the growth in demand for goods and services, or the complexity of the supply chain are just some of them.

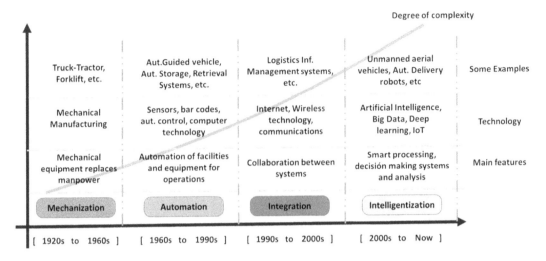

FIGURE 14.8 Generations of logistics.

Using technology, a direct digital image can be produced to subsequently establish, for example, real-time measures to increase the efficiency of networks throughout the company, as well as self-control, processing, and billing subsystems linking it with additional information from IT systems, cameras, or sensor systems. Therefore, the main objective of smart logistics is to reach a more efficient, decentralized, flexible, and agile order processing.

For sure, IoT technology and big data will continue to be implemented to manage transportation and product manufacturing. Benefiting the sector and multiplying its operational capacity, the activity in researching to maximize the efficiency of logistics networks means that they will be in continuous development.

14.4.6.1   *What Smart Logistics Is?*

Smart logistics [46] refers to a specific type of logistics characterized by a considerable improvement in efficiency in all the processes integrated into the development of the logistics activity; that is, it is not a single logistics system but rather refers to the fact that it is executed from the most efficient, sustainable, and profitable logistics perspective possible. In this sense, although there is no single aspect that must be taken into account when identifying intelligent logistics, there are certain common elements that are present in it:

- Sustainable logistics
- Social logistics
- Use of new technologies applied to traceability
- Process automation

These four elements are essential when we understand what smart logistics is since they are aspects that increase the efficiency of logistics activities as a whole and, at the same time, they respond to the demands of consumers who expect their purchase decisions to have an impact not only on their immediate economy but also on society as a whole. Figure 14.9 shows an example of a heterogeneous network dedicated to the logistics control of goods from the point of manufacture to delivery to the user.

14.4.6.2   *Benefits of Smart Logistics for Enterprises and Industry*

The benefits of using smart logistics for companies are numerous. For example, the quality and speed of transportation can be significantly improved based on more accurate diagnoses and reliable

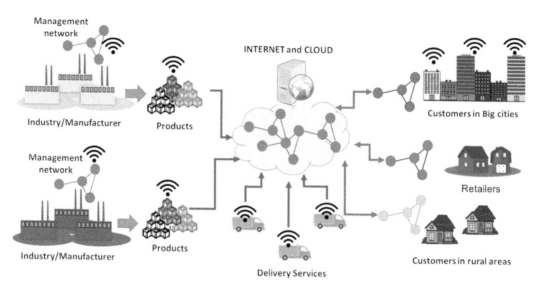

FIGURE 14.9   Example network in smart logistics.

forecasts. In addition, this step has the advantage of simplifying the sharing of interests with suppliers, warehouse personnel, and end customers through the exchange of visualizations and analysis [47].

Many logistics providers are already focusing their digitization strategies on interconnecting system data with sensor-collected vehicle data on a cloud platform. This is one of the positive consequences of smart logistics. In cooperation with the industry, this method will also facilitate the digital connection of existing installations and provide accurate information to ensure the stability of the entire infrastructure. Based on this approach, we can not only determine the maintenance strategy but also respond to intelligently exceptional situations. For example, when multiple error messages are received, they can decide which should take priority. The result is greater customer satisfaction thanks to smart logistics.

14.4.7   Smart Industry: Industrial Processing, Smart Manufacturing

Every day many industries join the Industrial Revolution, also known as Industry 4.0. Digital transformation has allowed physical elements to merge with digital ones and thus improve productivity. This gives rise to the smart industry and smart factory concepts [48].

Smart factory [49] refers to the intelligent industry, that is, disruptive technologies have been incorporated into its production processes and the result is a more flexible and modular production, thanks to these automation technologies.

The smart factory allows for minimizing time in the production processes, as well as the costs since they are capable of adapting and optimizing the processes in addition to storing and analyzing a large amount of data in real time. This gives rise to a more versatile, efficient, and autonomous production, making people focus on improving processes and not so much on repetitive tasks, providing great value [50].

Cloud computing in the smart industry [51] permits the storage of large volumes of data generated both in the plant (robots, sensors, etc.) and in specific tools (MES, ERP, etc.) and products manufactured. The following are the main features of the smart industry.

- **IoT in the Smart Industry**. The connectivity between the machines allows coordinating systems, capturing data, having remote control of production, as well as exchanging information between systems and products.

- **Big data**. The information generated through the connections between machines or plants and tools must be collected and analyzed considering two objectives: the first one refers to being able to identify patterns, and the second one is focused on preventing future events. Only big data enables working with a large volume of data at optimal times.
- **Cybersecurity** in a smart factory is one of the essential technologies since privacy and data protection are the most important requirements for industries.
- **Robots** facilitate tasks that require a high level of precision or all those that are repetitive. In each activity, a cognitive robot, an autonomous robot, or both are required.
- **Digital Twins** [52] allow increased efficiency, control, and planning of operations.
- **Virtual and augmented reality** help operators in the organization of products, production tasks, and the maintenance and repair of equipment. But we should not confuse both terms; when we talk about augmented reality (AR) we refer to the technology that allows us to superimpose, in real time, digital information to the information that is perceived through our eyes and we only require a smartphone. While virtual reality requires special glasses to transfer our person to the virtual world.

14.4.7.1 Benefits of Investing in Information and Communication Technology (ICT) for Smart Industry

Digitizing an industry brings numerous benefits that affect the planning, quality, and development of products and the logistics of the supply chain. Below, we list the most important competitive advantages [53]:

- Speed and flexibility in the event of unforeseen events
- Connection of digital and physical elements in real time through sensors and IoT devices
- Optimization of resources
- Reliability of stored data
- Bidirectional data flow between elements

In the long term, the smart industry will have other advantages such as the benefits provided by machine learning. We need time to collect and store enough data to draw up a demand forecast, carry out preventive and predictive maintenance, or generate digital twins, among many other actions that machine learning allows us [54].

14.4.8 Smart Energy: Smart Grid, Power Management

The energy generation and treatment approach, implemented traditionally since the 20th century, is a rigid and unidirectional model, based on a limited number of plants that supply top-down energy to customers, and is not sustainable in the medium and long term. According to the 2015 communication of the European Commission [55], it is necessary to invest 2,000 million euros each year, to generate savings of 9,000 million euros in the year 2030, which would be achieved by improving energy efficiency by 25%. Making the transition to smart energy brings with it a series of changes, greater energy efficiency, processing and final use of energy, and greater use of clean and renewable energy resources and smart energy systems [56].

What is intended with smart energy is to digitize the energy sector, which is working traditionally, to reach an increasingly decentralized and multidirectional model. The aim is to reach an adaptation of energy consumption to the real needs of the demand. Excess production will be avoided, from the traditional model, to adjust to what the consumer demands.

According to Dincer et al. [57], the key expectations in smart energy systems are energetically sound, energetically secure, environmentally benign, economically feasible, commercially viable, socially acceptable, integrable, and reliable. By implementing smart energy, not only cost savings will be acted on but also changes in the environment will arise, such as the reduction of the carbon footprint and reduction of water consumption.

In addition, some new concepts must be taken into account.

- New type of consumer, known as prosumer: A consumer of energy, which also produces it. The prosumer generates energy from its facilities and, in addition to consuming it, reinjects energy into the network.
- Smart grid: It is a type of network capable of ensuring a sustainable and efficient energy system, with very low losses, in addition to being able to supply supplies with high levels of quality and safety.
- Smart meters: They are the new energy meters. They must have telemanagement capabilities and allow time discrimination.
- Energy storage: The storage of energy, although very complicated, has become a necessity.

The search for maximum energy efficiency leads us toward smart grids, which are going to be networks equipped with intelligence, flexibility, efficiency, security, openness, and sustainability. They will be able to adapt quickly, thanks to the new monitoring and communication systems that are implemented on them.

From the beginning, energy transmission networks had meters to price the cost of each of the consumers that were connected. A new Smart grid must have characteristics such as:

- Monitoring systems allow the immediate location of any cut in the supply so that it is possible to send maintenance teams to carry out the appropriate repairs.
- Lifetime maintenance of energy generation equipment and systems, to control aging.
- Prevention will make it possible to detect and reduce power outages. This prevention will observe potential points of failure, which will be monitored, and based on the application of artificial intelligence to previous data, appropriate preventive actions will be carried out.
- Expenses will be optimized. Thanks to consumption monitoring, energy generation will be adjusted to needs in real time, so that energy waste is reduced.

One of the great problems facing the future of energy is its storage. A scale of the methods that allow the storage of energy would be the following:

- On a large scale: On the order of gigawatts (GW), it can be stored using reversible hydroelectric, or thermal storage.
- Network storage: On the order of megawatts (MW), it can be stored using cells and batteries; capacitors and superconductors; and flywheels.
- At the end-user level: On the order of kilowatts (kW), it can be stored using batteries, superconductors, and flywheels.

Another great challenge is to have smart meters, since the future form of pricing will be done on an hourly basis, and these meters will facilitate network management and control. It requires the replacement of outdated meters, for these new types of meters will be able to carry out remote measurements and remote management, which will allow the reading of the meter and the processing of information remotely.

For all the reasons stated above, the operation of the smart grid is based on a constant communication network capable of monitoring the consumption of its customers. Where it will be possible to continuously monitor and measure the behavior of all the devices that connect clients to the infrastructure. To implement this solution, an automated system must be available that is capable of regulating both generation and variations in customer demand. Figure 14.10 shows an example of

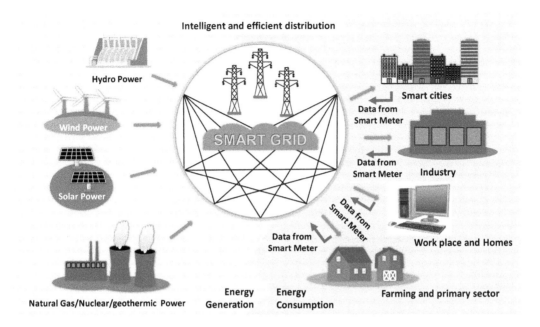

FIGURE 14.10 Smart energy distribution.

a smart distribution system where different sources of energy generation are shown on the left side while the right side shows some energy consumers.

14.4.9 Social Internet of Things (SIoT)

The concept of Social of Internet Things focuses on the integration of social networking with IoT, where objects interact with each other simulating human-to-human interactions and applying sociology concepts to their form of communication [58]. A social network comprised of objects is created to achieve common goals such as providing services or improving efficiency, functionality, and performance [59]. This way, things autonomously choose friendships or form friend-of-a-friend connections between the devices of a network. Thus, the interactions in SIoT are thing-to-thing or user-to-thing. The types of relationships that can be established within SIoT are depicted in Figure 14.11. As a result, SIoT can be utilized for coordination strategies, social gamification, and virtualized platforms, as well as to establish new forms of communication between the devices of other applications of IoT [58].

Relationship management is therefore one of the main tasks of SIoT. The benefit of socialized objects is the improvement in response time and accuracy obtained in comparison to objects that work on their own. Therefore, the tendency is for IoT to become more "social" as services and functionalities increase in complexity [59]. As SIoT can be implemented in other IoT use cases, the sensor devices of the applications of IoT can also be part of SIoT to establish a "social" form of communication with other devices. When an object is first introduced in a network, it needs to be assigned an ID, a profile with static and dynamic information about the other objects of the network, and the settings or permissions designated by the owner of the device to control its behavior [59]. This process is performed by the owner establishing communication with the server and creating an account [60].

The other main factor of interest in SIoT is trust management so as to determine which devices are malicious and which are benign. As a result, different types of trust with different characteristics have been identified depending on the trustworthiness of each object [59]. As a consequence of the trust system that establishes the social relationships between the objects, there are specific trust attacks that tamper with this system. Bad-mouthing attacks worsen the reputation of certain devices, reducing

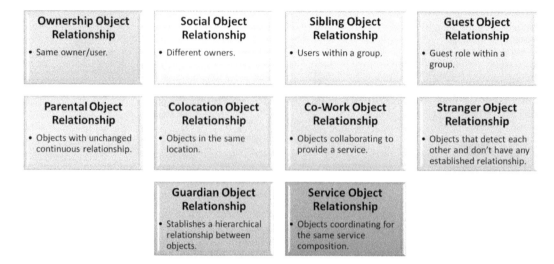

FIGURE 14.11 Types of relationships between SIoT devices.

their selection chances. Slandering attacks affect trust feedback. Whitewashing attacks clean the bad reputation of the device. Discriminatory attacks are directed to devices with weak connections within a group to isolate the device. Opportunistic service attacks are performed by malicious devices that usually provide bad services but improve their performance to gain trust and later participate in other types of attacks. Ballot stuffing attacks focus on recommending malicious objects so that they are chosen. Lastly, self-promoting attacks broadcast good feedback about themselves to gain the trust of other devices.

The advantages of SIoT rely on the ability of the objects to establish social relationships to find resources and provide more efficient results to complex problems [58]. Human social networks are emulated by objects to improve scalability, establish networks, and provide services. Security is increased by assigning labels such as "friend" to trusted devices and determining the interactions that can be performed with each device. Furthermore, existing social network tools can be applied to the relationships of the devices. However, there are some challenges to be considered. The deployment of SIoT networks implies a large number of devices generating large amounts of data that require efficient management. Furthermore, as the number of devices is incremented, some problems with scalability may arise. Managing heterogeneity of devices is a complicated task as things use different standards and forms of communication that may not be compatible with each other and create interoperability problems. And resource-constrained devices would require the system to provide effective resource management. Mobility also needs to be considered in dynamic environments as the state of the objects may change. Lastly, as security is one of the main challenges of SIoT, providing fault tolerance and good trust management is paramount.

14.4.10 Smart Education: eLearning

Smart education means the use of IoT solutions in smart building of educational entities, such as school buildings, classrooms, buses, and so on. With the growing popularity of devices like Amazon Alexa and Google Home, users have quickly integrated smart home solutions into their daily lives. As smart building solutions evolve, education experts and school administrators are beginning to recognize the benefits of using IoT technology on a large scale in school environments. Thus, the modernized electronic version of the teaching/learning processes is known as e-learning [61]. The introduction of sensor systems and IoT solutions can benefit both teachers and students. Smart education has nothing related to new devices. However, smart education should be considered a new educational paradigm designed for digital natives. The pioneers in this sense were some teachers from South Korea, such as ByeongGuk Ku [62], who encouraged his students to use their smartphones

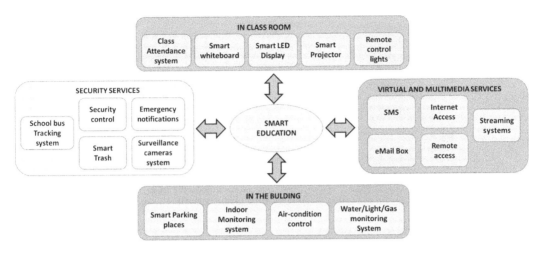

FIGURE 14.12 Uses of IoT in smart education.

in class when smartphones became popular. In 2011, Ku developed an interactive teaching/learning model that included social network services and cloud-based tools. After that, the South Korean government implemented a new educational plan called smart education. To do this, it increased investment intending to digitize learning environments in schools and commit to the use of new technologies in the classroom.

IoT solutions are capable of redefining the way that students, teachers/professors, and administrators can interact. Smart devices make possible the interconnection of the objects present in a classroom, improve experiences in the teaching/learning process, enhance educational results, and reduce costs. Some examples of IoT devices that can contribute to creating a smart education environment are:

- Smart whiteboards and other interactive digital media.
- Smart systems for monitoring environmental parameters such as temperature, ventilation, and air quality.
- Smart ID cards, attendance-tracking solutions, or school bus tracking systems.
- Wireless systems for locking doors and surveillance cameras with facial recognition systems, etc.

Figure 14.12 shows an example of an IoT integration for smart education [63, 64].

14.4.10.1 Smart Education Architecture

To start talking about smart learning environments, it is important to know and understand their architecture. It is possible to propose a layered model that contains the different elements and how these layers are communicated between them. We can define four basic layers, although these layers can be reduced if required [65]:

- **Core Layer:** Improved learning/teaching methods. The new learning/teaching processes required by a smart education system must include new teaching methods based on games, problem-based teaching methods, the study of real cases, flipped learning, or learning adapted to the needs of the target group. The global deployment of the Internet and the lowering of the cost of new technologies, such as computers, are the most influential innovations of the century. However, the simple support of these new methods through information and communication technologies cannot be considered smart education since it does not create a significant change in the educational paradigm. For this reason, new teaching/learning methods are at the bottom of the smart education model.

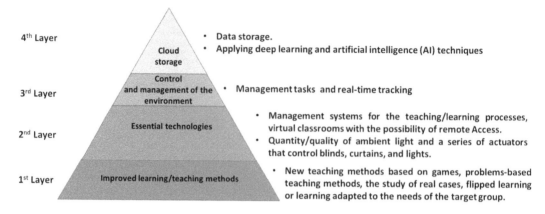

FIGURE 14.13 Layered model for smart education.

- **Second Layer:** Essential technologies. The use of technology is essential to the transformation of education as we commonly know it. These technologies should include management systems for the teaching/learning processes, virtual classrooms with the possibility of remote access, and self-managed monitored spaces. It is also possible to consider the incorporation of sensors and actuators, as well as communication technologies that allow communication within intelligent environments and elements. Some technologies that can be considered are the quantity/quality of ambient light and a series of actuators that control blinds, curtains, and lights. These will allow monitoring of the environment and the systems for learning performance analysis, educational data mining, electronic books, or books interactive. Likewise, all those technologies that favor remote access and virtual teaching, such as augmented reality, virtual reality, and interactive robots, can also be included in this layer.
- **Third layer:** Control and management of the environment. The techniques applied in this layer are capable of improving the experience in smart education. When there are several environments within the same organization, it is interesting to carry out the management tasks from a higher point of view (centralized or distributed, depending on the design). To perform real-time tracking of what is happening, it is important to monitor the events associated with the amount of movement in the classroom, the sound level, and the activity that is taking place. The environment management system can intelligently warn if it would be necessary to move a group to a specific classroom due to possible problems in the classroom parameters measured that endanger the comfort and performance of the students. These warnings can be sent directly through text messages or email.
- **Fourth layer:** Cloud storage. It is very interesting to store the collected data generated within intelligent environments. With this data and with the appropriate tools, it is possible to analyze the learning processes in a detailed and long-term way. In this layer, the most modern techniques of deep learning and artificial intelligence (AI) can be used, applying behavior analysis systems of people and correlating the results with the measurable parameters in the environments or the characteristics of the activities carried out. The conclusions obtained can be used to develop/improve the inference rules that manage the system.

Figure 14.13 shows the proposed layered model for smart education:

14.4.10.2 *Benefits of Smart Learning*

According to the study provided by Alcatel-Lucent Enterprise [66], the use of IoT applied to education can bring great benefits to the current education system:

- New customized methods for teaching through more dynamic learning experiences by using digital books and game-based learning techniques.
- Improving student performance by using new audiovisual equipment, digital video recorders, streaming platforms, and online tests.
- Simplify the tasks for the administrative team of the schools through the proactive supervision of the infrastructure and the creation of more efficient and profitable processes for the air conditioning, lighting, and management of the school.
- Safer environment for both students and teachers with modern surveillance systems, centralized lock doors, and tracking-based systems for school buses.
- Energy efficiency and cost savings with IoT in schools. IoT-connected lighting and other devices can be scheduled and automated. For example, lights can be set on a schedule or connected to occupancy sensors and programmed to turn off when a room is empty.

14.4.11   Internet of Nano Things (IoNT)

The concept of Internet of Nano Things (IoNT) has its origin in the concept of "nanotechnology." The origin of the term dates back to 1959 when R. Feynman cited the concept of nanotechnology for the first time in his publication entitled "There's Plenty of Room at the Bottom" [67]. In this manifesto, the author spoke about the possibility of miniaturizing already-known technology by creating smaller and more powerful devices with higher performance. In 1974, Taniguchi [68] tried to define nanotechnology as the process of manufacturing objects on scales between 1 to 100 nanometers.

M. Roco from US National Nanotechnology defined in [69] different generations in the development of nanotechnology. The first generation is related to the science of materials and the improvement of their properties which is achieved by incorporating "passive nanostructures." It can be done with coatings or with the use of carbon nanotubes to reinforce plastics. The second generation employs active nanostructures, for example, through bioactivity that allows a drug to be delivered to a specific cell or organ. It can be done by coating the nanoparticle with specific proteins. The complexity increases further in the third and fourth generations. The third generation starts from an advanced nano-system that includes "nanosystems of characteristics" that comprise thousands of interacting components, to finally reach the fourth generation, which is based on a molecular nano-system to control the development of artificial organs with nanomaterials. Finally, it is possible to include the fifth generation in nanotechnology by including artificial intelligence and cognitive awareness in those systems [70]. Figure 14.14 tries to identify each generation with the time.

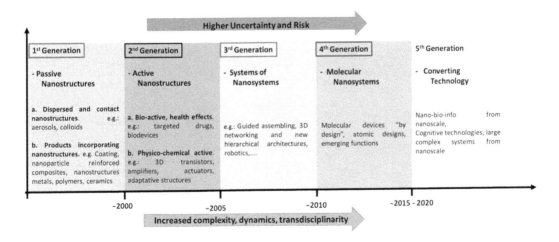

FIGURE 14.14   Nanotechnology generations.

The interconnection and coexistence of nano-scale devices with already existing networks and the Internet defines a novel networking paradigm known as "Internet of Nano-Things." The IoNT can be defined as a nano-scale network of physical tiny objects able to exchange data with each other by using Nano Communication.

IoNT infrastructure can be implemented by using nano-devices together with several other technologies such as IoT, sensors, and different computing techniques. The IoNT infrastructure mainly depends on the area of application and the constraints in bandwidth, the number of required connections/devices, or energy available. The improvement and the spread in the use of IoNT depend on the processing capabilities of devices, large storage at low costs, smart antennas, and smart RFID tag technology.

One of the major challenges to face with the IoNT is to ensure the privacy and security of users and their sensitive data. Because critical data is typically communicated between devices over the Internet (i.e., public networks), worries related to the privacy of the data have risen. Finally, another important factor that is hindering the growth of the IoNT market is the important economic investment required to permit the correct development and research in nanotechnology.

Currently, IoNT bases its development on two main areas of communication:

- Electromagnetic Nano Communication [71, 72] is related to the transmission/receiving of electromagnetic (EM) radiation from components based on nanomaterials.
- Molecular Communication [73, 74] refers to the transmission/receiving of data encoded in molecules.

14.4.11.1 Network Architecture of IoNT

In order to design and deploy IoNT, regardless of the application areas, the following devices and elements should be considered fundamental parts of an IoNT Architecture (see Figure 14.15 [75, 76]:

1. **Nano-nodes:** Nano-nodes are small devices, with limited storage capacities, installed in every-day objects such as keys, books, and gadgets. These devices are capable of performing simple tasks and calculations. The measured data is transmitted over short distances. Biological sensors installed in the human body can be considered nano-nodes.

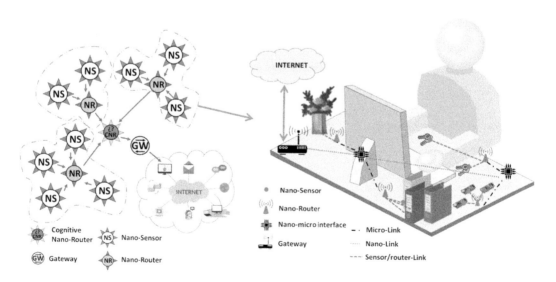

FIGURE 14.15 Network architecture of IoNT.

2. **Nano-Routers:** Nano-routers are devices with greater computational power responsible for interconnecting the different nano-nodes. Likewise, nano-routers are also capable of routing data between different nano-micro interfaces or sending data to a gateway with access to the Internet.

3. **Nano-micro interface devices:** They are devices in charge of adding the information coming from nano-routers to be transmitted to the gateway and vice versa. The gateway allows the connection of different things with the Internet and to other traditional communication networks with classic network protocols. These devices also communicate with other nano-micro interface devices.

4. **Gateway:** It allows access to the Internet of the entire network and the different objects and things present in the network.

5. **Links between devices:** The complete connection of all the nano-systems must be carried out with protocols and technologies appropriate to the environment and the requirements of the network.

14.4.11.2 *Uses and Benefits*

As this section has shown, nanotechnology will play an essential role in the development of innovation in science and engineering. Nanotechnology is present in many sectors such as energy, communication and information technology, aerospace, medicine, defense, and transportation.

Nanotechnology also promises important advancements in the industry of electrical vehicles creating energy-efficient batteries, solar panels, and fuel cells. Additionally, nanotechnology can provide interesting solutions to clean up pollution in crop soils and water bodies as well as provide enhancements in medicine and healthcare [77]. Some uses that can benefit from nanotechnology are:

- **Healthcare:** Nanotechnology can help to develop sophisticated tools for quick detection of diseases and new treatments to combat them.
- **Electronic devices** can benefit from advanced chips and personal electronic devices.
- In **Sports equipment**, nanotechnology can contribute to increasing the security of motorcycle helmets and other materials to build more durable baseball bats, tennis rackets, etc.
- **Fabrics** based on nanotechnology can resist staining and bacterial growth helping to improve air quality.
- **Household products** such as stain removers, antibacterial cleaners, paints, sealants, and air purifiers and filters can be improved with nanotechnology.
- **Energy innovations**, like more efficient solar panels, stronger, lightweight wind turbines, lighter car parts, and improved fuel efficiency, are powered by nanotechnology.
- **Industry and Food packaging** can benefit from nanotechnology to prevent contamination and to help food to stay fresher longer.

IoNT still presents some issues and challenges to be solved. Researchers should consider some problems in terms of context management, security, privacy, service composition, and discovery.

IoNT devices should develop new security and privacy mechanisms to ensure data is collected by nanosensors. Service-oriented architectures are more convenient for permitting nanosensors and nanonetworks to be compatible so as to hold large amounts of data with different formats.

14.5 Conclusion

IoT has been evolving and increasing its functionalities in recent years. Furthermore, it is expected to continue growing as the number of smart devices increases over time. This interest in connecting smart things that communicate and perform actions as a result of the changes in the environment surged as a consequence of the introduction of sensors in devices with the ability to communicate, usually wirelessly. Moreover, as technology has advanced, the size and precision of sensors have significantly improved. In this chapter, an overview of the domains of IoT and the role of sensor devices in each of them has been provided. The innovations and challenges of each IoT domain have been discussed as well. This way, the reader has obtained a general knowledge of the actual state of IoT and the sensor devices that enable IoT systems to provide their services.

The use of IoT in multiple areas leads us to think that its applicability will reach most aspects of life, providing a more sustainable [78], inclusive, and prosperous future [79]. This will lead to the deployment of millions of devices that will demand the improvement of wireless technologies to provide service and enable massive communications. Artificial intelligence is another technology that will be part of each IoT domain and will change the current paradigm regarding telemetry and the smart applications that feed from this data. Inevitably, this will lead to a great change in the ways of working and living of many people, which will require an increase in people with AI qualifications to manage these applications. As the use of IoT has extended, the cost of production has been substantially reduced, leading to a faster and further reach of this technology both in developed and developing countries looking for more efficient systems. Although the current geopolitical background has led to delays and cost increases in the supply chain, the overall tendency is for IoT devices and systems to reduce in cost and become more accessible as another of the services offered by service providers. It is thus in the best interest of service providers to improve communications and provide new cloud services to address the current limitations of the physical infrastructure deployed so far. 5G is currently one of the most popular wireless communication technologies to address the demands of future networks, but the cost of renovating the infrastructure is one of the principal reasons why the implementation of next-generation networks may take more time than what would be preferred. Nonetheless, the popularity of 5G is highlighted in the number of research works that keep being published. Therefore, it is expected that when 5G networks are deployed worldwide, they will include new and improved functionalities that are not part of the specifications followed by the 5G devices developed today. Securing these networks and the data that is transmitted through them is paramount for the successful implementation of next-generation IoT systems. As people and machines are more and more connected, the security mechanisms provided by IoT systems should ensure complete privacy and confidentiality so as to avoid wrong and fraudulent uses of the capabilities provided by IoT. Being aware of the improvements that IoT can bring to society and also the problems that can be derived from their wrong use can lead to realistic developments and aid policymakers in adapting the current legislation to the newer technological environment that is to come. Lastly, the new IoT paradigm contemplates applications such as the Internet of Nano Things (IoNT) that would require in-depth ethical assessments and updates concerning some domains of applications such as healthcare and agriculture. This area of IoT is nonetheless in its first steps and its first operative implementations will be part of a further future.

REFERENCES

1. Wang, J., Lim, M., Wang, C., Tseng, M., 2021. The evolution of the Internet of Things (IoT) over the past 20 years. *Computers & Industrial Engineering*. 155:107174.
2. Shifa, A., Asghar, M. N., Fleury, M. Multimedia Security Perspectives in IoT. In: 2016 Sixth International Conference on Innovative Computing Technology (INTECH). IEEE; 2016.
3. Hasan Alhafidh, B. M., Allen, W. Design and simulation of a smart home managed by an intelligent self-adaptive system. *International Journal of Engineering Research and Applications*. 2016 Aug; 6(8):64–90.
4. Aslam, S., Michaelides, M. P., Herodotou, H. Internet of ships: A survey on architectures, emerging applications, and challenges. *IEEE Internet of Things Journal*. 2020;7(10):9714–27.
5. Ali, O., Ishak, M. K., Bhatti, M. K. L. Emerging IoT domains, current standings and open research challenges: A review. *PeerJ Computer Science*. 2021;7(e659):e659.

6. Pekar, A., Mocnej, J., Seah, W. K. G., Zolotova, I. Application domain-based overview of IoT network traffic characteristics. *ACM Computing Surveys*. 2021;53(4):1–33.

7. Sendra, S., García, L., Lloret, J., Bosch, I., Vega-Rodríguez, R. LoRaWAN network for fire monitoring in rural environments. *Electronics (Basel)*. 2020;9(3):531.

8. Lin, B., Zhu, F., Zhang, J., Chen, J., Chen, X., Xiong, N. N., et al. A time-driven data placement strategy for a scientific workflow combining edge computing and cloud computing. *IEEE Transactions on Industrial Informatics*. 2019;15(7):4254–65.

9. Patel, K. K., Patel, S. M. Internet of Things-IOT: Definition, characteristics, architecture, enabling technologies, Application & Future Challenges. *International Journal of Engineering Science and Computing*. 2016 May;6(5):6122–31.

10. Sorri, K., Mustafee, N., Seppänen, M. Revisiting IoT definitions: A framework towards comprehensive use. *Technological Forecasting and Social Change*. 2022;179(121623):121623.

11. Xenofontos, C., Zografopoulos, I., Konstantinou, C., Jolfaei, A., Khan, M. K., Choo, K.-K. R. Consumer, commercial, and industrial IoT (in)security: Attack taxonomy and case studies. *IEEE Internet of Things Journal*. 2022;9(1):199–221.

12. Mega 2560 Rev3 [Internet]. *Arduino.cc*. Available from: https://docs.arduino.cc/hardware/mega-2560 [Accessed: Aug 10, 2022].

13. UNO R3 [Internet]. *Arduino.cc*. Available from: https://docs.arduino.cc/hardware/uno-rev3 [Accessed: Aug 10, 2022].

14. D1 mini — WEMOS documentation LOLIN [Internet]. *Wemos.cc*. Available from: https://www.wemos.cc/en/latest/d1/d1_mini.html [Accessed: Aug 10, 2022].

15. NodeMCU documentation [Internet]. *Readthedocs.io*. Available from: https://nodemcu.readthedocs.io/en/release/ [Accessed: Aug 10, 2022].

16. Datasheet of Raspberry Pi 2 Model B [Internet]. *Adafruit.com*. Available from: https://cdn-shop.adafruit.com/pdfs/raspberrypi2modelb.pdf [Accessed: Aug 10, 2022].

17. Raspberry Pi 3 Model B+ [Internet]. *Raspberrypi.org*. Available from: https://static.raspberrypi.org/files/product-briefs/Raspberry-Pi-Model-Bplus-Product-Brief.pdf [Accessed: Aug 10, 2022].

18. García, L., Parra, L., Jimenez, J. M., Lloret, J., Lorenz, P. IoT-based smart irrigation systems: An overview on the recent trends on sensors and IoT systems for irrigation in precision agriculture. *Sensors (Basel)*. 2020;20(4):1042.

19. Garcia, L., Jiménez, J. M., Taha, M., Lloret, J. Wireless technologies for IoT in smart cities. *Netw Protoc Algorithm*. 2018;10(1):23.

20. Durgin, G. D. RF Thermoelectric Generation for Passive RFID. In: 2016 IEEE International Conference on RFID (RFID). IEEE; 2016.

21. Heine, G., Sagkob, H. *GPRS: Gateway to Third Generation Mobile Networks*. Norwood, MA: Artech House; 2003.

22. Duelk, M., Zirngibl, M. 100 Gigabit Ethernet - Applications, Features, Challenges. In: Proceedings IEEE INFOCOM 2006 25TH IEEE International Conference on Computer Communications. IEEE; 2006.

23. Landrigan, P. J. , Fuller, R., Acosta, N. J. R., Adeyi, O., Arnold, R., Basu, N., et al., The Lancet commission on pollution and health. *The Lancet Commissions*. 2018;391(10119):462–512.

24. Microsoft's Planetary Computer Data Catalog. [Online] Available: https://planetarycomputer.microsoft.com/catalog. [Accessed: Aug 10, 2022].

25. Rai, A. C., Kumar, P., Pilla, F., Skouloudis, A. N., Di Sabatino, S., Ratti, C., Yasar, A., Rickerby, D. End-user perspective of low-cost sensors for outdoor air pollution monitoring. *Science of the Total Environment*. 2017;607–608:691–705.

26. Sampathkumar, A., Murugan, S., Elngar, A. A., Garg, L., Kanmani, R., Malar, A. C. J. A novel scheme for an IoT-based weather monitoring system using a wireless sensor network. *Integration of WSN and IoT for Smart Cities*. 2020, pp. 181–191.

27. Parra, L., Sendra, S., Jimenez, J. M., Lloret, J. Smart System to Detect and Track Pollution in Marine Environments. In: 2015 IEEE International Conference on Communication Workshop (ICCW), London, UK, 08–12 June 2015.

28. Lloret, J., Garcia, M., Bri, D., Sendra, S. A wireless sensor network deployment for rural and forest fire detection and verification. *Sensors*. 2009;9(11):8722–8747.

29. United Nations (UN). Global issues. *Population*. [On Line] Available: https://www.un.org/en/global-issues/population. [Accessed: Aug 10, 2022].

30. Food and Agriculture Organization of the United Nations. 2050: Increased investment in agricultural research essential. [On Line] Available: https://www.fao.org/news/story/en/item/35686/icode/. [Accessed: Aug 10, 2022].

31. García, L., Parra, L., Jimenez, J. M., Lloret, J., Mauri, P. V., Lorenz, P. L. DronAway: A proposal on the use of remote sensing drones as mobile gateway for WSN in precision agriculture. *Applied Sciences*, 2020;10(19):6668.

32. Gartner. Agricultural IOT will see a very rapid growth over the next 10 years. [On Line] Available: https://machinaresearch.com/news/agricultural-iot-will-see-a-very-rapid-growth-over-the-next-10-years/ [Accessed: Aug 10, 2022].

33. García, L., Parra, L., Jimenez, J. M., Lloret, J., Lorenz, P. IoT-based smart irrigation systems: An overview on the recent trends on sensors and IoT systems for irrigation in precision agriculture. *Sensors*. 2020;20(4):1042.

34. Lloret, J., Sendra, S., Garcia, L., Jimenez, J. M. A wireless sensor network deployment for soil moisture monitoring in precision agriculture. *Sensors*. 2021;21(21):7243.

35. Tian, S., Yang, W., Grange, J. M. L., Wang, P., Huang, W., Ye, Z. Smart healthcare: making medical care more intelligent. *Global Health Journal*. 2019;3(3):62–5.

36. Baker, S. B., Xiang, W., Atkinson, I, Internet of things for smart healthcare: Technologies, challenges, and opportunities. *IEEE Access*. 2017;5:26521–44.

37. Ghazal, T. M., Hasan, M. K., Alshurideh, M. T., Alzoubi, H. M., Ahmad, M., Akbar, S. S., et al. IoT for smart cities: Machine learning approaches in smart healthcare—A review. *Future internet*. 2021;13(8):218.

38. Kumar, A., Krishnamurthi, R., Nayyar, A., Sharma, K., Grover, V., Hossain, E. A novel smart healthcare design, simulation, and implementation using healthcare 4.0 processes. *IEEE Access*. 2020;8:118433–71.

39. Garcia-Sanchez, A.-J., Garcia Angosto, E., Llor, J. L., Serna Berna, A., Ramos, D. Machine learning techniques applied to dose prediction in computed tomography tests. *Sensors (Basel)*. 2019;19(23):5116.

40. SmartThings. Connected life with smart things [On Line] Available: https://www.samsung.com/es/apps/smartthings/ [Accessed: Aug 10, 2022].

41. Home Assistant. Awaken your home. [On Line] Available: https://www.home-assistant.io/ [Accessed: Aug 10, 2022].

42. United Nations. Revision of the world urbanization prospects. [On Line];2014. Available: https://www.un.org/en/development/desa/publications/2014-revision-world-urbanization-prospects.html [Accessed: Aug 10, 2022].

43. Townsend, A. *Smart Cities: Big Data Civic Hackers and the Quest for a New Utopia*. London: W. W. Norton & Company, Inc.; 2013.

44. Kogan, N., Lee, K. J. Exploratory research on success factors and challenges of smart city projects. *Asia Pacific Journal of Information Systems*. 2014;24(2):141–189.

45. Song, Y., Yu, F. R., Zhou, L., Yang, X., & He, Z. Applications of the Internet of things (IoT) in smart logistics: a comprehensive survey. *IEEE Internet of Things Journal*. 2020;8(6):4250–74.

46. Korczak, J., Kijewska, K. Smart Logistics in the development of smart cities. *Transportation Research Procedia*. 2019;39:201–1.

47. Ding, Y., Jin, M., Li, S., Feng, D. Smart logistics based on the internet of things technology: An overview. *International Journal of Logistics Research and Applications*. 2021;24(4):323–45.

48. Haverkort, B. R., Zimmermann, A. Smart industry: How ICT will change the game! *IEEE Internet Computer*. 2017;21(1):8–10.

49. Hozdić, E. Smart factory for industry 4.0: A review. *International Journal of Modern Manufacturing Technologies*. 2015;7(1):28–35.

50. Lom, M., Pribyl, O., Svitek, M. (2016). Industry 4.0 as a Part of Smart Cities. In: 2016 Smart Cities Symposium Prague (SCSP).

51. Serrano, M., Dimitropoulos, P. Smart Industry Services in Times of Internet of Things and Cloud Computing. In: Enterprise Interoperability: Interoperability for Agility, Resilience and Plasticity of Collaborations: I-ESA'14 Proceedings, 2015, 5–14.

52. Žídek, K., Pite¾, J., Adámek, M., Lazorík, P., Hošovský, A. Digital twin of experimental smart manufacturing assembly system for industry 4.0 concept. *Sustainability.* 2020;12(9):3658.

53. Shi, Z., Xie, Y., Xue, W., Chen, Y., Fu, L., Xu, X. Smart factory in Industry 4.0. *Systems Research and Behavioral Science.* 2020; 37(4):607–17.

54. Kalsoom, T., Ramzan, N., Ahmed, S., Ur-Rehman, M. Advances in sensor technologies in the era of smart factory and industry 4.0. *Sensors.* 2020;20(23):6783.

55. European Commission. A framework strategy for a resilient energy union with a forward-looking climate change policy. [On Line] Available: http://eur-lex.europa.eu/resource.html?uri=cellar: 1bd46c90-bdd4-11e4-bbe1-01aa75ed71a1.0001.03/DOC_1&format=PDF [Accessed: Aug 10, 2022]

56. Ellegård, K., Palm, J. Visualizing energy consumption activities as a tool for making everyday life more sustainable. *Applied Energy.* 2011;88(5):1920–6.

57. Dincer, I., Acar, C. Smart energy systems for a sustainable future. *Applied Energy.* 2017;194:225–235.

58. Shahab, S., Agarwal, P., Mufti, T., Obaid, A. J. SIoT (Social Internet of Things): A Review. In: S. Fong, N. Dey, A. Joshi (Eds.), *ICT Analysis and Applications.* Singapore: Springer Nature Singapore; 2022, pp. 289–97.

59. Malekshahi Rad, M., Rahmani, A. M., Sahafi, A., Nasih, Qader N. Social Internet of Things: Vision, challenges, and trends. *Human-centric Computing and Information Sciences.* 2020;10(1): 1–40.

60. Atzori, L., Iera, A., Morabito, G., Nitti, M. The Social Internet of Things (SIoT) – When social networks meet the Internet of Things: Concept, architecture and network characterization. *Computer Networks.* 2012;56(16):3594–608.

61. Prasanna, S. Combining internet of things and e-learning standards to provide pervasive learning experience. *International Journal of Advanced Research in Computer Science.* 2018;9(Special Issue 1):128.

62. Glasco, J. Smart education for smart cities: Visual, collaborative & interactive [Online article]. Published Feb 27, 2019. Available at: https://hub.beesmart.city/en/solutions/smart-people/smart-education/viewsonic-smart-education-for-smart-cities [Accessed: Aug 10, 2022].

63. Oda, T., Matsuo, K., Barolli, L., Yamada, M., Liu, Y. Design and implementation of an IoT-based e-learning testbed. *International Journal of Web and Grid Services.* 2017;13(2):228–241.

64. Zeeshan, K., Hämäläinen, T., Neittaanmäki, P. Internet of Things for sustainable smart education: An overview. *Sustainability.* 2022;14(7):4293.

65. Demir, K. A. Smart education framework. *Smart Learning Environments* 2021;8(1):1–36.

66. Alcatel Lucent Enterprise. The Internet of Things in education – Improve learning and teaching experiences by leveraging IoT on a secure foundation. Available at: https://www.al-enterprise.com/-/media/assets/internet/documents/iot-for-education-solutionbrief-en.pdf [Accessed: Aug 10, 2022].

67. Feynman, R. P. *There's Plenty of Room at the Bottom. Miniaturization* (H. D. Gilbert, ed.) New York: Reinhold; 1961.

68. Taniguchi, N. On the Basic Concept of Nano-Technology. In: Proceeding of the International Conference on Production Engineering, 1974.

69. Roco, M. C., Mirkin, C. A., Hersam, M. C. Nanotechnology Research Directions for Societal Needs in 2020: Retrospective and Outlook (Vol. 1). Springer Science & Business Media, 2011.

70. De Berardis, B., Marchetti, M., Risuglia, A. et al. Exposure to airborne gold nanoparticles: a review of current toxicological data on the respiratory tract. *Journal of Nanoparticle Research.* 2022;22:235.

71. Akyildiz, I. F., Jornet, J. M. Electromagnetic wireless nanosensor networks, *Nano Communication Networks Journal.* 2010;1(1):3–19.

72. Rutherglen, C., Burke, P. Nanoelectromagnetics: Circuit and electromagnetic properties of carbon nanotubes. *Small.* 2009;5(8):884–906.

73. Akyildiz, I. F., Jornet, J. M. The internet of nano-things. *IEEE Wireless Communications.* 2010;17(6):58–63.

74. Akyildiz, I. F., Brunetti, F., Blazquez, C., Nanonetworks: A new communication paradigm. *Computer Networks.* 2008;52(12):2260–79.

75. Al-Turjman, Fadi. A rational data delivery framework for disaster-inspired internet of nano-things (IoNT) in practice. *Cluster Computing.* 2019;22:1–13.

76. Nayyar, A., Puri, V., Le, D.-N., Internet of Nano Things (IoNT): Next evolutionary step in nanotechnology. *Nanoscience and Nanotechnology.* 2017;7(1):4–8.

77. Barbaza, M.. Le Sahel des "siècles obscurs": Données croisées de l'art rupestre, de l'archéologie,des chroniques et des traditions orales. Préhistoire, Art et Archéologie, 2005. Available at: https://hal. archives-ouvertes.fr/file/index/docid/370895/filename/PAS_2005_.pdf [Accessed: 2022, Aug 10].
78. Alvarado-Alcon, F.-J., Asorey-Cacheda, R., Garcia-Sanchez, A.-J., Garcia-Haro, J. (2022). Carbon footprint vs energy optimization in IoT network deployments. IEEE Access: Practical Innovations, Open Solutions, 10, 111297–111309. https://doi.org/10.1109/access.2022.3216377
79. Ahmed, S., Carr, M., Nouh, M., Merritt, J. (2023). State of the connected world 2023 edition. https://www3.weforum.org/docs/WEF_State_of_the_Connected_World_2023_Edition.pdf

15

An Energy-Aware Task Scheduling Method using the Meta-Heuristic Algorithm in IoT Environments

Fatemeh Bahrani-pour and Sepehr Ebrahimi Mood
Yazd University, Yazd, Iran

Alireza Souri
Halic University, İstanbul, Turkey

Mohammad Farshi
Yazd University, Yazd, Iran

15.1   Introduction

In recent years, with advances in technology, the emergence of the IoT has brought about major changes in the area of networked information technology [1]. The devices of the Internet of Things are sensors, smart appliances, thermostats, smart devices, and all sorts of devices that can connect to the Internet and send data. These devices are distributed geographically, and depending on the application, they sometimes require real-time processing and sometimes high security in data transfer. For example, data generated by health monitoring devices need to be processed in real time, and a delay in processing this information may cause irreparable damage. Resource limitation is one of the most important limitations of IoT devices. Most IoT devices have limitations when it comes to data processing, memory, and battery, so they need powerful resources to offload their tasks to those resources to process their information. There are powerful resources to treat in cloud and fog environments. The fog environment consists of a controller known as the fog controller and the fog network [2].

The fog resources have computing and storage capabilities, and the offloaded tasks that are temporarily stored in the buffer are executed in fog networks that include geographically distributed devices, such as advanced servers, personal computers, routers, and mobile phones. The fog controller manages the offloaded tasks, which require a method for scheduling tasks. There are different methods to perform this scheduling according to the importance of the tasks. The more intelligent and powerful the scheduling method is, the higher the quality of tasks processed is.

The cloud environment consists of a set of Virtual Machines (VMs), whose computational power and storage space are much more than the assets of the fog environment [3]. The more servers there are in cloud environments, the more important it is to have an intelligent approach to energy management. Therefore, it is a challenge to find a suitable strategy for the placement of VMs that has the least waste of resources and energy consumption.

Due to the enormous growth of IoT networks, energy management and finding new and up-to-date ways to optimize energy consumption have been important research topics in the field of IoT in recent years [4]. An approach to energy management is to allocate resources by scheduling requests. Finding an intelligent method for task scheduling can greatly increase the Quality of Service (QoS) provision in cloud and fog services. The goal of all scheduling algorithms is to identify the resources that must be allocated to process requests to complete task processing in the shortest possible overall task execution time [3].

Over the past few years, meta-heuristic algorithms have shown good performance in optimizing job scheduling and are improving rapidly. However, this approach faces a variety of challenges, including time to implement. Since in most applications, the scheduling algorithm must perform the scheduling operation in the shortest possible time, checking the execution time of a meta-heuristic scheduling algorithm is important. In most of the research, the execution time of the algorithm has not been considered an important parameter; only the focus of this research is on optimizing parameters such as delay or energy [5, 6]. As a result, a suitable method should not only perform well in optimization and find high-quality solutions but also be efficient in terms of execution time.

The use of machine learning (ML) and artificial intelligence (AI) techniques is another efficient method for scheduling tasks and assigning resource workloads. It has been proven that ML and AI techniques are helpful for applications like optimizing resources, optimizing energy, estimating workload, video gaming, task scheduling, and other applications that are often complex problems [7]. Collecting data, building ML models, and training and testing the built models, as well as checking their validity, are the steps that must be done before deploying the model in the cloud environment for applications such as resource management and task scheduling [8]. In this chapter, we propose an objective function by defining a system model for energy calculation using delay and maximum response time. By defining the objective function, we will have an optimization problem that must be solved using linear programming methods. In this chapter, while defining the objective function for the problem, we use a meta-heuristic algorithm inspired by nature, called Reptile Search Algorithm (RSA) algorithm. Considering the complex nature of the problem and the high efficiency of scaling methods in improving algorithms to solve complex problems, in this algorithm we use linear scaling to control selection pressure.

The remainder of the chapter is organized as follows: Section 15.2 provides a history of the work that has been done in this field. Section 15.3 presents the system model and formulated problems. Section 15.4 describes the improved RSA algorithm. Section 15.5 presents the simulation and results, and Section 15.6 presents conclusions and future works.

15.2 Background

In the study by Zhou et al. [9], the problem of scheduling tasks on a multi-processor system is considered to optimize the quality of security and energy in the IoT. To do this, a mixed-integer scheduling formula has been used, and after formulating the task scheduling problem with real-time and energy constraints, a two-stage scheme is presented to solve this problem. In this plan, in addition to maximizing the quality of security and reducing energy, the limitations of the system have also been met. This plan was tested to check the quality. The simulation results show that the proposed approach has good performance in solving the problem. In the study by Rajasoundaran et al. [10], a reinforcement learning approach was used. In this way, first, some tasks that endanger the security of the system are determined through a special validation approach. Second, these tasks are removed from the scheduling cycle to ensure security. Secure tasks are scheduled through reinforcement learning technique and Cat Swarm Optimization Based Job Servicing . The results show that the proposed approach has up to 8% better results compared to other approaches in this research.

In the study by Bao et al. [11], an ML system has been used for this purpose, and an online algorithm for scheduling tasks and decisions regarding resources has been presented to maximize overall utility. The online algorithm presented in this research has achieved polynomial time to solve this problem. The efficiency of the algorithm has been investigated by simulation and experiment. The results show that this online algorithm has obtained better results compared to several cloud computing algorithms reviewed in this article. In the study by Sugumaran et al. [12], a comprehensive review of scheduling strategies in the cloud environment is intended. This research examines the strengths and weaknesses of various methods. In particular, different scheduling approaches were studied to find out which features are more important. In general, in this research, the literature review has been done based on methods, applications, and parameters.

In study [13], first, the performance of different workload forecasting methods is compared. Then, a method for predicting workload is provided, and scheduling is done accordingly. To improve the accuracy of this article, a clustering method is used to categorize the tasks, then a predictive model is used and its training is done for each scheduling category. The results show that this method has reached 90% accuracy. In the study by Wang et al. [14], an online scheduling algorithm is presented. This algorithm has the capability of imitative learning and provides almost optimal performance. In this online algorithm, by solving the formulated optimization problem in an offline manner and finding the optimal scheduling strategy, online learning performed with an acceptable gap in performance. The results of this article show that the presented algorithm has improved by 50% compared to the comparative methods of this research.

In the study by Chobar et al. [15], a Hub-Spoke network is defined, and two goals of reducing network costs and reducing the emission of environmental pollutants are defined. A hybrid method based on meta-heuristic algorithms and ML techniques called (ML-MOAIS) has been used to solve the problem. MOAIS and NSGA-II algorithms have been used to evaluate the method. According to the results of this article, the use of ML methods has been able to converge to the optimal solution faster and limit the target space of the problem. The evaluation of the proposed method has been done with quantitative and qualitative indicators, and the results show that the proposed method has performed better than the two algorithms MOAIS and NSGA-II. The proposed method of the article has a Pareto optimal front with more dispersion and better solution quality. In the study by Tanha et al. [16], a hybrid algorithm based on genetics and simulated annealing is presented for task scheduling in the cloud environment. The combination of these two algorithms covers well the shortcomings in exploration and exploitation capabilities. The initial population in this algorithm was created by a new method. The crossover operator in genetics can increase exploration capability, and the simulated annealing algorithm increases the exploitation capability. Therefore, a balance is established between these two capabilities.

15.3 System Model

The architecture of the IoT network considered in this chapter consists of four parts. The first part is the IoT devices. The second part is the gateways, and the other parts are the fog and cloud environment. Figure 15.1 illustrates this IoT–Fog–Cloud architecture used in this chapter [2]. In this architecture, in the first layer, tasks generated by IoT devices are offloaded to the cloud or fog environment through gateways due to the limitations of these devices in memory and battery. According to parameters such as the deadline or processing priority of a task [17], the gateway decides which tasks should be processed in the fog network and which tasks should be processed in the cloud servers. In the fog environment, there is a set of resources for processing tasks. Tasks scheduling for processing in this environment enhances the Quality of Service (QoS) delivery.

15.3.1 Problem Formulation

- **Tasks:** We assume that a set of n tasks is generated by IoT devices; also we assume that cloud and fog resources are capable of processing these tasks. We denote the set of tasks that offloaded from IoT devices to the fog network by $R = \{r_1, r_2, \ldots, r_n\}$. We consider a set of features for each task. In such a way that each task has the characteristics $[Q_j, T_j, W_j, D_j]$. In the features set, Q_j is the size of the jth task and is usually determined by the number of packets. In this set, T_j is the initial time of the requested jth task. In this set, W_j represents the weight or priority of the jth task. We also assume that all tasks created by IoT devices are independent. Each task must be processed without interruption after it is assigned to a server. Each task could be processed on a single server, and it is not possible to process one task on multiple servers.

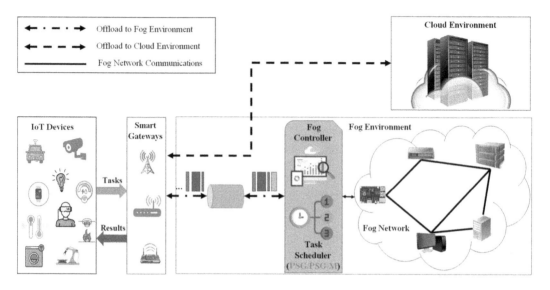

FIGURE 15.1 IoT system architecture.

- **Fog computing:** We assume that we have a set of *m* servers in the fog network that have different processing power. Some servers are more powerful and process tasks in less time, while some servers need more time. Processing power is usually specified in Million Instructions Per Second (MIPS). The fog network consists of several Fog Nodes (FNs) that have specific topologies. We denote the set of FNs servers by $S = \{s_1, s_2, \ldots, s_m\}$. We denote the processing power of *i*th FNs with p_i, so we have the set $P = \{p_1, p_2, \ldots, p_m\}$ that denotes the power processing of FNs. In addition to the processing power, each FN has another feature, which is energy consumption. When a server is in active mode and processing tasks, it consumes more energy in idle mode. Suppose the energy consumption of *i*th FNs in active mode is β_i and the energy consumption in the idle mode of these FNs is equal to α_i [19]. Therefore, according to the scenario, the tasks generated by the IoT devices were sent to the FNs through the gateways. Optimizing energy requires the scheduling algorithm. When a task is assigned to an FN, the processing time will be different according to the size of that task and the processing power of that FN. The Expected Time to Compute (ETC) matrix contains the expected time to process each task on different FN. Each element of this matrix is in the form of Q_j/P_i where Q_j is the size of the task in the packet for $1 \leq j \leq n$ and P_i is the power of FN in MIPS for $1 \leq i \leq m$.

15.3.2 Objective Function

First, we define the decision variable of the problem, then we describe the proposed model for calculating the response time and energy consumption. This decision variable is used to specify whether to assign a task to an FN or not. This variable is two-valued $x_{ij} \in \{0, 1\}$ and will affect calculations for values of 1.

$$x_{ij} = \begin{cases} 1 & \text{if task } j \text{ allocated to FN } i \\ 0 & \text{otherwise} \end{cases} \quad \forall j \in n, \forall i \in m \qquad (15.1)$$

Therefore, we can consider the X_{ij} matrix and call it the assignment matrix. In this matrix, it is determined which task is assigned to which FN, according to the decision variable; this happens in regions with a value of 1. To describe the model of energy, we need to calculate the response time that depends on the delay that the task may encounter in the process. The task requested by IoT devices experiences various delays from the start of processing until it ends. Examples of these delays are transmission and queuing delays. Transmission delay is calculated based on task size and link transfer speed, so the overall delay is designed in Equation 15.2 [18].

$$\text{delay} = d^{\text{tr}} + d^{q}, \tag{15.2}$$

where d^{tr} is the transmission delay and d^{q} is the queuing delay; therefore, the delay in processing jth task with ith FN is calculated using Equation 15.3 [18].

$$LT_{ij} = ST_{ij} + PT_{ij} + TQT_{ij}, \tag{15.3}$$

where ST_{ij} is the time at which task i starts processing on jth FN. PT_{ij} is the ijth element of matrix ETC. TQT_{ij} was calculated using Equation 15.4 [18].

$$TQT_{ij} = \sum_{i=1}^{n} \sum_{j=1}^{Q_j} d_{ij}^{q}, \tag{15.4}$$

where n is the number of tasks, Q_j is the size of the task by packet, and d_{ij}^{q} is queuing delay of the process ith task on jth FN. Now we can describe the energy model. For this, we first calculate the allocated workload for each node. Given that the amount of energy consumption in active and idle states is different, for each node, the duration of being active should be calculated, which is equal to the sum of the processing time for each task assigned to it, so we have the following equation [19].

$$ET_i = \sum_{i=1}^{n} \sum_{j=1}^{m} X_{ij} \times LT_{ij}, \tag{15.5}$$

where X_{ij} is the task assignment matrix, which is calculated in this function for values of 1, which means assigning a task to an FN and LT_{ij} is the overall delay that a task has to process. Now we can calculate the aggregate energy consumption from the following equation [19].

$$E(s_i) = [ET_i \times \beta_i + (M - ET_i) \times \alpha_i] \times p_i, \tag{15.6}$$

where M is the maximum execution time among all the FNs ($M = \max_{i \leq 1 \leq m} ET_i$), ET_i is the total execution time of all the tasks assigned to ith FNs, β_i and α_i are the energy consumption of FN in active and idle states, and p_i is the power of processing in MIPS. Now, we can define the objective function to minimize the energy consumption of scheduling as follows [19].

$$F = \text{argmin}_{X_{ij}} \sum_{i=1}^{m} E(s_i). \tag{15.7}$$

The objective function must be optimized according to the following constraints. In the first constraint presented in Equation 15.8, the task must be processed after transmitting to FN [18].

$$ST_{ij} \geq IT_j + TQT_j \, \forall j \in n, \, i \in m. \tag{15.8}$$

The constraint presented in Equation 15.9 indicates that each task must be processed by only one FN [18].

$$\sum_{i=1}^{n} \sum_{j=1}^{m} X_{ij} = 1 \, \forall j \in n, \, i \in m. \tag{15.9}$$

15.4 Improved Reptile Search Algorithm

In 2021, Laith Abualigah et al. introduced a meta-heuristic algorithm inspired by nature called RSA [20]. This algorithm is modeled on the behavior of crocodiles in courting and hunting. In this algorithm, the location of solutions is updated based on the behavior of crocodiles. The purpose of this update is to search better and find better quality solutions to make this algorithm ready to use on complex problems. Test functions and real-world engineering problems are used to investigate this issue [20]. The exploration and exploitation abilities of this algorithm are inspired by the mechanisms of confinement, hunting, and social behavior of crocodiles in nature. These behavioral mechanisms are modeled mathematically to be used in optimization operations. RSA, like most evolutionary algorithms, is population-based and could be used to solve optimization problems with certain constraints. In the following, we will fully examine the working method of this algorithm.

15.4.1 Phase 1

In the first phase, the optimization process begins with the construction of the initial population set that is randomly generated. The initial population is a set of possible solutions to the problem. An example of the initial population is shown in Equation 15.10 [20].

$$X = \begin{bmatrix} x_{1,1} & \cdots & x_{1,n} \\ \vdots & \ddots & \vdots \\ x_{n,1} & \cdots & x_{n,n} \end{bmatrix}, \tag{15.10}$$

where X is an initial population that is randomly generated according to the lower and upper bounds of the values that variables can take in the problem.

15.4.2 Phase 2 (Exploration)

Crocodiles have two evasive behaviors, and the idea of the algorithm to search in the problem solution space is to use this feature of crocodiles. The first behavior is high walking, and the second behavior is belly walking. These two movements of the crocodile ensure global exploration operations in the problem space. After the initial population is checked in the objective function and the values of the solutions calculated in the objective function, the position of the solutions should be updated. This update has been done according to Equation 15.11 [20].

$$x_{i,j}(t+1) = \begin{cases} \text{Best}_j(t) \times \eta_{i,j}(t) \times \beta - R_{i,j}(t) \times \text{rand}, & t < T/4 \\ \text{Best}_j(t) \times x_{r_1,j} \times \text{ES}(t) \times \text{rand}, & t \le 2T/4 \text{ and } t > T/4 \end{cases} \tag{15.11}$$

where $\text{Best}_j(t)$ is the position of the best-obtained so far solution, rand is a function that generates a random number in [0,1], t is the index of the current iteration, and T is the maximum number of iterations. The hunting operator is denoted by $\eta_{i,j}(t)$ for the jth position in the ith solution; this operator is obtained from Equation 15.12. The parameter that controls the accuracy of exploration is fixed $\beta = 0.1$. To decrease the search region, the function $R_{i,j}(t)$ is defined as in Equation 15.13. In this equation ε is a small random number. r_2 is a random number in [$1N$] that select a solution. The position of a selected solution, indicated by $x_{r_1,j}$, and N is the size of the initial population. Evolutionary Sense $ES(t)$ is calculated using Equation 15.14, which is a probability ratio. During the iterations of the algorithm, $ES(t)$ takes a random value in [$-2\,2$], and r_3 is a random number in [$-1\,1$].

$$\eta_{i,j}(t) = \text{Best}_j(t) \times P_{i,j}, \tag{15.12}$$

$$R_{i,j}(t) = \frac{\text{Best}_j(t) \times x_{r_2,j}}{\text{Best}_j(t) + \varepsilon}, \tag{15.13}$$

$$ES(t) = 2 \times r_3 \times (1 - \frac{1}{T}). \tag{15.14}$$

In Equation 15.12, $P_{i,j}$ is the difference between the position of the best-obtained solution and the current solution and is calculated using Equation 15.15.

$$P_{i,j} = \alpha + \frac{x_{i,j} - M(x_i)}{\text{Best}_j(t) \times (\text{UB}_j - \text{LB}_j) + \varepsilon}, \tag{15.15}$$

where $M(x_i)$ is the average of solution x_i and is calculated in Equation 15.16. UB(j) is the upper bound and LB(j) is the lower bound of variables in a solution. Fixed parameter $\alpha = 0.1$ is a parameter that controls the difference between solutions for the hunting cooperation over the iterations.

$$M(x_i) = \frac{1}{n} \sum_{j=1}^{n} x_{i,j}. \tag{15.16}$$

15.4.3 Phase 3 (Exploitation)

In this section, the efficiency of the algorithm is described using the behavior of crocodiles in hunting. Coordination and cooperation in hunting, which are among the hunting strategies of crocodiles, help in the exploitation search and convergence of the algorithm and getting closer to the optimal solution. These two strategies are modeled in Equation 15.17.

$$x_j(t+1) = \begin{cases} \text{Best}_j(t) \times P_{i,j}(t) \times \text{ rand}, t < {}^{3T}/_4 \text{ and } t > {}^{2T}/_4 \\ \text{Best}_j(t) - \eta_{i,j} \times \varepsilon - R_{i,j}(t) \times \text{ rand}, t \le T \text{ and } t > {}^{3T}/_4 \end{cases}, \tag{15.17}$$

In this equation $\text{Best}_j(t)$ is the position of the best-obtained so far solution; the hunting operator is denoted by $\eta_{i,j}(t)$ for the jth position in the ith solution; function $R_{i,j}(t)$ is the decrease function, which is calculated using Equation 15.13; $P_{i,j}$ is difference between the position of the best-obtained solution and the current solution, which is calculated using Equation 15.15; ε is a small random number; and rand is a function that produces a random number between 0 and 1. Therefore, after several iterations, the search is done near the optimal solution and the answers converge to the optimal solution. As a result, the algorithm can find an almost optimal solution. According to the explanations mentioned in this algorithm, until less than half of the iterations are done, the exploration phase is done, and when more than half of the iterations are done, the algorithm enters the exploit phase, and the search around the optimal solution is done until the algorithm converges.

These two phases are summarized in Figures 15.2 and 15.3. In these figures, the prey is shown in white color, and in the initial iterations (less than $T/2$), the reptiles, which are shown in different colors, search the entire problem space, and in the later iterations (more than $T/2$), the search is performed

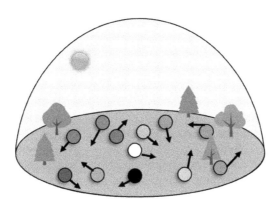

FIGURE 15.2 Exploration phase before T/2 iterations.

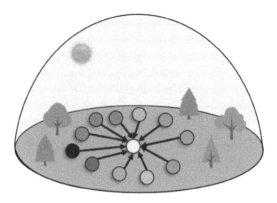

FIGURE 15.3 Exploitation phase after T/2 iterations.

Algorithm 1 Pseudo-code of the Reptile Search Algorithm (RSA)

---

1. Initialization phase
2. Initialize RSA parameters.
3. Initialize the solutions' positions randomly. $X : i = 1, \ldots N$.
4. *while* $(t < T)$ *do*
5. Calculate the fitness function for the candidate solutions (X).
6. Find the best solution so far.
7. Update the ES using Equation 15.14.
8. The beginning of the RSA
9. *for* $(i = 1 \, to \, N)$ *do*
10. *for* $(j = 1 \, to \, n)$ *do*
11. Update the $\eta, R, P,$ and values using Equation 15.12, Equation 15.13, and Equation 15.15 respectively.
12. *if* $(t \leq T/4)$ *then*
13. $x_{(i,j)}(t + 1) = Best_j(t) \times (-\eta_{i,j}(t)) \times \beta - R_{i,j}(t) \times rand.$ {*High walking*}
14. *else if* $t \leq 2T/4$ *and* $t > T/4$ *then*
15. $x_{(i,j)}(t + 1) = Best_j(t) \times x_{r_{1,j}} \times ES(t) \times rand.$ {*Belly walkingg*}
16. *else if* $t \leq 3T/4$ *and* $t > 2T/4$ *then*
17. $x_{(i,j)}(t + 1) = Best_j(t) \times P_{i,j}(t) \times rand$ {*Hunting cooperation*}
18. *else*
19. $x_{(i,j)}(t + 1) = Best_j(t) - \eta_{i,j}(t) \times \varepsilon - R_{i,j}(t) \times rand.$ {*Hunting cooperationg*}
20. *end if*
21. *end for*
22. *end for*
23. $t = t + 1$
24. *end while*
25. Return the best solution $(Best(X))$.

---

around the prey, which is the optimal solution, and then the convergence happens. The pseudo-code of the RSA is shown in Algorithm 1.

In the pseudo-code of the algorithm shown in Figure 15.4, it is clear that this algorithm, like most evolutionary algorithms, starts working with an initial population of candidate solutions. Then, during the iterations of the algorithm, they are guessed with the defined mechanisms to search for optimal solutions, and then they converge to the optimal solution in the last iterations of the algorithm.

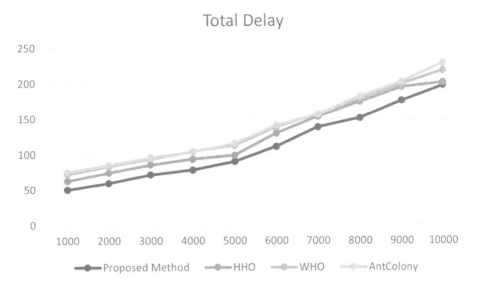

FIGURE 15.4 Total delay vs data size.

15.4.4 Phase 4 (Scaling)

To strengthen the capabilities of exploration and exploitation, which is one of the most important capabilities of evolutionary algorithms, we suggest the linear scaling method. In contrast to the advantages mentioned for the algorithm and its good capability in searching the problem space and finding the optimal solution, there are also disadvantages. Among them, we can mention early convergence and getting stuck in local optima, especially in complex problems with more constraints. To solve these disadvantages in this research, we used the idea of linear scaling. Linear scaling is one of the scaling methods that is known for its simple implementation and robust performance.

Scaling methods are widely used in real-world practical problems, especially the problems in which the scope of the definition of the fitness function is very small or very large. In such problems, due to the large scope of the definition of the values of the fitness function, the selection pressure increases, and, as a result, the probability of getting stuck in the local optimum and premature convergence increases. However, the smallness of the definition range of the fitness function results in low selection pressure, and as a result, the speed of convergence becomes extremely slow and the efficiency of the algorithm decreases. Using the linear scaling method in this algorithm causes the values of the fitness function to be changed by the scale functions; as a result, the range of values is scaled. In this case, while strengthening the capabilities of exploration and exploitation, the mentioned problems are completely solved. The output value of the fitness function for the ith agent in the tth iteration is calculated from Equation 15.18.

$$\text{fit}_i^s(t) = a(t) \times \text{fit}_i(t) + b(t), \tag{15.18}$$

In this equation $\text{fit}_i^s(t)$ is the scaled fitness function, $\text{fit}_i(t)$ is the output value of the fitness function of the ith agent before using the linear scaling method, and $a(t)$ and $b(t)$ are calculated from the following equations.

$$a(t) = \frac{(C_m - 1) \times \text{fit}^{\text{avg}}(t)}{\text{fit}^{\text{max}}(t) - \text{fit}^{\text{avg}}(t)} \tag{15.19}$$

$$b(t) = (1 - a(t)) \times \text{fit}^{\text{avg}}(t), \tag{15.20}$$

In Equation 15.19 and Equation 15.20, $\text{fit}^{\text{avg}}(t)$ is the average of output values of the population's fitness function at tth iteration and $\text{fit}^{\text{max}}(t)$ shows the highest value of the fitness function obtained

---

Algorithm 2 Pseudo-code of the Modified Reptile Search Algorithm (MRSA)

---

1. Initialization phase
2. Initialize RSA parameters.
3. Initialize the solutions' positions randomly. $X : i = 1, \ldots N$.
4. *while* $(t < T)$ *do*
5. Calculate the fitness function for the candidate solutions (X).
6. Find the best solution so far.
7. Update the ES using Equation 15.14.
8. The beginning of the RSA
9. *for* $(i = 1 \, to \, N)$ *do*
10. *for* $(j = 1 \, to \, n)$ *do*
11. Update the $\eta, R, P,$ and values using Equation 15.12, Equation 15.13 and Equation 15.15 respectively.
12. *if* $(t \leq T/4$ then
13. $x_{(i,j)}(t+1) = Best_j(t) \times (-\eta_{i,j}(t)) \times \beta - R_{i,j}(t) \times$ rand. {*High walking*}
14. *else if* $t \leq 2T/4$ *and* $t > T/4$ *then*
15. $x_{(i,j)}(t+1) = Best_j(t) \times x_{r_{1,j}} \times ES(t) \times$ rand. {*Belly walkingg*}
16. *else if* $t \leq 3T/4$ *and* $t > 2T/4$ *then*
17. $x_{(i,j)}(t+1) = Best_j(t) \times P_{i,j}(t) \times$ rand {*Hunting cooperation*}
18. *else*
19. $x_{(i,j)}(t+1) = Best_j(t) - \eta_{i,j}(t) \times \varepsilon - R_{i,j}(t) \times$ rand. {*Hunting cooperation*}
20. *end if*
21. *end for*
22. *end for*
23. Scale the values of the fitness function of solutions (X) using Equation 15.18.
24. $t = t + 1$
25. *end while*
26. Return the best solution $(Best(X))$.

---

among the members of the population at tth iteration, and C_m is the expected rate of choosing the best solution which calculated using Equation 15.21.

$$C_m = \frac{\text{fit}^{\text{avg}}(t)}{\text{fit}^{\text{max}}(t)} \tag{15.21}$$

C_m is a parameter and its value is defined in period [1, 2]. The value of 2 for this parameter means that the probability of choosing the best solution is twice the rate of choosing a solution with the average of the fitness function. In this position, there is the most selection pressure. The closer the value of this parameter is to 2, the more selection pressure there is. If the value of this parameter is closer to 1, it means that the probability of choosing the solution with the best fitness function will be equal to the rate of choosing the solution with the average fitness value. In this case, the selection pressure is at its lowest. So, by using the linear scaling method, the exploration and exploitation capabilities of the evolutionary algorithm can be controlled. The pseudo-code of the algorithm with linear scaling is shown in Algorithm 2.

15.5   Simulation and Results

To perform the simulation, we considered a three-layer architecture. IoT requests are generated by users in the first layer. Request generation follows a uniform distribution and is generated randomly. After creating requests for processing by cloud and fog resources, 16 cloud and fog servers are considered. The capabilities of cloud and fog servers are different. Therefore, in the initial model system, 100 requests are created randomly, which are different in terms of the number of packets. Ten fog servers and six cloud servers are produced, which are different in terms of processing power. Then, the proposed algorithm is used to schedule the requests to optimize energy according to the formulated problem. This algorithm schedules the requests in such a way that the delay in processing the requests is minimized and as a result, the minimum energy consumption in processing the request is used. It is clear that initially, all resources are available. With the passage of time and assigning requests to resources, the resources are busy processing, and some requests must spend time waiting for resources to be available for their processing. In this chapter, we consider the scheduling in static mode, so all the requests are initially available, and the initial time of creating the requests is zero. Server latency is set to an average of 5ms per packet and follows a uniform distribution between 1 and 9.7 ms. Request deadlines are set to 400 and 50 respectively with the mean and variance. To perform the test, we first consider the set of requests to be small enough in terms of the average number of packets that none of the requests miss their deadline. Then this average is increased and as a first test, we check the number of missed deadlines in different algorithms, while we control the amount of energy consumption with the resulting delay for each algorithm.

15.5.1 Missed Deadlines

To check the number of missed deadlines, we first check the total delay of each request in the schedule provided by each algorithm and consider the number of requests that experience a delay greater than the defined deadline. Figure 15.5 shows the overall delay for requests with an average between 1,000 and 10,000. In this figure, it is clear that the proposed RSA algorithm has obtained better results in optimization than other comparative algorithms.

The use of linear scaling in this algorithm increases the ability of the algorithm to explore the problem space despite constraints and has a significant effect on the timely convergence of the algorithm, which makes the results of the algorithm grow better than other algorithms in the incremental averages of requests. Now, according to the overall delay obtained, we examine and compare the algorithms in terms of the amount of missed deadlines. Figure 15.5 shows that the proposed algorithm starts to miss the deadline for requests after an average of 7,000 requests, while other algorithms miss the deadline for requests at lower averages. Figures 15.3 and 15.4 show that

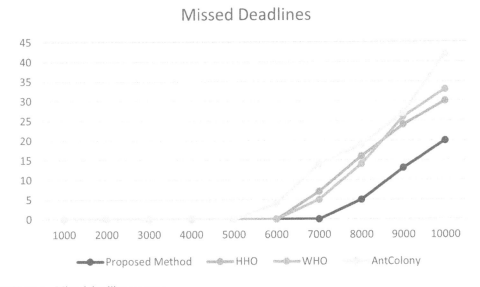

FIGURE 15.5 Missed deadline requests.

the algorithm performs better in delay optimization than other algorithms, which well shows the effect of using linear scaling.

15.5.2 Energy Consumption

To check the amount of energy consumption, according to the formulated problem, we compare the algorithms in terms of finding the optimal solution. The longer the processing delay, the higher the energy consumption as the response time increases. Figure 15.6 shows the performance of algorithms in finding optimal solutions in terms of energy consumption. The comparison of the results shows that with the increase in the average volume of requests, the proposed algorithm shows more robustness. This means that when the average volume of requests in terms of packets increases and the problem is more complex, the proposed algorithm can find the optimal solution better than other algorithms due to the scaling of the output values of the fitness function using the linear scaling method. The linear scaling method improves the performance of the algorithm by scaling the output parameters of the evaluation function.

To better examine the performance of linear scaling in the RSA algorithm and observe its effect on finding optimal solutions and balancing the exploration and exploitation capabilities of the algorithm, we examined the proposed method with various tests, including Fredman's test. In this test, algorithms are evaluated based on efficiency, and an algorithm that gets a better rating than other methods means that it has performed better compared to other methods. The results of Fredman's test with the available data on the performance of the algorithms are shown in Table 15.1.

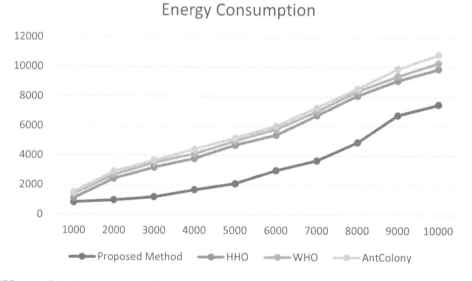

FIGURE 15.6 Overall energy consumption.

TABLE 15.1

Fredman's Test Result

Algorithm	Rank
Proposed method	14.56
HHO	17.78
WOA	18.67
Ant Colony	24.89
Pvalue ($\alpha = 0.05$)	0.00001 = Rejected

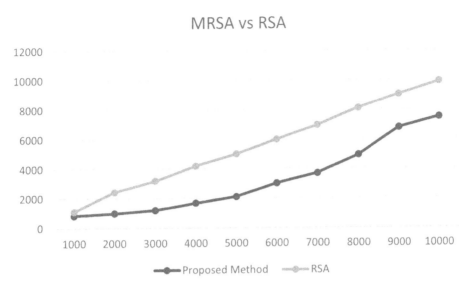

FIGURE 15.7   MRSA vs RSA.

The method that gets the first rank has the best performance compared to other methods. The p-value in this test is 0.00001 and indicates the statistical analysis of this test.

To observe the effect of linear scaling on the performance of the algorithm, we separately implemented the algorithm without linear scaling and with linear scaling on a fixed model system. We considered 50 repetitions of the algorithm execution and calculated the average values calculated by the algorithms. The results of the implementation of the algorithms show well that the use of linear scaling with the control of explore and exploit capabilities makes the algorithm explore the problem space well at the beginning, then at the end of the algorithm, it converges around the optimal solution by reducing the standard deviation.

15.6   Conclusion and Future Research

In general, in this chapter, for the problem of scheduling Internet of Things requests for energy optimization, we defined an objective function using delay and maximum response time, then to solve this problem, we used an improved evolutionary algorithm using linear scaling. Implementation results show that the use of linear scaling has a great effect in controlling the selection pressure and as a result strengthening the capabilities of exploring and exploiting the algorithm. In general, due to the complex nature of scheduling problems, especially problems that have multiple constraints and the range of values of the evaluation function is large, the use of the linear scaling method can reduce the selection pressure by scaling the output values.. This arrangement is that at the beginning of the algorithm implementation, that is, in the initial iterations, the standard deviation of the search factors' competence is high, so the solution space of the problem is well searched. Then, in the last iterations, to create a suitable convergence to the optimal solution, the standard deviation of the merit of the search factors is reduced; as a result, convergence to the optimal solution occurs. To continue the research, it is suggested to use multi-objective functions for optimization with parameters of delay, energy, security, bandwidth, etc. The use of intelligent methods and combining them with evolutionary algorithms is another suggestion. The use of neural networks and integration with evolutionary algorithms is suggested for scheduling. The proposed algorithm has some parameters, and the value of these parameters has a major role in the performance of the algorithm. In this chapter, we set the value of these parameters experimentally. However, fuzzy logic controller can be defined and used for calculating the value of these parameters in order to balance the abilities of the algorithm and improve the performance of the proposed method.

REFERENCES

1. J. A. Hulin and Z. B. Jin, "Real-time energy consumption detection simulation of network node in internet," *Sustainable Energy Technologies and Assessments,* vol. 44, 2021, p. 101004.
2. A. Sadoon, S. Mohammad, A. Jemal and B. Rajkumar, "Deadline-aware and energy-efficient IoT task scheduling in fog," *Journal of Network and Computer Applications,* vol. 201, 2021.
3. S. Bhambri and R. G. K. Pankaj, *Cloud and Fog Computing Platforms for Internet of Things* (P. Bhambri, S. Rani, G. Gupta, and A. Khang, Eds.). CRC Press, 2022.
4. B. Imran, A. Naeem Iqbal and D. H. Kim, "IoT Task Management Mechanism Based on Predictive Optimization for Efficient Energy Consumption in Smart Residential Buildings," *Energy & Buildings,* vol. 257, 2022.
5. C. Bu and J. Wang, "Computing Tasks Assignment Optimization among Edge Computing Servers via SDN," *Peer-to-Peer Netw,* vol. 14, pp. 1190–1206, 2021.
6. K. Gai, X. Qin and L. Zhu, "An Energy-Aware High Performance Task Allocation Strategy in Heterogeneous Fog Computing Environments," *IEEE Transactions on Computers,* vol. 70, pp. 626–639, 2021.
7. K. Yogesh, K. Surabhi and H. Yu-Chen, "Machine Learning for Energy-Resource Allocation, Workflow Scheduling and Live Migration In Cloud Computing: State-of-the-Art Survey," *Sustainable Computing: Informatics and Systems,* vol. 36, 2022.
8. A. Houssein and H. Essam, "Task Scheduling in Cloud Computing based on Meta-Heuristics: Review, Taxonomy, Open Challenges, and Future Trends," *Swarm and Meta-heuristics: Review, Taxonomy, Open Challenges, and Future Trends,* vol. 62, 2021.
9. J. Zhou, J. Sun, P. Cong, Z. Liu, X. Zhou, T. Wei and S. Hu, "Security-Critical Energy-Aware Task Scheduling for Heterogeneous Real-Time MPSoCs in IoT," *IEEE Transactions on Services Computing,* vol. 13, pp. 745–758, 2020.
10. S. Rajasoundaran, A. Prabu, R. Sidheswar, S. Santhosh Kumar, P. M. Prince, M. Suman, M. Amrit and G. Uttam, "Machine Learning Based Deep Job Exploration and Secure Transactions in Virtual Private Cloud Systems," *Computers & Security,* vol. 109, 2021.
11. Yixin Bao, Yanghua Peng, Chuan Wu and Zongpeng Li, "Online Job Scheduling in Distributed Machine Learning Clusters," in *IEEE INFOCOM 2018 - IEEE Conference on Computer Communications,* pp. 495–503, 2018.
12. A. Sugumaran, D. Manjula and Vijayan, "Task Scheduling Techniques in Cloud Computing: A Literature Survey," *Future Generation Computer Systems,* vol. 91, pp. 497–415, 2019.
13. J. Gao, H. Wang and H. Shen, "Machine Learning Based Workload Prediction in Cloud Computing," in *2020 29th International Conference on Computer Communications and Networks (ICCCN),* pp. 1–9, 2020.
14. X. Wang, Z. Ning, S. Guo and L. Wang, "Imitation Learning Enabled Task Scheduling for Online Vehicular Edge Computing," *IEEE Transactions on Mobile Computing,* vol. 21, 2022.
15. A. P. Chobar, M. A. Adibi and A. Kazemi, "Multi-Objective Hub-Spoke Network Design of Perishable Tourism Products Using Combination Machine Learning and Meta-Heuristic Algorithms," *Environment, Development and Sustainability,* 2022, pp. 1–28. DOI: 10.1007/s10668-022-02350-2
16. M. Tanha, S. Hosseini and A. Rahmani, "A Hybrid Meta-Heuristic Task Scheduling Algorithm Based on Genetic and Thermodynamic Simulated Annealing Algorithms in Cloud Computing Environments," *Neural Comput & Applic,* vol. 33, pp. 16951–16984, 2021.
17. M. Adhikari, M. Mukherjee and S. N. Srirama, "DPTO: A Deadline and Priority-Aware Task Offloading in Fog Computing Framework Leveraging Multilevel Feedback Queueing," *IEEE Internet of Things Journal,* vol. 7, pp. 5773–5782, 2020.
18. R. O. Aburukba, A. Mazin, L. Taha and E.-F. Khaled, "Scheduling Internet of Things Requests to Minimize Latency in Hybrid Fog–Cloud Computing," *Future Generation Computer Systems,* vol. 111, pp. 539–551, 2020.
19. S. K. Mishra, D. Puthal, J. Rodrigues, B. Sahoo and E. Dutkiewicz, "Sustainable Service Allocation Using a Metaheuristic Technique in a Fog Server for Industrial Applications," *IEEE Transactions on Industrial Informatics,* vol. 14, pp. 4497–4506, 2018.
20. A. Laith, A. E. Mohamed, S. Putra, W. G. Zong and A. H. Gandomi, "Reptile Search Algorithm (RSA): A Novel Nature-Inspired Meta-Heuristic," *Expert Systems with Applications,* vol. 192, p. 116158, 2022.

21. K. Yogesh, K. Surabhi and H. Yu-Chen, "Machine Learning for Energy-Resource Allocation, Work-flow Scheduling and Live Migration in Cloud Computing: State-of-the-Art Survey," *Sustainable Computing: Informatics and Systems,* vol. 36, 2022, p. 100780.

22. S.-H. Wu, Z.-H. Zhan and J. Zhang, "SAFE: Scale-Adaptive Fitness Evaluation Method for Expensive Optimization Problems," *IEEE Transactions on Evolutionary Computation,* vol. 25, pp. 478–491, 2021.

23. B. Pankaj, R. Sita, G. Gaurav and K. Alex, *Cloud and Fog Computing Platforms for Internet of Things*, 2022. CRC Press.

24. J. Z. Hulin Jin, "Real-time energy consumption detection simulation of network node in internet of things based on artificial intelligence," *Sustainable Energy Technologies and Assessments,* vol. 44, 2021, p. 101004.

25. S. Rajasoundaran, A. V. Prabu, R. Sidheswar, K. Santhosh, P. M. Prince, M. Suman, M. Amrit and Uttam Ghosh, "Machine Learning Based Deep Job Exploration and Secure Transactions in Virtual Private Cloud Systems," *Computers & Security,* vol. 109, 2021, p. 102379.

26. H. Essam, G. Ahmed, W. Yaser and S. Ponnuthurai Nagaratnam, "Task Scheduling in Cloud Computing Based on Meta-heuristics: Review, Taxonomy, Open Challenges, and Future Trends," *Swarm and Evolutionary Computation,* vol. 62, 2021, p. 100841.

27. Y. Bao, Y. Peng, C. Wu and Z. Li, "Online Job Scheduling in Distributed Machine Learning Clusters," *IEEE INFOCOM 2018 - IEEE Conference on Computer Communications,* pp. 495–503, 2018.

28. Imran, Naeem Iqbal and Do Hyeun Kim, "IoT Task Management Mechanism Based on Predictive Optimization for Efficient Energy Consumption in Smart Residential Buildings," *Energy & Buildings,* vol. 257, 2022, p. 111762.

16

Real-time Artificial Intelligence Applications in the IoT Based on Cloud Collaboration

Yu Guo, Yuanyan Xie, and Yue Chen
University of Science and Technology Beijing, China

16.1 Introduction

IoT aims to construct a type of real-time information-sharing Internet of global things using radio frequency identification technology and wireless communication technology. Currently, with the development of artificial intelligence (AI), historical and real-time data can be analyzed and used to judge user habits more accurately and make more intelligent behaviors to improve the user experience. Against this background, the word "AIoT" has appeared frequently since 2017 and has become a primary development direction in the IoT. AIoT means "AI + IoT," which refers to the integration of AI technology and IoT in practical applications, as shown in Figure 16.1. For example, smart homes allow people to automatically switch appliances on and off as desired and farmers can use the AIoT for analysis and automatic land management. According to a research report by "Markets and Markets," the global AIoT market is expected to grow to $16.2 billion by 2024.

The AIoT has some new features and requirements:

- Large scale of devices: Compared with millions of devices in cloud computing, the number of devices that will be supported by AIoT will likely reach billions in the future.
- Massive big data: More massive data will likely be generated.
- Low response delay: Different low delay requirements will likely exist according to different application scenarios.
- Data privacy: Ideal analysis results should be obtained without exposing the original data.

However, with limited hardware, low battery capacity, and high cost of IoT devices, it is difficult to ensure accuracy and real-time performance on IoT devices with complex AI algorithms, which hinders the development and practical application of AIoT. Although handing over the computing tasks directly to the cloud can reduce the processing pressure on IoT devices, the problems of time delay, communication energy consumption, packet loss, and even data leakage caused by transmitting a large amount of data are also brought in, which undoubtedly have a great impact on IoT systems, particularly for harsh application scenarios.

Taking a typical AI technology, natural speech interaction, which is divided into acoustics computing and natural language understanding (NLP), as an example, there is no doubt that the NLP parts (e.g., the device's understanding of user statements and the acquisition of information, like weather) must be solved in the cloud. However, for the conversion of a user's voice to text, such as "turn on the air conditioner and increase the temperature," some or even most calculations may

DOI:10.1201/9781003326236-16

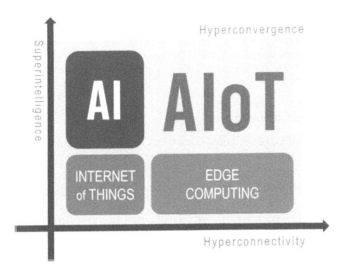

FIGURE 16.1 AIoT convergence technologies.

be completed locally on IoT devices. In this case, the data uploaded to the cloud will no longer be the compressed voice itself but a more concise result, and the response will be faster.

This chapter will describe the fundamental process to achieve real-time and complex AI applications in the IoT based on cloud collaboration and edge computing, which granulate the tasks and process them in the cloud and IoT devices cooperatively to markedly improve the computing power of the low-cost IoT devices and ensure the performance of the entire system. Typical case studies about implementing AI technology, such as computer vision (CV) and simultaneous localization and mapping (SLAM), on low-cost IoT devices are also described in this chapter from a design and development perspective.

16.2 Edge Computing

16.2.1 Evolution of Computing Form

In 1946, at the University of Pennsylvania, the electronic transistor computer ENIAC was introduced quietly with a large frame that covered 170 square meters and processors that contained 18,000 transistors. As a carrier of computing, the ENIAC opened the way for the development of modern computers. With the advent of electronic transistors, the form of computing has undergone several major changes to respond to increasingly abundant demands.

- **From collective to individual:** In the early days of computer development, due to high costs, computers were primarily used to perform large scientific experiments, and no personal computers existed. With the advent of integrated circuits, the size of computers continued to shrink, and costs have decreased. Now, many people can have personal computers to calculate and store data.
- **From local to the cloud:** With the continuous development of computer networks and Web technology, the computer is no longer just a carrier of storage or computing but is increasingly used for communication. A lot of information is migrated from the local to the Web server by the user. This process of "information networking" brings data to the server and gradually brings part of the computing process to the server, thus forming the current form of cloud computing step by step.
- **From cloud to edge:** With the popularization of smart devices, an increasing number of devices are connected to the network, which overwhelms cloud computing infrastructure.

The sync of computing resources from the operation center to the network edge devices near users has become an inevitable requirement to achieve large-scale real-time computing [1]. Thus, data transmission delays in the WAN can be completely avoided, and the level of data privacy security, access efficiency, and flexibility of service deployment and management can be improved.

16.2.2 Concept of Edge Computing

Edge computing is a hierarchical distributed computing model that primarily decentralizes computing from the center to the edge [2, 3]. By giving full play to the computing and storage capabilities of network edge devices, edge computing provides communication, storage, and computing resources at the edge of the network, forming a "device-edge-cloud" architecture to reduce application latency and network load.

As shown in Figure 16.2, for scenarios such as campuses and industrial parks, devices equipped with computing and storage resources can be used as edge devices; for urban block scenarios, communication base stations of mobile cellular networks can be used as edge computing devices to provide services [4]; and for residential scenarios, home routers can be used as edge computing devices.

16.2.3 Changes from Edge Computing

In edge computing, front-end devices send computing requests and necessary data to edge servers through different communication methods. Then, the edge server checks whether the computing service corresponding to the request is available: if yes, it will execute the computing task and return the calculation result to the front-end device; if no, it will request another edge server or cloud server to execute the task.

Compared with cloud computing, in edge computing, the distance between front-end devices and edge servers is usually fixed, and the transmission delay is markedly shortened, which can support various computing services with high real-time requirements.

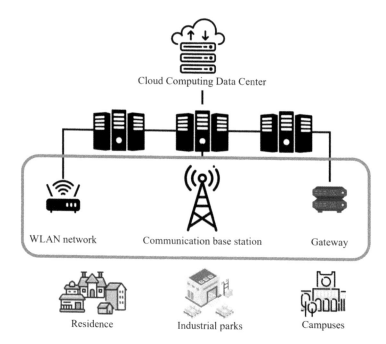

FIGURE 16.2 Schematic diagram of the edge computing system.

TABLE 16.1

Communication Delay and Energy Consumption of Different Communication Technologies

Application Scenarios	Communication Technologies	Communication Delay	Energy Consumption
Mobile computing	5G	<5 ms	High
Mobile computing	4G	<50 ms	High
Indoor short distance	Wi-Fi	<150 ms	Medium
Indoor short distance	Bluetooth	<200 ms	Medium
Embedded IoT	ZigBee	2s	Low
Embedded IoT	NB-IoT	1s	Low
Embedded IoT	SigFo6	2s	Low

TABLE 16.2

Delay Requirements for Various Computer and Mobile Applications

Service Type	Delay Requirement	Experience Feelings
AR	High	<10 ms
VR	High	<10 ms
Game	Medium	1–30 ms, very good
		31–100 ms, good
		100–200 ms, bad
		>200 ms, very bad
Video chat	Low	0.2–2s, very good
		2–6s, good
		6–18s, bad

Specifically, the edge computing model has the following characteristics:

- **Very low latency:** Edge computing is closer to front-end users than cloud computing. In a typical edge computing system, front-end users and edge servers are connected by a single-hop network, and the delay is directly related to the wireless transmission technology used. Table 16.1 summarizes the delay and energy consumption of different types of communication technologies. In the architecture of edge computing, the communication between front-end devices and edge servers will strongly affect the efficiency of edge computing [5]. For mobile devices, edge computing combined with 5G can provide low communication latency. For IoT devices, the latency of their cloud computing solutions is approximately 800–2000 ms. In such scenarios, edge computing is expected to reduce the end-to-end delay of the single-hop transmission delay and improve real-time performance by more than ten times.

  Table 16.2 shows the latency requirements of various computer and mobile applications. Under current conditions, AR/VR can only be executed by local computing. With the continuous development of wireless technology and the continuous optimization of edge computing architecture, more computing services will likely move from local to the edge, and an increasing number of application services that support ultralow latency will emerge.

- **Heterogeneous service objects:** Considering that the edge computing server primarily serves devices that are directly connected to it, the services carried on the edge server strongly depend on its service object devices and service requests. For example, the edge server targets in the smart home are primarily all types of smart homes and wearable devices; thus, most services running on the edge server will likely be data storage, data analysis, etc. However, the edge server that supports entertainment services will likely provide image rendering, image analysis, video caching, and other services.

- **Diversified service forms:** Different from the data center network in the cloud computing environment, the server of edge computing can be a variety of devices with relative resource advantages and low connection latency, providing services for other resource-constrained front-end devices. The difference between these forms primarily comes from the sinking degree of computing resources: when the service object is various smart devices in smart homes, the edge server can run computing services in the form of a home gateway; when the service object is mobile devices such as smartphones, the edge server can be integrated into mobile base stations to provide both communication and computing services.

- **Highly sensitive to mobility:** Edge computing serves users that are connected by a single hop, but the communication range of a single hop is usually limited, which makes edge computing highly sensitive to user movement. The mobility of users affects the quality of wireless transmission; conversely, users who move at high speeds are likely to switch between multiple edge servers. Such high switching frequency produces many challenges when using edge computing in mobile scenarios, and edge computing optimization technology under high mobility conditions has also become one of the current research hotspots in edge computing.

- **Privacy protection:** Because data are stored in edge devices near users, the network structure reduces or even eliminates the connectivity between user data and other network entities, making data privacy more secure. Due to the sinking of computing, more complex encryption and privacy protection algorithms can also be applied to more types of edge services to better protect user privacy. In addition, the reduction of data transmission delay has spawned new privacy-preserving computing models and more complex encryption algorithms, which markedly reduce the risk of privacy leakage.

16.2.4 Edge Computing Development Trends

- **Technology Development Trend:** Since 2017, edge computing has been listed on Gartner, an authoritative consulting institution in the field of technology, continuously, and its development has gradually entered the stage of high expectations from an innovation-driven perspective. With the development and maturity of 5G technology, edge computing has derived various subdivisions from the initial generalized concept, as shown in Table 16.3.

- **Academic Research:** In recent years, with the rise of edge computing research, an increasing number of scientific articles have been published. According to the statistics of articles using edge computing as a keyword in SCI journal sources in recent years, the number of research results has grown rapidly, as shown in Table 16.4.

TABLE 16.3

Changes in Edge Computing at Gartner

Year	Keywords	Location
2017	Edge computing	Innovation Trigger
2018	Edge AI	Innovation Trigger
2019	Edge AI/Analytics	Peak of inflated expectations
2020	Low-cost single board computers at the edge	Innovation Trigger

TABLE 16.4

Number of Academic Papers Related to Edge Computing (IEEE)

Year	2015	2016	2017	2018	2019
Number	500+	1,200+	2,000+	3,100+	5,000+

- **National strategy:** Each country's national strategy for the telecommunications network industry has promoted the development of edge computing to varying degrees. Edge computing acts as a lubricant between devices, systems, and decisions.

16.3 Principles of Edge Computing Architecture

In edge computing, front-end devices must offload computing tasks to edge servers, which are executed locally or offloaded to the cloud depending on the task. This process primarily involves three entities: front-end equipment, edge equipment, and cloud centers. The edge computing architecture refers to how these three entities are effectively organized and coordinated to operate through software and hardware.

16.3.1 Overall System Architecture

The network edge is a relative concept, which means far away from the center of the network. According to the current definition of edge computing and the characteristics of the real network architecture, we divide edge devices into two categories: backbone network edges and ubiquitous edges, as shown in Figure 16.3.

The edge devices of the backbone network are typically manageable and controllable and have relatively abundant resources, such as base stations of mobile cellular networks. Ubiquitous edge devices usually have strong instability, whether it is the availability of resources or the stability of connections, such as laptops and smartphones. Due to the characteristics of edge devices, it is difficult for edge computing to establish a general and fixed network architecture like cloud computing. The ideal edge computing architecture should be able to effectively use various edge resources, and the front-end computing tasks should be completed at the lowest cost under the premise of satisfying service and experience quality.

The current mainstream edge computing architectures discussed in academia and industry include the "cloud-edge-device" architecture, "edge-device" architecture, distributed D2D architecture, and elastic edge architecture, which are applied in different reference scenarios and face system challenges. These architectures are introduced below.

- **"Cloud-Edge-Device" architecture:** The "cloud-edge-device" three-layer architecture includes the cloud center layer, edge layer, and device layer, as shown in Figure 16.4. The user request that is sent from the front-end device will be accepted by the edge-layer device. If the edge-layer device can provide the corresponding edge service, the computing request will be processed,

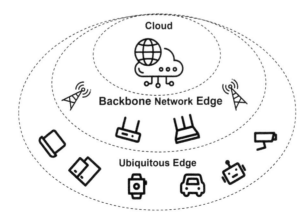

FIGURE 16.3 Backbone network edge and ubiquitous edge.

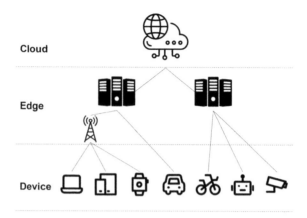

FIGURE 16.4 "Cloud-edge-device" architecture.

and the result will be returned to the front-end device. If there is no corresponding computing request on the devices at the edge layer, the task will be sent to related edge services or the cloud center for processing. Through this process, various computing tasks of front-end devices can be converted from local computing to requesting edge computing. Concurrently, front-end devices have markedly improved their computing capabilities by accessing more types of edge computing services. In this architecture, cloud computing primarily deals with tasks with a huge amount of calculation and a long-running period. As a useful supplement to the cloud center, edge devices are primarily used to deal with the following types of computing tasks: (a) the latency requirement is extremely low, and the cloud center cannot meet the required computing tasks; (b) the amount of data is large, and the transmission of task data to the cloud center will produce high bandwidth pressure; (c) the computing requests are frequent, the computing data are huge, and computing tasks in the cloud center may cause delays; and (d) computational tasks may require high privacy and cannot transmit data to the cloud center. The collaboration between edge and cloud involves resource collaboration between edge IaaS (infrastructure as a service) and cloud IaaS; edge PaaS (platform as a service) and cloud PaaS realize data sharing; intelligent collaboration and collaborative business orchestration; and edge SaaS (software as a service) and cloud SaaS to achieve service collaboration.

- **"Edge-Device" architecture:** In the edge-device architecture, a network composed of only edge servers (i.e., the edge network) and front-end devices is shown. Each server in the edge network is both an access point and a computing node, accepting and processing computing requests and task offloading from front-end devices. For a computing request, the connected edge node and the task processing node are not necessarily the same because there is no high-speed cloud center transmission channel. When the edge server receives a service type that it cannot handle, it must send the request to the other edge server with the corresponding service to achieve the effect of the coordinated operation on the entire. This architecture is usually used in highly customized scenarios, such as equipment communication and computing networks in industrial parks and experimental networks on university campuses. In these scenarios, the service objects and computing service types of edge networks are highly deterministic, and edge network deployment, resource allocation, and computing service orchestration must be performed according to specific application scenarios.

- **Multi-Access Edge Computing:** With the continuous generation of new applications and the increasing number of edge devices, ultra-dense networks have emerged as the times require. Each front-end device can access multiple edge servers; this architecture is called a multiaccess edge network. The multiaccess edge network can coexist with the above two architectures. The above architecture describes how the cloud and edge layers are implemented, while the multiaccess edge network emphasizes how the front-end device and the edge device layer are connected. When the front-end device changes from accessing one edge device to accessing multiple ones, it will have different impacts on the technical design and implementation in the above two architectures.

- **Distributed Device-to-Device/Device-for-Device Architecture (Ubiquitous Edge Architecture):** Device-to-Device (D2D) or Device-to-Device or Device-for-Device (D4D) edge computing means that the communication between edge devices no longer passes through the backbone network but forms an ad hoc network through direct device connection and multiple hops to complete information transmission between devices. Each device can offload computing to other devices and can also accept computing requests from other devices. Although the D2D architecture is relatively simple, due to the lack of global information, stable communication links, and physical topology, it is usually suitable for scenarios where infrastructure is lacking or the deployment of infrastructure is expensive, such as car networking scenarios and battlefield combat scenarios.

- **AIoT Architecture:** From the perspective of improving the capabilities of the Internet of Things, edge computing directly promotes the generation of the AIoT architecture – "Artificial Intelligence + Internet of Things." At the system level, the capabilities of AI will be provided through edge computing.

16.3.2 Challenges of Edge Computing Architecture Design

In edge computing, a front-end device offloads its computing tasks to an edge server, and the server executes these tasks locally or further to the cloud. This process involves front-end devices, edge devices, and the cloud. The work of edge computing architecture is to effectively organize and coordinate the three entities, and the challenges of edge computing architecture design are described below.

- **Diverse and customized scenarios:** Unlike cloud computing, edge computing is closer to the real computing scene, which makes edge computing more affected by specific scene requirements [6]. For example, industrial scenarios such as warehousing, the computing task type, task load, and user characteristics are highly deterministic. The edge computing setup for the scene must focus on data security, system reliability, connection stability, and other issues. For other scenarios (e.g., shopping malls, stations), due to the relatively complex computing types of front-end users, the diversity of users and services will have a completely different impact on the design of edge computing architecture. This scenario requires edge services to flexibly and quickly adjust service types and resource allocation strategies accordingly, which makes all aspects of edge architecture design an important issue for scene demand analysis.

- **Mobility of front-end users:** Edge computing markedly decreases the end-to-end delay of computing services by establishing direct communication between edge servers and front-end users, which also makes the mobility of front-end users directly affect edge service quality and service availability. Specifically, because edge computing is deployed closer to users, its coverage is relatively limited. For example, in the Internet of Vehicles scenario, a high-speed smart car must use multiple edge servers for coordination, which puts forward new requirements for the handover of access points, service migration and backup, and service resource allocation. Table 16.5 shows the mobility of users in different scenarios.

TABLE 16.5

User Mobility in Different Scenarios

Scenarios	Moving Speed	Edge Pointcut Switching Frequency (5G)
Autonomous driving + 5G edge gateway	60 km/h	5AP/m
High-speed rail multimedia service +5G edge gateway	300 km/h	25AP/m
Mobile AR/VR users + 5G edge gateway	4 km/h	0.33AP/m
Pedestrian + 5G edge gateway	4 km/h	1.33AP/m

- **Resource Constraints and Uncertainty for Multiple Infrastructures:** Due to the resource limitation of edge computing, a good edge collaboration mechanism should be formed at the edge service architecture level and should be able to support the rapid transformation between different tasks. However, the uncertainty of edge devices makes time-consuming computing tasks challenging. Reasonable resource allocation is required to avoid long task duration, and conversely, software architecture is required to support fine-grained and split task offloading to reduce the duration of service and reduce the computing and transmission pressure.
- **Diverse, massive, and heterogeneous edge services:** The diverse types of devices accessed by edge computing directly lead to various types of services [7]. Not only are the types of resources required for computing services diverse, but there are also large differences in the quality of experience and service quality requirements. For example, with video parsing, the required amount of video data is large, and the requirements for caching are high, but the requirements for the real-time result of video parsing are relatively low. For the automatic driving scenario, the real-time performance of video parsing results is high, but the requirement for the cache is low. Therefore, considering the diversity, mass, and heterogeneity of edge services, the edge architecture should be equipped with functions such as supporting edge device collaboration, resource sharing, and flexible configuration of services.

16.3.3   Edge Computing Operating System and Open-Source Framework

The operating system in edge computing is primarily to open up the business process between cloud, edge, and terminal; integrate resources of all parties; and provide open interfaces for developers and users to use. Compared with cloud computing operating systems, edge operating systems and frameworks primarily face three challenges: high heterogeneity, edge data analysis and processing, and edge optimization driven by business models.

Many types of edge operating systems and open-source frameworks are currently in use, such as AWS IoT (Greengrass) proposed by Amazon, Azure IoT Hub proposed by Microsoft, CORD (Central Office Rearchitecture as a Datacenter) proposed by AT&T, KubeEdge proposed by Huawei, Arduino IoT Cloud by Arduino, K3S proposed by Google, and OpenEdge proposed by Baidu.

The following will primarily introduce the EdgeX Foundry initiated by the Linux Foundation and the Starlingx project jointly initiated by Intel and Wind River.

- **EdgeX Foundry:** EdgeX Foundry (EdgeX for short) is an open-source project initiated by the Linux Foundation, which is primarily oriented to the application scenarios of the general industrial Internet of Things, focusing on the management of massive and heterogeneous front-end devices. EdgeX describes scenarios, such as device access and edge data transmission, but does not provide specifications for cloud-edge collaboration, cloud-based service, and application management. This software allows users to easily implement EdgeX-based edge systems for IoT application scenarios and resume their service management and application ecology on the edge system.
- **StarlingX:** The StarlingX project is an edge computing framework open-sourced by Intel and WindRiver and provides a software stack based on the OpenStack platform and VIM, automated service packaging, compilation, and configuration tools.

16.4   Computation Offloading in Edge Computing

16.4.1   Concept of Computation Offloading

Computation offloading is the core problem in edge computing [8] and refers to offloading computing tasks from users to edge servers, which can reduce task processing delay and equipment energy consumption. The computation offloading procedure includes three steps: task upload, task processing, and result return. Task upload refers to uploading tasks to edge servers through mobile access points, selecting the communication technology according to the characteristics of user services, and coordinating the upload policy. Task processing refers to allocating reasonable resources and processing the arriving tasks. Result return refers to sending the calculation results back to users.

Then, we will introduce the time delay model and energy consumption model of computation offloading. In cloud computing networks, the storage and forwarding delay of routers is dominant, while the wireless transmission delay of tasks is dominant at the access end. The "hop count" (i.e., the number of times data are forwarded on the network) of the router between the user and the core cloud is more than one. Cloud computing usually provides services for users with a large coverage area, and the interference between users on the front-end transmission is relatively small. In edge networks, wireless transmission delay at the access end dominates. The distance between the user and the edge server is often "one hop" (i.e., straight line connected). Edge servers provide services for users in the same area through A-Nodes, and the interference between channels is significant. The primary factors affecting the quality of wireless channels are multipath attenuation, signal-to-noise ratio, and co-frequency interference. The Shannon formula is used to estimate the theoretical channel transmission rate. Therefore, the task upload rate can be calculated by (16.1):

$$R_j = B \log_2 \left(1 + \frac{q_j g_j}{N + \sum_i q_i g_i} \right) \tag{16.1}$$

where B is the bandwidth allocated to the user, N is the ambient noise, q is the transmitted power of the user, and g is the channel gain.

The energy consumption of the data transmission can be calculated by (16.2), where *Input* is the amount of data to be uploaded during computation offloading R is the task upload rate; $\frac{Input}{R}$ is the time required for offloading the computing task; and q is the transmitted power of the user. Increasing the transmit power of the device increases the data transmission rate but also increases the energy consumption of the device:

$$E_t = q * \frac{Input}{R} \tag{16.2}$$

The task processing time can be discussed in two cases: (1) users request only a single task, and (2) users persistently request tasks. In the first case, when a single task is uploaded to the edge server, the processing time required by the edge server can be expressed as (16.3):

$$T = \frac{C}{S} \tag{16.3}$$

where C is the number of CPU cycles required to process the task, describing the complexity of the task, and S is the computing resources allocated to users by the edge server. In the second case, users continuously make requests for edge computing to the edge network (e.g., in AR applications, when the images collected by terminal devices change, the updated images must be continuously uploaded to the edge server for processing). When there are multiple tasks, part of the task will involve task waiting time. In general, we assume that two consecutive task arrival intervals are independent of each other and that the arrival times follow a Poisson distribution. Therefore, we formulate the task processing delay model as a queuing theoretic model, and the task processing delay can be calculated by (16.4):

$$T_e = \frac{1}{\mu - \lambda} \tag{16.4}$$

where μ is the strength of the user request (i.e., the mean value of the Poisson distribution) and λ is the average server processing time.

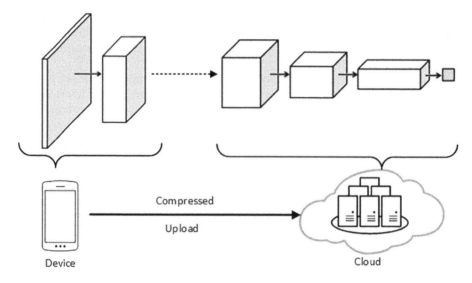

FIGURE 16.5   Deployment of a segmental network on the device-cloud system [12].

16.4.2   Computation Offloading Technologies

16.4.2.1   *Segmental Deployment of a Convolutional Neural Network Based on Computation Offloading*

Because ImageNet published a large-scale image classification and recognition dataset [9], the performance of deep convolutional neural networks has been continuously verified by various deep network models in image classification and recognition tasks, which has gradually attracted increasing attention from researchers and has led to the rapid development of deep learning. Existing methods deepen the network to enhance the performance of convolutional neural networks and have intensive computation and massive memory consumption, which are not affordable for low-cost mobile devices.

Computation offloading technologies can be used to accelerate the inference of convolutional neural networks by offloading computation-intensive tasks to the cloud [10, 11]. More specifically, by selecting the appropriate split point, the mobile device completes the processing of the front-end network and uploads the output feature value to the cloud, and the cloud completes the subsequent steps according to the feature value; thus, the low-performance robot can easily complete the image recognition task, as shown in Figure 16.5.

16.4.2.1.1   Methodology

Split point selection is the key problem that must be addressed, which should carefully balance computation on mobile devices and transmitted data between devices and the cloud. In this book, the size of the receptive field, the amount of computation, and the network transmission delay are jointly considered.

The receptive field is one of the important parameters to measure the ability of a layer to abstract the original image data, as shown in Figure 16.6. In convolutional neural networks, the receptive field can be computed by (16.5), where s_n is the stride of the current convolutional layer; j_n is the product of the strides of all layers before n; k_n is the kernel size; and r_n is the receptive field size. Also, $j_1 = 1, r_1 = 1$:

$$\begin{cases} j_n = j_{n-1}s_n \\ r_n = r_{n-1} + (k_n - 1)j_{n-1} \end{cases} \tag{16.5}$$

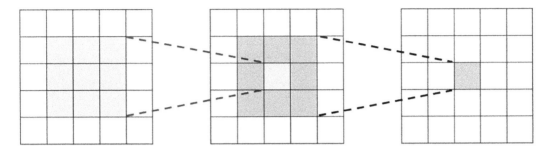

FIGURE 16.6 Receptive field of feature maps.

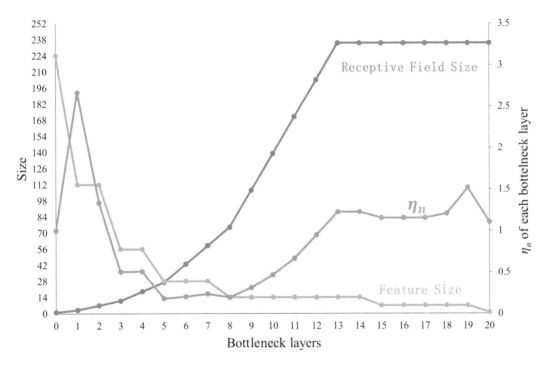

FIGURE 16.7 η_n diagram of standard MobileNetV2.

The amount of data transmitted to the cloud is determined by the output of the network at the split point, and the output data size of different layers in the network can be calculated by (16.6):

$$l_n = \frac{l_{n-1} + 2p_n - k_n}{s_n} + 1 \tag{16.6}$$

where l_n is the feature edge length of the current layer output, p_n is the padding, and k_n is the kernel size. To evaluate split point selection schemes, a metric η_n is defined as shown in (16.7), which refers to the sum of the compression ratio and the receptive field size ratio. In this study, l_0 is the length of the input images, and c_0 is the number of input channels. The smaller η_n is, the better the split point scheme. Concurrently, the front layer network must be as short as possible so that the computing cost of mobile devices can be decreased. In general, the proportion of the front-end network to the entire network is between 20% and 30%:

$$\eta_n = \frac{l_n^2 c_n}{l_0^2 c_0} + \frac{r_n^2}{l_0^2} = \frac{1}{l_0^2} \left(\frac{l_n^2 c_n}{c_0} + r_n^2 \right) \tag{16.7}$$

TABLE 16.6

Average MobileNet Deployment Time Across 50 Experiments, using Various Deployment Techniques

	Robot (ms)	Communication (ms)	Cloud (ms)	Total (ms)
MobileNet (Only robot)	513.5	—	—	513.5
Segmental-MobileNet	103.2	37.2	35.0	175.6
MobileNet (Only cloud)	43.6	206.7	54.3	302.4

FIGURE 16.8 Results of instance segmentation on the COCO test set. Bounding boxes, classes, and confidences are also displayed, along with colored masks.

Taking the standard MobileNetV2 as an example, we can obtain the result in Figure 16.7. The smallest η_n exists between the fifth and eighth layers. Thus, the fifth layer is selected as the final split point.

Table 16.6 shows the inference latency of MobileNetV2 with different deployment methods. The segmented deployment system can thus balance the execution efficiency of the robot and the cloud and consider the network transmission delay. Therefore, the overall delay of the system is the lowest, which meets the requirements of the real-time system.

16.4.2.2 *Real-Time Instance Segmentation Method Based on Computation Offloading*

One of the most difficult CV problems, instance segmentation [13–15] seeks to find the object instances in an image while localizing them using both bounding boxes and segmentation masks, as shown in Figure 16.8. Instance segmentation offers a wide range of application scenarios due to its ability to comprehend the environment through vision, which draws an increasing number of researchers from the field of robotics. Instance segmentation can help robots acquire the high-level

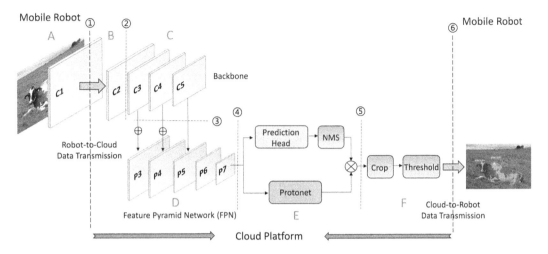

FIGURE 16.9 Computation offloading strategy for the instance segmentation network [15].

semantic information of environments and carry out more complicated interactions with environments, like navigation and grasping, as an addition to geometric robot perception approaches.

However, because they must maneuver in a confined location and therefore have a minimum volume and weight, mobile robots have limited onboard resources, including compute, memory, and battery capacity, in some specialized circumstances, such as disaster rescue, forest protection, and housekeeping. The broad use of mobile robots in daily life is hampered because of the huge cost of high-performance CPUs. These mobile robots cannot, therefore, afford the extensive computing and data requirements of instance segmentation techniques.

Offloading some of the instance segmentation network's computation to the cloud is a promising method, as shown in Figure 16.9. As a result, mobile robots can utilize strong cloud resources to hasten network execution. Mobile robots will process the data concurrently to remove unnecessary information and extract the important elements to speed up data transmission and improve data security [16, 17].

16.4.2.2.1 Methodology

Modeling the instance segmentation network as the directed acyclic graph $G = <M, D>$ is possible. The nodes $M = \{m_1, m_2, \ldots, m_K\}$ in the graph represent several network modules, such as the backbone network, which is utilized to extract the fundamental features, and other functional modules to carry out specific classification or segmentation tasks. Moreover, the backbone network can be divided into a number of convolutional layers, with each layer functioning as a separate module. In the instance segmentation network, two parallel components should be combined into a single module, and all modules must be sequential. The graph's edges $D = \{d_{ij} = (m_i, m_j)|m_i, m_j \in M\}$ signify the transmission of data between various modules, and the length of edge $|d_{ij}|$ reflects the volume of data transported from m_i to m_j.

16.4.2.2.2 Time Cost Model

Each module in the aforementioned directed acyclic graph can be installed on a mobile robot or cloud platform, and the hardware configuration determines how quickly it runs (e.g., CPU, GPU, and memory). The execution time on a mobile robot $t_r(m)$ is typically substantially longer than that on a cloud platform $t_c(m)$ for the same module. Robot-to-robot transmission (R2R) and robot-to-cloud transmission are the two different types of data transfer methods (R2C). The data transmission time in the R2C mode is dependent on the volume of data and the communication bandwidth, denoted as $t(d, R2, CB)$, where B is the communication bandwidth and is predicated on the assumption that the data transmission time in the R2R mode can be ignored (i.e., $t(d, R2R) = 0$).

The time cost of the full instance segmentation network can be expressed as (16.8) and includes both module execution time t_{exec} and data transmission time t_{trans}.

$$t_{\text{total}} = t_{\text{exec}} + t_{\text{trans}} \qquad (16.8)$$

We think about three scenarios: (1) Run a portion of the modules in the cloud; (2) Run the entire module in the cloud; (3) Run the entire module on the mobile robot.

The module execution time in the first scenario may be computed using the formula (16.9), where M_R denotes the set of modules processed on the mobile robot and M_C denotes the set of modules executed on the cloud platform. The data transmission time can be computed using the formula (16.10), where d is the intermediate outcome from the mobile robot's processing of the modules. As a result, (16.11) can be used to indicate the overall time cost:

$$t_{\text{exec}} = \sum_{m \in M_R} t_r(m) + \sum_{m \in M_C} t_c(m) \qquad (16.9)$$

$$t_{\text{trans}} = t(d, R2, CB) \qquad (16.10)$$

$$t_{\text{total}} = \sum_{m \in M_R} t_r(m) + \sum_{m \in M_C} t_c(m) + t(d, R2C, B) \qquad (16.11)$$

The module execution time in the second scenario can be estimated using (16.12), where M refers to all modules in the instance segmentation network. The data transmission time can alternatively be estimated using the formula (16.10), where d denotes the sensor-generated raw image or video data. As a result, the total time expenditure may be expressed as (16.13):

$$t_{\text{exec}} = \sum_{m \in M} t_c(m) \qquad (16.12)$$

$$t_{\text{total}} = \sum_{m \in M} t_c(m) + t(d, R2, CB) \qquad (16.13)$$

In the final scenario, the mobile robot executes the whole instance segmentation network, and the total time cost is (16.14):

$$t_{\text{total}} = \sum_{m \in M} t_r(m) \qquad (16.14)$$

16.4.2.2.3 Energy Consumption Model

Because mobile robot batteries have a limited capacity and energy consumption has a significant impact on the robots' standby time, this book only looks at the energy consumption of mobile robots. In contrast, cloud systems have a constant power source and can run continuously regardless of how much energy a particular process uses. The energy used by data transmission E_{trans} and module execution E_{exec} during the instance segmentation network's execution, as shown in (16.15), together account for the mobile robot's energy consumption.

$$E_{\text{robot}} = E_{\text{exec}} + E_{\text{trans}} \qquad (16.15)$$

The three situations described in Section 16.4.2.2.2 are also taken into account. The energy consumption in the first scenario may be estimated using (16.16), where $C(m)$ represents the battery consumption when the robot executes module m, and $C(d)$ represents the battery consumption when the robot sends data d to the cloud. Battery usage is measured in mAh, and 1mAh equals 0.001A*3600s, or 3.6As. In the second scenario, energy consumption is only caused by data transmission, and it may be computed by (16.17). In the third scenario, all modules are run on the

TABLE 16.7

The Average Time Cost of Yolact When Offloading Is Partly, Completely, or Not At All

Modules	Partly(s)	Completely(s)	Not at all(s)
C1	0.6271	0.0002	0.6271
C2	0.0013	0.0013	1.9786
C3+C4+C5	0.0058	0.0058	5.5642
FPN	0.0009	0.0009	0.9789
Proto+Pred_head	0.0303	0.0303	6.3138
Detect	0.0115	0.0115	0.2178
Data transmission	0.4800	4.0400	0.0000
Total	1.1569	4.0900	15.6804

mobile robot instead of using cloud resources. $E_{trans} = 0$. As a result, and the energy consumption can be estimated using Equation (16.18):

$$E_{robot} = \sum_{m \in M_R} 3.6 * (C(m) * U + C(d) * U) \tag{16.16}$$

$$E_{robot} = 3.6 * C(d) * U \tag{16.17}$$

$$E_{robot} = \sum_{m \in M} 3.6 * C(m) * U \tag{16.18}$$

The main issue to be solved is how to offload the computation of the instance segmentation network into the cloud in order to achieve real-time instance segmentation on a mobile robot with the help of clouds. With the aforementioned formulation, the computation offloading problem can be reduced to choosing which nodes in the directed acyclic graph should be executed on the mobile robot and which nodes should be executed on the cloud platform, with the aim of minimizing both the time and energy costs of the entire instance segmentation, as shown in (16.19):

$$\min_{M_R, M_C} \alpha t_{total} + \beta E_{robot}. \tag{16.19}$$

The Yolact results are shown in Table 16.7. It can be seen that our strategy, which involves partially offloading, completes the inference of a frame in the shortest amount of time – about one second – as opposed to completely offloading, which can take up to 15 seconds. We also display the time costs associated with each Yolact module, where C1, C2, C3, C4, and C5 denote the five blocks that make up the backbone network, FPN denotes the feature pyramid network, Proto + Pred Head denotes two concurrent subtasks (i.e., creating prototype masks and predicting mask coefficients), and Detect denotes the detection stage's conclusion and a number of post-processing steps. It has been discovered that partial offloading significantly reduces the time cost of C2, C3+C4+C5, FPN, Proto+Pred head, and Detect when compared to no offloading. This is due to the fact that these modules have been offloaded into the cloud, where execution times are far faster than they would be on a mobile robot.

16.5 AIoT Based on Edge Computing

Edge computing technology is one of the most important computing technologies, which aims to process and analyze industrial data at the edge of the network near the industrial site to meet the requirements of practical applications, including real-time performance, low device energy consumption, and data security [18–20]. Edge computing technology changes the paradigm of traditional manufacturing. In recent decades, the domestic and foreign industries have developed various edge computing architectures and models. In 2014, the European ETSI established the Mobile Edge Computing Standardization Working Group (MEC). In 2015, the OpenFog computing consortium (OFC) performed research on OpenFog architecture and computing models. The Domestic Edge Computing Industry Alliance and the Industrial Internet Industry Alliance jointly released the white paper "Edge Computing Reference Architecture 3.0" and more than 20 edge computing test beds. In terms of standard formulation, in 2020, the international standard of "Edge Computing Requirements and Capability Requirements" (ITU-TY.4208) promoted by China Unicom and other standards in ITU-T SG20 were officially released. Concurrently, the international standard of "Edge Computing Gateway" was steadily advancing. In October 2016, the IEEE/ACM Symposium on Edge Computing was officially established by IEEE and ACM. The Edge Computing Gateway formed an academic forum jointly recognized by academia, industry, and government (National Foundation of the United States). In 2017, Shenyang Institute of Automation, Chinese Academy of Sciences, led the establishment of the Edge Computing Committee of the Chinese Association of Automation. At Microsoft's 2018 Annual Developer Conference, Microsoft released "Azure IoT Edge" and other Edge products, which shifted its business focus from the Windows operating system to intelligent Edge computing. Concurrently, Amazon released its "AWS Greengrass" edge-side software that seamlessly extends AWS cloud services to devices. Ali Cloud announced that in 2018, it will strategically invest in the field of edge computing technology and launch the Edge computing product Link Edge.

The advantages of edge computing include the following three aspects:

1) The gateway on the edge side offers a variety of interfaces and protocols to field devices, which can solve the problem of network connections and communication among field devices, and integrate and converge a lot of data from different devices and sensors.

2) Business data can be uploaded to the cloud and can be processed at edge servers in real time, which markedly reduces the data transmission delay and network bandwidth consumption and ensures data security.

3) Edge computing is based on intelligent distributed architectures and platforms. System operation and maintenance personnel, decision-makers, and developers can cooperate with each other through the edge computing system.

16.5.1 Industrial Vision

Industrial vision is used to control and monitor production processes, including automatic inspection, workpiece processing, and assembly automation, as shown in Figure 16.10. Industrial vision can mostly replace manual inspection, reducing the labor costs of enterprises and improving the efficiency and precision of inspection. More specifically, a large amount of image information is collected from production lines by 4K, 8K, and other high-definition cameras and then must be

FIGURE 16.10 Industrial vision.

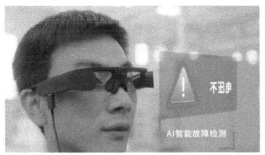

FIGURE 16.11   AR remote assistance.

processed and analyzed to support real-time feedback control. In industrial scenarios, these image data usually require a large bandwidth of 5–150 Mbps/300 Mbps for imaging data back and a low delay of 20–50 ms for PLC control feedback. Therefore, 5G+ edge computing can be a promising solution for industrial vision. Image information is transmitted through the high uplink bandwidth of 5G, which meets the demand of industrial vision with large bandwidth. With the machine vision AI algorithm deployed on the edge computing platform, real-time and intelligent production line inspection can also be achieved. In addition, it is necessary to cooperate with the cloud for big data storage and AI algorithm training.

16.5.2   AR Remote Assistance

AR remote assistance can support employee learning, training, and communication; provide operation demonstration and guidance; and remind production process precautions and operation details, as shown in Figure 16.11. The scene experienced by workers is directly transmitted to technical personnel, who can directly guide the workers through video, voice, marking, and other interactive means. AR applications aim at making users feel like they are there. If the rate of image rendering cannot keep pace with the user's moving speed, the picture will be shifted, causing a poor user experience. Therefore, low latency and real-time processing also must be ensured in AR remote assistance. Edge computing combined with 5G can achieve this goal, with various capabilities of transcoding, rendering, 3D reconstruction, object recognition, and AR content management.

16.5.3   Remote Driving

In recent years, remote driving has been applied in an increasing number of industrial scenarios, such as steel plant crane remote driving and underground mining truck remote driving, as shown in Figure 16.12. Usually, monitoring screen and control equipment are deployed in the central control room, and actuators (i.e., trucks or cranes) are deployed in industrial sites. This scenario requires precise control and low service delay (usually less than 20 ms). Edge computing can also be a promising solution for remote driving applications.

16.5.4   AI Video Surveillance

AI video surveillance has a wide range of applications, including park office monitoring, warehouse monitoring, park access monitoring, abnormal production line equipment, operator behavior, whether to wear a safety helmet, whether the workshop personnel walks according to the prescribed route, etc, as shown in Figure 16.13. In addition to security monitoring, it is also necessary to identify abnormal behavior of production line equipment and operators in the production process, enhancing the safety and reliability of the production line, as well as ensuring that key operations

FIGURE 16.12 Remote driving.

FIGURE 16.13 AI video surveillance.

are not omitted. In these scenarios, real-time data analysis and data privacy are important. With edge computing, video surveillance is deployed on-site to record workers' operations, and the data are transmitted to edge computing platforms and analyzed in real time to ensure production security and quality.

16.5.5 UAV Inspection

UAV inspection is widely used in smart logistics, smart parks, equipment inspection, and other fields to guarantee personnel, property, public security, and fire safety, as shown in Figure 16.14. The UAV transmits camera videos (visible high-definition, infrared, etc.) to the comprehensive control center of the factory in real time. Through the intelligent analysis (e.g., object recognition and pattern recognition) of videos, the control center can judge whether there are security anomalies or fire alarms in inspected locations and realize intelligent warnings to minimize the daily labor intensity of security personnel. Unfortunately, most front-end devices have sensing and simple processing capabilities and cannot perform the intensive computation of intelligent analysis. Data must be transferred to the data center for processing. Video analysis and processing services are deployed in the MEC platform near the sensing devices. The data collected by UAV cameras are transmitted to the MEC platform through a 5G base station for local analysis and preprocessing, which can reduce the bandwidth resource occupation of the core network and backbone network and shorten the total delay. AI training services are deployed in cloud data centers and rely on the powerful computing power of cloud computing to train data and obtain more accurate training models. The uplink rate of 5G can reach 200 Mbps and can support 4K, 8K, and even panoramic video transmission. The low delay and high reliability of the 5G millisecond level can effectively guarantee the precise control and positioning of the UAV.

FIGURE 16.14 UAV inspection.

FIGURE 16.15 AGV warehousing logistics.

16.5.6 AGV Warehousing Logistics

An automated guided vehicle (AGV) is a type of vehicle that is equipped with an electromagnetic or optical automatic guidance device that can follow the prescribed guidance path with safety protection and various load-shifting functions. The AGV system is one of the important components of a smart factory, realizing automatic delivery of goods and materials, and traceable production data collection throughout the process of production and manufacturing. In the AGV warehousing and logistics scenario, as shown in Figure 16.15, the AGV cart automatically goes to the corresponding position to work after receiving the instruction. In the workflow of AGV cars, it is necessary to locate their current position, detect roadblocks ahead through sensors, plan paths in real time, cooperate with other cars, etc.; thus, this workflow has high requirements on delay and concurrency. Through 5G+ edge computing, hundreds of AGV cars can be accessed concurrently, and the data collected by AGV sensors can be processed at the edge in real time to plan paths.

16.5.7 Discussion

AIoT is widely used in life, industry, agriculture, and other fields, and edge computing can solve the computing problems caused by the interconnection of a large number of devices. The advantages of edge computing in data processing capability and transmission delay can support "ubiquitous computing" and give the physical world the ability to "think" fluently. AIoT is providing more opportunities and new challenges.

16.6 Conclusions

AI is developing from "assisting manpower" and "replacing manpower" to "extending manpower," gradually completing the process of informatization and intelligence in the physical world. With the development of computer technology and communication technology, connections have transitioned from person-person to person-object and object-object. There are many challenges to implementing AI applications in real time due to the increasing number of AIoT connections and the powerful computing power to deploy the AI algorithm. This chapter introduces edge computing and computation offloading to solve the above problems. However, there are still challenges which should be solved in the future, such as unified technical specifications and standards, efficient and intelligent scheduling of offloading tasks, reliable network communication, load and cost balancing, intelligent collaborative AI between cloud and edge, real applications, hierarchical and multi-granularity privacy protection, and so on.

REFERENCES

1. P. Garcia Lopez, A. Montresor, D. H. J. Epema, A. Datta. "Edge-centric computing: Vision and challenges", *ACM SIGCOMM Computer Communication Review*, 45(5):37–42, 2015.
2. W. Shi, J. Cao. "Edge computing: Vision and challenges", *IEEE Internet of Things Journal*, 3(5):637–646, 2016.
3. J. Cao, Q. Zhang, W. Shi. "Challenges and opportunities in edge computing" In *Edge Computing: A Primer*, Cham, Switzerland: Springer, pp. 59–70, 2018.
4. D. Bradley, B. Lucia. "Orbital edge computing: Nanosatellite constellations as a new class of computer system", In *Proceedings of the Twenty-Fifth International Conference on Architectural Support for Programming Languages and Operating Systems* 2020, pp. 939–954.
5. J. Luo, X. Deng, H. Qi. "QoE-driven computation offloading for edge computing", *Journal of Systems Architecture*, 97:34–39, 2019.
6. M. Shahrad, J. Balkind, D. Wentzlaff. "Architectural implications of function-as-a-service computing", In *Proceedings of the 52nd Annual IEEE/ACM International Symposium on Microarchitecture* 2019, pp. 1063–1075.
7. A. Glikson, S. Nastic, S. Dustdar. "Deviceless edge computing: extending serverless computing to the edge of the network", In *Proceedings of the 10th ACM International Systems and Storage Conference*, pp. 1-1, 2017.
8. L. Xiao, X. Lu, T. Xu, X. Wan, W. Ji, Y. Zhang, "Reinforcement learning-based mobile offloading for edge computing against jamming and interference", *IEEE Transactions on Communications*, 68(10):6114–6126, 2020.
9. O. Russakovsky, J. Deng, H. Su, et al, "Imagenet large scale visual recognition challenge", *International Journal of Computer Vision*, 115(3):211–252, 2015.
10. C. Hu, W. Bao, D. Wang, and F. Liu, "Dynamic adaptive DNN surgery for inference acceleration on the edge", In *IEEE INFOCOM 2019-IEEE Conference on Computer Communications*, IEEE, 2019, pp. 1423–1431.
11. L. Jia, Z. Zhou, F. Xu, and H. Jin, "Cost-efficient continuous edge learning for artificial-intelligence-of-things (AIoT)", *IEEE Internet of Things Journal*, 9(10):7325–7337, 2021.
12. R. Liao, Y. Guo, Z. Mi and Y. Yang, "Segmental Deployment of Neural Network in Cloud Robotic System", In *Proceedings of 2018 IEEE 3rd International Conference on Cloud Computing and Internet of Things (CCIOT)*, 2018.
13. D. Bolya, C. Zhou, F. Xiao and Y. J. Lee, "YOLACT: Real-time instance segmentation", In *Proceedings of the 2019 IEEE/CVF International Conference on Computer Vision (ICCV)*, 2019.
14. H. Liu, R. A. R. Soto, F. Xiao, et al. "Yolactedge: Real-time instance segmentation on the edge." In *Proceedings of the 2021 IEEE International Conference on Robotics and Automation (ICRA)*. IEEE, 2021.
15. Y. Xie, Y. Guo, Z. Mi, Y. Yang and M. S. Obaidat, "Edge-assisted real-time instance segmentation for resource-limited IoT devices", *IEEE Internet of Things Journal*, 2022. DOI: 10.1109/JIOT.2022.3199921.

16. H. Wu, Z. Zhang, C. Guan, K. Wolter, M. Xu, "Collaborate edge and cloud computing with distributed deep learning for smart city internet of things", *IEEE Internet of Things Journal*, 7(9):8099–8110, 2020.

17. S. Deng, H. Zhao, W. Fang, J. Yin, S. Dustdar, A. Y. Zomaya, "Edge intelligence: The confluence of edge computing and artificial intelligence", *IEEE Internet of Things Journal*, 7(8):7457–7469, 2020.

18. Y. Xie, Y. Guo, Y. Chen, Z. Mi, "Real-Time Instance Segmentation for Low-Cost Mobile Robot Systems Based on Computation Offloading", In *Proceedings of 2021 International Conference on Communications, Computing, Cybersecurity, and Informatics (CCCI)*, 2021.

19. Y. Xie, Y. Guo, Z. Mi, Y. Yang, M. S. Obaidat, "Loosely coupled cloud robotic framework for qos-driven resource allocation-based web service composition", *IEEE Systems Journal*, 14(1):1245–1256, 2020.

20. Y. Guo, Z. Mi, Y. Yang, M. S. Obaidat, "An energy sensitive computation offloading strategy in cloud robotic network based on GA", *IEEE Systems Journal*, 13(3):3513–3523, 2019.

17

IoT-Supported Dynamic Emergency Evacuation: Modelling and Simulation

Jiacun Wang, Jordan Strobing, and Meghan Granit
Monmouth University, New Jersey, USA

17.1 Introduction

In teaching buildings, there must always be a plan for evacuation in the case of an emergency. While a teaching building may have an evacuation plan in place, the decision to choose a route to move out of a building for evacuees may be complicated due to the panic caused by emergency events such as fires and chemical spills. In general, many factors impact this decision-making process. Examples include the architecture and geometry of the building, number of exits and their locations, number of evacuees, and obstacles on the pathway [1–3]. The most commonly used strategy is distance-based, that is, people choose to walk to the nearest exit. This may not work if there is congestion on the pathway. Some people choose the exits that they are familiar with, or simply follow others [4, 5]. Therefore, it is important to develop a more scientific way to guide evacuation flow.

Many researchers have been trying to develop mathematical models for emergency evacuation, with the objective being to optimize evacuation paths and minimize total evacuation time [6–8]. These models can be classified into two groups: macroscopic and microscopic models [9]. Macroscopic models treat the systems as a whole. They study the characteristics of pedestrian movement, congestion, and cluster phenomena [10]. Regression models [11], route choice models [12], queuing models [13], and gas-kinetics models [14] are all macroscopic models. On the other hand, micromodel considers more details on pedestrian movement or human evacuation behaviour in different environments. Notable micromodels include social forces (particle systems) [15], rule-based [16], and cellular automata models [17]. For example, Zhang *et al.* presented evacuation simulations of occupants' flow in a tunnel fire via a modified cellular automaton model and developed corresponding optimized evacuation strategies in [18]. Cao et al. [19] studied the evacuation process from a room without visibility through both experimentation and modelling. Based on the experimental observation, a multi-grid model for evacuation without visibility is built for simulation. Li et al. [20] discussed the evacuation dynamics in an office building by experiment and simulation. A lattice gas (LG) model is developed for simulation of the dynamic process of orderly emergency evacuations.

Many researches focus on applications. For example, Mizuta et al. studied the preparedness of emergency evacuation for the leakage of toxic substances in chemical plants in [21]. A prediction model is designed that considers the wind speed, atmospheric conditions, and the leakage rate. In [22], a Petri Net-based approach to model and evaluate the performance of an evacuation plan related to a condensate storage tank fire scenario has been proposed. Simulation provides an efficient way of testing the safety of a building before construction. Pelechano *et al.* presented a review of crowd simulation models and selected commercial software tools for high-rise building evacuation simulation in [9]. Sheeba et al. [23] presented an analytical model of evacuation on fire

DOI:10.1201/9781003326236-17

using stochastic Petri nets (SPNs), which took into account some practical factors, such as human behaviours, and realistic situations, such as stampede in stairwells.

Petri nets are a powerful mathematical and graphic modelling and analysis tool [24, 25]. Since its inception in 1962 with the publication of Dr. Carl Petri's Ph.D. thesis [26], the Petri net model has been studied and put into application by scholars and industrial practitioners all over the world. Petri nets have been used to solve problems in various discrete event systems, such as manufacturing systems [27], healthcare systems [28], security architecture [29], and traffic control systems [30]. Petri nets have also been used by some researchers in evacuation modelling and simulation, such as the work reported in [22, 23] as discussed earlier. As another example, Danial *et al.* in [31] proposed a model of route learning in a new environment based on landmarks using generalized SPNs. The model considered information about landmarks along a route and associated navigation commands and then decided whether to save this information as part of the learned route or not. Petri nets are simple in concept, easy to learn, flexible to expand, and rigorous to support verifications of various system properties. The graphic representation makes a Petri net model easy to understand. Moreover, the development of timed Petri net models offers a powerful simulation tool for system performance analysis. Zhou *et al.* presented a stochastic timed Petri net-based simulation engine in [32] and applied it to emergency department performance evaluation. In the study by Wang [33], emergency healthcare workflow modelling and timing performance analysis based one-timed Petri nets have been proposed.

The Internet of Things (IoT) is an internet-based technology that integrates physical objects ("things") with sensors, software, and other technologies for the purpose of networking and data exchange. The connected objects can range from ordinary household electrical devices, such as TVs, lights, and robotic vacuums, to sophisticated industrial manufacturing tools, auto-driving vehicles, and power supply equipment. Cloud computing, machine learning, conversational artificial intelligence, and low-cost and low-power sensor access are among the key technologies that support IoT.

In this chapter, we aim to provide a way to decrease the total time spent evacuating a building. We do this by incorporating information technology that directs people to choose the right path during an evacuation. Advances in technology have impacted almost every industry; incorporating technology into the evacuation process helps deal with crowding and reduces evacuation time as a whole. The deployment of IoT in the building under consideration would enable evacuees to choose the most efficient route and, thus, leave the building in the least amount of time. The information collected by various sensors, such as video cameras and smoke detectors, can give a whole picture of the status of the building in a real-time manner. Such kind of data can be processed by dedicated servers in the local area or on the cloud and then be used to navigate the evacuation process. In particular, by instructing people when to change direction, we are able to avoid major crowding within the evacuation route. When there is less crowding within the hallways and exits, we are able to minimize the time it takes for a total evacuation of a teaching building.

We attempt to use IoT technology to dynamically direct evacuees as to which direction they should go when evacuating a teaching building. In practice, the evacuation process has not undergone any major changes in a long time. Adding technological aspects to this process is a change that positively impacts evacuation while providing a familiar feel to the original process. The new evacuation process is straightforward enough that students won't require new training on evacuation. In our study, we prove that IoT-based dynamic emergency evacuation can positively impact the evacuation time of teaching buildings. Every second in an evacuation is precious; even saving a few seconds can potentially save lives. An evacuation is a very high-tension process, our goal in this study is to let technology assist humans in their decision to choose the right route to exit a building quickly and safely.

The rest of the chapter is organized as follows: Section 17.2 briefly introduces Petri nets and timed Petri nets. Section 17.3 gives an overview of the IoT-supported dynamic evacuation. Section 17.4 presents a case study of the modelling and simulation of the dynamic evacuation and analyses the results. Section 17.5 briefly discusses multi-floor building evacuation. Section 17.6 concludes the chapter and explains the future plan of the work.

17.2 Petri Nets

This section introduces some fundamental concepts of Petri nets and timed Petri nets that are used in this study.

17.2.1 Petri Nets

A Petri net is a formal model for discrete event systems. It is a mathematical and graphic model. A Petri net has four types of elements: places, transitions, directed arcs, and tokens. It is formally defined as a 5-tuple $N = (P, T, I, O, M_0)$ where

- $P = \{p_1, p_2, \ldots, p_m\}$ is a finite set of *places*. A place can have *tokens*, which represent objects or conditions.
- $T = \{t_1, t_2, \ldots, t_n\}$ is a finite set of *transitions*. $P \cap T = \phi$ and $P \cup T \neq \phi$.
- $I : P \times T \to N$ defines the multiplicity of directed arcs from places to transitions. If $I(p, t) > 0$, then p is an *input place* of t.
- $O : P \times T \to N$ defines the multiplicity of directed arcs from transitions to places. If $O(p, t) > 0$, then p is an *output place* of t. I and O together specify token flow direction in a Petri net.
- $M_0 : P \to N$ defines the initial token distribution over places, called *initial marking*.

A place is said to be *marked* if it contains one or more tokens. A marking is an assignment of tokens to all places in a Petri net; it defines the *state* of a Petri net. A transition is an active element and can *fire*. When a transition fires, the token distribution over places may change, which results in a new marking or state. A transition can fire only if it is *enabled*. $M(p)$ denotes the number of tokens in p in the marking M. A transition t is enabled if each of its input places p has at least the number of tokens equal to the weight of the directed arc connecting p to t, that is, $M(p) \, \varepsilon \, I(p, t)$. The firing of t removes from each input place p the number of tokens equal to $I(p, t)$, and deposits in each output place p the number of tokens equal to $O(p, t)$. Firing t in M yields a new marking M', which is calculated as $M'(p) = M(p) - I(p, t) + O(p, t)$. $E(M)$ denotes the set of all enabled transitions in M.

Consider the simple Petri net in Figure 17.1(a). It has 4 places and 3 transitions, that is, $P = \{p_1, p_2, p_3, p_4\}$ and $T = \{t_1, t_2, t_3\}$. The initial marking is

$$M_0 = (1, 0, 0, 0).$$

Only t_1 is enabled in M_0. Firing of t_1 results in a new marking, say M_1:

$$M_1 = (0, 1, 1, 0).$$

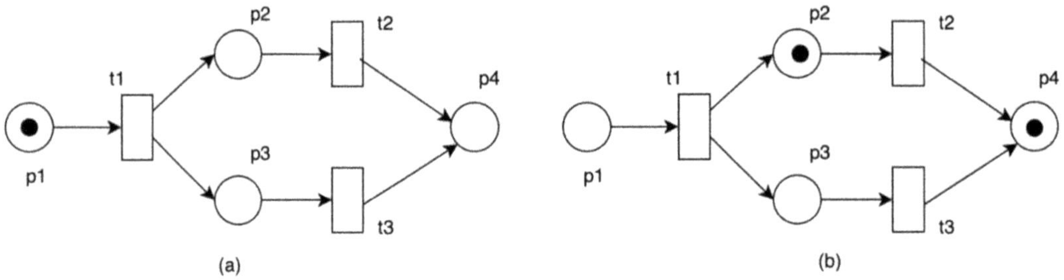

FIGURE 17.1 A simple Petri net and transition firing. (a) Initial marking. (b) The marking after firing t_1 and t_3.

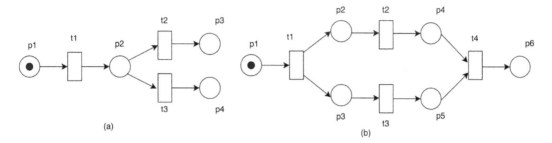

FIGURE 17.2 (a) t_2 and t_3 compete for the token in p_2. (b) t_4 is a synchronization transition.

M_1 enables t_2 and t_3. That is, $E(M_1) = \{t_2, t_3\}$. If t_2 is chosen to fire, the new marking, say M_2, is

$$M_2 = (0, 0, 1, 1).$$

If we fire t_3 instead of t_2 in M_1, we get

$$M_3 = (0, 1, 0, 1).$$

Figure 17.1(b) shows the token distribution after we t_1 and t_3 from the initial marking. Firing t_3 in M_2 or firing t_2 in M_3 will lead to

$$M_4 = (0, 0, 0, 2).$$

This is the final marking of this Petri net, because $E(M_4) = \emptyset$, that is, no transitions are enabled in this marking.

Petri nets can model sequential events, concurrent events, and decision-making or competition. In Figure 17.1(a), the sequence of $t_1 - t_2$ and $t_1 - t_3$ models two sequential events. In Figure 17.2(a), t_2 and t_3 form a *decision set*. They compete for the token in p_2 in order to fire. Firing one disables the other. In Figure 17.2(b), t_4 is a synchronization transition. It cannot fire until both p_4 and p_5 receive a token. It synchronizes the event sequence that injects a token to p_4 and the one that injects a token to p_5.

17.2.2 Stochastic Petri Nets (SPNs) and Generalized Stochastic Petri Nets

The basic Petri nets do not embed the notion of time. However, since in the real world, events always take time to complete, researchers extend Petri nets with event durations, which leads to various types of timed Petri nets. [24, 34]. One can associate time parameters with tokens, places, or transitions. As far as the value of time, it can be fixed or random. In the latter case, it can be uniformly distributed over an interval or following any probability distribution.

SPNs associate exponentially distributed firing time to each transition. Due to the memoryless property of exponential distributions, the marking process in the steady state of a recurrent SPN constitutes a *Markov chain*. Because of that, SPN model-based system performance evaluation becomes relatively easy.

An SPN is a six-tuple $(P, T, I, O, M_0, \Lambda)$, in which

- (P, T, I, O, M_0) is a regular Petri net and
- $\Lambda : T \rightarrow R$ is a set of firing rates whose entry λ is the rate of the individual exponential firing time distribution associated with each transition.

It has been proven that the marking process of an SPN is a continuous time Markov chain (CTMC) [24]. A CTMC is characterized by either a state transition rate diagram or a transition rate matrix, the latter is also called *infinitesimal generator matrix* and is denoted by Q. The state transition rate diagram is a labelled directed graph whose vertices are labelled with the CTMC states and whose arcs are labelled with the rate of the exponential distribution associated with the transition from one state to another. The infinitesimal generator is a matrix whose elements outside the main diagonal are the rates of the exponential distributions associated with the transitions from a state, while the elements on the main diagonal make the sum of the elements of each row equal to zero.

With the infinitesimal generator Q, the steady-state probability vector $\prod$ can be obtained as the solution of

$$\prod Q = 0$$
$$\sum_{i \in S} \pi_i = 1$$

If the state space S is finite, say $S = \{0, 1, \ldots, n - 1\}$, then $\prod$ is a $1 \times n$ vector, while Q is an $n \times n$ matrix. An individual term of $\prod Q = 0$ is given by

$$q_{ii}\pi_i + \sum_{j \in S, j \neq i} q_{ij}\pi_i = 0$$

where

$$\sum_{j \in S} q_{ij} = 0$$

A generalized stochastic Petri net (GSPN) is a special type of SPN, in which *immediate transitions* are introduced [35]. An immediate transition fires in 0 time, that is, when it is enabled and selected to fire, it fires with no delay. All other transitions are *timed transitions* and fire with an exponential delay. Given a marking M, if all transitions in $E(M)$ are timed transitions, and the firing rate of t is r, then the firing probability of t is determined by

$$\Pr(t) = \frac{r}{\sum_{t_j \in E(M)} r_j}$$

If all transitions in $E(M)$ are immediate transitions and a pre-defined probability distribution is defined for all these transitions, the next transition to fire is selected according to this probability distribution. If among enabled transitions there are immediate transitions and timed transitions, then we consider immediate transitions only [34, 35]. Please refer to [36] for how timed transitions and immediate transitions are handled in a real application.

17.3   Proposed Approach

Pedestrian evacuation is often addressed with cellular automata incorporating a floor field model that indicates promising movements to pedestrians. A static floor field represents the shortest path from each cell to an exit (and is usually combined with dynamic measures such as the density or distribution of pedestrians), and a dynamic one represents the fastest path from each cell to an exit [37]. We consider dynamic evacuation, that is, the evacuation path of an evacuee can be changed when it is necessary in case something unexpected happens during the process. This chapter presents an approach that leverages IoT technology to dynamically navigate evacuees during an evacuation process so that they can leave a building as soon as possible. We want to prove that managing which direction to evacuate while the evacuation is live can have a positive impact on the total evacuation time.

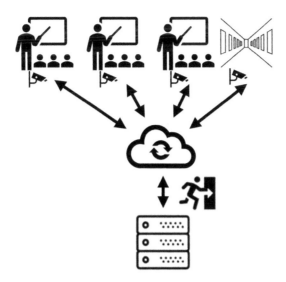

FIGURE 17.3 Illustration of dynamic teaching building evacuation. Sensors collect data (information about objects in each monitored cell) and send it to a server in the cloud periodically. The server performs situation assessment and sends evacuation instructions to evacuees through cellular network.

A key factor of the presented approach is the inclusion of technology at all stages of the evacuation process. The big idea of the approach is illustrated in Figure 17.3. Consider a teaching building in which several classes are in session. Each classroom is packed with teachers and students. When an emergency event such as a fire or chemical spill occurs, they are the evacuees. Assume that all students and teachers have smartphones. Sensors, such as cameras, are installed in each classroom and each section of hallways and stairs monitors object distribution and movement in the entire building. The sensors collect the data periodically and send it to a server in the cloud. The server identifies objects and object movement in the building, performs situation assessments, and calculates the best evacuation plan while notifying evacuees by sending the information to their smartphones. The server evaluates if there is potential crowding in any part of the building that is on the way to the exits. If a crowd is forming or is formed, the server will send a message to instruct evacuees to select their path towards the less-crowded side. By telling the evacuees to go to the less-crowded exit, crowds that delay evacuation are much less likely to occur.

Our original belief was that getting as much real-time information as possible could help us make informed decisions during evacuation time. By incorporating technology into the evacuation process, we are able to make live decisions based on what is going on inside the teaching building. This proved true during our evacuation experiment, as making live decisions significantly decreased evacuation time.

Being able to dynamically change what is happening in an evacuation is the main factor in bringing down evacuation time. It is a very different approach to traditional evacuation. Traditional evacuation gives a set of routes for each classroom. This does not factor in class size nor crowding, making it a static evacuation plan every time, no matter the circumstances.

The IoT-based dynamic evacuation process is modelled and simulated with GSPN, which will be discussed in detail in the next section.

17.4 Modelling and Simulation

We illustrate the modelling and simulation for our dynamic evacuation approach with a case study. We show the floor plan of the building under study first. We used a couple of software tools in the modelling and simulation. Among them, *GreatSPN* is a graphic editor and analyser for timed and

SPNs [38], and also a software package for the modelling, validation, and performance evaluation of distributed systems using STPN models. The tool is developed by the Università di Torino in Italy. The *GreatSPN* GUI is where we created our Petri net models and ran simulations on those models.

In addition to *GreatGPN*, we also used *Dash* and *Plotly*, two Python-based frameworks and libraries. *Dash* allows us to create web applications that can display data in various forms such as graphs. Due to the nature of our research, we accumulated a large amount of data. *Dash* is helpful in managing our data as well as providing us with a way to derive visual representations of our findings. For each test case that we will later explain, we imported the data into dash and created a line graph that shows the number of people evacuating the building over time. We used *Plotly* to graph the data of our simulation results and check for trends. *Plotly* is an extension of the *Dash* tool for data visualization.

17.4.1 Floor Plan of Evacuation Building

In order to depict an accurate representation of an evacuation process, we based our models on the second floor of Howard Hall within Monmouth University. This allowed us to utilize accurate measurements. The section of the building we modelled includes a six-foot-wide hallway with classrooms on each side. One side has two large classrooms with two exit doors each, while the opposite side has three smaller rooms with one exit door each. At each end of the hallway, there is an exit. Since there are two exits, this creates a decision-based evacuation. When walking out of a classroom, some people will choose to go left while others will go to the right. Because people walking out cannot see any exit, whether it is congested or not, they will take a particular exit based on their prior knowledge. Figure 17.4 shows the floor plan. The unit of measurement for each room and the hallway is in feet.

17.4.2 GSPN Modelling

Places are used to model individual regions or cells that people may be in. Each classroom is modelled by a place. For the hallway, we divided it into multiple cells, as illustrated in Figure 17.5. There are 14 cells, and each cell is modelled by a place in a Petri net model. Places $p_{10} - p_{16}$ are for people

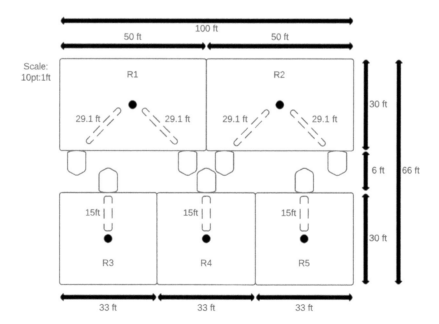

FIGURE 17.4 Floor plan of the teaching building. There are two large rooms (R1 and R2) and three small rooms (R3, R4, and R5). A large room has two doors while a small room has one door.

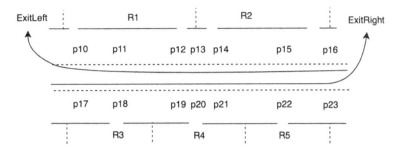

FIGURE 17.5 The hallway. It is divided into 14 cells to indicate where people are. For example, when someone walks out of the leftmost small room R3, if he chooses to turn left towards the left exit, he will be in the cell labelled p_{10}. If he turns right, he will be in the cell labelled p_{18}.

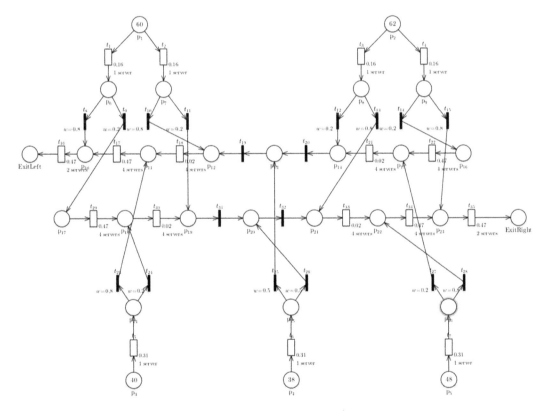

FIGURE 17.6 The Petri net model of the evacuation process. The token distribution indicates that there are 60 people in the classroom R1, 62 people in R2, 40 people in R3, 38 people in R4, and 48 people in R5. Nobody is in the hallway. The transition sequence $t_{16} - t_{22}$ represents people moving to the left exit, while the sequence $t_{29} - t_{35}$ represents people moving to the right exit.

who move towards the left exit, while $p_{17} - p_{23}$ are for people who move towards the tight exit. Take people moving out of the leftmost small room in R3 as an example. When people walk out of the room, they might choose to turn left and walk towards the left exit, or they can turn right and take the exit on the right end of the hallway. If they turn left, they will be an object in the cell marked as p_{10}. They can then continue to walk to the left exit. If they turn right, they will be in the cell marked with p_{18}. Then they move through $p_{19} - p_{23}$ and take the right exit.

The GSPN model that specifies the evacuation movement is shown in Figure 17.6. We will use this model to evaluate multiple evacuation scenarios. The first of which is designed to spread out the

TABLE 17.1

Description of Places in *n* Figure 17.3

Place	Description
p_1	Large classroom R1
p_2	Large classroom R2
p_3	Regular-sized classroom R3
p_4	Regular-sized classroom R4
p_5	Regular-sized classroom R5, has one door
p_6	The left-side door of R1
p_7	The right-side door of R1
p_8	The left-side door of R2
p_9	The right-side door of R2
p_{10}	The leftmost cell of the hallway when evacuating left
p_{11}	The 2nd leftmost cell of the hallway when evacuating left
p_{12}	The 3rd leftmost cell of the hallway when evacuating left
p_{13}	The 4th leftmost cell of the hallway when evacuating left
p_{14}	The 5th leftmost cell of the hallway when evacuating left
p_{15}	The 6th leftmost cell of the hallway when evacuating left
p_{16}	The 7th leftmost cell of the hallway when evacuating left
p_{17}	The 7th rightmost cell of the hallway when evacuating right
p_{18}	The 6th rightmost cell of the hallway when evacuating right
p_{19}	The 5th rightmost cell of the hallway when evacuating right
p_{20}	The 4th rightmost cell of the hallway when evacuating right
p_{21}	The 3rd rightmost cell of the hallway when evacuating right
p_{22}	The 2nd rightmost cell of the hallway when evacuating right
p_{23}	The rightmost cell of the hallway when evacuating right
p_{24}	The door of room R3
p_{25}	The door of room R4
p_{26}	The door of room R5
ExitLeft	The exit on the left-hand side of the hallway
ExitRight	The exit on the right-hand side of the hallway

students as much as possible towards the doors closest to their classrooms. This test case simulates an ideal evacuation where there are no obstacles, and everyone is going to the places they are instructed. Table 17.1 lists places and their descriptions. Table 17.2 lists all transitions in the model and their descriptions. Among the 35 transitions, 17 are timed transitions, and 18 are immediate transitions. Table 17.3 lists the firing rates of all timed transitions and the firing probabilities of all immediate transitions.

The two large classrooms are modelled by p_1 and p_2. The three small classrooms are modelled by p_3, p_4, and p_5. The model works as follows: Consider a student in the large classroom R1 (p_1). They might walk out of the room through the left door (t_1 fires and p_6 gets a token) or the right door (t_2 fires and p_7 gets a token). Assume they take the right door. When they move out of the door, they have the option to turn left (t_{10} fires and p_{12} gets a token) or turn right (t_{11} fires and p_{19} gets token). Assume they turn right. The token in p_{19} triggers the transition t_{31}. Firing of t_{31} injects a token to p_{20} that triggers t_{32}, and then $t_{33}, t_{34,}$ and t_{35}, and eventually the place ExitRight gets a token, meaning this student exited. We can analyse the model for all other evacuation options for an individual in any classroom.

Notice that in the model we use both timed transitions and immediate transitions. Timed transitions are used to model people moving from one cell to another cell. For example, in transitions $t_0 - t_6$ all model people walking out of a classroom, in which t_0 stands for people in the left large

TABLE 17.2

Description of Transitions in *n* Figure 17.3

Transition	Description
t_1	People walk out the classroom R1 through the left door
t_2	People walk out the classroom R1 through the right door
t_3	People walk out the classroom R2 through the left door
t_4	People walk out the classroom R2 through the right door
t_5	People walk out the classroom R3
t_6	People walk out the classroom R4
t_7	People walk out the classroom R5
t_8	Evacuee from the left door of R1 decides to leave towards the left
t_9	Evacuee from the left door of R1 decides to leave towards the right
t_{10}	Evacuee from the right door of R1 decides to leave towards the left
t_{11}	Evacuee from the right door of R1 decides to leave towards the right
t_{12}	Evacuee from the left door of R2 decides to leave towards the left
t_{13}	Evacuee from the left door of R2 decides to leave towards the right
t_{14}	Evacuee from the right door of R2 decides to leave towards the left
t_{15}	Evacuee from the right door of R2 decides to leave towards the right
t_{16}	Heading towards the left exit
t_{17}	Walking through the hallway, en route to the left exit
t_{18}	Walking through the hallway, en route to the left exit
t_{19}	Walking through the hallway, en route to the left exit
t_{20}	Walking through the hallway, en route to the left exit
t_{21}	Walking through the hallway, en route to the left exit
t_{22}	Walking through the hallway, en route to the left exit
t_{23}	Evacuee from room R3 decides to leave towards the left
t_{24}	Evacuee from room R3 decides to leave towards the right
t_{25}	Evacuee from room R4 decides to leave towards the left
t_{26}	Evacuee from room R4 decides to leave towards the right
t_{27}	Evacuee from room R5 decides to leave towards the left
t_{28}	Evacuee from room R5 decides to leave towards the right
t_{29}	Walking through the hallway, en route to the right exit
t_{30}	Walking through the hallway, en route to the right exit
t_{31}	Walking through the hallway, en route to the right exit
t_{32}	Walking through the hallway, en route to the right exit
t_{33}	Walking through the hallway, en route to the right exit
t_{34}	Walking through the hallway, en route to the right exit
t_{35}	Heading towards the left exit

room R1 walking out of the room through the left door, while t_1 stands for people in R1 walking out of the room through the right door. The immediate transitions model the decision to turn left or right. They are also used to model the movement between two cells that are very close to each other. For example, the three cells represented by p_{12}, p_{13} and p_{14} are almost the same area, and thus we ignore the time for evacuees to move among these three cells. This is also the case for cells p_{19}, $p_{20,}$ and p_{21}.

The exponential rate of each timed transition is calculated based on the classroom measurements shown in Figure 17.2. We assume that the average human moves 4.7 feet per second, so that is a key piece of data we used to calculate our rate. The transition firing rate is calculated by dividing 4.7 by the distance. This provides us with a realistic simulation that accurately captures human movement.

TABLE 17.3

Firing Rates of Timed Transitions and Firing Probabilities of Immediate Transitions

Timed Transition	Firing Rate	Immediate Transition	Probability
t_1	0.16	t_8	0.8
t_2	0.16	t_9	0.2
t_3	0.16	t_{10}	0.8
t_4	0.16	t_{11}	0.2
t_5	0.31	t_{12}	0.2
t_6	0.31	t_{13}	0.8
t_7	0.31	t_{14}	0.2
t_{16}	0.47	t_{15}	0.8
t_{17}	0.47	t_{19}	1
t_{18}	0.02	t_{20}	1
t_{21}	0.02	t_{23}	0.8
t_{22}	0.47	t_{24}	0.2
t_{29}	0.47	t_{25}	0.5
t_{30}	0.02	t_{26}	0.5
t_{33}	0.02	t_{27}	0.2
t_{34}	0.47	t_{28}	0.8
t_{35}	0.47	t_{31}	1
		t_{32}	1

An immediate transition's weight, that is, firing probability, is given based on what we thought the perfect evacuation route for each room would be. Table 17.3 lists default transition firing probabilities. The way our immediate transitions work are probabilities that add up to 1. For example, if one door has two exists, 0.8 is assigned to the left and 0.2 is assigned to the right. This means that 80% of tokens will go left while the remaining 20% will go right.

Transitions t_7 and t_8 form a decision set. t_7 models that when someone walks out of the large room R1 from the left door, they choose to turn left and walk towards the left exit. t_8 models that when someone walks out of R1 from the left door, they choose to turn right and walk towards the right exit. We can easily identify other decision sets: $\{t_{10}, t_{11}\}, \{t_{12}, t_{13}\}, \{t_{14}, t_{15}\}, \{t_{23}, t_{24}\}, \{t_{25}, t_{26}\}$, and $\{t_{27}, t_{28}\}$. There are seven such kinds of decision sets. We use α_i and $1 - \alpha_i$ to represent the probabilities of the two transitions in the i-th decision set, $i = 1, 2, \ldots, 7$.

17.4.3   Real-time Congestion Monitoring and Intervention

With the IoT technology in place, we can always get the distribution of evacuees in a building and therefore know if there is and where there is congestion. Based on some algorithms, we can also predict if there will be congestion. If we do foresee congestion, we take preventative action to stop it. In the Petri net model of Figure 17.6, each token represents an evacuee somewhere. For example, the initial marking indicates that there are 60 people in the classroom R1, 62 people in R2, 40 people in R3, 38 people in R4, and 48 people in R5. Nobody is in other places. When the evacuation simulation starts, the token distribution will change, representing people moving; each real-time snapshot of the token distribution is recorded by the marking of the Petri net. Therefore, by examining the marking of the GSPN model, we can analyse the evacuation status and see if intervention is needed to prevent any potential congestion from happening or worsening.

Notice that such a decision-making strategy should be made on a case-by-case basis. That is, the mechanism for the marking analysis and decision for intervention is contingent on the individual system or GSPN model. In general, we need to derive functions $f_i(M)$, such that

$$\alpha_i = f_i(M), i = 1, 2, \ldots, 7$$

This way, based on the current congestion status, we modify α_i and inform more people to move to a less congested exit. As far as the model in Figure 17.6, the total number of tokens in places $p_{10} - p_{16}$ is the number of people moving to the left exit, while the total number of tokens in places $p_{17} - p_{23}$ is the number of people moving to the right exit.

There are two decisions here. One is to decide when we need to adjust α_i. The second decision is how to adjust α_i. A simple way to decide if we need to adjust α_i is calculating the difference between the number of people moving towards each exit and see if it exceeds a threshold. Let

$$N_L = M(p_{10} \cup p_{11} \cup p_{12} \cup p_{13} \cup p_{14} \cup p_{15} \cup p_{16}),$$
$$N_R = M(p_{17} \cup p_{18} \cup p_{19} \cup p_{20} \cup p_{21} \cup p_{22} \cup p_{23}).$$

Denote the threshold of the difference by D. There are three cases. The first case is

$$|N_L - N_R| < D,$$

in which no action will be taken. In the second case,

$$N_L - N_R > D,$$

that is, too many people move to the left exit. We should instruct those who are still in the classrooms to move to the right exit when they walk out of a classroom. Similarly, in the third case,

$$N_R - N_L > D,$$

that is, too many people move to the right exit. We should instruct those who are still in the classrooms to move to the left exit when they walk out of the room. As far as how to adjust α_i, we can consider reducing α_i by a certain percentage in the second case and increasing α_i by a certain percentage in the third case. It is not a good idea to adjust α_i dramatically. We should consider all N_L, N_R, and D. For example, we can set the percentage to

$$D/\max\{N_L, N_R\}.$$

A more reasonable increment can be figured out through experiments.

A second way to decide if we need to adjust α_i is to track the change of N_L and N_R. If one increases much faster than the other, then we need to make an adjustment. The idea behind this is when the number of people moving towards one exit increases too fast, it is very likely a congestion will develop on the way to that exit. One can create an algorithm for this approach.

17.4.4   Simulation and Results

We designed three simulation scenarios to verify the effectiveness of the proposed dynamic evacuation mechanism. Scenario 1 corresponds to the simulation settings listed in Table 17.3. The initial token distribution of the Petri net, which is the initial evacuee distribution in the teaching building, is exactly as shown in Figure 17.6. Upon running the simulation of Scenario 1, we are provided with a near-perfect split of evacuees exiting between the left and right exits. The total evacuation time is 3089 seconds, which is an almost best-case scenario with the amount of people leaving the building. The result of the simulation is shown in Figure 17.7. The blue line represents people who left through the right exit, while the red line represents people who left through the left exit.

The second scenario we simulate is the one in which many more people are in a position to exit towards the right. The token distribution in the initial marking is changed as follows:

$$M(p_1) = 20; M(p_2) = 58; M(p_3) = 5; M(p_4) = 40; M(p_5) = 60.$$

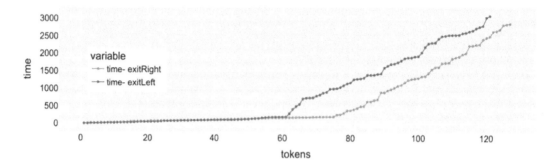

FIGURE 17.7 Result of simulation scenario 1. Evacuees are nearly evenly distributed in each classroom. The number of people who move to the two exits is almost the same. This is the ideal case.

TABLE 17.4

Scenario 2: Adjusted Immediate Transition Parameters

Transition	Probability	Transition	Probability
t_8	0.9	t_{20}	1
t_9	0.1	t_{23}	0.9
t_{10}	0.9	t_{24}	0.1
t_{11}	0.1	t_{25}	0.7
t_{12}	0.5	t_{26}	0.3
t_{13}	0.5	t_{27}	0.2
t_{14}	0.2	t_{28}	0.8
t_{15}	0.8	t_{31}	1
t_{19}	1	t_{32}	1

In this scenario, one side gradually becomes very crowded while the other side is letting people leave with ease. Our goal with this scenario is to direct the remaining evacuees to move towards the side that is less crowded. In our initial simulation, we simply let it run through without any intervention. The final time was 2921.392s to evacuate everyone. With intervention that makes the evacuation process dynamic, we hope that the total evacuation time will be reduced.

To test it out, we run the simulation again and dynamically shift the weights of the evacuees when there is crowding on one side. At time $t = 25$, the immediate transitions' firing probabilities are changed as listed in Table 17.4 to push more evacuees left due to crowding on the right side. At $t = 100$, the crowding is cleared up and the weights are reverted to their original form. By making these slight changes within a 75-second period, there are savings of 671.83 seconds on the total evacuation. That equates to over 11 minutes saved.

Figure 17.8 tracks the simulation result of this scenario in which the process is not intervened. The red plot tracks the evacuees that went through the left exit, while the blue plot tracks the evacuees that went through the right exit. Figure 17.9 shows the result with the dynamic navigation.

The third scenario is a variation of the second one. The number of people in each room is identical; however, the initial probabilities differ (see Table 17.5). With the majority of people being located on the right side of the hallway, this test case explores how sending most of them left will impact the overall evacuation time. The initial token distribution is as follows:

$$M(p_1) = 58; M(p_2) = 12; M(p_3) = 16; M(p_4) = 23; M(p_5) = 7.$$

As shown in Figure 17.10, when running the full simulation without altering any probabilities in the middle, the total evacuation time is 4216.85 seconds. This is a dramatic increase from the results

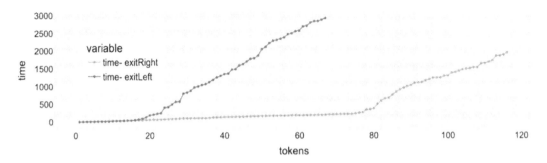

FIGURE 17.8 Simulation result of scenario 2: Static evacuation. The initial distribution of evacuees on the floor is not even and there are many more people on one side of the floor than on the other side. Without intervention, the evacuation takes 2921 seconds to complete.

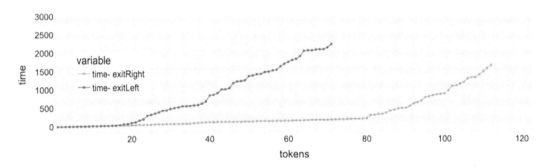

FIGURE 17.9 Simulation result of scenario 2: Dynamic evacuation. Initial evacuee distribution is the same as in Figure 17.8, but then dynamic intervention is adopted. The total evacuation time is reduced by 672 seconds.

TABLE 17.5

Scenario 3: Adjusted Immediate Transition Parameters

Transition	Probability	Transition	Probability
t_8	1	t_{20}	1
t_9	0	t_{23}	1
t_{10}	0.8	t_{24}	0
t_{11}	0.2	t_{25}	0.8
t_{12}	0.7	t_{26}	0.2
t_{13}	0.3	t_{27}	0.2
t_{14}	0.7	t_{28}	0.8
t_{15}	0.3	t_{31}	1
t_{19}	1	t_{32}	1

of test scenario 2. Based on the distribution of initial tokens in the model, it is predictable that the right side will quickly become overcrowded. However, by pushing more people towards the left exit, it ended up overcrowding the left exit. In order to resolve this, we changed the probabilities to $t = 30$ to push people towards the right exit. This resulted in a final evacuation time of 3414.613 seconds, as shown in Figure 17.11. It is a decrease of 802.237 seconds when compared to the static evacuation.

The above simulation results strongly suggest that with a dynamic navigation mechanism in place, we can monitor the evacuation status in real time and alter the evacuation flow in a timely manner if a congestion forms or is predicted to form. This process saves evacuation time.

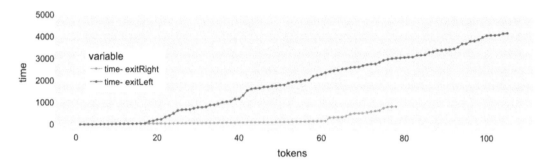

FIGURE 17.10 Simulation result of scenario 3: Static evacuation. The immediate transition probability settings force more evacuees to move to the left exit, which causes congestion on the path. The total evacuation time is 4217 seconds.

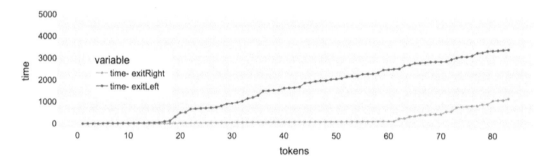

FIGURE 17.11 Simulation result of scenario 3: Dynamic evacuation. Same initial settings as in Figure 17.10, but intervention is taken in the middle of the process, which results in a decrease of evacuation time by 802 seconds.

17.5   Multi-floor Building Evacuation

We also applied the IoT-supported dynamic evacuation approach to multi-floor teaching building evacuation. Consider a building of two floors, for example. The entire GSPN model is composed of the model of the first floor and the model of the second floor, plus the model of stairs that connect the exits of the two floors. To get a sense of the impact of dynamic evacuation on multi-floor buildings, we assume the two floors have the exact same layout, and thus we use the GSPN of Figure 17.6 for each floor. We use a single transition to connect the two places representing the two left exits and another transition to connect the two places representing the two right exits. We measure the length of each stair and calculate the firing rate of the corresponding transition. The simulation parameters for each floor's model are the same as they are in Scenario 3, described in Section 17.4. The results are shown in Figure 17.12. The static evacuation took 4771 seconds, while the dynamic evacuation took 3219 seconds, resulting in savings of 1552 seconds.

17.6   Conclusion

In this study, we leverage the advanced IoT technique in emergency evacuation and propose to use dynamic navigation to help evacuees in the evacuation process and save evacuation time. We examine various evacuation scenarios in a teaching building to determine the effects that dynamic changes would have on final exit times through GSPN-based modelling and simulation. The results of our research support our theory that dynamically changing evacuation routes for individuals in a building would decrease the overall time to exit a building during an emergency, such as a fire

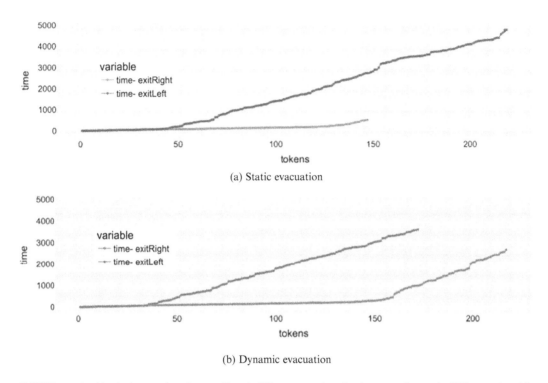

FIGURE 17.12 Simulation results of a two-floor building evacuation. Static evacuation took 4771 seconds, while dynamic evacuation took 3219 seconds. (a) Static evacuation. (b) Dynamic evacuation.

or chemical spill. This is especially important in a teaching building evacuation, as the number of students in each room heavily differs over the course of a day.

The results of our research could lead to enhanced evacuation procedures for teaching buildings of all types. Incorporating technology to make real-time evacuation decisions can help schools get students out of buildings safely in a much quicker timeframe. Since the primary goal of the school is to get students out safely, they might look to enact this approach to ensure the safest outcome in an evacuation.

Our future work will involve testing our evacuation process in hospitals, office buildings, and other types of densely populated buildings. Other potential future work can include incorporating machine learning techniques in capturing any abnormal behaviours with evacuees, such as falling down and special hand gestures from evacuees. For outdoor evacuation such as on streets, we can even use drones to monitor and track evacuation flows and identify traffic jams.

REFERENCES

1. H. Kurdi, A. Almuli, S. Al-Megrenb, and K. Youcef-Toumib, "A balanced evacuation algorithm for facilities with multiple exits." *European Journal of Operational Research*, 26(1), 285–296, 2021.
2. N. Bode, J. Miller, R. O'Gorman, and E. Codling, "Increased costs reduce reciprocal helping behaviour of humans in a virtual evacuation experiment." *Scientific Reports*, 5, 15896, 2015.
3. M. Lee, H. Nam, and C. Jun, "Multiple exits evacuation algorithm for real-time evacuation guidance." *Spatial Information Research*, 25, 261–270, 2017.
4. H. Kurdi, S. Al-Megren, R. Althunyan, and A. Almuli, "Effect of exit placement on evacuation plans." *European Journal of Operational Research*, 269, 749–759, 2018.
5. X. Pan, C. Han, K. Dauber, and K. Law, "Human and social behavior in computational modeling and analysis of egress." *Automation in Construction*, 15, 448–461, 2006.
6. M. Davidich, and G. Koster, "Towards automatics and robust adjustment of human behavioral parameters in a pedestrian stream model to measured data." *Safety Science*, 50, 1253–1260, 2012.

7. T. Dhamala, "A survey on models and algorithms for discrete evacuation planning network problems." *Journal of Industrial and Management Optimization*, 11, 265–289, 2015.
8. M. Yuksel, "Agent-based evacuation modeling with multiple exits using neuroevolution of augmenting topologies." *Advanced Engineering Informatics*, 35, 30–55, 2018.
9. N. Pelechano and A. Malkawi, "Evacuation simulation models: Challenges in modeling high rise building evacuation with cellular automata approaches." *Automation in Construction*, 17, 377–385, 2008.
10. Q. Xiao and J. Li, "Pedestrian evacuation model considering dynamic emotional update in direction perception domain." *Complexity*, 2021, 2021. https://doi.org/10.1155/2021/5530144
11. J.S. Milazzo, N.M. Rouphail, J.E. Hummer, and D.P. Allen, "Effect of pedestrians on the capacity of signalized intersections." *Transportation Research Record* 1646, Transportation Research Board, National Research Council, 1998.
12. S.P. Hoogendoorn, and P.H.L. Bovy, "Pedestrian travel behavior modeling." In: K. Axhausen (Ed.), Moving through nets: The physical and social dimensions of trave, *10th International Conference on Travel Behavior Research*, Lucerne (Switzerland), pp. 1–33, 2003.
13. G.C. Lovas, "Modeling and simulation of pedestrian traffic flow." *Transportation Research B*, 28(6), 429–443, 1994.
14. L.F. Henderson, "The statistics of crowd fluids." *Nature*, 229, pp. 381–383, 1971.
15. D. Helbing, I. Farkas, and T. Vicsek, "Simulating dynamical features of escape panic." *Nature*, 407, pp. 487–490, 2000.
16. C. Reynolds, "Flocks, herds, and schools: A distributed behavior model." *Proceedings of ACM SIGGRAPH '87*, pp. 25–34, 1987.
17. S. Wolfgram, "Statistical mechanics of cellular automata." *Reviews of Modern Physics*, 55, 601–644, 1983.
18. Y. Zhang, W. Li, Y. Rui, S. Wang, H. Zhu, and Z. Yan, "A modified cellular automaton model of pedestrian evacuation in a tunnel fire." *Tunnelling and Underground Space Technology*, 130, 2022. https://doi.org/10.1016/j.tust.2022.104673
19. S. Cao, W. Song, W. Lv, and Z. Fang, "A multi-grid model for pedestrian evacuation in a room without visibility." *Physica A: Statistical Mechanics and its Applications*, 436, 45–61, 2015.
20. X. Li, T. Chen, L. Pan, S. Shen, and H. Yuan, "Lattice gas simulation and experiment study of evacuation dynamics." *Physica A: Statistical Mechanics and its Applications*, 387(22), 5457–5465, 2008.
21. Y. Mizuta, M. Sumino, Y. Kunito, K. Shiota, Y. Izato, and A. Miyake. "Emergency evacuation model assuming leakage of toxic substances in a chemical plant." *Journal of Loss Prevention in the Process Industries*, 68, 104287, 2020.
22. R. Hamzi, F. Innala, M. Bouda, and M. Chati. "Performance assessment of an emergency plan using Petri nets." *Chemical Engineering Transactions*, 32, 235–240, 2013.
23. A. Sheeba Angel, and R. Jayaparvathy. "Performance modeling of an intelligent emergency evacuation system in buildings on accidental fire occurrence." *Safety Science*, 112, 196–205, 2019.
24. J. Wang, *Timed Petri Nets: Theory and Application*, Kluwer Academic Publishers, 1998.
25. J. Wang, and W. Tepfenhart, *Formal Methods in Computer Science*, CRC Press, 2019.
26. C.A. Petri, Kommunikation mit Automaten. Dissertation, Schriften des IIM 2, Rheinisch-Westfälisches Institut für Instrumentelle Mathematik an der Universität Bonn, Bonn, 1962.
27. J. Wang, M. Zhou, and Y. Deng, "Throughput analysis of discrete event systems based on stochastic Petri nets." *International Journal of Intelligent Control and Systems*, 3(3), 343–358, 1999.
28. J. Wang, J. Tian, and R. Sun, "Emergency healthcare resource requirement analysis: A stochastic timed Petri net approach." *IEEE International Conference on Network, Sensing and Control*, Zhuhai, China, March 30–April 2, 2018.
29. Y. Deng, J. Wang, J.J.P. Tsai, and K. Beznosov, "An approach for modeling and analysis of security system architectures." *IEEE Transactions on Knowledge and Data Engineering*, 15(5), 1099–1119, 2003.
30. J. Wang, Y. Deng, and C. Jin, "Performance analysis of traffic control systems based upon stochastic timed Petri net models." *International Journal of Software Engineering and Knowledge Engineering*, 10(6), 735–757, 2000.

31. S. Danial, F. Khan, and B. Veitch, "A Generalized Stochastic Petri Net model of route learning for emergency egress situations." *Engineering Applications of Artificial Intelligence*, 72, 170–182, 2018.
32. J. Zhou, J. Wang, and J. Wang, "A simulation engine for stochastic timed Petri nets and application to emergency healthcare systems." *IEEE/CAA Journal of Automatica Sinica*, 6(4), 969–980, July 2019.
33. J. Wang, "Emergency healthcare workflow modeling and timeliness analysis." *IEEE Transactions on Systems, Man and Cybernetics, Part A*, 42(6), 1323–1331, 2012.
34. M. Ajmone Marsan, G. Balbo, A. Bobbio, G. Chiola, G. Conte, and A. Cumani, "The effect of execution policies on the semantics and analysis of stochastic Petri nets." *IEEE Transactions on Software Engineering*, SE–15(7), 832–846, July 1989.
35. M. Ajmone Marsan, G. Conte, and G. Balbo, "A class of generalized stochastic Petri nets for the performance evaluation of multiprocessor systems." *ACM Transactions on Computer Systems*, 2(2), 93–122, 1984.
36. J. Wang, "Patient flow modeling and optimal staffing for emergency departments: A Petri net approach." *IEEE Transactions on Computational Social Systems*, 10(4), 2022–2032, 2023.
37. S. Galan, "Fast Evacuation Method: Using an effective dynamic floor field based on efficient pedestrian assignment." *Safety Science*, 120, 79–88, 2019.
38. E. Amparore, G. Balbo, M. Beccuti, S. Donatelli, and G. Franceschinis, "30 years of GreatSPN." *Principles of Performance and Reliability Modeling and Evaluation*, 227–254, Springer, 2016.

18

Networking Technologies for IoT

Anastasios Valkanis, Konstantinos Kantelis, Georgia Beletsioti, Vasileios Asteriou, Konstantina Spathi, Athanasios Tsakmakis, Petros Nicopolitidis, and Georgios Papadimitriou
Aristotle University of Thessaloniki, Thessaloniki, Greece

18.1 Introduction

IoT technology was developed with the purpose of transferring a huge amount of information, generated by humans or devices. This information can be used in a large number of applications (smart cities, smart homes, e-health, industrial monitoring), which in turn will help address many problems and challenges that concern modern societies. The cornerstone of IoT technology is networking, which is the interface between the generated information and the application layer. The main requirements in IoT networking are reliability, scalability, and security, which must be combined with high energy efficiency.

The diversity of applications that IoT networks are called upon to serve has led to the creation of many different networking technologies. These technologies in turn can be divided into two broad categories based on the coverage they provide: the Low Power Wide Area Networks (LPWAN) and short-range networks (Figure 18.1). In this chapter, the most important IoT networking technologies are presented and compared. Sections 18.2 and 18.3 offer insights pertaining to the short- and long-range networks, respectively, while a comparative analysis between these communication standards is demonstrated in Section 18.4 in detail. Finally, Section 18.5 refers to a set of the most used IoT application layer protocols, and Section 18.6 concludes the chapter.

18.2 Short-range Networks

For the short-range networking of IoT devices, several technologies are available, each having its own features. Choosing the appropriate one from the available technologies depends on the use case and the required networking specifications. The main factors that determine this choice are the energy consumption of the end devices, the offered range, data transmission rate, security and reliability, and the cost of the network deployment. In this section, the most important short-range communication protocols for IoT will be presented, which include Bluetooth, Zigbee, Z-Wave, Wi-Fi, and mesh networking.

18.2.1 802.15.1 (Bluetooth)

Bluetooth is a wireless communication technology that first appeared in 1999 with V.1, and in the following years it evolved, adapting to new networking requirements. A milestone year for its application in IoT networks was 2010, when Bluetooth low energy (BLE) was developed through V.4, which had energy efficiency as its main goal. The last version of the protocol, V.5, was developed

DOI:10.1201/9781003326236-18

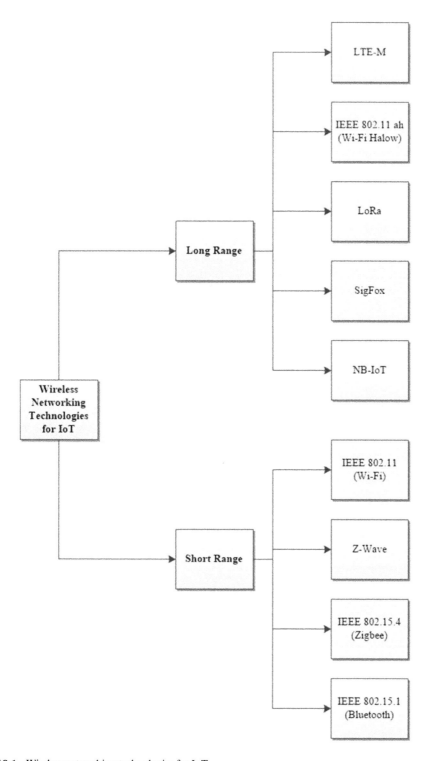

FIGURE 18.1 Wireless networking technologies for IoT.

in 2016 and apart from the improved operating features it featured in relation to its predecessors, it presented the first official specifications for its application in mesh topologies.

The operating band of Bluetooth is the industrial scientific and medical (ISM) from 2.400 to 2.4835 GHz. The 802.15.1 standard of operation is developed and evolved by the Bluetooth Special Interest Group, which defines the operating rules of both the physical and the MAC layers. Bluetooth supports the operation of two basic types of networks: the piconet and the scatternet. Piconet uses a star topology and consists of two to eight nodes, where one of them functions as a master, while the others as slaves. The master node is responsible for the synchronization and operation control of the network, while the communication of nodes is allowed only through the master node, a fact which prohibits direct communication between slave nodes. A scatternet consists of two or more piconets, where a node acts as the bridge between two piconets and can simultaneously be a member of them, as well as having the capability of having multiple roles. A scatternet increases both the number of nodes a Bluetooth network can consist of and its range, while improving the use of available spectrum resources.

The available spectrum is divided into 40 channels of 2 MHz, where 37 of them are used for data transmission and the remaining three for advertising events. The spectral resources are shared between network nodes, which means that a collision between concurrent transmissions can occur. For this reason, the medium access rules are determined by the combination of three well-known techniques. The first one is the time division multiple access (TDMA), where on the available channels fixed time slots of 0.625 msec are allocated to the nodes for data transmission. On the allocated time slots, frequency hopping (FH) is applied, in which a different channel is used by a node in each data transmission. Finally, the time division duplex (TTD) technique is applied where the available time of each time slot is separated and shared between the uplink and downlink.

The improvements of the latest version of Bluetooth are specifically proposed for BLE and include the doubling of the data transmission rate, which reaches 2 Mbps [1]. Another enhancement is the range increasing by applying the Forward Error Correction (FEC) technique, theoretically reaching 500 meters in an outdoor environment. Finally, another important improvement is the increase of the advertising capacity, since it is possible to use all 40 available channels for this purpose.

18.2.2   IEEE 802.15.4 (Zigbee)

Zigbee was developed with the main goal of creating short-range wireless networks that will combine low energy consumption, low complexity, and low operating costs but with low data transmission rate. The Zigbee networks consist of three types of devices: the coordinator and the router, which are characterized as full-function devices (FFD), and the end devices, which are characterized as reduced-function devices (RFC) (Figure 18.2a). The main function of the coordinator is to synchronize the network via beacon frames transmission and to select the network operation parameters such as channel selection and unique network identifier. The router's main function is to forward data between devices in order to extend network coverage. Both coordinators and routers typically are AC-powered because they must stay awake all the time. End devices on the other hand are battery powered, and their main function is to collect and transmit various information from sensors. Moreover, they are not able to relay information through the network, and they can be in a sleep state for energy saving.

The protocol stack of Zigbee consists of four layers, where physical and MAC layers are covered in IEEE 802.15.4 standard, while the network and application layers are covered in specifications published by the Zigbee alliance (Figure 18.2b). The physical layer is responsible for handling various tasks to assist channel selection, such as link quality estimation, energy detection measurement, and clear channel assessment. The available operating frequency bands are three, at 868 MHz with 1 available channel and a data rate of 20 Kbps using Binary Phase Shift Keying (BPSK) modulation, at 915 MHz with 10 available channels and a data rate of 40 Kbps using BPSK modulation and at 2.45 GHz with 16 available channels and a data rate of 250 Kbps using offset quadrature phase-shift

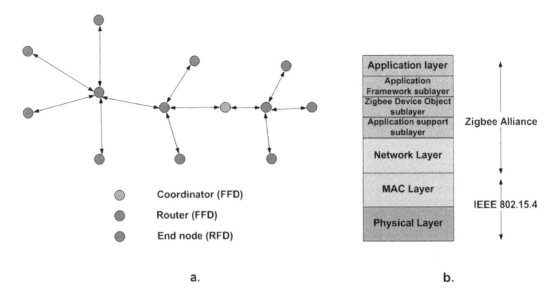

FIGURE 18.2 (a) Zigbee network and (b) Zigbee protocol stack.

keying (O-QPSK) modulation. The MAC layer acts as an interface between the physical and network layers. It uses four frame structures which are Beacon, Data, Acknowledge, and MAC command frame. It supports two methods of accessing the medium: the first one is beacon-initiated, where devices are synchronized and can transmit through contention in predefined time slots, while there is also the capability of contention-free periods through the allocation of guaranteed time slots by the coordinator. The second medium access method is the non-beacon, in which devices are not synchronized, thus there are no contention-free periods and no guaranteed slots. The second medium access method ensures better energy efficiency for end devices since it increases the time that they are in sleep mode, while the first medium access method improves the reliability of the network.

The network layer interfaces the application and MAC layers. Its main function is the formation of the network and the routing of information within it. The used topologies are star, tree, and mesh. The application layer according to the Zigbee specification is divided into three sublayers. The Application Framework sublayer manages the other layers through software that controls the hardware of a Zigbee device; the ZigBee device object sublayer, which is responsible for service discovery, security, and binding; and the Application Support sublayer, which acts as an interface between the network and application layers.

18.2.3 Z-Wave

Z-Wave, which appeared in 1999, is a wireless protocol that essentially focuses on connectivity within the smart home. It constitutes a low-power alternative compared to Wi-Fi but with a much bigger range than Bluetooth. The range of Z-Wave networks can be extended by enabling nodes to forward and relay messages with the help of routing tables. The maximum distance between the origin and the destination node is set to 4 hops by the protocol, so as to satisfy the trade-off between extended range and reliability in the network. The operating band of the Z-Wave device is dependent on the country that it is being used in; the United States uses 908.40, 908.42, and 916 MHz, whereas the UK and Europe use 868.40, 868.42, and 869.85 MHz.

The nodes of a Z-Wave network are divided into three basic categories based on the tasks and functionalities provided to them by the protocol. The first category consists of a single primary controller node, which is responsible for maintaining the routing tables of the network while being provided with the ability to communicate with every node in the network. Other important tasks of the primary controller are to include or exclude nodes in the network, as well as to assign roles (secondary controllers, slaves) and ID to network nodes. Secondary controller nodes have the same functionality as the primary controller node except for the ability to include or exclude nodes from the network. Slave nodes do not maintain routing tables and can act as repeaters provided that they are permanently powered. In case a slave node is battery powered, it is excluded from the central controller in the process of forming the routing table. Depending on the assigned functionality, slave nodes can have different roles within the network such as routing slave, frequently listening routing slave, or enhanced slave.

The protocol stack contains physical, MAC, network, and application layers. The physical layer defines the modulation parameters, with three available schemes, the first and most conservative one providing a transmission data rate of 9.6, the second with 40, and the third most aggressive with 100 Kbps. The medium access mechanism defined by the MAC layer is contention based using collision avoidance and backoff algorithms. It also supports up to 232 nodes per network and low power consumption mode for the nodes. Other functions of the network layer are to ensure the reliability of transmissions through retransmission, acknowledgment, and authentication mechanisms. Also, this layer defines four basic frame types, single cast, acknowledgment, multicast, and broadcast. Finally, the application layer is responsible for decoding and providing some network management functionalities to nodes.

18.2.4 IEEE 802.11 (Wi-Fi)

The Wi-Fi technology, based on the IEEE 802.11 protocols, is the most widespread way of connecting in wireless access networks. The spread of the technology is due both to the simplicity of connection it offers to end-users and devices and to the continuous evolution of the technologies it uses both in the physical and in the MAC layer. This development has allowed the multiplication of the provided transmission rates from the levels of Mbps to those of Gbps, as well as the improvement of reliability, energy efficiency, and provided security adapting to the evolution of the applications it is called to serve.

In IEEE 802.11, a station can be either an access point (AP) or a client which is an end device. A basic service set (BSS) is a group of stations communicating at the physical layer and depending upon the mode of operation can be in Infrastructure mode, where the devices communicate with other devices through APs or ad hoc, where the devices communicate on peer-to-peer basis in an ad hoc manner. Also, there is a capability of connection between BSS, which comprises an extended service set, via a distribution system that connects the APs of BSS.

The IEEE 802.11 consists of two layers: the data link and the physical. The data link layer consists of two sublayers: the link logical control (LLC), which provides an interface to higher layers and performs basic link layer functions such as error control and flow control, and the MAC, which defines two-channel access methods. The first one is the distributed coordination function, which uses the carrier sense multiple access with collision avoidance (CSMA/CA) with binary exponential backoff. CSMA/CA is a "listen before talk" access mechanism and requires an acknowledgment frame for each transmission. The second channel access method is the optional coordination function, where a centralized MAC algorithm provides contention-free service by polling mobile devices in turn. The operation bands of 802.11 are 2.4 and 5 GHz, where the physical layer defines channels of bandwidth up to 160 MHz, the modulation and coding scheme, and other details of transmissions.

The latest amendment of the protocol is the 802.11.ax, also called high efficiency. It mainly deals with the densification problem caused by the massive deployments of Wi-Fi networks, which degrades their overall performance due to cochannel interference between overlapped BSS [2]. The main improvements it offers are the better use of the available spectrum resources through the introduction of the aggressive 1024 QAM modulation, the application of orthogonal frequency division multiple access (OFDMA) technology to establish independently modulating subcarriers, and the use of advanced algorithms and techniques at the MAC layer that improve the spatial reuse of the available spectrum. Finally, in order to improve energy efficiency, the new amendment includes a mechanism for extended sleep states that reduce power consumption of end devices.

18.2.5   Mesh Networking for IoT

The diversity of scenarios that IoT networks are called upon to serve has created a great heterogeneity of technologies that are capable and suitable to serve them. Commonly used topologies are tree and star in which there is a hierarchy for the used devices with predefined roles. For example, there are devices that are responsible for collecting the information, while others forward or process the generated information, thus creating a centralized networking model. However, evolving IoT applications require more complex mesh topologies, which will adapt dynamically depending on the traffic conditions. The same also applies to network devices – they cannot have a predefined role and must serve different tasks on a case-by-case basis. The main advantages of mesh IoT networks are the reduction of installation and maintenance costs, the dynamic distribution of the network load, the increase of robustness to possible failures, and the capability of changing their topology [3].

A key procedure for the operation of IoT mesh networks is routing, which is divided into two categories: proactive and reactive. The main feature of proactive protocols is the use, maintenance, and update of routing tables by each device in the network for every possible route in it. This type of routing protocol is more suitable for small networks due to the limitation on the size of the routing tables. Reactive protocols, on the other hand, do not create routing tables proactively, as they only create routes after specific requests. Routing in this case includes both route discovery and route maintenance and is based on flooding.

The optimized link state routing (OLSR) is a proactive routing protocol. Its operation is based on periodic updates from all network nodes about the link status with neighboring nodes in order to maintain routing tables. The main flooding strategy is the assignment of topology control messages forwarding to specific neighbor nodes called multipoint relays (MPR), thereby minimizing unnecessary transmissions from the flooding process. The selection of 1-hop MPR nodes by the algorithm is done in such a way as to ensure the coverage of all neighboring 2-hop nodes. Figure 18.3 shows the MPR-selected nodes from node A to relay the topology control messages.

Dynamic source routing (DSR) is a reactive protocol whose operation is on a demand basis. Its function allows the distributed operation of the network without the need to maintain routing tables by the intermediate nodes that forward the packets. It uses the source routing technique, which does not require periodic routing advertisement. The protocol has two main functions. The first one is route discovery, which is initiated when a node does not have the route to the destination node in its

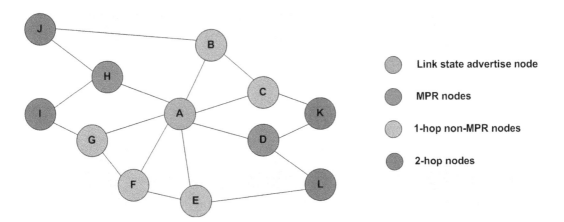

FIGURE 18.3   Selection of multipoint relay nodes by the optimized link state routing protocol.

cache. The second function of the protocol is route maintenance, which is activated when a route to a destination node is available in cache but is not valid anymore.

18.3 Long-range Networks

Low Power Wide Area Networks are wireless networks designed with a focus on Machine Type Communications (MTC) specifically for IoT, which means prioritizing low-cost, high-energy efficiency, and long communications range, at the expense of lower bandwidth. Most networks that are widely categorized as LPWANs across the literature have converged on some fundamental technical requirements that set this class of network apart from other networking technologies. The most important LPWAN requirements are [4]:

- *Energy Efficiency:* Given the need for massive IoT device deployments, often without access to a constant power source, LPWAN devices must support a target battery life in the order of ten years.
- *Range:* The target range for LPWANs spans from a few kilometers in urban areas to up to a few tens of kilometers for rural areas.
- *Scalability:* LPWAN networks must support large numbers of devices, in the order of at least a few tens of thousands of devices per base station.
- *Low Cost:* In order for the above range and scalability requirements to make economic sense, the deployment cost of an LPWAN network and its application must be kept sufficiently low. The target cost for an individual LPWAN device must be up to a few USD, while annual fees should not exceed 1 USD.

Some networks, especially cellular IoT networks, use licensed spectrum, while others use ISM bands for communications, highlighting the need for interference management. To reduce the impact of channel noise and interference, two main modulation approaches are employed: narrow band and spread spectrum. Common technical approaches across many LPWANs, but not all, are network operation over sub-GHz bands, to increase range at the expense of data rate, and extended periods in sleep mode for devices, to achieve long device lifetimes.

The general architecture of a long-range IoT network comprises a series of base station antennas that are connected to the core network servers and provide coverage to the IoT devices. Thus, the base stations relay messages between the devices and the core network, and no direct communication between IoT devices is required. The core network is then responsible for handling communication between the network's IoT devices and the various IoT applications and users. This architecture is illustrated in Figure 18.4.

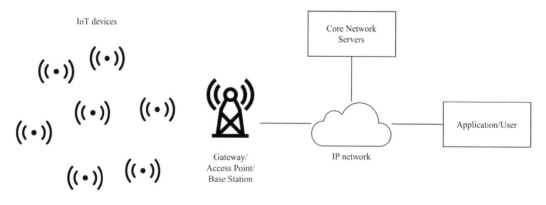

FIGURE 18.4   General architecture of a long-range IoT network.

18.3.1   IEEE 802.11ah (Wi-Fi HaLow)

The IEEE 802.11ah standard, also referred to as Wi-Fi HaLow, is a sub-GHz specification of Wi-Fi for IoT applications. In contrast to traditional Wi-Fi, the design objectives of Wi-Fi HaLow are low power consumption, higher node density, and higher range. Wi-Fi HaLow networks follow a star/tree architecture with a central AP, which acts as a gateway and with which the stations associate. In order to increase coverage, 802.11ah supports the use of relay nodes, which associate with the central root AP, and act as an AP themselves for other stations.

In the physical layer, IEEE 802.11ah uses OFDM. It operates in the sub-GHz ISM bands, while channel bandwidth varies from 1 to 16 MHz, allowing coverage of up to 1 km while being more energy efficient than conventional Wi-Fi. A diverse set of modulation schemes are specified in the standard, allowing flexibility in the data rate achieved, which ranges from 0.3 to about 230 Mbit/s. Thus, compared to other LPWANs, Wi-Fi HaLow achieves a higher data rate and a smaller range.

In the MAC layer, several adjustments to the CSMA/CA-based Wi-Fi protocol are introduced to enable large device numbers and energy-efficient operation. As in other Wi-Fi standards, network information is broadcast to active and potential devices using periodic beacons. Several optimizations aim to reduce overhead with shorter header lengths [5].

To reduce collisions in the association phase, two fast authentication schemes are defined: Centralized Authentication Control, where devices are randomly excluded from the association procedure until contention reduces, and Distributed Authentication Control, which is a backoff scheme. To manage collisions in dense deployments, the Restricted Access Window (RAW) is introduced, a limited contention protocol, illustrated in Figure 18.5. In this protocol, devices are grouped and airtime is divided into intervals, some of which may be reserved for specific groups. During reserved intervals, only stations in the corresponding group may contend for the channel, while the intervals are slotted and slots are assigned to stations in a round-robin – but not collision-free – way, based on their network ID [6].

The traffic indication map (TIM) mechanism is a method in IEEE 802.11 for advertising pending downlink traffic to the associated stations by transmitting a bitmap in the beacon frame. In Wi-Fi HaLow, a modification named TIM segmentation is introduced, in which the bitmap is sent in segments, reducing beacon duration, and allowing stations to skip multiple beacon receptions. Another method for enhanced power saving is the Target Wake Time method, in which the AP and the station negotiate extended sleeping periods, during which no reception of event the beacon frame is required. Another feature, aiming to manage overlap in the range of neighboring access points, is BSS coloring, where receptions from the wrong access point are terminated early.

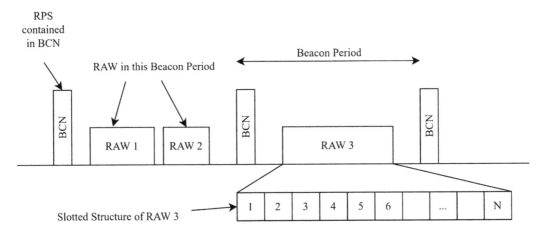

FIGURE 18.5   Example of the Restricted Access Window (RAW) protocol. The beacon frame (BCN) carries the RAW Parameter Set (RPS), which specifies the timing and corresponding group information for each RAW in the following Beacon Period. In each RAW, only the group of devices in the corresponding group can access the channel. Each RAW is slotted, and the slots are assigned evenly and pseudorandomly to devices in the corresponding group.

18.3.2   LTE-M and NB-IoT

The objective of Cellular IoT (CIoT) networks is to support IoT use cases, sometimes termed massive machine type communication (mMTC) in this context, over existing or new mobile network deployments. Requirements for mMTC have been a part of ITU's fifth generation mobile network vision since 2015 and CIoT technologies have been proposed and standardized by the 3GPP since Release 13 in 2015. The main challenge in CIoT is the support of IoT requirements in cost-effective ways that can be deployed on existing networks as well as in upcoming fifth-generation network deployments. The most important CIoT standards are LTE-M (also known as eMTC – enhanced MTC) and NB-IoT, both first standardized in 3GPP Release 13 and refined in later versions. The vision for these standards is for them to evolve in order to eventually satisfy the mMTC requirements laid by the ITU [4].

Two specifications that are important for achieving low power consumption are power saving mode (PSM) and enhanced discontinuous reception (eDRX), introduced in Releases 12 and 13, respectively. In PSM, the user equipment (UE) is allowed to enter deep sleep mode without losing its network registration, thus reducing power consumption as well as the overhead needed for re-connection to the network. In discontinuous reception (DRX) the UE, instead of listening continuously for paging signaling, only listens to it periodically and with increasing periodicity of up to about 10 s. In eDRX, this periodicity is extended further to up to a few hours.

NB-IoT is a long-range low-power networking standard based on a modified version of the LTE architecture. First introduced in Release 13, it removes several LTE core network features unnecessary for IoT, limits modulation techniques to QPSK and BPSK, and uses optimized signaling procedures while limiting uplink data rates to up to 158 kbps. A new lower hardware complexity and lower cost UE category, Cat-NB1 is defined. NB-IoT features three deployment modes, shown in Figure 18.6: in band, in which an LTE resource block is allocated for Cat-NB1 devices, guard band, in which spectrum is allocated for NB-IoT in LTE guard bands, and standalone, in which NB-IoT spectrum is allocated entirely independently of LTE spectrum. This last mode is intended for use in reclaimed 2G and 3G carriers. Release 14 introduced features such as a reduced transmission power class of 14 dBm (compared to the previous 20 and 23 dBm classes), enhanced positioning, the capability for multicast downlinks, and improved throughput, as well as a new UE category, Cat-NB2. Release 15 improvements include a wake-up mechanism, support for operation alongside 5G new radio (NR) and LTE-M – which is important for long-term deployment viability, and several other optimizations. Releases 16 and 17 have introduced further enhancements and protocol optimizations for improving throughput and power consumption [7, 8].

LTE-M aims towards higher performance IoT applications, with broadband-like network access requirements and supporting a smaller number of devices. Thus, it offers a complementary proposition to NB-IoT and other LPWANs, rather than a competitive one, while being backward compatible with LTE. It was first introduced in Release 13, which introduced UE Cat-M1, and featured positioning, and voice and video streaming capability, with a peak data rate of 1 Mbps. Release 14 introduced further energy optimizations and multicast capability, and defined UE Cat-M2, which can reach uplink data rates up to 7 Mbps.

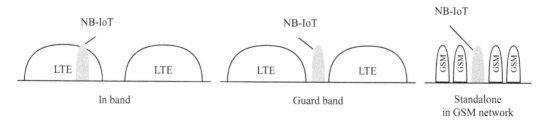

FIGURE 18.6   Illustration of NB-IoT deployment modes. In this example, the standalone deployment is assumed to utilize reclaimed GSM spectrum.

Another 3GPP specification targeting IoT applications is EC-GSM-IoT. This standard allows the provisioning of IoT connectivity services using existing GSM and GPRS mobile network deployments. Technical features of EC-GSM-IoT include a link budget increase of 20 dB, as well as PSM and eDRX, while data rates range from 0.35 up to 70 kbps for GMSK modulation and up to 240 kbps for 8PSK modulation.

18.3.3 LoRaWAN

LoRaWAN is an LPWAN standard developed by the LoRa Alliance. It is a star-of-stars network, with three types of devices: the network server, which is the network core backend connected to the Internet; the end devices, which are sensor/actuator IoT devices; and the gateways, which are BSs that relay traffic between the end devices and the network server. Although it uses the proprietary LoRa modulation on the physical layer, the networking architecture and the upper layers are open standards. The network operates in the sub-GHz ISM bands, on different frequencies in different regulatory regions. Due to the open nature of the LoRaWAN standard and the use of ISM bands, LoRaWAN can be deployed both as a public network service and as a private network [9].

In the physical layer, LoRaWAN uses LoRa modulation, a chirp spread spectrum scheme, and FSK modulation for higher data rates. A physical layer parameter, the spreading factor, controls the data rate and transmission duration trade-off, allowing extended coverage at the expense of higher power consumption. LoRaWAN operates on sub-GHz ISM bands, over 125, 250, and 500 kHz channels. A LoRaWAN gateway can achieve coverage of up to 5 km in urban areas, and there are reported coverages of up to 45 km in rural areas. The transmission data rate ranges from 0.3 to 37.5 kbps using LoRa and 50 kbps using FSK.

In the MAC layer, LoRaWAN supports three device classes, visualized in Figure 18.7. In Class A, which is the most energy efficient, devices transmit uplink data using random access in the TX window. Downlink frames may be received only on two reception windows (RX1, RX2) that the device opens after every uplink. Thus, in this case, a device can receive a message from the server only after transmitting an uplink message itself. In Class B, the devices synchronize with the network with the help of periodic beacon frames (BCN frame in Figure 18.7), and additional downlink reception windows (class B RX windows) open on ping slots at pseudorandom offsets from the beacon. This alleviates the above-mentioned downlink reception restriction of class A. In Class C, the device receiver is always on.

18.3.4 SigFox

SigFox is a proprietary LPWAN standard developed and operated by SigFox Corporation. The system features the IoT devices, the BSs, and the core network. The BSs are placed in the coverage area and connected to the core network through the Internet. The devices, after associating with the core network through a Registration Authority, can exchange small data frames with the core network Service Center through the BSs. The Service Center then exposes data and control functionality of the devices to customers.

SigFox features a number of design characteristics to support reduced energy consumption while achieving long range. At the physical level, the network operates in the sub-GHz unlicensed ISM bands. Communications take place over Ultra Narrow Band (UNB) channels of 100 Hz or 600 Hz, reducing the impact of white noise, while also reducing the data rate to 100 or 600 bps and increasing

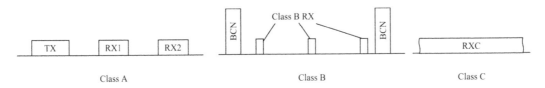

FIGURE 18.7 Illustration of LoRaWAN channel access modes for each device class.

transmission duration to 2s, and increasing the number of channels in a frequency band. Differential Binary Phase Shift Keying (D-BPSK) and Gaussian Frequency Shift Keying (GFSK) modulation are used, reducing hardware complexity.

At the MAC layer, the access method is random access based. No synchronization option is available. To increase network reliability, each frame is transmitted three times on randomly selected channels and time offsets, and it is received by multiple BSs whose receptions are used to reconstruct the original transmission. This strategy is termed time, frequency, and spatial diversity, respectively. Communication may be either unidirectional or bidirectional. Bidirectional communication happens only after uplink transmissions, on a reception window that opens at a predefined delay after the uplink. During that window, a downlink frame is received and then acknowledged by the device. Due to the combination of the UNB physical layer and the MAC layer diversity strategies, Sigfox base stations can achieve coverage of up to 10 km in urban areas and up to 50 km in rural areas [10].

18.4   Comparative Analysis

The correct choice of technology used in the IoT realm is crucial and challenging. Even though there are already deployed numerous wireless technologies that are based on similar principles and can fit the IoT concept, each of them has its own characteristics, advantages, and disadvantages. Thus, not all wireless technologies are suitable for all IoT applications. This section compares the short-range as well as long-range network technologies introduced and discussed in Sections 18.2 and 18.3, respectively, in terms of latency, energy consumption, cost, QoS, etc. In what follows, a comparison between the wireless technologies is made, while the appropriate wireless technology for a specific IoT application field is determined afterward.

The main characteristics of the short- as well as the long-range network technologies are shown in Table 18.1. Regarding short-range network technologies, Wi-Fi, which provides short-range coverage, was originally designed to offer high throughput to a small number of devices without special requirements in terms of energy consumption. These devices are mostly located indoors at short distances. Thus, Wi-Fi, with its variants, is not especially suitable for all IoT applications, especially for those that require low power and/or long-distance coverage. Therefore, to meet the low-power IoT requirements, technologies, and standards such as BLE, an enhancement to the classical Bluetooth, ZigBee, and Z-Wave has been introduced in the market. BLE and ZigBee for example

TABLE 18.1

Key Characteristics of Short/Long-Range Networks

Technology	Frequency	Range	Data Rate	Encryption	Modulation	Power	Network size
Bluetooth	2.4 GHz	10–100 m	1 Mbps	AES	GPSK	30 mA	Unlimited
ZigBee	2.4 GHz	10–100 m	250 kbps	AES	BPSK	30 mA	127
Z-Wave	~900 MHz	30–100 m	40–100 kbps	AES	BFSK	2.5 mA	232+
Wi-Fi	2.4 GHz, 5 and 6 GHz	<200 m	600 Mbps	AES	BPSK	High	255
Wi-Fi HaLow	~900 MHz	<1.5 km	150 kbps–346 Mbps	WPA	QPSK	Low	8000 devices supported
NB-IoT	Many	~10 km	200 kbps	LTE Encryption	QPSK	20/23 dBm	>100.000 devices supported
LoRaWAN	Many	1–10 km	0.3–50 kbps	AES	GFSK	20 dBm	>100.000 devices supported
SigFox	862–928 MHz	3–50 km	100–600 bps	Not built in	GFSK	13.5 dBm	>1.000.000 devices supported

TABLE 18.2

Comparison of Sigfox, NB-IoT, and LoRaWAN

	SigFox	LoRaWAN	NB-IoT
Scalability	2/5	3/5	5/5
Range	5/5	4/5	2/5
Coverage	5/5	4/5	1/5
Deployment	4/5	5/5	1/5
Cost efficiency	5/5	5/5	2/5
Battery life	5/5	5/5	3/5
QoS	2/5	2/5	5/5
Payload length	1/5	2/5	5/5
Latency performance	1/5	3/5	5/5

are low-cost technologies that consume considerably lower amounts of power, compared to Wi-FI, yet covering smaller distances between the devices, only up to 100 meters. In terms of data rate, BLE, Z-Wave, and ZigBee are limited to speeds lower than 1 Mbps rendering them appropriate technologies for applications using devices that have small bandwidth requirements and minimal traffic. Accordingly, for IoT applications, such as home automation, that require the deployment of fewer nodes with heavy traffic, WiFi 802.11 family appears to be the most suitable candidate. According to [11], ZigBee can support a large-scale network with many network devices (up to several hundreds), while on the contrary, Wi-Fi and BLE support a medium and a small number of devices, respectively.

Several IoT application scenarios require sending their data over long distances, a characteristic that cannot be served by the abovementioned short-range technologies. In order to overcome these constraints, Low Power Wide Area Network technology has been introduced. Numerous parameters can be used to compare LPWAN technology, and some of them are presented below to highlight which technology is superior, as also visually seen in Table 18.2 [12].

QoS: Quality of service is not provided by Sigfox or LoRaWAN. NB-IoT uses a licensed spectrum and an LTE-based synchronous protocol that is optimized for QoS at the expense of cost. Because of the QoS and cost trade-off, NB-IoT is preferable for applications that require guaranteed quality of service, whereas LoRaWAN or Sigfox should be used for applications that do not have this constraint. IEEE 802.11ah provides a medium-level QoS.

Battery life: End devices in Sigfox, LoRaWAN, and NB-IoT are in sleep mode for as long as the application requires, reducing the amount of energy spent as much as feasible. NB-IoT devices present increased energy consumption due to the need for synchronization, QoS processing, and OFDM/FDMA access using modes. When compared to Sigfox and LoRaWAN, the higher energy consumption reduces the NB-IoT end-device lifetime.

Latency: NB-IoT connectivity offers minimal IoT latency, while LoRaWAN class C devices also offer low bidirectional latency at the cost of high energy consumption. On the contrary, Sigfox and LoRaWAN class A devices show increased latency and are not recommended for IoT applications where low latency is required.

Cost and Scalability: When compared to NB-IoT, Sigfox and LoRaWAN have a cost advantage. One of the important advantages of Sigfox, LoRaWAN, and NB-IoT is their ability to support thousands of end devices. These cellular LPWANs provide a great degree of scalability. However, NB-IoT has far higher scalability than Sigfox and LoRaWAN since it can support more than 100K devices per base station.

18.4.1 Application Examples

The IoT realm covers a wide range of applications and devices. Which technology fits the best for a given application depends on the IoT application characteristics as well as the technological distinctions between the abovementioned wireless communication technologies, proving that there is not a single, universally effective communication standard for all applications. Thus, each solution is better suited for specific IoT use cases since it has varied strengths and limitations in terms of various network requirements. Smart meters and agricultural sensors, for example, have tiny payloads and infrequent message transmission requirements that LoRa can meet. NB-IoT, on the other hand, is better suited for public safety or ride-sharing apps that require frequent broadcasts of large payloads and mobility assistance. In what follows several application use cases are discussed, providing an overview of the technologies that are suitable in each application scenario [12–14].

IoT applications with high data-rate requirements such as streaming video are mostly supported by LTE and/ or Wi-Fi, while medium data-rate (smart home) and low data-rate (monitoring sensors) applications are accommodated by ZigBee, BLE, and LTE-M as well as LPWAN technologies, respectively. Wi-Fi, for example, is 20 to 30 times faster than BLE, making it a better alternative for large file transmissions. Pertaining to the latency, delay-sensitive applications, such as autonomous vehicles and health-care systems are best suited for Wi-Fi, BLE, Wi-FI HaLow, ZigBee, and LTE-M, while for delay-tolerant applications SigFox, NB-IoT, and LoRa technologies are better choices.

Furthermore, Bluetooth is the ideal choice for personal IoT devices such as fitness wearables and trackers. Bluetooth's capacity to continually broadcast massive volumes of data has long made it popular in the consumer electronics industry. Furthermore, BLE was created expressly for low-power IoT devices. Because the devices are designed to support sleep mode, BLE is best suited for devices that transfer low volumes of data in bursts.

On the other hand, mesh technologies are ideal for in-house applications and adjacent projects such as smart lighting, security systems, HVAC systems, and remote controls. ZigBee and Z-Wave which are able to use mesh topologies, transmit small packets over short to medium distances using a network of interconnected nodes.

Companies in electric metering application field often require frequent communication, low latency, and a large data rate. As electric meters provide a continuous power source, they do not require low energy usage or a lengthy battery life. Furthermore, enterprises want real-time grid monitoring in order to drive a time-critical decision mechanism. As a result, Sigfox presents high latency and is not the proper selection for time-sensitive applications. Electric meters, on the other hand, can be hooked up using LoRaWAN Class-C to ensure continuous observation. However, NB-IoT is the best choice for this kind of application, since it offers continuous and high data rate connectivity.

The battery life of sensor devices is very important in agricultural IoT applications. The use of critical information produced by sensors such as temperature, humidity, and alkalinity in order to adjust water supply could affect the yield. Because the environmental conditions have not altered significantly, devices sparsely update sensed data. As a result, Sigfox and LoRaWAN are excellent choices for agricultural applications. Furthermore, since many farms are not connected to LTE cellular service, the NB-IoT cloud will not be an agriculture option in the future.

Real-time machinery monitoring adjusts the operation parameters of industrial production lines and enables remote control for increased efficiency. In factory automation, the proper selection of IoT technology is dependent on the use-case requirements. NB-IoT performs better than Sigfox and LoRaWAN in applications where there is a demand for frequent communication and good service quality. Sigfox and LoRaWAN are a better fit than NB-IoT in applications that require low cost and energy efficiency such as asset tracking and status monitoring. Another option due to the diversity of requirements could be hybrid solutions.

Temperature, humidity, security, water flow, and electric outlet sensors alert property managers to prevent damage and respond to requests promptly without having to physically monitor the building. Building cleanliness and utilization could also be improved. These sensors necessitate a cheap cost and a long battery life. Because they do not demand high service quality or frequent communication, Sigfox and LoRaWAN are better suited for this type of application.

Sales point systems necessitate guaranteed quality of service because they manage regular communication. Because these devices use a constant electrical power supply, battery life is not limited.

There is also a major necessity for low latency (due to the fact that extended latency times limit the number of transactions that a store may make). As a result, NB-IoT is a superior match for this application.

18.5   Application Layer

Three-level architecture, containing the perception, network, and application layers, constitutes the most common architecture for IoT technology. In general, the perception layer represents the physical objects that are responsible for acquiring the appropriate information from the environment they are deployed, the network layer administers the transportation of data provided by the perception layer to the application layer, and finally, the application layer which includes all the necessary software to offer specific services, while determining a set of protocols for message passing at the application level. A set of the most used application layer protocols are discussed in this section.

18.5.1   Constrained Application Protocol (CoAP)

Constrained Application Protocol (CoAP) is a web transfer protocol designed specifically for small, constrained devices with low capability in RAM or CPU as well as constrained networks (i.e., low power, low data rate/throughput, high packet loss networks). CoAP is a request/response protocol similar to the client/server model of HTTP. Except for the lightweight nature of the protocol, which constitutes its main advantage, it supports unicast and multicast requests by taking advantage of UDP, while providing the capacity of asynchronous message exchanges [15]. Moreover, along with the low header overhead and parsing complexity, it also allows simple proxy and caching capabilities.

In general, a CoAP request is sent by a client to request an action, using a Method Code, on a resource (identified by a URI) on a server. Then, the server sends a response with a Response Code (Figure 18.8). CoAP is divided into two layers, namely the messaging and the request/response sub-layers, respectively, while its standard defines four types of messages: Confirmable, Non-confirmable, Acknowledgment, and Reset. Confirmable and Non-confirmable messages carry requests as well as responses, while the latter can also be piggybacked in Acknowledgment messages.

The lowest layer of CoAP deals with exchanging messages between endpoints using UDP. Each message, which can be either a Confirmable (CON) message or a Non-confirmable (NON) one, contains a unique ID to prevent message duplications. A CON message is a reliable message ensuring that the message will arrive at the server point. This confirmation is administered by the recipient of the initial message by sending an acknowledge message (ACK). Should one party have difficulties managing the incoming request, it can send back a Reset (RST) message instead of an ACK. In case of a NON message, no further actions are required from the receiver side. The upper layer of CoAP takes care of CON and NON messages requests. Acceptance of these requests depends on the server's availability. If the server can answer a CON request immediately, then he sends back an ACK

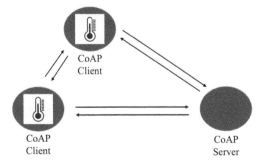

FIGURE 18.8   CoAP operation.

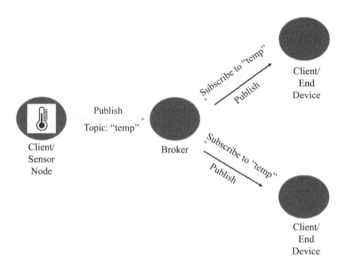

FIGURE 18.9 MQTT operation.

containing the response (piggybacked message). Otherwise, the server sends back an ACK with an empty response message. As soon as the response is available, the server sends back to the client a new CON message containing the response. In this scenario, the client sends an ACK message to the server. In case the request from the client uses a NON message request, then the server answers with a NON message response too.

18.5.2   Message Queue Telemetry Transport (MQTT)

Message Queue Telemetry Transport is a lightweight publish/subscribe message transport protocol, similar to the client/server model. It is designed for connecting remote devices with resource constraints and minimal network bandwidth, a feature that renders it ideal for IoT technology, while it is open, simple, and easy to implement.

MQTT communication, which uses TCP as a transport protocol and SSL/TLS for security, works using a publish/subscribe system, in which clients can publish messages on a specific topic and in turn all clients that are subscribed to that topic can receive the message (Figure 18.9) [16]. Except for the clients, the MQTT protocol defines one more network entity, namely the broker (or the server). The broker is responsible for orchestrating the communication between all the clients subscribed to the system. Clients can be either a subscriber or a publisher. In general, a publisher sends a message to the broker when he has an update or a periodic message, then the broker filters the incoming messages and distributes them accordingly to the correct subscribers. MQTT consists of 14 message types, with four of them used by the clients (CONNECT, PUBLISH, SUBSCRIBE, and UNSUBSCRIBE), while all the other types are used for internal mechanisms and message flows. According to reliability requirements and needs of each transmission, the MQTT determines three levels (0, 1, and 2) of Quality of Service (QoS).

18.5.3   Advanced Message Queuing Protocol (AMQP)

AMQP is a publish/subscribe model that relies on a dependable and efficient messaging queue. OASIS is in charge of standardization. AMQP is now widely utilized in commercial and business systems. The main advantage of the protocol is the offered scalability due to the used publish/subscribe method. AMQP also supports interoperability and heterogeneity between devices that support several communications languages. Messages can be exchanged between AMQP protocol applications. To accomplish reliability, security, and performance, the AMQP protocol defines a set of three message delivery guarantees: at most once, at least once, and exactly once.

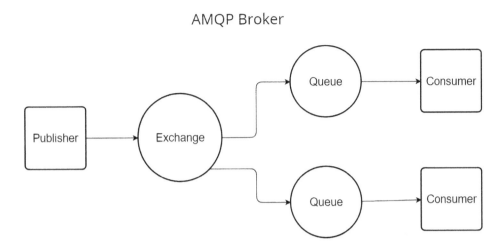

FIGURE 18.10 AMQP operation.

To ensure reliability, this protocol additionally employs a TCP transport layer. AMQP's publish/subscribe technique is made up of two parts: an exchange queue and a message queue (Figure 18.10). The exchange queue is in charge of routing messages to the appropriate order in the queue. Messages are stored in the message queue until they are transmitted to the receiver. To exchange messages between exchange components and message queues, a specialized method with a set of rules is used.

This protocol is extremely extensible and interoperable across platforms and environments; it is well suited to industrial environment applications. However, it is not ideal for limited environments or real-time applications, and it lacks an automation discovery mechanism.

18.5.4 Extensive Messaging and Presence Protocol (XMPP)

The IETF standardized the Extensible Messaging and Presence Protocol (XMPP), which is now one of the most common communication and messaging protocols in IoT. XMPP is a collection of open technologies that enable instant messaging, presence, multi-party chat, phone and video conversations, collaboration, lightweight middleware, content syndication, and generalized XML data routing.

This is a well-known protocol that was widely utilized in all networks. The XMPP protocol can satisfy IoT needs since it enables tiny messages, provides security, and has minimal latency; these properties make the XMPP protocol a strong choice for IoT communications and messaging. The decentralized nature of XMPP allows for high scalability. The XMPP protocol has various enhancements that allow it to work in an infrastructureless environment.

The XMPP protocol supports both the request/response and the publish/subscribe models (Figure 18.11). A client with a unique name communicates with another client with a unique name via an associated server in this architecture. The client form of the protocol is implemented by each client, while the server offers routing functionality. The request/response model allows for bidirectional communication, while the publish/subscribe model allows for multi-directional communication (push and pull data).

The XMPP protocol employs XML for text conversations, which may result in network traffic overhead, although this can be avoided by compressing XML with EXI. This protocol is uncomplicated and can be used in a variety of projects and applications. It is an extensible and adaptable protocol, and numerous extensions have been built on its basis. On the other hand, it has some flaws: it requires a lot of bandwidth and a lot of CPU power, there is no guarantee of QoS, and it is limited to simple data types [15].

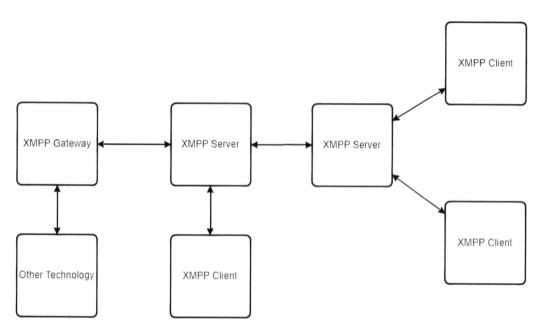

FIGURE 18.11 XMPP operation.

18.6 Conclusion

In recent years, both IoT connections and interconnected IoT devices have experienced a tremendous increase. Accomplishing the IoT vision can be realized only through the integration of various wireless communication technologies, motivated by the demands of various types of applications. To this end, this chapter provides an overview the most appropriate wireless communication networking technologies for the IoT industry, which are categorized as short and long range according to the transmission distance they cover. The key characteristics of each communication technology are thoroughly presented along with its advantages and disadvantages in terms of their performance regarding reliability, security, scalability, coverage, cost, and energy efficiency. An important considered future challenge is the design of architectures that will be able to support the heterogeneity of the presented network technologies. In this direction, it is important that future IoT networks have the ability to provide interoperability between different network protocols.

Acknowledgment

This work was supported by the European Union and Greek National Funds through the Operational Program Competitiveness, Entrepreneurship and Innovation, under the call RESEARCH–CREATE– INNOVATE 2 under Project T2EDK-02617.

REFERENCES

1. Cilfone, A., Davoli, L., Belli, L., & Ferrari, G. (2019). Wireless mesh networking: An IoT-oriented perspective survey on relevant technologies. *Future Internet*, 11(4), 99.
2. Darroudi, S. M., & Gomez, C. (2017). Bluetooth low energy mesh networks: A survey. *Sensors*, 17(7), 1467.
3. Qu, Q., Li, B., Yang, M., Yan, Z., Yang, A., Deng, D. J., & Chen, K. C. (2019). Survey and performance evaluation of the upcoming next generation WLANs standard-IEEE 802.11 ax. *Mobile Networks and Applications*, 24(5), 1461–1474.

4. Buurman, B., Kamruzzaman, J., Karmakar, G., & Islam, S. (2020). Low-power wide-area networks: Design goals, architecture, suitability to use cases and research challenges. *IEEE Access*, 8, 17179–17220.

5. Tian, L., Santi, S., Seferagić, A., Lan, J., & Famaey, J. (2021). Wi-Fi HaLow for the Internet of Things: An up-to-date survey on IEEE 802.11 ah research. *Journal of Network and Computer Applications*, 182, 103036.

6. Šljivo, A., Kerkhove, D., Tian, L., Famaey, J., Munteanu, A., Moerman, I., ...& De Poorter, E. (2018). Performance evaluation of IEEE 802.11 ah networks with high-throughput bidirectional traffic. *Sensors*, 18(2), 325.

7. Popli, S., Jha, R. K., & Jain, S. (2018). A survey on energy efficient narrowband internet of things (NBIoT): architecture, application and challenges. *IEEE Access*, 7, 16739–16776.

8. Díaz Zayas, A., Rivas Tocado, F. J., & Rodríguez, P. (2020). Evolution and testing of NB-IoT solutions. *Applied Sciences*, 10(21), 7903.

9. Almuhaya, M. A., Jabbar, W. A., Sulaiman, N., & Abdulmalek, S. (2022). A survey on Lorawan technology: Recent trends, opportunities, simulation tools and future directions. *Electronics*, 11(1), 164.

10. Gomez, C., Veras, J. C., Vidal, R., Casals, L., & Paradells, J. (2019). A sigfox energy consumption model. *Sensors*, 19(3), 681.

11. Elkhodr, M., Shahrestani, S., & Cheung, H. (2016). Emerging wireless technologies in the internet of things: a comparative study. arXiv preprint arXiv:1611.00861.

12. Mekki, K., Bajic, E., Chaxel, F., & Meyer, F. (2018, March). Overview of cellular LPWAN technologies for IoT deployment: Sigfox, LoRaWAN, and NB-IoT. In 2018 ieee international conference on pervasive computing and communications workshops (percom workshops) (pp. 197–202). IEEE.

13. [Online]. Available: https://www.iotworldtoday.com/2018/08/19/iot-connectivity-options-comparing-short-long-range-technologies/, accessed August 2022.

14. Ding, J., Nemati, M., Ranaweera, C., & Choi, J. (2020). IoT connectivity technologies and applications: A survey. arXiv preprint arXiv:2002.12646.

15. Shelby, Z., Hartke, K., Bormann, C., & Frank, B. (2012). Constrained application protocol (CoAP). draft-ietfcore-coap-12. Expires December, 27.

16. Yassein, M. B., & Shatnawi, M. Q. (2016, September). Application layer protocols for the Internet of Things: A survey. In 2016 International Conference on Engineering & MIS (ICEMIS) (pp. 1–4). IEEE.

19

Vulnerability Assessment of Industrial and Agricultural Control Systems within the IoT Framework

Roberto Caviglia, Franco Davoli, Alessandro Fausto, Giovanni Gaggero, Mario Marchese,
Aya Moheddine, Fabio Patrone, and Giancarlo Portomauro
University of Genoa, Genoa, Italy

19.1 Introduction

Industrial Control System (ICS) is a general term that encompasses different types of control systems, including Supervisory Control and Data Acquisition (SCADA) and Distributed Control Systems (DCS), but also different cyber-physical environments, such as, among others, transportation, dams, emergency services, healthcare, energy, and agricultural systems. An ICS consists of combinations of monitoring and control components that act together to achieve an industrial control objective. ICSs are increasingly relying on Information and Communication Technologies (ICTs). ICSs have evolved including ICT capabilities into existing physical systems, often replacing or supplementing physical control mechanisms. Internet of Things (IoT) communication technologies are part of this action.

From a cybersecurity perspective, a noteworthy step in the evolution of ICSs is the employment of different wireless technologies for monitoring and control purposes. The use of wireless technologies implies abandoning the so-called "security by obscurity" concept, which is the cyber defense philosophy that relies on the impossibility of the attacker gaining access to control networks. It will always be possible to try performing attacks against a wireless network if it is possible to physically be within its coverage range.

ICT technologies employed in the agricultural sector include sensor networks, as well as automation machines and autonomous vehicles. Due to the increasing number of new products, it is crucial to develop methods and tools to test the cybersecurity protection level of these objects. Defining proper procedures that can be followed by third-party entities to test their products in terms of specific requirements is also of primary importance. Software Defined Radio (SDR) is a very useful tool to test wireless communications. SDR allows the implementation of attacks on various protocols, known or unknown, without dedicated hardware and/or software. In this sense, SDR can be considered a fundamental security research technology.

The aim of this chapter is to present the application of SDR to implement attacks on two different technologies in the agricultural sector: sensor networks and autonomous teleoperated agricultural vehicles. The chapter is structured as follows. Section 19.2 provides an introduction to the SDR technology and its applications for penetration testing. Section 19.3 describes the implementation of security attacks in two real-world applications: a tractor that can operate autonomously or be remotely managed through a radio controller; and a sensor network based on the Long Range

DOI:10.1201/9781003326236-19

Wide Area Network (LoRaWAN) IoT communication protocol. Results show how the attacks are performed and their impact. Conclusions are drawn in Section 19.4.

19.2 SDR Applications in Cybersecurity

19.2.1 Introduction to SDR

SDR has no single, unified, globally recognized definition. With the term SDR, we generally identify the technologies that allow building radio equipment based on general-purpose hardware components and with software that can be flexibly configured to generate different kinds of radio signals. SDR can bring benefits both in the military sector, such as software upgradeable and reconfigurable military radio communications equipment, and in the commercial sector, such as multi-protocol multi-band base stations, mobile multi-standard terminals, and cognitive radios [1].

The role of SDR technology in cybersecurity can be two-fold [2]: on the "malicious" side, SDR can be used to perform active or passive attacks against potentially vulnerable systems with wireless communication interfaces; on the "protection" side, SDR can help develop security monitoring solutions against wireless cyberattacks.

19.2.2 SDR for Penetration Testing

SDR deeply influences the methods and tools used in the penetration testing community [3]. Historically, except for a few technologies, threats to wireless communication systems are confined to individuals with very specific knowledge or in possession of even more specific hardware. This condition makes it difficult to reliably assess the security of a particular wireless communication solution for an independent third party, especially in the presence of limited time or resources.

The use of SDR allows security researchers to perform attacks on a huge variety of wireless technologies by using the same relatively cheap hardware and open-source software, to discover new vulnerabilities. In the literature, several papers show the application of this methodology to various wireless solutions, such as cellular technologies, global navigation satellite systems, Radio Frequency Identifications (RFIDs), and IoT protocols. Ref. [4] utilizes a Universal Software Radio Peripheral (USRP) board and OpenBTS software to establish a rogue GSM base transceiver system and to show how it is possible to execute International Mobile Subscriber Identity (IMSI) catch-attack and impersonation of a mobile subscriber to send malicious SMSs by taking advantage of the lack of the two-way authentication. Attacks on an LTE network by using a USRP board are presented in Ref. [5] which shows how it is possible to locate an LTE device within a 2 km² urban area and to deny some or all services to a target LTE device. Ref. [6] contains the implementation of an attack on the Bluetooth 2.1+ secure simple pairing in passkey entry mode by using the GNU Radio software and USRP devices, while Ref. [7] presents the possibility of conducting RFID eavesdropping by using common SDR platforms.

Another fundamental field of application is Low-Power Wide Area (LPWA) protocols. A wide list of attacks that have been conducted in such networks will be presented in Section 19.3.2.

An interesting and peculiar application of SDR-based tools and methodologies is related to the ability to automatically perform attacks and discover vulnerabilities in devices that use unknown (proprietary) communication protocols with no publicly available information about how they work, how they format to send data, and which are their communication procedures. Traditionally, the analysis of unknown wireless protocols is a manual task involving ad-hoc defined and customized procedures typically hard to find in the literature and with non-well-described guidelines. The SDR technology allows third-party entities to perform security verification without having the protocol specifications and with more autonomous and generally defined procedures. For example, Ref. [8] exploits the HackRF One SDR card and GNU Radio software to study vulnerabilities in an IoT device whose communications are based on an unknown Radio Frequency (RF) protocol, by performing a series of tests that include demodulation and decoding of RF signals, jamming, and packet replaying. Another example is an open-source tool, called Universal Radio Hacker [9], which has been designed for protocol analysis and can perform operations in series, such as the recognition of signal modulation (Amplitude Shift Keying (ASK), Frequency Shift Keying (FSK), Phase Shift Keying (PSK), etc.), demodulation, and mapping of the signal to the bitstream. While this is a significant step toward the automation of wireless protocol analysis, additional work has to be done by the research community to develop affordable tools that can be universally used for a set of protocols as widely as possible.

19.3   Implementation of Security Attacks in Real World Applications

19.3.1   Use Case 1 - Autonomous Teleoperated Agricultural Machines

19.3.1.1   *State-of-the-Art of Modern Communication Technologies in the Agricultural Sector*

The growth of new technologies has taken place for the last 20 years in sectors such as agriculture [10] and construction [11], allowing them to achieve higher efficiency and safety. In the agricultural sector, new studies, such as Ref. [12], investigate how technologies can affect new cultivation techniques to achieve high sustainability in the entire food chain. This process leads to the so-called Agriculture 4.0. This term identifies a penetration of IoT and new kinds of technologies and techniques such as big data, artificial intelligence, and cloud computing in agriculture to improve the efficiency of the production chain. For example, Ref. [13] shows how IoT devices deployed in a homegrown crop field can improve the quality of the vegetables and minimize the use of water and time spent by farmers. Figure 19.1 shows an example of a control system architecture in Agriculture 4.0.

One of the main concerns of the last 20 years was (and still is) to ensure a high safety level of agricultural machines. Ref. [14] shows how the Rollover Protective Structure (ROPS) assembled on agricultural tractors reduces the probability of fatal accidents by 50%. To further reduce this probability, the use of remote or autonomous controls for agricultural machines is currently under

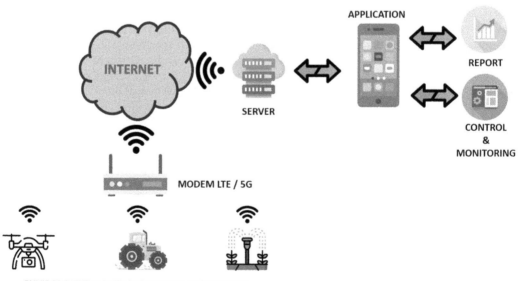

FIGURE 19.1   An example of a control system architecture in Agriculture 4.0.

study and development. Although the safety, efficiency, and quality of goods rise with the innovation of the agricultural sector, the likelihood of cyber attacks in this scenario rises too. Interconnections between sensors and actuators and, in particular, to the Internet are the key aspects making these systems prone to this kind of attack and easing malicious users to explore, find, and exploit new vulnerabilities.

Many studies are currently focused on autonomous vehicles, in particular tractors, to achieve the goals described in the Agriculture 4.0 definition. Ref. [15] compares different types of autonomous tractors and highlights the exploitation of technologies and algorithms also by developing an artificial intelligence algorithm based on a neural network aimed at improving self-learning. Ref. [16] describes an orchard management autonomous system that uses two autonomous tractors to mow grass, pick fruits, and spray verdigris and implements radio communications on a 1300-hectare orchard to control the agricultural vehicles through IoT sensors, such as laser scanners and color cameras, registered by GPS. Furthermore, Ref. [16] presents the design and implementation of a control room to analyze the system's behavior and send commands to the vehicles.

19.3.1.2   *State-of-the-Art of Cyber Attacks in the Agricultural Sector*

As described in Section 19.3.1.1, the growth of interconnected devices that monitor and act on agricultural devices by sending and receiving a big amount of data mainly through wireless channels and the use of control systems in Agriculture 4.0 are making agriculture scenarios more prone to a wider set of attacks and are increasing the number of vulnerabilities that could be exploited by attackers. There are different studies about cybersecurity in the agricultural sector. Ref. [17] analyzes six real farms in Finland and highlights the main threats and vulnerabilities of the communication architecture, concluding that one of the main problems is that farmers are not aware of the threats they are exposed to. Ref. [18] defines the main issues and cyber threats due to devices able to connect to the Internet in the agricultural sector and discusses cybersecurity challenges related to security, privacy, and safety in smart farming and the entire food supply chain. Ref. [19] shows the use of the LoRaWAN protocol in smart farming, highlights the vulnerabilities that can be exploited to perform cyber attacks and defines a method to prevent this kind of threat.

Many papers in the literature show the vulnerabilities of autonomous vehicles in the automotive sector, especially of the ones based on a CANbus network. Ref. [20] performs a penetration test over commercial cars demonstrating that it is possible to control the braking, steering, acceleration, and display systems of different vehicles. The same authors analyze the remote attack surface of a large variety of vehicles, estimating the difficulty of remotely compromising them in Ref. [21]. Automotive and agricultural vehicle control networks have many common elements, so some of the vulnerabilities found in the automotive sector can be present also in automated agricultural machines. Despite these similarities, just a few papers analyze the cybersecurity issues of agricultural vehicles. Ref. [22] presents a security testbed for agricultural vehicles as a potential solution to help the identification of cybersecurity vulnerabilities within commercially available off-the-shelf components, while Ref. [23] proposes a preliminary framework for network security verification of automated vehicles in the agricultural domain.

19.3.1.3   *Control Network of Agricultural Automated Vehicles*

Automated agricultural machines are usually equipped with a control network with multiple wireless interfaces that allow the machines to be monitored and controlled and/or to receive information from outside. A typical protocol used in these control networks is CANbus [24], which, originally developed by BOSCH for the automotive industry to replace the complex wiring harness, nowadays is an ISO standard employed in different sectors. CANbus has been designed as a multi-master message broadcast system that allows sending many short messages with extremely high reliability. Nevertheless, from a cybersecurity perspective, the protocol has severe vulnerabilities. Due to its design, it cannot assure the integrity, confidentiality, and availability of communications [24]. Still, it is considered an acceptable solution in many cases since it is employed in networks assumed

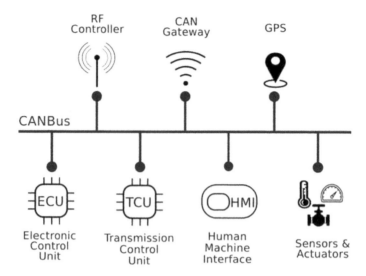

FIGURE 19.2   Typical autonomous vehicle internal CANbus network.

accessible only by physically reaching the network cables and so considered isolated. This assumption is only partially true. The security of the network depends on the security of its wireless interfaces.

The wireless interfaces that are connected to a CANbus network can vary depending on the network application field. In the field of automated agricultural vehicles, one can find three main cases:

- *Radio Frequency Controllers*: the vehicles can commonly be controlled remotely; in this case, the vehicle is equipped with a receiver that gets commands from a remote transmitter.
- *CANbus Gateways*: some agricultural automated vehicles use gateways that allow remote direct interaction with the control network. For example, CANbus can be interfaced with a wireless LAN through a web application.
- *Global Navigation Satellite System (GNSS)*: GNSS is typically used by autonomous vehicles to estimate their position.

Wireless interfaces may be connected to the same CANbus that connects vital components of the electronic systems, such as Electronic Control Units (ECUs), Transmission Control Units (TCUs), Human Machine Interface (HMI), and a set of sensors and actuators that directly communicate through CANbus. An overall scheme of a typical control network is shown in Figure 19.2.

Despite the differences in the practical use, a similar architecture of the control network can be found on each agricultural machine that we mentioned above. It is, therefore, necessary to develop procedures, guidelines, and tools to assess the vulnerabilities of these machines.

19.3.1.4 A Framework to Evaluate Cybersecurity of Agricultural Automated Vehicles

The proposed framework is composed of three main pillars:

- *Vulnerability assessment of the Gateway*: gateways can suffer from severe cybersecurity issues due to known vulnerabilities depending on the wireless technology they use, such as Wi-Fi. Web applications can be used by attackers to directly inject packets into the control network. Many packages and tools have been developed to evaluate the security level of gateways, such as the open-source framework provided by the OWASP foundation [25].

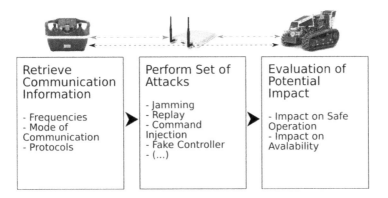

FIGURE 19.3   Proposed evaluation framework for agricultural automated vehicles.

- *Resilience to GNSS spoofing attacks*: GNSSs are prone to cyber attacks aimed at disrupting the service also by spoofing GNSS signals. GPS is prone to spoofing attacks [26]. Different algorithms for GPS spoofing detection have been presented in the literature [27], but very few of them, if none, can be implemented in a low computational power environment such as an agricultural vehicle. Another solution involves the possibility of jointly exploiting the information from both GNSS and Attitude and Heading Reference System (AHRS) sensors [28]. SDR can be employed to evaluate the system's resilience to such attacks and check the consequences: for example, if these attacks are sufficient to make the vehicle change its trajectory and to what extent, or if the vehicle can detect these attacks and enter a safe operational mode.

- *Vulnerability assessment of RF communications*: the first step is to identify the used communication protocol. In the case of well-known protocols, such as mobile communications or IoT non-proprietary protocols, the main vulnerabilities are already commonly known and analyzed in the state-of-the-art. SDR can therefore be used to implement attacks that exploit these vulnerabilities and to evaluate system responses. In the case of proprietary solutions, SDR can be used to get information about the communication protocol, data format, and communication parameters, such as the used modulation, before performing attacks.

Focusing on the last point, if the system under analysis does not use well-known protocols but proprietary solutions, proper and widely applicable procedures have to be developed to test the security level of these protocols and procedures to properly assess the impact and consequences of these attacks. For example, in case of a jamming attack, checking if it is possible to deny the communication is not sufficient. It is of paramount importance also to verify if the vehicle can operate in a safe mode under communication unavailability conditions and if the attack may threaten the safety of the system and the surrounding environment.

The proposed analysis of these systems' cybersecurity level follows three steps, as shown in Figure 19.3:

(1) *Retrieve communication information*: to analyze the used frequencies, communication mode (e.g., half duplex or full duplex), modulation, and all the information useful to properly set the attacks.

(2) *Perform a set of attacks*: to test the system by performing a set of defined attacks in sequence. Examples of attacks that can be included in this set are jamming (with different possible jammer configurations), replay, and protocol reverse engineering.

(3) *Evaluation of the impact*: to evaluate the impact that each attack has on the physical behavior of the system and the risk of damage to the system and the surrounding environment and objects.

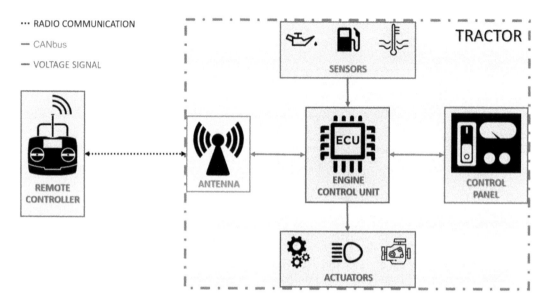

FIGURE 19.4   The communication system architecture of the considered agricultural automated vehicle.

19.3.1.5 Internal Architecture of Agricultural Automated Vehicles

The considered case study is a utility tractor that can move in autonomous mode or be moved through a Remote Controller (RC). Our testbed consists of the control and communication system of a commercial model of the tractor and is shown in Figure 19.4.

It is made of the following components:

- *Sensors*: multiple sensors to monitor, for example, water temperature, oil, and gasoline levels, are connected to the ECU by electric wires. Measures are encoded as proper voltage values.
- *Actuators*: multiple actuators, such as the motor, hydraulic valves, and power take-off, are, as the sensors, connected to the ECU through cables. Received commands are encoded as voltage values.
- *Engine Control Unit (ECU)*: the ECU is the core of internal communications. It reads data from sensors and receives information about the status of the remote controller's switches. It periodically creates, on one hand, CANbus messages to send to the control panel and antenna, and, on the other hand, proper voltage values to send to the actuators.
- *Control panel*: the control panel allows to manage the basic functions of the tractor, such as turning on/off lights, starting and stopping the engine and emergency stop switch. Inside the control panel, there are also warning lights for parameters such as battery charge state, gasoline level, water temperature, and oil level. A diagnostic display is also present to allow viewing some information such as error messages and the total working time of the vehicle. These data are sent and received by CANbus.
- *Antenna*: the antenna allows transmitting and receiving CANbus messages as data packets through the related radio interface.
- *Remote controller*: the remote controller allows an authorized operator to remotely drive the tractor. It has buttons, switches, and potentiometers that allow managing different parameters, such as speed, direction, and activation of the rotor. Besides, a small screen displays some information about the radio communication link status and allows the operator to monitor the tractor's conditions.

19.3.1.6 Considered Cyber Attacks

19.3.1.6.1 Jamming Attack

Jamming attacks aim to deny the communication between the controller and tractor. For test purposes, we implement a jamming attack by using an SDR card configured to generate a proper jamming signal by using the GNU radio software. It is extremely important to evaluate the impact of this attack to understand if the vehicle can continue to operate in a safe mode even if the communication with the remote controller is disrupted or starts behaving dangerously for itself and the objects and people in the surrounding environment.

The system may be prone to jamming attacks depending on the configuration of the internal software and the sophistication of the attacks. Regarding the attack model, we made our tests by using three different kinds of jamming:

- Fixed jamming with white noise: the jamming signal is a white noise signal with fixed central frequency and bandwidth.
- Reactive jamming with white noise: the jamming signal is a white noise signal with variable central frequency and fixed bandwidth. The jammer just turns on as soon as it "hears" something on the monitored channels. It can automatically adjust the central frequency of the jamming signal "chasing" the original signal.
- Jamming with fake controller packets: the jamming signal is composed of a series of packets formatted as the packets sent by the remote controller but without meaningful data. In this way, the jammer is "mimicking" the remote controller by sending fake commands that might be interpreted as trustworthy commands.

The system can react differently to the considered types of attacks. Figure 19.5 shows the effect of fixed jamming. It can be noticed that the system can react by using a frequency hopping mechanism that switches the signal central frequency whenever the previously used channel is busy.

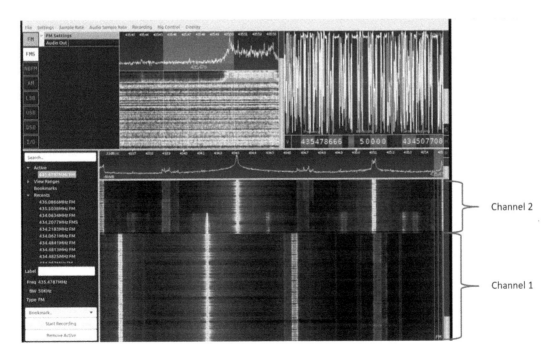

FIGURE 19.5 Fixed jamming attack with white noise.

While this specific attack has no impact on our testbed, it is not so for the other ones. If the reactive jammer is sufficiently fast, it can completely disrupt the communication even in the case the transmitter implements a frequency hopping mechanism.

Besides, considering the jamming with fake packets, the receiver immediately stops receiving commands. For this attack, we collect packets, truncate some of them so to remove part of the data, and transmit them as a replay. In this case, the receiver behaves differently from the jamming with white noise: it immediately interrupts the communication. The joystick can then try again to establish a new communication on another channel.

19.3.1.6.2   Replay Attack

The replay attack consists in recording legitimate packets sent by the remote controller and re-transmitting them to the vehicle by using an SDR card. If the system does not implement any authentication mechanism, a replay attack may let the attacker partially or even completely control the vehicle. A replay attack can be carried out even if the attacker is not able to isolate single packets: depending on the communication, the raw re-transmission of recorded communications may be sufficient to perform the attack.

Figure 19.6 shows the effect of a replay attack on our testbed.

We can identify 4 main phases:

(1)   Normal operation.

(2)   Start of the replay attack: the signal by the rogue controller overlaps the legitimate signal. The receiver starts following the indications of the rogue controller instead of the ones of the legitimate user.

(3)   Re-connection: it is still possible for the authorized human operator to try reconnecting to the receiver by choosing another channel.

(4)   Normal operation again.

Figure 19.7 shows a representation of the information that flows into the CANbus network.

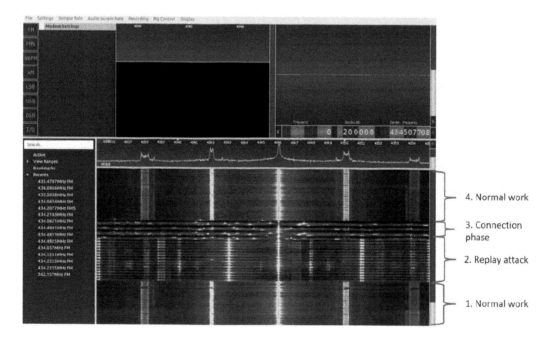

FIGURE 19.6   Ongoing replay attack: frequency spectrum.

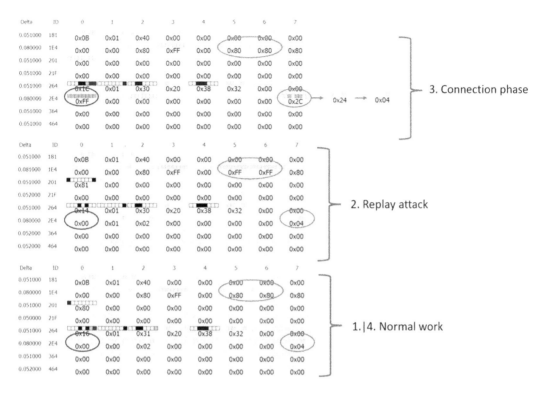

FIGURE 19.7   Ongoing replay attack: packets received by the tractor.

The light blue circles highlight the data bytes related to tractor's movement commands. When the value is 80, the tractor is stopped (normal work and re-connection phases). When the value is FF, the tractor is moving straight due to commands contained in the replay packets (replay attack phase). It is possible to see how the receiver recognizes the SDR device as the remote controller during the attack by looking at the 0 values evidenced by red circles, which means that the controller is online (attack and normal work phases). The value is FF when the controller is offline. The green circles identify how the values have changed during the re-connection phase. To summarize, the output is that the tractor is moving ahead while the authorized operator sets the tractor state on stop.

19.3.1.6.3   Reverse Engineering

A more complete control of the wireless communication can be obtained if the attacker is able to understand the features of the protocol and reproduce packets containing malicious information. If the system does not implement any authentication mechanism and the attacker is able to reverse-engineer the protocol, he/she can take the complete control of the vehicle.

The process of reverse engineering an unknown wireless protocol can hardly be formalized in a strict procedure and automatized. Still, we can identify some fundamental steps:

(1) *Identification of the modulation*: it allows obtaining a string of bits from the raw signal. The identification of the modulation can be done by computing some parameters of the signal. For example, Figure 19.8 shows the modulation constellation of the radio signals of our testbed, which helped us identify that, in this case, the modulation is the Gaussian Minimum-Shift Keying (GMSK).

(2) *Identification of each packet*: it allows obtaining the single packets from the string of bits. Figure 19.9 shows the sniffed radio signal generated by the remote controller highlighting, in the bottom part, a single packet.

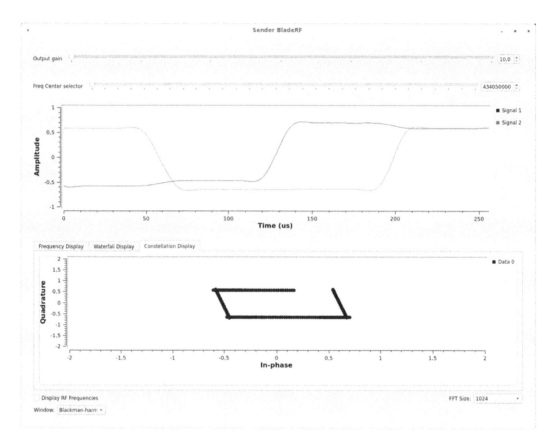

FIGURE 19.8 Modulation constellation of the remote controller's radio signal.

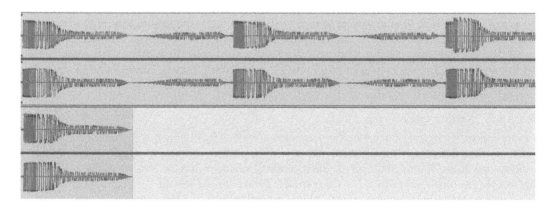

FIGURE 19.9 Remote controller's radio signal intensity over time.

(3) *Identification of the meaning of each bit*: it allows identifying the structure of each retrieved packet and so the meaning of each single bit or subset of bits. This can be done, for example, by comparing packets over time. This last step is typically the most manual and time-consuming: it is necessary to record multiple packets over time; packets vary in a known way, such as when clicking on a single button or moving a single lever on the remote controller; in practice if the action changes the packet changes accordingly so allowing to associate bits and actions.

These tests highlight some severe vulnerabilities that afflict the system under test. The system also has several similarities with many other off-the-shelf products for autonomous agricultural vehicles, but also with other automated machines. This suggests that similar vulnerabilities could be found in many other systems and should be seriously taken care of. This analysis also strengthens the need for procedures and tools to test the cybersecurity of these kinds of apparatus considering a wide set of possible cyber attacks.

19.3.2   Use Case 2 - Sensor Networks in the Agricultural Sector

19.3.2.1   *IoT System Architecture and Layers*

IoT has been gaining great interest and attention in many domains for the last few years. The term IoT was introduced in 1999 by Kevin Ashton and associated with the concept of connecting anything, anytime, and anywhere so allowing objects to communicate with each other and with the Internet [29].

The typical IoT architecture consists of three main layers, as shown in Figure 19.10: *perception*, *network*, and *application* layers.

The first layer corresponds to IoT devices, such as sensors and actuators which interact with the surrounding environment and collect data to be transmitted and processed. Ensuring security in this layer is of primary importance, also because the generated data are transferred to the upper network layer and can cause damage to the rest of the network, especially in the case IoT devices are unmonitored and prone to cyberattacks [30]. The network layer is responsible for data transmission through the network. Various communication protocols have been designed for this purpose depending on the performance requirement of the related IoT application, such as short-range or long-range, delay-sensitive or delay-tolerant, and high or low required reliability. This layer has the ability to manage and control the massive amount of exchanged traffic. However, since its function is similar to the network and transport layers of the OSI model, this layer is susceptible to different cyberattacks, such as Man-in-the-Middle (MITM) or Denial of Service (DoS) [31]. The application layer represents the IoT application and differs depending on the IoT service and manufacturer. Its role is to connect end users to their IoT devices through a specific user interface and to ensure authentication. It is a critical layer since it typically deals with a massive amount of data transactions making it prone to data or software attacks, such as data breaching, malicious script injection, and phishing [31–33].

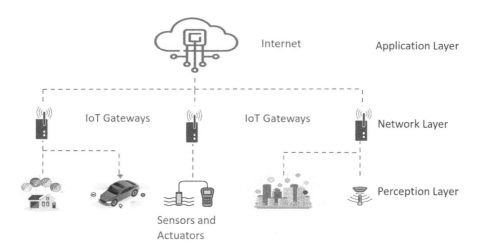

FIGURE 19.10   IoT three layers architecture.

19.3.2.2   Security Challenges in IoT Networks

The dynamic nature, heterogeneity of hardware, wide accessibility, and global connectivity make the IoT world critical and challenging from a security perspective. As a consequence, various security challenges and threats can affect the IoT world by targeting IoT devices and communication channels [34]. Moreover, the IoT concept is based on the interaction of a huge number of objects with end users and virtual entities making it essential to ensure security and privacy [35]. Due to these reasons, multiple attacks are available and security assurance is a significant issue. One of the most important challenges in any IoT system is to ensure the confidentiality of the transferred data and information. Different encryption techniques are used to guarantee data secrecy between different entities, such as AES (Advanced Encryption Standard) cipher or Triple DES (Data Encryption Standard). However, such techniques are not enough to properly guarantee data privacy. Sensitive information can be retrieved by using traffic analysis of the monitored and eavesdropped data. In addition, such data can be released and compromised when a malicious node is introduced into the network. On the other hand, even if confidentiality is guaranteed, data integrity may not be. This can be done by introducing a malicious node that injects false data into the network by altering the communication packets and even causing disruptions to the offered service [36]. The effect is damaged data packets and data loss. Moreover, data authentication needs to be ensured in any IoT network, since IoT devices typically share the wireless communication medium with the server [37]. The end-to-end nodes need to be authenticated in order to both verify the source node and avoid any malicious node or spoofed packet. Availability is another aspect considered as a critical challenge in IoT systems. It can be violated through the presence of compromised nodes or failures in the IoT gateway, which cause mistakes and disruptions in receiving data by the end entity [38].

19.3.2.3   Attacks Performed on IoT Networks

IoT networks are known for their low-cost installation and ease of programming and deployment. This makes it easier to perform different attacks that can affect the network and its behavior. Security attacks are increasing against IoT networks causing degradation in their performance regarding power consumption, delay, and throughput. Two types of attacks can be performed on any IoT network: (I) cyber and (II) physical attacks. Cyber attacks include all attacks that are typically performed remotely (even if, in some cases, a cyber attack can begin with a physical action), whereas physical attacks aim to compromise or damage entities of the IoT network by using a more "traditional" and physical approach [39]. Attacks may also be classified into passive or active ones [40].

Each IoT layer has its own security concerns regarding threats and attacks, as summarized in Figure 19.11.

Starting with the perception layer, the attacks target IoT devices to destroy them or alter their behavior. The main attacks on this layer are:

- *Jamming*: the attacker generates a powerful disturbing signal aimed at disrupting all legitimate communications within its coverage range.
- *Node Tampering*: the attacker takes full control of the IoT sensor or device and can modify it or even replace it with a malicious device. Considering that the device is integrated within the IoT network, this attack can cause security issues for the whole IoT system [41].
- *Malicious code injection*: the attacker injects some malicious code that can force the IoT device to perform unexpected and unplanned functions. This attack may be carried out in different situations, such as during the periodic update/upgrade of the device firmware typically done over the air.
- *False data injection*: the attacker injects erroneous data into the IoT device memory once it has the device control. This attack may affect the user behavior as a consequence of faulty data.
- *Eavesdropping*: the attacker monitors and eavesdrops on the data generated by or destined to the IoT devices staying within their coverage range [42]. This attack is often aimed at getting

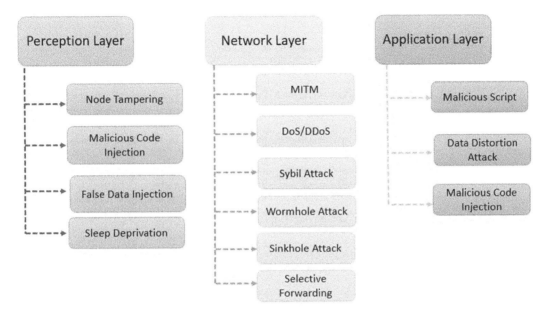

FIGURE 19.11   Summary of the attacks that can be performed on each layer of IoT network.

information about formats, actions, and processes and also for possible use in future node tampering and false data injection.

- *Sleep deprivation*: the attacker aims to drain the IoT device battery forcing it to do useless and power-consuming tasks.

Regarding the second layer, the main attacks that target the network layer are:

- *Sinkhole / Wormhole*: the attacker inserts a malicious listening device and a malicious IoT node in the network. The listening device intercepts data packets coming from the IoT device to be attacked and forwards them to the malicious IoT device through a separate communication channel. The malicious IoT device sends these packets to the IoT gateway pretending to be the real device. If the attack is successful, any downlink communication can be re-routed toward the malicious device [43]. This attack may also cause network congestion and impact the network performance [44].
- *Selective forwarding*: the attacker enters the network between the attacked IoT device and the user and "filters" the communication, that is, it may decide, for example, to forward just some packets and drop the others [45, 46].
- *Denial of Service (DoS) / Distributed DoS (DDoS)*: the attacker aims to disable the system's services by continuously generating requests aimed at saturating system resources that will not be able to process the rightful packets anymore. If the fake packets destined to the IoT devices aim to trigger some responses, another consequence of this attack is the devices' battery drain [47].
- *Man-in-the-Middle (MITM)*: the attacker monitors and intercepts the communications between the IoT device and gateways/servers in order to collect data and exploit information, such as the one that is exchanged to secure data transmissions and authenticate the device [48].
- *Sybil*: the attacker tries creating or using different fake identities to gain the system's trust and violate users' privacy [49].

The application layer directly deals with the end users. The main attacks that target the application layer are:

TABLE 19.1

Summary of Attacks Against IoT Systems

Attack	Layer	Action	Effect
Jamming	Perception	to generate a disturbing signal to disrupt legitimate communications	IoT devices are unable to communicate with the IoT system
Node tampering	Perception	to gain physical control of IoT devices	to change sensitive information/ to replace the device
Malicious code injection	Perception	to insert malicious code within the IoT devices	to force the IoT node to perform unplanned operations
False data injection	Perception	to introduce false data into the IoT device memory	to change the data delivered to the user
Eavesdropping	Perception	to monitor and intercept IoT device data	to intercept private data
Sleep deprivation	Perception	to force IoT devices to perform useless but power-consuming tasks	to drain IoT device battery
Sinkhole / Wormhole	Network	to re-route data packets generated by IoT devices	to change routing information for downlink communications
Selective forwarding	Network	to "filter" IoT device communications	packet loss
DoS/DDoS	Network	to send a very high number of fake requests	disruption of the network operations
MITM	Network	to connect to the IoT network between the IoT devices and the users	to access private data and information, to disrupt communications
Sybil	Network	to create different identities for the same malicious node	to gain the system's trust and violate users' privacy
Malicious script	Application	to inject malicious scripts	effects ranging from data theft to system failure
Data distortion	Application	to inject fake data	to change the stored user data

- *Malicious script*: the attacker exploits a remote connection with the attacked IoT device to inject a script that looks like legitimate code and is automatically executed by the device software. After accessing the device, the user is exposed to consequences ranging from data theft to system failure [50].
- *Data distortion*: the attacker changes the data generated by the IoT devices acting on the IoT system's server where data are typically stored to be retrieved by the users [48, 50].

Table 19.1 summarizes all these mentioned attacks and their impact on an IoT network.

19.3.2.4   LoRa and LoRaWAN Communication Protocols

We decided to focus our security analysis on one of the wireless communication protocols better suitable for this use case: the LoRaWAN communication protocol. Long Range or LoRa is a modulation technique designed for IoT applications. This technology offers long-range connectivity, low-power consumption for IoT nodes, and noise and interference robust communications at the cost of low data rates. It uses a Chirp Spread Spectrum (CSS) modulation technique to make it more robust to noise, the signal is spread over a wide bandwidth thus reducing the Signal to Noise Ratio (SNR) and increasing the range. LoRa communications use the unlicensed ISM frequency band which reduces the deployment costs with different sets of frequencies per region [51].

LoRaWAN is the application protocol that enables the end-to-end communications between IoT devices and users connected to the Internet. It is one of the most adopted IoT communication protocols since it offers both a low-cost and a low-power solution. It is considered an ideal solution for outdoor IoT applications that require wide coverage. This feature makes it more prone to

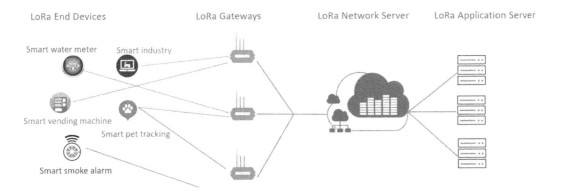

LoRa End Devices · LoRa Gateways · LoRa Network Server · LoRa Application Server

Smart water meter · Smart industry · Smart vending machine · Smart pet tracking · Smart smoke alarm

FIGURE 19.12 LoRaWAN network architecture.

interference and attacks. A LoRaWAN network adopts the star-of-stars network topology and is formed mainly of four components: (1) end devices, (2) LoRa gateways, (3) Network servers and (4) Application servers. LoRa gateways are responsible of packet forwarding, are equipped with a LoRa interface toward the LoRa devices and are also connected to the network server typically located on the Internet. The Network server transfers packets by using the standard IP technology to the Application server and also sends downlink messages and MAC commands back to end devices [52, 53]. Figure 19.12 shows a representation of the typical LoRaWAN network architecture.

19.3.2.5 Jamming Attacks in LoRaWAN Networks

The Jamming attack is considered the most performed one in Wireless Sensor Networks (WSNs) and IoT systems. There are four main kinds of jamming attacks [54–57]:

- *Constant jammer*: this jammer broadcasts a powerful signal interfering with the legitimate user's signals. It is always active and it blocks the users from accessing the channel since it is continuously occupied by the attacker. The attacker can perform this attack on the entire spectrum used by LoRaWAN communications or only on some channels [55, 57, 58].
- *Deceptive jammer*: the attacker sends strings of bits corresponding to LoRaWAN packets mimicking a legitimate node [57].
- *Reactive jammer*: it is similar to the constant jammer but it follows the concept of listening and then jamming instead of being always active. It listens to the LoRaWAN channels and transmits the interfering radio signal only when it detects legitimate packet transmissions [57, 59, 60]. It is more power efficient than the previous two jamming techniques but it has to be faster to react as soon as it detects packet transmissions.
- *Random jammer*: it is similar to the reactive jammer but it turns itself on at random time intervals instead of listening to the channels and acting accordingly and staying active for a fixed duration. It is considered a less destructive and more power-efficient jammer compared to the constant one.

Various studies in the literature analyze the behaviors of the LoRaWAN protocol under jamming attacks. Ref. [61] evaluates the behavior of LoRaWAN under channel-aware jamming (a reactive jamming), and channel-oblivious jamming (a continuous jamming). Simulation results show that the LoRaWAN protocol is vulnerable to such jamming with degradation in both end device throughput and gateway performance. A reactive jammer was designed in [62] by using special hardware components to provide LoRaWAN connectivity. The jammer introduced in Ref. [62] is based on two parameters: (1) Channel Active Detection (CAD) and (2) Received Signal Strength Indicator (RSSI). The jammer consists of two parts: the detector and the jammer. The detector examines the CAD for preamble checking, and, once detected, the jammer checks the RSSI value before deciding whether to jam the signal or not. A similar reactive jammer is presented in Ref. [63]: it uses the concept of CAD detection on a specific channel and a spreading factor causing collisions at the gateway level by transmitting a jamming signal with higher power. Ref. [64] presents a LoRaWAN jammer based on low-cost commercial devices and able to transmit a signal with a higher signal strength than the legitimate one. A selective jamming and a combination of selective and wormhole jamming are introduced in Ref. [65]: the selective jammer detects and receives the LoRaWAN packets and then jams the channel immediately; the integrated selective and wormhole jammer is composed of a sniffer and jammer, the sniffer detects, receives, and records the LoRaWAN packets and then triggers the jammer when enough content is received. Once the signal is received by the jammer, it launches the attack.

19.3.2.6 *Reactive LoRa Jammer Design and Test*

To assess the robustness of a LoRaWAN IoT network against jamming attacks, we designed a reactive jammer aimed at interrupting LoRa signals and packet transmissions generated by a LoRa device before being received by the gateway. Figure 19.13 shows the logical structure of the LoRa jammer.

The jammer is composed of two SDR cards and a Linux system equipped with GNU Radio software that can be used also alone depending on the test purpose, as shown in Figure 19.14.

In detail, the Linux-based PC equipped with GNU radio and two SDR cards acts as the LoRa signal jammer (red part). The PC runs the GNU radio software with the gr-LoRa module.[1] This software can perform different actions depending on the executed GNU radio script, whether it is a LoRa decoder (RX) or a LoRa bit-flipper (RX/TX). The jammer uses a HackRF SDR card to transmit the jamming signal and one RTL-SDR card to monitor the activity in the LoRa RF channels. The LoRa gateway is based on a COTS Linux LoRa gateway with special live monitoring software for offline analysis (blue part). LoRa devices are based on Arduino and can generate data manually by setting different LoRa parameters, such as the packet inter-generation time.

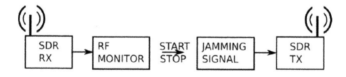

FIGURE 19.13 Logical structure of the developed LoRa jammer.

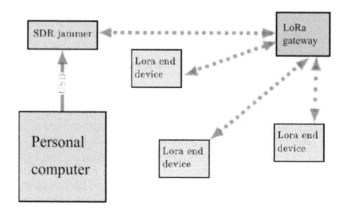

FIGURE 19.14 LoRa jammer testbed scheme.

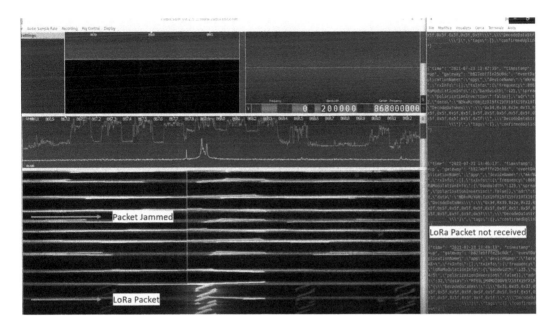

FIGURE 19.15 RF spectrum of a successfully jammed LoRa packet.

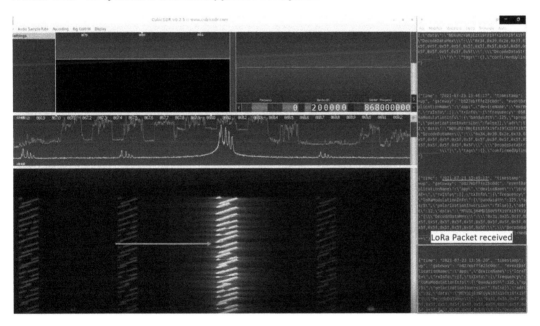

FIGURE 19.16 RF spectrum of a successfully received LoRa packet

The LoRa reactive jammer can interfere with the LoRa signal and completely disrupt the communication between end devices and the gateway. The jamming signal is based on continuous up-chirp and down-chirp signals sent for 1 second after a LoRa transmission is detected.

Figure 19.15 shows a successfully jammed LoRa signal which is not received by the gateway.

The performance of the jammer may depend on different factors, such as the distance between the jammer and end devices and/or gateway, which affects the jammer's reliability. We carried out other tests by increasing the distance between the jammer and attacked IoT device and sometimes a packet can pass through, as shown in Figure 19.16.

19.4 Conclusions

This work shows a practical use of Software Defined Radio in the vulnerability assessment process of wireless communications in the field of industrial and agricultural systems. We present two main use cases and show how it is possible to develop a procedure to test the security of teleoperated agricultural vehicles that rely on proprietary solutions for wireless communications. The obtained results show how these devices can suffer from severe vulnerabilities. It is therefore necessary to properly assess the security of new products by considering minimum security requirements. We have also developed an SDR-based jammer for LoRaWAN-based sensor networks to show how a reactive jammer can completely disrupt IoT device communications. The impact of the denial of communication must be taken into account while deploying LoRaWAN-based sensor networks for monitoring and control purposes. Future developments will include the evaluation of the impact of the distance between the attacker and the victim on the effectiveness of the attacks. A great distance of the attacker may cause not the complete failure of the attack, but rather a decrease of performances basing on different parameter, such as the packet delivery ratio in the case of a jamming attack. A deeper analysis of this impact would be significant, because the distance of the attacker can have very practical consequences on the implementation of the attack.

Note

[1] https://github.com/rpp0/gr-LoRa.git

REFERENCES

1. Ulversoy T. Software defined radio: Challenges and opportunities. *IEEE Communications Surveys & Tutorials*. 2010;12(4):531–550.
2. Uribe JdJR, Guillen EP, Cardoso LS. A technical review of wireless security for the internet of things: Software defined radio perspective. *Journal of King Saud University-Computer and Information Sciences*. 2021;34(7):4122–4134.
3. Picod JM, Lebrun A, Demay JC. Bringing software defined radio to the penetration testing community. In: Black Hat USA Conference; 2014.
4. Dubey A, Vohra D, Vachhani K, et al. Demonstration of vulnerabilities in GSM security with USRP B200 and open-source penetration tools. In: 22nd Pacific Conference on Communications (APCC); IEEE; 2016. pp. 496–501.
5. Shaik A, Borgaonkar R, Asokan N, et al. Practical attacks against privacy and availability in 4G/LTE mobile communication systems. arXiv preprint arXiv:151007563. 2015.
6. Barnickel J, Wang J, Meyer U. Implementing an attack on Bluetooth 2.1+ secure simple pairing in passkey entry mode. In: IEEE 11th International Conference on Trust, Security and Privacy in Computing and Communications; IEEE; 2012. pp. 17–24.
7. Le Roy F, Quiniou T, Mansour A, et al. RFID eavesdropping using SDR platforms. In: International Conference on Applications in Electronics Pervading Industry, Environment and Society; Springer; 2016. pp. 208–214.
8. Hung PD, Vinh BT. Vulnerabilities in IoT devices with software-defined radio. In: IEEE 4th International Conference on Computer and Communication Systems (ICCCS); IEEE; 2019. pp. 664–668.
9. Pohl J, Noack A. Universal radio hacker: A suite for analyzing and attacking stateful wireless protocols. In: 12th USENIX Workshop on Offensive Technologies (WOOT); 2018.
10. Kour VP, Arora S. Recent developments of the internet of things in agriculture: A survey. *IEEE Access*. 2020;8:129924–129957.
11. Kanan R, Elhassan O, Bensalem R. An IoT-based autonomous system for workers' safety in construction sites with real-time alarming, monitoring, and positioning strategies. *Automation in Construction*. 2018;88:73–86.

12. Ahmad A, Ordonez J, Cartujo P, et al. Remotely piloted aircraft (RPA) in agriculture: A pursuit of sustainability. *Agronomy*. 2020;11(1):7.

13. Muangprathub J, Boonnam N, Kajornkasirat S, et al. IoT and agriculture data analysis for smart farm. *Computers and Electronics in Agriculture*. 2019;156:467–474.

14. Rondelli V, Casazza C, Martelli R. Tractor rollover fatalities, analyzing accident scenario. *Journal of Safety Research*. 2018;67:99–106.

15. Roshanianfard A, Noguchi N, Okamoto H, et al. A review of autonomous agricultural vehicles (The experience of Hokkaido University). *Journal of Terramechanics*. 2020;91:155–183.

16. Moorehead SJ, Wellington CK, Gilmore BJ, et al. Automating orchards: A system of autonomous tractors for orchard maintenance. In: IEEE International Conference of Intelligent Robots and Systems, Workshop on Agricultural Robotics; 2012.

17. Nikander J, Manninen O, Laajalahti M. Requirements for cybersecurity in agricultural communication networks. *Computers and Electronics in Agriculture*. 2020;179:105776.

18. Gupta M, Abdelsalam M, Khorsandroo S, et al. Security and privacy in smart farming: Challenges and opportunities. *IEEE Access*. 2020;8:34564–34584.

19. Kuntke F, Romanenko V, Linsner S, et al. LoRaWAN security issues and mitigation options by the example of agricultural IoT scenarios. *Transactions on Emerging Telecommunications Technologies*. 2022;33(5):e4452.

20. Miller C, Valasek C. Adventures in automotive networks and control units. *Def Con*. 2013;21:260–264.

21. Miller C, Valasek C. A survey of remote automotive attack surfaces. In: Black Hat USA Conference; 2014. p. 94.

22. Freyhof M, Grispos G, Pitla S, et al. Towards a cybersecurity testbed for agricultural vehicles and environments. arXiv preprint arXiv:220505866. 2022.

23. Gaggero GB, Fausto A, Patrone F, et al. A framework for network security verification of automated vehicles in the agricultural domain. In: 2th International Conference Electronics; IEEE; 2022. pp. 1–5.

24. Bozdal M, Samie M, Aslam S, et al. Evaluation of can bus security challenges. *Sensors*. 2020;20(8):2364.

25. Meucci M, Muller A. OWASP Testing Guide V. 4.0. *Open Web Application Security Project*. 2014;4:165–166.

26. Zeng KC, Liu S, Shu Y, et al. All your GPS are belong to us: Towards stealthy manipulation of road navigation systems. In: 27th USENIX Security Symposium; 2018. pp. 1527–1544.

27. Jafarnia-Jahromi A, Broumandan A, Nielsen J, et al. GPS vulnerability to spoofing threats and a review of antispoofing techniques. *International Journal of Navigation and Observation*. 2012; 2012:1–16.

28. Kwon KC, Shim DS. Performance analysis of direct GPS spoofing detection method with AHRS/accelerometer. *Sensors*. 2020;20(4):954.

29. Balaji S, Nathani K, Santhakumar R. IoT technology, applications and challenges: A contemporary survey. *Wireless Personal Communications*. 2019;108(1):363–388.

30. Liang X, Kim Y. A survey on security attacks and solutions in the IoT network. In: IEEE 11th Annual Computing and Communication Workshop and Conference (CCWC); IEEE; 2021. pp. 0853–0859.

31. Deogirikar J, Vidhate A. Security attacks in IoT: A survey. In: International Conference on I-SMAC (IoT in Social, Mobile, Analytics and Cloud)(I-SMAC); IEEE; 2017. pp. 32–37.

32. Hassija V, Chamola V, Saxena V, et al. A survey on IoT security: Application areas, security threats, and solution architectures. *IEEE Access*. 2019;7:82721–82743.

33. Mohanty J, Mishra S, Patra S, et al. IoT security, challenges, and solutions: A review. *Progress in Advanced Computing and Intelligent Engineering*. 2021;493–504. DOI: 10.1007/978-981-15-6353-9_46

34. Alkhalil A, Ramadan RA. IoT data provenance implementation challenges. *Procedia Computer Science*. 2017;109:1134–1139.

35. Roman R, Zhou J, Lopez J. On the features and challenges of security and privacy in distributed internet of things. *Computer Networks*. 2013;57(10):2266–2279.

36. Padmavathi DG, Shanmugapriya M, et al. A survey of attacks, security mechanisms and challenges in wireless sensor networks. arXiv preprint arXiv:09090576. 2009.

37. Hassan WH, et al. Current research on Internet of Things (IoT) security: A survey. *Computer Networks*. 2019;148:283–294.

38. Burhanuddin M, Mohammed AAJ, Ismail R, et al. A review on security challenges and features in wireless sensor networks: IoT perspective. *Journal of Telecommunication, Electronic and Computer Engineering (JTEC)*. 2018;10(1–7):17–21.

39. Tahsien SM, Karimipour H, Spachos P. Machine learning based solutions for security of Internet of Things (IoT): A survey. *Journal of Network and Computer Applications*. 2020;161:102630.

40. Rong C, Çayırcı E. *Security Attacks in Ad Hoc, Sensor and Mesh Networks*. Book Security in Wireless Ad Hoc and Sensor Networks (Chapter 8). 2009. DOI: 10.1002/9780470516782.ch8

41. Kumar S, Sahoo S, Mahapatra A, et al. Security enhancements to system on chip devices for IoT perception layer. In: IEEE International Symposium on Nanoelectronic and Information Systems (iNIS); IEEE; 2017. pp. 151–156.

42. Liao CH, Shuai HH, Wang LC. Eavesdropping prevention for heterogeneous Internet of Things systems. In: 15th IEEE Annual Consumer Communications & Networking Conference (CCNC); IEEE; 2018. pp. 1–2.

43. Hu YC, Perrig A, Johnson DB. Packet leashes: A defense against wormhole attacks in wireless networks. In: IEEE International Conference on Computer Communications (INFOCOM); Vol. 3; IEEE; 2003. pp. 1976–1986.

44. Butun I, Österberg P, Song H. Security of the Internet of Things: Vulnerabilities, attacks, and countermeasures. *IEEE Communications Surveys & Tutorials*. 2019;22(1):616–644.

45. Wallgren L, Raza S, Voigt T. Routing attacks and countermeasures in the RPL-based internet of things. *International Journal of Distributed Sensor Networks*. 2013;9(8):794326.

46. Krishna RR, Priyadarshini A, Jha AV, et al. State-of-the-art review on IoT threats and attacks: Taxonomy, challenges and solutions. *Sustainability*. 2021;13(16):9463.

47. Haji SH, Ameen SY. Attack and anomaly detection in IoT networks using machine learning techniques: A review. *Asian Journal of Research in Computer Science*. 2021;9(2):30–46.

48. Abosata N, Al-Rubaye S, Inalhan G, et al. Internet of things for system integrity: A comprehensive survey on security, attacks and countermeasures for industrial applications. *Sensors*. 2021;21(11):3654.

49. Abdul-Ghani HA, Konstantas D, Mahyoub M. A comprehensive IoT attacks survey based on a building-blocked reference model. *International Journal of Advanced Computer Science and Applications*. 2018;9(3):355–373.

50. Gautam S, Malik A, Singh N, et al. Recent advances and countermeasures against various attacks in IoT environment. In: 2nd International Conference on Signal Processing and Communication (ICSPC); IEEE; 2019. pp. 315–319.

51. Alliance L. Lora regional parameters. https://lora-alliance.org/resource_hub/rp2-1-0-3-lorawan-regional-parameters/; 2021.

52. Haxhibeqiri J, De Poorter E, Moerman I, et al. A survey of lorawan for IoT: From technology to application. *Sensors*. 2018;18(11):3995.

53. Ertürk MA, Aydın MA, Büyükakkaşlar MT, et al. A survey on lorawan architecture, protocol and technologies. *Future Internet*. 2019;11(10):216.

54. Mpitziopoulos A, Gavalas D, Konstantopoulos C, et al. A survey on jamming attacks and countermeasures in WSNs. *IEEE Communications Surveys & Tutorials*. 2009;11(4):42–56.

55. Pelechrinis K, Iliofotou M, Krishnamurthy SV. Denial of service attacks in wireless networks: The case of jammers. *IEEE Communications Surveys & Tutorials*. 2010;13(2):245–257.

56. Wang L, Wyglinski AM. A combined approach for distinguishing different types of jamming attacks against wireless networks. In: IEEE Pacific Rim Conference on Communications, Computers and Signal Processing; IEEE; 2011. pp. 809–814.

57. Xu W, Trappe W, Zhang Y, et al. The feasibility of launching and detecting jamming attacks in wireless networks. In: 6th ACM International Symposium on Mobile Ad Hoc Networking and Computing; 2005. pp. 46–57.

58. Grover K, Lim A, Yang Q. Jamming and anti-jamming techniques in wireless networks: A survey. *International Journal of Ad Hoc and Ubiquitous Computing*. 2014;17(4):197–215.

59. Cai Y, Pelechrinis K, Wang X, et al. Joint reactive jammer detection and localization in an enterprise WiFi network. *Computer Networks*. 2013;57(18):3799–3811.

60. Vadlamani S, Eksioglu B, Medal H, et al. Jamming attacks on wireless networks: A taxonomic survey. *International Journal of Production Economics*. 2016;172:76–94.

61. Martinez I, Tanguy P, Nouvel F. On the performance evaluation of LoRaWAN under Jamming. In: 12th IFIP Wireless and Mobile Networking Conference (WMNC); IEEE; 2019. pp. 141–145.

62. Huang CY, Lin CW, Cheng RG, et al. Experimental evaluation of jamming threat in LoRaWAN. In: IEEE 89th Vehicular Technology Conference (VTC2019-Spring); IEEE; 2019. pp. 1–6.

63. Perković T, Rudeš H, Damjanović S, et al. Low-cost implementation of reactive jammer on LoRaWAN network. *Electronics*. 2021;10(7):864.

64. Perković T, Siriščević D. Low-cost LoRaWAN jammer. In: 5th International Conference on Smart and Sustainable Technologies (SpliTech); IEEE; 2020. pp. 1–6.

65. Aras E, Small N, Ramachandran GS, et al. Selective jamming of LoRaWAN using commodity hardware. In: 14th EAI International Conference on Mobile and Ubiquitous Systems: Computing, Networking and Services; 2017. pp. 363–372.

20

Intrusion Detection in IoT with Machine Learning and Deep Learning: A Systematic Review

Manjit Kumar Nayak and Debasis Gountia
Odisha University of Technology and Research, Bhubaneswar, India

Niranjan K. Ray
KIIT University, Bhubaneswar, India

20.1 Introduction

The security of IoT, particularly intrusion detection system (IDS) based on machine learning (ML) and deep learning (DL) techniques. We systematically study and analyze different mechanisms proposed in intrusion detection to identify their limitations and strengths. These techniques are evolving as emerging systems in the arena of network security.

The Internet of Things (IoT) has become evident since late 1999 [1]. It has been growing significantly with millions and millions of wearable devices, sensors, actuators, medical equipment, home appliances, etc. Worldwide, there is a huge number of linked devices; 7 million IoT devices are expected to grow to more than 22 billion in the coming years [2]. Most of the IoT devices are not designed with security features that provide safety and privacy to the users [3]. In 2019, more than 105 million attacks on honeypot servers were found [4]. An IDS is a blend of several methods to detect malicious actions both at the host and network levels [5, 6]. In spite of a huge body of research on network intrusion, there is a lot of scope for advancement in detecting intrusion and its prevention [1]. An intrusion is a deliberate attempt or threat to retrieve data, (ii) modify information, and (iii) provide an untrustworthy and ineffectual system. For example, attacks like DoS keep the server busy with a queue of unnecessary requests which keep the legitimate user from getting intended services. Anomaly-based intrusion discovery is the problem of recognizing infrequent patterns in network traffic that do not match with regular traffic. These unusual patterns are called anomalies, outliers, peculiarities, etc. [2, 3]. Anomaly discovery has wide applications in areas like credit card fraud detection, cyber security, and military surveillance. Unusual traffic in an IoT network indicates that a hacked system is sending delicate information to an illegitimate device.

Researchers of statistics have been investigating the detection of irregularities since the 19th century [2]. In the past decades, ML and DL have shown a major role in anomaly detection. Most of the surveys do not discuss individual methods that contributed to better performance [2, 5, 6]. In this chapter, we discuss in detail what is intrusion detection, different attack types in an IoT network, and different methods to detect these attacks and datasets used. Sensors collect data in an IoT network and transmit the data through wired and wireless community mediums. The IoT system must handle an enormous capacity of information from a large number of sensors without losing data while also providing secure communication [7]. IoT is exposed to safety matters as it is connected to the network for the transmission of information [8]. Reliable authentication mechanisms, integrity, and confidentiality of the data are the required security objectives in an IoT environment. If any of these

DOI:10.1201/9781003326236-20

issues are violated, it creates an insecure network. IoT equipment has insufficient resources, that is, battery, storage capacity, bandwidth, and computing ability. So highly complex and configurable security models are not useful [9]. For the security of IoT systems ML and DL-based security models are promising alternatives. The machine can be trained using methods of ML and DL to detect different attacks and provide the required defense mechanism. The attacks can be noticed at an initial stage and new kinds of attacks may be detected using new skills to lever them cleverly. ML and DL models deliver better safety mechanisms for IoT networks than ever before.

20.2 Detection of Intrusion

It is the group of activities performed to hamper the security and privacy of network and authorized users with respect to confidentiality, integrity, and availability [10]. This is generally achieved by an external agent to have illegal access and regulate the system. IDSs provide well-defined mechanisms to protect the infrastructure of the system, which collects network information and analyzes it to detect possible security attacks.

The functions of intrusion detection include:

(i) Tracking and analyzing different users of the network, network activities, and the network.
(ii) Developing mechanisms that identify different attacks.
(iii) Analyzing file systems and integrity.
(iv) Analysis of deviation of network activities from normal activities.
(v) Monitoring user violations.

20.2.1 Concept of Anomaly Detection

The concept of normality is required to provide a solution in network anomaly detection. The idea of normality is expressed as a relationship among basic variables influencing the system dynamics. A reinvent or object is noticed as irregular if its notch of aberration in terms of profile or conduct of the system stated by regularity models.

20.2.2 Classification of Attacks

There are two types of intruders: (a) outsider and (b) insider. Outsider intruders are illegal operators of the system. Insider intruders are authorized users who do not have rights to the source or super user mode.

20.2.2.1 *Previous Research on Network Intrusion Detection*

For detection of anomalies, a survey based on statistics and ML has been done [11, 12]. For numeric and symbolic data, an extensive review has been done [13]. A survey on specifically cyber intrusion detection has been done by Patcha, Park [14], and Synder [15]. The complete review of methods of detection of anomalies is depicted by Zhang et al [16]. The concept of intrusion detection with flow techniques and categorized attacks and thorough debate of discovery methods for DoS attacks, botnets, and viruses is presented by Sperotto et al [17].

A survey has been done by Sun et al [18] to detect intrusion for Mobile Ad hoc networks (MANET) and wireless sensor networks (WSN). They have also discussed many issues and research problems in the situation of making IDS by mixing different facets of mobility.

Markov Chain and Hotelling T2 IDS models for MANET are introduced by Sun et al [18]. The classification technique is used to detect anomalies. The application of computational intelligence methods for intrusion detection is presented by Wu and Banzhaf [19]. Various methods like neural networks, fuzzy, evolutionary computing, and immune systems that are artificial have been included. DoS and DDoS attack detection techniques are extremely surveyed [20].

20.2.3   Different Types of Attack

The IoT has been experiencing different kinds of attacks since the past decade. So, manufacturers of IoT devices are more careful about their development and usage. Attacks on IoT can be classified as physical attacks and cyber attacks. The act of hacking the system to steal, delete, modify, and manipulate the user's information is called a cyber attack. In physical attacks, the attackers do not any network rather they physically harm different IoT devices like sensors, cameras, and routers and succeed in disrupting the network [21].

20.2.3.1   *Active Attacks*

In active attacks, the intruder somehow intervenes in the system with the objective to disturb the configuration, halt, or cause malfunction in the network. Sometimes, he tries to steal and modify the information. Active attacks include DoS, jamming, hole attacks, and spoofing sybil attacks.

20.2.3.1.1   *Denial of Service*

Here the attacker continuously transmits redundant requests to the system. As a result, the devices remain busy and are unable to provide the required service to the actual users of the system. So, the attacker disrupts the system and the system becomes dysfunctional. Due to this particular reason, the devices remain in the active state and gradually lose their battery life. A special type of DOS attack is called a DDOS attack in which several requests are being made from different IPs at the same time to a server, thus making the server busy. So, it is very tough to distinguish normal traffic and attack traffic [22]. Recently a botnet attack popularly known as "Mirai" has made a destructive DDOS attack and has devastated thousands of IoT devices [23].

20.2.3.1.2   *Spoofing and Sybil Attacks*

To illegally access the data, these attacks mostly aim for the credentials, that is, the RFID, MAC address. As TCP/IP protocols do not have a reliable mechanism, spoofing attacks are more vulnerable. These two attacks recruit many serious attacks.

20.2.3.1.3   *Jamming Attack*

By transferring undesirable indications to the IoT equipment of an active wireless network, the network is kept busy. The performance of the network is degraded by this attack, which consumes more energy, bandwidth, and memory.

20.2.3.1.4   *Man in the Middle Attack*

In this type of attack, the attacker cleverly intrudes into the system and behaves as if he is an authorized user. This enables him to create problems in the network, and he may steal and misuse the information [22]. This kind of attack allows the assailant to capture delicate data such as login credentials and credit card information. This attack is also referred to as monkey-in-the-middle and monster-in-the-middle attacks.

20.2.3.1.5   *Selective Forwarding Attack*

In this type of attack, the attacker acts as a node in the network that allows to drop different packets creating holes in the network. It is very hard to identify and prevent such attacks in the network.

20.2.3.1.6   *Data Tinkering*

The assailants intentionally employ the user's data to deliberately disturb the secrecy of the user. The important information carried by IoT devices like location, billing price, and fitness is under great threat due to these data tinkering attacks [24].

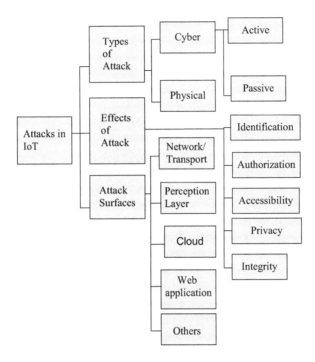

FIGURE 20.1 Different types of attacks, attack surfaces, and attack effects.

20.2.3.2 *Passive Attack*

The attackers collect user's data without their approval and try to decrypt their private secured information [25]. In an IoT network, eavesdropping and traffic investigation are the two ways to execute inactive attacks. IoT device of a user is deployed as a sensor in eavesdropping to gather and mismanage their private data and position [26–29].

20.2.4 Different Consequences of Attacks

The consequences of attacks on IoT networks on the user's identity, authorization, validation, and privacy. A group of different kinds of attacks and their consequences on an IoT network are given in Figure 20.1. The subsequent effects must be taken into account to prevent these effects while developing a new security protocol for the IoT network.

20.2.4.1 *Identification*

Identification signifies authorization of users of the IoT network, restricting only authorized users to access the network and the cloud server. The urge to maintain robustness and trade-off of IoT networks is creating challenges for identification [30]. Attacks like Sybil and Spoofing destroy the security of the network and allow unauthorized users to enter the network without proper identification. Therefore, an effective and strong security mechanism is required to be developed, which restricts unauthorized users from entering the system [31].

20.2.4.2 *Authorization*

Authorization refers to the approachability of the user. Only authorized users are allowed to access, monitor, and use the information. It is very difficult to maintain the log of the users and requests and provide information according to the needs of the requests as not only humans are the users but

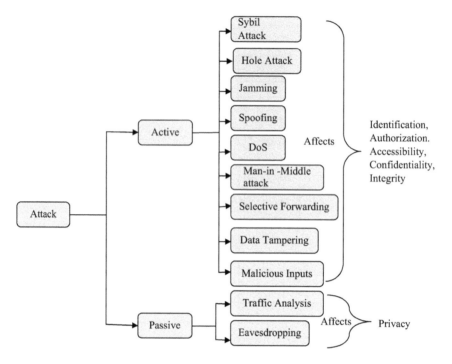

FIGURE 20.2 Different attacks and their effects.

also sensors and different machines act as the users [32]. While processing large datasets, it is very difficult to maintain a strong protective environment [33]. This is shown in Fig. 20.2.

20.2.4.3 Accessibility

Accessibility ensures that only authorized users get the services rendered by IoT systems. It is very important to create an effective secured network as attacks like DoS and jamming send unnecessary requests. As a result, the server remains busy always. Therefore, there is a requirement for strong protocols that ensure the facilities of the IoT are provided to authorize users without any interruption [34].

20.2.4.4 Privacy

Privacy of the IoT network is hampered due to both active and passive attacks. Sensitive information like personal identity, location, health records, and national security data stored in IoT devices must not be disclosed to any unauthorized users [35]. However, it's very hard to preserve the privacy of the network since the attackers track the location of IoT devices to decrypt the information and misuse it [36].

20.2.4.5 Integrity

Integrity assures only legal users can alter any data of IoT equipment. This particular requirement is very much essential for any IoT network. The SQL query injection attack is a malicious attack to disturb the integrity of the network. This affects the functionality of the IoT network if this particular feature is compromised. It not only reveals delicate data but also sacrifices human lives [36].

20.3 Intrusion Detection System (IDS)

The method to protect a network where alarms are used to inform an attack, and it takes a measured act and blocks the attacker [37]. Many IDSs have been developed, and it is divided into three main categories.

(i) HIDS (Host-based IDS) – It tracks vital operating system files and detects internal movement such as which program retrieves which resources and does prohibited entry. It observes the state of the system and the stored facts maybe in RAM, file systems, or log files. HIDS acts like an agent that monitors whether anything or anyone has tried to breach the security policy informed by the operating system [38].

(ii) NIDS (network-based IDS) – It analyzes data flowing across the network. Intrusion is identified when there is a deviation in the pattern of traffic as models model the data in a sequential fashion to detect deviations from that pattern [38]. The main reason for these attacks is to have illegal use of the network with the intention to steal or gain data or to disturb the functioning of a network.

A network is associated with the world through the Internet. The NIDS captures all inward traffic so as to detect deviations in the traffic pattern. For example, if it is observed that there is a huge amount of TCP linking appeals for a huge quantity of dissimilar ports in a short span of time, it can be assumed that some attacker is intentionally doing a "PORT SCAN" in some specific computers in the network. To detect port scanning of incoming shell, codes must be done similarly to the IDS. Along with the analysis of inward traffic, NIDS also delivers valuable information about the intrusion from outward traffic. There are three functional mechanisms in the existing IDS [39].

(a) Source of information – The source of event information about inward packets or information used to determine the intrusion.

(b) Analysis – It is the most important mechanism where it is analyzed from composed actions that intrusions are happening or already happened.

(c) Response – After the detection of intrusion response is of two kinds: active and passive. In active response, the system intervenes by itself. In passive response, the details of the detection are reported to the administrator, who intervenes.

20.3.1 Machine Learning and Deep Learning in Intrusion Detection

Machine learning is a part of artificial intelligence which systematically applies its algorithms to synthesize the inherent relationship between data and information. In 1959 Samuel defined ML as the area of study that empowers computers the ability to learn without explicit programming [40]. ML is a combination of numerous disciplines such as statistics, probability, linear algebra, information theory, and theory of algorithms [41]. ML algorithms are classified into three types – supervised, unsupervised, and reinforcement learning. Supervised output variables can be predicted from Learning. An output variable is not estimated by unsupervised learning. The machine educates itself in reinforcement learning in a continuous way, from past knowledge it learns and tries to apprehend the finest possible data for creating precise decisions. Linear regression, logistic regression, decision tree, random forest, artificial neural network (ANN), k-nearest neighbor (KNN), support vector machine (SVM), and Naive Bayes are the best-known algorithms [42]. Limitations of ML exist. It has some limits to activate regular records in their raw form. It requires a huge experience to design a feature extractor, which transforms raw information into an appropriate depiction from which the classifier can classify or detect patterns [43]. Deep learning offers simple representations [44]. For better efficiency, ML algorithms like SVM and DT are widely used. "IoT" and "ICN" are very popular in unsupervised learning models.

The effectiveness of ML and DL models is reduced significantly in the case of an adversarial environment. By some means the actual performance of the network is prevented in an adversarial environment. Adversarial examples are generated using evolutionary computing and DL [45]. High misclassification rates in many ML models and classifiers are achieved by their adversarial environments. A reinforcement learning algorithm for intrusion detection in adversarial environments has been proposed [46].

To obtain better results, an adversarial agent strategy is added to the training, which increases false predictions in classifiers, and it is forced to learn the most difficult cases. However, in these environments, more research needs to be done to study intrusion detection.

20.3.1.1 The Decision Tree

It is a tree model comprised of decisions and their outcomes and helps to make decisions. It is a mutually administered learning classification technique mainly used for classification activity in IDS. Features of a packet are selected by a trained DT to determine its class. Most of the data is contained by an optimal DT with the minimum number of levels [47]. ID3 [48], C4.5 [49], and Classification and Regression Tree (CART) [50] are a few algorithms for general optimal trees. Different metrics are used to measure DT performance. The selection of attributes with the highest information is called "entropy." The decision is made by the algorithm ID3 based on entropy. However, the applicability limitation of ID3 is its failure to identify missed values with continuity in features. C4.5 utilizes a ratio of information gain of ID3 and trims leaf nodes, which does not help. ID3 does not handle regression tasks which CART does using Gini impurity as a metric.

DT is a common model of intrusion detection with an exclusive classifying approach which is modest to apply and interpret, and pruning can be done after construction for better generalization. A three-layer mechanism called IDS has been proposed in [51] that recognizes IoT equipment relying on MAC addresses, categorizes messages as genuine and false, and then applies DT for the classification of attacks. DTs are used distinctively for classified records as malicious in [52]. The system identified DoS attacks, botnets, and scanning and produced good results. The formation of K number of clusters is done by K-means algorithm depending on the similarity of Euclidean distance implementing C4.5 to every group that constructs decision trees for bonafide and malicious messages in [53].

The limitation of DT is it is feeble in sturdiness. When few modifications in training records are done, it produces an entirely dissimilar DT. Large DTs require manual pruning as data gain is influenced by characteristics with extra levels [54].

20.3.1.2 Support Vector Machines (SVM)

To classify data optimally, an N-dimensional hyperplane is made [55]. SVM is of two types: linear and nonlinear. When this model is employed for data separable linearly, it is alienated into two groups by a straight line. If it is a nonlinear data then nonlinear SVM is used. The kernel method is used that sets data points in higher dimensions separated using planes or functions.

The problem of high dimension can be simplified by SVM. It has the ability of good generalization depending on small simple statistical theory and is frequently used in intrusion detection. A lightweight attack detection strategy is developed by [56] using SVM which detects attacks caused by the injection of unwanted data into the IoT network. A feature pool is obtained and used with a label vector by this strategy. This technique has a good cataloging strategy and discovery times. A four-stage SVM detection method is constructed on the structure of DT [57]. Detection of regular data, denial of service attacks, probing, R2L, or U2R is achieved by SVM1, SVM2, SVM3, and SVM4. Experimentally it is shown that this model exceeds in performance compared to single-stage SVM models. To distinguish normal traffic and malicious traffic across statistical methods and self-organized map (S-O-M), this method has been proposed in [58]. To differentiate regular and malicious traffic, this method also employs PCA and Fisher Discriminant Ratio (FDR) for noise removal and selection of features. PSOM (Probabilistic Self-organizing Mapping) is also used.

20.3.1.3 Clustering

It groups objects of similar types from other types. There is a wide variety of clustering algorithms. Depending on the matching criteria between Objects and Clusters, they are categorized as hard or soft clusters. K-means clustering and KNN are widely used algorithms from which Euclidean distance between objects can be calculated. Every object's belongingness to a group is measured by the degree of probability.

Different categories of clustering algorithms are connectivity based, K-means based (centroid-based), distribution based, density based, and grid based. The limitations of algorithms are simple to implement and interpret. The influence on the results is too much depending on the outliers and early values of parameters.

To obtain clustering and reduce similarity, a small batch K-means and PCA to decrease dimension [59] for intrusion detection is employed.

The results shown by experiment and time complexity analysis of this method are found to be effective. An unsupervised intrusion detection system (UIDS) [60] detects unknown attacks.

20.3.1.4 The DNN

For the investigation of very huge-scale information and real-time processing, a DNN (distributed DL) for the detection of intrusion has been discussed [61]. An IDS involving RNN with Gated Recurrent Units (GRUs), Multilayer Perceptron (MLP), and SOFTMAX has been proposed [62]. DNN is found to be efficient for very large-scale data and real-time processing. With multiple layers between input and output layers, DNN is an efficient ANN [63]. An entirely linked neural network is a model parallel to MLP.

20.3.1.5 The CNN

It has shown excellent performance in computer vision [64]. These methods have shown good results [65, 66]. Convolutional neural network (CNN) is inspired by biological processes. It is a shared model of neural networks. It also involves convolutional kernels.

CNN has the ability to extract resident characteristics, can detect masses, and also reduces computational complexity, so it improves training and computational speed.

20.3.1.6 The RNN

When data consists of frequently incessant data streams, recurrent neural network (RNNs) are widely applied in IDS [67]. However, RNNs do not handle activation functions efficiently. Gradient vanishing happens when the number of layers of the networks is large. The difficulty of fitting data that changes temporally by DNN is solved by RNN.

20.3.1.7 LSTM

The classical problem of RNN known as the gradient vanishing problem is solved by long short-term memory networks (LSTM) by introducing additional storage states [68]. The degree of gradient vanishing problem is controlled effectively by LSTM by means of a gate function as the activation function. The vanishing gradients problem is a kind of unstable behavior that is encountered during the training of network. It pronounces the condition when a neural network is incapable of spreading valuable gradient data from the output of the prototype back to the layers near the input of the system.

The result is the general incapability of models with many layers to acquire the available dataset.

Forgetting gates have been introduced that enable LSTM to reorganize its state by simulation of failing to recall process of memory using the original LSTM architecture [68] Because of its efficiency, it is measured as the most traditional LSTM architecture. The performance of LSTM is maintained with few parameters by the GRU containing the reorganized gate and update gate [69].

The greatest deviation of RNN is LSTM as it resolves the gradient-disappearing phenomenon of classical RNN. LSTM is used by many IDS studies [70, 71]. LSTM networks are very applicable for cataloging and forecast-based time series data and fail to recall mechanisms. LSTM networks are improved in detecting data streams.

LSTM models are often too costly to run as architecture cannot be trained in equivalent due to the innate nature of RNNs [72].

20.3.1.8   Naive Bayes (NB)

NB algorithms are a collection of information-collecting algorithms that use Bayes theorem of probability assuming naive uniqueness between every pair of features. Naive Bayes algorithm is a supervised learning algorithm on the Bayes theorem.

Intrusion detection problems are affected by high network data stream dimensionality, and highly correlated features founded on hidden Naive Bayes (HNB) model [73]. A mutual relationship between two or more things is known as a correlation.

$$P(A|B) = \frac{P(B|A)P(A)}{P(B)}$$
(20.1)

And

$$P(A|B) = P(B1|A) \times P(B2|A) \times \cdots \cdots \times P(Bn|A) \times P(B)$$
(20.2)

In intrusion detection the probability of an attack can be calculated by the probability of an attack occurring by initially estimating the probability that some preceding data were part of that type of attack and then multiplying the probability of occurrence of that type of attack.

Naive Intrusion detection problems are affected by high network data stream, dimensionality, and highly correlated features based on the HNB model [73]. A common relationship among two or more things is known as correlation if there are certain points$(x_i, y_i), i = 1, 2, 3 \ldots n$ in a dataset. Correlation observes if huge values of "x" are combined with huge values of "y" and small values of "x" are combined with small values of "y," also if minor values of "x" are combined with huge values of "y" and vice versa. Correlation coefficient is computed by

$$\sum_{i=1}^{n} \frac{(x_i - \underline{x})(y_i - \underline{y})}{\sqrt{\sum_{i=1}^{n}(x_i - \underline{x})^2 \sum_{i=1}^{n}(y_i - \underline{y})^2}}$$

The conditional independence approach of the Naive Bayes model is relaxed by the HNB data mining model. Greater efficiency is achieved in terms of accuracy, error rate, and misclassification cost by the HNB model than the traditional NB model. A multi-agent IDS Naive algorithm called NB-MAIDS specifies possible pressures of DDoS threats in the IoT and applied multi-agents in the entire network [74]. In this model, the information is gathered by different agents through sensors. Then further processing is done through the analysis of gathered information. The attacks and illegal activities may be prevented by disseminating the gathered information of malicious traffic to either the connected IoTs or the administrator. Serious security issues in IoT are DoS and DDoS. In these attacks, the network services are disturbed by flooding unwanted, meaningless huge traffic over the network. DDoS attacks are massive and hazardous. It tries to capture the bandwidth and prevent legitimate users from receiving the required service from the intended network. Mostly there exist two mechanisms to initiate DDoS threats on IoT. (i) The attacker sends some faulty packets to the victim to create some hindrance to the protocol or application running on it. (ii) The attacker tries to execute one or both of the following. (a) Application-level flooding attack is done by overloading the resources of the server. By this, the attacker blocks and delays the services to a legitimate valid

TABLE 20.1

DDoS Attacks on IoT Network

Layers		Threats
Perception Layer	(a)	Jamming
	(b)	Kill command
	(c)	De-Synchronizing attack
Perception Layer – 802.15.4	(a)	Boot-strapping attack
	(b)	Node-specific and message-specific denial
	(c)	Wide-band denial and pulse denial
Network Layer – Wifi	(a)	ICMB flooding attack
	(b)	IP Spoofing
Network Layer – ZigBee	(a)	Hello – flooding
	(b)	Homing attack
	(c)	Black-Hole attack
Application Layer	(a)	Reprogramming attack
	(b)	Path-based DoS

user [75]. (b) The network resources, router processing capability, and bandwidth are exhausted by the attacker to hamper valid user services [76]. The DDoS Attacks on IoT Network is shown in Table 20.1.

20.3.1.9 Multi-Agent System (MAS)

To achieve a common goal, the agents independently collect data and information in a coordinating and supportive way. All agents work on a common algorithm and communicate with other agents when required. The workload on nodes can be reduced drastically by distributing the load among multi-agents in case of intrusion detection. In a distributed system, implementing MAS is most appropriate.

20.4 Intrusion Detection Datasets

From the beginning of DARPA 1998, new datasets started appearing in the research community. From 2009 the intrusion discovery datasets started to surge rapidly. More than half of the datasets as given in Table 9 have been obtained from simulation experiments. The precision and validity of such datasets are a big issue [77]. The intrusion discovery models built based on these datasets are observed to be inefficient.

From Table 20.2 it is seen that KDD-99 and NSL-KDD are mostly used datasets even though they are obtained by simulated experiments. These datasets have been widely available for a long time. Whenever researchers propose any new intrusion technique that wants to be compared with previous techniques which were previously developed, it requires KDD-99 and NSL-KDD datasets. The contents of these datasets are found to be obsolete.

In future research, it is recommended to apply new datasets for intrusion detection such as CIRA-CID-DoHBrw 2020. The researchers should also apply some real-time datasets like ISOT CId, IoT-23, and SDN datasets for the validation of their models.

DARPA has created many datasets in an emulated environment at the MIT Lincoln lab, which are very popular for intrusion detection research. DARPA 1998 and DARPA 1999 contain network traffic data for five to seven weeks in packet format. Attacks like DoS, buffer overflow, port scans, and rootkits have been emulated in these datasets. These datasets are widely distributed and often criticized for redundancy and artificial attack injection.

TABLE 20.2

Use of Datasets by Different Researchers

Dataset	No. of Times Used
KDD-99	Forty-six
NSL-KDD	Thirty-five
U N S W-N B 15	Eight
I S C X 2012	Six
Kyoto 2006+	Two
Botnet	Two

- **KDD99:** From DARPA network dataset files KDD99 dataset was created. For preprocessing of the data and to investigate the structures of the DARPA datasets constructed through data mining. Seven weeks of network traffic data is contained in this dataset. Approximately 4.9 billion vectors are contained in this dataset. The different types of attacks in this dataset are User-to-Root (U2R), Remote-to-Local (R2L), Probing, and DoS. Each occurrence of the dataset is described by numerous structures in collections like basic, traffic, and content. From TCP/IP connections Basic features are extracted. Features of traffic belong to the same Host or specific service. The malicious behavior of the data part belongs to content part. To appraise intrusion discovery models KDD99 dataset has been extensively used.

- **NSL-KDD:** This dataset is suggested to solve the problems in KDD99. This new dataset also suffers from many problems [78]. Different intrusion detection models can be compared using this dataset. The advantage of this dataset is it can be used for complete experiments without using some portions of the records. This dataset helps in research for consistent and comparable results.

- **UNSW-NB15:** The Cyber Range Laboratory of the Australian cyber security center has created this dataset. Because of its variation of new attacks, it is widely used. Fuzzers, Backdoor, DoS, Generic, Reconnaissance, Shellcode Exploits, and Worms are the types of attacks analyzed using this dataset. This dataset contains 82,332 training records and 1,75341 testing records.

- **CICIDS2017:** Data from the source and results of analysis, that is, CSV files with time periods, IP addresses of sender and receiver, different ports, procedures, and token movements of threats, and all benign and common attacks are analyzed by dataset. The B-profile system is used by researchers to examine the illegal behavior of users to create benign traffic in the background. This dataset from the Canadian Institute for Cybersecurity is available online for intrusion discovery datasets for Application layer DoS/DDoS attacks. Eight DoS attacks have been executed by the authors at the application layer. A combination of results with attack-free traffic and results traces of ISCX 2012 dataset was done to generate normal user behavior. A network traffic of 24 hours in packet setup is available in the dataset.

- **CICIDDoS2019:** The latest DDoS attacks are contained by **CICIDDoS2019**. This dataset is similar to real-world data. CICFLOWMeter-V3 is used by this dataset, which contains the consequences of network traffic analysis, and token flow based on timestamp sender, and receiver.

- **KDD – CUP-99:** A small range realistic and user behavior data is contained by honeypot dataset Kyoto 2006+, which is publicly available. The packet-based traffic is converted into sessions by the developers. Every session is a collection of 24 categories; 14 numbers are statistical structures taken from **KDD to CUP-99** dataset, and the remaining 10 are normal traffic characteristics. The dataset contains 93 million sessions collected over three years.

- **NDSEC-1:** The dataset **NDSEC-1** shows attacks like botnet and brute force type, which are in contradiction of SSH, FTP, HTTP, and DoS based on UDP flooding, HTTP, SYN, and Exploits, portscans, spoofing, and XSS/SQL injection. It was taken from packet-based setup in 2016 and available online. The researchers have extracted trace and log files from the network.

- **CTU-13:** In 2013 the researchers generated a dataset **CTU-13**, which is presented in packet format. Where the flow of data is unidirectional and bidirectional. This dataset was taken from the network of a university, and its 13 setups are from botnet attacks. The data regarding infected hosts was presented in the form of a web portal. Traffic has been labeled as three types. (i) All communication details to and from infested hosts are considered as a botnet. (ii) The traffic that matches specific filters is labeled as normal traffic. (iii) The rest of the communication is considered as related in this dataset, which may be infected or normal.

- **BOT-IoT:** A realistic network environment was designed in the Cyber Range Lab of the center of UNSW Canberra Cyber to create the **BOT-IoT** dataset. The situation is a blend of regular and botnet traffic. The dataset source files are presented in different formats in the form of pcap files, the generated argus files, and csv files. For better labeling, the files were separated based on attack categories and subcategories. It includes attacks like keylogging, DDoS, data infiltration attacks, DoS, and Service scan. A tool called Node-red tool is used to simulate IoT networks. A lightweight communication protocol MQTT is used for machine-to-machine (M2M) communication. The test scenario for the IoT was a smart fridge, weather station, motion-activated lights, remote-controlled garage door, and smart thermostat.

- **IoT-23:** The network traffic was extracted from faulty scenarios from the network of some actual devices: a smart LED lamp, echo home intelligent personal assistant, and Somfy Smart Door Lock for the dataset **IoT-23**. It consists of 20 PCAP files and 23 network scenarios of IoT traffic. In each malicious scenario, Raspberry Pi malware was executed using a different protocol. Both infected and benign scenarios of IoT traffic were run on an undisturbed Internet connection. It was first available in January 2020, with detentions ranging from 2018 to 2019. This IoT network traffic was captured in the Stratosphere Laboratory, AIC group, FEL, CTU University, Czech Republic. Its goal is to offer a large dataset of real and labeled IoT malware infections and IoT benign traffic for researchers to develop ML algorithms. This dataset and its research are funded by Avast Software, Prague. The goal of this dataset is to make the two types of datasets available for the community: the first type contains malicious network traffic and the second one benign IoT traffic only. Both benign and malicious traffic flows have two new columns for network behavior description labels. These labels are assigned following the next process. The original .pcap file is analyzed manually. The suspicious flows are detected, and labels are assigned in an analysis dashboard. A labels.csv file is generated by the analyst.

- **LBNL:** In an enterprise network, LBNL dataset was developed to analyze network traffic characteristics. The dataset contains almost normal user behavior and is used for security research purposes. The dataset exists in packet setup, anonymized and obtainable with a maximum hundred hours of network data.

20.5   Evaluation Metrics in IDS

The efficiency of intrusion detection techniques can be measured using different evaluation metrics. The commonly used metrics are being discussed. The most common of them are accuracy, precision, recall, F1, and false alarm rate (FAR). The detection rate or True Positive Rate (TPR) is also called Recall. TPR is the ratio of properly categorized attacks to total attacks. The accuracy of classification in recognizing attacks is called Recall. Accuracy is the fraction of properly anticipated samples to the overall number of anticipated samples. FAR is a precarious metric in intrusion discovery. False Alarms are consequences of wrong positives. The huge number of FARs increases the weight of the network.

Afterward, arrangement information is separated into four groups: True Positive (TP), False Positive (FP), True Negative (TN), and False Negative (FN). When the model correctly predicts the positive class, it is True Positive. When the model correctly predicts the negative class, it is called True Negative.

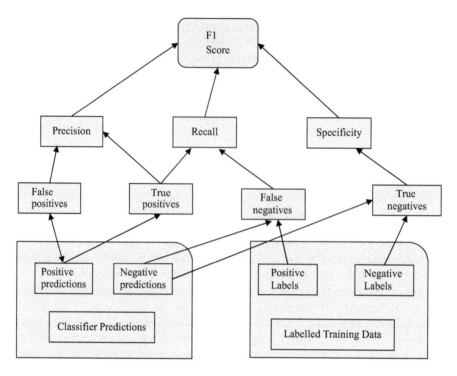

FIGURE 20.3 Hierarchy of metrics.

When the model incorrectly predicts the positive class, it is called False Positive. When the model incorrectly predicts the negative class, it is called False Negative.

All the metrics give a fine-grained idea of how well a classifier is working. An overview of these metrics can be shown in Figure 20.3.

Confusion Matrix

A confusion matrix is used to illustrate classifier performance.

		Actual Values	
		Positive	**Negative**
Predicted Values	Positive	TP	FP
	Negative	FN	TN

$$\text{Accuracy} = \frac{TP + TN}{TP + TN + FP + FN}$$

$$= \frac{\text{No. of correct predictions}}{\text{No. of all predictions}}$$

$$= \frac{\text{No. of correct predictions}}{\text{size of Dataset}}$$

Precision

Precision is a measure of how many of the positive predictions made are correct (True Positive).

$$\text{Precision} = \frac{TP}{TP+FP} = \frac{\text{No. of Correct predicitons}}{\text{No. of total positive predicitons}}$$

Recall/Sensitivity

It is the number of positive cases the classifier projected correctly over all the positive cases in the data.

$$\text{Sensitivity} = \frac{\text{True positives}}{\text{True positives} + \text{False Negative}}$$

$$= \frac{\text{No. of correctly predicted positive instances}}{\text{No. of total positive instances in the Dataset}}$$

Specificity (FAR)

It measures the total no. of correctly predicted negative predictions.

$$\text{Sensitivity} = \frac{\text{True Negatives (TN)}}{\text{True Negatives} + \text{False Positives}}$$

$$= \frac{\text{No. of correctly predicted negative instances}}{\text{No. of total negative instances in the dataset}}$$

$$F1 = \frac{2 \times \text{Precision} \times \text{Recall}}{\text{Precision} + \text{Recall}}$$

A mutual assessment metric is the detection time in the arena of intrusion detection. It means it is the total period consumed to categorize a model with an already trained model. The research of IDS often faces the problem of dimensional disaster and causes high detection time due to complications of communication even with s feature collection for reduction of dimensions. The core area of intrusion detection is to accomplish a suitable rate of detection with negligible expense of resources. High detection period of proposed prototype means that time complexity of the algorithm is too high.

In the case of big data, DL-based models take a long time. The computation time complexity of some algorithms is hard to compute, which has a direct influence on detection time. So there is still a requirement for a cohesive complexity assessment in the present IDS research other than detection time.

20.6 Conclusion

IoT is a widely spreading technology across the world that is bringing changes to human lives. People can store information, communicate, and carry out different day-to-day activities with the help of smart IoT devices.

The IoT equipment should be configured in different areas starting from home, agriculture, offices, industries, etc., with all security and safety measures Although people get connected to the virtual world and life becomes comfortable, smooth, and easy with the help of smart devices, the security issues connected with the confidentiality of information and privacy are a major concern. To enhance the security of IoT networks, there is a huge demand for reliable and efficient security protocols from the research community. There is a challenge for the researchers to further diagnose the available security mechanisms and protocols; identify their limitations; and develop efficient, secured robust security mechanisms for IoT networks. In this chapter, we have attempted to do extensive literature survey of previous research to explain intrusion detection, different types of attacks in an IoT network, ML/DL models of intrusion detection, different datasets with their limitations, and performance metrics being used. We also identify different limitations of the existing mechanisms and specify different research challenges and issues. We expect this would immensely help the researchers proceeding in this area to extend and fix their objectives.

REFERENCES

1. Ashton, Kevin. 2009. That 'Internet of Things' Thing - 2009-06-22 - Page 1 - RFID Journal. Journal. [Online]. Available: https://www.rfidjournal.com/articles/view?4986

2. State of the IoT 2018: Number of IoT devices now at 7B – Market accelerating. [Online]. Available: https://iot-analytics.com/state-ofthe-iot-update-q1-q2-2018-number-of-iot-devices-now-7b/

3. Hossain, M. M., Fotouhi, M., and Hasan, R. 2015. Towards an Analysis of Security Issues, Challenges, and Open Problems in the Internet of Things. Proceedings - 2015 IEEE World Congress on Services, SERVICES 2015, pp. 21–28.

4. IoT under fire: Kaspersky detects more than 100 million attacks on smart devices in H1 2019 | Kaspersky. [Online]. Available: https://www.kaspersky.com/about/press-releases/2019_iot-underfire-kaspersky-detects-more-than-100-million-attacks-on-smartdevices-in-h1-2019

5. Kwon, D., Kim, H., Kim, J., Suh, S. C., Kim, I., and Kim, K. J. Jan. 2019. A survey of deep learning-based network anomaly detection. *Cluster Computing*, 22, 949–961.

6. Malik, A. J., Shahzad, W., and Khan, F. A. Nov. 2015. Network intrusion detection using hybrid binary PSO and random forests algorithm, *Secure Communication Networks*, 8(16), 2646–2660.

7. Khan, Rafiullah, Khan, Sarmadullah, Zaheer, Rifaqat, and Khan, Shahid. 2012. Future internet: The internet of things architecture. Possible Applications and Key Challenges. 257–260. https://doi.org/10.1109/FIT.2012.53

8. Borgohain, T., Kumar, U., and Sanyal, S. 2015. Survey of security and privacy issues of internet of things. *International Journal of Advanced Networking Applications*, 6, 2372–2378.

9. Zhou, J., Cap, Z., Dong, X. and Vasilakos, A.V. 2017. Security and privacy for cloud-based IoT: Challenges. *IEEE Communications Magazine*, 55, 26–33. https://doi.org/10.1109/MCOM.2017.1600363CM

10. Axelsson, S. 2000. *Intrusion detection systems: a survey and taxonomy*, Chalmers University of Technology, Sweden, Technical Report 99-15, pp. 1–27.

11. Hodge, V., and Austin, J. 2004. A survey of outlier detection methodologies. *Artificial Intelligence Review*, 22(2), 85–126.

12. Nguyen, T., and Armitage, G. 2008. A survey of techniques for internet traffic classification using machine learning. *IEEE Commun. Surveys Tutorials*, 10(4), 56–76.

13. Agyemang, M., Barker, K., and Alhajj, R. 2006. A comprehensive survey of numeric and symbolic outlier mining techniques. *Intelligence Data Analysis*, 10(6), 521–538.

14. Patcha, A., and Park, J. M. 2007. An overview of anomaly detection techniques: Existing solutions and latest technological trends. *Computer Networks*, 51(12), 3448–3470.

15. Snyder, D. 2001. Online intrusion detection using sequences of system calls. Master's thesis, Department of Computer Science, Florida State University.

16. Zhang, Z., Li, J., Manolopoulos, C. N., Jorgenson, J., and Ucles, J. 2001. HIDE: A Hierarchical Network Intrusion Detection System Using Statistical Preprocessing and Neural Network Classification. Proceedings IEEE Man Systems and Cybernetics Information Assurance Workshop.

17. Sperotto, A., Schaffrath, G., Sadre,R., Morariu, C., Pras, A., and Stiller, B. quarter 2010. An overview of IP flow-based intrusion detection. *IEEE Commun. Surveys Tutorials*, 12(3), 343–356.

18. Sun, B., Osborne, L., Xiao, Y., and Guizani, S. October 2007. Intrusion detection techniques in mobile ad hoc and wireless sensor networks. *IEEE Wireless Commun.*, 14(5), 56–63.

19. Wu, S. X. and Banzhaf, W. January 2010. The use of computational intelligence in intrusion detection systems: A review. *Applied Soft Computing*, 10(1), 1–35.

20. Peng, T., Leckie, C., and Ramamohanarao, K. April 2007. Survey of network-based defense mechanisms countering the DoS and DDoS problems. *ACM Computing Surveys*, 39(1), 1–42.

21. Roman, R., Zhou, J., and Lopez, J., 2013. On the features and challenges of security and privacy in distributed internet of things. *Comput. Network.*, 57(10), 2266–2279.

22. Andrea, I., Chrysostomou, C., and Hadjichristofi, G. Feb. 2015. "Internet of things: Security Vulnerabilities and Challenges. Proceedings IEEE Symp. Computers and Communication, Larnaca, Cyprus, pp. 180–187.

23. Bertino, E., and Islam, N. 2017. Botnets and internet of things security. *Computer*, 50(2), 76–79.

24. Bekara, C. 2014. Security issues and challenges for the IoT based smart grid. *Procedia Comput. Sci.*, 34, 532–537.

25. AlTawy, R., and Youssef, A.M. Jan 2016. Security tradeoffs in cyber physical systems: A case study survey on implantable medical devices. *IEEE Access*, 26(4), 959–979.

26. Wamba, S.F., Anand, A., and Carter, L. 2013. A literature review of RFIDenabled healthcare applications and issues. *Int. J. Inf. Manag.*, 33(5), 875–891.

27. Malasri, K., and Wang, L., 2009. Securing wireless implantable devices for healthcare: Ideas and challenges. *IEEE Commun. Mag.*, 47(7), 74–80.

28. Wang, N., Jiang, T., Lv, S., and Xiao, L., 2017a. Physical layer authentication based on an extreme learning machine. *IEEE Commun. Lett.*, 21(7), 1557–1560.

29. Spachos, P., Papapanagiotou, I., and Plataniotis, K.N. Sept. 2018. Microlocation for smart buildings in the era of the internet of things: A survey of technologies, techniques, and approaches. *IEEE Signal Process. Mag.*, 35(5), 140–152.

30. Bose, T., Bandyopadhyay, S., Ukil, A., Bhattacharyya, A., and Pal, A., 2015. Why Not Keep Your Personal Data Secure Yet Private in IoT?: Our Lightweight Approach. Intelligent Sensors, Sensor Networks and Information Processing (ISSNIP), 2015 IEEE Tenth International Conference on. IEEE, pp. 1–6.

31. Yao, X, Farha, F, Li, R, Psychoula, I, Chen, L, and Ning, H. Aug 1 2021. Security and privacy issues of physical objects in the IoT: Challenges and opportunities. *Digital Communications and Networks*, 7(3), 373–384.

32. Ahmed, E., et al. 2017. The role of big data analytics in the Internet of Things. *Comput. Network.* 129, 459–471.

33. Moosavi, S.R., et al., 2015. SEA: a secure and efficient authentication and authorization architecture for IoTbased healthcare using smart gateways. *Procedia Comput. Sci.* 52, 452–459.

34. Restuccia, F., Daro, S., and Melodia, T., Dec. 2018. Securing the internet of things in the age of machine learning and softwaredefined networking. *IEEE Internet Things J.* 5(6), 4829–4842.

35. Roman, R., Zhou, J., and Lopez, J., 2013. On the features and challenges of security and privacy in distributed internet of things. *Comput. Network.*, 57(10), 2266–2279.

36. Camara, C., Peris-Lopez, P., and Tapiador, J.E., 2015. Security and privacy issues in implantable medical devices: A comprehensive survey. *J. Biomed. Inf.*, 55, 272–289.

37. Axelsson, S. 2000. Intrusion detection systems: a survey and taxonomy, Chalmers University of Technology, Sweden, Technical Report 99-15, pp. 1–27.

38. F. Wikimedia. Intrusion detection system. http://en.wikipedia.org/wiki/Intrusion-detectionsystem, Feb 2009.

39. Al-Garadi, M. A., Mohamed, A., Al-Ali, A., Du, X., Ali, I., and Guizani, M. Apr. 2020. A survey of machine and deep learning methods for internet of things (IoT) security. *IEEE Commun. Surv. Tutorials*, 22(3), 1646–85.

40. Awad, M., and Khanna, R. 2015. Machine learning. In *Efficient Learning Machines: Theories, Concepts, and Applications for Engineers and System Designers* (pp. 1–18). Apress.

41. Munoz, A. Machine learning and optimization. [Online]. Available: https://www.cims.nyu.edu/~munoz/files/ml_optimization.pdf [WebCite Cache ID 6fiLfZvnG]

42. Commonly used machine learning algorithms | Data Science. Online]. Available: https://www.analyticsvidhya.com/blog/2017/09/common-machinelearning-algorithms/. [Accessed: Jun 09, 2020].

43. Lecun, Y., Bengio, Y., and Hinton, G. 27 May 2015. Deep learning, *Nature*, 521(7553), 436–444.

44. Goodfellow, I., Bengio, Y., and Courville, A. 2016. *Deep learning*. MIT Press.

45. Alhajjar, E., Maxwell, P., and Bastian, N., 2021. Adversarial machine learning in network intrusion detection systems. *Expert Syst Appl*, 186, 115782.

46. Caminero, G., Lopez-Martin, M., and Carro, B., 2019. Adversarial environment reinforcement learning algorithm for intrusion detection. *Comput. Netw.*, 159, 96–109.

47. Quinlan, J.R. 1983. Learning efficient classification procedures and their application to chess end games. In Machine learning 1983 Jan 1 (pp. 463–482). Morgan Kaufmann.

48. Quinlan, J.R. 1986. Induction of decision trees. *Mach. Learn.*, 1(1), 81–106.

49. Quinlan, J.R., 2014. *C4. 5: Programs for Machine Learning*. Elsevier.

50. Loh, W.-Y., 2011. Classification and regression trees. *Wiley Interdiscip. Rev. Data Min.Knowl. Discov.*, 1(1), 14–23.

51. Anthi, E., Williams, L., Słow inska, M., Theodorakopoulos, G., and Burnap, P. 2019. A supervised intrusion detection system for smart home IoT devices. *IEEE Internet Things J.*, 6(5), 9042–9053.

52. Abbes, T., Bouhoula, A., and Rusinowitch, M. 2010. Efficient decision tree for protocol analysis in intrusion detection. *Int. J. Secur. Netw.*, 5(4), 220–235.

53. Muniyandi, A.P., Rajeswari, R., and Rajaram, R. 2012. Network anomaly detection by cas- cading k-means clustering and C4. 5 decision tree algorithm. *Procedia Eng.*, 30, 174–182.

54. Deng, H., Runger, G., and Tuv, E., 2011. Bias of Importance Measures for Multi-Valued Attributes and Solutions. International Conference on Artificial Neural Networks, pp. 293–300.

55. Özgür, A., Erdem, H., 2016. A review of KDD99 dataset usage in intrusion detection and machine learning between 2010 and 2015. *PeerJ*. Preprints 4, e1954v1. https:doi.org/10.7287/PEERJ.PREPRINTS.1954.

56. Jan, S.U., Ahmed, S., Shakhov, V., and Koo, I. 2019. Toward a lightweight intrusion detection system for the internet of things. *IEEE Access*, 7, 42450–42471.

57. Teng, S., Wu, N., Zhu, H., Teng, L., and Zhang, W. 2017. SVM-DT-based adaptive and collaborative intrusion detection. *IEEE/CAA J. Autom. Sin.*, 5(1), 108–118.

58. De la Hoz, E., De La Hoz, E., Ortiz, A., Ortega, J., and Prieto, B. 21 Sep 2015. PCA filtering and probabilistic SOM for network intrusion detection. *Neurocomputing*, 164, 71–81.

59. Peng, K., Leung, V.C., Huang, Q. 2018. Clustering approach based on mini batch Kmeans for intrusion detection system over big data. *IEEE Access*, 6, 11897–11906.

60. Casas, P., Mazel, J., and Owezarski, P. 2012. Unsupervised network intrusion detection systems: Detecting the unknown without knowledge. *Comput. Commun.*, 35(7), 772–783.

61. Vinayakumar, R., Alazab, M., Soman, K., Poornachandran, P., Al-Nemrat, A., and Venkatra-man, S. 2019. Deep learning approach for intelligent intrusion detection system. *IEEE Access*, 7, 41525–41550.

62. Xu, C., Shen, J., Du, X., and Zhang, F. 2018. An intrusion detection system using a deep neural network with gated recurrent units. *IEEE Access*, 6, 4 8697–4 8707.

63. Bengio, Y., 2009. *Learning Deep Architectures for AI*. Now Publishers Inc.

64. He, H., Bai, Y., Garcia, E.A., and Li, S. 2008. ADASYN: Adaptive Synthetic Sampling Approach for Imbalanced Learning. 2008 IEEE International Joint Conference on Neural Networks (IEEE World Congress on Computational Intelligence), pp. 1322–1328.

65. Dong, Y., Wang, R., and He, J. 2019. Real-Time Network Intrusion Detection System Based on Deep Learning. 2019 IEEE 10th International Conference on Software Engineering and Service Science (ICSESS), pp. 1–4.

66. Vinayakumar, R., Soman, K., and Poornachandran, P. 2017. Applying Convolutional Neural Net-work for Network Intrusion Detection. 2017 International Conference on Advances in Computing, Communications and Informatics (ICACCI), pp. 1222–1228.

67. Yin, C., Zhu, Y., Fei, J., and He, X. 2017. A deep learning approach for intrusion detection using recurrent neural networks. *IEEE Access*, 5, 21954–21961.

68. Gers, F.A., Schmidhuber, J., and Cummins, F., 2000. Learning to Forget: Continual Prediction with LSTM. *Neural Comput.*, 12(10), 2451–2471.

69. Cho, K., Van Merriënboer, B., Gulcehre, C., Bahdanau, D., Bougares, F., Schwenk, H., and Bengio, Y. 2014. Learning phrase representations using RNN encoder-decoder for statistical machine translation. arXiv preprint arXiv:1406.1078.

70. Bontemps, L., McDermott, J., Le-Khac, N.-A., et al., 2016. Collective Anomaly Detection Based on Long Short-Term Memory Recurrent Neural Networks. International Conference on Future Data and Security Engineering, pp. 141–152.

71. Roy, S.S., Mallik, A., Gulati, R., Obaidat, M.S., and Krishna, P.V. 2017. A Deep Learning Based Artificial Neural Network Approach for Intrusion Detection. International Conference on Mathematics and Computing, pp. 44–53.

72. Bai, S., Kolter, J.Z., and Koltun, V. 2018. An empirical evaluation of generic convolutional and recurrent networks for sequence modeling. arXiv preprint arXiv: 1803.01271.

73. Koc, L., Mazzuchi, T.A., and Sarkani, S., 2012. A network intrusion detection system based on a hidden Naïve Bayes multiclass classifier. *Expert Syst. Appl.*, 39(18), 13492–13500.

74. Mehmood, A., Mukherjee, M., Ahmed, S.H., Song, H., and Malik, K.M. 2018. NBC-MAIDS: Naïve Bayesian classification technique in multi-agent system-enriched IDS for securing IoT against DDoS attacks. *J. Supercomput*, 74(10), 5156–5170.

75. Zargar, S.T., Jyoti, J., and Tipper, D. 2013. A survey of defense mechanisms against distributed denial of service (DDoS) flooding attacks. *IEEE Commun Surv Tutor*, 15(4), 2046–2069.

76. Prasad, K.M., Reddy, A.R.M., and Rao, K.V. 2014. DoS and DDoS attacks: Defense, detection and traceback mechanisms—A survey. *Glob J Comput Sci Technol*, 14(7), 1–19.

77. Mahoney, Matthew, Philip, V., and Chan, K. 2003. An Analysis of the 1999 DARPA/Lincoln Laboratory Evaluation Data for Network Anomaly Detection. International Workshop on Recent Advances in Intrusion Detection, Springer, Berlin, Heidelberg, pp. 220–237.

78. Tavallaee, M., Bagheri, E., Lu, W., and Ghorbani, A.A. 2009. A Detailed Analysis of the KDD CUP 99 Data Set. 2009 IEEE Symposium on Computational Intelligence for Security and Defense Applications, pp. 1–6.

21

An Enhanced Effective Methodology to Detect Intrusions Using Machine Learning

Devishree Naidu, Shubhangi Tirpude, Sandesh Sachdev, and Vaidik Murarka
Shri Ramdeobaba College of Engineering and Management, Nagpur, India
Kalinga Institute of Industrial Technology, Odisha, India

Niranjan K. Ray
Kalinga Institute of Industrial Technology, Odisha, India

21.1   Introduction

Network security is critical in today's world of linked networks. Despite businesses' and organisations' best attempts to safeguard their networks, no device is totally secure, especially if it is linked to the Internet. This is due to the fact that hackers are continually developing new and sophisticated types of malware, with MAcfee claiming that over 300,000 new pieces of malware are developed every day.

Businesses and organisations invest millions of dollars to air-gap their networks in order to resist these dangers. To limit the danger of prospective assaults, air-gapping entails physically disconnecting the network from the Internet. However, this strategy is not infallible, as air-gapped networks have been infiltrated in the past.

This is when intrusion detection steps in. Intrusion detection is a model-based strategy for detecting possible network intrusions. The approach works by continually monitoring network traffic for suspicious or unusual behavior. If a breach is found, the model will notify system administrators, who may then take the required mitigation procedures.

Because it gives early notice of prospective assaults, intrusion detection is an effective technique to protect network security. This allows system administrators to take action and repair any vulnerabilities before they cause substantial damage. The use of an intrusion detection system (IDS) may also assist firms in meeting numerous security rules and standards, such as the Payment Card Industry Data Security Standard (PCI DSS).

Accordingly, network security is an important concern in today's linked society. Despite the greatest attempts to safeguard networks, no device, especially one linked to the Internet, is completely secure. Intrusion detection is a model-based way to detectect possible network breaches and provide early warning of future assaults. This allows system administrators to intervene and patch any flaws before they do major damage, making intrusion detection a critical tool for safeguarding network security.

21.2   Related Work

The NSL-KDD dataset is used in this chapter to compare several classification methods for identifying aberrant network traffic patterns. It is an enhanced version of its predecessor, KDD'99. [1]

DOI:10.1201/9781003326236-21

Intrusion detection has emerged as a critical area of concern over the past decade, with researchers focusing on different datasets to enhance system accuracy and reduce false positives in line with the DAPRA'98 initiative. Machine learning-based anomaly-based attack detection systems can be trained to increase their detection performance. However, because not all forms of attacks can be accurately recognized, current anomaly detection approaches frequently produce large false positive rates and only modest accuracy and detection rates. The NSL-KDD dataset has already been examined in earlier works. An extensive literature review of numerous research studies that have used either the KDD'99 or NSL-KDD security datasets to investigate IDS or implement IDS models using machine learning techniques is included in the study "A Survey on Machine Learning based Intrusion Detection System on NSL-KDD Dataset." The survey covers a variety of classification methods and classifiers that have been used for the security dataset, such as K-Nearest Neighbor (KNN), K-means SVM, Deep Belief Network, Genetic Algorithm, and Deep Convolution Neural Network (DCNN). The study's conclusions demonstrate the possibility of a hybrid strategy to improve machine learning-based intrusion detection technologies. [2] In the year 2015, author presented performance evaluation of NSL-KDD dataset using Artificial Neural Network (ANN). The chapter recommends using Tansig transfer function, Levenberg-Marquardt (LM), and BFGS quasi-Newton Backpropagation (BFG) algorithms when using ANNs on the NSL-KDD dataset. [3]The neural network architecture is designed to modify the values of neurons and layers during the learning process. The proposed approach outperforms other reported techniques for binary class classification, exhibiting superior accuracy in detecting attacks. Additionally, the study finds that the system has the ability to effectively identify attacks for specific classes within the NSL-KDD dataset during five-class classification. Pervez et al. [4, 5] presented NSL-KDD Cup 99 dataset feature selection and intrusion classification using. Support Vector Machines (SVMs), which are reliable machine learning algorithms frequently used for image classification, pattern recognition, and biometric analysis, are suggested to be employed in the research work. The suggested strategy uses fewer input features from the training data while maintaining the high accuracy of the SVM classifier. The chapter makes use of the NSL-KDD Cup 99 dataset, a multi-class classification issue that includes both normal and attack network connections. The suggested approach achieves classification accuracies of 91% using only three input features, 99% using 36 input features, and 99% when all 41 input features are utilized. These results demonstrate the effectiveness of the proposed method in accurately classifying network connections.

21.3 Dataset

The NSL-KDD dataset, an improved version of the KDD'99 dataset, has been extensively utilized by researchers to develop effective IDSs. Its superior performance over its predecessor can be attributed to the rectification of several issues. The NSL-KDD dataset is built upon the DARPA '98 dataset produced by the MIT Lincoln Laboratory's Cyber Systems and Technological group.

The NSL-KDD dataset has been subjected to various analyzes, using a range of methodologies and tools, with the ultimate goal of developing an efficient IDS. In this context, The NSL-KDD dataset has been thoroughly examined by the WEKA program using a variety of machine learning techniques. In particular, several attacks, both known and undiscovered, have been trained and tested using the K-means clustering technique.

In summary, the NSL-KDD dataset has served as a significant benchmark in the field of intrusion detection, facilitating the development of effective and efficient machine learning algorithms for detecting attacks. The utilization of such techniques has significantly advanced the ability to safeguard computer systems against malicious activities. [6]

The NSL-KDD data set is an improved version of the one that came before. It includes all of the crucial KDD data set records. The researchers have access to a variety of files that can be downloaded.

Although the NSL-KDD data collection has several issues, it is still a highly useful data set that may be used for study. [6, 7] NSL-KDDDataset Files List is shown in Table 21.1 and data records are referred in Figures 21.1 and 21.2.

Dataset	Number of Records					
	Normal	DoS	Probe	U2R	R2L	Total
KDD Train	67343	45927	11656	52	995	125973
KDD Test	9711	7458	2421	200	2654	22444

FIGURE 21.1   NSL-KDD dataset referred data records.

TABLE 21.1

NSL-KDD Dataset Files List with Their Description

Sr. No.	File Name	Explanation
1	KDDTrain+.ARFF	The full NSL-KDD train set with binary labels in ARFF format
2	KDDTrain+.TXT	The full NSL-KDD train set including attack-type labels and difficulty level in CSV format
3	KDDTrain+_20Percent.ARFF	A 20% KDDTrain+.arff file
4	KDDTrain+_20Percent.TXT	A 20% KDDTrain+.txt file
5	KDDTest+.ARFF	The full NSL-KDD test set with binary labels in ARFF format
6	KDDTest+.TXT	The full NSL-KDD test set including attack-type labels and difficulty level in CSV format
7	KDDTest-21.ARFF	A subset of the KDDTest+.arff file which does not include records with difficulty level of 21 out of 21
8	KDDTest-21.TXT	A subset of the KDDTest+.txt file which does not include records with difficulty level of 21 out of 21

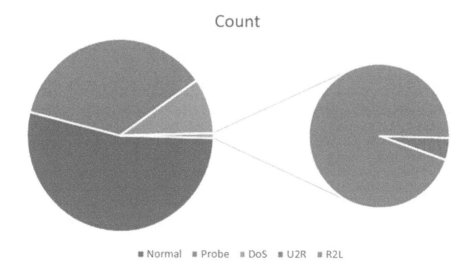

FIGURE 21.2   The figure shows the data records in the NSL-KDD dataset on attacks class in the form of a Pie Chart.

21.4   Proposed Methodology

21.4.1   Machine Learning Methodologies and Prediction Techniques: Model Training

The process of training a model on a collection of data so that it can make predictions or judgements based on fresh data is known as machine learning. Several steps are involved in the model training process:

1. Data collection: The first stage in model training is to collect data relevant to the situation at hand.
2. Data cleaning and preprocessing: Once the data has been acquired, it must be cleaned and preprocessed to guarantee that it can be used by machine learning algorithms.
3. Feature engineering is the process of identifying and developing meaningful features from data that the machine learning model can use.
4. Model selection: To train a model, numerous machine learning techniques can be utilized. The method you choose is determined by the problem you are attempting to answer as well as the qualities of the data.
5. Model training: Once you've decided on an algorithm, you must train it on data. This entails putting the data into the algorithm and modifying the model's parameters to optimize its performance.
6. Model evaluation: The model must be tested against a set of test data after it has been trained to ensure that it is reliable and accurate.
7. Model deployment: Once the model has been trained and assessed, it may be put into production and make predictions or judgements based on fresh data.

21.4.2   Data Preprocessing

Data preprocessing is an important stage in the data mining and assessment process that includes turning raw data into an organized and standardized format that computers and machine learning algorithms can readily comprehend and analyze. Raw data in many forms, such as text and photos, is typically jumbled, with mistakes and inconsistencies. Furthermore, the data is frequently inadequate and lacks a clear and standard format. This data may be turned into a usable format for accurate analysis and decision-making through preprocessing.

21.4.3   Data Visualization

Data visualization, or the depiction of data in graphical or pictorial representations, is an important part of machine learning. It is an effective tool for comprehending large datasets, recognizing patterns and trends, and making data-driven decisions. In this chapter, we will look at the significance of data visualization in machine learning, as well as the stages needed in developing good visualizations.

Step 1: Cleanup and Preprocessing of Data

Cleaning and preparing the data is the initial stage in data visualization. This includes deleting missing numbers, outliers, and other abnormalities that might degrade the visualization's quality. The data should be translated into a visually appealing format, such as a table, matrix, or graph.

Step 2: Choose the Best Visualization Technique

The proper visualization approach must be used to deliver the intended message to the audience. Scatter plots, line charts, bar charts, histograms, and heatmaps are some of the visualization techniques accessible. The approach used is determined by the type of data, the research topic, and the audience.

Step 3: Create the Visualization

Once the approach has been chosen, the visualization should be devised to properly portray the information. This includes selecting the appropriate colors, labels, titles, and comments to improve data comprehension. The visualization should be simple to understand, aesthetically appealing, and effectively convey the idea.

Step 4: Visualization Interactive

The interactive visualization allows the viewer to interact with the visualization and study the data in real time. This may be accomplished by use tools like as zooming, panning, filtering, and highlighting. Interactive visualization gives a more engaging experience and can aid in the discovery of fresh insights that static visualizations may not provide.

21.4.4 Feature Engineering

Feature engineering is an important part of machine learning that includes developing additional variables or features to improve the performance of a prediction model. This chapter will give an in-depth description of feature engineering, covering the many phases required.

The feature engineering process consists of four major steps: feature development, transformation, extraction, and selection. The initial stage is to discover and pick variables that will be most beneficial in the prediction model. This phase is subjective and needs domain understanding as well as imagination. This step's features should capture the significant qualities of the data that might aid in forecasting the target variable.

The next phase is transformation after the features have been built. This stage entails modifying the predictor variables in order to improve model performance. For example, we may use scaling or normalization to increase the model's performance by making the data more consistent.

The third stage is to extract features. Feature extraction is an automated technique that includes extracting new variables from raw data to create new variables. The goal of this stage is to lower the dataset's dimensionality and make it more manageable for modeling. Principal component analysis (PCA), linear discriminant analysis (LDA), and independent component analysis (ICA) are all methodologies for extracting features.

21.4.5 Experimenting Random Forest Classifier

It includes the creation of decision trees using various samples, followed by an analysis of the results and a prediction based on the decision trees' majority votes. To enhance its performance, Random Forest generates a huge number of decision trees rather than only using one. As compared to the decision tree algorithm, it is more accurate. It offers a practical method for dealing with missing data, also without hyperparameter adjustment, it can generate a reasonable prediction. It fixes the overfitting problem with decision trees. At the node's splitting point in every Random Forest tree, a subset of features is chosen at random.

21.4.6 Experimenting KNN Classifier

Based on commonalities, data points are categorized. Because it does not create a learning algorithm to forecast the outcome, it is frequently referred to as a lazy algorithm. It makes no assumptions about how the model will be built using the provided data. This is beneficial for carrying out pattern recognition tasks that categorize things based on various traits.

21.4.6.1 *Intrusion Detection Mechanism*

21.4.6.2 *Data Preprocessing*

Prior to importing the dataset, it is essential to import useful libraries like Pandas, Numpy, Matplotlib, Seaborn, and SK Learn in order to facilitate machine learning classification and regression algorithms. In comparison to the KDD'99 dataset, the NSL-KDD dataset has a substantial benefit because it has cleaner records, which eliminates the need for preprocessing. This is shown in Figure 21.3.

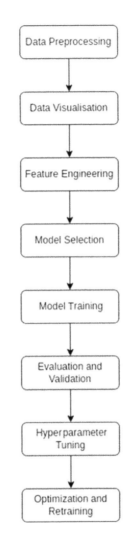

FIGURE 21.3 Development phases in the machine learning.

21.4.6.3 *Exploratory Data Analysis*

21.4.6.4 *Encoding*

The dataset has 42 properties, which were discovered when studying it. The final of them, the actual attack class, is one of 41 criteria that determine the packet information.

Following further investigation, it was discovered that three of the characteristics were of the type object, i.e., string values. These object values have to be translated into numerical values in order for the classification models to cope with this data. To do so, the object values were converted using hot-encoding and label encoding when needed.

21.4.6.5 *Data Visualization*

In this analysis, graphical representations were added to visualize the records from the dataset. Upon examining the graphs, each protocol type was seen to differ from the others. The protocol might be beneficial in determining the kind of traffic being watched, according to our original theory. Therefore, a deeper investigation was performed to see if the flag followed a similar pattern.

To summarize, the addition of graphical representations allowed for a visual representation of the records in the dataset. Upon examination, it was observed that there was a difference in each protocol type, leading to the hypothesis that the protocol could be useful in identifying the type of traffic being observed. Further investigation was conducted to see if the flag followed a similar pattern.

From the perspective of a network administrator, analyzing the combination of protocol, flag, and service in network traffic can yield valuable insights into the nature of that traffic. These parameters provide crucial information about the type of communication occurring within the network, allowing for a deeper understanding of network behavior and potential security threats. By leveraging this data, administrators can employ more effective strategies for network monitoring, intrusion detection, and incident response. Furthermore, with the aid of machine learning algorithms, the identification of anomalous traffic patterns can be automated, providing a scalable and efficient means of protecting network infrastructure.

21.4.7   Feature Engineering

To commence the process of feature building, it appears that the protocol type, service, and flag are promising starting points. These elements exhibit sufficient diversity to facilitate a fundamental level of identification. In addition, we intend to incorporate basic numerical data such as duration, source bytes, and destination bytes. These metrics are readily obtainable from contemporary network equipment and are expected to provide valuable insights into the nature of network activity.

21.4.7.1   Feature Selection

Feature selection [8, 9] is a crucial process in machine learning that involves identifying and selecting a subset of relevant features from a larger set of available features. This is achieved by applying specific evaluation criteria to determine the most valuable features for a given task or application. The feature selection process typically comprises three main phases, which include the selection of an initial subset of features, followed by an evaluation of each feature's worth within the subset. The final phase involves selecting the most valuable features that will be used for model training and prediction. This process helps to improve model performance by reducing the complexity of the feature space, minimizing overfitting, and improving model interpretability. The importance of feature selection cannot be overemphasized, particularly in scenarios where large volumes of data are involved.

21.4.7.2   Feature Extraction

To enhance the performance and accuracy of our model, we endeavored to engineer artificial features, eliminate redundant features, and selectively retain only pertinent ones. Specifically, we decided to remove the "numOutboundCmds" feature because it had redundant values in every row of the dataset. Additionally, we avoided using the whole collection of features for training by using the scikit-learn feature selection package to find and incorporate only the most important features into our model.

21.4.8   Train-Test Split

The provided dataset is comprised of separate train and test datasets, with a split size of 0.3 for both training and testing. The prediction model relies on two distinct features: attack identification and attack type classification. This approach employs machine learning techniques to detect intrusion attempts and mitigate the risks associated with malicious activities in a given system or network environment. The utilization of a split dataset enables the model to train on a subset of the available data and test on an independent subset, providing a more accurate evaluation of the model's predictive capabilities. By leveraging the insights gained from the trained model, system administrators and cybersecurity professionals can take proactive measures to enhance the security posture of their organization and prevent cyberattacks. The details is presented through Figures 21.4, 21.5 and 21.6.

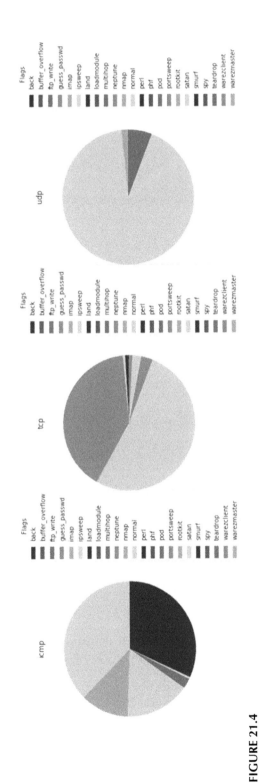

FIGURE 21.4

The figure presents a dataset comprising records that have been stratified according to their transport layer protocol and the corresponding attack patterns they exhibit.

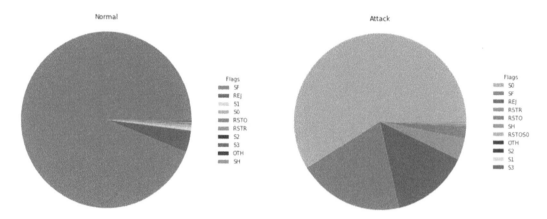

FIGURE 21.5 The figure provides a visualization of network packets, categorized as either "Normal" or "Attack" based on the flags that are active on the packet.

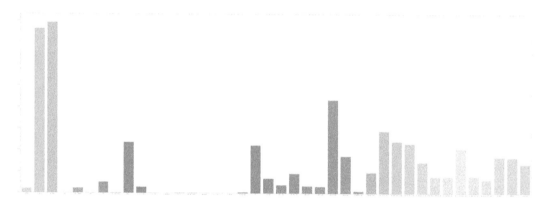

FIGURE 21.6 The figure shows the feature which are selected by using Random Forest feature selection function for important attribute.

21.4.8.1 Model for Training and Testing

Trained Model uses three classifiers:

1. Random Forest Model
2. KNN Model
3. Logistic Regression Model

During the model training phase, the splits generated from the dataset are provided to the classifiers for further analysis. The training split is utilized to train the model, whereas the test split is used to evaluate the model's predictive capabilities.

Given the characteristics of the dataset, decision trees are deemed to be a suitable starting point for constructing predictive models. Accordingly, a Random Forest technique is employed to create and consolidate multiple decision trees.

In order to assess the model's performance, a confusion matrix is constructed to identify the number of false positives. The model's accuracy is then evaluated, and if it is discovered to be poor, hyperparameter tuning is carried out to improve the accuracy. After hyperparameter adjustment, the model is retrained on the dataset splits. This is shown in Figures 21.7 and 21.8.

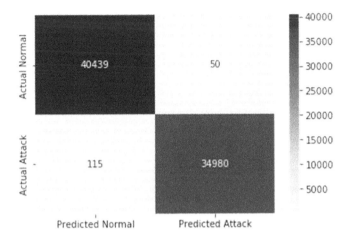

FIGURE 21.7 This figure displays binary classification-based confusion matrix using training dataset.

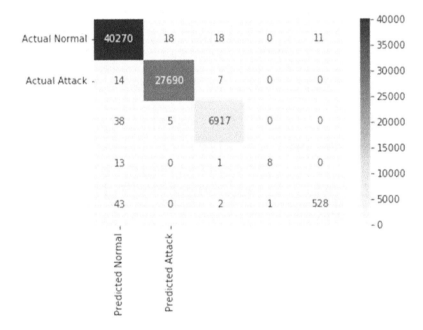

FIGURE 21.8 The given figure displays the multi-class classification confusion matrix experimented on the training dataset, which illustrates the ability of a machine learning model to accurately classify instances into multiple classes.

21.5 Result and Discussion

The goal of this study was to improve model performance by reducing the dimensionality of the data and using a feature selection technique. The NSL-KDD dataset was used, and a random feature selection technique was applied to lessen model complexity and training time. While this approach proved effective in the current study, its efficacy may be dependent on the specific characteristics of the data.

	F1		Fbeta	
Binary Score	0.9976471		0.998202	
	Macro	Micro	Macro	Micro
Multi Score	0.8914191	0.997738	0.929808	0.997738

FIGURE 21.9 The depicted graph illustrates the scores for both binary and multi-class classifications achieved through the implementation of a Random Forest classifier.

	F1		Fbeta	
Binary Score	0.9976471		0.998202	
	Macro	Micro	Macro	Micro
Multi Score	0.8463801	0.991189	0.862354	0.991189

FIGURE 21.10 The figure depicts the classification scores for both binary and multi-class classification tasks using the KNN algorithm.

The usage of a Random Forest technique, which can handle irregularly dispersed data, allowed for accuracy rates above 98%. A bootstrap procedure is used in the Random Forest approach to increase minority class representation, which reduces data misclassification and improves model accuracy. The Random Forest approach is very good at identifying data imbalance. This is shown in Figures 21.9 and 21.10.

Below are the results for all three classifications:

21.5.1 Random Forest Classifier

Among all the classifiers evaluated, the Random Forest classifier demonstrated the highest prediction accuracy, achieving a F1 Score of 99.76% and a F-Beta Score of 99.8%. Additionally, the multi-score prediction through this classifier yielded a F1 Score of 89.14% (Macro) and 99.77% (Micro), and a F-Beta Score of 92.98% (Macro) and 99.77%, respectively. These findings suggest that the Random Forest classifier is a highly effective approach for intrusion detection tasks.

21.5.2 KNN

The KNN algorithm exhibited an impressive accuracy rate, with 99.76% and 99.8% F1 Score and F-Beta Score, respectively. Furthermore, The KNN classifier's multi-score prediction showed an 84.63% (Macro) and 99.11% (Micro) F1 Score and an 86.23% (Macro) and 99.11% (Micro) F-Beta Score. These results showcase the efficacy of KNN in accurately predicting intrusions.

21.5.3 Logistic Regression

The logistic regression model exhibited a high level of accuracy in predicting intrusions, with F1 and F-Beta scores of 86.83% and 88.389%, respectively. When employing the classifier for multi-score prediction, the model achieved a Micro F1 Score and Micro F-Beta Score of 84.52%. These results demonstrate the effectiveness of logistic regression in identifying intrusions and highlight the potential for its application in IDSs.

According to experimental findings, the suggested technique achieves classification accuracy of 91% with just three features and 99% with all 36 characteristics plus 41 training features. These findings support the efficacy of the approach, demonstrating the ability to achieve high classification accuracy rates of up to 99%. The results are shown in Figures 21.11, 21.12 and 21.13.

	F1		Fbeta	
Binary Score	0.8683753		0.88389	
	Macro	Micro	Macro	Micro
Multi Score	0.3565048	0.845219	0.349988	0.845219

FIGURE 21.11 The figure illustrates the performance metrics of binary and multi-class classification utilizing logistic regression.

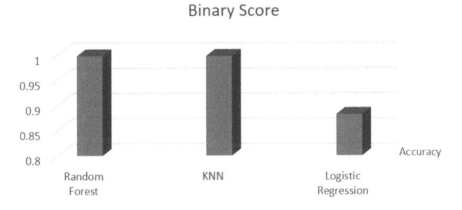

FIGURE 21.12 The presented figure illustrates a bar graph depicting the binary score obtained from all three classifiers utilized in the project.

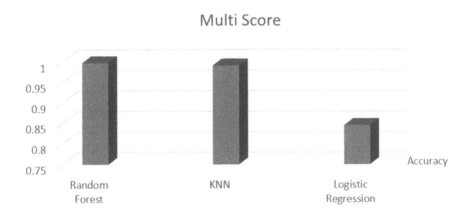

FIGURE 21.13 The figure presents a bar graph depicting the multi-scores of the three classifiers employed in the project.

21.6 Conclusion and Future Scope

In our study, we conducted an in-depth analysis of the NSL-KDD dataset and evaluated its performance using three classifiers, namely Random Forest, KNN, and Logistic Regression. Our training results exhibited commendable accuracy levels that were consistent with previous research conducted using a popular dataset. Our findings were extensively illustrated in the result section.

It was observed that although the prominent classifiers used in the well-renowned NSL-KDD data set produced promising results for the training set, their accuracy levels were suboptimal for the test set. This observation highlights the need for further research in developing classifiers that can accurately detect intrusions in the test set. The current intrusion detection model is experiencing a lag in performance on the test dataset, despite exhibiting high accuracy in the training dataset, with true accurate prediction almost reaching 99.8%. The reason behind this under-performance is the presence of outliers in the test dataset. In the forthcoming research, it is suggested to employ techniques with improved optimization to explore the ability to develop a more precise and effective IDS. One promising avenue of investigation involves the use of ensemble-based techniques, where multiple algorithms are combined to generate more robust and accurate results. Moreover, the exploration of alternative classifiers and techniques, such as deep learning models like Artificial Neural Networks (ANNs), Convolutional Neural Networks (CNNs), Recurrent Neural Networks (RNNs), and clustering algorithms like K-means, could be fruitful. These models can be analyzed and evaluated to identify the most appropriate and effective approach for developing an improved IDS. Ultimately, the success of the IDS model will hinge on its ability to perform well on the test dataset, indicating its reliability and practical utility in real-world settings. There is a critical security challenge as a result of the growth of unauthorized access to and use of network resources. Rapid identification of intrusions is crucial to mitigate the impact on system networks as attacks continue to pose a serious threat. Machine learning classifiers have gained prominence in IDSs due to their flexibility, capacity for generalization, and resilience. Deploying such models on network servers would enhance their robustness and accuracy in detecting attacks on the system.

REFERENCES

1. Revathi, S., Malathi, A.: A detailed analysis on nsl-kdd dataset using various machine learning techniques for intrusion detection. *International Journal of Engineering Research & Technology (IJERT)* **2**(12), 1848–1853 (2013).
2. Solanki, S., Gupta, C., Rai, K.: A survey on machine learning based intrusion detection system on nsl-kdd dataset. *International Journal of Computers and Applications* **176**, 36–39 (2020).
3. Ingre, B., Yadav, A.: Performance analysis of nsl-kdd dataset using ann. In: 2015 International Conference on Signal Processing and Communication Engineering Systems, pp. 92–96 (2015). IEEE.
4. Buczak, A.L., Guven, E.: A survey of data mining and machine learning methods for cyber security intrusion detection. *IEEE Communications Surveys & Tutorials* **18**(2), 1153–1176 (2015).
5. Pervez, M.S., Farid, D.M.: Feature selection and intrusion classification in nsl-kdd cup 99 dataset employing svms. In: The 8th International Conference on Software, Knowledge, Information Management and Applications (SKIMA 2014), pp. 1–6 (2014). IEEE.
6. Dhanabal, L., Shantharajah, S.: A study on nsl-kdd dataset for intrusion detection system based on classification algorithms. *International Journal of Advanced Research in Computer and Communication Engineering* **4**(6), 446–452 (2015).
7. Aljawarneh, S., Aldwairi, M., Yassein, M.B.: Anomaly-based intrusion detection system through feature selection analysis and building hybrid efficient model. *Journal of Computational Science* **25**, 152–160 (2018).
8. Deshmukh, D.H., Ghorpade, T., Padiya, P.: Improving classification using preprocessing and machine learning algorithms on nsl-kdd dataset. In: 2015 International Conference on Communication, Information & Computing Technology (ICCICT), pp. 1–6 (2015). IEEE.
9. Nguyen, H.A., Choi, D.: Application of data mining to network intrusion detection: classifier selection model. In: Asia-Pacific Network Operations and Management Symposium, pp. 399–408 (2008). Springer.

Index

Pages in *italics* refer to figures, pages in **bold** refer to tables, and pages followed by "n" refer to notes.